19th Edition

Deskbook Encyclopedia of Public Employment Law

Center for
Education & Employment Law

Center for Education & Employment Law
P.O. Box 3008
Malvern, Pennsylvania 19355

Copyright © 2009 by Center for Education & Employment Law
All rights reserved. No part of this publication may be reproduced by any means, electronic or mechanical, including photocopying, without prior written permission from the publisher.
First edition 1991
Nineteenth edition 2009
Printed in the United States of America

> "This publication is designed to provide accurate and authoritative information in regard to the subject matter covered. It is sold with the understanding that the publisher is not engaged in rendering legal, accounting or other professional service. If legal advice or other expert assistance is required, the service of a competent professional person should be sought." -*from a Declaration of Principles jointly adopted by a Committee of the American Bar Association and a Committee of Publishers and associations.*

The Library of Congress has catalogued this book as follows:

Deskbook Encyclopedia of Public Employment Law - 19th ed.
    p.   cm.
    Includes bibliographical references and index.
    ISBN 978-1-933043-37-1
    1. Civil Service – United States – Digests. 2. Employee-management relations in government – Law and legislation – United States – Digests. Center for Education & Employment Law (Malvern, Pa.)

KF4220.A59P75   2002
344.73'072—dc20
[347.30472]   94-441
                                          CIP

Library of Congress Catalog Card Number: 93-70613
ISBN 978-1-933043-37-1

Cover Design by Patricia Jacoby

Other Titles Published by Center for Education & Employment Law:

    Deskbook Encyclopedia of American School Law
    Deskbook Encyclopedia of Employment Law
    Higher Education Law in America
    Keeping Your School Safe & Secure: A Practical Guide
    Private School Law in America
    Students with Disabilities and Special Education

TABLE OF CONTENTS

INTRODUCTION I

ABOUT THE EDITORS III

HOW TO USE YOUR DESKBOOK V

TABLE OF ABBREVIATIONS IX

TABLE OF CASES XI

TABLE OF CASES BY STATE XXVII

CHAPTER ONE
Employment Discrimination

I. AGE DISCRIMINATION 2
   A. Burden of Proof Under ADEA 2
      1. Age Factor 3
      2. Adverse Employment Action 6
      3. Pretext for Discrimination 7
   B. Procedural Issues 9
   C. Defenses 12
      1. Maximum Age Limitations 13
      2. Mandatory Retirement 14

II. DISABILITY DISCRIMINATION 16
   A. The Rehabilitation Act and ADA 17
      1. Physical or Mental Impairment 17
      2. Substantial Limitation 20
      3. Essential Job Functions 23
      4. Procedural Issues 25
      5. Defenses 26
      6. Regarded as Disabled 29
   B. Reasonable Accommodation 30
      1. Types of Accommodation 31
      2. Unreasonable Accommodations 33
   C. Drug and Alcohol Use 35
   D. State Statutes 37

III. RACE AND NATIONAL ORIGIN DISCRIMINATION 40
   A. Race Discrimination 40
      1. Burden of Proof 40
      2. Racial Harassment 46
      3. Judgments and Settlement Decrees 48
   B. National Origin Discrimination 51

TABLE OF CONTENTS

- IV. SEX DISCRIMINATION 54
  - A. Generally..54
    - 1. Burden of Proof..54
    - 2. Legitimate Reasons 58
    - 3. Defenses...60
  - B. Equal Pay..62
  - C. Pregnancy 66
  - D. Harassment...67
    - 1. Burden of Proof..68
    - 2. Defenses...72
    - 3. Same-Sex and Sexual Orientation Issues 75
    - 4. 42 U.S.C. § 1983 77
    - 5. State Statutes 78

- V. RELIGIOUS DISCRIMINATION 80
  - A. Burden of Proof..80
  - B. Reasonable Accommodations 82
  - C. Seniority Systems 86

- VI. RETALIATORY DISCRIMINATION 87

- VII. AFFIRMATIVE ACTION 93
  - A. Affirmative Action Programs....................................93
    - 1. Hiring Decisions 93
    - 2. Promotions 95
    - 3. Employment Terminations...................................97
  - B. Procedural Issues 98
  - C. Termination and Modification of Programs 99

- VIII. PROCEDURAL MATTERS 101
  - A. Generally..101
  - B. Continuing Violation Doctrine................................103

CHAPTER TWO
Discipline, Suspension and Termination

- I. EMPLOYEE DUE PROCESS RIGHTS 106
  - A. Hearing Rights 106
    - 1. Notice and Opportunity to Respond 108
    - 2. Evidentiary Issues...110
    - 3. Impartial Decision Maker 113
  - B. Property and Liberty Interests................................115
    - 1. Probationary Employees.....................................117
    - 2. Transfers 119
    - 3. Reputation Interests 121
    - 4. Property Interests 123
  - C. Employment Handbooks and Policies 126
    - 1. Procedures 126

TABLE OF CONTENTS

       2. Employment Status 128
    D. Statutes and Ordinances 129
       1. Procedures 129
       2. Employment Status 132
    E. Collective Bargaining Agreements 133
       1. Procedures 134
       2. Investigatory Interviews 136

II. EMPLOYMENT ABANDONMENT AND RESIGNATION 138
    A. Abandonment 138
    B. Resignation 140
       1. Voluntary Resignation 140
       2. Withdrawal of Resignation 142

III. EMPLOYEE MISCONDUCT 143
    A. Official Misconduct 143
       1. Ethics Codes 143
       2. Neglect of Duty 145
    B. Criminal Violations 147
    C. Violations of Employer Rules and Policies 149
       1. Rules and Policies 149
       2. Refusal to Follow Orders 153
    D. Off-Duty Misconduct 156

IV. LAYOFFS FOR FINANCIAL REASONS 159

V. RETALIATION 162
    A. Whistleblower Protection Acts 162
       1. Retaliatory Actions 162
       2. Employment Termination 166
    B. Wrongful Discharge 170

VI. NATIONAL SECURITY 173

CHAPTER THREE
Freedom of Expression and Privacy

I. FREEDOM OF SPEECH 177
    A. Supreme Court Cases 178
    B. The *Garcetti v. Ceballos* Issue 181
    C. Protected Speech 183
       1. Matters of Public Concern 184
       2. Speaker's Interest Outweighs Government's Interest .. 186
       3. Speech Reporting Criminal Activity 190
       4. Prior Restraint 192
    D. Unprotected Speech 193
       1. Government's Interest Outweighs Speaker's Interest .. 194
       2. Speech of a Personal Nature 199

TABLE OF CONTENTS

        3. Qualified Immunity and Other Defenses...................204
    E. Freedom of Association 207
    F. Defamation...210

II. UNION AND POLITICAL ACTIVITY..214
    A. Union Activities..215
    B. Political Activities...218
        1. Managerial and Discretionary Positions 219
        2. Participation in the Political Process........................224
        3. Running for Public Office 227
        4. Retaliation Against Same Party Members 229
    C. Loyalty Oaths...230

III. PERSONAL APPEARANCE AND DRESS CODES 233

IV. RELIGIOUS FREEDOM...238

V. PRIVACY...242

CHAPTER FOUR
Governmental Immunity and Tort Liability

I. SOVEREIGN IMMUNITY...252
    A. Generally..252
    B. Insurance as Waiver 256

II. GOVERNMENTAL EMPLOYEE IMMUNITY..........................258
    A. Absolute Immunity 258
    B. Qualified Immunity 262
        1. Supreme Court Cases 262
        2. Emergency Calls...264
        3. Improper Office Behavior 265
        4. Police Misconduct...267
        5. Other Employee Misconduct.....................................270
    C. Constitutional Violations...271
        1. First Amendment Speech Rights 271
        2. Fourteenth Amendment Rights 273
        3. Fourth Amendment Rights 276
        4. Eighth Amendment Rights 278
        5. Fifth Amendment Rights 279
    D. Special Duty to Protect 279
        1. Supreme Court Case 279
        2. Police Officers...280
        3. Other Public Employees 281

III. GOVERNMENTAL AND EMPLOYEE LIABILITY....................283
    A. Generally..284

TABLE OF CONTENTS

      1. Suicides 284
      2. Domestic Disputes 285
      3. The Firefighter's Rule 287
      4. Vicarious Liability 288
      5. Other Liability Cases..291
  B. 42 U.S.C. § 1983 293
      1. Supreme Court Cases 293
      2. Police Officers' Actions 295
      3. Firefighters' and Other Employees' Actions 300
  C. The Federal Tort Claims Act 303
  D. State Tort Claims Acts..305

CHAPTER FIVE
Searches and Seizures

I. SEARCHES OF HOMES, OFFICES AND PERSONS 311
  A. Applicable Standard of Reasonableness......................312
  B. Expectations of Privacy..317

II. BLOOD AND DRUG TESTING..321
  A. Balancing Public and Individual Rights.........................321
      1. Assertions of Overbroad Policies 322
      2. Safety-Sensitive Positions 325
      3. Random Testing 330
      4. Direct Observation 333
      5. Post-Accident Testing 336
  B. Standards for Reasonable Suspicion 337
      1. Police Officers and Firefighters................................338
      2. Corrections Officers and Court Employees 340
      3. Transportation Employees 342
  C. Testing and Unemployment Benefits 344
  D. Adequacy of Testing Procedures 346

CHAPTER SIX
Employee Benefits

I. PENSION BENEFITS 352
  A. Eligibility...352
  B. Statutory Amendments...354
  C. Benefit Calculations 357
  D. Misconduct Disqualification..361

II. DISABILITY AND WELFARE BENEFITS 364
  A. Eligibility...364
  B. Modification and Termination 368
  C. Vacation and Sick Leave 372

III. EXEMPTIONS...376

TABLE OF CONTENTS

- A. Age Restrictions 376
- B. Service Retirement 379
- C. ERISA 379

IV. UNEMPLOYMENT AND WORKERS' COMPENSATION 380
- A. Unemployment Compensation 380
- B. Workers' Compensation 385
  1. Arising From Employment 386
  2. Exclusivity 391
  3. Off-Duty Occurrences 393
  4. Amount of Compensation 397

V. FAMILY AND MEDICAL LEAVE ACT OF 1993 400
- A. Eligibility Issues 402
- B. Documentation and Notice Issues 404
- C. Intermittent Leave 406
- D. Procedural Issues 407
  1. Post-Leave Problems 407
  2. Concurrent Paid Leave 408
  3. Other Procedural Issues 409

VI. OTHER EMPLOYMENT BENEFITS CASES 411
- A. Coordination of Benefits 411
- B. Contribution Rates 413
- C. Taxation 416

CHAPTER SEVEN
Labor Relations

I. FAIR LABOR STANDARDS ACT 419
- A. Covered Employees 419
- B. Overtime Wages 422
  1. Exempt Salaried Employees 423
  2. Method of Calculation 427
  3. Comp and Flex Time 432
  4. Compensable Activities 434
  5. Commuting Expenses 437
  6. Procedural Issues 439

II. PRIVACY OF EMPLOYEE INFORMATION 441

III. WAGE DISCRIMINATION 443

IV. UNION REPRESENTATION 445
- A. Duty of Fair Representation 447
- B. Collective Bargaining Fees 451

TABLE OF CONTENTS

- V. UNFAIR LABOR PRACTICES 454
  - A. Right to Organize 454
  - B. Terms and Conditions 457
    1. Wages and Hours 457
    2. Employer Policies 459
    3. Procedural Issues 464
  - C. Arbitration 467

CHAPTER EIGHT
Employment Practices

- I. APPOINTMENTS AND PROMOTIONS 471
  - A. Eligibility Lists 472
    1. Examinations 474
    2. Review of Test Materials 476
    3. Preference Points and Credits 477
  - B. Classifications 479
    1. Creation of Classifications 480
    2. Temporary Assignments 481
    3. Reclassification 483
  - C. Privatization 486
  - D. Nepotism 489

- II. RESIDENCY REQUIREMENTS 491

- III. VETERANS' RIGHTS AND PREFERENCES 495

- IV. EMPLOYER POLICIES AND RESTRICTIONS 500
  - A. Secondary Employment 501
  - B. Employment Testing 504
  - C. Legal Fees Reimbursement 506
  - D. Marital Restrictions 508

APPENDIX A
United States Constitution - Relevant Provisions 511

APPENDIX B
Table of Recent and Important United States
Supreme Court Employment Cases 517

THE JUDICIAL SYSTEM 525

HOW TO READ A CASE CITATION 529

GLOSSARY 531

INDEX 537

INTRODUCTION

The *Deskbook Encyclopedia of Public Employment Law* provides an encyclopedic compilation of state and federal court decisions that affect public employment. It covers a wide range of important topics, including discrimination, discipline and termination, and immunity and liability. Our editorial staff reviews court decisions from the past year for inclusion in the deskbook and arranges them topically so you can locate them easily. Within each chapter, the subsections contain explanatory passages to help you develop an overall understanding of the legal issues in that particular area. More importantly, each case summary has been written in everyday language, with boldface type to emphasize important facts, issues and holdings.

For your convenience, we have also included relevant provisions of the U.S. Constitution, compiled a topical list of U.S. Supreme Court decisions, and provided a Glossary of legal terms. Of course, we have also included an index at the back of the book, as well as a Table of Contents, a Table of Cases and a Table of Cases by State.

We have designed the *Deskbook Encyclopedia of Public Employment Law* to provide professionals involved in all areas of public employment law with access to important case law. Our aim has been to make the law accessible to you regardless of your level of understanding of the legal system.

Steve McEllistrem, Esq.
Senior Legal Editor
Center for Education & Employment Law

ABOUT THE EDITORS

Steve McEllistrem is the senior legal editor at the Center for Education & Employment Law. He is a co-author of *Students with Disabilities and Special Education Law* and *Higher Education Law in America*, and is the former managing editor of the monthly newsletter *Special Education Law Update*. He graduated *cum laude* from William Mitchell College of Law and received his undergraduate degree from the University of Minnesota. Mr. McEllistrem is admitted to the Minnesota Bar.

Thomas D'Agostino is a managing editor at the Center for Education & Employment Law and is the editor of *Higher Education Legal Alert* and *School Safety & Security Alert*. He graduated from the Duquesne University School of Law and received his undergraduate degree from Ramapo College of New Jersey. He is a past member of the American Bar Association's Section of Individual Rights and Responsibilities as well as the Pennsylvania Bar Association's Legal Services to Persons with Disabilities Committee. Mr. D'Agostino is admitted to the Pennsylvania bar.

Laurel Kalser is the editor of the monthly newsletters *Employment Law Report* and *Public Employment Law Report*. Ms. Kalser graduated *cum laude* from the University of Pennsylvania, and received her law degree from the University of Miami in Coral Gables, Florida, where she was a member of the Moot Court Board for outstanding appellate advocacy. Ms. Kalser is admitted to the Florida Bar.

Curt J. Brown is the Group Publisher of the Center for Education & Employment Law. Prior to assuming his present position, he gained extensive experience in business-to-business publishing, including management of well-known publications such as *What's Working in Human Resources*, *What's New in Benefits & Compensation*, *Keep Up to Date with Payroll*, *Supervisors Legal Update*, and *Facility Manager's Alert*. Mr. Brown graduated from Villanova University School of Law and graduated *magna cum laude* from Bloomsburg University with a B.S. in Business Administration. He is admitted to the Pennsylvania bar.

HOW TO USE YOUR DESKBOOK

We have designed your *Deskbook Encyclopedia of Public Employment Law* in an accessible format for both attorneys and non-attorneys to use as a research and reference tool toward prevention of legal problems.

Research Tool

As a research tool, our deskbook allows you to conduct your research on two different levels – by topics or by cases.

Topic Research

◆ If you have a general interest in a particular **topic** area, our **table of contents** provides descriptive section headings with detailed subheadings for each chapter.

> ✓ For your convenience, we also include the chapter table of contents at the beginning of each chapter.

Example:
For information on protected speech, the table of contents indicates that a discussion of that subject takes place in Chapter Three under the section heading, Freedom of Speech, and begins on page 183. The table also shows that protected speech has been divided into subheadings.

I. FREEDOM OF SPEECH 177
   A. Supreme Court Cases 178
   B. The *Garcetti v. Ceballos* Issue. 181
➔ C. Protected Speech 183
      1. Matters of Public Concern. 184
      2. Speaker's Interest Outweighs
         Government's Interest. 186
      3. Speech Reporting Criminal Activity 190

HOW TO USE YOUR DESKBOOK

◆ If you have a specific interest in a particular **issue**, our comprehensive **index** collects all of the relevant page references to particular issues.

> **Example:**
> For cases involving harassment, the index refers you to the page numbers where that issue is discussed.
> → Harassment
>   Racial, 46-48
>   Sexual, 67-80
>   42 U.S.C. § 1983, 77-78
>   Same-sex and sexual orientation issues, 75-77
>   State statutes, 78-80

Case Research

◆ If you know the **name** of a particular case, our **table of cases** will allow you to quickly reference the location of the case.

> **Example:**
> If you wanted to look up the case *Stewart v. Evans*, you would look in the table of cases, which has been arranged alphabetically, under S.
>
> **S**
> Stevens v. Dep't of the Treasury, 10
> → Stewart v. Evans, 318
> Storm v. McClung, 308
> Stover v. Martinez, 92
> Stratman v. Brent, 212
> Stratton v. Dep't for the Aging for the City
>   of New York, 9

✓ Each of the cases summarized in the deskbook also contains the case citation, which will allow you to access the full text of the case from a law library. *See How to Read a Case Citation, p. 529.*

HOW TO USE YOUR DESKBOOK

◆ If your interest lies in cases from a **particular state**, our **table of cases by state** will identify the cases from your state and direct you to the page numbers where they are located.

> **Example:**
> If cases from Massachusetts are of interest, the table of cases by state, arranged alphabetically, lists all of the cases from Massachusetts that have been summarized in the book.
>
> **MASSACHUSETTS**
>
> Ahern v. O'Donnell, 316
> Alake v. City of Boston, 271
> Andrews v. Civil Service Comm'n, 496
> Baron v. Suffolk County Sheriff's Dep't, 300
> Belhumeur v. Labor Relations Comm'n, 454
> Bennett v. City of Holyoke, 163
> Billings v. Town of Grafton, 68
> Bogan v. Scott-Harris, 260, 261
> Bracket v. Civil Service Comm'n, 96

✓ Remember, the judicial system has two court systems – state and federal – which generally function independently of each other. *See The Judicial System, p. 525.* We have included the federal court cases in the table of cases by state according to the state in which the court resides. However, federal court decisions often impact other federal courts within that particular circuit. Therefore, it may be helpful to review cases from all of the states contained in a particular circuit.

Reference Tool

As a reference tool, the deskbook includes information of a general nature that can be helpful in determining legal rights and responsibilities. For example:

◆ **Appendix A** contains provisions of the **U.S. Constitution** that are relevant to employment law. The Commerce Clause, for instance, located on page 511, grants Congress the right to regulate commerce and is the source of power for most of the laws enacted by the legislature.

HOW TO USE YOUR DESKBOOK

◆ **Appendix B** contains a list of recent and important **U.S. Supreme Court employment cases**. The cases are arranged by subject matter and have been placed in reverse chronological order (from newest to oldest).

We hope you benefit from the use of your *Deskbook Encyclopedia of Public Employment Law*. If you have any questions about how to use the book, please contact Steve McEllistrem at smcellistrem@pbp.com.

TABLE OF ABBREVIATIONS

The following abbreviations are used in your *Deskbook Encyclopedia of Public Employment Law*.

ADA – Americans with Disabilities Act

ADEA – Age Discrimination in Employment Act

ALJ – Administrative Law Judge

BFOQ – bona fide occupational qualification

CBA – collective bargaining agreement

DOL – Department of Labor

DOT – Department of Transportation

DUI – driving under the influence

EEO – equal employment opportunity

EEOC – Equal Employment Opportunity Commission

EPA – Equal Pay Act

ERISA – Employee Retirement Income Security Act

FBI – Federal Bureau of Investigation

FDIC – Federal Deposit Insurance Corporation

FLSA – Fair Labor Standards Act

FMLA – Family and Medical Leave Act

FTCA – Federal Tort Claims Act

HIPAA – Health Insurance Portability and Accountability Act

HR – human resources

HUD – U.S. Department of Housing and Urban Development

IRS – Internal Revenue Service

OSHA – Occupational Safety and Health Administration

OWBPA – Older Workers Benefit Protection Act

USERRA – Uniformed Services Employment and Reemployment Rights Act

VA – Veterans Affairs

TABLE OF CASES

A

AARP v. EEOC, 377, 412
Abbamont v. Piscataway Board of Educ., 173
Abendschein v. Montgomery County, Maryland, 436
Aberle v. City of Aberdeen, 126
Abernathy v. City of Albany, Georgia, 390
Abrahamson v. Board of Educ. of Wappingers Falls Cent. School Dist., 379
Acton v. City of Columbia, 428
Adair v. Charter County of Wayne, 433
Adair v. City of Kirkland, 431
Adams v. City of Norfolk, 425
Adams v. Rice, 18
Adarand Constructors, Inc. v. Pena, 94
AFSCME Local 2623 v. Dep't of Corrections, 342
AFSCME v. City of Benton, 369
AFSCME, Council 17 v. State of Louisiana, 133
AFSCME, Council 4, Local 1565 v. Dep't of Correction, 134
Agwiak v. U.S., 438
Ahalt v. Montgomery County, Maryland, 368
Ahart v. Dep't of Corrections, 340
Ahern v. O'Donnell, 316
Akers v. Caperton, 224
Akins v. Fulton County, 204, 273
Alake v. City of Boston, 271
Alden v. Maine, 252
Alderfer v. Board of Trustees of Edwards County Hospital and Healthcare Center, 108
Alderman by Alderman v. U.S., 305
Allegheny County Airport Authority v. Construction General Laborers and Material Handlers Union, 150
Allen v. Board of Public Educ. for Bibb County, 439
Allen v. City of Pocahontas, 197
Allison-LeBlanc v. Louisiana Dep't of Public Safety, 67
Almerico v. Harahan Municipal Fire and Police Civil Service Board, 153
Altamore v. Barrios-Paoli, 478
Altman v. Minnesota Dep't of Corrections, 241
Amalgamated Transit Union Local 757 v. Tri-County Metropolitan Transportation Dist., 346
American Federation of Government Employees Local 1 v. Stone, 207
American Federation of Government Employees v. Derwinski, 329
American Federation of Government Employees v. Roberts, 341
American Federation of Government Employees v. Skinner, 328
American Federation of Government Employees v. Sullivan, 332
American Federation of Government Employees, AFL-CIO v. Dep't of Housing & Urban Development, 248
American Federation of Government Employees, National Veterans Affairs Council 53 v. FLRA, 461
Americanos v. Carter, 223
Anchorage Police Dep't Employees Ass'n v. Municipality of Anchorage, 326
Anderson v. Bessemer City, 55
Anderson v. Burke County, 197
Anderson v. Creighton, 263
Anderson v. Dep't of Public Safety and Corrections, 313
Anderson v. Independent School Dist., 211
Anderson v. North Dakota State Hospital, 19
Anderson v. Sedgwick County, 490
Andrews v. Anne Arundel County, Maryland, 357
Andrews v. Civil Service Comm'n, 496
Aneja v. Triborough Bridge and Tunnel Authority, 425
Angara v. City of Chicago, 317
Angell v. The Union Fire Dist. of South Kingstown, 391
Ansonia Board of Educ. v. Philbrook, 83
Antisdel v. City of Oak Creek Police & Fire Comm'n, 118
Antonelli v. State of New Jersey, 49
Apgar v. State Employees' Retirement System, 363
Aponte v. U.S. Dep't of Treasury, 412
Appeal of Barry, 370
Appeal of City of Portsmouth, Board of Fire Commissioners, 456
Appeal of Hillsboro-Deering School Dist., 462
Appeal of Merrimack County Board of Commissioners, 469
Appeal of Nashua Police Comm'n, 458
Appelbaum v. Milwaukee Metropolitan Sewerage Dist., 8
Appleton v. Stonington Board of Educ., 292
Arkansas Dep't of Correction v. Holybee, 399
Arline v. School Board of Nassau County, 18
Arraleh v. County of Ramsey, 51
Ascolese v. SEPTA, 89
Ash v. Tyson Foods, Inc., 42
Ass'n for Los Angeles Deputy Sheriffs v. County of Los Angeles, 372
Ass'n of Cleveland Firefighters v. City of Cleveland, Ohio, 492
Atterberry v. Sherman, 120
Auction v. City of Clarksville, 47
Auer v. Robbins, 424, 426, 427

B

Backlund v. Hessen, 491
Baggett v. Bullitt, 231

TABLE OF CASES

Bahr v. Council Bluffs Civil Service Comm'n, 505
Bailey v. Dep't of Public Safety and Corrections, 156
Baker v. City of Detroit, 282
Baker v. Runyon, 256
Balint v. Carson City, Nevada, 86
Ballerino v. WCAB, 369
Balton v. City of Milwaukee, 209
Bannister v. Dep't of Streets, 139
Baqir v. Principi, 52
Barbera v. New York City Employees' Retirement System, 371
Barefield v. Village of Winnetka, 432
Barnes v. Gorman, 291
Barnes v. U.S., 303
Barnette v. Chertoff, 4
Barney v. Haveman, 379
Barnhart v. Thomas, 364
Barnthouse v. City of Edmond, 474
Baron v. City of Highland Park, 9
Baron v. Suffolk County Sheriff's Dep't, 300
Barr v. Crosson, 445
Barr v. Great Falls Int'l Airport, 244
Barrow v. Greenville Independent School Dist., 240
Barrows v. Wiley, 124
Bartlik v. U.S. Dep't of Labor, 166
Bass v. Florida Dep't of Law Enforcement, 348
Bass v. Potter, 404
Bates v. Dep't of Corrections of Kansas, 437
Bauers v. City of Lincoln, 355
Beadle v. City of Tampa, 86
Beardsley v. Webb, 78
Beck v. City of Cleveland, 433
Becker v. City of New York, 359
Beckley v. Crabtree, 309
Beecham v. Henderson County, 207
Belhumeur v. Labor Relations Comm'n, 454
Bellevue John Does 1-11 v. Bellevue School Dist. 405, 442
Benn v. First Judicial Dist. of Pennsylvania, 26
Bennett v. City of Holyoke, 163
Bennett v. Watters, 5
Benningfield v. City of Houston, 191
Benshoff v. City of Virginia Beach, 421
Benson v. New York State Dep't of Civil Service, 476
Berini v. Federal Reserve Bank of St. Louis, 380
Berry v. Dep't of Social Services, 195
Berube v. Conley, 306
Bessard v. California Community Colleges, 232
Beyer v. County of Nassau, 56
Billings v. Town of Grafton, 68
Billings v. U.S., 440
Birch v. Cuyahoga County Probate Court, 64
Bisbal-Ramos v. City of Mayaguez, 229
Bishop v. Wood, 116

Bivens v. Six Unknown Named Agents of Federal Bureau of Narcotics, 292
Bivens v. Trent, 182
Bizzarro v. Miranda, 154
Blair v. City of Pomona, 190
Blake v. Wright, 246
Blakey v. U.S.S. Iowa, 305
Blanken v. Ohio Dep't of Rehabilitation & Correction, 235
Blizzard v. Dalton, 500
Block v. Orange County Employees Retirement System, 411
Boaden v. Dep't of Law Enforcement, 509
Board of County Commissioners of Bryan County v. Brown, 253
Board of Regents v. Roth, 115, 116
Board of Trustees of Univ. of Alabama v. Garrett, 17
Boddie v. City of Columbus, Mississippi, 218
Bogan v. Scott-Harris, 260, 261
Bolden v. State of Washington Dep't of Transportation, 389
Bolton v. City of Dallas, 124
Bond v. Sheahan, 32
Bonner v. County of San Diego, 484
Booker v. City of St. Louis, 334
Borough of Ellwood City v. Pennsylvania Labor Relations Board, 460
Borough of Glassboro v. Fraternal Order of Police Lodge No. 108, 492
Borough of Heidelberg v. Workers' Compensation Appeal Board (Selva), 398
Borough of Lewistown v. Pennsylvania Labor Relations Board, 468
Borough of Wilkinsburg v. Colella, 474
Botke v. Chippewa County, 396
Bottari v. Sarasota Springs City School Dist., 151
Bourdais v. New Orleans, 98
Bowen v. U.S. Postal Service, 448
Boyd v. Constantine, 113
Boyle v. Maryland-National Capital Park and Planning Comm'n, 501
Bracket v. Civil Service Comm'n, 96
Braddy v. Florida Dep't of Labor and Employment Security, 266
Bradshaw v. School Board of Broward County, Florida, 78
Brady v. Dep't of Personnel, 477
Bragdon v. Abbott, 18
Brame v. Western State Hospital, 392
Brandon v. City of Providence, 265
Brazil v. U.S. Dep't of Navy, 175
Breitigan v. New Castle County, 377
Brennan v. Norton, 164
Bridenbaugh v. O'Bannon, 500
Brimage v. City of Boston, 306
Bristol County Retirement Board v. Contributory Retirement Appeal Board, 358
Brittel v. Dep't of Correction, 79

TABLE OF CASES

Brockman v. Snow, 66
Brockman v. Wyoming DFS, 255
Broderick v. Donaldson, 92
Brodie v. WCAB, 397
Brotherhood of Midwest Guardians v. City of Omaha, 101
Brouwer v. Metropolitan Dade County, 422
Brown v. Bryan County, 253
Brown v. Dep't of Health and Rehabilitative Services, 283
Brown v. Dep't of Navy, 157
Brown v. New Mexico State Personnel Office, 125
Brown v. Snow, 58
BRV, Inc. v. Superior Court, 442
Buffalo Teachers Federation v. Tobe, 458
Buford v. Runyon, 449
Bulloch v. City of Pascagoula, 141
Bunch v. Board of Review, 384
Burcham v. City of Van Buren, 476
Burella v. City of Philadelphia, 274
Burka v. New York City Transit Authority, 344
Burke v. Utah Transit Authority and Local 382, 448
Burke-Fowler v. Orange County, Florida, 508
Burkett v. Wicomico County, 117
Burks v. Wisconsin Dep't of Transportation, 45
Burlington Northern and Santa Fe Railway Co. v. White, 88
Burrell v. City of Mattoon, 472
Burrus v. Vegliante, 228
Burton v. Hillsborough County, Florida, 437
Burton v. Town of Littleton, 122
Busbee v. State of Florida, 362
Butera v. District of Columbia, 298
Butler v. Alabama Dep't of Transportation, 42
Buzzi v. Gomez, 269
Bybee v. State of Idaho, Industrial Special Indemnity Fund, 391
Bynum v. City of Magee, Mississippi, 284
Byrd v. City of Philadelphia, 43

C

Caggiano v. Fontoura, 104
Cain v. Jefferson Parish Dep't of Fleet Management, 347
Calhoun v. Commissioner of Baltimore Police, 506
California Correctional Peace Officers Ass'n v. Schwarzenegger, 486
Callison v. City of Philadelphia, 405
Calovecchi v. Michigan, 388
Canfield v. West Virginia Division of Corrections, 373
Capobianco v. City of New York, 19
Carberry v. State of New Jersey, Division of State Police, 397
Cardenas v. Massey, 53

Carleton v. Massachusetts, 27
Carlow v. Mruk, 260
Carlucci v. Doe, 174
Carney v. City of Shawnee, Kansas, 203
Carpenter v. City & County of Denver, Colorado, 427
Carr v. City of Fort Worth, 472
Carreon v. Illinois Dep't of Human Services, 200
Carriero v. Borough of Naugatuck, 412
Carroll v. City of Westminster, 339
Carver v. Sheriff of La Salle County, 292
Casamasino v. City of Jersey City, 131
Casey v. Town of Portsmouth, 4
Cash v. Granville County Board of Educ., 440
Cassimy v. Board of Educ. of Rockford Public Schools, 21
Castellano v. Board of Trustees of Police Officers' Variable Supplements Fund, 416
Catletti v. Rampe, 188
CBOCS West, Inc. v. Humphries, 42
Cedeno v. Montclair State Univ., 152
Centola v. Potter, 76
Central State Univ. v. American Ass'n of Univ. Professors, CSU Chapter, 460
Cepero-Rivera v. Fagundo, 170
Chan v. Wodnicki, 270
Chandler v. Miller, 323
Charles v. Grief, 181
Chen v. County of Orange, 508
Chenoweth v. Hillsborough County, 22
Chesler v. City of Derby, 386
Chevron U.S.A. v. Echazabal, 26
Chicago Teachers Union v. Hudson, 453
Chrisanthis v. County of Atlantic, 79
Christensen v. Harris County, 432
Chubb v. City of Omaha, 409
Chudasama v. Metropolitan Government of Nashville and Davidson County, 307
Cicchetti v. Morris County Sheriff's Office, 102
City of Belvidere v. Illinois State Labor Relations Board, 488
City of Boerne, Texas v. Flores, 232
City of Boston v. Labor Relations Comm'n, 459
City of Cedar Rapids v. Board of Trustees, 367
City of Cincinnati v. Dixon, 238
City of Delray Beach v. Professional Firefighters, 459
City of East Providence v. United Steelworkers of America, Local 15509, 109
City of El Paso v. Higginbotham, 264
City of Erie v. Workers' Compensation Appeal Board, 398
City of Fort Wayne v. Moore, 289
City of Hialeah v. Rojas, 104
City of Hildalgo v. Prado, 269
City of Kansas City v. Arthur, 494
City of Kissimmee v. Dickson, 396
City of Lawrence v. Civil Service Comm'n, 475

TABLE OF CASES

City of Los Angeles Dep't of Water v. Manhart, 414
City of Midwest City, Oklahoma v. Public Employees Relations Board, 461
City of Muskogee v. Grayson, 483
City of Newark v. Newark Council 21, 485
City of Odessa, Texas v. Barton, 129
City of Palo Alto v. SEIU, Local 715, 467
City of Philadelphia v. WCAB (Cospelich), 387
City of Philadelphia v. WCAB, 389
City of Pittsburgh v. Bachner, 473
City of Pittsburgh v. Brentley, 138
City of Richmond v. J.A. Croson Co., 93
City of San Diego v. Roe, 194
City of St. Louis v. Praprotnik, 294
City of Sweetwater Florida v. St. Germain, 507
City of Thornton v. Replogle, 372
City of Virginia Beach v. Harris, 171
City of Woonsocket v. Int'l Brotherhood of Police Officers, 353
Civil Service Comm'n v. City of Kelso, 135
Clamor v. U.S., 304
Clark County School Dist. v. Breeden, 88
Clark v. Alston, 508
Clark v. Riverview Fire Protection Dist., 103
Clark v. State of Idaho, 118
Clay v. City of Cedar Rapids, 154
Cleburne County Comm'n v. Norton, 444
Cleveland Board of Educ. v. LaFleur, 66
Cleveland Board of Educ. v. Loudermill, 107
Cleveland Branch, NAACP v. City of Parma, 494
Cleveland Police Patrolmen's Ass'n v. City of Cleveland, 470
Cleveland v. City of Elmendorf, Texas, 439
Cleveland v. City of Los Angeles, 428
Clifton v. Massachusetts Bay Transportation Authority, 103
Clue v. Johnson, 216
Coahoma County v. Mississippi Employment Security Comm'n, 383
Coastal Florida Police Benevolent Ass'n v. Williams, 455
Coats v. City of Columbus, 284
Cobb v. Pozzi, 215
Coddington v. Evanko, 318
Coffey v. Chattanooga-Hamilton County Hospital Authority, 171
Coker v. McFaul, 406
Coleman v. Lane, 303
Coleman v. Loudoun, 43
Collins v. City of Harker Heights, 294
Collins v. City of Manchester, 446
Communication Workers of America v. Ector County Hospital Dist., 234
Comwlth. of Kentucky v. Gobert, 485
Comwlth. of Pennsylvania v. PLRB, 461
Comwlth. of Pennsylvania, Dep't of Corrections v. Krempowsky, 479

Comwlth., Justice and Public Safety Cabinet, Dep't of Corrections v. Searcy, 142
Comwlth., Labor Cabinet v. Hasken, 427
Cone v. Nevada Service Employees Union, 449
Conner v. City of Forest Acres, 170
Connick v. Myers, 178, 180
Conroy v. New York State Dep't of Corrections, 26
Cook County v. U.S. ex rel. Chandler, 254
Cook v. Gwinnett County School Dist., 273
Coolidge v. Consolidated City of Indianapolis and Marion County, 69
Cooper v. City of New York, 288
Cooper v. Federal Reserve Bank of Richmond, 49
Cooper v. Lee County Board of Supervisors, 222
Cooper v. Smith, 191
Copeland v. County of Macon, 289
Correctional Services Corp. v. Malesko, 292
Corvelli v. Board of Trustees, 363
Cossifos v. New York and Local Employees' Retirement System, 366
Costilla v. State of Minnesota, 80
Cotarelo v. Village of Sleepy Hollow Police Dep't, 184
Council 13 v. Comwlth. of Pennsylvania, 421
Counts v. South Carolina Electric & Gas Co., 425
County of Cook v. Licensed Practical Nurses Ass'n of Illinois, 463
County of Sacramento v. AFSCME Local 146, 464
County of Sacramento v. Lewis, 295
County of Washington v. Gunther, 63
Cowles v. State of Alaska, 318
Cox v. Mississippi Dep't of Corrections, 145
Cragg v. City of Osawatomie, Kansas, 226
Cramp v. Board of Public Instruction of Orange County, 231
Crawford v. City of Fairburn, 91
Crawford v. Metropolitan Government of Nashville, 87
Crawford-El v. Britton, 295
Cripe v. City of San Jose, 24
Criscolo v. Vagianelis, 483
Cross v. New York City Transit Authority, 7
Crumpacker v. State of Kansas Dep't of Human Resources, 57
Cruz-Gomez v. Rivera-Hernandez, 484
Cudd v. Aldrich, 222
Cullen v. Retirement Board of Policeman's Annuity and Benefit Fund, 363
Cullom v. Brown, 46
Culton v. Missouri Dep't of Corrections, 89
Cummings v. Connell, 453
Cunliffe v. Industrial Claims Appeals Office, 382
Curinga v. City of Clairton, 221
Curlee v. Kootenai County Fire & Rescue, 166
Cutler v. Dorn, 81

TABLE OF CASES

D

D'Amico v. City of New York, 36
Daily Gazette Co. v. City of Schenectady, 443
Daleiden v. Jefferson County Joint School Dist., 392
Damiano v. Contributory Retirement Appeal Board, 352
Danahy v. Buscaglia, 267
Daniel v. Michigan Dep't of Corrections, 385
Daniels v. City of Arlington, 201
Danskine v. Miami-Dade County Fire Dep't, 95
Dargis v. Sheahan, 23
Dark v. Curry County, 34
Davenport v. Washington Educ. Ass'n, 452
Davidson v. City of Elkhart, Indiana, 199
Davidson v. Office of Employee Appeals, 135
Davis v. Indiana State Police, 11
Davis v. Lambert-St. Louis Int'l Airport, 264
Davis v. Michigan Dep't of Treasury, 416
Davis v. Workers' Compensation Appeals Board, 385
Davoll v. Webb, 33
De Franks v. City of Buffalo, 495
Decker v. Campus, 299
DeCorte v. Jordan, 98
DeLaMater v. Marion Civil Service Comm'n, 477
Delaraba v. Nassau County Police Dep't, 332
Delaware County Lodge No. 27, Fraternal Order of Police v. Township of Tinicum, 109
DeLisa v. County of Bergen, 168
DeMaagd v. City of Southfield, 167
Demoret v. Zegarelli, 74
Demos v. City of Indianapolis, 429
Denhof v. City of Grand Rapids, 90
Denton v. Civil Service Comm'n of the State of Illinois, 498
Dep't of Business and Professional Regulation v. Doyle, 145
Dep't of Corrections, SCI-Camp Hill v. Unemployment Compensation Board of Review, 381
Dep't of Public Safety and Correctional Services v. Palmer, 435
Dep't of the Navy v. Egan, 173, 175
Dep't of Transportation v. Comm'n on Human Rights, 45
Dermott Special School Dist. v. Johnson, 257
Deschenie v. Board of Educ., 204
DeShaney v. Winnebago County DSS, 268, 280
DeVeaux v. City of Philadelphia, 239
DeVittorio v. Hall, 317
Devoney v. Retirement Board of Policemen's Annuity & Benefit Fund, 362
Dew v. City of Scappoose, 184
Dewey v. Tacoma School Dist., 169
Dibble v. City of Chandler, 194
Diesel v. Town of Lewisboro, 157
Dillon v. Maryland-National Capital Park and Planning Comm'n, 402
Dinsdale v. Comwlth., 262
Dishon v. Maine State Retirement System, 413
District of Columbia v. Tarlosky, 415
Dobbins v. County of San Diego Civil Service Comm'n, 120
Dodaro v. Village of Glendale Heights, 404
Doe v. Cheney, 174
Doe v. City of Stamford, 399
Doe v. Dep't of Mental Health, Mental Retardation, and Substance Abuse Services, 248
Doe v. Gates, 174
Doe v. Southeastern Pennsylvania Transportation Authority, 250
Doe v. U.S. Postal Service, 245
Doe v. U.S., 433, 439
Doherty v. Retirement Board of Medford, 362
Dominguez-Curry v. Nevada Dep't of Transportation, 58
Donaldson v. Taylor, 375
Donovan v. Broward County Board of County Commissioners, 89
Dorris v. Absher, 247
Dothard v. Rawlinson, 61
Downey v. Strain, 404
Drake v. County of Essex, 341
Draper v. Logan County Public Library, 233
Draper v. Walsh, 278
Duffey v. Bryant, 278
Dumont v. Administrative Officer, 14
Duncan v. Kelly, 132
Duncan v. WMATA, 21
Dunn v. Telfair County, 256
Dunn v. Washington County Hospital, 70
Dupont v. Commissioners of Essex County, 160
Durgins v. City of East St. Louis, Illinois, 201
Dwan v. City of Boston, 279
Dykes v. Southeastern Pennsylvania Transportation Authority, 343
Dyson v. California State Personnel Board, 321

E

Eaves v. Florida Division of Retirement, 354
Edelman v. Lynchburg College, 102
Edgerton v. State Personnel Board, 342
Edwards v. City of Goldsboro, 190, 503
EEOC v. Baltimore County, 377
EEOC v. Board of Regents of Univ. of Wisconsin System, 12
EEOC v. City of Independence, 11
EEOC v. Comwlth. of Massachusetts, 378
EEOC v. Liberal R-II School Dist., 8
EEOC v. Union Independente de la Autoridad de Acueductos y Alcantarillados de Puerto Rico, 84

TABLE OF CASES

EEOC v. Waffle House, Inc., 101
Ehlers v. Jackson County Sheriff's Merit Comm'n, 137
Eich v. Board of Regents for Cent. Missouri State Univ., Dep't of Public Safety, 70
El v. Southeastern Pennsylvania Transportation Authority, 44
Elfbrandt v. Russell, 232
Elgabi v. Toledo Area Regional Transit Authority, 51
Elliott v. Maryland Dep't of Human Resources, 43
Ellis v. Sheahan, 301
Elmore v. Cleary, 129
Elrod v. Burns, 220
Elsensohn v. St. Tammany Parish Sheriff's Office, 409
Elvin v. Oregon Public Employees Union, 454
Employees' Retirement System of Georgia v. Melton, 444
Employers Insurance Co. of Nevada v. Daniels, 386
Employment Division, Dep't of Human Resources of Oregon v. Smith, 238, 239
Endres v. Indiana State Police, 84
Engber v. New York State Comptroller, 352
Engel v. Rapid City School Dist., 69
Engquist v. Oregon Dep't of Agriculture, 102, 117
Enriquez v. West Jersey Health Systems, 38
Epperson v. Utah State Retirement Board, 354
Epps v. City of Pine Lawn, 257
Etsitty v. Utah Transit Authority, 61
Etter v. Spencer, 121
Evans v. City of Bishop, 8
Evans v. Port Authority of New York and New Jersey, 49
Everson v. Michigan Dep't of Corrections, 61

F

Faculty Rights Coalition v. Shahrokhi, 195
Fain v. Wayne County Auditor's Office, 410
Fairfax County Fire and Rescue Dep't v. Mottram, 387
Falken v. Glynn County, 430
Faragher v. City of Boca Raton, 73
Farm Labor Organizing Committee v. Ohio State Highway Patrol, 268
Fazio v. City and County of San Francisco, 223
FDIC v. Meyer, 253
Feingold v. State of New York, 81
Feliciano v. City of Cleveland, 350
Feola v. Carroll, 147
Fernandez v. New York State and Local Retirement Systems, 358
Fettke v. City of Wichita, 247
Fewer v. City and County of San Francisco, 119

Fielder v. Stonack, 308
Fincher v. State of Georgia, 247
First v. Stark County Board of Commissioners, 315
Fitzpatrick v. City of Atlanta, 237
Flaherty v. Giambra, 444
Flechsig v. U.S., 304
Florian v. State Civil Service Comm'n, 151
Floyd v. Missouri Dep't of Social Services, 54
Fontaine v. Clermont County Board of Commissioners, 323
Ford v. West, 48
Forest Service Employees for Environmental Ethics v. U.S. Forest Service, 243
Foster v. Mahdesian, 453
Fowler v. Unemployment Appeals Comm'n, 346
Fox v. District of Columbia, 191
Fraternal Order of Police v. City of Newark, 85
Fraternal Order of Police v. Mayor and City Council of Ocean City Maryland, 218
Fraternal Order of Police v. Williams, 160
Fraternal Order of Police, Montgomery County Lodge No. 35 v. Mehrling, 502
Frazier v. Badger, 266
Frazier v. Simmons, 24
Freeman v. Fallin, 323
Freitag v. Ayers, 69
Fryman v. Harrison, 283
Fuerschbach v. Southwest Airlines, 277
Funderburke v. New York State Dep't of Civil Service, 365

G

Gabriele v. Metropolitan Suburban Bus Authority, 491
Galdamez v. Potter, 47
Gallagher v. Manatee County, 254
Galli v. New Jersey Meadowlands Comm'n, 225
Galvin v. State of Washington, Employment Security Dep't, 384
Gamble v. Gregg County, 375
Garcetti v. Ceballos, 119, 181, 183
Garcia v. City of Albuquerque, 140
Garcia v. Kankakee County Housing Authority, 197
Garcia v. San Antonio Metropolitan Transit Authority, 420
Gardner v. Insura Property and Casualty Insurance Co., 280
Garner v. Missouri Dep't of Health, 44
Garraghty v. Comwlth. of Virginia, 126
Garrett v. Univ. of Alabama at Birmingham Board of Trustees, 20
Gasser v. District of Columbia, 27
Genas v. State of New York Correctional Services, 242
General Dynamics Land Systems, Inc. v. Cline, 3

TABLE OF CASES

Gentilli v. Board of Police and Fire Commissioners, 148
Gentry v. Lowndes County, Mississippi, 225
George v. Dep't of Fire, 337
George v. Fairfield Metropolitan Housing Authority, 489
Gierschick v. State Employees' Retirement Board, 362
Gilbert v. Dep't of Corrections, 384
Gilbert v. Homar, 107
Gilbrook v. City of Westminster, 189
Gillis v. Georgia Dep't of Corrections, 45
Giordano v. City of New York, 30
Glover v. City of North Charleston, South Carolina, 422
Gobin v. New York City Health and Hospitals Corp., 52
Goldstein v. Chestnut Ridge Volunteer Fire Co., 302
Golembiewski v. City of Milwaukee, 494
Gomez v. Toledo, 262
Goncalves v. City of Boston, 472
Goncalves v. Labor Relations Comm'n, 450
Gonzalez v. Florida Dep't of Highway Safety, 53
Gordon v. Brown, 348
Gorski v. New Hampshire Dep't of Corrections, 71
Gossmeyer v. McDonald, 316
Gouveia v. Sears, 490
Govea v. City of Norcross, 289
Grabicki v. Dep't of Retirement Systems, 360
Graham v. City of Philadelphia, 123
Grandville Municipal Executive Ass'n v. City of Grandville, 456
Grantham v. Trickey, 206
Gray v. Marinette County, 450
Greater Community Hospital v. PERB, 466
Grech v. Clayton County, 296
Green Township Educ. Ass'n v. Rowe, 198
Green v. Board of County Commissioners, 183
Green v. City of St. Louis, 162
Green v. City of Wichita, 398
Green v. State of California, 38
Greer v. Amesqua, 198
Greer v. Board of Educ., 50
Griffin v. City of Opa-Locka, 72
Griffin v. Kemper County School Dist., 128
Griffis v. Pinal County, 243
Griffith v. Lanier, 455
Grossman v. South Shore Public School Dist., 239
Gu v. Boston Police Dep't, 60
Guilloty Perez v. Pieluisi, 164
Guiney v. Police Commissioner of Boston, 332
Gummo v. Village of Depew, New York, 500
Gunter v. Morrison, 186
Gurnari v. Luzerne County Housing Authority, 254
Gusewelle v. City of Wood River, 493
Gustafson v. Jones, 121

H

Haas v. San Bernardino County, 114
Haber v. Evans, 245
Hack v. Gillespie, 288
Haddon v. Executive Residence at the White House, 196
Hadfield v. McDonough, 220
Hafer v. Melo, 263
Haines v. Fisher, 290
Hale v. Mann, 256
Hall v. Johnson, 350
Hamera v. County of Berks, 81
Hamilton County Sheriff v. State Employment Relations Board, 462
Hammer v. City of Osage Beach, 211
Hammond v. Monmouth County Sheriff's Dep't, 111
Hamner v. St. Vincent Hospital & Health Care Center, 76
Hanger v. Lake County, Minnesota, 408
Hanrahan v. City of Atlanta, 503
Hansen v. California Dep't of Corrections, 335
Hanson v. Hancock County Memorial Hospital, 249
Hardeman v. City of Albuquerque, 186
Harden v. Ohio Attorney General, 374
Hardy v. City of Berkeley, 118
Harlow v. Fitzgerald, 258
Harman v. City of New York, 193
Harmon v. Thornburgh, 333
Harrell v. U.S. Postal Service, 405
Harris v. Beedle, 204
Hart v. City of Little Rock, 275
Hartsfield v. Miami-Dade County, 32
Hassan v. City of Minneapolis, 268
Hassler v. State Retirement Comm'n, 368
Hawkins v. Holloway, 276
Hayes v. North State Law Enforcement Officers Ass'n, 100
Haynes v. City of Circleville, Ohio, 183
Haynes v. Police Board of Chicago, 155
Haynes v. Williams, 19
Haynie v. State, 38
Heckmann v. City of Detroit, 162
Henry v. Jones, 43
Henry v. Oklahoma County Board of County Commissioners, 205
Herman v. City of Allentown, 37
Herman v. Dep't of Justice, 165
Hervey v. County of Koochiching, 56
Hess v. Port Authority Trans-Hudson Corp., 253
Hesse v. Town of Jackson, Wyoming, 271
Hester v. City of Flint, 166
Hetman v. State Civil Service Comm'n, 227

TABLE OF CASES

Heuton v. Anderson, 304
Hicks v. St. Mary's Honor Center, 41
Hill v. City of Scranton, 493
Hill v. KCATA, 35
Hiller v. County of Suffolk, 50
Hillig v. Rumsfeld, 93
Hinshaw v. Smith, 195
Hoffler v. State of Colorado, 152
Holiday v. City of Chattanooga, 20
Holland v. City of Chicago, 415
Holloman v. Greater Cleveland Regional Transit Authority, 337
Holt v. Albemarle Regional Health Services Board, 167
Hopp v. City of Pittsburgh, 95
Houston Police Officers Union v. City of Houston, 434
Howard County Police Officers Ass'n, Inc. v. Howard County, 502
Hoyt v. Andreucci, 215
Hudson v. City of Chicago, 109
Huff v. DeKalb County, 424
Hufford v. McEnaney, 189
Hughes v. City of North Olmsted, 250

I

I.B.E.W., Local 1245 v. Skinner, 329
IAFF, Local 3808 v. Kansas City, 208
Ieyoub v. Polito, 503
Imada v. City of Hercules, California, 438
In re Amalgamated Transit Union, Local 717, 127
In re City of Manchester, 135
In re Code Enforcement Officer, 482
In re Exeter Police Ass'n, 137
In re Hruska, 474
In re Lincoln-Woodstock Cooperative School Dist., 136
In re Martinez, 473
In re New Hampshire Dep't of HHS, 388
In re Queen, 141
In re Subryan, 144
In re Tulko, 475
Ingram v. County of Bucks, 436
Int'l Ass'n of Fire Fighters, Local 2665 v. City of Clayton, 355
Int'l Ass'n of Fire Fighters, Local 27 v. City of Seattle, 356
Int'l Ass'n of Firefighters, Local No. 64 v. City of Kansas City, 415
Int'l Union v. Winters, 330
Inturri v. City of Hartford, 234
Irby v. Bittick, 65

J

Jackson v. City of Chicago, 23
Jackson v. County of Racine, 74
Jackson v. Gates, 340
Jackson v. Hudspeth Mental Retardation Center, 156
Jackson v. Retirement Board, 370
James v. Tablerion, 148
Jana-Rock Construction, Inc. v. New York State Dep't of Economic Development, 94
Jankovitz v. Des Moines Independent Community School Dist., 352
Jaramillo v. City of Albuquerque, 324
Jaramillo v. Colorado Judicial Dep't, 60
Jaso v. Travis County Juvenile Board, 6
Jennings v. State of Illinois Dep't of Corrections, 51
Jensen v. Henderson, 104
Johanson v. Dep't of Social & Health Services, 486
Johnson v. Labor & Industry Review Comm'n, 13
Johnson v. Lodge #93 of the Fraternal Order of Police, 49
Johnson v. Rumsfeld, 90
Johnson v. State of Minnesota, 283
Johnson v. Transportation Agency, Santa Clara County, 96
Johnson v. Unified Government of Wyandotte County/Kansas City, Kansas, 421
Johnson v. Univ. of Iowa State Board of Regents, 59
Jones v. Board of Trustees of the Police Pension Fund, 365
Jones v. City of Houston, 481
Jones v. Denver Public Schools, 403
Jones v. Johanns, 91
Jones v. Kerrville State Hospital, 35
Jones v. Reynolds, 280
Jones v. Smith, 501
Jordan v. City of Gary, 151
Jordan v. Jones, 499
Jordan v. U.S. Postal Service, 410
Jubic v. City of Troy City Corp., 14

K

Kalina v. Fletcher, 260
Kapche v. City of San Antonio, 24
Kaplan v. City of North Las Vegas, 28
Kara B. by Albert v. Dane County, Wisconsin, 282
Karahalios v. National Federation of Federal Employees, Local 1263, 447
Kari v. City of Maplewood, 265
Kaske v. City of Rockford, 504
Katz v. Univ. of California Board of Regents, 5
Kaucher v. County of Bucks, 291
Keaveney v. Town of Brookline, 331
Keever v. City of Middletown, 33
Keller v. PERC, 498
Kelley v. Johnson, 233

TABLE OF CASES

Kelley v. Sheriff's Merit Com'n of Kane County, 504
Kells v. Town of Lincoln, 130
Kelly v. City of New Haven, 475
Kelly v. Civil Service Comm'n, 112
Kemp v. Clairborne County Hospital, 336
Kennedy v. District of Columbia, 237
Kennell v. Gates, 298
Kent v. Maryland Transportation Authority, 404
Kentucky Retirement Systems v. EEOC, 364
Keyser v. Sacramento City Unified School Dist., 205
Kidwell v. WCAB, 397
Kimel v. Florida Board of Regents, 10
Kincaid v. City of Omaha, 28
Kincel v. Pennsylvania, 392
King County v. Sheehan, 245
King v. City of Boston, 56
Kirby v. City of Elizabeth City, 201
Kirk v. City of New York, 36
Kitchings v. Jenkins, 480
Klem v. Santa Clara County, 426
Knapp v. State, Dep't of Prisons, 158
Knickerbocker v. City of Stockton, 155
Knight v. Connecticut Dep't of Health, 241
Konits v. Valley Stream Cent. High School, 185
Konno v. County of Hawaii, 487
Kosan v. Utah Dep't of Corrections, 239
Kotch v. Board of River Port Pilot Commissioners, 491
Kozisek v. County of Seward, Nebraska, 29
Krentz v. Robertson Fire Protection Dist., 110
Kreutzer v. City and County of San Francisco, 122
Krieg v. Seybold, 326, 330
Krocka v. City of Chicago, 22
Krohn v. New York City Police Dep't, 255
Krupp v. Dep't of Fire, 347
Kuhr v. City of Billings, 458
Kunzie v. City of Olivette, 257
Kupstas v. City of Greenwood, 30
Kvorjak v. Maine, 24

L

LaChance v. Erickson, 107
Lake City Police Club v. City of Oswego, 480
Lamb v. City of Decatur, Illinois, 278
Lamb v. Town of Esopus, 159
Lane v. City of LaFollette, 224
Lane v. Industrial Comm'n of Arizona, 393
Lang v. City of Omaha, 436
Langley v. Hot Spring County, Arkansas, 225
Lanman v. Johnson County, Kansas, 30
Lanman v. Oklahoma County Sheriff's Office, 395

Lapides v. Board of Regents of Univ. System of Georgia, 254
Larsen v. Municipality of Anchorage, 482
Larson v. City of Tomah, 171
Las Cruces Professional Fire Fighters v. City of Las Cruces, 463
Las Vegas Metropolitan Police Dep't v. Berni, 147
Lash v. City of Traverse City, 492
Latino Officers Ass'n City of New York v. City of New York, 235
Lawrence v. City of Philadelphia, 421
Lawson v. South Carolina Dep't of Corrections, 168
Lawson v. Umatilla County, 128
Layman v. State, 414
Leach v. Commissioner of the Massachusetts Rehabilitation Comm'n, 38
Leadbetter v. Gilley, 62
Ledbetter v. Goodyear Tire & Rubber Co., Inc., 63
Lee v. Employment Appeal Board, 382
Leeds v. Potter, 25
Leever v. Carson City, 429
Leggio v. Suffolk County Police Dep't, 388
Lehnert v. Ferris Faculty Ass'n, 452
Leibovitz v. New York City Transit Authority, 72
Leisen v. City of Shelbyville, 23
LeMaitre v. Massachusetts Turnpike Authority, 357
Letner v. City of Oliver Springs, 434
Levine v. City of Alameda, 108
Lewis v. City of Chicago, 57
Lewis v. City of Kinston, 495
Lewis v. School Dist. #70, 407
Lindsey v. City of Orrick, Missouri, 183
Lister v. Defense Logistics Agency, 184
Littrell v. City of Kansas City, 163
Lloyd v. City of Bethlehem, 186
Local 21, Int'l Federation of Professional & Technical Engineers v. City and County of San Francisco, 366
Locke v. Karass, 451
Locurto v. Guiliani, 195
Loder v. City of Glendale, California, 324
Logan v. Personnel Board of Jefferson County, 349
Longo v. Dolce, 336
Los Angeles Police Protective League v. City of Los Angeles, 506
Love-Lane v. Martin, 188
Lowery v. Klemm, 79
Lubke v. City of Arlington, 405
Lucas v. Murray City Civil Service Comm'n, 114
Lumpkin v. City of Lafayette, Alabama, 261
Lybrook v. Farmington Municipal Schools Board of Educ., 216
Lytle v. Carl, 301

TABLE OF CASES

M

MacSuga v. County of Spokane, 35
Maestas v. Segura, 159
Magaw v. Middletown Board of Educ., 389
Maggio v. Sipple, 202
Mahoney v. City of Chicago, 99
Maine-Endwell Teachers' Ass'n v. Board of Educ., 240
Majeske v. City of Chicago, 97
Malahoff v. Saito, 457
Malley v. Briggs, 259
Mallick v. Pennsylvania State Police, 4
Mandel v. Allen, 161
Mandell v. County of Suffolk, 240
Mannix v. County of Monroe, 129
Mantone v. Board of Trustees of Teachers' Pension and Annuity Fund, 361
Marceaux v. State of Louisiana, 445
Mard v. Town of Amherst, 370
Markos v. City of Atlanta, Texas, 187
Martin v. Barnesville Exempted School Dist. Board of Educ., 36
Martin v. Brevard County Public Schools, 402
Martin v. City of O'Fallon, 470
Martin v. Wilks, 99
Martinez v. County of Monroe, 54
Martinez v. State Univ. of New York–College at Oswego, 142
Martinez v. Texas Dep't of Criminal Justice, 256
Maryland Troopers Ass'n v. Evans, 101
Mason v. Retirement Board of City and County of San Francisco, 359
Massachi v. AHL Services, Inc., 264
Massachusetts Bay Transportation Authority v. Massachusetts Comm'n Against Discrimination, 83
Massachusetts Board of Retirement v. Murgia, 14
Massachusetts Correction Officers Federated Union v. Labor Relations Comm'n, 137
Mastroianni v. Bowers, 261
Mathes v. City of Omaha, 112
Matter of Division of Criminal Justice State Investigators, 457
Matter of Jackson, 39
Matter of Tavani, 481
Matthews v. Columbia County, 301
Mauder v. Metropolitan Transit Authority, 403
Mazares v. Dep't of the Navy, 154
McCann v. Tillman, 156
McCarthy v. New York City Technical College, 9
McClead v. Pima County, 417
McClendon v. City of Columbia, 268
McCloskey v. Honolulu Police Dep't, 325
McCloud v. Testa, 230
McClure v. Independent School Dist. No. 16, 111
McCrary v. City of Biloxi, 385
McCulloch v. Glendening, 456
McCurdy v. Arkansas State Police, 75
McDade v. West, 302
McDonnell Douglas Corp. v. Green, 40, 41
McElroy v. City of Temple, 481
McFall v. Bednar, 187
McFaul v. Randall-Owens, 282
McGeshick v. Principi, 27
McGowan v. City of Eufala, 91
McGrath v. Rhode Island Retirement Board, 357
McKee v. Hart, 272
McKenzie v. Dovala, 19
McMillian v. Monroe County, Alabama, 294
McPherson v. City of Waukegan, 75
McQuirk v. Donnelley, 212
McWilliams v. Jefferson County, 21
Meacham v. Knolls Atomic Power Laboratory, 3
Means v. Baltimore County, Maryland, 391
Meek v. Springfield Police Dep't, 113
Melanson v. Town of West Hartford, 392
Mendenhall v. North Carolina Dep't of Human Resources, 155
Meredith v. Louisiana Federation of Teachers, 447
Merheb v. Illinois State Toll Highway Authority, 143
Metropolitan Milwaukee Ass'n of Commerce v. Milwaukee County, 465
Michael v. St. Joseph County, 202
Michalowicz v. Village of Bedford Park, 113
Michigan AFSCME Council 25 v. Livingston County Road Comm'n, 144
Michigan State AFL-CIO v. Michigan Civil Service Comm'n, 217
Michigan State Police Troopers Ass'n v. Michigan Dep't of State Police, 314
Middlebrooks v. Wayne County, 330
Middletown Township Policemen's Benevolent Ass'n v. Township of Middletown, 367
Mikels v. City of Durham, 78
Miller v. Administrative Office of the Courts, 199
Miller v. California Dep't of Corrections, 70
Miller v. City of Indianapolis, 497
Miller v. City of Nederland By and Through Wimer, 133
Miller v. City of West Columbia, South Carolina, 213
Miller v. Clinton County, 199
Miller v. Sioux Gateway Fire Dep't, 40
Miller v. Vanderburgh County, 342
Mills v. City of Evansville, Indiana, 200
Mills v. Meadows, 222
Milwaukee County v. Juneau County, 387
Milwaukee Dist. Council 48 v. Milwaukee County, 353
Milwaukee Police Ass'n and Julie Horter v. Jones, 192
Milwaukee Professional Fire Fighters Ass'n v. City of Milwaukee, 378

TABLE OF CASES

Mincey v. U.S. Postal Service, 451
Minch v. City of Chicago, 15
Miron v. Univ. of New Haven Police Dep't, 211
Mississippi Employment Security Comm'n v. Marion County Sheriff's Dep't, 382
Missouri Dep't of Natural Resources v. Lossos, 383
Mitchell v. Dep't of Corrections, 320
Mitchell v. Forsyth, 259
Miyler v. Village of East Galesburg, 124
Modica v. Taylor, 272
Molloy v. City of Bellevue, 39
Molnar v. Booth, 77
Molsness v. City of Walla Walla, Washington, 141
Monahan v. Girouard, 109
Mondt v. Cheyenne Police Dep't, 133
Monell v. Dep't of Social Services, 301
Montana Public Employee's Ass'n v. Dep't of Transportation, 439
Montegue v. City of New Orleans Fire Dep't, 327
Montgomery County v. Krieger, 153
Montgomery County v. Wade, 395
Montgomery v. Stefaniak, 208
Montgomery v. West Virginia State Police, 111
Moore v. Board of County Commissioners of County of Leavenworth, 305
Moore v. State, Dep't of Transportation, 489
Moore v. Town of Collierville, 366
Moreau v. Klevenhagen, 433
Morgan v. McCotter, 131
Morris v. City of Chillicothe, 153
Morris v. Lindau, 192
Mortenson v. County of Sacramento, 434
Moser v. Indiana Dep't of Corrections, 60
Moss v. Martin, 220
Motarie v. Northern Montana Joint Refuse Disposal Dist., 172
Mothersell v. City of Syracuse, New York, 507
Moy v. County of Cook, 291
Mt. Healthy City School Dist. v. Doyle, 179
Mueller v. County of Westchester, New York, 293
Mullins v. City of New York, 424
Mutschler v. Housing Authority of Raleigh, North Carolina, 206
Myers v. Hasara, 186

N

Nagy v. Employees' Review Board, 374
National Ass'n of Government Employees, Inc. v. Barrett, 149
National League of Cities v. Usery, 419, 420
National Pride At Work, Inc. v. Governor of Michigan, 365
National Railroad Passenger Corp. v. Morgan, 46, 103
National Treasury Employees Union v. Dep't of Treasury, 325
National Treasury Employees Union v. King, 218
National Treasury Employees Union v. Von Raab, 321, 322, 330, 332
Navarro v. Block, 286
Navlet v. Port of Seattle, 380
Neal v. Roche, 45
Nelson v. Gillette, 289
Nelson v. Salem State College, 243
Nessel v. Board of Fire and Police Commissioners of Northlake, Illinois, 146
Nevada Dep't of Human Resources v. Hibbs, 401, 409
New Jersey State Firemen's Mutual Benevolent Ass'n v. North Hudson Regional Fire & Rescue, 446
New Jersey Transit PBA Local 304 v. New Jersey Transit Corp., 326, 504
New Jersey Turnpike Authority v. Local 196, 148
New Jersey v. T.L.O., 312, 313
New York City Transit Authority v. New York State PERB, 136, 465
New York City Transit Authority v. State of New York, 87
Ney v. City of Hoisington, 409
NFFE, Local 1309 v. Dep't of the Interior, 448
NLRB v. Weingarten, 136
Nolan v. City of Anaheim, 366
Nord Community Mental Health Center v. Lorain County, 380
Novak v. City of Pittsburgh, 501

O

O'Brien v. Dep't of Agriculture, 47
O'Brien v. Town of Agawam, 429
O'Connor v. City of Newark, 163
O'Connor v. Consolidated Coin Caterers Corp., 4
O'Connor v. Ortega, 313, 315
O'Connor v. Pierson, 244
O'Keefe v. Utah State Retirement Board, 360
O'Rourke v. City of Providence, 72
O'Rourke v. Comwlth. of Pennsylvania Dep't of Corrections, 165
Oak Park Public Safety Officers Ass'n v. City of Oak Park, 461
Oakley v. Cowan, 77
Office & Professional Employees Int'l Union, Local 32 v. Camden County Municipal Utilities Authority, 440
Office of Personnel Management v. Richmond, 369
Okazaki v. Dep't of Children and Families, Florida, 59
Olsen v. Town of Loudon, 435
Oncale v. Sundowner Offshore Services, Inc., 76
Oregon Police Officers' Ass'n v. State of Oregon, 361

TABLE OF CASES

Ortiz v. Los Angeles Police Relief Ass'n, 246
Osborn v. Haley, 130
Otto v. Pennsylvania State Educ. Ass'n, 453
Oubre v. Entergy Operations, Inc., 10
Owen v. City of Independence, 293

P

Painter v. Graley, 172
Paresi v. City of Portland, 441
Parker v. Wakelin, 356
Parks v. City of Warner Robins, Georgia, 509
Paterson v. State of Idaho, 80
Patterson v. Balsamico, 291
Patterson v. Board of Trustees, State Police Retirement System, 365
Patterson v. City of Utica, 211
Peeper v. Callaway County Ambulance Dist., 209
Pena v. DePrisco, 275
Pennsylvania Game Comm'n v. State Civil Service Comm'n, 478
Pennsylvania State Corrections Officers Ass'n v. State Civil Service Comm'n, 479
Pennsylvania State Police v. Suders, 73
Pennsylvania State Univ. v. State Employees' Retirement Board, 442
Pennyfeather v. Tessler, 244
People ex rel. Sklodowski v. State of Illinois, 356
People v. Coutu, 149
Pereira v. Commissioner of Social Services, 202
Perez v. Unified Government of Wyandotte County, 274
Perrodin v. City of Lafayette, 375
Perry v. Sindermann, 115, 116
Perry v. Woodward, 46
Peters v. City of Mauston, 30
Petersen v. City of Mesa, 331
Peterson v. District of Columbia, 44
Peterson v. Scott County, 12
Petit v. City of Chicago, 96
Petty v. Metropolitan Government of Nashville-Davidson County, 496
Pfifer v. Town of Edinburgh, 160
Phelan v. City of Chicago, 408
Phelan v. Cook County, 69
Philadelphia Gas Works v. Unemployment Compensation Board, 345
Philadelphia Housing Authority v. AFSCME, 467
Philbrook v. Ansonia Board of Educ., 83
Phillips v. City of Livingston, 136
Phillips v. Collings, 82
Phillips v. County of Allegheny, 285
Pickering v. Board of Educ., 178, 179
Piercy v. Maketa, 56
Pietras v. Board of Fire Commissioners of the Farmingville Fire Dist., 58
Pike v. Osborne, 226
Pima County v. Pima County Merit System Comm'n, 146
Piotrowski v. City of Houston, 297
Pirant v. U.S. Postal Service, 402
Piroglu v. Coleman, 335
Piscottano v. Murphy, 207
Pleva v. Norquist, 221
Polanco v. Industrial Commission of Arizona, 398
Poland v. Chertoff, 6
Police Ass'n of New Orleans v. City of New Orleans, 100
Pollard v. E.I. du Pont de Nemours & Co., 68
Polomski v. Mayor & City Council of Baltimore, Maryland, 413
Poole v. Waterbury, 354
Port Edwards School Dist. v. Reissmann, 407
Porter v. City of Royal Oak, 214
Porter v. Osborn, 274
Powell v. Alexander, 300
Prescott v. Higgins, 43
Presti v. Farrell, 140
Price v. Industrial Claim Appeals Office, 396
Prince George's County, Maryland v. Fraternal Order of Police, Lodge 89, 473
Proksa v. Arizona State Schools for the Deaf and the Blind, 125
Providence Teachers' Union, Local 958 v. City of Council of City of Providence, 493
Pruitt v. City of Chicago, 103
Public Employees' Retirement System v. Gallant, 444

Q

Quiles v. Henderson, 29
Quon v. Arch Wireless Operating Co., 276

R

Raad v. Fairbanks North Star Borough School Dist., 52
Radecki v. Barela, 276
Rafferty v. City of Youngstown, 99
Rafi v. Thompson, 6
Ragsdale v. Wolverine World Wide, Inc., 402
Ramirez v. Arlequin, 219
Rankin v. McPherson, 178, 180
Raspa v. Office of the Sheriff of the County of Gloucester, 34
Rawlings v. Police Dep't of Jersey City, 339
Rawls v. Public Employees Relations Comm'n, 145
Ray v. City of Maple Grove, 399
Raygor v. Regents of Univ. of Minnesota, 11
Razor v. New Orleans Dep't of Police, 338
Reames v. Dep't of Public Works, 331
Reeves v. Sanderson Plumbing Products, 3
Regents of the Univ. of California v. John Doe, 252
Reich v. Collins, 417

TABLE OF CASES

Reilly v. City of Atlantic City, 182
Relford v. Lexington-Fayette Urban County Government, 338
Renaud v. Wyoming Dep't of Family Services, 302
Reninger v. State Dep't of Corrections, 120
Retirement Board of the Employees' Retirement System v. DiPrete, 361
Reyes v. Maschmeier, 277
Rhode Island Brotherhood of Correctional Officers v. State of Rhode Island, 445
Riback v. Las Vegas Metropolitan Police Dep't, 81
Ricco v. Potter, 407
Rice v. Ohio Dep't of Transportation, 223
Richard v. Lafayette Fire and Police Civil Service Board, 338
Richardson v. McKnight, 263
Richey v. City of Independence, 150
Richmond v. Thompson, 213
Rios v. Rossotti, 53
Rioux v. City of Atlanta, 42
Riva v. Comwlth. of Massachusetts, 378
Riveros v. City of Los Angeles, 119
Riverside Sheriff's Ass'n v. County of Riverside, 467
Roberts v. Ward, 234
Robertson v. City of New England, 388
Robertson v. Fiore, 230
Robinson v. City of Philadelphia, 270
Robinson v. Sappington, 71
Robinson v. Shell Oil Co., 88
Robinson v. Winslow Township, 299
Roche v. Town of Wareham, 490
Rochester Fire Fighters Ass'n v. Griffith, 466
Rodgers v. City of Des Moines, 406
Rodriguez v. City of Chicago, 85
Roebuck v. Washington, 75
Rogers v. City of San Antonio, 497
Rogers v. Miller, 227
Rogers v. Powell, 277
Rolon v. Henneman, 260
Roseman v. Firemen and Policemen's Fund, 416
Ross v. Denver Dep't of Health & Hospitals, 376
Ross v. Douglas County, Nebraska, 47
Rossbach v. City of Miami, 21
Rourke v. New York State Dep't of Correctional Services, 237
Rowland v. Perry, 300
Roy v. County of Lexington, South Carolina, 431
Roy v. Inhabitants of City of Lewiston, 287
Ruiz v. Mero, 287
Ruotolo v. City of New York, 182
Rupp v. Phillips, 198
Rutan v. Republican Party of Illinois, 219
Rutherford v. City of Albuquerque, 343
Rutherford v. City of Flint, 358
Ryduchowski v. Port Authority of New York & New Jersey, 65

S

Saavedra v. City of Albuquerque, 328
Sacramento County Deputy Sheriffs' Ass'n v. Sacramento County, 249
Sagendorf-Teal v. County of Rensselaer, New York, 206
Salazar v. Ballesteros, 393
San Diego County Deputy Sheriffs Ass'n v. San Diego County Sheriffs Dep't, 131
Santana v. City and County of Denver, 59
Sasse v. U.S. Dep't of Labor, 163
Saucier v. Katz, 267
Saunders v. Village of Dixmoor, 48
Savage v. Glendale Union High School Dist., 255
Saxe v. Board of Trustees of Metropolitan State College of Denver, 128
Scarbrough v. Board of Trustees Florida A&M Univ., 90
Schlicher v. Board of Fire and Police Commissioners of Village of Westmont, 473
School Board of Nassau County v. Arline, 18
School Committee of Norton v. Massachusetts Comm'n Against Discrimination, 31
Schorr v. Borough of Lemoyne, 297
Schroer v. Billington, 55
Schulte v. Potter, 6
Sciolino v. City of Newport News, 122
Sciortino v. Dep't of Police, 349
Scott v. Boston Housing Authority, 5
Scott v. Harris, 295
See v. City of Elyria, 272
Seegmiller v. Laverkin City, 273
Seelig v. Koehler, 333
Sehie v. City of Aurora, 435
Seiber v. Town of Oliver Springs, 145
Sellers v. Mineta, 157
Seminole Tribe of Florida v. Florida, 252
Semple v. City of Moundsville, 281
Senger v. City of Aberdeen, 427
Senior v. City of Edina, 39
SEPTA v. WCAB, 394
Service Employees Int'l Union, Local 509 v. Labor Relations Comm'n, 466
Shaffer v. Potter, 57
Shahar v. Bowers, 82
Shapiro v. Township of Lakewood, 32
Sharp v. City of Houston, 298
Sheikh v. Dep't of Public Safety, 67
Shelton v. Tucker, 231
Shelton v. Univ. of Medicine & Dentistry of New Jersey, 85
Sher v. U.S. Dep't of Veterans Affairs, 144
Sheriff of Suffolk County v. AFSCME Council 93, Local 419, 372
Sherin v. Florida Dep't of Human Resources, 267
Shoemaker v. Handel, 321

TABLE OF CASES

Shortess v. Dep't of Public Safety & Corrections, 149
Shrum v. City of Coweta, Oklahoma, 272
Sicuro v. City of Pittsburgh, 499
Sigsworth v. City of Aurora, Illinois, 183
Silberstein v. City of Dayton, 275
Silk v. City of Chicago, 28
Silverman v. Campbell, 241
Simonton v. Runyon, 77
Sims-Fingers v. City of Indianapolis, 63
Singer v. City of Waco, 430
Singh v. City of New York, 437
Singhas v. New Mexico State Highway Dep't, 393
Sircy v. Metropolitan Government of Nashville and Davidson County, 484
Sisca v. City of Fall River, 138
Siwek v. Police Board of City of Chicago, 150
Skaarup v. City of North Las Vegas, 196
Skinner v. Railway Labor Executives' Ass'n, 321, 322
Slentz v. City of Republic, 408
Smith v. City of Des Moines, Iowa, 13
Smith v. City of Hemet, 296
Smith v. City of Jackson, 3
Smith v. County of Kern, 308
Smith v. Danielczyk, 210
Smith v. District of Columbia, 92
Smith v. East Baton Rouge Parish School Board, 408
Smith v. Fresno Irrigation Dist., 327
Smith v. Henderson, 34
Smith v. Howard County, 386
Smith v. Kingsboro Psychiatric Center (KPC), 117
Smith v. Northeastern Illinois Univ., 47
Smith v. State of Oklahoma, 59
Snider v. Belvidere Township, 64
Snyder v. City of Moab, 221
Soelter v. King County, 223
Soto v. Schembri, 227
Spades v. City of Walnut Ridge, 22
Spain v. City of Mansfield, 193
Speer v. City of Wynne, 123
Spradling v. City of Tulsa, 426
Springfield v. Dep't of Environmental Protection, 139
Sprint/United Management Co. v. Mendelsohn, 10
St. Mary's Honor Center v. Hicks, 41
Stachowski v. Town of Cicero, 144
Stallworth v. City of Evergreen, Alabama, 115
Stalnaker v. M.L.D., 367
Stamps v. City of Taylor, 286
Stanfield v. Peregoy, 271
Stanziale v. Jargowsky, 13
State Dep't of Corrections v. Harris, 345
State Dep't of Social & Rehabilitation Services v. PERB, 443
State ex rel. Fern v. Cincinnati, 476
State ex rel. Glass Workers v. SERB, 457
State of Arizona v. McLamb, 236
State of Florida, Times Publishing Co. v. City of Clearwater, 244
State of Montana v. Schnittgen, 158
State of New Jersey v. Communications Workers of America, AFL-CIO, 464
State of New Jersey v. Perez, 148
State of New York v. Kinsella, 489
State of Rhode Island v. Rhode Island Council 94, 469
State of West Virginia v. Lincoln County Comm'n, 229
State Personnel Board v. Adams, 16
State Personnel Board v. Wallace, 485
State Police for Automatic Retirement Ass'n v. DiFava, 15
State v. Int'l Federation of Professional and Technical Engineers, Local 195, 430
State v. Rhode Island Employment Security Alliance, Local 401, SEIU, 465
Stationary Engineers Local 39 v. County of Sacramento, 479
Staveley v. City of Lowell, 102
Steadman v. Texas Rangers, 205
Steenken v. Campbell County, 496
Stein v. City of Toledo, 319
Steinhauer v. Degolier, 60
Sterling v. Borough of Minersville, 297
Stevens v. California Dep't of Corrections, 406
Stevens v. Dep't of the Treasury, 10
Stewart v. Evans, 318
Storm v. McClung, 308
Stover v. Martinez, 92
Stratman v. Brent, 212
Stratton v. Dep't for the Aging for the City of New York, 9
Strickland v. Water Works and Sewer Board of Birmingham, 406
Stueart v. Arkansas State Police Comm'n, 348
Suppan v. Dadonna, 216
Sutherland v. Michigan Dep't of Treasury, 97
Swepston v. Board of Tax Appeals of Ohio, 161
Syrie v. Schilhab, 281

T

Tanner v. Oregon Health Sciences Univ., 367
Teague v. City of Flower Mound, 203
Teigen v. Renfrow, 130
Tennessee v. Garner, 295
Texarkana School Dist. v. Conner, 394
Texas Dep't of Community Affairs v. Burdine, 55
Tharling v. City of Port Lavaca, 194
Theater v. Palm Beach County Sheriff's Office, 200
Thomas v. City of Beaverton, 187

TABLE OF CASES

Thomas v. Corwin, 27
Thomas v. County of Camden, 78
Thomas v. National Ass'n of Letter Carriers, 84
Thomas v. Straub, 504
Thomas v. Town of Hammonton, 71
Thompson v. Adams, 125
Thompson v. Bi-State Development Agency, 91
Thompson v. District of Columbia, 119, 185
Thorn v. City of Glendale, 290
Thornton v. Univ. Civil Service Merit Board, 320
Throneberry v. McGehee Desha County Hospital, 410
Thurber v. City of Burlington, 157
Tice v. Centre Area Transportation Authority, 19
Tillman v. City of West Point, Mississippi, 210
Timmer v. Michigan Dep't of Commerce, 65
Tindle v. Caudell, 159
Todd v. City of Cincinnati, 29
Toeller v. Wisconsin Dep't of Corrections, 410
Tomlinson v. Dep't of Health & Rehabilitative Services, 139
Torain v. U.S. Postal Service, 161
Torres v. Wisconsin Dep't of Health and Social Services, 62
Town of Castle Rock v. Gonzales, 285
Town of Dedham v. Dedham Police Ass'n, 374
Town of Hudson v. Labor Relations Comm'n, 464
Town of Newton v. Rumery, 286
Town of Plymouth v. Civil Service Comm'n, 152
Toyota Motor Manufacturing v. Williams, 20
Tran v. Trustees of the State Colleges of Colorado, 75
Tripp v. Cole, 200
Troster v. Pennsylvania State Dep't of Corrections, 236
Trustees of Health and Hospitals of City of Boston, Inc. v. Massachusetts Comm'n Against Discrimination, 44
Tucker v. State of California Dep't of Educ., 82
Tuggle v. Mangan, 70
Turner v. Unemployment Compensation Board of Review, 381
Tuttle v. Metropolitan Government of Nashville and Davidson County, Tennessee, 7
Tuttle v. Missouri Dep't of Agriculture, 7
Twisdale v. Snow, 93
Tysinger v. Police Dep't of the City of Zanesville, 66

U

U.S. Civil Service Comm'n v. National Ass'n of Letter Carriers, 228
U.S. Dep't of Defense v. Federal Labor Relations Authority, 441
U.S. Postal Service Board of Governors v. Aikens, 41
U.S. Postal Service v. Gregory, 110
U.S. v. Barrows, 317
U.S. v. City of Miami, 97, 100
U.S. v. Massey, 146
U.S. v. National Treasury Employees Union, 181
U.S. v. Paradise, 94
U.S. v. Simons, 315
Uniform Firefighters of Cohoes v. City of Cohoes, 371
United Public Workers of America v. Mitchell, 228
Univ. of Alaska v. Univ. of Alaska Classified Employees Ass'n, 463
Univ. of Texas Medical Branch at Galveston v. Savoy, 167
Urofsky v. Gilmore, 199
US Airways v. Barnett, 31
Utah Educ. Ass'n v. Shurtleff, 224

V

Valenzuela v. California State Personnel Board, 110
Van Vleet v. Montana Ass'n of Counties Workers' Compensation Trust, 394
Van Voorhis v. Hillsborough County Board of County Commissioners, 11
Vance v. Bradley, 15
Vaughn v. Lawrenceburg Power System, 208
Velez v. City of Chicago, 52
Velez v. Levy, 123
Vera Cruz v. City of Escondido, 296
Vermont State Employees' Ass'n v. Vermont Criminal Justice Training Council, 487
Vernon v. City of Los Angeles, 242
Verri v. Nanna, 319
Victor v. Administrator, Office of Employment Security, 385
Villegas v. Board of Fire & Police Commissioners, 132
Virgili v. Gilbert, 314
Vollemans v. Town of Wallingford, 12

W

Wade v. Ohio Bureau of Workers' Compensation, 169
Wadewitz v. Montgomery, 307
Wager v. City of Ladue, 74
Wagner v. City of Memphis, 115
Wagstaff v. Dep't of Employment Security, 345
Wainscott v. Henry, 188
Walker v. Board of Trustees of North Carolina Local Governmental Employees' Retirement System, 353
Walker v. Elmore County Board of Educ., 403
Wallace v. City of San Diego, 496
Wallace v. County of Comal, 185

TABLE OF CASES

Wallace v. Estate of Davies by Davies, 285
Walsh v. Heilmann, 220
Walsh v. Nevada Dep't of Human Resources, 25
Walsh v. Unemployment Compensation Board of Review, 381
Walters v. Metropolitan Educ. Enterprises, Inc., 88
Warda v. City Council of City of Flushing, 506
Washington Metropolitan Area Transit Authority v. Local 2, Office Professional Employees Int'l Union, 460
Washington State Dep't of Labor & Industries v. Johnson, 395
Washington v. Illinois Dep't of Revenue, 92
Waters v. Churchill, 180
Waters v. City of Morristown, 301
Watkins v. Board of Managers of City of Birmingham Retirement & Relief System, 411
Watson v. Dep't of Justice, 170
Watson v. District of Columbia Water and Sewer Authority, 142
Watts v. Dep't of Health & Human Resources, 486
Weaver v. Henderson, 238
Webb v. City of Philadelphia, 83
Webb v. State Civil Service Comm'n, 150
Webb-Edwards v. Orange County Sheriff's Office, 74
Webster v. Doe, 174
Webster v. Public School Employees of Washington, Inc., 426
Weicherding v. Riegel, 209
Weiss v. City of Milwaukee, 390
Wells v. North Carolina Dep't of Corrections, 164
Wernsing v. Dep't of Human Services, 64
Westbrook v. City of Omaha, 314
Westmoreland County v. Westmoreland County Detectives, 134
Westmoreland Intermediate Unit #7 v. WIU #7 Classroom Assistants Educ. Support Personnel Ass'n PSEA/NEA, 134
Wheatley v. Wicomico County, 64
Wheeler v. Hampton Township, 428
Wheeling Park Comm'n v. Hotel Union, 217
White v. City of Boston, 371
White v. St. Louis Teachers Union, Division of Employment Security, 381
White v. Village of Homewood, Illinois, 307
Whitehill v. Elkins, 232
Whitener v. McWatters, 261
Whittington v. City of Crisfield, 126
Widow v. City of Kansas City, 57
Wilbur v. Mahan, 229
Wilcher v. City of Wilmington, 334
Wiley v. Doory, 279
Will v. Michigan Dep't of State Police, 263

Williams v. Berney, 274
Williams v. City of Jacksonville, 270
Williams v. Garraghty, 214
Williams v. London Utility Comm'n, 132
Williams v. Riverside Community Corrections Corp., 373
Williams v. Widnall, 37
Wilson v. City of Norwich, 295
Wilson v. Municipality of Anchorage, 449
Wilson-Simmons v. Lake County Sheriff's Dep't, 50
Winskowski v. City of Stephen, 122
Wishkin v. Potter, 25
Wittmer v. Peters, 95
Wolf v. Williamson, 214
Wolfe v. Anne Arundel County, 257
Wollman v. Cleveland, 482
Wood v. Irving, 483
Wood v. Wabash County, 127
Wooden v. Maryland Dep't of Public Safety, 90
Woodruff v. Peters, 34
Woods v. State Civil Service Comm'n, 147
Wright v. City of Danville, Illinois, 507
Wright v. Rolette County, 268
Wright v. Universal Maritime Service Corp., 25
Wyche v. Dep't of Labor, 140
Wygant v. Jackson Board of Educ., 98

X

X-Men Security v. Pataki, 270

Y

Yin v. State of California, 29
Yoder v. Town of Middleton, 143
Young v. City of Providence, 296
Yunus v. Dep't of Veterans Affairs, 168

Z

Zalewska v. County of Sullivan, 234
Zanghi v. Niagara Frontier Transportation Comm'n, 288
Zirkle v. District of Columbia, 167

TABLE OF CASES BY STATE

ALABAMA

Ash v. Tyson Foods, Inc., 42
Board of Trustees of Univ. of Alabama v. Garrett, 17
Butler v. Alabama Dep't of Transportation, 42
Cleburne County Comm'n v. Norton, 444
Dothard v. Rawlinson, 61
Garrett v. Univ. of Alabama at Birmingham Board of Trustees, 20
Ledbetter v. Goodyear Tire & Rubber Co., Inc., 63
Logan v. Personnel Board of Jefferson County, 349
Lumpkin v. City of Lafayette, Alabama, 261
Martin v. Wilks, 99
McCann v. Tillman, 156
McMillian v. Monroe County, Alabama, 294
Stallworth v. City of Evergreen, Alabama, 115
State Dep't of Corrections v. Harris, 345
State Personnel Board v. Wallace, 485
Strickland v. Water Works and Sewer Board of Birmingham, 406
U.S. v. Paradise, 94
Walker v. Elmore County Board of Educ., 403
Watkins v. Board of Managers of City of Birmingham Retirement & Relief System, 411

ALASKA

Agwiak v. U.S., 438
Anchorage Police Dep't Employees Ass'n v. Municipality of Anchorage, 326
Cowles v. State of Alaska, 318
Larsen v. Municipality of Anchorage, 482
Moore v. State, Dep't of Transportation, 489
Porter v. Osborn, 274
Public Employees' Retirement System v. Gallant, 444
Raad v. Fairbanks North Star Borough School Dist., 52
Stalnaker v. M.L.D., 367
Univ. of Alaska v. Univ. of Alaska Classified Employees Ass'n, 463
Wilson v. Municipality of Anchorage, 449

ARIZONA

Dibble v. City of Chandler, 194
Elfbrandt v. Russell, 232
Griffis v. Pinal County, 243
James v. Tablerion, 148
Lane v. Industrial Comm'n of Arizona, 393
McClead v. Pima County, 417
Petersen v. City of Mesa, 331
Pima County v. Pima County Merit System Comm'n, 146
Polanco v. Industrial Commission of Arizona, 398
Proksa v. Arizona State Schools for the Deaf and the Blind, 125
Savage v. Glendale Union High School Dist., 255
State of Arizona v. McLamb, 236
Watson v. Dep't of Justice, 170

ARKANSAS

AFSCME v. City of Benton, 369
Allen v. City of Pocahontas, 197
Arkansas Dep't of Correction v. Holybee, 399
Bennett v. Watters, 5
Burcham v. City of Van Buren, 476
Dermott Special School Dist. v. Johnson, 257
Donaldson v. Taylor, 375
Hart v. City of Little Rock, 275
Hinshaw v. Smith, 195
Langley v. Hot Spring County, Arkansas, 225
McCurdy v. Arkansas State Police, 75
O'Brien v. Dep't of Agriculture, 47
Ragsdale v. Wolverine World Wide, Inc., 402
Shelton v. Tucker, 231
Spades v. City of Walnut Ridge, 22
Speer v. City of Wynne, 123
Stueart v. Arkansas State Police Comm'n, 348
Texarkana School Dist. v. Conner, 394
Thompson v. Adams, 125
Throneberry v. McGehee Desha County Hospital, 410
Tindle v. Caudell, 159
U.S. v. Massey, 146

CALIFORNIA

American Federation of Government Employees Local 1 v. Stone, 207
American Federation of Government Employees v. Derwinski, 329
American Federation of Government Employees v. Roberts, 341
Ass'n for Los Angeles Deputy Sheriffs v. County of Los Angeles, 372
Berry v. Dep't of Social Services, 195
Bessard v. California Community Colleges, 232
Billings v. U.S., 440
Blair v. City of Pomona, 190
Block v. Orange County Employees Retirement System, 411
Bonner v. County of San Diego, 484
Brazil v. U.S. Dep't of Navy, 175
Brodie v. WCAB, 397
BRV, Inc. v. Superior Court, 442
California Correctional Peace Officers Ass'n v. Schwarzenegger, 486
Chen v. County of Orange, 508
Chevron U.S.A. v. Echazabal, 26
City of Los Angeles Dep't of Water v. Manhart, 414

TABLE OF CASES BY STATE

City of Palo Alto v. SEIU, Local 715, 467
City of San Diego v. Roe, 194
Cleveland v. City of Los Angeles, 428
County of Sacramento v. AFSCME Local 146, 464
County of Sacramento v. Lewis, 295
Cripe v. City of San Jose, 24
Cummings v. Connell, 453
Dobbins v. County of San Diego Civil Service Comm'n, 120
Dyson v. California State Personnel Board, 321
Edgerton v. State Personnel Board, 342
Fazio v. City and County of San Francisco, 223
Fewer v. City and County of San Francisco, 119
FDIC v. Meyer, 253
Foster v. Mahdesian, 453
Freitag v. Ayers, 69
Garcetti v. Ceballos, 119, 181, 183
Gilbrook v. City of Westminster, 189
Green v. State of California, 38
Haas v. San Bernardino County, 114
Hansen v. California Dep't of Corrections, 335
I.B.E.W., Local 1245 v. Skinner, 329
Imada v. City of Hercules, California, 438
Jackson v. Gates, 340
Johnson v. Transportation Agency, Santa Clara County, 96
Karahalios v. National Federation of Federal Employees, Local 1263, 447
Katz v. Univ. of California Board of Regents, 5
Keyser v. Sacramento City Unified School Dist., 205
Kidwell v. WCAB, 397
Klem v. Santa Clara County, 426
Knickerbocker v. City of Stockton, 155
Kreutzer v. City and County of San Francisco, 122
Levine v. City of Alameda, 108
Local 21, Int'l Federation of Professional & Technical Engineers v. City and County of San Francisco, 366
Loder v. City of Glendale, California, 324
Los Angeles Police Protective League v. City of Los Angeles, 506
Mason v. Retirement Board of City and County of San Francisco, 359
Mazares v. Dep't of the Navy, 154
McDade v. West, 302
McQuirk v. Donnelley, 212
Miller v. California Dep't of Corrections, 70
Mortenson v. County of Sacramento, 434
National Railroad Passenger Corp. v. Morgan, 46, 103
Navarro v. Block, 286
Nolan v. City of Anaheim, 366
O'Connor v. Ortega, 313, 315
Ortiz v. Los Angeles Police Relief Ass'n, 246
Quon v. Arch Wireless Operating Co., 276

Regents of the Univ. of California v. John Doe, 252
Riveros v. City of Los Angeles, 119
Riverside Sheriff's Ass'n v. County of Riverside, 467
Sacramento County Deputy Sheriffs' Ass'n v. Sacramento County, 249
San Diego County Deputy Sheriffs Ass'n v. San Diego County Sheriffs Dep't, 131
Saucier v. Katz, 267
Skinner v. Railway Labor Executives' Ass'n, 321, 322
Smith v. County of Kern, 308
Smith v. Fresno Irrigation Dist., 327
Smith v. City of Hemet, 296
Stationary Engineers Local 39 v. County of Sacramento, 479
Stevens v. California Dep't of Corrections, 406
Thorn v. City of Glendale, 290
Tucker v. State of California Dep't of Educ., 82
US Airways v. Barnett, 31
Valenzuela v. California State Personnel Board, 110
Vera Cruz v. City of Escondido, 296
Vernon v. City of Los Angeles, 242
Wallace v. City of San Diego, 496
Yin v. State of California, 29

COLORADO

Adarand Constructors, Inc. v. Pena, 94
Ahart v. Dep't of Corrections, 340
Carpenter v. City & County of Denver, Colorado, 427
City of Thornton v. Replogle, 372
Cunliffe v. Industrial Claims Appeals Office, 382
Davoll v. Webb, 33
Ford v. West, 48
Hillig v. Rumsfeld, 93
Hoffler v. State of Colorado, 152
Jaramillo v. Colorado Judicial Dep't, 60
Jones v. Denver Public Schools, 403
McWilliams v. Jefferson County, 21
National League of Cities v. Usery, 419, 420
Piercy v. Maketa, 56
Price v. Industrial Claim Appeals Office, 396
Ross v. Denver Dep't of Health & Hospitals, 376
Santana v. City and County of Denver, 59
Saxe v. Board of Trustees of Metropolitan State College of Denver, 128
Stover v. Martinez, 92
Teigen v. Renfrow, 130
Town of Castle Rock v. Gonzales, 285
Tran v. Trustees of the State Colleges of Colorado, 75
Vance v. Bradley, 15
Williams v. Berney, 274

TABLE OF CASES BY STATE

CONNECTICUT

AFSCME, Council 4, Local 1565 v. Dep't of Correction, 134
Ansonia Board of Educ. v. Philbrook, 83
Appleton v. Stonington Board of Educ., 292
Brittel v. Dep't of Correction, 79
Carriero v. Borough of Naugatuck, 412
Chesler v. City of Derby, 386
Dep't of Transportation v. Comm'n on Human Rights, 45
Doe v. City of Stamford, 399
Inturri v. City of Hartford, 234
Kelly v. City of New Haven, 475
Knight v. Connecticut Dep't of Health, 241
Melanson v. Town of West Hartford, 392
Miron v. Univ. of New Haven Police Dep't, 211
Nagy v. Employees' Review Board, 374
O'Connor v. Pierson, 244
Philbrook v. Ansonia Board of Educ., 83
Piscottano v. Murphy, 207
Poole v. Waterbury, 354
Vollemans v. Town of Wallingford, 12
Wilson v. City of Norwich, 295

DELAWARE

Breitigan v. New Castle County, 377
Wilcher v. City of Wilmington, 334

DISTRICT OF COLUMBIA

Adams v. Rice, 18
American Federation of Government Employees, AFL-CIO v. Dep't of Housing & Urban Development, 248
American Federation of Government Employees, National Veterans Affairs Council 53 v. FLRA, 461
American Federation of Government Employees v. Skinner, 328
American Federation of Government Employees v. Sullivan, 332
Barnette v. Chertoff, 4
Broderick v. Donaldson, 92
Butera v. District of Columbia, 298
Carlucci v. Doe, 174
Crawford-El v. Britton, 295
Davidson v. Office of Employee Appeals, 135
District of Columbia v. Tarlosky, 415
Doe v. Cheney, 174
Doe v. Gates, 174
Doe v. U.S., 433, 439
Doe v. U.S. Postal Service, 245
Duncan v. WMATA, 21
Fox v. District of Columbia, 191
Fraternal Order of Police v. Williams, 160
Freeman v. Fallin, 323
Gasser v. District of Columbia, 27
Griffith v. Lanier, 455
Haddon v. Executive Residence at the White House, 196
Harlow v. Fitzgerald, 258
Harmon v. Thornburgh, 333
Haynes v. Williams, 19
Kennedy v. District of Columbia, 237
LaChance v. Erickson, 107
National Treasury Employees Union v. King, 218
NFFE, Local 1309 v. Dep't of the Interior, 448
Office of Personnel Management v. Richmond, 369
Peterson v. District of Columbia, 44
Piroglu v. Coleman, 335
Rafi v. Thompson, 6
Roebuck v. Washington, 75
Schroer v. Billington, 55
Smith v. District of Columbia, 92
Stewart v. Evans, 318
Thompson v. District of Columbia, 119, 185
United Public Workers of America v. Mitchell, 228
U.S. Civil Service Comm'n v. National Ass'n of Letter Carriers, 228
U.S. v. National Treasury Employees Union, 181
U.S. Postal Service Board of Governors v. Aikens, 41
U.S. Postal Service v. Gregory, 110
Watson v. District of Columbia Water and Sewer Authority, 142
Webster v. Doe, 174
Woodruff v. Peters, 34
Wyche v. Dep't of Labor, 140
Zirkle v. District of Columbia, 167

FLORIDA

Arline v. School Board of Nassau County, 18
Bass v. Florida Dep't of Law Enforcement, 348
Beadle v. City of Tampa, 86
Braddy v. Florida Dep't of Labor and Employment Security, 266
Bradshaw v. School Board of Broward County, Florida, 78
Brouwer v. Metropolitan Dade County, 422
Brown v. Dep't of Health and Rehabilitative Services, 283
Burke-Fowler v. Orange County, Florida, 508
Burton v. Hillsborough County, Florida, 437
Busbee v. State of Florida, 362
Buzzi v. Gomez, 269
Chenoweth v. Hillsborough County, 22
City of Delray Beach v. Professional Firefighters, 459
City of Hialeah v. Rojas, 104
City of Kissimmee v. Dickson, 396
City of Sweetwater Florida v. St. Germain, 507

TABLE OF CASES BY STATE

Coastal Florida Police Benevolent Ass'n v. Williams, 455
Cramp v. Board of Public Instruction of Orange County, 231
Danskine v. Miami-Dade County Fire Dep't, 95
Dep't of Business and Professional Regulation v. Doyle, 145
Donovan v. Broward County Board of County Commissioners, 89
Eaves v. Florida Division of Retirement, 354
Faragher v. City of Boca Raton, 73
Fowler v. Unemployment Appeals Comm'n, 346
Gallagher v. Manatee County, 254
Gilbert v. Dep't of Corrections, 384
Gonzalez v. Florida Dep't of Highway Safety, 53
Griffin v. City of Opa-Locka, 72
Hartsfield v. Miami-Dade County, 32
Hassler v. State Retirement Comm'n, 368
Herman v. Dep't of Justice, 165
Keller v. PERC, 498
Kimel v. Florida Board of Regents, 10
Maggio v. Sipple, 202
Martin v. Brevard County Public Schools, 402
Mitchell v. Dep't of Corrections, 320
Okazaki v. Dep't of Children and Families, Florida, 59
Rawls v. Public Employees Relations Comm'n, 145
Reyes v. Maschmeier, 277
Rogers v. Miller, 227
Rossbach v. City of Miami, 21
Scarbrough v. Board of Trustees Florida A&M Univ., 90
School Board of Nassau County v. Arline, 18
Seminole Tribe of Florida v. Florida, 252
Springfield v. Dep't of Environmental Protection, 139
State of Florida, Times Publishing Co. v. City of Clearwater, 244
Theater v. Palm Beach County Sheriff's Office, 200
Tomlinson v. Dep't of Health & Rehabilitative Services, 139
U.S. v. City of Miami, 97, 100
Van Voorhis v. Hillsborough County Board of County Commissioners, 11
Webb-Edwards v. Orange County Sheriff's Office, 74
Williams v. City of Jacksonville, 270
Yunus v. Dep't of Veterans Affairs, 168

GEORGIA

Abernathy v. City of Albany, Georgia, 390
Akins v. Fulton County, 204, 273
Allen v. Board of Public Educ. for Bibb County, 439
Anderson v. Burke County, 197
Brown v. Snow, 58
Chandler v. Miller, 323
Cook v. Gwinnett County School Dist., 273
Cooper v. Smith, 191
Crawford v. City of Fairburn, 91
Duffey v. Bryant, 278
Dunn v. Telfair County, 256
Employees' Retirement System of Georgia v. Melton, 444
Falken v. Glynn County, 430
Fincher v. State of Georgia, 247
Fitzpatrick v. City of Atlanta, 237
Gillis v. Georgia Dep't of Corrections, 45
Govea v. City of Norcross, 289
Grech v. Clayton County, 296
Hanrahan v. City of Atlanta, 503
Huff v. DeKalb County, 424
Irby v. Bittick, 65
Lapides v. Board of Regents of Univ. System of Georgia, 254
Mastroianni v. Bowers, 261
Matthews v. Columbia County, 301
National Ass'n of Government Employees, Inc. v. Barrett, 149
Parks v. City of Warner Robins, Georgia, 509
Reich v. Collins, 417
Rioux v. City of Atlanta, 42
Scott v. Harris, 295
Shahar v. Bowers, 82
Sherin v. Florida Dep't of Human Resources, 267
State Personnel Board v. Adams, 16

HAWAII

Clamor v. U.S., 304
Konno v. County of Hawaii, 487
Malahoff v. Saito, 457
McCloskey v. Honolulu Police Dep't, 325

IDAHO

Bybee v. State of Idaho, Industrial Special Indemnity Fund, 391
Clark v. State of Idaho, 118
Curlee v. Kootenai County Fire & Rescue, 166
Daleiden v. Jefferson County Joint School Dist., 392
Hufford v. McEnaney, 189
Paterson v. State of Idaho, 80

ILLINOIS

Angara v. City of Chicago, 317
Atterberry v. Sherman, 120
Baker v. Runyon, 256
Barefield v. Village of Winnetka, 432
Baron v. City of Highland Park, 9

TABLE OF CASES BY STATE

Bivens v. Trent, 182
Boaden v. Dep't of Law Enforcement, 509
Bond v. Sheahan, 32
Burrell v. City of Mattoon, 472
Carreon v. Illinois Dep't of Human Services, 200
Carver v. Sheriff of La Salle County, 292
Cassimy v. Board of Educ. of Rockford Public Schools, 21
CBOCS West, Inc. v. Humphries, 42
Chan v. Wodnicki, 270
Chicago Teachers Union v. Hudson, 453
City of Belvidere v. Illinois State Labor Relations Board, 488
Coleman v. Lane, 303
Cook County v. U.S. ex rel. Chandler, 254
Copeland v. County of Macon, 289
County of Cook v. Licensed Practical Nurses Ass'n of Illinois, 463
Cullen v. Retirement Board of Policeman's Annuity and Benefit Fund, 363
Cullom v. Brown, 46
Dargis v. Sheahan, 23
Denton v. Civil Service Comm'n of the State of Illinois, 498
Devoney v. Retirement Board of Policemen's Annuity & Benefit Fund, 362
Dodaro v. Village of Glendale Heights, 404
Dunn v. Washington County Hospital, 70
Durgins v. City of East St. Louis, Illinois, 201
Ehlers v. Jackson County Sheriff's Merit Comm'n, 137
Ellis v. Sheahan, 301
Elrod v. Burns, 220
Garcia v. Kankakee County Housing Authority, 197
Gossmeyer v. McDonald, 316
Greer v. Board of Educ., 50
Gusewelle v. City of Wood River, 493
Harrell v. U.S. Postal Service, 405
Haynes v. Police Board of Chicago, 155
Holland v. City of Chicago, 415
Hudson v. City of Chicago, 109
Jackson v. City of Chicago, 23
Jackson v. Retirement Board, 370
Jennings v. State of Illinois Dep't of Corrections, 51
Jones v. Board of Trustees of the Police Pension Fund, 365
Kaske v. City of Rockford, 504
Kelley v. Sheriff's Merit Com'n of Kane County, 504
Krocka v. City of Chicago, 22
Lamb v. City of Decatur, Illinois, 278
Lewis v. City of Chicago, 57
Lewis v. School Dist. #70, 407
Mahoney v. City of Chicago, 99
Majeske v. City of Chicago, 97
Martin v. City of O'Fallon, 470

McPherson v. City of Waukegan, 75
Meek v. Springfield Police Dep't, 113
Merheb v. Illinois State Toll Highway Authority, 143
Michalowicz v. Village of Bedford Park, 113
Minch v. City of Chicago, 15
Miyler v. Village of East Galesburg, 124
Moss v. Martin, 220
Moy v. County of Cook, 291
Myers v. Hasara, 186
Nessel v. Board of Fire and Police Commissioners of Northlake, Illinois, 146
Oakley v. Cowan, 77
People ex rel. Sklodowski v. State of Illinois, 356
Petit v. City of Chicago, 96
Phelan v. City of Chicago, 408
Phelan v. Cook County, 69
Pickering v. Board of Educ., 178, 179
Pirant v. U.S. Postal Service, 402
Pruitt v. City of Chicago, 103
Robinson v. Sappington, 71
Rodriguez v. City of Chicago, 85
Rutan v. Republican Party of Illinois, 219
Saunders v. Village of Dixmoor, 48
Schlicher v. Board of Fire and Police Commissioners of Village of Westmont, 473
Sehie v. City of Aurora, 435
Sigsworth v. City of Aurora, Illinois, 183
Silk v. City of Chicago, 28
Siwek v. Police Board of City of Chicago, 150
Smith v. Northeastern Illinois Univ., 47
Snider v. Belvidere Township, 64
Stachowski v. Town of Cicero, 144
Stratman v. Brent, 212
Thornton v. Univ. Civil Service Merit Board, 320
Velez v. City of Chicago, 52
Villegas v. Board of Fire & Police Commissioners, 132
Walsh v. Heilmann, 220
Walters v. Metropolitan Educ. Enterprises, Inc., 88
Washington v. Illinois Dep't of Revenue, 92
Waters v. Churchill, 180
Weicherding v. Riegel, 209
Wernsing v. Dep't of Human Services, 64
White v. Village of Homewood, Illinois, 307
Wilbur v. Mahan, 229
Wittmer v. Peters, 95
Wood v. Wabash County, 127
Wright v. City of Danville, Illinois, 507

INDIANA

Americanos v. Carter, 223
Bridenbaugh v. O'Bannon, 500
City of Fort Wayne v. Moore, 289
Coolidge v. Consolidated City of Indianapolis and Marion County, 69

TABLE OF CASES BY STATE

Davidson v. City of Elkhart, Indiana, 199
Davis v. Indiana State Police, 11
Demos v. City of Indianapolis, 429
Endres v. Indiana State Police, 84
Fain v. Wayne County Auditor's Office, 410
Hamner v. St. Vincent Hospital & Health Care Center, 76
Jordan v. City of Gary, 151
Krieg v. Seybold, 326, 330
Kupstas v. City of Greenwood, 30
Leisen v. City of Shelbyville, 23
Michael v. St. Joseph County, 202
Miller v. City of Indianapolis, 497
Miller v. Vanderburgh County, 342
Mills v. City of Evansville, Indiana, 200
Molnar v. Booth, 77
Montgomery v. Stefaniak, 208
Moser v. Indiana Dep't of Corrections, 60
Pfifer v. Town of Edinburgh, 160
Sims-Fingers v. City of Indianapolis, 63
Twisdale v. Snow, 93
Wainscott v. Henry, 188
Wallace v. Estate of Davies by Davies, 285
Williams v. Riverside Community Corrections Corp., 373

IOWA

Bahr v. Council Bluffs Civil Service Comm'n, 505
City of Cedar Rapids v. Board of Trustees, 367
Clay v. City of Cedar Rapids, 154
DeLaMater v. Marion Civil Service Comm'n, 477
Greater Community Hospital v. PERB, 466
Hanson v. Hancock County Memorial Hospital, 249
Heuton v. Anderson, 304
Jankovitz v. Des Moines Independent Community School Dist., 352
Johnson v. Univ. of Iowa State Board of Regents, 59
Lee v. Employment Appeal Board, 382
Miller v. Sioux Gateway Fire Dep't, 40
Rodgers v. City of Des Moines, 406
Shaffer v. Potter, 57
Smith v. City of Des Moines, Iowa, 13

KANSAS

Alderfer v. Board of Trustees of Edwards County Hospital and Healthcare Center, 108
Anderson v. Sedgwick County, 490
Barnes v. Gorman, 291
Bates v. Dep't of Corrections of Kansas, 437
Carney v. City of Shawnee, Kansas, 203
Cragg v. City of Osawatomie, Kansas, 226
Crumpacker v. State of Kansas Dep't of Human Resources, 57
Fettke v. City of Wichita, 247

Frazier v. Simmons, 24
Green v. City of Wichita, 398
IAFF, Local 3808 v. Kansas City, 208
Int'l Ass'n of Firefighters, Local No. 64 v. City of Kansas City, 415
Johnson v. Unified Government of Wyandotte County/Kansas City, Kansas, 421
Lanman v. Johnson County, Kansas, 30
Moore v. Board of County Commissioners of County of Leavenworth, 305
Ney v. City of Hoisington, 409
Perez v. Unified Government of Wyandotte County, 274
Rupp v. Phillips, 198
Sprint/United Management Co. v. Mendelsohn, 10
State Dep't of Social & Rehabilitation Services v. PERB, 443
Thomas v. National Ass'n of Letter Carriers, 84

KENTUCKY

Comwlth., Justice and Public Safety Cabinet, Dep't of Corrections v. Searcy, 142
Comwlth., Labor Cabinet v. Hasken, 427
Comwlth. of Kentucky v. Gobert, 485
Draper v. Logan County Public Library, 233
Flechsig v. U.S., 304
Fryman v. Harrison, 283
Kentucky Retirement Systems v. EEOC, 364
Miller v. Administrative Office of the Courts, 199
Osborn v. Haley, 130
Relford v. Lexington-Fayette Urban County Government, 338
Roberts v. Ward, 234
Smith v. Henderson, 34
Steenken v. Campbell County, 496
Toyota Motor Manufacturing v. Williams, 20
Williams v. London Utility Comm'n, 132

LOUISIANA

AFSCME, Council 17 v. State of Louisiana, 133
Allison-LeBlanc v. Louisiana Dep't of Public Safety, 67
Almerico v. Harahan Municipal Fire and Police Civil Service Board, 153
Anderson v. Dep't of Public Safety and Corrections, 313
Bailey v. Dep't of Public Safety and Corrections, 156
Bannister v. Dep't of Streets, 139
Bourdais v. New Orleans, 98
Cain v. Jefferson Parish Dep't of Fleet Management, 347
Connick v. Myers, 178, 180
DeCorte v. Jordan, 98
Downey v. Strain, 404

TABLE OF CASES BY STATE

Elsensohn v. St. Tammany Parish Sheriff's Office, 409
George v. Dep't of Fire, 337
Ieyoub v. Polito, 503
Kotch v. Board of River Port Pilot Commissioners, 491
Krupp v. Dep't of Fire, 347
Marceaux v. State of Louisiana, 445
Meredith v. Louisiana Federation of Teachers, 447
Montegue v. City of New Orleans Fire Dep't, 327
National Treasury Employees Union v. Von Raab, 321, 322, 330, 332
Oncale v. Sundowner Offshore Services, Inc., 76
Oubre v. Entergy Operations, Inc., 10
Perrodin v. City of Lafayette, 375
Police Ass'n of New Orleans v. City of New Orleans, 100
Razor v. New Orleans Dep't of Police, 338
Richard v. Lafayette Fire and Police Civil Service Board, 338
Sciortino v. Dep't of Police, 349
Shortess v. Dep't of Public Safety & Corrections, 149
Smith v. East Baton Rouge Parish School Board, 408
Syrie v. Schilhab, 281
Victor v. Administrator, Office of Employment Security, 385

MAINE

Alden v. Maine, 252
Berube v. Conley, 306
Bragdon v. Abbott, 18
Dishon v. Maine State Retirement System, 413
Doe v. Dep't of Mental Health, Mental Retardation, and Substance Abuse Services, 248
Kvorjak v. Maine, 24
Locke v. Karass, 451
Parker v. Wakelin, 356
Roy v. Inhabitants of City of Lewiston, 287
Sher v. U.S. Dep't of Veterans Affairs, 144
Tripp v. Cole, 200

MARYLAND

Abendschein v. Montgomery County, Maryland, 436
Ahalt v. Montgomery County, Maryland, 368
Andrews v. Anne Arundel County, Maryland, 357
Boyle v. Maryland-National Capital Park and Planning Comm'n, 501
Brockman v. Snow, 66
Burkett v. Wicomico County, 117
Calhoun v. Commissioner of Baltimore Police, 506
Carroll v. City of Westminster, 339
Dep't of Public Safety and Correctional Services v. Palmer, 435
Dillon v. Maryland-National Capital Park and Planning Comm'n, 402
EEOC v. Baltimore County, 377
Elliott v. Maryland Dep't of Human Resources, 43
Fraternal Order of Police, Montgomery County Lodge No. 35 v. Mehrling, 502
Fraternal Order of Police v. Mayor and City Council of Ocean City Maryland, 218
Goldstein v. Chestnut Ridge Volunteer Fire Co., 302
Howard County Police Officers Ass'n, Inc. v. Howard County, 502
Kent v. Maryland Transportation Authority, 404
Maryland Troopers Ass'n v. Evans, 101
McCulloch v. Glendening, 456
Means v. Baltimore County, Maryland, 391
Mills v. Meadows, 222
Montgomery County v. Krieger, 153
Montgomery County v. Wade, 395
Polomski v. Mayor & City Council of Baltimore, Maryland, 413
Prince George's County, Maryland v. Fraternal Order of Police, Lodge 89, 473
Robinson v. Shell Oil Co., 88
Smith v. Danielczyk, 210
Smith v. Howard County, 386
Wheatley v. Wicomico County, 64
Whitehill v. Elkins, 232
Whittington v. City of Crisfield, 126
Wiley v. Doory, 279
Wolfe v. Anne Arundel County, 257
Wooden v. Maryland Dep't of Public Safety, 90

MASSACHUSETTS

Ahern v. O'Donnell, 316
Alake v. City of Boston, 271
Andrews v. Civil Service Comm'n, 496
Baron v. Suffolk County Sheriff's Dep't, 300
Belhumeur v. Labor Relations Comm'n, 454
Bennett v. City of Holyoke, 163
Billings v. Town of Grafton, 68
Bogan v. Scott-Harris, 260, 261
Bracket v. Civil Service Comm'n, 96
Brimage v. City of Boston, 306
Bristol County Retirement Board v. Contributory Retirement Appeal Board, 358
Burton v. Town of Littleton, 122
Carleton v. Massachusetts, 27
Centola v. Potter, 76
City of Boston v. Labor Relations Comm'n, 459
City of Lawrence v. Civil Service Comm'n, 475
Clifton v. Massachusetts Bay Transportation Authority, 103

TABLE OF CASES BY STATE

Damiano v. Contributory Retirement Appeal Board, 352
Dinsdale v. Comwlth., 262
Doherty v. Retirement Board of Medford, 362
Dupont v. Commissioners of Essex County, 160
Dwan v. City of Boston, 279
EEOC v. Comwlth. of Massachusetts, 378
Goncalves v. City of Boston, 472
Goncalves v. Labor Relations Comm'n, 450
Guiney v. Police Commissioner of Boston, 332
Gu v. Boston Police Dep't, 60
Hadfield v. McDonough, 220
Keaveney v. Town of Brookline, 331
Kelly v. Civil Service Comm'n, 112
King v. City of Boston, 56
Leach v. Commissioner of the Massachusetts Rehabilitation Comm'n, 38
LeMaitre v. Massachusetts Turnpike Authority, 357
Lowery v. Klemm, 79
Mard v. Town of Amherst, 370
Massachusetts Bay Transportation Authority v. Massachusetts Comm'n Against Discrimination, 83
Massachusetts Board of Retirement v. Murgia, 14
Massachusetts Correction Officers Federated Union v. Labor Relations Comm'n, 137
Nelson v. Salem State College, 243
O'Brien v. Town of Agawam, 429
Pereira v. Commissioner of Social Services, 202
Powell v. Alexander, 300
Prescott v. Higgins, 43
Riva v. Comwlth. of Massachusetts, 378
Roche v. Town of Wareham, 490
School Committee of Norton v. Massachusetts Comm'n Against Discrimination, 31
Scott v. Boston Housing Authority, 5
Service Employees Int'l Union, Local 509 v. Labor Relations Comm'n, 466
Sheriff of Suffolk County v. AFSCME Council 93, Local 419, 372
Sisca v. City of Fall River, 138
State Police for Automatic Retirement Ass'n v. DiFava, 15
Staveley v. City of Lowell, 102
Town of Dedham v. Dedham Police Ass'n, 374
Town of Hudson v. Labor Relations Comm'n, 464
Town of Plymouth v. Civil Service Comm'n, 152
Trustees of Health and Hospitals of City of Boston, Inc. v. Massachusetts Comm'n Against Discrimination, 44
Weaver v. Henderson, 238
White v. City of Boston, 371

MICHIGAN

Adair v. Charter County of Wayne, 433
Baker v. City of Detroit, 282
Barney v. Haveman, 379
Botke v. Chippewa County, 396
Calovecchi v. Michigan, 388
Clark v. Alston, 508
Daniel v. Michigan Dep't of Corrections, 385
Davis v. Michigan Dep't of Treasury, 416
DeMaagd v. City of Southfield, 167
Denhof v. City of Grand Rapids, 90
Everson v. Michigan Dep't of Corrections, 61
Grandville Municipal Executive Ass'n v. City of Grandville, 456
Haynie v. State, 38
Heckmann v. City of Detroit, 162
Hester v. City of Flint, 166
Int'l Union v. Winters, 330
Jones v. Reynolds, 280
Lash v. City of Traverse City, 492
Lehnert v. Ferris Faculty Ass'n, 452
Mannix v. County of Monroe, 129
McFaul v. Randall-Owens, 282
Michigan AFSCME Council 25 v. Livingston County Road Comm'n, 144
Michigan State AFL-CIO v. Michigan Civil Service Comm'n, 217
Michigan State Police Troopers Ass'n v. Michigan Dep't of State Police, 314
Middlebrooks v. Wayne County, 330
National Pride At Work, Inc. v. Governor of Michigan, 365
Oak Park Public Safety Officers Ass'n v. City of Oak Park, 461
People v. Coutu, 149
Porter v. City of Royal Oak, 214
Rutherford v. City of Flint, 358
Stamps v. City of Taylor, 286
Sutherland v. Michigan Dep't of Treasury, 97
Timmer v. Michigan Dep't of Commerce, 65
Will v. Michigan Dep't of State Police, 263
Warda v. City Council of City of Flushing, 506
Wygant v. Jackson Board of Educ., 98

MINNESOTA

Altman v. Minnesota Dep't of Corrections, 241
Anderson v. Creighton, 263
Anderson v. Independent School Dist., 211
Arraleh v. County of Ramsey, 51
Backlund v. Hessen, 491
Costilla v. State of Minnesota, 80
Hanger v. Lake County, Minnesota, 408
Hassan v. City of Minneapolis, 268
Hervey v. County of Koochiching, 56
Johnson v. State of Minnesota, 283
Kari v. City of Maplewood, 265

TABLE OF CASES BY STATE

Peterson v. Scott County, 12
Ray v. City of Maple Grove, 399
Raygor v. Regents of Univ. of Minnesota, 11
Senior v. City of Edina, 39
Winskowski v. City of Stephen, 122

MISSISSIPPI

Boddie v. City of Columbus, Mississippi, 218
Bulloch v. City of Pascagoula, 141
Bynum v. City of Magee, Mississippi, 284
Coahoma County v. Mississippi Employment Security Comm'n, 383
Cox v. Mississippi Dep't of Corrections, 145
Gentry v. Lowndes County, Mississippi, 225
Griffin v. Kemper County School Dist., 128
Jackson v. Hudspeth Mental Retardation Center, 156
Kemp v. Clairborne County Hospital, 336
McClendon v. City of Columbia, 268
McCrary v. City of Biloxi, 385
Mississippi Employment Security Comm'n v. Marion County Sheriff's Dep't, 382
Reeves v. Sanderson Plumbing Products, 3
Smith v. City of Jackson, 3
Tillman v. City of West Point, Mississippi, 210
U.S. Dep't of Defense v. Federal Labor Relations Authority, 441

MISSOURI

Acton v. City of Columbia, 428
Auer v. Robbins, 424, 426, 427
Berini v. Federal Reserve Bank of St. Louis, 380
Booker v. City of St. Louis, 334
Buford v. Runyon, 449
City of Kansas City v. Arthur, 494
City of St. Louis v. Praprotnik, 294
Clark v. Riverview Fire Protection Dist., 103
Culton v. Missouri Dep't of Corrections, 89
Davis v. Lambert-St. Louis Int'l Airport, 264
EEOC v. City of Independence, 11
EEOC v. Liberal R-II School Dist., 8
Eich v. Board of Regents for Cent. Missouri State Univ., Dep't of Public Safety, 70
Epps v. City of Pine Lawn, 257
Floyd v. Missouri Dep't of Social Services, 54
Garner v. Missouri Dep't of Health, 44
Grantham v. Trickey, 206
Green v. City of St. Louis, 162
Gunter v. Morrison, 186
Hammer v. City of Osage Beach, 211
Hardy v. City of Berkeley, 118
Hawkins v. Holloway, 276
Hicks v. St. Mary's Honor Center, 41
Hill v. KCATA, 35
Int'l Ass'n of Fire Fighters, Local 2665 v. City of Clayton, 355

Kennell v. Gates, 298
Krentz v. Robertson Fire Protection Dist., 110
Kunzie v. City of Olivette, 257
Lindsey v. City of Orrick, Missouri, 183
Littrell v. City of Kansas City, 163
McDonnell Douglas Corp. v. Green, 40, 41
Missouri Dep't of Natural Resources v. Lossos, 383
Morris v. City of Chillicothe, 153
Owen v. City of Independence, 293
Peeper v. Callaway County Ambulance Dist., 209
Phillips v. Collings, 82
Richey v. City of Independence, 150
Sellers v. Mineta, 157
Slentz v. City of Republic, 408
St. Mary's Honor Center v. Hicks, 41
Thomas v. Corwin, 27
Thompson v. Bi-State Development Agency, 91
Tuggle v. Mangan, 70
Tuttle v. Missouri Dep't of Agriculture, 7
Wager v. City of Ladue, 74
White v. St. Louis Teachers Union, Division of Employment Security, 381
Widow v. City of Kansas City, 57

MONTANA

Barr v. Great Falls Int'l Airport, 244
Kuhr v. City of Billings, 458
Montana Public Employee's Ass'n v. Dep't of Transportation, 439
Motarie v. Northern Montana Joint Refuse Disposal Dist., 172
Phillips v. City of Livingston, 136
State of Montana v. Schnittgen, 158
Van Vleet v. Montana Ass'n of Counties Workers' Compensation Trust, 394
Wolf v. Williamson, 214

NEBRASKA

Bauers v. City of Lincoln, 355
Brotherhood of Midwest Guardians v. City of Omaha, 101
Chubb v. City of Omaha, 409
Kincaid v. City of Omaha, 28
Kozisek v. County of Seward, Nebraska, 29
Lang v. City of Omaha, 436
Mathes v. City of Omaha, 112
Ross v. Douglas County, Nebraska, 47
Westbrook v. City of Omaha, 314

NEVADA

Balint v. Carson City, Nevada, 86
Clark County School Dist. v. Breeden, 88
Cone v. Nevada Service Employees Union, 449
Dominguez-Curry v. Nevada Dep't of Transportation, 58

TABLE OF CASES BY STATE

Employers Insurance Co. of Nevada v. Daniels, 386
Kaplan v. City of North Las Vegas, 28
Knapp v. State, Dep't of Prisons, 158
Las Vegas Metropolitan Police Dep't v. Berni, 147
Leever v. Carson City, 429
Lytle v. Carl, 301
Nevada Dep't of Human Resources v. Hibbs, 401, 409
Riback v. Las Vegas Metropolitan Police Dep't, 81
Skaarup v. City of North Las Vegas, 196
Walsh v. Nevada Dep't of Human Resources, 25

NEW HAMPSHIRE

Appeal of Barry, 370
Appeal of City of Portsmouth, Board of Fire Commissioners, 456
Appeal of Hillsboro-Deering School Dist., 462
Appeal of Merrimack County Board of Commissioners, 469
Appeal of Nashua Police Comm'n, 458
Collins v. City of Manchester, 446
Gorski v. New Hampshire Dep't of Corrections, 71
In re Amalgamated Transit Union, Local 717, 127
In re City of Manchester, 135
In re Exeter Police Ass'n, 137
In re Lincoln-Woodstock Cooperative School Dist., 136
In re New Hampshire Dep't of HHS, 388
Olsen v. Town of Loudon, 435
Town of Newton v. Rumery, 286
Yoder v. Town of Middleton, 143

NEW JERSEY

Abbamont v. Piscataway Board of Educ., 173
Antonelli v. State of New Jersey, 49
Barnhart v. Thomas, 364
Borough of Glassboro v. Fraternal Order of Police Lodge No. 108, 492
Brady v. Dep't of Personnel, 477
Brennan v. Norton, 164
Caggiano v. Fontoura, 104
Carberry v. State of New Jersey, Division of State Police, 397
Cardenas v. Massey, 53
Casamasino v. City of Jersey City, 131
Cedeno v. Montclair State Univ., 152
Chrisanthis v. County of Atlantic, 79
Cicchetti v. Morris County Sheriff's Office, 102
City of Newark v. Newark Council 21, 485
Corvelli v. Board of Trustees, 363
Cutler v. Dorn, 81

DeLisa v. County of Bergen, 168
Drake v. County of Essex, 341
Enriquez v. West Jersey Health Systems, 38
Evans v. Port Authority of New York and New Jersey, 49
Fielder v. Stonack, 308
Fraternal Order of Police v. City of Newark, 85
Galli v. New Jersey Meadowlands Comm'n, 225
Green Township Educ. Ass'n v. Rowe, 198
Hammond v. Monmouth County Sheriff's Dep't, 111
Hess v. Port Authority Trans-Hudson Corp., 253
In re Code Enforcement Officer, 482
In re Hruska, 474
In re Martinez, 473
In re Subryan, 144
In re Tulko, 475
Magaw v. Middletown Board of Educ., 389
Mantone v. Board of Trustees of Teachers' Pension and Annuity Fund, 361
Massachi v. AHL Services, Inc., 264
Matter of Division of Criminal Justice State Investigators, 457
Matter of Jackson, 39
Matter of Tavani, 481
Middletown Township Policemen's Benevolent Ass'n v. Township of Middletown, 367
New Jersey State Firemen's Mutual Benevolent Ass'n v. North Hudson Regional Fire & Rescue, 446
New Jersey Transit PBA Local 304 v. New Jersey Transit Corp., 326, 504
New Jersey Turnpike Authority v. Local 196, 148
New Jersey v. T.L.O., 312, 313
Patterson v. Board of Trustees, State Police Retirement System, 365
O'Connor v. City of Newark, 163
Office & Professional Employees Int'l Union, Local 32 v. Camden County Municipal Utilities Authority, 440
Raspa v. Office of the Sheriff of the County of Gloucester, 34
Rawlings v. Police Dep't of Jersey City, 339
Reames v. Dep't of Public Works, 331
Reilly v. City of Atlantic City, 182
Robertson v. Fiore, 230
Robinson v. Winslow Township, 299
Ruiz v. Mero, 287
Ryduchowski v. Port Authority of New York & New Jersey, 65
Shapiro v. Township of Lakewood, 32
Shoemaker v. Handel, 321
Shelton v. Univ. of Medicine & Dentistry of New Jersey, 85
Stanziale v. Jargowsky, 13
State of New Jersey v. Communications Workers of America, AFL-CIO, 464
State of New Jersey v. Perez, 148

TABLE OF CASES BY STATE

State v. Int'l Federation of Professional and Technical Engineers, Local 195, 430
Thomas v. County of Camden, 78
Thomas v. Town of Hammonton, 71
Thurber v. City of Burlington, 157

NEW MEXICO

Brown v. New Mexico State Personnel Office, 125
Deschenie v. Board of Educ., 204
Fuerschbach v. Southwest Airlines, 277
Garcia v. City of Albuquerque, 140
Hardeman v. City of Albuquerque, 186
Jaramillo v. City of Albuquerque, 324
Las Cruces Professional Fire Fighters v. City of Las Cruces, 463
Lybrook v. Farmington Municipal Schools Board of Educ., 216
Maestas v. Segura, 159
McGeshick v. Principi, 27
Perry v. Woodward, 46
Radecki v. Barela, 276
Rutherford v. City of Albuquerque, 343
Saavedra v. City of Albuquerque, 328
Singhas v. New Mexico State Highway Dep't, 393

NEW YORK

Abrahamson v. Board of Educ. of Wappingers Falls Cent. School Dist., 379
Altamore v. Barrios-Paoli, 478
Aneja v. Triborough Bridge and Tunnel Authority, 425
Barbera v. New York City Employees' Retirement System, 371
Barr v. Crosson, 445
Becker v. City of New York, 359
Benson v. New York State Dep't of Civil Service, 476
Beyer v. County of Nassau, 56
Bivens v. Six Unknown Named Agents of Federal Bureau of Narcotics, 292
Bizzarro v. Miranda, 154
Bottari v. Sarasota Springs City School Dist., 151
Boyd v. Constantine, 113
Buffalo Teachers Federation v. Tobe, 458
Burka v. New York City Transit Authority, 344
Burrus v. Vegliante, 228
Capobianco v. City of New York, 19
Castellano v. Board of Trustees of Police Officers' Variable Supplements Fund, 416
Catletti v. Rampe, 188
Clue v. Johnson, 216
Cobb v. Pozzi, 215
Conroy v. New York State Dep't of Corrections, 26

Cooper v. City of New York, 288
Correctional Services Corp. v. Malesko, 292
Cossifos v. New York and Local Employees' Retirement System, 366
Cotarelo v. Village of Sleepy Hollow Police Dep't, 184
Criscolo v. Vagianelis, 483
Cross v. New York City Transit Authority, 7
Daily Gazette Co. v. City of Schenectady, 443
D'Amico v. City of New York, 36
Danahy v. Buscaglia, 267
De Franks v. City of Buffalo, 495
Decker v. Campus, 299
Delaraba v. Nassau County Police Dep't, 332
Demoret v. Zegarelli, 74
DeVittorio v. Hall, 317
Diesel v. Town of Lewisboro, 157
Dumont v. Administrative Officer, 14
Duncan v. Kelly, 132
Engber v. New York State Comptroller, 352
Feingold v. State of New York, 81
Feola v. Carroll, 147
Fernandez v. New York State and Local Retirement Systems, 358
Flaherty v. Giambra, 444
Funderburke v. New York State Dep't of Civil Service, 365
Gabriele v. Metropolitan Suburban Bus Authority, 491
Genas v. State of New York Correctional Services, 242
Giordano v. City of New York, 30
Gobin v. New York City Health and Hospitals Corp., 52
Gordon v. Brown, 348
Gummo v. Village of Depew, New York, 500
Hale v. Mann, 256
Harman v. City of New York, 193
Harris v. Beedle, 204
Hess v. Port Authority Trans-Hudson Corp., 253
Hiller v. County of Suffolk, 50
Hoyt v. Andreucci, 215
Jana-Rock Construction, Inc. v. New York State Dep't of Economic Development, 94
Jubic v. City of Troy City Corp., 14
Kelley v. Johnson, 233
Kirk v. City of New York, 36
Kitchings v. Jenkins, 480
Konits v. Valley Stream Cent. High School, 185
Krohn v. New York City Police Dep't, 255
Lake City Police Club v. City of Oswego, 480
Lamb v. Town of Esopus, 159
Latino Officers Ass'n City of New York v. City of New York, 235
Leggio v. Suffolk County Police Dep't, 388
Leibovitz v. New York City Transit Authority, 72
Locurto v. Guiliani, 195
Longo v. Dolce, 336

TABLE OF CASES BY STATE

Maine-Endwell Teachers' Ass'n v. Board of Educ., 240
Mandell v. County of Suffolk, 240
Martinez v. County of Monroe, 54
Martinez v. State Univ. of New York–College at Oswego, 142
McCarthy v. New York City Technical College, 9
Meacham v. Knolls Atomic Power Laboratory, 3
Monell v. Dep't of Social Services, 301
Morris v. Lindau, 192
Mothersell v. City of Syracuse, New York, 507
Mueller v. County of Westchester, New York, 293
Mullins v. City of New York, 424
New York City Transit Authority v. New York State PERB, 136, 465
New York City Transit Authority v. State of New York, 87
Patterson v. Balsamico, 291
Patterson v. City of Utica, 211
Pena v. DePrisco, 275
Pennyfeather v. Tessler, 244
Pietras v. Board of Fire Commissioners of the Farmingville Fire Dist., 58
Presti v. Farrell, 140
Rochester Fire Fighters Ass'n v. Griffith, 466
Rolon v. Henneman, 260
Rourke v. New York State Dep't of Correctional Services, 237
Ruotolo v. City of New York, 182
Ryduchowski v. Port Authority of New York & New Jersey, 65
Sagendorf-Teal v. County of Rensselaer, New York, 206
Seelig v. Koehler, 333
Simonton v. Runyon, 77
Singh v. City of New York, 437
Smith v. Kingsboro Psychiatric Center (KPC), 117
Soto v. Schembri, 227
State of New York v. Kinsella, 489
Stratton v. Dep't for the Aging for the City of New York, 9
Thomas v. Straub, 504
Torain v. U.S. Postal Service, 161
Uniform Firefighters of Cohoes v. City of Cohoes, 371
Velez v. Levy, 123
Verri v. Nanna, 319
Wood v. Irving, 483
X-Men Security v. Pataki, 270
Zalewska v. County of Sullivan, 234
Zanghi v. Niagara Frontier Transportation Comm'n, 288

NORTH CAROLINA

Anderson v. Bessemer City, 55
Aponte v. U.S. Dep't of Treasury, 412
Baqir v. Principi, 52
Bishop v. Wood, 116
Brown v. Dep't of Navy, 157
Cash v. Granville County Board of Educ., 440
Edwards v. City of Goldsboro, 190, 503
Hayes v. North State Law Enforcement Officers Ass'n, 100
Holt v. Albemarle Regional Health Services Board, 167
Kirby v. City of Elizabeth City, 201
Lewis v. City of Kinston, 495
Love-Lane v. Martin, 188
Mendenhall v. North Carolina Dep't of Human Resources, 155
Mikels v. City of Durham, 78
Mutschler v. Housing Authority of Raleigh, North Carolina, 206
O'Connor v. Consolidated Coin Caterers Corp., 4
Rowland v. Perry, 300
Walker v. Board of Trustees of North Carolina Local Governmental Employees' Retirement System, 353
Wells v. North Carolina Dep't of Corrections, 164

NORTH DAKOTA

Anderson v. North Dakota State Hospital, 19
Jensen v. Henderson, 104
Nelson v. Gillette, 289
Robertson v. City of New England, 388
Wright v. Rolette County, 268

OHIO

Ass'n of Cleveland Firefighters v. City of Cleveland, Ohio, 492
Beck v. City of Cleveland, 433
Birch v. Cuyahoga County Probate Court, 64
Blake v. Wright, 246
Blanken v. Ohio Dep't of Rehabilitation & Correction, 235
Central State Univ. v. American Ass'n of Univ. Professors, CSU Chapter, 460
City of Cincinnati v. Dixon, 238
Cleveland Board of Educ. v. LaFleur, 66
Cleveland Board of Educ. v. Loudermill, 107
Cleveland Branch, NAACP v. City of Parma, 494
Cleveland Police Patrolmen's Ass'n v. City of Cleveland, 470
Coats v. City of Columbus, 284
Coker v. McFaul, 406
Elgabi v. Toledo Area Regional Transit Authority, 51

TABLE OF CASES BY STATE

Farm Labor Organizing Committee v. Ohio State Highway Patrol, 268
Feliciano v. City of Cleveland, 350
First v. Stark County Board of Commissioners, 315
Fontaine v. Clermont County Board of Commissioners, 323
General Dynamics Land Systems, Inc. v. Cline, 3
George v. Fairfield Metropolitan Housing Authority, 489
Hack v. Gillespie, 288
Hall v. Johnson, 350
Hamilton County Sheriff v. State Employment Relations Board, 462
Harden v. Ohio Attorney General, 374
Haynes v. City of Circleville, Ohio, 183
Holloman v. Greater Cleveland Regional Transit Authority, 337
Hughes v. City of North Olmsted, 250
Johnson v. Rumsfeld, 90
Keever v. City of Middletown, 33
Leeds v. Potter, 25
Lister v. Defense Logistics Agency, 184
Martin v. Barnesville Exempted School Dist. Board of Educ., 36
McCloud v. Testa, 230
Mt. Healthy City School Dist. v. Doyle, 179
Nord Community Mental Health Center v. Lorain County, 380
Painter v. Graley, 172
Rafferty v. City of Youngstown, 99
Ricco v. Potter, 407
Rice v. Ohio Dep't of Transportation, 223
Roseman v. Firemen and Policemen's Fund, 416
Sasse v. U.S. Dep't of Labor, 163
See v. City of Elyria, 272
Silberstein v. City of Dayton, 275
Spain v. City of Mansfield, 193
State ex rel. Fern v. Cincinnati, 476
State ex rel. Glass Workers v. SERB, 457
Stein v. City of Toledo, 319
Swepston v. Board of Tax Appeals of Ohio, 161
Todd v. City of Cincinnati, 29
Tysinger v. Police Dep't of the City of Zanesville, 66
Virgili v. Gilbert, 314
Wade v. Ohio Bureau of Workers' Compensation, 169
Wilson-Simmons v. Lake County Sheriff's Dep't, 50
Wollman v. Cleveland, 482

OKLAHOMA

Barnthouse v. City of Edmond, 474
Bass v. Potter, 404
City of Midwest City, Oklahoma v. Public Employees Relations Board, 461
City of Muskogee v. Grayson, 483
Draper v. Walsh, 278
Green v. Board of County Commissioners, 183
Henry v. Oklahoma County Board of County Commissioners, 205
Johnson v. Lodge #93 of the Fraternal Order of Police, 49
Jordan v. U.S. Postal Service, 410
Lanman v. Oklahoma County Sheriff's Office, 395
McClure v. Independent School Dist. No. 16, 111
McFall v. Bednar, 187
McGowan v. City of Eufala, 91
Neal v. Roche, 45
Schulte v. Potter, 6
Shrum v. City of Coweta, Oklahoma, 272
Smith v. State of Oklahoma, 59
Spradling v. City of Tulsa, 426
U.S. v. Barrows, 317
Williams v. Widnall, 37

OREGON

AFSCME Local 2623 v. Dep't of Corrections, 342
Amalgamated Transit Union Local 757 v. Tri-County Metropolitan Transportation Dist., 346
County of Washington v. Gunther, 63
Dark v. Curry County, 34
Dew v. City of Scappoose, 184
Elvin v. Oregon Public Employees Union, 454
Employment Division, Dep't of Human Resources of Oregon v. Smith, 238, 239
Engquist v. Oregon Dep't of Agriculture, 102, 117
Forest Service Employees for Environmental Ethics v. U.S. Forest Service, 243
Galdamez v. Potter, 47
Gouveia v. Sears, 490
Lawson v. Umatilla County, 128
Oregon Police Officers' Ass'n v. State of Oregon, 361
Paresi v. City of Portland, 441
Poland v. Chertoff, 6
Storm v. McClung, 308
Tanner v. Oregon Health Sciences Univ., 367
Thomas v. City of Beaverton, 187

PENNSYLVANIA

AARP v. EEOC, 377, 412
Allegheny County Airport Authority v. Construction General Laborers and Material Handlers Union, 150
Apgar v. State Employees' Retirement System, 363
Ascolese v. SEPTA, 89

TABLE OF CASES BY STATE

Ballerino v. WCAB, 369
Benn v. First Judicial Dist. of Pennsylvania, 26
Borough of Ellwood City v. Pennsylvania Labor Relations Board, 460
Borough of Heidelberg v. Workers' Compensation Appeal Board (Selva), 398
Borough of Lewistown v. Pennsylvania Labor Relations Board, 468
Borough of Wilkinsburg v. Colella, 474
Burella v. City of Philadelphia, 274
Byrd v. City of Philadelphia, 43
Callison v. City of Philadelphia, 405
City of Erie v. Workers' Compensation Appeal Board, 398
City of Philadelphia v. WCAB, 389
City of Philadelphia v. WCAB (Cospelich), 387
City of Pittsburgh v. Bachner, 473
City of Pittsburgh v. Brentley, 138
Coddington v. Evanko, 318
Comwlth. of Pennsylvania, Dep't of Corrections v. Krempowsky, 479
Comwlth. of Pennsylvania v. PLRB, 461
Council 13 v. Comwlth. of Pennsylvania, 421
Curinga v. City of Clairton, 221
Davis v. Workers' Compensation Appeals Board, 385
Delaware County Lodge No. 27, Fraternal Order of Police v. Township of Tinicum, 109
Dep't of Corrections, SCI-Camp Hill v. Unemployment Compensation Board of Review, 381
DeVeaux v. City of Philadelphia, 239
Doe v. Southeastern Pennsylvania Transportation Authority, 250
Dykes v. Southeastern Pennsylvania Transportation Authority, 343
El v. Southeastern Pennsylvania Transportation Authority, 44
Elmore v. Cleary, 129
Florian v. State Civil Service Comm'n, 151
Gierschick v. State Employees' Retirement Board, 362
Gilbert v. Homar, 107
Graham v. City of Philadelphia, 123
Gurnari v. Luzerne County Housing Authority, 254
Haber v. Evans, 245
Hafer v. Melo, 263
Hamera v. County of Berks, 81
Herman v. City of Allentown, 37
Hetman v. State Civil Service Comm'n, 227
Hill v. City of Scranton, 493
Hopp v. City of Pittsburgh, 95
Ingram v. County of Bucks, 436
Kaucher v. County of Bucks, 291
Kincel v. Pennsylvania, 392
Lawrence v. City of Philadelphia, 421

Lloyd v. City of Bethlehem, 186
Mallick v. Pennsylvania State Police, 4
McKee v. Hart, 272
Miller v. Clinton County, 199
Mitchell v. Forsyth, 259
Novak v. City of Pittsburgh, 501
O'Rourke v. Comwlth. of Pennsylvania Dep't of Corrections, 165
Otto v. Pennsylvania State Educ. Ass'n, 453
Pennsylvania Game Comm'n v. State Civil Service Comm'n, 478
Pennsylvania State Corrections Officers Ass'n v. State Civil Service Comm'n, 479
Pennsylvania State Police v. Suders, 73
Pennsylvania State Univ. v. State Employees' Retirement Board, 442
Philadelphia Gas Works v. Unemployment Compensation Board, 345
Philadelphia Housing Authority v. AFSCME, 467
Phillips v. County of Allegheny, 285
Robinson v. City of Philadelphia, 270
Rogers v. Powell, 277
Schorr v. Borough of Lemoyne, 297
SEPTA v. WCAB, 394
Sicuro v. City of Pittsburgh, 499
Sterling v. Borough of Minersville, 297
Suppan v. Dadonna, 216
Tice v. Centre Area Transportation Authority, 19
Troster v. Pennsylvania State Dep't of Corrections, 236
Turner v. Unemployment Compensation Board of Review, 381
Walsh v. Unemployment Compensation Board of Review, 381
Webb v. City of Philadelphia, 83
Webb v. State Civil Service Comm'n, 150
Westmoreland County v. Westmoreland County Detectives, 134
Westmoreland Intermediate Unit #7 v. WIU #7 Classroom Assistants Educ. Support Personnel Ass'n PSEA/NEA, 134
Wheeler v. Hampton Township, 428
Wishkin v. Potter, 25
Woods v. State Civil Service Comm'n, 147

PUERTO RICO

Bisbal-Ramos v. City of Mayaguez, 229
Cepero-Rivera v. Fagundo, 170
Cruz-Gomez v. Rivera-Hernandez, 484
EEOC v. Union Independente de la Autoridad de Acueductos y Alcantarillados de Puerto Rico, 84
Gomez v. Toledo, 262
Guilloty Perez v. Pieluisi, 164
Quiles v. Henderson, 29
Ramirez v. Arlequin, 219

TABLE OF CASES BY STATE

RHODE ISLAND

Angell v. The Union Fire Dist. of South Kingstown, 391
Brandon v. City of Providence, 265
Bunch v. Board of Review, 384
Casey v. Town of Portsmouth, 4
Carlow v. Mruk, 260
City of East Providence v. United Steelworkers of America, Local 15509, 109
City of Woonsocket v. Int'l Brotherhood of Police Officers, 353
Kells v. Town of Lincoln, 130
Malley v. Briggs, 259
McGrath v. Rhode Island Retirement Board, 357
Monahan v. Girouard, 109
O'Rourke v. City of Providence, 72
Providence Teachers' Union, Local 958 v. City of Council of City of Providence, 493
Retirement Board of the Employees' Retirement System v. DiPrete, 361
Rhode Island Brotherhood of Correctional Officers v. State of Rhode Island, 445
State of Rhode Island v. Rhode Island Council 94, 469
State v. Rhode Island Employment Security Alliance, Local 401, SEIU, 465
Young v. City of Providence, 296

SOUTH CAROLINA

Conner v. City of Forest Acres, 170
Counts v. South Carolina Electric & Gas Co., 425
EEOC v. Waffle House, Inc., 101
Frazier v. Badger, 266
Glover v. City of North Charleston, South Carolina, 422
Lawson v. South Carolina Dep't of Corrections, 168
Layman v. State, 414
Miller v. City of West Columbia, South Carolina, 213
Mincey v. U.S. Postal Service, 451
Roy v. County of Lexington, South Carolina, 431
Silverman v. Campbell, 241
Wright v. Universal Maritime Service Corp., 25

SOUTH DAKOTA

Aberle v. City of Aberdeen, 126
Engel v. Rapid City School Dist., 69
Senger v. City of Aberdeen, 427

TENNESSEE

Auction v. City of Clarksville, 47
Barnes v. U.S., 303
Bartlik v. U.S. Dep't of Labor, 166
Beecham v. Henderson County, 207
Burlington Northern and Santa Fe Railway Co. v. White, 88
Crawford v. Metropolitan Government of Nashville, 87
Chudasama v. Metropolitan Government of Nashville and Davidson County, 307
Coffey v. Chattanooga-Hamilton County Hospital Authority, 171
Dorris v. Absher, 247
Gardner v. Insura Property and Casualty Insurance Co., 280
Holiday v. City of Chattanooga, 20
Jones v. Johanns, 91
Jones v. Smith, 501
Lane v. City of LaFollette, 224
Leadbetter v. Gilley, 62
Letner v. City of Oliver Springs, 434
Moore v. Town of Collierville, 366
Petty v. Metropolitan Government of Nashville-Davidson County, 496
Pollard v. E.I. du Pont de Nemours & Co., 68
Richardson v. McKnight, 263
Seiber v. Town of Oliver Springs, 145
Sircy v. Metropolitan Government of Nashville and Davidson County, 484
Tennessee v. Garner, 295
Tuttle v. Metropolitan Government of Nashville and Davidson County, Tennessee, 7
Vaughn v. Lawrenceburg Power System, 208
Wagner v. City of Memphis, 115
Waters v. City of Morristown, 301

TEXAS

Barrow v. Greenville Independent School Dist., 240
Benningfield v. City of Houston, 191
Board of County Commissioners of Bryan County v. Brown, 253
Bolton v. City of Dallas, 124
Brown v. Bryan County, 253
Carr v. City of Fort Worth, 472
Charles v. Grief, 181
Christensen v. Harris County, 432
City of Boerne, Texas v. Flores, 232
City of El Paso v. Higginbotham, 264
City of Hildalgo v. Prado, 269
City of Odessa, Texas v. Barton, 129
Cleveland v. City of Elmendorf, Texas, 439
Collins v. City of Harker Heights, 294
Communication Workers of America v. Ector County Hospital Dist., 234
Cudd v. Aldrich, 222
Daniels v. City of Arlington, 201
Evans v. City of Bishop, 8
Faculty Rights Coalition v. Shahrokhi, 195
Gamble v. Gregg County, 375

TABLE OF CASES BY STATE

Garcia v. San Antonio Metropolitan Transit Authority, 420
Houston Police Officers Union v. City of Houston, 434
Jaso v. Travis County Juvenile Board, 6
Jones v. City of Houston, 481
Jones v. Kerrville State Hospital, 35
Jordan v. Jones, 499
Kapche v. City of San Antonio, 24
Lubke v. City of Arlington, 405
Markos v. City of Atlanta, Texas, 187
Martinez v. Texas Dep't of Criminal Justice, 256
Mauder v. Metropolitan Transit Authority, 403
McElroy v. City of Temple, 481
Miller v. City of Nederland By and Through Wimer, 133
Modica v. Taylor, 272
Moreau v. Klevenhagen, 433
NLRB v. Weingarten, 136
National Treasury Employees Union v. Dep't of Treasury, 325
Perry v. Sindermann, 115, 116
Piotrowski v. City of Houston, 297
Rankin v. McPherson, 178, 180
Rios v. Rossotti, 53
Rogers v. City of San Antonio, 497
Sharp v. City of Houston, 298
Steadman v. Texas Rangers, 205
Stevens v. Dep't of the Treasury, 10
Singer v. City of Waco, 430
Teague v. City of Flower Mound, 203
Texas Dep't of Community Affairs v. Burdine, 55
Tharling v. City of Port Lavaca, 194
Univ. of Texas Medical Branch at Galveston v. Savoy, 167
Wadewitz v. Montgomery, 307
Wallace v. County of Comal, 185

UTAH

Burke v. Utah Transit Authority and Local 382, 448
Epperson v. Utah State Retirement Board, 354
Etsitty v. Utah Transit Authority, 61
Kosan v. Utah Dep't of Corrections, 239
Lucas v. Murray City Civil Service Comm'n, 114
Morgan v. McCotter, 131
O'Keefe v. Utah State Retirement Board, 360
Seegmiller v. Laverkin City, 273
Sheikh v. Dep't of Public Safety, 67
Snyder v. City of Moab, 221
Utah Educ. Ass'n v. Shurtleff, 224
Wagstaff v. Dep't of Employment Security, 345

VERMONT

Vermont State Employees' Ass'n v. Vermont Criminal Justice Training Council, 487

VIRGINIA

Adams v. City of Norfolk, 425
Alderman by Alderman v. U.S., 305
Beardsley v. Webb, 78
Benshoff v. City of Virginia Beach, 421
Blakey v. U.S.S. Iowa, 305
Blizzard v. Dalton, 500
Bowen v. U.S. Postal Service, 448
City of Richmond v. J.A. Croson Co., 93
City of Virginia Beach v. Harris, 171
Coleman v. Loudoun, 43
Cooper v. Federal Reserve Bank of Richmond, 49
Cooper v. Lee County Board of Supervisors, 222
Edelman v. Lynchburg College, 102
Etter v. Spencer, 121
Fairfax County Fire and Rescue Dep't v. Mottram, 387
Garraghty v. Comwlth. of Virginia, 126
Mandel v. Allen, 161
Office of Personnel Management v. Richmond, 369
Pike v. Osborne, 226
Salazar v. Ballesteros, 393
Sciolino v. City of Newport News, 122
Stanfield v. Peregoy, 271
U.S. v. Simons, 315
Urofsky v. Gilmore, 199
Washington Metropolitan Area Transit Authority v. Local 2, Office Professional Employees Int'l Union, 460
Whitener v. McWatters, 261
Williams v. Garraghty, 214

WASHINGTON

Adair v. City of Kirkland, 431
Baggett v. Bullitt, 231
Bellevue John Does 1-11 v. Bellevue School Dist. 405, 442
Bolden v. State of Washington Dep't of Transportation, 389
Brame v. Western State Hospital, 392
Civil Service Comm'n v. City of Kelso, 135
Davenport v. Washington Educ. Ass'n, 452
Dep't of the Navy v. Egan, 173, 175
Dewey v. Tacoma School Dist., 169
Galvin v. State of Washington, Employment Security Dep't, 384
Grabicki v. Dep't of Retirement Systems, 360

TABLE OF CASES BY STATE

Int'l Ass'n of Fire Fighters, Local 27 v. City of Seattle, 356
Johanson v. Dep't of Social & Health Services, 486
Kalina v. Fletcher, 260
King County v. Sheehan, 245
MacSuga v. County of Spokane, 35
Molloy v. City of Bellevue, 39
Molsness v. City of Walla Walla, Washington, 141
Navlet v. Port of Seattle, 380
Reninger v. State Dep't of Corrections, 120
Richmond v. Thompson, 213
Soelter v. King County, 223
Washington State Dep't of Labor & Industries v. Johnson, 395
Webster v. Public School Employees of Washington, Inc., 426

WEST VIRGINIA

Akers v. Caperton, 224
Beckley v. Crabtree, 309
Canfield v. West Virginia Division of Corrections, 373
In re Queen, 141
Montgomery v. West Virginia State Police, 111
Semple v. City of Moundsville, 281
State of West Virginia v. Lincoln County Comm'n, 229
Watts v. Dep't of Health & Human Resources, 486
Wheeling Park Comm'n v. Hotel Union, 217

WISCONSIN

Antisdel v. City of Oak Creek Police & Fire Comm'n, 118
Appelbaum v. Milwaukee Metropolitan Sewerage Dist., 8
Balton v. City of Milwaukee, 209
Barrows v. Wiley, 124
Board of Regents v. Roth, 115, 116
Burks v. Wisconsin Dep't of Transportation, 45
DeShaney v. Winnebago County DSS, 268, 280
EEOC v. Board of Regents of Univ. of Wisconsin System, 12
Gentilli v. Board of Police and Fire Commissioners, 148
Golembiewski v. City of Milwaukee, 494
Gray v. Marinette County, 450
Greer v. Amesqua, 198
Grossman v. South Shore Public School Dist., 239
Gustafson v. Jones, 121
Henry v. Jones, 43
Jackson v. County of Racine, 74

Johnson v. Labor & Industry Review Comm'n, 13
Kara B. by Albert v. Dane County, Wisconsin, 282
Larson v. City of Tomah, 171
Metropolitan Milwaukee Ass'n of Commerce v. Milwaukee County, 465
Milwaukee County v. Juneau County, 387
Milwaukee Dist. Council 48 v. Milwaukee County, 353
Milwaukee Police Ass'n and Julie Horter v. Jones, 192
Milwaukee Professional Fire Fighters Ass'n v. City of Milwaukee, 378
Peters v. City of Mauston, 30
Pleva v. Norquist, 221
Port Edwards School Dist. v. Reissmann, 407
Steinhauer v. Degolier, 60
Toeller v. Wisconsin Dep't of Corrections, 410
Torres v. Wisconsin Dep't of Health and Social Services, 62
Weiss v. City of Milwaukee, 390

WYOMING

Brockman v. Wyoming DFS, 255
Haines v. Fisher, 290
Hesse v. Town of Jackson, Wyoming, 271
McKenzie v. Dovala, 19
Mondt v. Cheyenne Police Dep't, 133
Renaud v. Wyoming Dep't of Family Services, 302

CHAPTER ONE

Employment Discrimination

                                                                                Page

I. AGE DISCRIMINATION 2
    A. Burden of Proof Under ADEA 2
        1. Age Factor 3
        2. Adverse Employment Action..6
        3. Pretext for Discrimination 7
    B. Procedural Issues 9
    C. Defenses...12
        1. Maximum Age Limitations..13
        2. Mandatory Retirement 14

II. DISABILITY DISCRIMINATION 16
    A. The Rehabilitation Act and ADA...17
        1. Physical or Mental Impairment 17
        2. Substantial Limitation 20
        3. Essential Job Functions 23
        4. Procedural Issues 25
        5. Defenses..26
        6. Regarded as Disabled 29
    B. Reasonable Accommodation 30
        1. Types of Accommodation 31
        2. Unreasonable Accommodations 33
    C. Drug and Alcohol Use 35
    D. State Statutes 37

III. RACE AND NATIONAL ORIGIN DISCRIMINATION...............40
    A. Race Discrimination 40
        1. Burden of Proof..40
        2. Racial Harassment 46
        3. Judgments and Settlement Decrees 48
    B. National Origin Discrimination..51

IV. SEX DISCRIMINATION 54
    A. Generally..54
        1. Burden of Proof..54
        2. Legitimate Reasons 58
        3. Defenses..60
    B. Equal Pay...62
    C. Pregnancy..66
    D. Harassment..67
        1. Burden of Proof..68
        2. Defenses..72

3. Same-Sex and Sexual Orientation Issues 75
4. 42 U.S.C. § 1983 77
5. State Statutes 78

V. **RELIGIOUS DISCRIMINATION** 80
   A. Burden of Proof..80
   B. Reasonable Accommodations 82
   C. Seniority Systems 86

VI. **RETALIATORY DISCRIMINATION** 87

VII. **AFFIRMATIVE ACTION** 93
   A. Affirmative Action Programs.......................................93
      1. Hiring Decisions 93
      2. Promotions 95
      3. Employment Terminations...................................97
   B. Procedural Issues 98
   C. Termination and Modification of Programs 99

VIII. **PROCEDURAL MATTERS** 101
   A. Generally...101
   B. Continuing Violation Doctrine...................................103

I. AGE DISCRIMINATION

The Age Discrimination in Employment Act, 29 U.S.C. § 621 et seq. (ADEA), prohibits employment discrimination based upon age. It limits its protection to individuals who are at least <u>40 years old</u>. However, state laws may provide protections for persons younger than 40.

The ADEA's protections apply not only to hiring and firing decisions but also to <u>adverse actions</u> and the provision of compensation and benefits. Adverse action can include such things as negative performance reviews, suspensions, transfers to undesirable positions, harassment and other actions taken by management or even co-workers.

In 1990, the ADEA was amended by the Older Workers Benefit Protection Act (OWBPA), which prohibits discrimination against older workers in all employee benefits "except when age-based reductions in employee benefit plans are justified by significant cost considerations."

A. Burden of Proof Under ADEA

The U.S. Supreme Court has held that once an employee has presented a *prima facie* case of discrimination under the ADEA and shown that the employer's asserted reasons for its adverse action are false, intentional discrimination may be inferred without further evidence of discrimination. *Reeves v. Sanderson Plumbing Products*, 530 U.S. 133 (2000).

Although the ADEA prohibits employers from favoring younger employees over older ones, it does not protect younger employees from actions favoring older workers. See *General Dynamics Land Systems, Inc. v. Cline*, 540 U.S. 581 (2004).

* After the Navy ordered the Knolls Atomic Power Lab to reduce its workforce, 100 employees took the lab's buyout offer. The lab then had 31 jobs to cut. It told managers to score employees in three categories: job performance, flexibility and criticality. The flexibility factor assessed whether the employees' skills were transferable to other assignments. The criticality factor assessed the importance of the employees' skills to the lab. When 30 of the 31 people laid off were age 40 or older, an ADEA lawsuit ensued. A New York jury ruled that the layoff process had a disparate impact on older employees, but the Second Circuit reversed, finding the employees should have been required to prove that the selection process was unreasonable. The Supreme Court vacated and remanded the case. **The burden should have been on the employer to prove that its layoff process used reasonable factors other than age.** *Meacham v. Knolls Atomic Power Laboratory*, 128 S.Ct. 2395 (U.S. 2008).

1. Age Factor

Where age is proven to be a factor in an adverse action, an employer will become liable under the ADEA. However, where a factor other than age is used to make an adverse decision – even if that factor sometimes correlates with age – no liability will attach.

* A group of senior, longtime police officers with a Mississippi city challenged the city's revised pay policy because it gave proportionately higher raises to officers with less than five years of tenure. They claimed that the revised policy had a disparate impact on them. In other words, a facially neutral policy had an adverse effect on them. The case reached the U.S. Supreme Court, which held that **the officers could sue for disparate impact discrimination under the ADEA**. To win, the officers would have to identify a "specific test, requirement, or practice with the pay plan that ha[d] an adverse impact on older workers." The city claimed that the differential was justified by the need to make junior officers' salaries competitive with comparable positions in the market. Here, the Court determined that the policy was based on reasonable factors other than age and therefore did not violate the ADEA. *Smith v. City of Jackson*, 544 U.S. 228, 125 S.Ct. 1536, 161 L.Ed.2d 410 (2005).

* **A North Carolina employer fired a 56-year-old employee and replaced him with a 40-year-old man.** The employee sued, alleging age discrimination in violation of the ADEA even though he was replaced by a person within the protected class. The case reached the U.S. Supreme Court, which held that he could sue under the ADEA. The Court noted that because the ADEA prohibits discrimination on the basis of age, and not on the basis of class membership, the

replacement of an employee by a substantially younger employee was a far more reliable indicator of age discrimination than was the status of the respective employees. *O'Connor v. Consolidated Coin Caterers Corp.*, 517 U.S. 308, 116 S.Ct. 1307, 134 L.Ed.2d 433 (1996).

♦ A 50-year-old African-American Department of Homeland Security employee was passed over for a promotion in favor of a 35-year-old white woman. A lawsuit resulted, and the U.S. Court of Appeals, D.C. Circuit, ruled that the promotion did not violate Title VII or the ADEA. The selected candidate had less supervisory experience, but more operations experience, and was only one grade classification below the rejected candidate, while still fulfilling the requirements for promotion. **The two candidates were not so significantly different as to suggest that race or age was the true reason for the non-promotion.** *Barnette v. Chertoff*, 453 F.3d 513 (D.C. Cir. 2006).

♦ The Pennsylvania State Police generally offered overtime to state troopers in descending order of seniority, so troopers who were close to retirement were favored for overtime assignments. This resulted in higher pay for troopers close to retirement, which in turn resulted in higher retirement and pension benefits. After reviewing overtime assignments, the head of the state police became concerned about safety issues and sent out a directive ordering bureau chiefs to stop favoring troopers close to retirement for overtime assignments. Retiring troopers sued for age discrimination, but the Commonwealth Court ruled against them. It noted that **decisions based on years of service were not necessarily correlated with age.** *Mallick v. Pennsylvania State Police*, 862 A.2d 739 (Pa. Commw. Ct. 2004).

♦ A Rhode Island town passed over a 51-year-old town resident for a public works position, even though he tied for the highest score on the exam, because he seemed surly during the interview. It hired a 28-year-old. Later, the town passed him over for another job and hired a 38-year-old who scored much lower on the test and who was not a town resident, despite a hiring policy that gave a preference for town residents. Again, the applicant's attitude seemed antagonistic during the interview. He sued for discrimination under state law, and the Supreme Court of Rhode Island ruled against him. **The town's reason for not hiring him – bad attitude – was consistent and legitimate.** *Casey v. Town of Portsmouth*, 861 A.2d 1032 (R.I. 2004).

♦ The Boston Housing Authority contracted with a window glazier to work on apartments it managed. It renewed the contracts annually until it determined that it had no more funds for his position. The general contract superintendent stated that the reason for not renewing the contract was that the rehabilitation fund was out of money and that personnel cuts had to be made. However, he kept three brothers-in-law and a cousin employed during this time. When the glazier sued for age discrimination under state law, a jury found in his favor and awarded him more than $700,000. The Appeals Court of Massachusetts affirmed. Here, even though the evidence of age discrimination was not overwhelming, and **the real reason for not renewing the contract was likely**

nepotism, the jury was allowed to credit the glazier's testimony over the evidence presented by the authority. *Scott v. Boston Housing Authority*, 777 N.E.2d 174 (Mass. App. Ct. 2002).

* A records clerk for an Arkansas police department obtained a note from her doctor advising her not to work for two weeks while she recuperated from a bladder infection, depression and work-related anxiety. The police chief approved her medical leave, and her supervisor informed her that she was required to see the department's physician. However, she failed to keep two appointments with the department's doctor and was fired for insubordination. She sued the department and the chief for violating the ADEA, alleging that the chief had hired a large percentage of employees under the age of 40 after he became chief. A federal court ruled in favor of the defendants, and the Eighth Circuit affirmed. Here, the department had a legitimate reason for terminating her employment – her insubordination. Also, **the hiring statistics did not prove age discrimination**, but only that younger people tended to be looking for jobs while older people tended to be leaving jobs. *Bennett v. Watters*, 260 F.3d 925 (8th Cir. 2001).

* California decided to create a voluntary retirement incentive program for eligible members of the University of California Retirement Plan (UCRP) (4,425 eligible members with an average age of 55). It chose not to offer the early retirement incentive to university employees who were members of the Public Employees Retirement System (PERS) (440 potentially eligible members with an average age of 60). Surplus funds in the UCRP covered the costs of the voluntary incentive program for its members. However, the cost of offering the program to PERS members would have been $30 million. When the PERS members sued the university under the ADEA, a federal court refused to let them pursue their theory of disparate impact – that outwardly neutral employment practices had an adverse effect on persons of a particular age. After a jury ruled for the university, the Ninth Circuit Court of Appeals affirmed. **The university's refusal to offer a voluntary retirement incentive program to PERS members could not be considered disparate impact discrimination.** Only 238 of the 895 employees age 60 or older were adversely affected by the decision. This was not enough to show disparate impact discrimination. *Katz v. Univ. of California Board of Regents*, 229 F.3d 831 (9th Cir. 2000).

* An assistant chief juvenile probation officer was one of three finalists for the chief juvenile probation officer position. He had worked for the department for 30 years. However, a 40-year-old assistant chief juvenile probation officer from another county was selected for the job, and a lawsuit arose under state law. **The assistant claimed that he had been treated unfavorably during the interview process** – for example, he had not been invited to a "lunch and tour" with the other two candidates. The Texas Court of Appeals found, however, that since the employee had worked at the facility for 30 years, he already was familiar with its operations and staff. Also, a stray remark by the board chair (that if she had been with the county for 30 years, she would retire) was not made during the discussion of the employee's qualifications and preceded the

screening interview that actually led to his selection as a finalist. *Jaso v. Travis County Juvenile Board*, 6 S.W.3d 324 (Tex. Ct. App. 1999).

2. Adverse Employment Action

Different jurisdictions have different rules about what constitutes adverse action. Some consider termination the only adverse action upon which a lawsuit can be based. Others allow lawsuits for constructive discharge, suspensions, demotions and even negative performance evaluations.

♦ A 60-year-old Oklahoma postal carrier was turned down for two promotions, then suspended for 22 days because she improperly recirculated mail she was supposed to deliver. She sued under the ADEA. A federal court and the Tenth Circuit Court of Appeals ruled against her. Here, the postal service had a legitimate reason for rejecting her for the promotions – other candidates fared better on the interview and test. Also, **the suspension was justified because a clerk saw her improperly return the mail**. The carrier failed to prove age discrimination by the postal service. *Schulte v. Potter*, 218 Fed.Appx. 703 (10th Cir. 2007).

♦ A doctor was rejected for a volunteer position with the National Institutes of Health (NIH) in a medical genetics program. Working as a volunteer could lead to permanent employment with the NIH. He sued under Title VII and the ADEA. The NIH sought pretrial judgment, claiming the volunteer position did not qualify as federal employment for purposes of the statutes. A D.C. federal court refused to dismiss the case. **Volunteer work that provides a clear pathway to employment amounts to employment for purposes of Title VII and the ADEA.** However, the doctor had to show that he was qualified for the position. He did not fit into the two types of candidates generally considered for volunteer positions. He was not a graduate student, and he did not come to the NIH with an independent source of funding. *Rafi v. Thompson*, 2006 WL 3091483 (D.D.C. 10/30/06).

♦ A supervisor with the U.S. Customs Service in Oregon had a bias against older employees. He initiated an investigation of a 53-year-old manager under his supervision who had filed an EEO complaint 14 months earlier. He alleged that the manager was disrespectful toward other workers in the office. He selected the witnesses who would be testifying without input from the manager. After a hearing before an independent panel, the manager was stripped of his managerial duties and reassigned. He resigned after six months, then sued for retaliation and constructive discharge under the ADEA. The case reached the Ninth Circuit, which held that **the Customs Service could be liable for the biased supervisor's retaliatory conduct even though the hearing panel's decision was not biased**. Here, the biased supervisor influenced the panel's decision-making process. The court remanded the case for a determination of damages. *Poland v. Chertoff*, 494 F.3d 1174 (9th Cir. 2007).

◆ Two New York City Transit Authority employees (ages 59 and 62) brought ADEA claims after their boss hesitated to promote them, then **refused to give them any training** and finally demoted them after they refused to be tested on equipment they had not been properly trained on. Three under-40 employees were trained on the equipment. A jury decided in favor of the employees, awarding one employee $134,000 and the other $55,000. The Second Circuit upheld the awards. The jury reasonably discredited the testimony of their boss as self-serving and obviously false. *Cross v. New York City Transit Authority*, 417 F.3d 241 (2d Cir. 2005).

◆ A 51-year-old grain inspector for the Missouri Department of Agriculture was fired as part of a reduction in force. He declined an offer to work part time in the lower classification of grain sampler and sued under the ADEA. A jury held in his favor, but the trial judge vacated the verdict, ruling that there was insufficient evidence of age discrimination. The Eighth Circuit affirmed, rejecting the inspector's argument that discrimination could be inferred from the department's offer of voluntary early retirement. The court also refused to find discriminatory intent in a manager's statement that retirement of personnel would be beneficial to the department. Nor was it persuasive that the department refused to promote the inspector or that all of the other terminated inspectors were over 40 and had been with the department for a number of years. The employer could **eliminate the least versatile class of employees, whose work could be distributed to lower-paid part-time employees**. *Tuttle v. Missouri Dep't of Agriculture*, 172 F.3d 1025 (8th Cir. 1999).

3. Pretext for Discrimination

Most employers are smart enough to avoid using age as the reason for an adverse action. But when the employer asserts an explanation that seems phony to a jury, it may decide that the real motive was discrimination.

◆ After making several accounting errors and receiving an evaluation stating that she needed to work on getting along with her peers, a 63-year-old Nashville public works employee was transferred to a position weighing garbage trucks, then fired. She sued under the ADEA, and a jury awarded her $192,000. The court wiped out the award, but the Sixth Circuit reversed that decision. Here, the department supervisor failed to track whether the employee's younger replacement made accounting errors and also **failed to discharge a second younger co-worker who received a similar warning** about getting along with her co-workers. Finally, several age-related comments, though not insidious, permitted the jury to decide that the real reason for the termination was age. *Tuttle v. Metropolitan Government of Nashville and Davidson County, Tennessee*, 474 F.3d 307 (6th Cir. 2007).

◆ A 59-year-old secretary in the HR department of the Milwaukee sewer district was targeted for layoff in a reduction in force despite inferior performance by a younger secretary. She managed to keep her job when another secretary resigned. The following year, the secretary was fired for breaching the department's confidentiality rule, as well as for poor job performance. The district changed its explanation for the firing several times, sometimes asserting just the breach of confidentiality and sometimes asserting poor performance as a factor. When the secretary sued under the ADEA, a jury ruled in her favor and awarded her $87,000 in back pay, $87,000 in liquidated damages, and $27,000 in front pay. The Seventh Circuit affirmed the award, noting that **the shifting explanations for the firing** and the prior attempt to lay off the secretary allowed the jury to infer that age was a motivating factor in the termination decision. *Appelbaum v. Milwaukee Metropolitan Sewerage Dist.*, 340 F.3d 573 (7th Cir. 2003).

◆ After a 70-year-old school bus driver was not rehired, he filed a charge with the Equal Employment Opportunity Commission (EEOC) for age discrimination. He alleged that the school superintendent told him the reason for the non-renewal of his contract was his age. The superintendent denied making the statement. The EEOC sued the school district on the driver's behalf, but a Missouri federal court granted pretrial judgment to the school district. The Eighth Circuit Court of Appeals reversed. It held that the driver could proceed with his age discrimination lawsuit because there were issues of fact as to whether age had been the real reason for the contract non-renewal. Despite the superintendent's assertion that age was not the reason for refusing to rehire the driver, he had made an age-based statement in opposing the driver's claim for unemployment benefits. He stated that the driver was not approved for the following year because **he was "70 years of age" and "the public had voiced concerns about his driving safety."** A jury would have to determine whether age was the real reason for the refusal to rehire. *EEOC v. Liberal R-II School Dist.*, 314 F.3d 920 (8th Cir. 2002).

◆ A Texas mayor received between 5 and 10 applications for a new administrative position, including one from a 60-year-old black former council member, and one from a Hispanic municipal court clerk under 40 years old. After receiving the clerk's application, **the mayor changed the qualifications for the job without telling anyone and hired the clerk** without interviewing anyone. When the former council member sued the city for age, race and gender discrimination, a federal court granted pretrial judgment to the city. The Fifth Circuit Court of Appeals reversed, finding that the former council member had established a *prima facie* case of discrimination plus the existence of pretext, which was enough for a jury to find in his favor. The Title VII and ADEA lawsuit would have to go to trial. *Evans v. City of Bishop*, 238 F.3d 586 (5th Cir. 2000).

◆ When a New York public college refused to reappoint a 62-year-old campus security director and his 54-year-old assistant, there was no discrimination under the ADEA. The college never sought or hired a replacement for the assistant, which lent credence to its assertion that **it fired him for budgetary reasons.** Also, the person hired to replace the director actually was older than he was. Thus, even though the replacement left after a brief employment period, no inference could be made that he had been hired to insulate the college from

ADEA liability and to disguise age discrimination. *McCarthy v. New York City Technical College*, 202 F.3d 161 (2d Cir. 2000).

• After 22 years on the job, a 47-year-old Illinois firefighter applied unsuccessfully for a promotion to lieutenant. The two men selected for the position were ages 30 and 31. The 30-year-old had received the same low score as the 47-year-old on the written exam but was ranked much higher in his oral interview. The 31-year-old ranked much higher on both the written exam and the interview. The rejected firefighter sued under the ADEA. The district court ruled for the city, and the U.S. Court of Appeals, Seventh Circuit, affirmed. **The city could legitimately refuse to promote the firefighter because of the interviewers' observations that he was deficient in his communication skills and poise**, that he came across as being uninterested in the position, and that would not be able to command the requisite respect from the people he supervised. *Baron v. City of Highland Park*, 195 F.3d 333 (7th Cir. 1999).

• A 61-year-old bureau director with the New York City Department for the Aging always received excellent job reviews. Things changed when a 39-year-old became her supervisor and the average age of department employees dropped from 50 to 45. She was then not consulted on major changes, lost her secretarial staff, and her performance evaluation was lowered. She was laid off during a "budget crisis." When the department recalled a number of previously laid-off employees, it did not call her back. Later, the department advertised for a new position, which encompassed the same duties as her previous position. However, it never considered her for the job and hired a person 17 years younger. She sued for age discrimination, and a jury awarded her $1.5 million. The Second Circuit upheld the award, finding that **the department's proffered reason for her termination was merely pretext**. The court rejected the city's contention that budget cuts justified the discharge. *Stratton v. Dep't for the Aging for the City of New York*, 132 F.3d 869 (2d Cir. 1997).

B. Procedural Issues

The ADEA and its implementing regulations have set forth specific procedures for pursuing an age discrimination complaint. In particular, the Equal Employment Opportunity Commission (EEOC) has established several regulations governing ADEA claims such as filing deadlines for complaints.

The Older Workers Benefit Protection Act also identifies specific procedures that govern potential age discrimination complaints. More specifically, the Supreme Court has held that an employer's failure to follow the specific statutory requirements for waiver of ADEA claims renders the employee's waiver invalid.

• A Sprint employee, fired in a reduction in force, sued in a Kansas federal court under the ADEA. She sought to introduce "me too" testimony from five other Sprint employees who claimed that their supervisors had also discriminated against them because of age. The case reached the U.S. Supreme

Court, which held that the evidence was neither per se admissible nor inadmissible. It required a fact-intensive determination of its relevance and its prejudicial effect before it could be admitted. The Court remanded the case for further proceedings. *Sprint/United Management Co. v. Mendelsohn*, 128 S.Ct. 1140 (U.S. 2008).

♦   A group of faculty members at Florida State University sued for age discrimination when the board of regents refused to require the university to allocate funds for previously agreed-upon salary adjustments. The case reached the Supreme Court, which held that **Congress had no authority under Section 5 of the Fourteenth Amendment to abrogate (eliminate) states' immunity from lawsuits under the ADEA.** Thus, state employers would have to be sued under state law for age discrimination; however, local governmental employers would still be subject to the ADEA. *Kimel v. Florida Board of Regents*, 528 U.S. 62, 120 S.Ct. 631, 145 L.Ed.2d 522 (2000).

♦   The U.S. Supreme Court held that the Older Workers Benefit Protection Act (OWBPA) amended the ADEA by prohibiting employers from obtaining waivers under the act unless the statutory requirements were met. In a Louisiana case where an employer obtained a release from an employee for all claims against it, the Court found that the release violated the ADEA because it did not give her 20 days to consider the waiver before signing it; it failed to give her seven days after signing the waiver to change her mind; and it made no reference to the ADEA. When the employee sued under the ADEA, the employer tried to defend by asserting that the employee had kept the money she received for signing the release. The Court stated that **the employee's failure to tender back the severance pay award did not excuse the employer's failure to comply with the OWBPA.** *Oubre v. Entergy Operations, Inc.*, 522 U.S. 422, 118 S.Ct. 838, 139 L.Ed.2d 849 (1998).

♦   A 63-year-old IRS employee claimed that he was discharged because of his age. A federal court dismissed his case because he filed it over 180 days after the adverse action. The Fifth Circuit held that he was not required to bring suit within 180 days of the employer's action; he only needed to serve notice within that time. However, the dismissal was upheld because his notice to the EEOC was not filed within 30 days of his filing suit in a federal court. The case then reached the U.S. Supreme Court, which ruled that the requirement of notice to the EEOC had been incorrectly applied. **The ADEA allows a federal employee to proceed directly to federal court by serving notice of the alleged unlawful practice on the employer within 180 days** and requires only that the employee notify the EEOC (of the intent to sue) not less than 30 days from when the suit is brought. The employee had met this requirement. The case was reversed and remanded for trial. *Stevens v. Dep't of the Treasury*, 500 U.S. 1, 111 S.Ct. 1562, 114 L.Ed.2d 1 (1991).

♦   Two employees of the University of Minnesota claimed that the university tried to force them to accept early retirement at the age of 52. When they refused to retire, the university reclassified their jobs to lower their salaries. They sued the university in federal court under the ADEA and also alleged age discrimination under the Minnesota Human Rights Act. Based on *Kimel*, above, which made states immune to lawsuits brought by individuals under the ADEA, a federal court dismissed their lawsuit. They then sought to sue the university in state court under state law, alleging that the statute of limitations was tolled during the time they were pursuing their federal court action. The case reached the U.S. Supreme Court, which ruled against them. **Since the state had immunity in the federal action, there was no tolling of the state action up until the time the federal action was dismissed.** *Raygor v. Regents of Univ. of Minnesota*, 534 U.S. 533, 122 S.Ct. 999, 152 L.Ed.2d 27 (2002).

♦ A 42-year-old state police officer in Indiana resigned to take another job. Two months later, he sought to be rehired in his old job but the state police rehiring board refused to do so. He then sued under the ADEA. Although the ADEA allows law enforcement agencies to hire on the basis of age "pursuant to a bona fide" hiring or retirement rule, **the officer here claimed that the rule was not bona fide because he would have been able to work until age 65 under state law had he not resigned two months earlier**. A federal court dismissed his lawsuit, but the Seventh Circuit reinstated it. The state statute at issue was ambiguous and seemed to suggest that "rehire" decisions weren't always made "pursuant to" it. The case was remanded for further action. *Davis v. Indiana State Police*, 541 F.3d 760 (7th Cir. 2008).

♦ Along with a number of other over-40 applicants, a 50-year-old pilot with 5,000 hours of agricultural spraying experience applied for a job with a Florida county for its mosquito control section. The manager of the section allegedly told two employees that he didn't want to interview the qualified applicants because he didn't want to "hire an old pilot." Instead, he changed the qualifications for the position so that applicants no longer had to have at least 100 hours of agricultural spraying experience. He then hired a 40-year-old woman who didn't meet the earlier requirements. When the 50-year-old applicant sued under the ADEA, a federal court granted pretrial judgment to the county. The Eleventh Circuit reversed, ruling that **the manager's alleged comments were direct evidence of age discrimination**. The case required a trial. *Van Voorhis v. Hillsborough County Board of County Commissioners*, 512 F.3d 1296 (11th Cir. 2008).

♦ A Missouri city employee who was over 60 had health problems that required him to take a leave. His co-workers began donating vacation and sick leave to him, but the city's HR administrator and his supervisor allegedly told him he couldn't participate in the donation leave program because he was too old. The city's policy prohibited employees eligible for regular retirement from participating. He retired, and the EEOC sued on his behalf, claiming the city violated the ADEA. A federal court granted pretrial judgment to the city, but the Eighth Circuit reversed. Here, the **comments about his age were direct evidence that the city was motivated by age** when it denied him the right to participate in the donation leave program. A jury would have to decide the case. *EEOC v. City of Independence*, 471 F.3d 891 (8th Cir. 2006).

♦ A city employee who worked at a power plant was notified that the plant would be closing, eliminating his position. Four months later, the plant closed, but he stayed on another two and a half years to help with the transition. Six months later, he filed discrimination charges with the state human rights commission. Eventually, he sued for age discrimination. A state court ruled that he waited too long, but the Connecticut Court of Appeals reversed. Unlike Title VII, which starts the statute of limitations running at the time an employee receives notice that the job is ending, **Connecticut law starts the statute of limitations on the last day of work**. Thus, the lawsuit was timely filed. *Vollemans v. Town of Wallingford*, 928 A.2d 586 (Conn. Ct. App. 2007).

♦ A 51-year-old female applicant for a corrections officer position in Minnesota had nine years of experience. However, she was only offered an intermittent position, while three men younger than 40 were hired full time. Two other men who initially lacked the minimum qualifications were also hired full time ahead of her. She sued for age and gender discrimination under the ADEA and Title VII. A federal court granted pretrial judgment to the county, but the Eighth Circuit reversed. It noted that an issue of fact existed as to whether **the county's "changing hiring process" and "fluid standards for applicants"** were really ways to discriminate against her. *Peterson v. Scott County*, 406 F.3d 515 (8th Cir. 2005).

♦ The University of Wisconsin Press, a nonprofit publishing company affiliated with the university's graduate school, laid off four workers between the ages of 46 and 54. All were replaced by younger workers. When the four workers complained to the EEOC, the EEOC agreed to prosecute the case. A federal jury concluded that the university willfully violated the ADEA, and it awarded money damages. The Seventh Circuit affirmed. Even though the university was immune to lawsuits under the ADEA brought by individual workers, it was not immune to a lawsuit brought by the EEOC. Ample evidence supported the jury's verdict. The decision to lay off the employees was made without any consideration of their respective job skills, without input from supervisors, and without any discussion with the employees. Further, **the jury's finding that the violation was willful was upheld** because university officials were not educated on their obligations under the ADEA. *EEOC v. Board of Regents of Univ. of Wisconsin System*, 288 F.3d 296 (7th Cir. 2002).

C. Defenses

In some instances, age may constitute a <u>bona fide occupational qualification</u> reasonably necessary to the normal operation of the particular business. Additionally, many state and local laws impose age limitations on certain public employees, such as police officers and firefighters.

♦ **A New Jersey county could pay a younger sanitary inspector more than an older inspector** based on the younger inspector's better education, certifications and computer skills. The difference in pay did not violate the ADEA because the reason given for the pay disparity was legitimate and nondiscriminatory. Even though the younger inspector's qualifications went beyond what was minimally required for the position, the county could take those qualifications into account in determining her salary. The older inspector failed to show that the younger inspector's qualifications were so unrelated to the job that compensating her for them was a pretext for discrimination. *Stanziale v. Jargowsky*, 200 F.3d 101 (3d Cir. 2000).

1. Maximum Age Limitations

♦ A 59-year-old Wisconsin man applied for a job as an entry-level firefighter with a city fire department. He passed the tests, including a strenuous physical test, and was placed on the list of qualified candidates. Several positions opened; however, the applicant never received a job offer. The positions were all filled by candidates under 40 years of age. The applicant filed an age discrimination suit against the fire department. After a hearing at the Department of Industry, Labor and Human Relations, the administrative law judge (ALJ) dismissed the suit on the grounds that a state statute exempted the occupation of firefighting from age discrimination suits. The Labor and Industry Review Commission affirmed, as did the Court of Appeals of Wisconsin. The statutory firefighter exemption precluded the applicant's age discrimination suit. The court adopted the commission's conclusion that **the legislature deemed age to be a bona fide occupational qualification reasonably necessary in jobs such as firefighting.** *Johnson v. Labor & Industry Review Comm'n*, 547 N.W.2d 783 (Wis. Ct. App. 1996).

♦ A city in Iowa instituted annual testing of its firefighters to determine whether they could safely fight fires while wearing a self-contained breathing apparatus (SCBA). One firefighter captain failed the tests and was not approved to wear a SCBA. Although several physicians concluded that he was capable of fighting fires, he failed to meet the minimum fitness standard, and the city eventually discharged him. He sued under the ADEA and the Iowa Civil Rights Act. The Eighth Circuit Court of Appeals determined that the city had established a business necessity defense. On job-relatedness, the city presented undisputed evidence that the captain was frequently involved in fire suppression activities that required wearing a SCBA. Also, the fitness standard was necessary to ensure safe and effective job performance. The city had developed appropriate standards based on a review of the relevant medical literature and had applied the best test available for measuring fitness. **The law does not require a city to risk firefighters' lives by taking the chance that a particular firefighter is fit for duty** when solid scientific studies indicate that persons with similar test results are not. Because the captain failed to show that an alternative test would have less of a disparate impact on older firefighters, the court affirmed the district court's grant of pretrial judgment. *Smith v. City of Des Moines, Iowa*, 99 F.3d 1466 (8th Cir. 1996).

♦ A 43-year-old man submitted an application for the position of federal probation officer with a New York federal court. The United States failed to process his application based on its requirement that first-time candidates for the position be under 37 years of age at the time of the appointment. The applicant challenged the United States' policy of refusing to appoint older applicants, alleging that the maximum age limitation violated the Equal Protection Clause. The district court held that **the government policy of maintaining a vigorous staff was a legitimate government objective.** The maximum hiring age of 36 was rationally related to that purpose. The age policy kept the average age of the probation officer low, and in the majority of cases, a younger individual would be more physically vigorous and thus better suited to the potential dangers associated with supervising criminals. While the classification was both under- and over-inclusive, the provision did not offend the Constitution simply because it was not mathematically precise. *Dumont v. Administrative Officer*, 915 F.Supp. 671 (S.D.N.Y. 1996).

♦   A New York city fire department posted a notice for an examination to qualify for a firefighter vacancy. The notice provided that candidates turning 35 by the date of the exam were not eligible for the position. After a 34-year-old applicant passed the written examination, the department offered him a position contingent on his passing a physical fitness test. The applicant took and passed the test but was not permitted to report to duty because he had just turned 35. He sued the city. The court noted that the New York Civil Service Law sanctioned **reasonable age restrictions for open competitive examinations when dealing with the positions of police officers, firefighters or prison guards**. The age restriction, to the extent that it attempted to disqualify applicants who had passed the competitive examination before they turned 35, was void under the civil service law. Consequently, the court instated the firefighter to the position with full and complete seniority rights. *Jubic v. City of Troy City Corp.*, 633 N.Y.S.2d 720 (N.Y. Sup. Ct. 1995).

2. Mandatory Retirement

♦   A Massachusetts law required **automatic retirement at the age of 50** for its uniformed state police officers. An officer who was automatically retired sued the state board of retirement in a federal district court, asserting that the law denied him equal protection. Four months before his retirement, he had passed a rigorous examination, and he stated that his mental and physical health still rendered him capable of performing the duties of a uniformed officer. The district court agreed with the officer that compulsory retirement at age 50 was irrational and violated equal protection. The board then appealed to the U.S. Supreme Court, which first determined that officers over 50 are not a suspect class of persons requiring heightened judicial scrutiny. It then noted that the Massachusetts law was rationally related to a legitimate state interest, because physical ability generally declines with age. Further, the state's needs in protecting the public outweighed the interests of the few officers who still were capable of performing their duties after age 50. Although the state could have chosen a more individualized means to determine fitness than an arbitrary cutoff at age 50, its law did not violate equal protection. The Court upheld the mandatory retirement law. *Massachusetts Board of Retirement v. Murgia*, 427 U.S. 307, 96 S.Ct. 2562, 49 L.Ed.2d 520 (1976).

* The U.S. Congress enacted a mandatory retirement age of 60 for participants in the foreign service retirement system. Employees covered by the civil service retirement system were not required to retire until age 70. A group of past and present foreign service employees sued in a Colorado federal court, challenging the constitutionality of the classification requiring earlier retirement, and a special three-judge court was convened to hear the case. It held that the law was violative of equal protection and that no distinction should be made between civil service and foreign service employees. The U.S. Supreme Court noted that so long as there was a rational basis for the law, it would be upheld, because foreign service personnel over age 60 were not members of a suspect class of people who required strict judicial scrutiny. The Court then determined that **an earlier mandatory retirement age furthered a legitimate governmental interest** in two ways. First, it created incentives to morale and performance by assuring more predictable promotions. Second, it removed from service those who might be less able to face the rigors of overseas duty. Even if the decision by Congress was not wise, Congress had chosen a rational means to achieve a legitimate end. The Court refused to find the law unconstitutional. *Vance v. Bradley*, 440 U.S. 93, 99 S.Ct. 939, 59 L.Ed.2d 171 (1979).

* In 2000, four years after Congress authorized age caps for local public safety personnel for the second time, the city of Chicago reinstated its mandatory retirement age of 63 for firefighters. Two firefighters sued, claiming that the collective bargaining agreement prevented the city from forcing any firefighter to retire based solely on age, and also gave them a protected property interest in continued employment past age 63 unless the city had good cause to fire them. The Seventh Circuit rejected their due process argument. **The bargaining agreement's "just cause" provision applied to disciplinary discharge, not involuntary retirement**, and did not create a property right to continued employment after age 63. *Minch v. City of Chicago*, 486 F.3d 294 (7th Cir. 2007).

* As part of the reorganization of the Massachusetts State Police, three separate police departments were merged, and a law was passed mandating retirement for police officers at the age of 55. A group of officers facing mandatory retirement challenged the law under the ADEA, and the First Circuit Court of Appeals entered a preliminary injunction prohibiting the state from enforcing the mandatory retirement provision. In a subsequent action, a federal court ruled that the ADEA preempted and superseded the state mandatory retirement law. It permanently enjoined the state from forcing officers to retire solely on the basis of age. The state did not appeal that ruling. Later, a group and a number of individuals sued to have the injunction declared invalid. The First Circuit upheld the injunction, noting that even though individuals cannot sue states in federal court for money damages under the ADEA, **the ADEA remains in full force against the states**. And Massachusetts could be sued for injunctive relief under the ADEA. As a result, the injunction preventing the state from enforcing mandatory retirement was still in effect. *State Police for Automatic Retirement Ass'n v. DiFava*, 317 F.3d 6 (1st Cir. 2003).

♦ A law enforcement conservation ranger employed by the Georgia Department of Natural Resources was automatically retired at 55. He applied for a waiver of mandatory retirement as authorized by state statute. The Board of Natural Resources denied his application pursuant to departmental policy. An administrative law judge and the state personnel board dismissed the ranger's request for a hearing on the issue, and he appealed to a Georgia trial court. The court ruled that the department was required to consider the ranger's application for waiver of mandatory retirement. The department appealed to the Court of Appeals of Georgia, which noted that trial courts may reverse board decisions if an applicant's substantial rights have been prejudiced. The relevant state law provided that **the board "may waive the [specified] mandatory retirement ages ... for conservation officers in supervisory classifications."** The court held that the board improperly failed to consider the ranger's application, whether favorably or unfavorably. Because the ranger's mandatory retirement was without the benefit of a right conferred by state statute, the board was required to consider his application. The court affirmed the trial court judgment. *State Personnel Board v. Adams*, 453 S.E.2d 821 (Ga. Ct. App. 1995).

II. DISABILITY DISCRIMINATION

The Rehabilitation Act of 1973, 29 U.S.C. § 701 et seq., proscribes discrimination against individuals with disabilities by the federal government, federal contractors and recipients of federal financial assistance. Section 504 of the act prohibits discrimination solely by reason of disability in programs or activities receiving federal financial assistance.

The Americans with Disabilities Act (ADA), 42 U.S.C. § 12101 et seq., provides broader protection in that it covers employers, including governments, governmental agencies, and political subdivisions who are engaged in an industry affecting commerce and who have 15 or more employees. In addition to the Rehabilitation Act and the ADA, states also have enacted similar statutes that prohibit discrimination on the basis of disability.

The ADA Amendments Act of 2008 requires that mitigating measures, such as medication, not be considered when determining if a person is "substantially limited" in a major life activity. It also expands the definition of "major life activity" to include a non-exhaustive list of physical activities such as reading, bending and communicating, as well as a non-exhaustive list of major bodily functions like immune system and bowel, bladder, brain and respiratory.

The Amendments also clarify that an episodic impairment or one in remission is a disability if it substantially limits a major life activity when active. And it provides that people covered only under the "regarded as disabled" prong are not entitled to reasonable accommodation.

In 2001, the U.S. Supreme Court held that states are immune to lawsuits seeking money damages under the ADA because Congress exceeded its authority in eliminating states' immunity. However, states still must comply with the ADA. They can be sued by the Equal Employment Opportunity Commission for failing to do so, and individuals still can sue for injunctive relief under the act. Further, almost every state anti-discrimination law allows for lawsuits seeking money damages.

• When a nurse at a state university hospital was diagnosed with breast cancer, she took a leave of absence. Upon her return to work, she was demoted. She sued under the ADA. The university sought to dismiss the case on the grounds of Eleventh Amendment immunity. The U.S. Supreme Court held that **states (including the university here) were immune to lawsuits seeking money damages in federal court under the ADA**. Congress exceeded its authority in eliminating states' immunity under the law because there was no pattern of discrimination by states against persons with disabilities. Under the Fourteenth Amendment, state employers may discriminate against people with disabilities so long as the discrimination is rationally related to a legitimate governmental purpose. People with disabilities are not a suspect class (like race or sex) deserving of increased protections. *Board of Trustees of Univ. of Alabama v. Garrett*, 531 U.S. 356, 121 S.Ct. 955, 148 L.Ed.2d 866 (2001).

A. The Rehabilitation Act and ADA

The Rehabilitation Act and ADA prohibit discrimination against any qualified individual with a disability because of disability. A "qualified individual with a disability" is one who, with or without reasonable accommodation, can perform the essential functions of the job.

Employers have a duty to engage in an interactive process with employees to determine whether a reasonable accommodation can be reached to allow the employees to continue in the job.

1. Physical or Mental Impairment

For an impairment to be a disability under the ADA or Section 504, it must be sufficiently severe to substantially limit the employee in a major life activity. An employee with an impairment that is only inconvenient or temporary will not be protected by the ADA.

• A Maine dentist refused to fill the cavity of an asymptomatic HIV-positive patient in his office, but offered to perform the work at a hospital. The patient sued him under the ADA, which prohibits discrimination against individuals with disabilities by a variety of services and public accommodations, including most employers. The case reached the U.S. Supreme Court, which held that **asymptomatic HIV is a physical impairment that substantially limits the major life activity of reproduction**. Accordingly, the patient was disabled within the meaning of the ADA. The Court remanded the case to the court of appeals for a determination of whether the patient's HIV infection posed a significant threat to the health and safety of others that might justify the dentist's refusal to treat her in his office. *Bragdon v. Abbott*, 524 U.S. 624, 118 S.Ct. 2196, 141 L.Ed.2d 540 (1998).

• The U.S. Supreme Court ruled that tuberculosis and other contagious diseases are to be considered disabilities under Section 504 of the Rehabilitation Act. The case involved a Florida elementary school teacher who was discharged because of the continued recurrence of tuberculosis. The teacher sued the school board under Section 504 but a federal court dismissed her claims. The Eleventh Circuit reversed, holding that persons with contagious diseases fall within Section 504's coverage. The school board appealed. The U.S. Supreme Court ruled that **tuberculosis was a handicap under Section 504 because it affected the respiratory system and affected the teacher's ability to work**. Allowing discrimination based on the contagious effects of a physical impairment would be inconsistent with the underlying purpose of Section 504. Contagion cannot remove a person from Section 504 coverage. The Court remanded the case to the district court to determine whether the teacher was otherwise qualified for her job and whether the school board could reasonably accommodate her as an employee. *School Board of Nassau County v. Arline*, 408 U.S. 273, 107 S.Ct. 1123, 94 L.Ed.2d 307 (1987).

On remand, the Florida federal district court held that the teacher was otherwise qualified to teach. The teacher posed no threat of tuberculosis to her students. At the time the teacher was on medication, medical tests indicated a limited number of negative cultures. Her family members tested negative, and she had limited contact with students. The court ordered her reinstatement or a front-pay award of $768,724, representing her earnings until retirement. *Arline v. School Board of Nassau County*, 692 F.Supp. 1286 (M.D. Fla. 1988).

• An applicant for a position with the Foreign Service received an unlimited medical clearance for an assignment anywhere in the world. The next month, she was diagnosed with breast cancer. She had a mastectomy, and she also had her ovaries and fallopian tubes removed. After learning that she was ranked seventh out of 200 candidates and that she would receive an appointment in three months, she informed the State Department of her diagnosis. Although her doctor stated that she could go anywhere in the world, the State Department's medical officer revoked her clearance. She sued under the Rehabilitation Act. A federal court granted pretrial judgment to the State Department, but the U.S. Court of Appeals, D.C. Circuit, reversed. **The State Department discriminated against the applicant because she had a record of a disability.** *Adams v. Rice*, 531 F.3d 936 (D.C. Cir. 2008).

• An employee of the New York City sanitation department was diagnosed with **night blindness**, which prevented him from driving at night or in dim light, and from safely walking, running or riding a bicycle at night, except in the most familiar and well-lit situations. The city stopped assigning him night duty and for eight months switched him back and forth between a clerical job and a safety/training job. It later fired him. When he sued under the ADA, a federal court granted pretrial judgment to the city. However, the Second Circuit reversed, finding issues of fact as to whether the employee was disabled and whether he could be accommodated reasonably. *Capobianco v. City of New York*, 422 F.3d 47 (2d Cir. 2005).

• A budget analyst for the District of Columbia suffered from severe itching, probably caused by a skin allergy to something in his office. As a result, he could not get to sleep until around 4 a.m. and was frequently late for work. Eventually, he was fired for lateness and sued under the ADA. A federal court and the District of Columbia Circuit Court of Appeals ruled against him. He did not qualify for ADA protection because **he could not show that any location other than his office triggered his allergy**. And if his impairment could be eliminated by changing his work address, then it was neither permanent nor long term. *Haynes v. Williams*, 392 F.3d 478 (D.C. Cir. 2004).

• The Eighth Circuit held that **an employee failed to show that her fear of snakes was a disability** under the ADA. Here, a snake had been seen in the employee's work area, causing her to take a leave of absence for several months. When she was transferred to a lower-paying position in another building, she sued. The court held that her temporary hysteria did not prevent her from either working or driving. *Anderson v. North Dakota State Hospital*, 232 F.3d 634 (8th Cir. 2000).

• During her 10 years in a county sheriff's office, a deputy rose to the rank of sergeant. However, she began to suffer psychological problems, including post-traumatic stress disorder related to childhood sexual abuse by her father. She later fired six shots into the ground at her father's grave and was placed on administrative leave. When her leave expired, she resigned. A month later, her doctor cleared her to return to work. She reapplied for a job with the sheriff's office, but was rejected for every position she sought. She then sued the sheriff under the ADA, asserting that he had refused to rehire her because he regarded her as disabled. A Wyoming federal court granted pretrial judgment to the sheriff, but the Tenth Circuit reversed. Here, **she had presented evidence that the sheriff perceived her as disabled**. For example, the sheriff refused to let her undergo a fitness-for-duty evaluation, and the undersheriff sought to have her decertified by the Wyoming POST Commission. As a result, her lawsuit under the ADA for discrimination on the basis of a perceived disability could proceed. *McKenzie v. Dovala*, 242 F.3d 967 (10th Cir. 2001).

• A bus driver with a recurring back problem went on medical leave for almost two years. He contemplated surgery, but his doctor determined that he could return to work with exercise and medication. However, his employer informed him that he would have to undergo an independent medical exam before he could be reinstated. **He sued under the ADA, asserting that the employer regarded him as disabled.** A Pennsylvania federal court ruled in favor of the employer, and the Third Circuit Court of Appeals affirmed. The bus driver could be required to submit to an independent medical exam to determine his fitness to return to duty. Having doubts about his ability to do the job was not the same as regarding him as disabled under the ADA. *Tice v. Centre Area Transportation Authority*, 247 F.3d 506 (3d Cir. 2001).

♦ A police officer candidate passed a physical agility test and was given a conditional offer of employment. When he took his physical exam, **he voluntarily informed the doctor that he was HIV-positive. The doctor then failed him.** He sued under the ADA. After his case was dismissed, the Sixth Circuit reversed, finding that he had raised genuine issues of material fact about whether he was not hired because of his HIV status. Here, the officer had passed the physical agility test (including various tests of strength and endurance) and had served as a police officer elsewhere after being rejected by the city. *Holiday v. City of Chattanooga*, 206 F.3d 637 (6th Cir. 2000).

2. Substantial Limitation

Some impairments are inherently substantially limiting, like blindness and HIV infection. Others are more questionable. Many impairments only limit an employee in the performance of one particular job, which is not sufficient to prove a protected disability under the ADA.

The ADA Amendments Act of 2008 provides that the effect of medication or other corrective measures on an individual's impairment cannot be taken into consideration when determining whether an individual is disabled. Also, courts must look to more than just the employee's ability to perform job duties when determining if the employee is substantially limited in a major life activity.

♦ In *Toyota Motor Manufacturing v. Williams*, 534 U.S. 184 (2002), the U.S. Supreme Court held that the ADA requires a person to be substantially limited in a "major" life activity, and that an employee's inability to perform a manufacturing job did not qualify her as disabled under the act. If the employee was substantially limited in the ability to perform the types of tasks that are **centrally important** to people's daily lives (household chores, bathing and brushing her teeth), then she would be disabled under the ADA.

♦ A nurse at a public university hospital in Alabama took leave to treat her breast cancer, then returned to work and underwent chemotherapy and radiation. She had difficulty completing her duties due to side effects – fatigue, hot flashes and burns on her arms – of her treatment. Eventually she was forced to transfer to a lower-paying position. When she sued under the ADA and the Rehabilitation Act, the Eleventh Circuit held that she was not disabled under the acts because the "substantial limitation to major life activities" she suffered was temporary and did not exist at the time she was forced to transfer to a lower-paying position. *Garrett v. Univ. of Alabama at Birmingham Board of Trustees*, 507 F.3d 1306 (11th Cir. 2007).

♦ An Illinois principal claimed that disciplinary problems, parental complaints and a lack of support from the school board caused him to become depressed. He took a leave of absence for stress. Three weeks later, he was released to return to work, and the board decided to place him in the classroom as a teacher. However, he did not have an Illinois teacher's certificate. The board told him he would have to get a certificate. Instead, he began teaching in the

New York school system and filed a lawsuit for disability discrimination. He then moved back to Illinois to teach there. The Seventh Circuit held that **he was not disabled under the ADA because his stress and depression did not substantially limit his ability to work.** *Cassimy v. Board of Educ. of Rockford Public Schools*, 461 F.3d 932 (7th Cir. 2006).

- A computer support specialist for a Colorado county claimed that her rude behavior and unexcused absences were caused by her depression. After several negative performance reviews, the county fired her and she sued for disability discrimination. The case reached the Tenth Circuit Court of Appeals, which ruled against her, finding that she did not have a disability under the ADA. **The irritability she exhibited did not demonstrate that she was substantially limited in a major life activity.** She also failed to show that retaliation under the FMLA was a factor in her termination. The county had documented the reasons for firing her before she took FMLA leave. *McWilliams v. Jefferson County*, 463 F.3d 1113 (10th Cir. 2006).

- Five Miami police officers assigned to light-duty work because of on-the-job injuries were denied the opportunity to take off-duty assignments because they were not "combat ready." For public safety reasons, only combat-ready police officers could accept off-duty employment. The officers sued the city under the ADA, and a jury awarded them $160,000. However, the court then found as a matter of law that the city could not be liable to them. The Eleventh Circuit Court of Appeals agreed. Here, although the officers' injuries were uncomfortable and inconvenient, they did not substantially limit the officers in a major life activity. The city also did not regard the officers as disabled because it only regarded them as unable to perform the particular job of combat-ready police officer. *Rossbach v. City of Miami*, 371 F.3d 1354 (11th Cir. 2004).

- A transit authority employee whose job required him to lift heavy weights injured his back on a number of occasions and was given a 50-pound lifting restriction. Because his job required him to lift more than that amount, he was eventually discharged when no light-duty positions became available. His lawsuit under the ADA failed because **he did not show that he was substantially limited in the major life activity of working**. Although he was unable to perform the essential functions of the position he held, he did not prove that he could not work in a class of jobs or a broad range of jobs in various classes. *Duncan v. WMATA*, 240 F.3d 1110 (D.C. Cir. 2001).

- A nurse worked for a Florida county where she reviewed the files of hospital patients for whom the county was financially responsible. After suffering a seizure, she was diagnosed with epilepsy and began taking medication. However, as a result of her condition, she was ineligible to drive a car until she had gone six months without a seizure. She asked to work at home two days a week with a varied schedule at the office so she could find alternative transportation. She also asked that she not be required to drive to other sites to check files. The county granted the latter request, but rejected the former, and she sued under the ADA. A federal court ruled for the county, and the Eleventh

Circuit affirmed. **Driving was not a "major life activity" under the statute.** Thus, even though her ability to drive was substantially limited, she was not an otherwise qualified individual with a disability under the ADA because she was not substantially limited in a major life activity. *Chenoweth v. Hillsborough County*, 250 F.3d 1328 (11th Cir. 2001).

♦ A police officer taking Prozac for severe depression was ordered to take a blood test to determine the amount of the drug in his system. He sued under the ADA and lost, because the Seventh Circuit Court of Appeals found that he was not substantially limited in the major life activity of working. In fact, he continued to work. The court also determined that he was not regarded as disabled. Even if the department overreacted to the news that he was taking Prozac by forcing him to take the blood test, it did not regard him as disabled because **it continued to let him perform his job without any restrictions, and it continued to allow him to carry a weapon.** *Krocka v. City of Chicago*, 203 F.3d 507 (7th Cir. 2000).

♦ An Arkansas city learned that one of its police officers, who was on medical leave for depression, attempted suicide by trying to shoot himself in the head. The officer had used his city-issued handgun to inflict the wound, and the city, concerned that his continued employment would increase its exposure to legal liability, terminated him. The officer sued under the ADA, claiming that the city had discriminated against him on the basis of his depression. He conceded that he was receiving medication and counseling for the depression, which allowed him to function without limitation and made him capable of returning to work. The district court entered pretrial judgment for the city, and the officer appealed. The U.S. Court of Appeals, Eighth Circuit, held that the officer did not have an ADA-protected disability because medication and counseling controlled his depression. The court also held that **the increased potential liability associated with the employee's past activities was a legitimate nondiscriminatory reason for the termination.** *Spades v. City of Walnut Ridge*, 186 F.3d 897 (8th Cir. 1999).

♦ A firefighter had been hired by an Indiana city fire department that required all new hires to be either certified paramedics or to achieve that status within three years of their date of hire. After four failed attempts to successfully complete a paramedic certification program by the three-year deadline, the firefighter requested an extension so she could enroll in yet another paramedic course. She claimed that job stress and treatment by her co-workers caused her failures. After she was fired, she sued the city for disability discrimination. She later passed a paramedic certification course in Ohio. In her lawsuit, the city argued that the firefighter did not have a disability and that, even if she did, it did not breach its duty to accommodate her. The Seventh Circuit held that **the firefighter failed to show that her depression "substantially limited" one of her major life activities** (caring for oneself, performing manual tasks, walking, seeing, hearing, speaking, breathing, learning, or working). Her difficulty in passing the paramedic certification course did not prove that she was substantially limited in the major life activity of learning. Nor was she substantially limited in the major life activity of working. *Leisen v. City of Shelbyville*, 153 F.3d 805 (7th Cir. 1998).

3. Essential Job Functions

Essential job functions are the tasks that need to be performed every day, or that the employee potentially needs to be able to perform every day. For example, being able to fire a gun, pursue fleeing suspects and make forcible arrests might be essential job functions for a police officer. On the other hand, if certain desk jobs are made available to some officers, those skill sets might not be essential to the job.

♦ A sergeant with an Illinois county sheriff's office suffered a stroke while on duty and went on disability leave. His doctor later released him for duty so long as he had no physical contact with inmates and no lifting, kneeling, stooping or running. The assistant executive director determined that the sergeant could no longer perform the essential functions of a correctional officer and placed him on "zero pay status." He sued under the ADA and also claimed due process violations, asserting that he should have been granted a hearing before being put on unpaid status. A federal court and the Seventh Circuit agreed that he was deprived of due process. It ordered the sheriff to provide him with a hearing. However, as to the ADA claim, **he could not be accommodated because he could not rotate through all the assignments – an essential job function**. *Dargis v. Sheahan*, 526 F.3d 981 (7th Cir. 2008).

♦ A Chicago police officer with fibromyalgia applied for total disability benefits and then sought to be returned to active duty. The city asked her to clarify her medical restrictions but she failed to do so, insisting that the city already had her medical information on file. After she was fired, she sued under the ADA. A federal court and the Seventh Circuit Court of Appeals ruled against her. Here, her own doctor believed she would be **a danger to herself or others if allowed to carry a gun**, which was an essential function of the job. Further, she thwarted the interactive process by failing to respond to the request for information on her medical restrictions. *Jackson v. City of Chicago*, 414 F.3d 806 (7th Cir. 2005).

♦ A California city refused to allow disabled officers to compete for special assignment positions. Instead, those desirable positions were awarded under an "officer transfer policy" negotiated with the police officers' union. That policy required officers to work on beat patrol before and after the special assignment. Disabled officers who could not make forcible arrests or pursue fleeing suspects were placed in modified-duty positions that they claimed were degrading. Six disabled officers sued the city for violating the ADA, and a federal court granted pretrial judgment to the city. The Ninth Circuit Court of Appeals reversed, noting that **the officers raised questions of fact over whether making forcible arrests and pursuing fleeing suspects were essential functions of the job** so as to disqualify them from the special assignment positions. It rejected the city's argument that "readiness for patrol duty" justified denying disabled officers the opportunity to compete for the special assignment positions. *Cripe v. City of San Jose*, 261 F.3d 877 (9th Cir. 2001).

• An insulin-dependent diabetic applied for a police officer position and passed the written exam as well as the background check. However, the city disqualified him from the force on the grounds that he could not drive a police vehicle, an essential function of the job. He sued the city in a Texas federal court, which granted pretrial judgment to the city, holding that the applicant posed a direct threat to the health and safety of others that could not be eliminated by reasonable accommodation. The Fifth Circuit Court of Appeals reversed, noting that the district court **failed to make an individualized assessment of the applicant's ability to perform the essential function of driving**. Here, evidence of medical advancements such as portable glucose monitors, routine hemoglobin testing, improved insulin-delivery systems and improved insulin needed to be considered. The case was remanded. *Kapche v. City of San Antonio*, 304 F.3d 493 (5th Cir. 2002).

• An employee with the unemployment division of the Maine Department of Labor suffered from spina bifida, which caused him problems with incontinence and triggered substantial pain if he sat too long. When the department closed the office where the employee worked, he refused a transfer to another location because he could not make the 90-minute commute each way. He also refused to relocate. Instead, he sought to be allowed to work from home. The department refused his request on the grounds that he would not be able to provide technical advice to office staff if he were working at home, and this job responsibility was essential. He sued under Section 504 of the Rehabilitation Act and the Maine Human Rights Act, asserting that the department failed to reasonably accommodate his disability. A federal court ruled for the state, and the First Circuit affirmed. Because **the employee could not perform the essential functions of the job from home**, he could not succeed on his claims. *Kvorjak v. Maine*, 259 F.3d 48 (1st Cir. 2001).

• An investigator with the Kansas Department of Corrections was diagnosed with multiple sclerosis and eventually became unable to engage in strenuous physical activity. He also could not safely operate a gun. After taking an extended leave of absence, he asserted that his condition had improved and asked to be reinstated to his former position. His supervisors determined that he could not perform the essential functions of the job and instead fired him. He sued under the ADA, seeking reinstatement or reassignment. The court refused to grant Eleventh Amendment immunity to the department, but otherwise ruled in its favor. The Tenth Circuit Court of Appeals affirmed. It noted that **even though using a gun and restraining prisoners were infrequent activities, they were essential to the position**, and his inability to perform those functions even with an accommodation made him unqualified under the ADA. Further, all the positions to which he could be reassigned still required him to be able to use a gun and restrain people if necessary. *Frazier v. Simmons*, 254 F.3d 1247 (10th Cir. 2001).

4. Procedural Issues

◆ The Supreme Court held that an employee covered by a collective bargaining agreement (CBA) could sue under the ADA without first using the grievance procedure contained in the CBA. **He was not required to follow the grievance procedures** because the dispute here involved the meaning of a federal statute – not the CBA – and because the arbitration clause did not provide a clear and unmistakable waiver of the right to sue. *Wright v. Universal Maritime Service Corp.*, 525 U.S. 70, 119 S.Ct. 391, 142 L.Ed.2d 361 (1998).

◆ An Ohio postal worker injured his back and was transferred to a non-restricted forklift operator position. After he was involved in an accident on the forklift, his forklift license was suspended for between 30 and 90 days pursuant to postal service procedures. He was then sent to work on the sack sorter machine. He told the department manager and another supervisor that the job was "kicking [his] ass." The manager and supervisor told him to "hang in there" and be careful. After a few days on the sack sorter, he had to go to an urgent care facility. He was placed under severe medical restrictions and never returned to work. He then sued the postal service for discrimination under the Rehabilitation Act. The Sixth Circuit ruled against him. **His single comment was not sufficient to inform his superiors that he needed an accommodation**, and he conceded that they did not know about his disability. *Leeds v. Potter*, 249 Fed.Appx. 442 (6th Cir. 2007).

◆ An employee of the Nevada Department of Human Resources who suffered from obsessive compulsive disorder claimed that her supervisors gave her baseless reprimands once they learned of her condition. She eventually stopped going to work per her doctor's orders and was then fired. She sued the department and her supervisors under the ADA. The Ninth Circuit Court of Appeals held that **individual supervisors could not be held liable under the ADA**. Also, she was not entitled to injunctive relief because she no longer worked for the department and showed no interest in returning to her former job. Finally, the department was not liable for money damages because it was a state entity. *Walsh v. Nevada Dep't of Human Resources*, 471 F.3d 1033 (9th Cir. 2006).

◆ A Postal Service supervisor ordered a disabled employee to undergo a fitness-for-duty exam, and a postal service doctor examined him for three hours, finding him fit for duty. The supervisor then called the doctor, who changed the form to "unfit for duty" without re-examining the employee. When the employee sued under the Rehabilitation Act, a Pennsylvania federal court granted pretrial judgment to the Postal Service. The Third Circuit reversed, finding issues of fact that required a trial. In addition to the sudden change to the medical evaluation, the scheduling of a number of disabled employees for fitness exams on the same day, contrary to standard practice, raised questions about whether discrimination had been behind the decision. *Wishkin v. Potter*, 476 F.3d 180 (3d Cir. 2007).

♦ A Philadelphia court probation officer suffered from job-related anxieties after being transferred to a new assignment that required him to carry a firearm, wear a bullet-proof vest, and locate and apprehend dangerous criminals. After seeing a co-worker assaulted, he took a medical leave until he was fired. He sued for discrimination under the ADA. A federal court and the Third Circuit ruled against him, holding that **the court system was an arm of the state that was immune from individual ADA lawsuits** under the Eleventh Amendment and not a local entity that could be sued. *Benn v. First Judicial Dist. of Pennsylvania*, 426 F.3d 233 (3d Cir. 2005).

♦ The New York State Department of Correctional Services had a sick leave policy that required employees to submit medical certification of their illness if they were absent for four or more days. The policy also allowed, "in exceptional cases," a supervisor to request certification for any absence charged to sick leave or family sick leave regardless of duration in order to control unauthorized or unexcused absences. An employee with severe asthma and pulmonary obstructive disease requested accommodations for her illness and challenged the sick leave policy under the ADA. A federal court granted her pretrial judgment, but the Second Circuit reversed. Here, **the certification was a medical inquiry under the ADA**, so the department had to prove job-relatedness and business necessity to justify its use. The department argued that the policy allowed it to determine whether a corrections officer who had been absent because of illness could perform her duties safely, without infecting inmates or co-workers, and also allowed it to curb the conduct of known attendance abusers. The case would have to go to a jury on these issues. *Conroy v. New York State Dep't of Corrections*, 333 F.3d 88 (2d Cir. 2003).

5. Defenses

Common defenses to an action brought under the ADA include: that the employee is not sufficiently impaired as to be "disabled" under the law; that the employee cannot perform the job's essential functions with or without a reasonable accommodation; and that any accommodation would cause an undue hardship to the employer.

♦ In a private sector case, the U.S. Supreme Court held that a California refinery could reject an applicant for a position where the applicant suffered from hepatitis C and could die from prolonged exposure to chemicals in the refinery. The Supreme Court stated that **the "direct threat" defense could be applied to prevent harm to the individual seeking a job**. It was not limited to preventing harm to "others" in the workplace. If a person's disability would create a direct threat of harm to himself in the workplace, the employer need not hire the person, even if the individual is willing to take the risk. *Chevron U.S.A. v. Echazabal*, 536 U.S. 73, 122 S.Ct. 2045, 153 L.Ed.2d 82 (2002).

♦ An administrative aide for the juvenile unit of the Kansas City, Missouri, Police Department engaged in troubling behavior, including hiding her computer screen from others, sleeping at her desk and going into a back room to talk on the phone. After a performance evaluation criticizing her conduct, she was diagnosed with job-related stress and took three weeks off, but refused to tell her superiors what work-related pressures she experienced. The department ordered her to undergo a fitness-for-duty evaluation, where it was learned that she was taking anti-depressants. She claimed she was on the medication for fatigue. The psychologist sought her medical records. She refused to release them and was fired. When she sued under the ADA, she lost. The Eighth Circuit held that **the department's request for a fitness evaluation was consistent with business necessity**. The department had legitimate doubts about her ability to perform the job safely. *Thomas v. Corwin*, 483 F.3d 516 (8th Cir. 2007).

• A Massachusetts EMT who wore a hearing aid sought to become a firefighter but was turned down because of standards that required him to pass the hearing test unaided. He sued the state for disability discrimination. The Massachusetts Supreme Judicial Court ruled against him. The state's anti-discrimination law allows employers to adopt physical or mental job qualification requirements consistent with safe and lawful job performance. Here, **there would be risk to the EMT and others if his hearing aid failed while fighting a fire**. *Carleton v. Massachusetts*, 858 N.E.2d 258 (Mass. 2006).

• A District of Columbia sergeant who took medication for a blood-clotting condition was placed on limited duty because of the possibility of trauma-associated bleeding in responding to emergency situations. When the department sought to involuntarily retire him, he sued under the ADA, claiming he was regarded as disabled. A federal jury ruled in his favor, but the court of appeals reversed. Department policy required all officers to be "street ready." Here, **the officer's condition created a safety risk that the department properly took into account**, and he failed to show that he was regarded as disabled from performing a wide range of jobs. *Gasser v. District of Columbia*, 442 F.3d 758 (D.C. Cir. 2006).

• An applicant for a VA housekeeping aide job in New Mexico suffered from Meniere's disease, a progressive disorder of the inner ear most commonly characterized by dizziness. VA physicians said he should not be hired because his symptoms would create a safety hazard to himself and others in performing the job's heavy manual labor, which included climbing stairs and ladders and carrying up to 50 pounds. He sued under the Rehabilitation Act, alleging that the VA illegally regarded him as disabled when it rejected him for the job. A federal court ruled against him, and the Tenth Circuit affirmed. Here, the VA's decision not to hire the applicant was grounded on the advice of doctors who believed he **posed a direct threat to the safety of himself and others**. Further, it only regarded him as unable to perform the particular job of housekeeping aide. *McGeshick v. Principi*, 357 F.3d 1146 (10th Cir. 2004).

• A detention supervisor at a jail in Nebraska suffered a work-related shoulder injury that required surgery. Before her doctor cleared her to return to work, she inquired about a detention manager position that would not involve physical confrontations with prisoners. The city did not promote her because she was not cleared to return to work. After returning to work in a light-duty position, she suffered another shoulder injury that required surgery. Although she could work in a non-confrontational position following that surgery, the city again failed to promote her when the detention manager job opened up for a second time. She sued for disability discrimination under the ADA and lost because **the person who got the job (a retired police lieutenant) was at least as well qualified as she was.** *Kincaid v. City of Omaha*, 378 F.3d 799 (8th Cir. 2004).

♦ A Las Vegas police officer injured his right wrist and thumb during a training exercise. Two doctors diagnosed him with rheumatoid arthritis not related to his injury. He was placed in a civilian light-duty position because he could not perform the essential functions of his job, including grasping and gripping a handgun and grasping and detaining suspects if he had to use his right hand. After the city terminated his employment, he re-qualified in the use of a handgun and sued under the ADA. He later learned that he never suffered from rheumatoid arthritis. A Nevada federal court ruled that he was not a qualified individual with a disability entitled to the protections of the ADA, and the Ninth Circuit Court of Appeals upheld the ruling for the city. Here, the officer could not perform the essential functions of the job without an accommodation, and, **because he was not actually disabled, he was not entitled to a reasonable accommodation.** *Kaplan v. City of North Las Vegas*, 323 F.3d 1226 (9th Cir. 2003).

♦ After being diagnosed with sleep apnea, a condition characterized by interruptions in breathing during sleep, a Chicago police sergeant was accommodated in his request not to work the midnight to 8 a.m. watch. Later, he was put on limited-duty status and allowed to work only the 8 a.m. to 4 p.m. watch. However, the officer, who had a Ph.D. in public administration, also kept his second job teaching an early evening class at a local university. This was a violation of departmental rules prohibiting limited-duty officers from engaging in secondary employment. The Internal Affairs director ordered the sergeant to stop teaching and issued him a five-day suspension. The director told the officer that **because he was medically unable to work the evening shift for the department, there was no justification for him working any part of that shift for a secondary employer.** The sergeant sued under the ADA and the Rehabilitation Act, and the case reached the U.S. Court of Appeals, Seventh Circuit, which held that the director's reasons for issuing the order were legitimate. Finding no evidence of discrimination, the court ruled for the city. *Silk v. City of Chicago*, 194 F.3d 788 (7th Cir. 1999).

♦ Over the course of five years, a tax auditor for the state of California had excessive absences and incidents of being sick at work. As a result, her productivity declined. When one of her supervisors requested that she provide a copy of her medical records, she refused. She later refused to submit to an independent medical examination and retained a lawyer. She sued to keep the state from requiring her to release her medical records, submit to an examination, or discipline her for refusing. The court ruled for the state, and the Ninth Circuit affirmed, holding that **the medical examination fell within the business necessity exception of the ADA**. The proposed medical exam was job-related, designed to determine whether the auditor was capable of doing her job. *Yin v. State of California*, 95 F.3d 864 (9th Cir. 1996).

6. Regarded as Disabled

It is unlawful under the ADA to discriminate against employees because of the perception that they cannot do the job. However, employers can take action against employees whom they believe cannot perform the essential functions of one particular job.

• A Nebraska county employee (and Vietnam veteran) left work early one day, began drinking, shot some animals on his family's farm and threatened his wife. Based on the incident, he agreed to get a psychological and substance abuse evaluation. A VA mental health practitioner recommended an inpatient treatment program, but the employee wanted to do an outpatient program combined with Alcoholics Anonymous. He refused to enroll in the inpatient program and was fired, after which he sued for discrimination under the ADA. A federal court and the Eighth Circuit ruled against him, finding **no evidence that the county illegally regarded him as disabled**. *Kozisek v. County of Seward, Nebraska*, 539 F.3d 930 (8th Cir. 2008).

• A postal employee in Puerto Rico suffered panic attacks and anxiety about his job. **His supervisors referred to him as "crazy"** and believed he posed a risk because of his treatment by a psychiatrist. They made numerous jokes and insulted him in front of co-workers and customers. He sued under the Rehabilitation Act and won a jury verdict of $300,000. The First Circuit upheld the award. There was sufficient evidence for a jury to find that he was illegally regarded as disabled by the postal service and that he was subjected to a hostile work environment as a result. *Quiles v. Henderson*, 439 F.3d 1 (1st Cir. 2006).

• A Cincinnati captain and a sergeant **refused to hire a firearms instructor applicant because he had retired from the police department with a disability pension and a bad back**. They told the applicant about their doubts when they denied him the job. He sued under the ADA, and a federal court granted pretrial judgment to the city. The Sixth Circuit reversed, finding issues of fact over whether they illegally regarded the applicant as disabled in violation of the ADA. *Todd v. City of Cincinnati*, 436 F.3d 635 (6th Cir. 2006).

• An Indiana city laborer/truck driver hurt his back and had surgery, after which he was put on certain restrictions. His department head and the city's HR director mistakenly believed that his restrictions prevented him from performing certain aspects of the job, and when they could find no other job for him to perform, they fired him. He sued for discrimination under the ADA, but a federal court and the Seventh Circuit ruled against him. Here, the city **only regarded him as unable to perform one particular job**, not as substantially limited in the major life activity of working. Thus, its actions did not violate the ADA. *Kupstas v. City of Greenwood*, 398 F.3d 609 (7th Cir. 2005).

♦ A sheriff's deputy in Kansas who classified inmates for processing at a county jail made some serious classification mistakes. She had been called "nuts" and "crazy" by some co-workers, and admitted that some of the comments were good-natured teasing. After the county decided to transfer her to another unit, a co-worker complained that she made him feel uncomfortable. The county ordered a fitness-for-duty test, which she passed. However, she resigned after taking a month of medical leave. She then sued the county for disability discrimination and lost. The Tenth Circuit ruled that when the county **required her to take the fitness-for-duty exam**, it did not illegally regard her as disabled. The name-calling by her co-workers was more a personality conflict than a perception of disability. *Lanman v. Johnson County, Kansas*, 393 F.3d 1151 (10th Cir. 2004).

♦ A city worker performed a wide variety of construction tasks, most of which involved heavy lifting. After suffering two work-related injuries, the city administrator asked him to undergo a functional capacity evaluation. His doctor examined him and erroneously placed permanent lifting restrictions on him. The city then fired him. He sued the city under the Rehabilitation Act. A Wisconsin federal court ruled for the city, and the Seventh Circuit affirmed. Here, the 50-pound lifting restriction did not amount to a disability under Section 504. Also, **the city only regarded him as unable to perform the particular job he was doing**, and it refused to transfer him because there were no job vacancies at the time. Even though his doctor erroneously reported that he had permanent lifting restrictions, the city could rely on that information when it discharged him. *Peters v. City of Mauston*, 311 F.3d 835 (7th Cir. 2002).

♦ A 34-year-old, 14-year veteran of the New York Police Department was diagnosed with an aneurysm. He underwent corrective surgery and was prescribed a blood thinner that he would likely have to take for the rest of his life. After his surgery, the police commissioner authorized him to return to "restricted duty." Although he was temporarily restored to patrol duty, a police medical board determined that he should be retired because he could bleed to death in the event of a blow or physical attack. When he was discharged, he sued the city under the ADA and state law, asserting that he was fired because the city regarded him as disabled. A federal court dismissed his claims, and the Second Circuit affirmed in part. Here, **at most, the city regarded the officer as unable to perform one particular job – that of patrol officer**. As a result, he was not entitled to the protections of the ADA. However, state law was broader than the ADA, and the officer was entitled to have those claims heard by a state court. *Giordano v. City of New York*, 274 F.3d 740 (2d Cir. 2001).

B. Reasonable Accommodation

Reasonable accommodation includes: making existing facilities accessible; job restructuring; modified work schedules; reassignment to a vacant position;

acquisition or modification of equipment or devices; modification of examinations, training materials or policies; and the provision of qualified readers or interpreters.

If a worker with a disability can perform the essential functions of the job upon the employer's taking one of the above-stated actions, the employer will probably have to make such an accommodation.

However, if providing an accommodation to a worker with a disability will cause <u>undue hardship</u>, then the employer will not be required to make the accommodation. The factors used in determining whether accommodation will amount to undue hardship include the nature and cost of the accommodation needed; the overall financial resources of the employer; and the impact of the accommodation on the operations of the employer.

1. Types of Accommodation

Employers need not accept the particular accommodation suggested by an employee. However, they must be flexible. Where they choose not to accede to a suggested accommodation, they should propose one or more accommodations that will work for them.

- In a private sector case that reached the Supreme Court, a customer service employee for an airline injured his back and sought a mailroom position even though he was not entitled to it by virtue of the seniority rules. The airline decided not to make an exception to its seniority policy, and the employee sued under the ADA, claiming that the airline should have accommodated his request. The U.S. Supreme Court held that while **a seniority system trumps a disabled worker's accommodation request for a particular job in ordinary cases**, the worker still may show that special circumstances make the accommodation request reasonable in his situation. *US Airways v. Barnett*, 535 U.S. 391, 122 S.Ct. 1516, 152 L.Ed.2d 589 (2002).

- An elementary school cafeteria worker in Massachusetts injured her back, had surgery, then informed the cafeteria director that her doctor had placed a lifting restriction on her of 25 pounds. The director told her she could not return to work with the lifting restriction. Her attorney then wrote the school board, suggesting an accommodation of having another employee lift a 31-pound milk crate – a task she had to perform once a day. The board stated that this would require hiring another person and would create an undue hardship. After she was fired, she sued under state law. The Massachusetts Court of Appeals upheld a $158,000 award in her favor, finding that the school board and cafeteria director **should have engaged her in discussions about possible accommodations** rather than simply rejecting her suggestion. Her duties could have been accommodated without an undue financial or administrative hardship. *School Committee of Norton v. Massachusetts Comm'n Against Discrimination*, 830 N.E.2d 1090 (Mass. App. Ct. 2005).

♦ A New Jersey emergency medical technician (who formerly worked as a police dispatcher) injured his back while lifting an elderly patient. He worked for six months on light duty in the EMS department, then was placed on out-of-work status and given temporary disability leave for one month. He made repeated requests for a job accommodation that would allow him to continue to work, but he failed to apply for a transfer to a vacant police dispatcher position under the disability-neutral procedure the township had in place. Instead, he asked either for the dispatcher job or for advice about what sort of training he should pursue for a job transfer. The township did not offer him the dispatcher job or tell him what sort of training to pursue. When he sued under the ADA, a federal court granted pretrial judgment to the township because of his failure to follow the disability-neutral procedures. However, the Third Circuit reversed, holding that **he could prevail if he could show that special circumstances existed that would make his exemption from the disability-neutral transfer policy reasonable.** *Shapiro v. Township of Lakewood*, 292 F.3d 356 (3d Cir. 2002).

♦ A 20-year employee with the Cook County Department of Corrections **suffered from asthma and asked the department to accommodate her by enforcing its no-smoking policy.** Rather than enforce the policy, the department transferred her to another division. When she learned that she would no longer be able to work overtime in her new position, she asked for a transfer back to her old job even though the area was still not smoke-free. The department refused her request, and she sued it under the ADA. The department sought to have the case dismissed. Instead, the Illinois federal court ruled that there were issues of fact as to whether she was disabled under the ADA, whether the department failed to reasonably accommodate her, and whether the reassignment was an adverse employment action (because of her inability to work overtime in the new position). The case would have to proceed to trial. *Bond v. Sheahan*, 152 F.Supp.2d 1055 (N.D. Ill. 2001).

♦ An analyst with a Florida county evaluated information about the county's airports for the aviation department. She suffered from Stargardt's disease, a progressive condition that causes loss of central vision in its early stages. She could see peripherally and used a hand-held high power magnifier to read from a computer. **After she requested a closed-circuit TV to help her read more quickly and provided documentation from her physician, the request was apparently lost.** She did not receive the TV until 10 months later. When she sued under the ADA, a Florida federal court ruled for the county. It noted that when the county discovered the request had been lost, it acted promptly to forward a second request through the appropriate administrative channels. In addition, during the delay, it allowed her to take breaks and leaves of absence when necessary. Thus, the county could not be said to have failed in its duty to reasonably accommodate her under the ADA. *Hartsfield v. Miami-Dade County*, 90 F.Supp.2d 1363 (S.D. Fla. 2000).

♦ Three Denver police officers suffered severe on-the-job injuries that prevented them from using a gun or making an arrest. After being told he had to retire, one requested permanent reassignment to his light-duty juvenile intake position. Another inquired generally about Career Service positions. The third did not pursue reassignment after a sergeant told her that neither the department nor the city would help find her another job. Because the city had a policy of refusing to transfer police officers from the Classified Service into vacant Career Service positions, the officers were forced to retire. They sued the city and county under the ADA and the Equal Protection Clause. A jury awarded the officers $800,000 in compensatory damages as well as other relief, and the city appealed. The Tenth Circuit upheld the verdict because of the police department's refusal, in accordance with the policy, to consider reassigning the officers. **A qualified individual with a disability includes a person who desires and can perform – with or without reasonable accommodation – an available reassignment job within the organization**, even if the person cannot perform the essential functions of his or her current job. Also, reassignment of an employee to a vacant position is a reasonable accommodation that *must* be considered and, if appropriate, offered to an employee who is unable to perform his or her current job. *Davoll v. Webb*, 194 F.3d 1116 (10th Cir. 1999).

• An Ohio police officer suffered various job-related injuries, which had both physical and mental effects on him. Subsequently, he missed an excessive amount of work, and disputes arose about the legitimacy of his absences. He agreed to resign, obtained disability benefits and a permanent disability retirement, then sued the city under the ADA. The case reached the Sixth Circuit, which found that the officer was not "otherwise qualified" because he had rejected a reasonable accommodation that would have enabled him to perform the duties of an officer by working a desk job. The court rejected his contention that the desk job involved diminished material responsibilities and was demeaning, and therefore was an unreasonable accommodation. Although he desired a different position, under ADA regulations **the employer has the ultimate discretion to choose between effective accommodations**. *Keever v. City of Middletown*, 145 F.3d 809 (6th Cir. 1998).

2. Unreasonable Accommodations

Where no reasonable accommodation can be made, employers may fire, demote or refuse to hire disabled employees/applicants. However, they must engage in the interactive process to determine whether a reasonable accommodation can be made.

• After 13 years on the job, a New Jersey corrections officer developed a hyperactive thyroid, making it unsafe for him to have contact with inmates. The sheriff placed him in various light-duty positions for the next few years, but then issued a new policy limiting light-duty assignments to 30 days. When the officer's doctor stated that the officer needed to be in an environment with minimal or no inmate contact, the sheriff decided that he could no longer assure the officer's safety. He placed the officer on disability retirement. The officer sued under the Law Against Discrimination, but the New Jersey Supreme Court ruled against him, reversing the jury award of $236,000 he had obtained.

Maintaining inmate contact was an essential function of a corrections officer's job, and the sheriff was not required to create a permanent light-duty job for the officer. *Raspa v. Office of the Sheriff of the County of Gloucester*, 924 A.2d 435 (N.J. 2007).

• A team supervisor for the Federal Aviation Administration (FAA) injured his back at work and was then allowed to telecommute up to two days per week. He later took medical leave to have back surgery. He returned to work in stages, working from home much of the time and being allowed to choose office hours that shortened his commute. However, his new superior refused to let him handle supervisory responsibilities during this time. He filed an EEOC complaint and a month later, received a memo from his new superior revoking the telecommuting arrangement. When he sued for disability discrimination, a federal court granted pretrial judgment to the defendants. The U.S. Court of Appeals, D.C. Circuit, reversed. It found issues of fact as to **whether the telecommuting arrangement posed an undue hardship** for the FAA, especially given that he had been allowed to telecommute for several months. *Woodruff v. Peters*, 482 F.3d 521 (D.C. Cir. 2007).

• An Oregon county employee who suffered from epilepsy blacked out while driving a county truck. His co-worker was able to bring the truck to a safe halt. The county had the employee evaluated by a neurologist, who concluded his disease precluded him from working around machinery. The county then fired him. When he sued under the ADA, the Ninth Circuit ruled that his case could continue to trial because he raised issues of fact about the real reason for his firing. **The county failed to engage in the interactive process** to determine if a reasonable accommodation (like reassignment) was possible. *Dark v. Curry County*, 451 F.3d 1078 (9th Cir. 2006).

• Managers at a postal service branch in Kentucky promoted a female employee with rheumatoid arthritis to a supervisory position and told her that her 40-hour per week medical restriction no longer applied because she was now exempt from overtime compensation. They also refused to let her delegate accounting duties to a subordinate even though she had performed those duties for her male supervisor when she was a subordinate. She had difficulty with the increased hours and eventually quit, then sued for discrimination under the Rehabilitation Act and Title VII. A federal court granted pretrial judgment to the postal service, but the Sixth Circuit reversed. A jury could infer that the employee was forced to quit because of her supervisor's actions (constructive discharge), and that the postal service's **failure to engage in the Rehabilitation Act's interactive process was a failure to accommodate** her condition. A jury could also find that male supervisors were treated more favorably than females. *Smith v. Henderson*, 376 F.3d 529 (6th Cir. 2004).

• A paralegal for the Spokane County, Washington, Public Defender's Office injured her neck and shoulder in an off-duty car accident. Her primary job responsibility was to conduct interviews with clients in jail and make handwritten notes, which the lawyers then used during criminal proceedings.

After the accident, the paralegal asked for an accommodation to reduce the handwriting, and various ideas were discussed and rejected as impracticable. The county eventually fired her. She sued under state law and the Family and Medical Leave Act, and the jury returned a verdict for the county. In affirming, the appeals court said that **an employer is obligated to do no more than make reasonable efforts to find an accommodation**, which the paralegal's supervisors did. *MacSuga v. County of Spokane*, 983 P.2d 1167 (Wash. Ct. App. 1999).

• A bus driver was discharged for twice falling asleep while assigned to a bus route, but not while operating the bus. She sued, claiming that her on-the-job drowsiness was caused by a combination of medication she was taking to remedy hypertension and to relieve pain caused by job-related injuries. She claimed that the transportation authority should have accommodated her disability under the ADA. The district court granted pretrial judgment for the authority, and the Eighth Circuit affirmed. The court found **no evidence in the record that the driver's physical condition** *compelled* **her to take a combination of medications** that persistently affected her ability to stay awake on the job. Moreover, the Kansas City, Missouri, Area Transportation Authority had no obligation to provide the bus driver with a drug screening that would identify a combination pain and hypertension medication that would not cause drowsiness. *Hill v. KCATA*, 181 F.3d 891 (8th Cir. 1999).

• A Texas licensed vocational nurse who suffered from physical disabilities was hired by a state mental hospital. As part of her employment, she had to complete a training course and annual refresher courses in the prevention and management of aggressive behavior (PMAB), including a physical portion. When the hospital refused to grant her an exemption from the physical portion, she sued under the ADA. The Fifth Circuit Court of Appeals held that **it is an unreasonable accommodation for an employer to have to exempt an employee from performing an essential function of the job**. The nurse did not present any evidence that she could have performed the physical portion of the PMAB course either with or without a reasonable accommodation. Accordingly, she was not an otherwise qualified individual under the ADA. *Jones v. Kerrville State Hospital*, 142 F.3d 263 (5th Cir. 1998).

C. Drug and Alcohol Use

Under the Rehabilitation Act and the ADA, an employee or applicant currently engaged in the illegal use of drugs is not a qualified individual with a disability. However, once rehabilitated, the employee or applicant can receive protection from the statutes.

• A New York firefighter was terminated after he tested positive for cocaine during a random drug test. He sued, claiming that the random drug test was unconstitutional and that he was discriminated against because of his alcohol dependency. The Supreme Court, Appellate Division, ruled that he was properly fired. Although alcohol dependency qualified as a disability under state law, drug abuse did not, and **he failed to establish that his drug use was causally** connected to his alcohol dependency. *Kirk v. City of New York*, 848 N.Y.S.2d 169 (N.Y. App. Div. 2008).

♦ A school board hired a bus driver, who later obtained a custodial position. He was then spotted drinking beer while on duty. He signed a last chance agreement that allowed him to keep his job. Subsequently, he submitted bids for a part-time bus driver position and a part-time garage worker position. The school board rejected him because of the drinking incident, and he filed a grievance. After binding arbitration, he was awarded the positions. He then sued under the ADA. The case reached the Sixth Circuit Court of Appeals, which held that **the school board had not violated the ADA by refusing him the positions because he had been caught drinking on the job three years earlier**. Even if the board perceived the employee to have a drinking problem, it had presented a legitimate nondiscriminatory reason for denying him the jobs – the serious risk he posed to the children's safety and to the board's financial liability. Since there was no ADA violation, the employee was not entitled to damages. *Martin v. Barnesville Exempted School Dist. Board of Educ.*, 209 F.3d 931 (6th Cir. 2000).

♦ A New York firefighter tested positive for cocaine. He was suspended and ordered to complete treatment, which he eventually did. But he was later fired because of his drug use. He sued the city in a New York federal court under Section 504 of the Rehabilitation Act. The court ruled for the employer, and the U.S. Court of Appeals, Second Circuit, affirmed. In order to establish a *prima facie* case under the act, the firefighter had to prove that he was an individual with a disability, that he was otherwise qualified for the position, that he was denied the position on the basis of his disability, and that the employer received federal funds. **The firefighter was not otherwise qualified for the job given his history of cocaine use** and the inherent danger to himself and others that could occur due to a lapse of judgment. Given the fact that the firefighter had admitted using drugs after his termination, the employer properly believed that a relapse was likely. Also, he never previously sought any accommodations for his disability. The court found that the firefighter had not established a *prima facie* case of discrimination under the Rehabilitation Act. *D'Amico v. City of New York*, 132 F.3d 145 (2d Cir. 1998).

♦ A civilian employee of the Air Force suffered from alcoholism. While at work, he made threats against his supervisor and co-workers. The Air Force began sending him to treatment and, one week into the program, he made another threat and was fired. He filed suit in an Oklahoma federal court against the Secretary of the Air Force under the Rehabilitation Act. The court granted the Secretary's motion to dismiss, and the employee appealed. The Tenth Circuit Court of Appeals held that alcoholism qualifies as a disability. However, the employee was not qualified to perform the essential functions of his job. Although being given time off for treatment is a reasonable accommodation, **the employer did not have to wait until treatment was completed where the threats continued even during treatment**. The employer was unable to reasonably accommodate the employee without exposing its other employees to potential harm. Employers need not accept threatening behavior from a disabled employee when the same behavior from a non-disabled employee would result in termination. The dismissal was affirmed. *Williams v. Widnall*, 79 F.3d 1003 (10th Cir. 1996).

* A Pennsylvania firefighter was fired after he was arrested for altering a painkiller prescription. He entered into a reinstatement agreement with the city that required him to pass a drug test and be cleared by the city's doctor before returning to work. When the firefighter took the drug test, he informed the test administrator that he was taking cough medicine prescribed by his family doctor. The drug test was positive for cough medicine. The city doctor cleared him to return to work with five conditions. The city's drug expert also found no painkiller abuse and cleared him for work. When city officials learned of the positive drug test for cough medicine, they became disgusted with him and told the city doctor that the firefighter had failed a second drug test even though he never took a second drug test. Based on those statements, the doctor added an additional condition to the firefighter's return: that he complete a $7,000 treatment program not covered by his insurance. The city refused the firefighter's request to complete a comparable program that was covered by his insurance. He sued the city under the ADA, requesting reinstatement.

The court found that since he was a qualified person with a disability, the firefighter was protected under the ADA. The city had intentionally discriminated against the firefighter by agreeing to rehire him on certain conditions and then adding the requirement that he participate in a treatment program that city officials knew he could not afford. He should have at least been allowed to participate in the comparable program covered by his insurance. The basis for the new requirement was not that the firefighter was still abusing drugs, but that he tested positive for cough medicine. **Once the city agreed to rehire the firefighter, it could not discriminate against him in the rehiring process.** The court reinstated the firefighter. *Herman v. City of Allentown*, 985 F.Supp. 569 (E.D. Pa. 1997).

D. State Statutes

Many states also have enacted statutes prohibiting employment discrimination based on disability. Although the statutes often parallel the Rehabilitation Act and the ADA, some statutes provide additional coverage for individuals with disabilities by recognizing a broader range of disabilities or providing for other forms of relief.

* A California corrections department employee contracted hepatitis C and began taking a drug that caused fatigue, as well as headaches and difficulty sleeping. After he injured his back on the job, the workers' compensation doctor recommended that he work only in a light-duty position. Since the prison had **a policy limiting light-duty assignments**, he was forced to take disability retirement. He sued for disability discrimination under the Fair Employment and Housing Act (FEHA), and a jury awarded him $597,000 in economic damages and $2 million in noneconomic damages. The California Supreme

Court then held that the jury should have been instructed that he had to prove he was qualified for the job to recover under the FEHA. The language of the state law closely tracked the ADA. A new trial was required. *Green v. State of California*, 165 P.3d 118 (Cal. 2007).

♦ A hearing-impaired vocational rehabilitation counselor for a Massachusetts agency began experiencing repetitive stress injury symptoms but did not report them to her superiors until six months later. She then left work for six months. When she returned, the agency tried to accommodate her impairment with an ergonomic desk, a split keyboard and a wrist pad. It also provided other employees to help her with her workload. She nevertheless became unable to work a full-time day or type on her keyboard and she left work again. She sued the agency for disability discrimination under state law, but lost. Here, she waited six months to notify the agency of her injuries and when she did, it tried to accommodate her. Further, **the agency had no duty to foresee her injuries and provide preventative accommodations** even though it knew of an increased risk of repetitive stress injuries for hearing-impaired individuals. *Leach v. Commissioner of the Massachusetts Rehabilitation Comm'n*, 827 N.E.2d 745 (Mass. App. Ct. 2005).

♦ Two capitol security officers with the Michigan State Police (a male and a female) shot and killed each other while on duty. The female's estate filed a lawsuit, claiming that the male had sexually harassed the female by making hostile and offensive comments about her gender, thus creating a hostile work environment. The estate claimed that when the female complained to her superiors, no action was taken. The case reached the Supreme Court of Michigan, which ruled that **gender-based harassment that was not sexual in nature was not sexual harassment under the state's Civil Rights Act**. No recovery was possible. *Haynie v. State*, 664 N.W.2d 129 (Mich. 2003).

♦ **A doctor hired by West Jersey Health Systems began to grow breasts and long hair as part of gender reassignment treatment.** He was then diagnosed with gender dysphoria and changed his name to Carla. Shortly thereafter, West Jersey told the doctor that it was not going to renew her contract because another company was taking over the program for which she had been hired. She sued under the Law Against Discrimination (LAD), but the case was dismissed. The New Jersey Superior Court, Appellate Division, reversed. It found that she had raised issues of fact as to whether she was subjected to gender discrimination because of her transsexualism. There also was the possibility that she had been subjected to disability discrimination under the law. A trial would have to be held to determine if she was disabled under the LAD, and whether the employer discriminated against her because of her gender. *Enriquez v. West Jersey Health Systems*, 777 A.2d 365 (N.J. Super. Ct. App. Div. 2001).

♦ A Minnesota city firefighter who weighed approximately 307 pounds was unable to fit into essential equipment and had difficulty climbing a ladder while wearing his standard firefighting apparel. He was placed on extended personal leave and was informed that his performance was unsatisfactory because he had not participated in enough training exercises and had not responded to enough fire calls. He was eventually fired for not maintaining adequate physical standards. The firefighter was told that he would be considered for rehire if he reduced his weight to 240 pounds and completed the new recruit testing. After two evidentiary hearings, at which the city manager determined that the firefighter had gained approximately 50 pounds, the discharge decision was affirmed. The city council upheld the decision, and the firefighter appealed. The Court of Appeals of Minnesota affirmed, noting that a high level of physical fitness was required to work safely as a firefighter. Flexibility, agility and high cardiovascular functioning were all crucial to the job. Even absent precise data defining the connection between the firefighter's degree of obesity and poor firefighting ability, **the city council had properly determined that the firefighter was not capable of performing the job safely at his present weight.** *Senior v. City of Edina*, 547 N.W.2d 411 (Minn. Ct. App. 1996).

* A New Jersey city firefighter was suspended for illegal drug use. After completing a rehabilitation program, he was allowed to return to work. Pursuant to the collective bargaining agreement, he agreed to several conditions and acknowledged that another drug use violation would cause him to forfeit his position. Subsequently, the firefighter tested positive for cocaine. He completed another rehabilitation program, but the city terminated his employment. The Merit System Board upheld the termination. The Superior Court of New Jersey affirmed, finding that although the firefighter was a handicapped person under the state Law Against Discrimination, **the city could nevertheless remove him if it could no longer reasonably accommodate his drug addiction.** A firefighter under the influence was a hazard to both the fire department and the general public. The collective bargaining agreement did not provide or specify that a firefighter was entitled to two attempts at rehabilitation. Accordingly, the city had reasonably accommodated the firefighter's condition. *Matter of Jackson,* 683 A.2d 203 (N.J. Super. Ct. App. Div. 1996).

* A Washington police officer slipped and fractured his left ankle while responding to a call. He underwent surgery but sustained a 25% permanent partial impairment. The department discharged him and offered him a position as a dispatcher. The officer refused the position and indicated that he was moving to California to obtain his teaching credentials. He then sued for wrongful termination and failure to accommodate his disability. The court granted pretrial judgment to the department on the wrongful termination claim but not on the department's alleged failure to accommodate. The Court of Appeals of Washington noted that the officer's disability admittedly precluded his employment as a police officer. Consequently, he had been legally fired. **Department policy requiring officers to be able to perform all the duties of a police officer rendered the officer ineligible for any police employment.** Further, his expressed intent to move to California ended the department's obligation to notify him of any available civilian employment opportunities. Thus, the department did not fail to accommodate him. *Molloy v. City of Bellevue,* 859 P.2d 613 (Wash. Ct. App. 1993).

• A probationary member of a fire department operated by the Iowa Air National Guard suffered from diabetes mellitus. He reported to work extremely tired on three occasions and later had an insulin reaction while at work. As requested by the department, he obtained medical approval before returning to work. However, the department discharged him for less-than-competent job performance. He sued, alleging wrongful discharge because of his handicap. The Supreme Court of Iowa held that the firefighter was not disabled under the state Civil Rights Act. First, although his diabetes limited a major life activity, he was not otherwise qualified to retain his position. The National Fire Protection Agency deemed diabetes mellitus "a reasonable reason for rejection from the position of firefighter." Given the lack of time to obtain nourishment or insulin during an emergency situation, **many lives would be put at risk if he suffered from an insulin reaction** at such a time. *Miller v. Sioux Gateway Fire Dep't,* 497 N.W.2d 838 (Iowa 1993).

III. RACE AND NATIONAL ORIGIN DISCRIMINATION

Title VII of the Civil Rights Act of 1964 prohibits employment discrimination on the basis of race, color, national origin, sex and religion. Most of the cases in the remaining sections of this chapter involve Title VII claims.

A. Race Discrimination

It is never appropriate to take adverse action against an employee because of race. Every employer knows this. Thus, there is rarely direct evidence of race discrimination. Complaining parties are typically forced to rely on indirect evidence to prove race discrimination.

1. Burden of Proof

In Title VII employment discrimination cases, courts first allocate the burden of proof to the employee to show that the employer has taken adverse employment action and that the employee has protected status. The employer must then articulate a nondiscriminatory motive for the action.

If the employer provides a legitimate reason, the complaining party then has to establish that the employer's explanation for the adverse action is a pretext for impermissible discrimination. The ultimate burden of proof remains with the employee. The U.S. Supreme Court case, *McDonnell Douglas Corp. v. Green,* 411 U.S. 792 (1973), established the shifting burden of proof in Title VII lawsuits.

• A black Washington, D.C. postal employee was turned down for a promotion. Although he possessed the minimum qualifications necessary, the postal service selected a non-minority candidate. It asserted that he was not promoted because he had turned down several lateral transfers that would have broadened his experience. He sued under Title VII, 42 U.S.C. § 2000e *et seq.,* claiming he had been discriminated against because of race. A federal court ruled in favor of the postal service, but the court of appeals reversed. It held that the district court had erred in requiring the employee to offer direct proof of discriminatory intent. On appeal, the U.S. Supreme Court noted that once the employee established a *prima facie* case that the postal service had discriminated against him, and the service had produced a legitimate, nondiscriminatory reason for not promoting him, **the burden fell on the employee to show that the reason given for rejecting him was pretextual**. However, it was not necessary for him to submit direct evidence of discriminatory intent. He merely had to persuade the judge that the postal service's reason was not the real reason for his rejection. Because the district court had used the wrong standard to determine whether the postal service was liable, the Court vacated the decision and remanded the case to the district court for a proper determination. *U.S. Postal Service Board of Governors v. Aikens*, 460 U.S. 711, 103 S.Ct. 1478, 75 L.Ed.2d 403 (1983).

◆ A Missouri halfway house employed an African-American man as a correctional officer. After being demoted and ultimately discharged, the officer sued, alleging race discrimination under Title VII. The district court held that the officer had failed to carry his ultimate burden of proving that the adverse actions were racially motivated and found for the halfway house. The Eighth Circuit reversed and held that the officer was entitled to judgment as a matter of law once he proved that all of the employer's stated nondiscriminatory reasons for the discharge were pretextual. The halfway house appealed.

The U.S. Supreme Court reinstated the district court's decision, stating that the judge's rejection of an employer's asserted reasons for its actions does not entitle a plaintiff to judgment as a matter of law. However, **if a plaintiff states a *prima facie* case and the trier of fact disbelieves the defendant's proffered nondiscriminatory reasons, no further proof of intentional discrimination is required**. Therefore, rejection of the defendant's nondiscriminatory reasons permits but does not compel an inference of intentional discrimination. Under *McDonnell Douglas Corp v. Green*, above, the ultimate burden of persuasion remains at all times with the employee. The trier of fact is required to decide the ultimate question of fact: whether the employee has proven that the employer intentionally discriminated against him because of his race. In short, "it is not enough to disbelieve the employer; the factfinder must believe the plaintiff's explanation of intentional discrimination." *St. Mary's Honor Center v. Hicks*, 509 U.S. 502, 113 S.Ct. 2742, 125 L.Ed.2d 407 (1993).

On remand, the district court ruled against the officer, and the U.S. Court of Appeals, Eighth Circuit, affirmed. The officer's unfair treatment was because of personal animosity and was not race-related. *Hicks v. St. Mary's Honor Center*, 90 F.3d 285 (8th Cir. 1996).

◆ Two African-American employees in Alabama sued under Title VII when they were passed over for promotions in favor of two white employees. They introduced evidence that the plant manager called them "boy" when talking to them. A jury ruled in their favor, but the Eleventh Circuit held that the use of the word "boy" by itself was not evidence of discrimination. The case reached the

U.S. Supreme Court, which held that **the use of the word "boy" by itself could evidence racial animus**, given the context of the remark, inflection or tone of voice, local custom and historical usage. Also, the employees did not have to prove that their qualifications were so superior to the white employees' that the difference virtually jumped off the page and slapped the court in the face. A better test was needed for determining pretext in the qualifications context – e.g., were the plaintiff's qualifications "clearly superior"? Or could no reasonable person have chosen the selected candidate over the plaintiff? The Court remanded the case for further proceedings. *Ash v. Tyson Foods, Inc.*, 546 U.S. 454, 126 S.Ct. 1195, 163 L.Ed.2d 1053 (2006).

♦ A black assistant manager at an Illinois restaurant claimed he was fired because he complained to his superiors that a white assistant manager was harassing black employees. He sued under 42 U.S.C. § 1981, and the case reached the Supreme Court, which held that **Section 1981 prohibits retaliation** in the making and enjoyment of contractual relationships even though it doesn't expressly say so. *CBOCS West, Inc. v. Humphries*, 128 S.Ct. 1951 (U.S. 2008).

♦ A white deputy fire chief in Georgia was demoted after he grabbed a firefighter by the lapel to chastise him for arriving late to a fire. The deputy chief sued the fire chief and the city's chief operating officer (COO) under 42 U.S.C. § 1983, alleging that the real reason for his demotion was that the chief wanted to open up more spots for racial minorities. He claimed this violated his equal protection rights. A federal court held that the chief and the COO were entitled to immunity for their actions, and the Eleventh Circuit affirmed. **The deputy chief violated workplace violence rules, justifying his demotion.** *Rioux v. City of Atlanta*, 520 F.3d 1269 (11th Cir. 2008).

♦ A black Alabama state employee was riding in a white co-worker's pickup truck on the way back from lunch when a vehicle driven by a black male hit their truck. The white co-worker made two racial slurs about the black driver, neither one directed at the employee. The employee tried to tell her supervisor about it at the hospital but was told not to bring it up. She then began to tell other co-workers about the slurs. The co-worker learned of her discussions and confronted her. Their blow-up stopped work, and the employee was reprimanded; the co-worker was not. After the employee received a negative job evaluation, she retired, then sued for race discrimination and retaliation. A jury awarded her $200,000, but the Eleventh Circuit reversed the award. **None of the actions the employee suffered rose to the level of an "adverse employment action."** *Butler v. Alabama Dep't of Transportation*, 536 F.3d 1209 (11th Cir. 2008).

♦ Boston's public works department used a four-person committee (two white males, one white female, one black male) to conduct interviews when it needed a new general foreman for its fleet division. It asked the same questions of four applicants, focusing on federal vehicle safety regulations rather than education or knowledge of mechanics. The department selected a white candidate, and a black candidate sued for discrimination. A federal court and the

First Circuit ruled against him. The selected candidate answered every question correctly and had 10 more years' experience. It did not matter that the candidate thought the committee should have asked other questions. *Prescott v. Higgins*, 538 F.3d 32 (1st Cir. 2008).

- An African-American Virginia school board employee was fired after two-and-a-half months. She sued, claiming she was fired for complaining that the board failed to hire a black woman she had recommended for another position. The Fourth Circuit ruled against her, noting that the board had offered a legitimate reason for rejecting the other candidate. So **even if the employee believed the firing was retaliatory, that belief was not objectively reasonable**. Further, the board offered a legitimate reason for firing her too – that she was not getting her work done. *Coleman v. Loudoun*, 2008 WL 4412111 (4th Cir. 9/29/08).

- A white Milwaukee police officer was fired after a local TV station aired a video of him shoving an unarmed black man waiting to be booked on charges. The officer was reinstated after a board review found insufficient evidence that he had mistreated the arrestee, and the district attorney's office decided not to press civil rights charges against the officer. He then sued the chief under Title VII, **alleging that the chief had political aspirations and that the firing was racially biased**. A Wisconsin federal court and the Seventh Circuit ruled against the officer, noting that he failed to present evidence that race was behind his termination. *Henry v. Jones*, 507 F.3d 558 (7th Cir. 2007).

- Philadelphia officials chose to appoint the white operations manager of a city-run health care center to a temporary director position rather than the black health services administrator who was the highest on the promotion eligibility list. It did so despite the fact that the white employee did not qualify for the position. Later, she passed the exam, making her eligible behind the black candidate, and she was awarded the permanent position after the interview process. The black candidate sued for race discrimination and the city sought to dismiss the case. A federal court refused to do so, finding that **a jury could infer discrimination from the city's failure to follow its own policies**. *Byrd v. City of Philadelphia*, 2007 WL 3231696 (E.D. Pa. 10/30/07).

- A black assistant director in a division of Maryland's Department of Human Resources was fired because of her failure to quell racial tension among her subordinates. Among the problems was the perception that she treated black employees more favorably than white ones. She believed the real reason for the discharge was her race, and sued under Title VII. A federal court ruled against her, noting that **her mere belief that she was properly managing the office was not sufficient** to override the department's stated reason for her firing. *Elliott v. Maryland Dep't of Human Resources*, 2007 WL 627864 (D. Md. 2/22/07).

- The directors of a Massachusetts agency running Boston's city hospitals learned of budget restrictions and decided to lay off eight employees – five black employees; one white; one Hispanic; and a city employee assigned to the agency. They also decided to give the employees no notice. However, in fact, they gave the white employee a day's notice so he could pack his things and say goodbye to co-workers. The Hispanic employee was not given notice, but was not monitored when she packed up her things. Yet the five black employees, in addition to receiving no notice, were monitored as they packed their things and were not allowed to say goodbye to co-workers. The black employees sued for discrimination, and the Supreme Judicial Court ruled in their favor. Here, **the directors deviated from their neutral layoff policy** and treated the black employees more harshly. *Trustees of Health and Hospitals of City of Boston, Inc. v. Massachusetts Comm'n Against Discrimination*, 871 N.E.2d 444 (Mass. 2007).

♦ An African-American program coordinator for a District of Columbia hospital heard rumors that certain administrators wanted to transfer her out of her job. After she took a few days' medical leave, she learned that she had in fact been transferred from the psychiatric residency training program to the engineering and maintenance department, with the same compensation and benefits. She sued the District under 42 U.S.C. § 1981 and the D.C. Human Rights Act. A federal court refused to allow her case to proceed to trial. She could prove **no adverse action**, nor could she show that the transfer was racially motivated. *Peterson v. District of Columbia*, 2007 WL 1307889 (D.D.C. 5/3/07).

♦ A black, 62-year-old Pennsylvania man who had been convicted of murder at the age of 15 was hired by a subcontractor to drive paratransit buses for disabled people on behalf of the Southeastern Pennsylvania Transportation Authority (SEPTA). He listed the conviction on his application, but the HR department apparently didn't notice it. He was fired when the subcontractor received his criminal background report. He sued SEPTA under Title VII, claiming race discrimination. A federal court and the Third Circuit ruled against him, crediting SEPTA's expert testimony that **a person with a prior violent conviction is more likely to commit a future violent act than a person with no such history**. *El v. Southeastern Pennsylvania Transportation Authority*, 479 F.3d 232 (3d Cir. 2007).

♦ An African-American drug counselor for a Missouri mental health center was accused of accepting money from a patient's Social Security check – a violation of the center's rules. The center's superintendent placed her on administrative leave and ordered an investigation, during which the counselor admitted receiving gifts and buying items from patients – also a violation of the center's rules. The superintendent fired her. When she sued for discrimination under Title VII and 42 U.S.C. § 1981, the Eighth Circuit ruled against her. Even though she was fired when some white employees who bought items from patients were not, there was no discrimination because the superintendent had had a legitimate reason for the firing – the investigation results plus the **admitted infraction of rules**. *Garner v. Missouri Dep't of Health*, 439 F.3d 958 (8th Cir. 2006).

Sec. III   RACE AND NATIONAL ORIGIN DISCRIMINATION   45

• An African-American probationary employee of the Wisconsin DOT received a positive performance review after three months. However, her performance declined by her six-month review and her probationary period was extended. She was fired shortly thereafter and sued for race discrimination under Title VII. A federal court and the Seventh Circuit ruled against her, noting that **the department had documented her performance in weekly progress reports** that supported the department's decision to fire her. She failed to meet deadlines, take initiative or stay in contact with officials whose applications she processed – all job requirements. *Burks v. Wisconsin Dep't of Transportation*, 464 F.3d 744 (7th Cir. 2006).

• An African-American probation officer was given a "meets expectations" evaluation and a 3% raise rather than an "exceeds expectations" rating and a 5% raise. Two white males were given the 5% raises. When she sued the state under Title VII, a Georgia federal court held that no adverse action was taken against her. The Eleventh Circuit, however, reversed. It noted that **where a lower evaluation was tied to a raise, it could be considered adverse action** under Title VII. The court of appeals remanded the case for a determination of whether the state could show it had a legitimate, nondiscriminatory reason for giving her the lower evaluation. *Gillis v. Georgia Dep't of Corrections*, 400 F.3d 883 (11th Cir. 2005).

• A Sri Lankan employee of a Connecticut agency did not have a professional engineer license. When he applied for a promotion to a position that required such a license, he failed to get the job. He was told that in addition to the license problem, he did not interview well. He sued for race discrimination under Title VII, claiming pretext. The case reached the Connecticut Supreme Court, which ruled that even if the agency had some bias against the employee, **his failure to obtain a professional engineer license was an absolute bar to his promotion**. *Dep't of Transportation v. Comm'n on Human Rights*, 863 A.2d 204 (Conn. 2005).

• An African-American medical data technician with the Air Force sought a promotion to an analyst position. She contended that the captain overseeing the selection instead chose a white employee in violation of her Title VII rights. She conceded that the real reason for the decision was to protect the white employee from losing her civilian purchasing agent position, which was to be converted to a military job at the end of the year. An Oklahoma federal court granted pretrial judgment to the Secretary of the Air Force, and the Tenth Circuit affirmed. The Air Force did not commit race discrimination when it **promoted the white employee to protect her from losing her job**. Even though the black employee was better qualified, and the reason for the promotion was emotional, Title VII was not violated because the reason for the action was not racial animus. *Neal v. Roche*, 349 F.3d 1246 (10th Cir. 2003).

• A black employee with an Illinois VA hospital filed a number of Equal Employment Opportunity (EEO) complaints against the VA. Although he performed poorly in the job, his supervisors were afraid to rate him as anything other than "fully successful" because they believed he would file further EEO complaints. However, they informed him that he needed to improve his performance. This resulted in the employee filing another EEO complaint. The employee continued to get "fully successful" ratings despite his poor performance. When he was later denied a promotion despite his ratings, he sued for race discrimination and retaliation under Title VII. The case reached the Seventh Circuit, which noted that **the VA did not violate Title VII by overrating the employee's performance** as a means of keeping him from suing for race discrimination. Artificially high performance ratings were not adverse employment actions. *Cullom v. Brown*, 209 F.3d 1035 (7th Cir. 2000).

◆ The Tenth Circuit joined the Fourth and Fifth Circuits in holding that **an at-will employee can sue for race discrimination under 42 U.S.C. § 1981**. Here, the court held that a Hispanic deputy county clerk could sue her employer for race discrimination under Section 1981 despite her at-will status and the fact that she had no written employment contract with the county. *Perry v. Woodward*, 199 F.3d 1126 (10th Cir. 1999).

2. Racial Harassment

Like sexual harassment, racial harassment is prohibited by Title VII. And it's important to note that teasing, even when intended to be in jest, can be construed as harassment.

◆ An Amtrak employee alleged that he was consistently harassed and disciplined more harshly than other employees because he was black. After filing a claim with the Equal Employment Opportunity Commission (EEOC), he sued under Title VII. Amtrak maintained that it could not be liable for conduct that occurred more than 300 days prior to the employee's filing of charges with the EEOC, and a California federal court agreed. The case reached the U.S. Supreme Court, which held that courts can consider the entire scope of a hostile work environment claim, even if some of the allegedly harassing conduct occurred outside the 300-day limitations period. The only necessity is that at least one act occurred within the 300-day period. Since a hostile work environment generally consists of a series of harassing acts, the **"continuing violation doctrine" allows acts outside the limitations period to be included** in the determination of whether a hostile work environment existed and what kind of liability ought to be imposed. *National Railroad Passenger Corp. v. Morgan*, 536 U.S. 101, 122 S.Ct. 2061, 153 L.Ed.2d 106 (2002).

◆ After being demoted from the vice/narcotics unit, an African-American police officer was turned down for promotion to sergeant. Also, a noose was hung in the station for four months, and a Caucasian officer called another black officer a "n-----." When the officer sued for discrimination under Title VII and Tennessee law, a jury awarded him $100,000 for the demotion and non-promotion, $100,000 for harassment, and $100,000 for retaliation. The Sixth Circuit upheld the latter two awards, but reversed the demotion and non-promotion award, holding that those events occurred outside the limitations period. However, the jury properly heard evidence of those claims as part of the officer's hostile work environment action. *Auction v. City of Clarksville*, 244 Fed.Appx. 639 (6th Cir. 2007).

• Two white Department of Agriculture employees in Arkansas had a black supervisor who regularly interfered with their work, ostracized them, and subjected their work to close scrutiny and frequent criticism. They sued the department under Title VII, alleging that the supervisor created a racially hostile work environment. A federal court and the Eighth Circuit ruled against them, noting that **the sheer number of alleged instances of harassment did not equate to a racially hostile work environment**. The incidents were neither severe nor pervasive enough to constitute race discrimination. *O'Brien v. Dep't of Agriculture*, 532 F.3d 805 (8th Cir. 2008).

• A Hispanic Postal employee in rural Oregon was promoted to the position of Postmaster. She then began experiencing **harassment from customers**, some of whom described themselves as "rednecks." She notified her superiors about the treatment and asked for assistance. Instead, she was placed on disciplinary leave based on customer complaints. She sued the Postal Service for wrongful discharge and harassment under Title VII. A federal court refused to let her harassment claim go to the jury, which ruled for the Postal Service on the wrongful discharge claim. The Ninth Circuit reversed on the harassment claim. A jury would have to consider it, even though it would be difficult to prove what the Postal Service could have done to stop the harassment. *Galdamez v. Potter*, 415 F.3d 1015 (9th Cir. 2005).

• Four university police officers in Illinois sued the university and individual defendants under Title VII, alleging a hostile work environment on the basis of race. The Seventh Circuit ruled against them, noting that **while the work environment was far from ideal, it did not sink to the level of what is barred by Title VII**. There were undoubtedly personality clashes and favorable treatment as well as deplorable language, but the university hired two separate outside entities to address the issue of race discrimination, and the outside entities concluded that personality clashes were largely to blame for the tensions in the office. *Smith v. Northeastern Illinois Univ.*, 388 F.3d 559 (7th Cir. 2004).

• **A black corrections officer could recover for racial harassment where the supervisor who was harassing him also was black.** The Eighth Circuit rejected the county's argument that because the supervisor was black, he could not have had the racial animus required to support a hostile work environment claim under Title VII. Here, the supervisor called the officer "nigger" and "black boy," and referred to the officer's white wife as "whitey." The officer resigned after being given one of the most difficult assignments (allegedly in retaliation for filing a race discrimination complaint with the Nebraska EOC). When he sued, a jury awarded him backpay and $100,000 in emotional damages. The court of appeals upheld the award. *Ross v. Douglas County, Nebraska*, 234 F.3d 391 (8th Cir. 2000).

♦   A black civilian tractor operator for an Army medical center in Colorado filed several complaints of racial harassment with the federal sector EEO office. One day **he saw a noose hanging from the ceiling of an employee break room and believed it had been put there to harass him**. He complained to a union steward and an investigation resulted. Ultimately a work-release prisoner admitted to hanging the noose as a practical joke directed at the employee's co-worker, who had commented that he should be hung for losing a game of dominoes. After his confession, he was returned to prison. The employee nevertheless sued, believing that the investigation had been a cover-up to hide the racial motivation behind the noose incident. The Tenth Circuit Court of Appeals upheld the lower court's ruling for the Army, finding that it had responded reasonably to the report of the noose by conducting the investigation and removing the prisoner. Further, the Army and the employee had agreed on a transfer for the employee after the EEO complaint was filed. *Ford v. West*, 222 F.3d 767 (10th Cir. 2000).

♦   An African-American police officer worked part time for an Illinois village for six years. After a new police chief was selected, the officer interrupted a discussion between the old and new chief, demanding to know what the new scheduling arrangements would be. The new chief told the officer that he could not discuss them, but the officer persisted. After a heated exchange, the new chief blurted out, "Nigger, you're suspended." The new chief then ordered the officer to leave the station, and when the officer refused, the new chief suspended him for 90 days. The officer quit and sued the village under Title VII. A federal court ruled for the village, and the Seventh Circuit Court of Appeals affirmed. It agreed with the lower court that **"this one instance of racial harassment was not sufficiently severe or pervasive to alter the conditions of employment** and create an objectively hostile work environment." *Saunders v. Village of Dixmoor*, 178 F.3d 869 (7th Cir. 1999).

3. Judgments and Settlement Decrees

♦   The EEOC sued the Federal Reserve Bank of Richmond, Virginia, alleging that one of the bank's branches violated Title VII by engaging in discriminatory employment practices. Four black employees were allowed to intervene and received certification as a class. They then notified other class members who joined in the suit. The court found discrimination with respect to employees in certain specified pay grades, but not with respect to employees above those grades. The court denied other employees' motions to intervene because they were in the higher grades, and they then filed separate actions under 42 U.S.C. § 1981. The Fourth Circuit reversed the district court's finding of discrimination in the class action and determined that the judgment in the class action precluded the individual suits from being litigated. The U.S. Supreme Court reversed, noting that **while the class members were bound by the judgment against them in the class action, they were not precluded from bringing individual claims against the bank**. Even though it had not been shown that the bank had systematically engaged in a discriminatory pattern of conduct, the individuals might be able to show isolated cases of discrimination. The Court allowed the individual claims to be brought. *Cooper v. Federal Reserve Bank of Richmond,* 467 U.S. 867, 104 S.Ct. 2794, 81 L.Ed.2d 718 (1984).

• An Oklahoma city entered into a consent decree with a federal court after a class action lawsuit was brought against it for race discrimination. The police officers union challenged the consent decree, asserting that it conflicted with the collective bargaining agreement currently in place. A federal court and the Tenth Circuit approved the consent decree. Here, the bargaining agreement contained a broad management rights clause that allowed the city to assign working hours, hire and promote, and discipline officers without first bargaining over those matters. Although the consent decree required the police department to adopt certain race-neutral policies, it did not prevent the city from bargaining in good faith with respect to future negotiations, and it was **narrowly tailored to address the Title VII violations raised** in the lawsuit. *Johnson v. Lodge #93 of the Fraternal Order of Police,* 393 F.3d 1096 (10th Cir. 2004).

• After a 1990 consent decree, New Jersey developed a new firefighter exam that contained three parts: a cognitive element, a physical test and a biographical questionnaire, which was intended to measure the teamwork component. The judge ordered that each of the three parts should be weighed equally. After a number of white applicants failed the test due to the teamwork component, they sued for discrimination under the Equal Protection Clause. The case reached the Third Circuit Court of Appeals, which held that **the test was not discriminatory**. The test was scored in keeping with the judge's order. Further, the passing rate for the teamwork component was remarkably similar for African-American, Hispanic and white applicants. *Antonelli v. State of New Jersey,* 419 F.3d 267 (3d Cir. 2005).

• A black, female port authority employee applied for a client manager position that was eventually offered to a white female. She then learned that a white male had been promoted to a senior information officer position, an opening that had not been advertised and of which she was not aware. She filed a complaint with the Equal Employment Opportunity Commission, then sued the authority in a New Jersey federal court under Title VII and 42 U.S.C. §§ 1981 and 1983. A jury found in her favor, awarding her **compensatory damages of $1.15 million for emotional distress, backpay of $148,000 and front pay of $182,000**. The court refused to submit the issue of punitive damages to the jury, reduced the compensatory damages award to $375,000 and awarded the employee $635,555 in attorneys' fees. The Third Circuit Court of Appeals affirmed in part. However, it found the attorneys' fee award to be excessive. Also, punitive damages were not appropriate against the port authority. *Evans v. Port Authority of New York and New Jersey,* 273 F.3d 346 (3d Cir. 2001).

• A black English teacher worked for a Chicago school for seven years until shifting student enrollment prompted the principal to eliminate his position, subjecting him to reassignment anywhere in the school district. After filing a union grievance, he was retained temporarily as a part-time substitute and was given 10 months to secure a permanent teaching position. He applied for a position at another district school, but **was not hired because of a consent decree designed to achieve racial integration among students and teachers**. The school already had a disproportionate number of minority teachers on staff. After he was honorably terminated, an arbitrator ordered the school board to reinstate him. It refused to do so, and a lawsuit ensued. The case reached the Seventh Circuit, which held that the school district did not violate Title VII by complying in good faith with the consent decree. It did not have to reinstate the teacher. *Greer v. Board of Educ.*, 267 F.3d 723 (7th Cir. 2001).

♦ An African-American corrections officer complained to her supervisor after a co-worker allegedly told her that another corrections officer had sent a racist e-mail about her to a third officer. However, she refused to identify the co-worker or to provide any details about the e-mail message. When she asked to see the e-mails sent by every corrections officer for the entire month, her supervisor told her that they would need to be reconstructed and that it would cost her $2,500 to pay for the department's computer specialist to do so. She sued under 42 U.S.C. §§ 1981 and 1983, asserting race discrimination and retaliation, and claiming that she should have been charged only $3 – the price of a public record. An Ohio federal court **dismissed her lawsuit as frivolous** and ordered her to pay the department's attorneys' fees. The court also made her attorneys jointly and severally liable for the award. The Sixth Circuit affirmed. *Wilson-Simmons v. Lake County Sheriff's Dep't*, 207 F.3d 818 (6th Cir. 2000).

♦ In 1986, a New York county and the United States settled an action alleging that the county had engaged in a pattern or practice of employment discrimination against women, blacks and Hispanics with respect to job opportunities in the police department. However, despite a massive recruitment effort under the consent decree and the administration of two open competitive examinations, the county failed to achieve a true representation of the minority community. Accordingly, it advised the Justice Department that it was creating a cadet program to benefit the disadvantaged groups. The program essentially selected black and Hispanic candidates to complete a two-year criminal justice degree program, tuition-free, and to work for the police department as service aides for $10 per hour. They were then given the standard police officer examination, and a passing grade entitled them to a "promotion" to the rank of police officer. All qualified cadets would be considered for appointment before any other candidate on the eligible list, regardless of examination grade. A group of non-minority applicants sued the county, alleging that they had been denied admittance to the program because of their race.

A New York federal court noted that **the cadet program was discriminatory and in direct violation of the express terms of the consent decree** because employment decisions were not made on a nondiscriminatory basis. Although the county had acted in good faith, the program was a voluntary undertaking that contravened the express terms of the consent decree. Because the program did not pass the strict scrutiny test applicable to all racially motivated governmental programs, it violated 42 U.S.C. § 1983 and Title VII. *Hiller v. County of Suffolk*, 977 F.Supp. 202 (E.D.N.Y. 1997).

B. National Origin Discrimination

Title VII also prohibits discrimination based on national origin. Employees asserting a claim of national origin discrimination must follow the burden-shifting analysis that applies to race discrimination claims.

Since 9/11/2001, claims of national origin discrimination have been much higher than they were historically. Often, the discriminatory acts come not from managers but from fellow employees who tease and harass those who are different. These actions can lead to liability.

♦ A Mexican-American corrections officer at an Illinois prison was investigated for smuggling contraband cigars into the prison and trading them with inmates for goods from the commissary. An independent investigator concluded that the officer smuggled and traded in cigars, and an employee review board recommended a 30-day suspension pending discharge. The Illinois Department of Central Management then approved the termination without offering a last-chance agreement. The officer alleged national origin discrimination under Title VII, citing anti-Hispanic slurs made by the warden and a major at the prison. A federal court and the Seventh Circuit ruled in favor of the prison. Here, **independent agencies were involved in the decision to fire the officer**, and there was no evidence that the warden or major had sufficient influence over that outcome. It was not enough that some non-Hispanic officers caught bringing electronic equipment into the prison for inmates to repair were given last-chance agreements. *Jennings v. State of Illinois Dep't of Corrections*, 496 F.3d 764 (7th Cir. 2007).

♦ An Ohio man of Egyptian heritage worked for the Toledo Area Regional Transit Authority (TARTA) as a probationary bus driver. He failed to disclose on his application that he had been convicted of domestic violence or that he had been arrested on a firearms violation. When TARTA learned of the conviction, it fired him. He sued under Title VII for national origin discrimination, but lost. The Sixth Circuit held that **he was not similarly situated to other drivers who had also lied on their job applications**. The other employees failed to disclose moving violations, not domestic violence. Further, none of the other drivers who were retained were probationary employees. *Elgabi v. Toledo Area Regional Transit Authority*, 228 Fed.Appx. 537 (6th Cir. 2007).

♦ When his temporary position as a county counselor ended, a Somalian applied for one of the permanent openings. Because he had been reprimanded for missing client meetings, he was not hired. He sued for national origin discrimination under Title VII and the Minnesota Human Rights Act. A federal court and the Eighth Circuit ruled against him. He provided no proof that white employees had been treated better. Further, **another Somalian, two African-Americans and a white male were hired** into the permanent openings. Thus, he failed to show that the hiring decision was discriminatory. *Arraleh v. County of Ramsey*, 461 F.3d 967 (8th Cir. 2006).

♦ A Hindu from Guyana worked for a New York City-run hospital and was subjected to comments about her religion and national origin by her black supervisor and others. After she was fired for misconduct involving unauthorized changes to performance evaluations, she sued for discrimination and harassment. A federal court ruled against her, noting that **the comments she was subjected to occurred over two years and did not permeate her work conditions**. Also, even though she disagreed with her employer over the reason for her termination, she could not show that it was a pretext for discrimination. *Gobin v. New York City Health and Hospitals Corp.*, No. 2: 06CV0004MLM, 2006 WL 2038621 (S.D.N.Y. 7/19/06).

♦ Two Chicago paramedics of Puerto Rican descent complained to their superiors that a commander made them perform menial tasks, prohibited them from speaking Spanish and took them out of the chain of command. However, they never specified that the commander harassed them because of their national origin. He was also not their supervisor under the law because he did not have the authority to fire, demote, transfer or discipline them. When they sued for discrimination and hostile work environment under Title VII, a federal court and the Seventh Circuit ruled against them. **They failed to show that the city knew or should have known about the harassment** by the commander. *Velez v. City of Chicago*, 442 F.3d 1043 (7th Cir. 2006).

♦ A Pakistani-born cardiologist obtained a probationary position at a VA hospital in North Carolina. During that period, he was observed by several cardiologists who all concluded that he lacked the necessary skills for the job. The VA hospital then fired him. He sued for discrimination under Title VII and the ADEA, but lost his lawsuit when he failed to show that he was fired because of his national origin, race, religion or age. **The VA hospital offered a legitimate reason for his discharge – that he was unable to perform at the level of competence his superiors expected.** *Baqir v. Principi*, 434 F.3d 733 (4th Cir. 2006).

♦ A teacher who was born in Lebanon worked as a substitute and temporary full-time teacher in the Fairbanks, Alaska, school district. Although she spoke English with an accent, there was no evidence that her accent ever interfered with her performance. She sought and was recommended for a full-time position, but did not receive an offer. Two school district officials informed her that the reason was because of her accent. When she sued the district under Title VII for national origin discrimination, a federal court granted pretrial judgment against her. The Ninth Circuit Court of Appeals reversed, noting that a jury had to determine whether the district had actually refused to hire the teacher because of her national origin. A 2002 guidance on national origin discrimination provides that in taking adverse action against an employee, "**an employer may consider an employee's foreign accent if the individual's accent materially interferes with the ability to perform job duties.**" However, where the evidence here seemed to indicate that her accent did not interfere with her ability to perform her duties, there was an issue of fact that had to be tried. *Raad v. Fairbanks North Star Borough School Dist.*, 323 F.3d 1185 (9th Cir. 2003).

- Florida Highway Patrol troopers are allowed to supplement their salaries by working off-duty for private employers, but they must get permission to do so and are limited in the number of hours they can work. A lawsuit arose when a number of Hispanic troopers alleged that they were discriminated against in violation of Title VII because they suffered adverse employment actions for failing to report their off-duty hours while non-Hispanic troopers were not so disciplined. They also asserted that they were subjected to a hostile work environment. The Eleventh Circuit ruled against them, finding that one of the troopers did not suffer an adverse employment action because he was only given a negative evaluation (which was not used as the basis for any action against him), and the troopers who were disciplined failed to show that non-Hispanics were not disciplined for similar offenses. Also, **the derogatory comments at issue (made over a period of 20 years) were not sufficiently severe to amount to a hostile work environment**. *Gonzalez v. Florida Dep't of Highway Safety*, 45 Fed.Appx. 886 (11th Cir. 2002).

- A Hispanic manager for New Jersey's Administrative Office of the Courts was paid less than his predecessor even though he performed additional duties. He also claimed that his supervisor subjected him to ethnic slurs whenever the two had a professional disagreement, that his supervisor rounded down his performance review ratings while rounding up the ratings for non-Hispanic employees, and that he was set up to fail in his work projects (by the assignment of projects that were too complicated for his unit). He claimed that he was forced to resign because of the hostile work environment and sued under state and federal law. A New Jersey federal court granted pretrial judgment to the defendants, but the Third Circuit Court of Appeals reversed. There were issues of fact as to whether the defendants had discriminated against him; and he could pursue his unequal pay claim because even though his pay may have been improperly set over six years ago (outside the statute of limitations), **each paycheck constituted a distinct violation that would be covered by the continuing violation doctrine**. *Cardenas v. Massey*, 269 F.3d 251 (3d Cir. 2001).

- A Hispanic employee with the Internal Revenue Service (IRS) in Texas filed a grievance after the IRS tried to fire her and managed to keep her job, albeit in a demoted position. She was later promoted to accounting aide, then applied for another promotion to tax auditor. When she failed to get the job, she sued the IRS under Title VII for national origin discrimination. A federal court ruled for the IRS, and the Fifth Circuit affirmed. Here, even though the employee had shown that some IRS managers in Texas were hostile toward Hispanic employees, **none of the people involved in the promotion process were alleged to have made negative comments to or about Hispanics**. Further, the process used had two objective components (performance review scores and any awards received) and only one subjective component ("potential for success," which looked at whether the applicant had recent experience performing in very technical positions and whether the applicant received high ratings for performing technical functions). Also, she failed to show that the supervisor who gave her a poor performance review did so for discriminatory or retaliatory reasons. *Rios v. Rossotti*, 252 F.3d 375 (5th Cir. 2001).

♦ A blind Turkish Muslim worked as a teacher for the Missouri Department of Social Services and consistently received exemplary evaluations. When a supervisory job opened up, she applied for the position and received the highest rating, but the department decided to develop a more qualified applicant pool and recruited three more candidates. A deputy director made an informal offer to one candidate. The candidate declined the position, and instead of offering it to the teacher or the remaining candidate, the deputy director sought other applicants. The teacher sued for discrimination based on disability, religion and national origin. The court held for the department, and the Eighth Circuit affirmed. Here, **the department had articulated three nondiscriminatory reasons for its action**. First, the teacher tended to take matters outside the department if she did not like the way her supervisors handled a particular case. Second, she did not have the willingness or supervisory skills to manage the staff. Third, one of the consumer agencies opposed her appointment. *Floyd v. Missouri Dep't of Social Services*, 188 F.3d 932 (8th Cir. 1999).

IV. SEX DISCRIMINATION

Sex, or gender, discrimination encompasses several different types of claims including unequal pay, pregnancy discrimination, and harassment. Title VII generally provides the framework for sex discrimination claims; however, states also have enacted similar laws prohibiting sex discrimination.

A. Generally

As in race discrimination cases, once an employee or applicant establishes a *prima facie* case of discrimination by the employer, and the employer articulates a legitimate nondiscriminatory reason for its actions, the employee or applicant must then prove that the employer's reason was pretextual.

♦ A New York community college employee **married her same-sex partner in Canada, then sought spousal health benefits** for her in New York. The college refused to recognize the Canadian marriage, and a lawsuit resulted. An appellate court noted that an executive law forbids employers in the state from discriminating against an employee on the basis of sexual orientation. Further, the college was not protected by governmental immunity. Since New York recognizes valid marriages from outside the state, the employee was entitled to get spousal health benefits. *Martinez v. County of Monroe*, 850 N.Y.S.2d 740 (N.Y. App. Div. 2008).

1. Burden of Proof

♦ A Texas woman with several years experience in employment training was hired by the state department of community affairs. She received one promotion and subsequently applied for a supervisor's position, which she did not receive. The department then fired her in a staff reduction. However, it later rehired, transferred and promoted her, keeping her salary commensurate with what she would have received had she gotten the first promotion. She nevertheless sued, asserting that the failure to promote and the decision to fire her were based on gender discrimination. The case reached the U.S. Supreme Court, which held that the employee had the burden of showing a *prima facie* case of discrimination, namely: that she belonged to a protected minority, that she was qualified for the job, that she was rejected despite her qualifications, and that after her rejection the department continued to look at candidates with the same qualifications. The burden would then shift to the department to articulate some legitimate, nondiscriminatory reason for the employee's rejection. If it was successful, **the employee would then have to prove that the reasons given by the department were a pretext for discrimination**. Because the court of appeals had not used this standard, the Court vacated its decision and remanded the case. *Texas Dep't of Community Affairs v. Burdine,* 450 U.S. 248, 101 S.Ct. 1089, 67 L.Ed.2d 207 (1981).

• A North Carolina city developed a new job for managing the city's recreational facilities. Four men and one woman composed the mayoral committee responsible for selecting an applicant. After considering eight applicants, the four men voted to hire a 24-year-old man who had recently graduated from college with a physical education degree. The sole female committee member voted to hire the only female applicant, a 39-year-old teacher with degrees in social studies and education. The female applicant sued the city under Title VII. A federal court held in the applicant's favor, finding that she had a broader range of experience than the selected applicant. Also, male committee members were biased against the female applicant, and the committee had actively solicited male applicants but had made no attempt to recruit females. Finally, the reasons given for hiring the male applicant were pretextual. The Fourth Circuit reversed, but the U.S. Supreme Court reinstated the district court's holding. **The court of appeals had improperly attempted to conduct a new evaluation of the evidence.** There was sufficient evidence of sex bias and discrimination in the district court record. *Anderson v. Bessemer City,* 470 U.S. 564, 105 S.Ct. 1504, 84 L.Ed.2d 518 (1985).

• An applicant for a terrorism specialist position at the Library of Congress had a long and distinguished military career but also was in the process of transitioning from male to female. After being offered the job, the applicant informed the employer of the transition. The hiring official then rescinded the job offer, expressing concern that the applicant couldn't obtain a timely security clearance. The applicant sued under Title VII, and a federal court ruled in her favor, finding that **the employer discriminated "because of sex" when it revoked the offer.** *Schroer v. Billington,* 577 F.Supp.2d 293 (D.D.C. 2008).

• A longtime employee of a Minnesota sheriff's office got a new supervisor and immediately began to butt heads with him. At one point, she sought legal advice from the county attorney rather than through the office. Later, she earned a mixed review and was told that when she left her position, it was going to be eliminated. She was then suspended twice for refusing to meet with her supervisor on a daily basis. She sued under Title VII and state law, alleging sex discrimination. A federal court and the Eighth Circuit ruled against her. Even though **the management structure seemed dysfunctional** and the workplace was hostile, she failed to show that the discipline she received for insubordination was because of her gender. *Hervey v. County of Koochiching*, 527 F.3d 711 (8th Cir. 2008).

* A female police detective with a master's degree in forensic science sought to transfer to the latent fingerprint section after the serology section where she worked began to be outsourced. When she interviewed for the transfer, she was told that the latent fingerprint section was about "taking care of the guys that did the right thing." After she was denied a transfer on two separate occasions, she sued for gender discrimination. A federal court granted pretrial judgment to the county on the grounds that she did not suffer an adverse employment action. However, the Second Circuit reversed, noting that **the denial of a transfer could be a materially adverse action**. A transfer would allow the detective career advancement opportunities not available if she stayed in the serology section. *Beyer v. County of Nassau*, 524 F.3d 160 (2d Cir. 2008).

* A female police lieutenant in Boston complained that although the city had separate locker rooms for all its superior male officers, it did not have separate locker rooms for all its superior female officers. In her station, she was given the option of using a locked closet in the female patrol officers' locker room or using the office of the drug control unit. The police commissioner then took steps to eliminate the rank-specific locker rooms, but the union objected, asserting that the locker rooms were a mandatory subject of collective bargaining. In the lawsuit that followed, the Massachusetts Court of Appeals reversed the grant of pretrial judgment for the city, finding issues of fact over **whether the failure to provide rank-specific locker rooms for female superior officers was discriminatory**. There was also an issue of retaliation that had to be addressed. *King v. City of Boston*, 883 N.E.2d 316 (Mass. App. Ct. 2008).

* A female deputy sheriff at a Colorado coed prison sought a transfer to an all-male prison that was smaller and did not allow prisoners direct access to the staff at all times. When she was not allowed to transfer, she complained of discrimination. Meanwhile, she had earlier been told that her tongue-piercing might violate the dress code and that she shouldn't wear a tongue stud on duty. Two weeks after she filed a formal complaint with the EEOC, the undersheriff requested an investigation into the tongue-piercing matter. This resulted in the deputy's firing for insubordination and violation of the dress code. The deputy sued for discrimination and retaliation. She lost on the retaliation claim because the sheriff's office offered a legitimate reason for firing her. However, **the refusal to grant the transfer was an adverse action** because of the substantial differences in the two jobs. That claim required a trial. *Piercy v. Maketa*, 480 F.3d 1192 (10th Cir. 2007).

Sec. IV   SEX DISCRIMINATION   57

• The Secretary of the Kansas Department of Human Resources (a political appointee) selected an employee of the governor's office to work as the Director of Employment and Training. Later, the secretary fired the director, who sued the department for sex discrimination under Title VII. A jury awarded her $200,000, and the department appealed. The Tenth Circuit affirmed. Here, **the director was not a political appointee exempted from Title VII's protection** because the secretary who appointed her was not an elected official (but rather a political appointee himself). Also, the fact that the governor had to consent to her appointment did not make her a political appointee. *Crumpacker v. State of Kansas Dep't of Human Resources*, 474 F.3d 747 (10th Cir. 2007).

• A female postal worker in Iowa began an affair with a married co-worker. She later called the postal inspector to complain that the co-worker's wife and son were trespassing in the employee parking lot. At that time, the inspector became aware of the affair. He told the employee that allowing her personal problems to come into the workplace could affect her job. Later, the employee threatened the co-worker with whom she was having the affair. After an investigation, the postal inspector swore out a complaint against the employee and she was arrested. She was fired, but the male co-worker was not. When she sued for sex discrimination, she lost. The Eighth Circuit stated that **she was legitimately fired for making threats against her co-worker**. Since he made no threats, he could be retained. *Shaffer v. Potter*, 499 F.3d 900 (8th Cir. 2007).

• When the Washington, D.C. police department sought help from other departments to handle demonstrations at an upcoming event, Chicago's police chief issued a memo requesting volunteers. The memo stated that a "lone female officer" would not be sent since there would be two persons to each room. A female officer who qualified for the detail was not sent to Washington and complained. She was then transferred to the gang unit, where she would have fewer opportunities for advancement. She sued under Title VII. An Illinois federal court granted pretrial judgment to the city, but the Seventh Circuit reversed. Here, **the memo didn't use the gender-neutral phrase "lone officer,"** and the officers actually sent to Washington all had individual rooms. Further, the reassignment could be construed as retaliation. Questions of fact required a trial. *Lewis v. City of Chicago*, 496 F.3d 645 (7th Cir. 2007).

• Two female firefighters in Kansas City, Missouri complained repeatedly about being required to wear men's firefighting gear, as well as the scarcity and inadequacy of female restrooms. The men's gear didn't fit properly and where female restrooms existed, they often didn't have showers or could be accessed only through male bunkrooms. Eventually they sued the city for sex discrimination under Title VII and a jury awarded them $335,000. The Eighth Circuit upheld the awards, finding that **those conditions jeopardized the firefighters' ability to do their jobs in a safe and efficient manner**. *Widow v. City of Kansas City*, 442 F.3d 661 (8th Cir. 2006).

• An IRS employee in Georgia received a performance evaluation rating of 3.67 out of 5, as well as a "fully successful" designation. He then was assigned a new female supervisor who allegedly made advances that he rejected. She lowered his rating to 3.33 and threatened to "get back" at him, but did not change the "fully successful" designation. After he was denied several promotions, he filed an EEOC complaint, then sued under Title VII. A federal court and the Eleventh Circuit ruled against him because **he failed to show that the lower performance evaluation cost him the promotions.** *Brown v. Snow*, 440 F.3d 1259 (11th Cir. 2006).

♦ A supervisor with the Nevada Department of Transportation (DOT) repeatedly made demeaning comments about women and about how he would rather work with men. He also stated that if he ever became a permanent manager he would hire a man for the program officer III position. When he became a permanent manager and was involved in hiring a new program officer III, he and the chief engineer selected a male. A female employee sued for sex discrimination under Title VII, and a federal court granted pretrial judgment to the DOT. The Ninth Circuit reversed, finding issues of fact that required a trial. Here, **even if the man who was hired was more qualified, the DOT could still be liable if an illegitimate reason was a motivating factor** in the decision-making process. Under the mixed-motive theory of liability, if the DOT could show that it would have made the same decision absent the supervisor's bias, the female employee's remedies would be limited, but the DOT would not escape liability altogether. *Dominguez-Curry v. Nevada Dep't of Transportation*, 424 F.3d 1027 (9th Cir. 2005).

♦ An employment relationship can exist within Title VII's scope, even when a firefighter receives no salary, "so long as he or she gets numerous job-related benefits." Here, a female probationary **volunteer firefighter** was terminated after she repeatedly failed to pass the department's physical agility test (24 men took and passed the test; both women who took the test failed). She sued, claiming that the test had a disparate impact on women. The Second Circuit rejected the city's argument that she wasn't an employee under Title VII. Under state law, she was entitled to numerous benefits, including a retirement pension, life insurance, death benefits and disability insurance. Thus, she was an employee for purposes of Title VII. Also, **the physical agility test flunked the EEOC's "four-fifths" rule,** which reasons that a pass rate for women that is less than four-fifths of the pass rate for men typically establishes disparate impact. *Pietras v. Board of Fire Commissioners of the Farmingville Fire Dist.*, 180 F.3d 468 (2d Cir. 1999).

2. Legitimate Reasons

Employees must show more than that they disagree with their employer's decision to take adverse action against them. For example, an employee who believes she was unfairly demoted must prove that other similarly situated male employees were not demoted.

♦ A psychologist at a Florida state hospital sued for gender discrimination under Title VII and the Equal Pay Act, asserting that she was paid less than male employees holding the same or a similar position. However, she lost at trial because **the hospital showed that it based its salary decisions on years of experience, market conditions, current salary and the need to fill vacant positions**. These were factors other than sex so as to justify them under the Equal Pay Act. She also lost her Title VII claim because she could not show any discriminatory intent. *Okazaki v. Dep't of Children and Families, Florida*, 2008 WL 4525333 (N.D. Fla. 10/3/08).

- After an Oklahoma District Attorney's (DA's) office suffered budget cuts, a female investigator was fired. She filed an EEOC complaint, then sued under Title VII. A federal court and the Tenth Circuit ruled against her, noting that **the DA's office could terminate underperforming employees that it would have kept around had economic decisions not been forced upon it**. Further, the female employee was not in the same position as three male investigators who were given a chance to improve their performance before being fired because their firings were not the result of budget cuts. *Smith v. State of Oklahoma*, 245 Fed.Appx. 807 (10th Cir. 2007).

- A female police sergeant in Colorado applied for a promotion to captain and scored 93.3 out of 100 on the required skills assessment test. However, during the interview with the three-member panel, she became emotional and couldn't answer some of the questions due to stress. **The panel became concerned about her ability to handle the stress of a captaincy and selected a male candidate** for the opening. The sergeant sued for sex discrimination under Title VII and lost. The Tenth Circuit held that the city had a legitimate nondiscriminatory reason for refusing to promote her. It asked the same questions of each candidate. However, the court allowed her to pursue a disparate impact claim against the city and county. *Santana v. City and County of Denver*, 488 F.3d 860 (10th Cir. 2007).

- The University of Iowa allowed new biological mothers to use accrued sick leave of up to six weeks to stay home after their baby was born, but **did not provide the same benefit to new biological fathers**. It also allowed adoptive parents of both sexes to use up to five days of accrued sick leave. A new biological father sued the university under Title VII, alleging sex discrimination. A federal court and the Eighth Circuit ruled against him. The policy was not discriminatory because new biological mothers need more time to recover from the physical trauma of giving birth – a valid reason wholly separate from gender. Also, adoptive parents face demands on their time and finances that are different than those of biological parents. For example, there is no insurance coverage for adoption. *Johnson v. Univ. of Iowa State Board of Regents*, 431 F.3d 325 (8th Cir. 2005).

- A Denver Probation Officer I applied for a level II position but failed to get the job. She was initially told that she scored lower on the evaluating test but in fact she scored higher (by less than a point). When she sued for sex discrimination under Title VII, she lost. The Tenth Circuit held that the employer had given legitimate, nondiscriminatory reasons for its decision to promote the other candidate – he was certified in drug and alcohol counseling, he was fluent in Spanish and he had experience working at the INS detention facility. Also, **the incorrect statement about her test score was not sufficient evidence of pretext**. It could have been a mistake or an effort to spare her feelings. *Jaramillo v. Colorado Judicial Dep't*, 427 F.3d 1303 (10th Cir. 2005).

♦ The affirmative action coordinator at a boot camp for juvenile offenders in Indiana was fired after she **used the "f word"** and engaged in other inappropriate behavior. She sued the department of corrections for sex discrimination under Title VII. A federal court and the Seventh Circuit ruled against her. Fatal to her claim was the fact that she failed to meet the department's legitimate performance expectations. Accordingly, she could not prove that the real reason for her termination was sex discrimination. *Moser v. Indiana Dep't of Corrections*, 406 F.3d 895 (7th Cir. 2005).

♦ The newly appointed head of the Wisconsin Conservation Corps had an authoritative, hands-on management style and butted heads with a number of project managers about their performance. She hired a male assistant, but six months later, on the day before his probationary period ended, she fired him. He sued for sex discrimination under Title VII, but the Seventh Circuit ruled against him. Here, the head of the Corps did not have a discriminatory attitude about men; rather, she vehemently disagreed with her predecessor over how to run the agency. She belittled women as well as men who disagreed with her way of running things. Further, it seemed unlikely she would hire a man only to fire him six months later because of his gender. *Steinhauer v. Degolier*, 359 F.3d 481 (7th Cir. 2004).

♦ Two female analysts in the Boston Police Department applied for a newly created, higher-ranking position, for which neither was qualified. After they interviewed for the job, a male from another police department was selected. They sued for sex discrimination under Title VII. A Massachusetts federal court ruled against them, and the First Circuit affirmed. Here, **the male candidate met all the required qualifications** and most of the preferred qualifications on the job posting. Even though the analysts were the most senior employees in the department, they had no specific experience in the computer research field required by the job. *Gu v. Boston Police Dep't*, 312 F.3d 6 (1st Cir. 2002).

3. Defenses

Gender can be a bona fide occupational qualification, but for most jobs – including police officer and firefighter – gender cannot be a factor in an employment decision.

♦ An Alabama woman sought employment as a prison guard with the state board of corrections. The board rejected her application. Although she had graduated from college with a degree in correctional psychology, the applicant failed to meet the department's minimum height and weight requirements, which were five feet two inches and 120 pounds. The applicant filed a Title VII discrimination complaint with the Equal Employment Opportunity Commission, which resulted in a federal court decision in her favor. The court found that the state's restrictions would exclude 40% of all female applicants but only 10% of male applicants. This constituted unlawful sex discrimination by the corrections department. The state appealed to the U.S. Supreme Court, which noted that the district court had properly found that the height and weight restrictions were discriminatory as applied to female applicants. The state had failed to justify the correlation between height and weight and strength or to show that height and weight were essential to job performance. However, the Court noted that a state regulation enacted after the commencement of the lawsuit did not violate Title VII. The regulation, which described prisoner contact jobs in male penitentiaries as too dangerous for women, was permissible as a measure of controlling inmates and safety at male prisons. The Court held that **the state regulation outlined a bona fide occupational qualification** and reversed that part of the district court's judgment. *Dothard v. Rawlinson*, 433 U.S. 321, 97 S.Ct. 2720, 53 L.Ed.2d 786 (1977).

♦ A Utah bus driver had begun taking hormones prior to gender reassignment surgery and dressed as a woman. She wanted to use female public restrooms along her route even though she still had male genitalia. A superior became concerned about potential liability if a transit authority employee with male genitalia was observed using a female restroom. She met with the driver and her supervisor, and ultimately discharged the driver, who sued for discrimination under Title VII and the Equal Protection Clause. A federal court and the Tenth Circuit ruled against her, noting that **transsexuals are not a protected class** under either Title VII or the Equal Protection Clause. Further, the Transit Authority had a legitimate reason for terminating her employment – the fact that she was a biological male who intended to use women's public restrooms. *Etsitty v. Utah Transit Authority*, 502 F.3d 1215 (10th Cir. 2007).

♦ After allegations of rampant sexual abuse and harassment at Michigan prisons by male corrections officers and resident unit officers, two lawsuits were filed – one by the Department of Justice and the other by female inmates. Subsequently, the head of the Department of Corrections decided to remove all male officers from female housing units. A group of male officers sued for sex discrimination under Title VII, and a federal court ruled in their favor. However, the Sixth Circuit reversed, noting that gender was a bona fide occupational qualification given the state's "deplorable record regarding the care of its female inmates." **The use of female officers was better for security reasons as well as inmate safety and privacy**, and there were no reasonable alternatives. *Everson v. Michigan Dep't of Corrections*, 391 F.3d 737 (6th Cir. 2004).

♦ When the University of Tennessee's General Counsel retired, the president selected a female deputy general counsel to replace him. A male employee in a lower-level position sued for reverse discrimination under 42 U.S.C. § 1983. He claimed that the president had a policy of favoring females and minorities over white males. A federal court granted pretrial judgment to the president, and the Sixth Circuit affirmed. Here, the female employee was more qualified than the male employee in every aspect of the job. She had **more experience and better credentials**. And even if the president had sent an e-mail asserting that the university had a policy of "in-breeding" white males for advancement to the detriment of others, this was not enough to allow the claim to proceed to trial. *Leadbetter v. Gilley*, 385 F.3d 683 (6th Cir. 2004).

♦ A Wisconsin women's maximum security prison promoted its treatment director to the position of superintendent. She then began discussions with her superiors and personnel regarding the prison's staffing needs. She felt that many of the positions at the prison should be staffed only by female correctional officers. Ultimately, her plan was adopted and three male officers were reassigned with no loss in pay. They sued the superintendent and the Department of Health and Social Services for sex discrimination under Title VII. The district court found that the department and supervisor had not established a bona fide occupational qualification (BFOQ) and ordered the male officers reinstated. The Seventh Circuit reversed. **So long as it was reasonably necessary to the normal operation of the prison, a classification based on sex would be upheld as a valid BFOQ.** Because rehabilitation of the female inmates was essential to the "business" of running the prison, and because the superintendent and department believed female correctional officers were reasonably necessary to achieve that goal, a valid BFOQ had been demonstrated. The court remanded the case for a full consideration of the superintendent's decision to be certain the BFOQ was valid. *Torres v. Wisconsin Dep't of Health and Social Services*, 859 F.2d 1523 (7th Cir. 1988).

B. Equal Pay

The Equal Pay Act (EPA), 29 U.S.C. § 206(d), enacted as part of the Fair Labor Standards Act, prohibits wage discrimination between employees on the basis of sex for substantially equal work. States have enacted similar laws prohibiting unequal pay. For cases dealing with wage discrimination in general, refer to Chapter Seven, Labor Relations.

♦ Female guards at an Oregon county jail were paid substantially less than male guards at the same facility. The county eliminated the female section of the jail, transferred its prisoners to a neighboring county and terminated the employment of the female guards. The guards sued the county in a federal district court under Title VII, seeking back pay and alleging that they had been unlawfully paid unequal wages for substantially similar work as that performed by the male guards. The court held that the male guards supervised over 10 times as many prisoners and did less clerical work than their female counterparts. It ruled that the female guards were not entitled to equal pay because they did not perform substantially similar work and that the pay inequity was not attributable to sex discrimination. The court held that because the females had not met the standard of the 1963 Equal Pay Act, no Title VII action was possible. The female employees appealed to the Ninth Circuit, which reversed, holding that alleged sex discrimination victims were entitled to Title VII protection. The county appealed to the U.S. Supreme Court.

The Court noted that Title VII wage discrimination claims could be brought in this situation and that the female guards were not limited to remedies under the Equal Pay Act. **Title VII barred sex-based wage discrimination but permitted differentials that could be justified under the Equal Pay Act.** This included seniority, merit, quantity or quality of work or other bona fide factors. Title VII claims for sex-based wage discrimination were thus permissible. Here, the county had evaluated the female guards' job worth at 95% of the male guards, yet had paid them only 70% as much. The court of appeals had correctly ruled that this presented a viable Title VII complaint for sex discrimination. *County of Washington v. Gunther*, 452 U.S. 161, 101 S.Ct. 2242, 68 L.Ed.2d 751 (1981).

• A female area manager for an Alabama plant received raises based on her supervisors' evaluations of her job performance. Initially, her salary was in line with the salaries of male area managers, but over time her pay slipped in comparison. She alleged that the pay disparity began in the 1980s as retaliation because she rejected a supervisor's sexual advances. She also claimed that another supervisor gave her a poor evaluation because of her gender. However, she didn't complain to the EEOC until March 1998. When she finally sued under Title VII, the U.S. Supreme Court held that **she waited too long to sue**. She could not prove that the most current raises she received were the result of any discriminatory intent. She should have filed an EEOC charge within 180 days after each of the earlier poor evaluations. *Ledbetter v. Goodyear Tire & Rubber Co., Inc.*, 127 S.Ct. 2162, 167 L.Ed.2d 982 (U.S. 2007).

• A female parks manager in Indiana brought a lawsuit under the Equal Pay Act, claiming she was paid less than a number of male managers. A federal court and the Seventh Circuit ruled against her, noting that she was paid more than 7 of the 16 male managers and that another eight male managers ran parks that were larger and either had water facilities (requiring more responsibility) or generated significantly more income and patronage. The remaining male manager was assigned to a park that had not yet opened but which was designed to be 100 acres, compared to the female manager's six-acre park. He had extensive duties in preparing the park for opening and had a master's degree in human relations – a relevant credential for operating an extensive outreach program. Accordingly, the female manager was not working a job that required "equal skill, effort and responsibility" under similar working conditions. Further, the difference between her pay and his was less than 2%. He made $35,000 annually and she made $34,373. **That small differential easily justified the difference between the two managers' duties.** *Sims-Fingers v. City of Indianapolis*, 493 F.3d 768 (7th Cir. 2007).

• The Illinois Department of Human Services hired a female investigator who had made $1,928 per month in the private sector and paid her $2,478 per month. It also hired a male investigator at the rate of $3,739 per month, a 10% increase from his previous job with the Department of Children and Family Services ($3,399 per month). The female sued under the Equal Pay Act and lost. The Seventh Circuit Court of Appeals explained that **the employer could use prior** salary as a way to determine the starting salary for new hires. This did not violate the Equal Pay Act even though the job market generally paid males more than females. Using prior salary to determine the starting wage was a legitimate factor other than sex. *Wernsing v. Dep't of Human Services*, 427 F.3d 466 (7th Cir. 2005).

♦ The director and deputy director of a Maryland county's emergency services department brought an Equal Pay Act lawsuit against the county, alleging that male directors and deputy directors earned on average $25,000 more per year than they did. The case reached the Fourth Circuit Court of Appeals, which noted that they failed to identify a male director or deputy director whose job involved the same responsibilities as theirs did. Here, they held similar titles and performed some of the same general duties but **the Equal Pay Act requires more than similarity between jobs**. The jobs must be substantially equal – they must demand equal skills and equal responsibilities. The county did not have to pay them the higher wages they sought. *Wheatley v. Wicomico County*, 390 F.3d 328 (4th Cir. 2004).

♦ A female magistrate for an Ohio county probate court was the lowest-paid magistrate in any of the county court's divisions. Also, the highest-paid female magistrate made less than the lowest-paid male magistrate. When several female magistrates met with the presiding judge to learn how to close the salary gap, he allegedly stated that females should be paid less because of their gender. A female magistrate sued the county for sex discrimination under the Ohio Civil Rights Act (OCRA). A federal court dismissed the case, but the Sixth Circuit reinstated it, noting that she deserved a trial. **The OCRA, like Title VII, did not require her to prove that she performed "equal" work to male employees** who were paid more. And the presiding judge's alleged comments were direct evidence of discrimination. *Birch v. Cuyahoga County Probate Court*, 392 F.3d 151 (6th Cir. 2004).

♦ A female deputy assessor for an Illinois township went to a board meeting to find out what her raise would be. At the meeting, she learned that a new male assessor was being hired and that he was going to be paid more than she was currently making. She also was going to be receiving a raise to that same amount. She expressed her displeasure to the board, asserting that she should be paid more because she had six years' seniority and was more qualified. Two days later, her supervisor called a departmental meeting, at which the deputy assessor accused the supervisor of paying men in the office more than women. The supervisor fired her and she sued under the Equal Pay Act, Title VII and the First Amendment. A federal court ruled for the township, and the Seventh Circuit affirmed. The Equal Pay Act claim failed because **as of the male's starting date, both males and females were being paid the same wage**. The Title VII claim failed because it was not timely filed, and the First Amendment claim failed because the assessor's statements had not been on a matter of public concern. They were merely complaints about her salary. *Snider v. Belvidere Township*, 216 F.3d 616 (7th Cir. 2000).

- A female engineer sued her employer under the Equal Pay Act, claiming that she received smaller pay increases than a similarly situated male colleague. The Second Circuit upheld a jury verdict in her favor, finding that the employer failed to abide by a written policy requiring it to take into account certain factors when granting merit increases. **Even though the employer had a merit system policy in place, it had given the engineer (and others) a merit raise outside the acceptable range.** This indicated that the merit system was not validly implemented and that it was not systematically applied to all employees. The court also noted that evidence had been presented of discriminatory animus by the engineer's supervisors. *Ryduchowski v. Port Authority of New York & New Jersey*, 203 F.3d 135 (2d Cir. 2000).

- A female analyst in the insurance bureau of the Michigan Department of Commerce was classified as a Departmental Specialist VII. A man who also worked as an analyst, but with a different type of insurance, was classified at level VIII and paid at a higher rate. The woman sought reclassification of her position. However, the department determined that it had erred in classifying the man's position. It then "restricted" the man's position, continuing his current salary level, but providing that the next person who moved into his job would be classified and receive pay as a level VII. The woman sued under the Equal Pay Act (EPA) and lost. The Sixth Circuit found that the department established an affirmative defense. **The wage disparity was due to a mistake – a factor other than sex** – because it had made a sex-neutral error based on advice that the man's position involved more complex insurance policies. The restriction policy also amounted to a "red circle" rate, defined as certain unusual, higher-than-normal wage rates that are maintained for reasons unrelated to sex. The department had remedied the mistake in accordance with civil service sex-neutral rules. *Timmer v. Michigan Dep't of Commerce*, 104 F.3d 833 (6th Cir. 1997).

- A Georgia county contracted for the services of two male investigators employed by a nearby city beginning in 1983. The county employed several full-time investigators in its own criminal investigations division, including a female appointed in 1989. The city rescinded the contract in 1989, and the county hired the two male officers at salaries substantially greater than that of the female investigator. All of the investigators employed by the county performed the same work involving identical skill, effort, responsibility and working conditions. The female investigator sued, alleging that the pay disparity violated the Equal Pay Act. The district court held for the county, and the investigator appealed to the Eleventh Circuit, which ruled that the county's pay disparity was not justified by a valid seniority system. Even though the investigators had more experience than the female officer, they had not been promoted to a rank above her so as to justify a higher salary. Also, their previously higher salaries with the city, alone, could not justify the pay disparity. However, **the county's reliance on the investigators' greater experience and their previously higher salaries constituted a valid affirmative defense for sex discrimination**. Consequently, the district court's ruling was affirmed. *Irby v. Bittick*, 44 F.3d 949 (11th Cir. 1995).

C. Pregnancy

Discrimination on the basis of pregnancy violates Title VII of the Civil Rights Act. The Pregnancy Discrimination Act is a definitional amendment to Title VII to include pregnancy-based discrimination. In particular, the prohibition extends to pregnancy, childbirth, and related medical conditions as outlined in the definition. States have enacted similar laws barring pregnancy discrimination.

♦ The U.S. Supreme Court held that rules of school boards requiring that maternity leaves be taken at mandatory and fixed time periods violate the Due Process Clause of the Fourteenth Amendment to the U.S. Constitution. Two cases were involved in this appeal to the Supreme Court. In both cases school district rules required mandatory leaves at a fixed time early in pregnancy. The Court said that the rules were unconstitutional. The test in this case and other similar cases is that **the maternity policy, in order to be valid, must bear a rational relationship to legitimate school interests**. If there is such a relationship, the rules pass constitutional examination; if not, they are unconstitutional and cannot be enforced. *Cleveland Board of Educ. v. LaFleur*, 414 U.S. 632, 94 S.Ct. 791, 39 L.Ed.2d 52 (1974).

♦ A pregnant IRS employee in Maryland was hospitalized for acute pregnancy complications, including bleeding and threatened abortion. Her doctor gave her a medical certificate endorsing her ability to work from home if she remained on bed rest until further notice. The employee called her supervisor to request that she be allowed to work from home. She also faxed her medical certificate and a note to her supervisor, again requesting permission to work from home. The supervisor offered sick leave but denied the request because of the employee's failure to provide medical documentation that she could do her job from home during her prescribed bed rest, the difficulties involved in communicating with the employee, and security concerns about having customer information in the employee's home. The employee returned to work. When she sued for pregnancy discrimination, she lost. The Fourth Circuit held that **she suffered no adverse action. She was not denied leave. She simply wanted to avoid taking sick leave.** *Brockman v. Snow*, 217 Fed.Appx. 201 (4th Cir. 2007).

♦ A pregnant Ohio police officer, after an altercation with a suspect, obtained a note from her doctor limiting her to light-duty work. Because there were no light-duty positions available, the chief placed her on a leave of absence until she could return to the full-time job. After she gave birth, she returned to work, then filed charges under the Pregnancy Discrimination Act. The case reached the Sixth Circuit, which noted that her lawsuit failed because **she could not show she was treated differently than male police officers injured off the job**. Although two officers with leg injuries had not been placed on leave, they had also not requested restricted duty assignments, assuming the risk that they would be able to handle the demands of the job until their injuries healed. *Tysinger v. Police Dep't of the City of Zanesville*, 463 F.3d 569 (6th Cir. 2006).

- A pregnant dispatcher employed by a Utah county sheriff's department went on maternity leave. A fellow dispatcher quit, and the department was forced to adjust the schedule because new employees were not allowed to work graveyard shifts. Shortly before the pregnant dispatcher's return, she was informed that she had been scheduled for graveyard shifts that a new employee could not work. The dispatcher resigned, citing her inability to obtain a babysitter during the graveyard shift. However, she had never informed her supervisors of this problem. The dispatcher sued for constructive discharge based on pregnancy discrimination. The case reached the Court of Appeals of Utah, which noted that the dispatcher never complained about the schedule until she quit. It also noted that no one else had been given a similar schedule because the dispatch office had changed from a two-week to a three-week rotational schedule shortly after the employee returned so that such difficult schedules would not occur anymore. **Although the dispatcher was a qualified member of a protected class, the schedule change had been necessary** to avoid placing a new employee on the graveyard shift and was in keeping with a long-standing policy. The dispatcher had not been constructively discharged. *Sheikh v. Dep't of Public Safety*, 904 P.2d 1103 (Utah App. 1995).

- A Louisiana probationary state police officer informed her troop commander that she was pregnant. In accordance with a State Police Procedural Order, a captain placed her on involuntary sick leave. She had received satisfactory ratings on her performance evaluations throughout her first six months and was favorably cited for her on-duty conduct. However, the captain "disapproved" her promotion to permanent status, noting that he did not have sufficient time to fully evaluate her because of her pregnancy. She was prevented from continuing her probationary duties and eventually was fired. The State Police Commission ordered her reinstatement, and the state appealed. The Court of Appeal of Louisiana held that **the procedural order improperly excluded pregnant officers at the onset of pregnancy regardless of their ability to perform their regular duties**. Non-pregnant female officers and all male officers who were diagnosed with a medical condition were not relieved of their regular duties without an evaluation to determine the extent of the disability. The order unlawfully assumed pregnant police officers were disabled without such an evaluation. The court affirmed the reinstatement of the officer providing that she complete the same type of training and supervision received by all probationary troopers after graduation from the academy. *Allison-LeBlanc v. Louisiana Dep't of Public Safety*, 671 So.2d 448 (La. Ct. App. 1995).

D. Harassment

Sexual harassment is a form of sex discrimination prohibited by Title VII. The U.S. Supreme Court has determined that employers may be held vicariously liable for sexual harassment committed by supervisors and has established an affirmative defense for employers where there is no tangible employment action taken against the employee. Further, the U.S. Supreme Court has extended Title VII protections to same-sex sexual harassment.

- When a Tennessee worker sued her employer under Title VII for subjecting her to a hostile work environment, a federal court awarded her over $107,000 in back pay and benefits as well as $300,000 in compensatory damages – the maximum permitted by 42 U.S.C. § 1981a(b)(3). The court determined that it was bound by a previous case, which held that front pay was subject to the statutory cap. The Sixth Circuit affirmed. However, the U.S. Supreme Court reversed, holding that **front pay was not an element of compensatory damages within the meaning of the Civil Rights Act of 1991**. As a result, the worker could be awarded $300,000 in compensatory damages as well as an additional amount in front pay (money awarded for lost pay between the time of the judgment and when the employee is reinstated, or as here, money awarded in lieu of reinstatement). *Pollard v. E.I. du Pont de Nemours & Co.*, 532 U.S. 843, 121 S.Ct. 1946, 150 L.Ed.2d 62 (2001).

1. Burden of Proof

The courts have recognized two theories of sexual harassment under Title VII and analogous state anti-discrimination laws. The first, *quid pro quo* harassment, occurs when a supervisor conditions tangible employment benefits such as raises, promotions or even continued employment on submission to sexual demands.

The second, hostile work environment harassment, requires proof of pervasive and unwelcome verbal or physical harassment of the complaining party due to his or her membership in a protected class. An employer may be deemed to have knowledge of sexual harassment if a supervisor perpetrates sexual harassment or fails to take remedial action when harassment is reported.

- A secretary for a Massachusetts town administrator complained that when she talked to him, he would initially look her in the eye, then lower his gaze to her chest. She filed charges with the EEOC. During the investigation, the administrator learned that he had "alternating intermittent exotropia," a condition that made his eyes lose focus when someone looked at him. The administrator then suffered a heart attack. When he returned to work, he asked for an accommodation for his stress, and the town transferred the secretary to another position that had previously been part-time. She sued for sexual harassment and retaliation, and a federal court granted pretrial judgment to the town. The First Circuit reversed, holding that a trial was required. Harassing conduct need not be motivated by sexual desire, and **a man's repeated staring at a woman's breasts is sexual**. *Billings v. Town of Grafton*, 515 F.3d 39 (1st Cir. 2008).

- A South Dakota school district employee complained that a co-worker sexually harassed her. The co-worker was suspended and warned that if he harassed anyone in the future, he would be fired. When he returned to work, he continued to leer at the employee, who complained again. The district suspended the co-worker again and gave him another warning, but without the threat of immediate termination. When the employee quit and then sued under

Title VII, a federal court granted pretrial judgment to the district. The Eighth Circuit reversed and remanded the case for a trial. **The district's alleged backtracking on its discipline of the co-worker may have emboldened him to continue his inappropriate behavior.** *Engel v. Rapid City School Dist.*, 506 F.3d 1118 (8th Cir. 2007).

◆ A female employee of an Indiana crime lab sued for sexual harassment by her supervisor and received an award of $300,000. A year after her supervisor retired, while going through a cabinet, she discovered pornographic videotapes, including one depicting necrophilia. She took the tapes to her lawyer to make copies, then returned them to the lab. Shortly thereafter she was fired for that act, as well as for failing to take a blood stain sample from a rape kit, and for taking her lawyer a page from the rape case file. She sued for harassment again, and also asserted a claim for retaliation. A federal court and the Seventh Circuit ruled against her. **The videotapes in the cabinet did not rise to the level of harassment**, and she was properly fired. *Coolidge v. Consolidated City of Indianapolis and Marion County*, 505 F.3d 731 (7th Cir. 2007).

◆ A female corrections officer in California complained to the warden about male inmates' sexually harassing behavior, including masturbating in front of her. She wrote a number of incident reports about the harassment and also wrote a letter to the director of the Department of Corrections and Rehabilitation. **She was then ordered to undergo a psychiatric evaluation.** After she filed a formal complaint of sexual harassment and wrote a letter to a state senator, the inspector general's (IG's) office began an investigation. She was fired before the IG issued its report. When she sued under Title VII and the First Amendment, a jury awarded her $600,000 in compensatory damages. The Ninth Circuit upheld the ruling that the prison officials were liable for failing to take action on the sexual harassment. However, her internal reports were not protected speech because they were part of her job. The court remanded the case for a re-determination of damages. *Freitag v. Ayers*, 468 F.3d 528 (9th Cir. 2006).

◆ A woman working for Cook County Hospital in the boiler room allegedly endured harassment and even physical assaults at her co-workers' hands. She was offered a transfer to another area, but the harassment continued and her supervisors allegedly did nothing about it. She was finally diagnosed with post-traumatic stress disorder and was fired when she failed to report to work. She filed discrimination charges with the EEOC and was reinstated with back pay two days later. When she sued, a federal court granted pretrial judgment to the county. The Seventh Circuit reversed, holding that **the termination counted as an adverse action even though she was reinstated**. Also, a jury could find the county knew about the harassment and ignored it. *Phelan v. Cook County*, 463 F.3d 773 (7th Cir. 2006).

◆ A nurse at an Illinois county hospital alleged that she and other female employees were sexually harassed by a doctor who was an independent contractor, and that he threatened her with professional and personal harm if she did not withdraw her complaint. She sued the county for sexual harassment under Title VII. A federal court granted pretrial judgment to the county, but the Seventh Circuit reversed. **It did not matter that the harassing acts were committed by an independent contractor.** The county had a duty to provide its employees with nondiscriminatory working conditions. The case required a trial. *Dunn v. Washington County Hospital*, 429 F.3d 689 (7th Cir. 2005).

♦ Two former corrections employees in California filed a lawsuit claiming they were sexually harassed by a warden who was having affairs with other women. His favoritism for his paramours was on public display and sent the message that women could get ahead only by sexually pleasing their superiors. Also, one of the paramours harassed the two women and even assaulted one of them, all without being disciplined. The California Supreme Court reversed pretrial judgment for the corrections department and held that a trial was necessary. **Widespread sexual favoritism can create a hostile work environment**, and a jury would have to determine whether that was the case here. *Miller v. California Dep't of Corrections*, 115 P.3d 77 (Cal. 2005).

♦ Over a two-year period, the only female employee in a Missouri Department of Transportation signal shop was subjected to sexually offensive comments from her boss. He told her that "women are better secretaries" and that he wished she could be his personal secretary. He also made other comments about her office work and secretarial skills, and gave her less favorable assignments than the male employees. She filed a grievance, and the demeaning comments stopped. She was also given better assignments and was promoted within six months. She nevertheless sued for sexual harassment under Title VII. The Eighth Circuit ruled against her. Although she was subjected to harassing conduct, it was not so extreme as to change the terms and conditions of her employment. *Tuggle v. Mangan*, 348 F.3d 714 (8th Cir. 2003).

♦ A female police detective sergeant for a state university documented at least 16 instances of harassing behavior and reported them to the chief numerous times over a seven-year period. The harassment included offensive touching, simulated sexual acts and explicit sexual remarks. Despite her reports, the offensive conduct continued until she went on administrative leave and filed a discrimination charge with the Equal Employment Opportunity Commission and the Missouri Commission on Human Rights. The university investigated and concluded that no sexual harassment had occurred. She was ordered back to work, but refused when she was told no changes to her work environment would be made. She was fired, and sued under Title VII. A jury awarded her $240,000. The Eighth Circuit upheld the award. The behavior here went far beyond gender-related jokes and occasional teasing, and **the university failed to do anything about the employee's repeated complaints**. *Eich v. Board of Regents for Central Missouri State Univ., Dep't of Public Safety*, 350 F.3d 752 (8th Cir. 2003).

♦ A female 911 police dispatcher for a New Jersey town claimed that her instructor during her probationary period groped himself and made sexually explicit comments to her while training her on how to handle emergency calls.

She complained to her lieutenant, and was told she did not have to take the class on days the instructor was teaching. She missed most of the rest of the month with an upset stomach, and was terminated one day before the end of her probationary period. She sued for harassment and retaliation. A federal court granted summary judgment to the town, but the Third Circuit reversed in part. Although she failed to show that her termination was in retaliation for complaining about the instructor, a jury could determine that the town failed to take effective measures to stop the instructor's conduct. Here, the evidence suggested the dispatcher would be a poor risk as far as dependability was concerned, but a trial was required on the sexual harassment issue. *Thomas v. Town of Hammonton*, 351 F.3d 108 (3d Cir. 2003).

♦   A judicial clerk in Illinois was subjected to sexual harassment by the judge for whom she worked. When she complained to the supervising judge, he told her that the only way he could protect both her and the judge would be to reassign her to another judge who was opposed to the transfer. He also suggested that she could resign. The clerk resigned after her boss left her a voice mail asking her out. She sued for hostile work environment under Title VII, and a federal court granted pretrial judgment to the defendants. The Seventh Circuit reversed. Here, there was sufficient evidence for a jury to find that the workplace was hostile, and **the supervising judge's official actions could be construed to make the employment intolerable** such that the "constructive discharge" of the clerk was a tangible employment action. A trial was required. *Robinson v. Sappington*, 351 F.3d 317 (7th Cir. 2003).

♦   A New Hampshire woman worked in a secure psychiatric unit in the men's state prison in Concord. After she became pregnant, she alleged that two male supervisors made a number of derogatory comments to her and denied her a transfer, forcing her to quit two months later. In her complaint, she listed seven separate examples of what she claimed were hostile or abusive remarks. When she sued under Title VII for sexual harassment and pregnancy discrimination, a federal court dismissed the harassment claim. It then conducted discovery on the pregnancy claim before dismissing that one as well. The First Circuit Court of Appeals held that the lower court **erred in dismissing the harassment claim** because, in doing so, the lower court assessed how extreme the comments were. This was an evaluative judgment that should have been left to a trier of fact. *Gorski v. New Hampshire Dep't of Corrections*, 290 F.3d 466 (1st Cir. 2002).

♦   A Florida city clerk was subjected to a series of harassing acts by her manager, and eventually resigned. Before she actually stopped working for the city, she attended a Rotary Club event (all city employees were expected to attend). She arranged for the police chief to give her a ride home, but her manager told the chief he would take her. When they arrived at her place, the manager followed her inside and raped her. She sued the city under Title VII and obtained $500,000 for the harassment. She also was awarded $1.5 million for the rape. On appeal, the Eleventh Circuit Court of Appeals reversed the $1.5 million rape award because the city did not have a policy or custom of tolerating or ignoring rape. However, **because city officials knew of the harassment and** did nothing to stop it, the court of appeals upheld the **$500,000 harassment award**. There was repeated testimony at the trial that the manager regularly discussed his sex life in front of co-workers, and that he would discuss with other male employees what it would be like to have sex with female employees. *Griffin v. City of Opa-Locka*, 261 F.3d 1295 (11th Cir. 2001).

♦ A female deputy superintendent for the New York City Transit Authority learned that a male co-worker was harassing women who were under his supervision. She did not see the harassment happening and only became aware of it after the fact. While management investigated the alleged harassment, the deputy superintendent developed major depression, which she claimed stemmed from her efforts to secure a remedy for the harassed women. She sued the transit authority under Title VII, and a jury awarded her $60,000 for the authority's deliberate indifference to sexual harassment. She also obtained over $142,000 in attorneys' fees and costs. The Second Circuit Court of Appeals reversed the award in her favor. It held that **she could not recover for harassment she had never witnessed or endured**. Allowing a recovery would expose employers to almost limitless liability. *Leibovitz v. New York City Transit Authority*, 252 F.3d 179 (2d Cir. 2001).

♦ A female firefighter in Rhode Island was entitled to a $275,000 jury award where she demonstrated a continuing violation of Title VII by a series of individual acts that went back more than 300 days. The acts themselves may not have been sufficiently severe or discriminatory, but together they added up to actionable discrimination. Here, her co-workers violated the chief's policy against sexually explicit materials and discussed their sex lives in front of her. They also made offensive sexual remarks to her and ostracized her. Her car was vandalized, her locker was glued shut, and co-workers often referred to her food as "lesbian food." The First Circuit noted that although she filed the charge of sexual harassment more than 300 days after the first acts of discrimination against her, **the continuing violation doctrine allowed her to recover for all the harassing activity against her**, not just the harassment that occurred over the last 300 days. *O'Rourke v. City of Providence*, 235 F.3d 713 (1st Cir. 2001).

2. Defenses

The Supreme Court set forth the primary defense to a claim of sexual harassment: that the employer had a sexual harassment policy in place, and the employee failed to avail herself of its protections. But this defense does not work if tangible adverse action is taken against the employee.

♦ A Florida woman worked as a lifeguard for a city. She had two male supervisors who controlled all aspects of her job, including work assignments and discipline. The lifeguard was subjected to severe and pervasive unwelcome touching, sexual comments, and other offensive behavior from the two supervisors. Although the city had a policy against sexual harassment, it failed to disseminate the policy to the lifeguard's department. Also, the policy did not assure that harassing supervisors could be bypassed in registering complaints.

The employee did not report the harassment to higher management. She instead resigned and sued the city for sexual harassment under Title VII and 42 U.S.C. § 1983. The district court found the city liable for the harassment. The Eleventh Circuit Court of Appeals reversed.

The U.S. Supreme Court held that Title VII imposes vicarious liability on an employer for actionable discrimination caused by a supervisor with authority over an employee. When a supervisor discriminates in the terms and conditions of a subordinate's employment, his actions draw upon his superior position over the subordinate. In cases where there is no tangible employment action taken against the employee, **the employer may first prove that it exercised reasonable care to prevent and promptly correct any sexual harassment, and second, that the employee unreasonably failed to avail herself of any employer remedies or failed to avoid harm otherwise**. However, the defense is not available to the employer when the supervisor's harassment culminates in a tangible employment act such as discharge or demotion. The Court found the city vicariously liable for the hostile environment created by the lifeguard's supervisors. It reversed and remanded the case. *Faragher v. City of Boca Raton*, 524 U.S. 775, 118 S.Ct. 2275, 141 L.Ed.2d 662 (1998).

♦ A communications officer with the Pennsylvania State Police was allegedly subjected to sexually offensive comments and gestures from her supervisors. She also asserted that the state police's EEO officer failed to do anything about her complaints. She resigned, then sued the state police for sexual harassment under Title VII, alleging that she had been constructively discharged. A federal court found that the defendants were entitled to pretrial judgment based on the *Ellerth/Faragher* defense – no liability for a supervisor's harassment where no tangible action was taken against the employee, and 1) the employer exercised reasonable care to prevent the harassment, and 2) the employee did not avail herself of the employer's preventive opportunities.

The Third Circuit Court of Appeals reversed, holding that constructive discharge amounts to a tangible employment action such that the *Ellerth/Faragher* defense is not available. The U.S. Supreme Court then held that **if the constructive discharge was not the result of employer-sanctioned action, but instead the misconduct of a rogue supervisor, the employer could assert the *Ellerth/Faragher* defense**. Employer-sanctioned adverse actions occur when a supervisor subjects the victim to a humiliating demotion, extreme cut in pay, or transfer to a position with unbearable working conditions. Here, the employee presented enough evidence to warrant a trial. The Court remanded the case. *Pennsylvania State Police v. Suders*, 542 U.S. 129, 124 S.Ct. 2342, 159 L.Ed.2d 204 (2004).

♦ A Florida police sergeant made weekly comments to a female deputy, telling her "she looked hot, but it would be better if [she'd] wear tighter clothes." When she reported his comments to a superior, she was allowed to move to a different office while an investigation was conducted. Within a month the sergeant apologized, and she did not complain again. Later she sued for harassment under Title VII and lost. The Eleventh Circuit Court of Appeals held that **the sergeant's remarks, while taunting, boorish and unmistakably** gender-based, did not rise to the level of illegal sexual harassment under Title VII. *Webb-Edwards v. Orange County Sheriff's Office*, 525 F.3d 1013 (11th Cir. 2008).

♦ Two female dispatchers for a Missouri police department endured sexually harassing behavior by a captain for about a year before reporting it to a lieutenant, who informed the chief. The harassment ended immediately, though the chief's investigation resulted in a finding that no harassment occurred. The chief also allegedly intimidated witnesses and shared confidential results with his friend, the captain. The two dispatchers sued the city under Title VII. The city claimed it was not liable under *Ellerth* and *Faragher* because the two dispatchers waited unreasonably long to report the harassment and, in any event, it stopped immediately upon their report of it. A federal court and the Eighth Circuit held for the city. **Even though the investigation was flawed, the harassment stopped**, no retaliation occurred, and the dispatchers were unreasonably afraid to report the harassment to the chief because of his friendship with the captain. *Wager v. City of Ladue*, 500 F.3d 710 (8th Cir. 2007).

♦ Four female employees of a Wisconsin county endured unwanted touching and inappropriate comments by their male supervisor. They complained to the HR manager about his behavior, but refused to file a formal complaint. The HR manager investigated the matter and conveyed a meeting of the anti-harassment committee, which counseled the supervisor about his behavior. Two months later, the women formally complained about the supervisor's behavior. Within days, an investigation resulted in the supervisor's demotion and transfer. When the women sued under Title VII, they lost. The Seventh Circuit held that the *Faragher/Ellerth* defense applied because **the county took reasonable steps to prevent the harassment as soon as it learned of the situation**. *Jackson v. County of Racine*, 474 F.3d 493 (7th Cir. 2006).

♦ A female employee of a New York village claimed that her boss was condescending to her even though he did not behave the same way toward male co-workers. He also micromanaged her work and gave some of her duties to a male college intern. When she sued for sexual harassment under Title VII and state law, a federal court refused to grant immunity to the defendants. However, the Second Circuit Court of Appeals reversed, finding insufficient evidence that the employee was subjected to a sexually hostile work environment. Also, **the disparate treatment she received was not so severe or abusive that it altered the terms or conditions of her job**. *Demoret v. Zegarelli*, 451 F.3d 140 (2d Cir. 2006).

♦ An administrative assistant with the District of Columbia Department of Corrections put up with sexual harassment from her supervisor for months before making a complaint. When she finally did complain, the warden initially recommended she be reassigned to the "relief pool," an undesirable transfer, but later told her she would be switching duties with another administrative assistant. Instead, she took a sick leave. While she was gone, her supervisor was demoted and transferred. She sued the department anyway under Title VII, but a jury found that **she waited an unreasonably long time to complain** and thus was not entitled to relief. The D.C. Circuit Court of Appeals affirmed. *Roebuck v. Washington*, 408 F.3d 790 (D.C. Cir. 2005).

• A clerk in the building department of an Illinois city endured harassing behavior and comments by her supervisor over a period of two years but never mentioned it to anyone until he put his hand under her shirt and pants. At that point, she complained to the mayor's daughter. That same afternoon, the mayor met with the city attorney and the supervisor, who resigned. The city gave the clerk 52 days of paid leave. She refused to return from leave even though the harasser was gone, and sued the city for sexual harassment. The Seventh Circuit held that **the city was not liable because it quickly responded once the clerk reported the harassment**. The supervisor's previous behavior and comments were not sufficiently severe to create a hostile work environment. Further, the city had no way of knowing about the earlier harassment because the clerk did not report it. *McPherson v. City of Waukegan*, 379 F.3d 430 (7th Cir. 2004).

• A radio dispatcher for the Arkansas State Police worked the night shift from 3-11 p.m. One night, a supervisor allegedly made offensive remarks to her for about an hour, also brushing up against her. When she reported the offensive behavior, the agency immediately interviewed witnesses, insulated the dispatcher from the supervisor, then transferred and demoted the supervisor. She sued for sexual harassment under Title VII but lost because the agency had a reporting policy in place and responded immediately to the dispatcher's complaint. Whether she unreasonably failed to avail herself of the agency's reporting procedures did not matter. **The agency's quick response relieved it of liability.** *McCurdy v. Arkansas State Police*, 375 F.3d 762 (8th Cir. 2004).

• A computer programmer at a Colorado college complained about her supervisor's sexual harassment. College officials promptly gave her a new assignment to a prestigious "web team." However, she had trouble adjusting to that position. They then reassigned her to a third position that was also considered a plum job. Nevertheless, she had problems adjusting there as well. Her performance slipped; she received a low evaluation; and she quit. She sued for retaliation under Title VII, and a federal court ruled for the college. The Tenth Circuit affirmed. Here, the college officials' **good-faith belief that they were transferring the programmer to desirable positions**, even though she later claimed she had not wanted the jobs, could not be construed as adverse employment actions or retaliation. *Tran v. Trustees of the State Colleges of Colorado*, 355 F.3d 1263 (10th Cir. 2004).

3. Same-Sex and Sexual Orientation Issues

Some states provide protection against sexual orientation harassment. Title VII does not. However, it does protect against same-sex harassment where that harassment is "because of gender." In other words, if a male employee is harassed because he seems too effeminate, he would be protected.

♦ A Louisiana man, working as a roustabout on an oil platform in the Gulf of Mexico, claimed that his male co-workers physically assaulted him in a sexual manner and threatened him with rape. When he complained to the employer's safety compliance clerk, the clerk did nothing. Eventually, he quit and sued for sex discrimination under Title VII. A federal court granted pretrial judgment to the employer, holding that the employee had no cause of action under Title VII for harassment by male co-workers. The Fifth Circuit affirmed. The U.S. Supreme Court stated that **sex discrimination consisting of same-sex harassment was actionable under Title VII**. The statute's prohibition of discrimination "because of ... sex" in the terms or conditions of employment protects men as well as women. Not all verbal or physical harassment in the workplace is prohibited by Title VII. Rather, where members of one sex are exposed to disadvantageous terms or conditions of employment to which members of the opposite sex are not exposed, the harassment violates the statute. Further, conduct that is not severe or pervasive enough to create an objectively hostile or abusive work environment – one that a reasonable person would find hostile or abusive – is not covered by Title VII. The Court reversed the lower court decisions and remanded the case. *Oncale v. Sundowner Offshore Services, Inc.*, 523 U.S. 75, 118 S.Ct. 998, 140 L.Ed.2d 201 (1998).

♦ A letter carrier was subjected to a number of harassing episodes by co-workers and supervisors who thought he was gay. Even though he never told them he was a homosexual, they inferred the fact from his behavior and mannerisms. When he complained about the harassment, he claimed that he was subjected to additional harassment and retaliation. He sued under Title VII for sex discrimination and discrimination on the basis of sexual orientation. A federal court refused to dismiss the lawsuit, noting that if the harassment occurred because **he was too effeminate and did not meet gender stereotypes of what a man should look or act like**, then the postal service could be liable under Title VII. However, the employee still had to show that the harassment was so severe as to alter the conditions of employment. The case would proceed to trial. *Centola v. Potter*, 183 F.Supp.2d 403 (D. Mass. 2002).

♦ A nurse at an Indiana hospital claimed that he was subjected to harassment by the hospital's medical director because of his sexual orientation. He filed a written grievance. Subsequently, the hospital fired him for making an improper notation on a patient's admission sheet. He sued under Title VII, asserting that the termination had been in retaliation for the grievance. The Seventh Circuit disagreed. It noted that **Title VII does not protect against harassment on the basis of sexual orientation**. Here, even if the firing occurred as a retaliatory measure, there could be no Title VII violation because the underlying conduct was not unlawful. The director had not harassed the nurse because of his sex but because of his sexual orientation. *Hamner v. St. Vincent Hospital & Health Care Center*, 224 F.3d 701 (7th Cir. 2000).

♦ A postal service employee in New York endured a great deal of abuse and harassment as a result of his sexual orientation. He claimed that it even caused him to suffer a heart attack. When he sued under Title VII, the Second Circuit ruled against him, noting that **he was not protected against harassment because of sexual orientation**. If he had been harassed because he did not conform to sexual stereotypes (for example, if he behaved in a stereotypically feminine manner), he might have had a claim. But he made no such allegation here. *Simonton v. Runyon*, 232 F.3d 33 (2d Cir. 2000).

4. 42 U.S.C. § 1983

When a manager, acting "under color of" state law, deprives an employee of a federally guaranteed right, the public entity can be held liable under Section 1983. Those guaranteed rights can arise under either the Constitution or a federal statute.

* A male corrections officer in Illinois was fired for violating the department's sexual harassment policy and standards of conduct. He allegedly grabbed women's breasts and buttocks, among other acts. He sued the warden and two other superior officers under 42 U.S.C. § 1983, claiming they denied him equal protection by firing him, but not female officers who had engaged in similar or worse conduct. A federal court granted pretrial judgment to the defendants, and the Seventh Circuit affirmed. Here, despite the officer's allegations, **he presented no evidence that female officers engaged in sexual harassment or that, if they did, their behavior was reported up the chain of command**. The only evidence he proffered was his own testimony, and his knowledge was admittedly limited to secondhand accounts. Further, two of the superiors were not involved in the decision to fire him. *Oakley v. Cowan*, 187 Fed.Appx. 635 (7th Cir. 2006).

* On her first day of work, an intern art teacher at an Indiana junior high school was approached by the principal, invited into his office and asked for her phone number. She was also told that he could get her a permanent art room (a perk other junior art teachers did not have) and supplies. She perceived this as a sexual advance and became uncomfortable. Over the next month, he continued to engage her in personal talk and even invited her onto his boat. She rejected all his advances, causing him to take back the supplies he had given her. He then gave her what could be construed as a failing evaluation. When she complained to union officials, a formal grievance was filed, but the school board took no action against the principal. It did, however, overturn the decision that she had flunked her internship. When she sued under Title VII and 42 U.S.C. § 1983, a jury ruled in her favor. The Seventh Circuit affirmed, noting that **the principal's action in removing her art supplies was a tangible employment action that would support a finding of sexual harassment**. It upheld the jury's verdict in her favor, including the award of $25,000 in punitive damages. *Molnar v. Booth*, 229 F.3d 593 (7th Cir. 2000).

* A North Carolina police corporal grabbed a female member of his squad and kissed her. The squad supervisor, who witnessed the incident, immediately issued the corporal an oral reprimand. On the next shift, a department captain issued a formal written reprimand. The supervisor then met with the squad and warned

that this "horseplay" and the like would not be tolerated in the future. The supervisor and the captain also met with female members of the squad to determine whether they had experienced comparable conduct. After the officer filed a formal charge against the corporal, the police chief suspended the corporal for two months without pay, demoted him and reassigned him to another division. The city manager's office later set aside the demotion. When the officer's co-workers openly voiced their resentment toward her, she resigned, then sued under Title VII and Section 1983. The district court ruled for the city. The Fourth Circuit affirmed, finding that **the city had taken prompt and adequate remedial measures**. *Mikels v. City of Durham*, 183 F.3d 323 (4th Cir. 1999).

♦ A female second lieutenant for a Virginia county sheriff's office accused her supervisor of sexual harassment. He allegedly massaged her shoulders during roll call, accused her of having an affair with a deputy, asked her what type of underwear she wore, ordered her to drive him to a repair shop, and then told her it was his "turn to make out in the parking lot." After she filed a complaint against him, he stated that she had chosen to work in a male-dominated field and that if she did not like it she could "just get out." He then refused to talk with her, regularly criticized her performance and generally undermined her efforts to run her shift. The lieutenant filed a 42 U.S.C. § 1983 lawsuit against the supervisor, alleging sexual harassment, discrimination and retaliation. The district court held for the lieutenant and awarded damages, and the Fourth Circuit affirmed. **The supervisor's acts altered the conditions of the lieutenant's employment and created an objectively abusive working environment.** *Beardsley v. Webb*, 30 F.3d 524 (4th Cir. 1994).

5. State Statutes

♦ A federal jury determined that a school district supervisor sexually harassed a female employee and awarded her $500,000 in her lawsuit under Title VII and the Florida Civil Rights Act. Because of statutory caps on damages, a question arose as to how much she was due. **She asserted that she should get the $300,000 cap from Title VII and the $100,000 cap from state law.** The Eleventh Circuit disagreed, holding that she was only entitled to the $300,000 from Title VII. Where Title VII authorizes an amount greater than $100,000 (as here), the victim is entitled only to the higher amount. *Bradshaw v. School Board of Broward County, Florida*, 486 F.3d 1205 (11th Cir. 2007).

♦ A New Jersey town radio dispatcher was required to obtain a 911 certification and took the class at the county's training center. She claimed that the trainer subjected her to sexually harassing remarks and obscene recordings of supposedly emergency calls. After complaining to her superiors, she was allowed to complete her certification via other means. When she failed to report to work due to illness, she was fired. She then sued the county for violating the state's Law Against Discrimination. A state court granted pretrial judgment to the county, but the appellate division reversed. **Even though the county was not her employer, it could be liable for the harassment as a place of public accommodation.** *Thomas v. County of Camden*, 902 A.2d 327 (N.J. Super. Ct. App. Div. 2006).

- A Massachusetts woman volunteered at a swap shop owned by a town. For three years, she endured harassment at the hands of a supervisor, despite her repeated requests that he leave her alone. After she was let go, she filed a complaint under a state law that guaranteed "persons" the right to be free from sexual harassment. The case reached the Supreme Judicial Court of Massachusetts, which held that she could not proceed under the law. **The law was enacted to protect employees, not volunteers.** Thus, she would have to proceed under the state's civil rights act or bring a common law claim for harassment. *Lowery v. Klemm*, 845 N.E.2d 1124 (Mass. 2006).

- A New Jersey county jail entered into a contract with a private health care business to provide medical services to inmates. Under the contract, the jail could, if dissatisfied with any individual employee's performance, have the business remove the employee from the county jail assignment. However, it could not require the business to fire the employee. Two years after a nurse was hired to work at the jail, she reported that a corrections officer touched her in a sexually inappropriate way. The subsequent investigation could not support the allegations. Later that year, the business informed the nurse that its contract was expiring and that her services would no longer be needed. She sued the county under the state's Law Against Discrimination (LAD). The New Jersey Superior Court, Appellate Division, ruled that **she was not an employee of the county and thus was not entitled to the protections of the LAD** with respect to the county. She was an employee of the health care business, which exercised control over her work and pay. She could not sue the county. *Chrisanthis v. County of Atlantic*, 825 A.2d 1192 (N.J. Super. Ct. App. Div. 2003).

- An employee filed a claim under Connecticut's Fair Employment Practices Act alleging that she was constructively discharged when the Department of Corrections failed to remedy harassment from inmates and staff. She had been offered a transfer to other facilities after an investigation could not turn up who had begun rumors about her. She refused the transfer and went on medical leave, but was deemed to have resigned after failing to submit necessary medical documentation. A trial court ruled in favor of the Department, and the Supreme Court of Connecticut affirmed. Because the identity of inmates and staff responsible for harassing acts and rumors about the employee could not be discovered quickly, **the offer to transfer her constituted an appropriate response reasonably designed to end the harassment**, and fairly accommodated the legitimate interests and concerns of the employee. Thus, the employee could not establish the existence of an intolerable work atmosphere that would compel a reasonable person to resign. *Brittel v. Dep't of Correction*, 247 Conn. 148, 717 A.2d 1254 (Conn. 1998).

- A Minnesota state employee, who was required to work with a federal employee, was subjected to numerous acts of sexual harassment. The employee notified her supervisors on at least two occasions about the harassment. On one occasion, the employee's supervisor did not act upon learning of the information. On the second occasion, a state affirmative action officer spoke to the employee and offered some services. Also, the federal employee's supervisor was contacted and took action against the federal employee. However, the sexual harassment continued. The employee sued the state under the Human Rights Act for sexual harassment and intentional infliction of emotional distress. The Minnesota Court of Appeals noted that the act recognized a cause of action where an employee is sexually harassed by a non-employee. **An employer may be liable if it is aware of a non-employee's sexual harassment toward its employee and fails to take timely and appropriate action** to protect the employee. However because the state took some action to address the harassment when it learned of the situation, it could not be liable for intentional infliction of emotional distress. *Costilla v. State of Minnesota*, 571 N.W.2d 587 (Minn. Ct. App. 1997).

♦ An information specialist for the state of Idaho was constantly subjected to crude language on the job. She later testified to over 275 individual examples of sexually charged or degrading comments. An investigation resulted in insufficient proof of wrongdoing, and no disciplinary action was taken against the perpetrators. She was then transferred to a poorly equipped office with less work. She sued the state and her supervisor, alleging violations of the Idaho Human Rights Act (IHRA). The jury found that the supervisor violated the IHRA 75 times and imposed a $500 penalty for each violation. It found that the state violated the IHRA 98 times, imposing a $1,000 penalty for each violation. The Supreme Court of Idaho found that the district court had incorrectly allowed every incident of harassment to be a violation of the IHRA. **The very nature of a hostile work environment claim under the IHRA entails proof of numerous incidents.** Thus, the jury should not have awarded separate penalties for each violation. Also, the supervisor was not subject to individual liability. *Paterson v. State of Idaho*, 915 P.2d 724 (Idaho 1996).

V. RELIGIOUS DISCRIMINATION

Religious discrimination is prohibited by Title VII of the Civil Rights Act. However, public employers need make only reasonable accommodation for an employee's or applicant's religious beliefs and practices. If accommodating the employee would impose an undue hardship on the employer, then the employer will not have to accommodate the employee. States also have enacted similar laws prohibiting religious discrimination. Please see Chapter Three for cases involving First Amendment religious issues.

A. Burden of Proof

♦ A Jewish police officer in New Jersey endured numerous anti-Semitic comments, including being called "the Jew" by the chief twice a month and having a German flag sticker placed on his locker. He eventually filed an internal complaint, then sued under the state's law against discrimination. A jury found the borough liable for religious harassment, but an appeals panel reversed. The New Jersey Supreme Court reversed the appellate court and reinstated the liability verdict. **It was the cumulative effect of the incidents** that made the harassment actionable even though isolated incidents weren't sufficient by themselves to reach the level necessary to create liability. *Cutler v. Dorn*, 955 A.2d 917 (N.J. 2008).

• A Las Vegas police officer began observing Orthodox Judaism and sought to wear a beard as well as a head covering. While he was undercover, he wore a beard and a baseball cap, but that required him to work on the Sabbath. He transferred to a non-uniformed quality assurance unit, but shortly thereafter was told that he could not wear a beard and yarmulke. He sued the department under Title VII and also alleged constitutional violations. He sought pretrial judgment. The court found issues of fact that required a trial. **If the department made an exception for medical conditions with respect to beards, it could not deny him the right to wear a closely shaved beard.** However, the yarmulke was a religious symbol and could undermine the department's image as religiously neutral. The department might not have to accommodate this request. *Riback v. Las Vegas Metropolitan Police Dep't*, 2008 WL 3211279 (D. Nev. 8/6/08).

• A former priest who worked as a corrections officer was subjected to five comments about homosexual pedophiles and abusive priests over a 12-year period. He sued the county in a Pennsylvania federal court for religious discrimination in violation of Title VII. The case reached the Third Circuit, which ruled for the county, finding that **even though the comments may have been humiliating, they were limited in number**, made by different people and spread out over a long time, with long gaps in between. Thus, they did not amount to harassment severe and pervasive enough to violate Title VII. *Hamera v. County of Berks*, 248 Fed.Appx. 422 (3d Cir. 2007).

• An administrative law judge (ALJ) for the New York Department of Motor Vehicles claimed that he was subjected to a hostile work environment because he was Jewish. He asserted that four of the five senior ALJs were African-American Christians, and the fifth (a supervising judge) was a white, female Christian. He alleged that the four ALJs made derogatory remarks about his religion and **called him "Jewish-sounding" names**. When he sued under Title VII, a federal court granted pretrial judgment to the state. The Second Circuit reversed, finding sufficient facts to warrant a trial. A jury could decide that the religious animosity of the remarks directed at him altered his working conditions for the worse. *Feingold v. State of New York*, 366 F.3d 138 (2d Cir. 2004).

• A Missouri social worker told his supervisor that his religious beliefs prevented him from approving foster parent licenses for individuals living in openly homosexual relationships. His supervisor recommended that he be fired, in large part because she believed he could not perform his job as a result of his religious views. When the Division of Family Services refused to fire him, she re-wrote the worker's evaluation and turned it from a four-page document into a 53-page criticism of almost every aspect of his job performance. She delivered the evaluation to him even though he had since transferred to another position no longer under her supervision. **He sued her for religious discrimination under 42 U.S.C. § 1983**, and a jury awarded him $1,500 in compensatory damages and $25,000 in punitive damages. The Eighth Circuit Court of Appeals upheld the award, noting that the cumulative effect of the supervisor's conduct amounted to an adverse employment action. Further, the supervisor was not entitled to qualified immunity. *Phillips v. Collings*, 256 F.3d 843 (8th Cir. 2001).

* A California computer analyst with the state department of education displayed a religious phrase and acronym on software programs and other materials. One of his supervisors instructed him not to use the acronym; however, the analyst continued and was eventually suspended for five days. He then received a specific written order to refrain from: 1) using a name, acronym, or symbol with religious connotations on any document in the workplace, 2) initiating or promoting religious discussions during the workday except for breaks and lunch periods outside the workplace, and 3) displaying or promoting religious books, pamphlets, etc., outside his workspace. Later, a supervisor issued a similar order to all employees in the division. The analyst sued, alleging both constitutional and Title VII claims. The Ninth Circuit held that the religious bans violated the First Amendment. **The religious advocacy ban lacked any substantial governmental interests sufficient to outweigh the employee's interests in free expression.** *Tucker v. State of California Dep't of Educ.*, 97 F.3d 1204 (9th Cir. 1996).

* The Georgia Department of Law offered a permanent position as a department attorney to a homosexual female with an outstanding academic record. The applicant completed a standard personnel form on which she showed her marital status as engaged and indicated that her future spouse was a woman. After the attorney general learned that the planned wedding was to another woman and that the wedding was to be performed by a rabbi who performed homosexual marriages, he withdrew the offer of employment. He stated that inaction on his part would constitute "tacit approval" of the purported marriage and jeopardize the proper function of his office. The applicant sued the attorney general for violating her rights to intimate and expressive association, freedom of religion, equal protection, and substantive due process. The court ruled for the attorney general, and the Eleventh Circuit affirmed. Under the *Pickering* balancing test, **the attorney general did not violate the applicant's First Amendment right of association by withdrawing the job offer.** The attorney general's interest in promoting the efficiency of important public service outweighed the applicant's personal associational interests. *Shahar v. Bowers*, 114 F.3d 1097 (11th Cir. 1997).

B. Reasonable Accommodations

* A Connecticut high school teacher sued his school district under Title VII. He belonged to a church that required members to refrain from secular employment during designated holy days. This required the teacher to miss approximately six school days each year for religious purposes. The district's collective bargaining agreement allowed only three days of paid leave for religious observation. The agreement also allowed three days paid leave for necessary personal business which, the district said, could not be used for

religious purposes. The teacher asked to use three days of necessary personal business leave for religious purposes. He also offered to pay for a substitute teacher if the school board would pay him for the extra days he missed. These alternatives were turned down by the school board. When all administrative alternatives were exhausted, he filed a lawsuit alleging that the school board's policy was discriminatory on the basis of religion. A U.S. district court dismissed the teacher's lawsuit, and he appealed.

The Second Circuit held that the school board was bound to accept one of the teacher's proposed solutions unless that accommodation caused undue hardship. On further appeal, the U.S. Supreme Court decided that **the school district was not required to accept the teacher's proposals even if acceptance would not result in undue hardship**. The school board was only bound to offer a fair and reasonable accommodation of the teacher's religious needs. The bargaining agreement policy of allowing three days paid leave for religious purposes, but excluding additional days of necessary personal business leave if needed for religious purposes, would not be reasonable if paid leave was provided for all purposes except religious ones. Because none of the lower courts had decided whether the necessary personal business leave policy had been administered fairly in the past, the case was remanded. *Ansonia Board of Educ. v. Philbrook*, 479 U.S. 60, 107 S.Ct. 367, 93 L.Ed.2d 305 (1986).

On remand, it was determined that the school board's policy reasonably accommodated the teacher. *Philbrook v. Ansonia Board of Educ.*, 925 F.2d 47 (2d Cir. 1991).

♦ A Seventh-Day Adventist applied for a job as a part-time bus driver in Massachusetts. He told transit officials that he could not work from sundown Friday to sundown Saturday. After passing the written exam and the background checks, as well as a physical exam and drug screening, he was given a conditional offer of employment. However, the offer was withdrawn because of his inability to work the Friday rush hour after sunsets. No offer of accommodation was made. He filed a complaint of religious discrimination. The Supreme Judicial Court of Massachusetts ruled in his favor, finding that **the transit authority failed to even engage in the interactive process of seeking an accommodation**. It could not claim that merely looking into the possibility of voluntary shift swaps would impose an undue burden on it. *Massachusetts Bay Transportation Authority v. Massachusetts Comm'n Against Discrimination*, 879 N.E.2d 36 (Mass. 2008).

♦ A Philadelphia police department directive prohibited officers from wearing religious symbols or religious apparel while in uniform. When a Muslim officer sought to wear a khimar (a religious headpiece covering hair, forehead, sides of the head, neck, shoulders and chest), permission was denied. She filed a charge with the EEOC and attempted to wear the khimar on duty. The department suspended her. When she sued for discrimination under Title VII, she lost. A federal court held that **allowing her to wear the khimar would be an undue burden because of the department's need to maintain religious neutrality** among its officers and in the eyes of the diverse community it served. *Webb v. City of Philadelphia*, 2007 WL 1866763 (E.D. Pa. 6/27/07).

♦ A Baptist officer with the Indiana State Police was assigned as a gaming agent at a local casino. He asserted that the assignment conflicted with his religious beliefs against gambling. When he requested another assignment, his employer refused to accommodate him. He failed to report for duty and was fired. When the case reached the Seventh Circuit, it held that **the officer was not entitled to the accommodation he had requested because it was not reasonable**. Further, he was not fired because of his religious beliefs; he was fired for his refusal to report for duty, a fate that would have befallen him if he had refused to work for secular reasons. *Endres v. Indiana State Police*, 349 F.3d 922 (7th Cir. 2003).

♦ A water management authority offered permanent status to a temporary employee who also was a Seventh Day Adventist. The employee did not disclose that his religious beliefs prevented him from becoming a member of a labor organization. However, a union security clause required all permanent employees to be union members. The employee first objected to meeting on Saturdays, to the loyalty oath he had to take, and to paying union dues. But when the union agreed to accommodate him on these matters, the employee claimed he could not join a union at all. After the employee was fired, the Equal Employment Opportunity Commission (EEOC) sued the water authority under Title VII. A Puerto Rico federal court granted pretrial judgment to the EEOC, but the First Circuit reversed. Here, there were questions of fact as to **whether the employee really objected to joining a union for religious reasons**, or only did so after the authority agreed to accommodate his objections to aspects of union membership. The issue of a bona fide religious belief required a trial. *EEOC v. Union Independente de la Autoridad de Acueductos y Alcantarillados de Puerto Rico*, 279 F.3d 49 (1st Cir. 2002).

♦ An agreement between the postal service and the letter carriers' union provided that mail carriers would have to work five out of every six Saturdays. When a Kansas letter carrier became a member of the Church of God, he sought to be excused from the requirement that he work on Saturdays (the Sabbath). He suggested five accommodations that would have permanently excused him. The union refused to agree to the accommodations on the ground that doing so would violate the Local Memorandum of Understanding it had with the postal service. **The postal service did, however, approve nearly all his requests to take annual leave on Saturdays.** It also allowed him to trade shifts with other letter carriers who were willing to do so. The employee nevertheless missed a number of Saturdays and was eventually dismissed. He sued the postal service under Title VII for religious discrimination. A Kansas federal court and the Tenth Circuit Court of Appeals ruled against him, finding that the postal service had taken reasonable steps to accommodate his religious beliefs. Thus, it had fulfilled its obligations under Title VII. *Thomas v. National Ass'n of Letter Carriers*, 225 F.3d 1149 (10th Cir. 2000).

♦ An emergency room nurse for a New Jersey university medical center was a member of the Pentecostal faith. Because of her religious beliefs, she refused to participate in any procedure that would end a fetus's life. For a number of years, the center accommodated her by allowing her to trade assignments with other nurses. However, after two incidents in which she refused to treat pregnant patients with life-threatening conditions, the center informed her that she would have to transfer out of the emergency room. It offered her a position in the newborn intensive care unit, which she refused. She also refused to work with the human resource department to find another appropriate position. After the center fired her, she sued under Title VII for religious discrimination. The Third Circuit upheld the dismissal of her lawsuit. **The center did not have to provide her with the best possible accommodation or even the accommodation she preferred.** It merely had to provide her with an accommodation that was reasonable. It had done so here. *Shelton v. Univ. of Medicine & Dentistry of New Jersey*, 223 F.3d 220 (3d Cir. 2000).

• The Third Circuit Court of Appeals held that the Newark police department discriminated against two Muslim officers when it threatened to fire them for violating its no-beard policy. The policy permitted mustaches and sideburns but not goatees and full beards. Undercover officers were exempted, as their assignments required. The department also had made an exception for officers who suffered from pseudo folliculitis barbae, a skin condition in which follicles become infected when the hair is shaved. The officers asserted that the Koran commands the wearing of a beard, and that the refusal by a male to grow a beard if he can is a major sin. But the department refused to allow the officers to wear beards. The city claimed the police department needed to foster a uniform appearance and that allowing the officers to wear beards would undermine the force's morale and *esprit de corps*, as well as the public's confidence in the department. But the court found these reasons superficial. Because **the standard for granting a reasonable accommodation request under Title VII is the same as it is under the Americans with Disabilities Act**, if the department permitted one it had to permit the other. *Fraternal Order of Police v. City of Newark*, 170 F.3d 359 (3d Cir. 1999).

• An anti-abortion police officer believed that guarding abortion clinics was a violation of his religious beliefs and sued to be taken off such duty. An Illinois federal court held for the city, finding that under the collective bargaining agreement, various options existed that would have resolved the conflict between the officer's faith and his job assignments and thus the city had satisfied its duty of accommodation. Generally, the officer's supervisors tried to avoid assigning him to clinic duties. Moreover, the officer frequently avoided such assignments himself by applying for "special function assignments," changing his shift, changing his start time, using time due and using unpaid leave. Finally, the officer had the option of transferring to a district that did not contain any abortion clinics. The officer appealed to the Seventh Circuit, arguing that the city should exempt him from clinic duty while permitting him to stay in the 14th District because that accommodation would not be an undue hardship. The appeals court disagreed. **By providing at least one reasonable accommodation, the city discharged its duty under Title VII.** The fact that the officer chose not to accept a transfer did not make the option any less reasonable. *Rodriguez v. City of Chicago*, 156 F.3d 771 (7th Cir. 1998).

♦ A Florida Seventh Day Adventist police recruit began his 16-week field training session. The department knew of his religious beliefs and knew that he had a religious discrimination claim pending against his prior employer, but it made no promises that he would not be required to work on his Sabbath. Each officer worked four 10-hour days followed by three days off. Every eight weeks, the shift schedules rotated forward one day. The recruit was randomly assigned to work Friday through Monday. No recruit was allowed to use vacation or sick leave during their first six months on duty, and the department denied his request for Saturday off. He sued the department for religious discrimination. A federal court held for the department, and the Eleventh Circuit affirmed. Title VII mandates accommodation of an employee's religious practices unless it causes the employer undue hardship. **Undue hardship is any act requiring an employer to bear more than a *de minimis* (minimal) cost in accommodating an employee's religious beliefs.** Here, requiring the department to grant shift exceptions would improperly jeopardize citizens' health and welfare by interfering with the department's scheduling and training programs. Because such an accommodation would result in a greater than *de minimis* cost, the city's refusal to accommodate the recruit did not violate Title VII. *Beadle v. City of Tampa*, 42 F.3d 633 (11th Cir. 1995).

C. Seniority Systems

♦ A member of the Worldwide Church of God, which strictly forbids all forms of secular work from sundown Friday to sundown Saturday, was offered a position with a Nevada sheriff's department. On her application, she did not mention any religious or other objections to working certain shifts. The sheriff's department deputies were scheduled pursuant to a longstanding, seniority-based shift-bidding system. There also was an unwritten rule prohibiting deputies from trading shifts on a regular basis. When she reported to work, she learned that she was assigned to a swing shift that began on a Friday. She informed her supervisor that she could not work on her Sabbath and requested that her schedule be adjusted to accommodate her religious practices. After the supervisor informed her that there would be no accommodation, she sued for religious discrimination under Title VII. The district court granted the city's motion for pretrial judgment. The Ninth Circuit reversed. It noted that **the mere existence of a seniority system did not relieve the employer of the duty to attempt a reasonable accommodation of the employee's religious practices**, if such an accommodation can be accomplished without modification of the seniority system and with no more than a minimal cost. Here, there was a question of fact as to whether the accommodation of implementing a split-shift schedule would create an undue hardship for the employer. A trial would have to be held. *Balint v. Carson City, Nevada*, 180 F.3d 1047 (9th Cir. 1999).

♦ A newly hired bus driver, employed by the New York City Transit Authority, was a Seventh Day Adventist who could not work from sundown Friday to sundown Saturday. However, the authority regularly scheduled her to work on her Sabbath. Under the collective bargaining agreement between the authority and the Transport Workers Union, the privilege of selecting weekly days off was allocated in accordance with a strict seniority system. Unable to obtain any accommodation, the driver took unauthorized days off and was eventually fired. She filed a complaint with the state human rights division, alleging that the authority and union both violated state law prohibiting employers from engaging in religious discrimination. The case reached the Court of Appeals of New York, which dismissed the union as a party. However, the authority had a statutory duty to take reasonable steps short of those involving "undue economic hardship" to accommodate the operator's religious needs. **The court rejected the authority's argument that it was excused from its duty because of the seniority system's preference for days off.** Good faith requires the employer to show that it exerted reasonable efforts to accommodate, not that an accommodation was actually found. Here, the authority failed to show it made a reasonable effort. *New York City Transit Authority v. State of New York*, 674 N.E.2d 305 (N.Y. 1996).

VI. RETALIATORY DISCRIMINATION

Pursuant to Title VII, an employer may not retaliate against a current or former employee for filing a charge of discrimination. The U.S. Supreme Court has decided that an employer "has" an employee if an employment relationship between the parties exists. Moreover, the Court has extended Title VII protection to former employees.

♦ A Tennessee school district began an internal investigation into alleged harassment by its employee relations director. During an interview, a female employee informed the investigator of several instances of harassment she had endured. Shortly thereafter, the district fired the employee while taking no action against the director. The employee filed a charge with the EEOC, then sued under Title VII, claiming retaliation for her report of the director's harassment. A federal court granted pretrial judgment to the district because the employee had not initiated any action against the district but merely responded to an internal investigation. The Sixth Circuit affirmed, but the U.S. Supreme Court reversed, holding that **Title VII's anti-retaliation provision applies to employees who speak out during an internal investigation.** *Crawford v. Metropolitan Government of Nashville and Davidson County*, 2009 WL 160424 (U.S. 1/26/09).

♦ In a private sector case, a female forklift operator complained of harassment, then was taken off forklift duties. She filed a retaliation charge with the EEOC and was then suspended for insubordination. After she filed a grievance, the company found she had not been insubordinate and reinstated her with back pay. She sued for retaliation and a jury awarded her $46,750. The U.S. Supreme Court upheld the award, noting that **reassignment of job duties can be retaliation if it is "materially adverse" to an employee**. It defined materially adverse as a harmful action that could dissuade a reasonable worker from making a charge of discrimination. The suspension was also materially adverse even though she was reinstated with back pay because a reasonable employee might choose not to file a discrimination charge knowing she could be out of work indefinitely. *Burlington Northern and Santa Fe Railway Co. v. White*, 548 U.S. 53, 126 S.Ct. 2405, 165 L.Ed.2d 345 (U.S. 2006).

♦ A female school district employee met with her male supervisor and a male employee to review psychological evaluation reports from job applicants seeking employment in the district. She alleged that during the meeting, her supervisor read from a report that an applicant had once commented to a co-worker, "I hear making love to you is like making love to the Grand Canyon." The supervisor said he didn't know what that meant, and the male employee said he would explain it to him later. Then both male employees chuckled. She asserted that when she complained about the incident, she was transferred to another position in retaliation. She sued the district under Title VII. A Nevada federal court ruled against her, but the Ninth Circuit reversed.

The U.S. Supreme Court reversed the appellate court, finding that **the employee failed to show any causality between the incident and the transfer, which occurred some 20 months later**. There must be a very close proximity in time between an employer's knowledge of an employee's protected conduct and an adverse employment action if that is the only evidence of retaliation. Here, the supervisor's comment and the male employee's response were at worst an isolated incident that was not sufficiently severe or pervasive to amount to sexual harassment. Simple teasing, offhand comments and isolated incidents that are not extremely serious are not discriminatory changes in the terms and conditions of employment. *Clark County School Dist. v. Breeden*, 532 U.S. 268, 121 S.Ct. 1508, 149 L.Ed.2d 509 (2001).

♦ An employee filed a sex discrimination complaint against her employer with the EEOC, asserting that she should have received a promotion. The employer then fired her. The EEOC sued the employer for unlawful retaliation under Title VII. The employer moved to dismiss, stating that it did not have 15 employees during 20 weeks in the past two years and thus did not come within the coverage of the act. The case reached the U.S. Supreme Court, which agreed with the EEOC that **the appropriate test for when an employer has an employee is whether the parties have an employment relationship on the day in question**. Applying this test, the employer had employment relationships with 15 or more employees for 38 weeks of the calendar year in question and was an employer under Title VII. *Walters v. Metropolitan Educ. Enterprises, Inc.*, 519 U.S. 202, 117 S.Ct. 660, 136 L.Ed.2d 644 (1997).

♦ An oil corporation fired an African-American employee, who then filed a complaint against it with the EEOC. When the oil corporation gave him a negative employment reference, allegedly in retaliation for having filed the EEOC charge, the former employee sued for retaliation under Title VII. A Maryland federal court dismissed the case, and the Fourth Circuit affirmed. The U.S. Supreme Court reversed, finding that **Title VII protected former employees from retaliatory action by former employers**. *Robinson v. Shell Oil Co.*, 519 U.S. 337, 117 S.Ct. 843, 136 L.Ed.2d 808 (1997).

- A female transit officer in Philadelphia complained to a sergeant about hostile treatment she was subjected to by a fellow officer, but she declined to file a formal complaint. The transit authority conducted an investigation but decided not to transfer either officer. After the hostility with the fellow officer continued, another investigation was conducted. The other officer was suspended for 10 days but had the suspension reduced to one day. The female officer was transferred to a station farther away from her home. She sued for harassment and retaliation, and the transit authority sought pretrial judgment. The federal court refused to grant the motion, finding issues of fact that required a trial. **A jury could find that the reduced discipline was not reasonably calculated to end the harassment, and that the transfer was retaliatory.** *Ascolese v. SEPTA*, 2008 WL 2165102 (E.D. Pa. 5/22/08).

- A Missouri corrections officer responsible for the armory told his captain to stop harassing his girlfriend, also a Department of Corrections employee, or else he would inform the captain's wife about the behavior. Around that same time, the major who supervised the officer began questioning the officer's performance and learned that the officer was not conducting the required monthly inventories. When the major reassigned the officer to a lower-skilled position, citing the officer's attitude problems with the captain as one of the reasons, the officer told him about the harassment. After the officer was docked pay for an unscheduled absence, he sued for retaliation under Title VII. A federal court and the Eighth Circuit ruled against him. **The reassignment could not be retaliatory because the major did not know of the harassment until afterwards**, and the docked pay was legitimate because of the absence. *Culton v. Missouri Dep't of Corrections*, 515 F.3d 828 (8th Cir. 2008).

- A Florida county had a policy of ending investigations into allegations of discrimination where employees filed charges with the EEOC or the Florida Commission on Human Relations. After a white bus driver filed a complaint of race discrimination, the county initiated an investigation. But when the bus driver filed charges with the EEOC, the county stopped its investigation. The Florida District Court of Appeal held that this action could be deemed retaliatory. **Even though the policy was not adopted for retaliatory reasons, it had the effect of potentially letting the statute of limitations run** because it required the investigations to be sequential rather than concurrent. This might discourage a reasonable employee from filing a complaint in the first place. *Donovan v. Broward County Board of County Commissioners*, 974 So.2d 458 (Fla. Dist. Ct. App. 2008).

- A Florida state university employee filed a sexual harassment complaint against his supervisor. According to him, she then confronted him in his office, swearing at him and threatening violence. He called campus police, then went to court to get an injunction against her. The dean fired him after receiving the injunction papers, maintaining that his involving the police was unnecessarily disruptive and therefore adequate grounds for firing him. He sued, and a federal court granted pretrial judgment to the university. The Eleventh Circuit reversed, finding the call to the police was protected activity under Title VII. **If he was fired solely for involving the police, he was improperly fired in retaliation for protected activity. The court remanded the case for further proceedings. *Scarbrough v. Board of Trustees Florida A&M Univ.*, 504 F.3d 1220 (11th Cir. 2007).

♦   A female corrections officer in Maryland applied for a promotion to captain and did not get it. She filed discrimination charges, which were settled, and she received the next captaincy position that became available. She was later promoted to acting major and was transferred several times. She sued for retaliation, but lost when a federal court determined that **she couldn't prove the transfers were caused by her earlier charges of discrimination**. More than two years elapsed between the two events. Also, it was uncertain the transfers were adverse actions. *Wooden v. Maryland Dep't of Public Safety*, 2007 WL 2768905 (D. Md. 9/17/07).

♦   After an Ohio Defense Department employee won a sexual harassment lawsuit, she was transferred to another division. She claimed that she then suffered multiple harassing comments by co-workers about her lawsuit. However, none of the comments were physically threatening and she presented no evidence relating to the frequency of the remarks other than to say that she was continually harassed. She retired after a superior mentioned that there would no longer be any GS-11 positions, which she took to mean that her job was being eliminated. When she sued for retaliation and constructive discharge, she lost. **The insults did not amount to actionable harassment**, and she quit without checking to see if the superior's comment was true. *Johnson v. Rumsfeld*, 238 Fed.Appx. 105 (6th Cir. 2007).

♦   Nine female police officers in Michigan sued for discrimination. Ten days after a judge ruled for the city, the chief requested fitness for duty examinations for two of the female officers. One had "threatened" to kill anyone who broke into her house and believed an earlier break-in had been done by male officers. The other had post-traumatic stress resulting from a shooting. The city's doctor found both officers unfit for duty, even though the officers' doctors had found them both able to work. The two officers sued for retaliation and won an award of $300,000. The Sixth Circuit held that **the city officials ignored the officers' doctors** and inexplicably believed the officers were refusing treatment despite their doctors' reports that they were stable. *Denhof v. City of Grand Rapids*, 494 F.3d 534 (6th Cir. 2007).

♦   A Georgia police officer, whose primary duty was to clean up management problems and improve morale, investigated a sexual harassment complaint by a female officer and expanded the investigation to include allegations of insubordination, rumors and gossip. The city administrator chastised him for opening a can of worms. Shortly after he found no merit to the harassment claims, the city council approved his termination and he resigned. He sued under Title VII for retaliation, but the Eleventh Circuit ruled against him. Here, the city gave five reasons for its decision to fire him, including poor morale and what it believed was an inaccurate investigation, as well as poor management and scheduling, and displeasure with a traffic enforcement unit he set up. **Even if retaliation was a factor in his discharge, the city showed he would have been fired anyway.** *Crawford v. City of Fairburn*, 482 F.3d 1305 (11th Cir. 2007).

• An African-American employee of the Department of Agriculture was responsible for providing conservation-related advice to 1,600 landowners in Tennessee. He got into a number of disputes, and met with his white supervisors several times. Eventually he was reassigned to a new position, keeping his classification level and same pay. However, he perceived that his promotional opportunities had narrowed, and filed charges with the EEOC, alleging discrimination and retaliation. Over the next three years, he received three letters asking him to stop contacting employees regarding his claim, which was still pending. After the EEOC found no evidence of discrimination or retaliation, he sued. The Sixth Circuit Court of Appeals ruled against him. **The three letters came too far apart to be connected to the charges of discrimination**, and in any event they did not amount to adverse action. *Jones v. Johanns*, 264 Fed.Appx. 463 (6th Cir. 2007).

• An Oklahoma jailer/dispatcher testified on behalf of an African-American officer who was claiming discrimination. She then claimed retaliation by her co-workers and sued the city under Title VII. While that lawsuit was pending, she failed to look in on an arrestee once an hour (as required by the job) and the arrestee hung himself with his belt, which the arresting officer had forgotten to confiscate. She then falsified a log book to make it look like she had checked on the arrestee every hour. The officer was suspended and later fired (the day after she testified in her retaliation lawsuit against the city). She claimed she was fired for testifying against the city. A federal court and the Tenth Circuit ruled against her. Her offense was greater than the arresting officer's and **her firing was legitimate despite coming the day after her testimony**. *McGowan v. City of Eufala*, 472 F.3d 736 (10th Cir. 2006).

• A Missouri bus driver who had sued his employer for discrimination got into an accident. He claimed he "blanked out" right before his bus hit a truck, so he was placed on sick leave. When a psychiatrist determined that he could return to work, the employer, having found that the accident was preventable, initiated disciplinary proceedings against him. He was given a standard five-day suspension and took a disability retirement rather than return to work. He then sued the employer for retaliation. A federal court and the Eighth Circuit ruled against him. **He was not constructively discharged because he quit without giving the employer a chance to address any work issues he had.** *Thompson v. Bi-State Development Agency*, 463 F.3d 821 (8th Cir. 2006).

• An attorney with the Securities and Exchange Commission won a sexual harassment lawsuit and was promoted two levels. However, for the next 10 years, she continued to handle the same kinds of duties she had before. She asked for a promotion, which was denied, then sued for retaliation, claiming she should have been allowed to submit her briefs to a more senior attorney. A federal court and the D.C. Circuit ruled against her. **The denial of her request** to have fewer people supervising her did not amount to adverse action under Title VII. *Broderick v. Donaldson*, 437 F.3d 1226 (D.C. Cir. 2006).

♦ A District of Columbia mental health specialist was supposed to visit patients' homes, but suffered from injuries and illness that made it difficult to accomplish that task. After she requested accommodations, her superiors informed her that making home visits was an essential function of the job. She was then ordered to report to a hospital for a 120-day detail at a psychiatric hotline. She refused to do so on the grounds that it was too far from her home. When she was fired, she sued for retaliation. A federal court and the U.S. Court of Appeals, D.C. Circuit, ruled against her. **Even if the reassignment was an adverse action, the agency had a legitimate reason for making it** – her inability to perform an essential job function. *Smith v. District of Columbia*, 430 F.3d 450 (D.C. Cir. 2005).

♦ Over two years after testifying in a colleague's case, a female, Jewish attorney for the U.S. Department of Housing and Urban Development (HUD) was reassigned to a newly created position where she kept her salary and benefits but no longer had supervisory powers. She filed two EEOC complaints, then was given a lower performance evaluation, denied a supervisory position, and rejected for a promotion. She sued HUD under Title VII, and a Colorado federal court ruled against her. The Tenth Circuit affirmed. Here, the lower performance evaluation was completed a week before she filed the EEOC complaints. Further, **lower performance evaluations do not constitute adverse actions for the purpose of proving retaliation**. Also, she never officially applied for the supervisory position, and HUD had a legitimate reason for promoting someone else to head the Denver office – avoiding the competitive application process to fill the vacancy before the next election. *Stover v. Martinez*, 382 F.3d 1064 (10th Cir. 2004).

♦ An executive secretary with the Illinois Department of Revenue was allowed to work a flex time schedule so she could be home after school to take care of her Down syndrome-afflicted son. After she filed charges of race discrimination, claiming her duties were being reassigned to others, her position was abolished and a new executive secretary position was given to her. She then had to reapply for flex time. Her request was denied, forcing her to use vacation or sick leave for two hours each day until those benefits were exhausted. She sued for retaliation under Title VII, but a federal court dismissed the case, holding that no adverse action had been taken against her. The Seventh Circuit reversed, finding that **the denial of flex time could be considered adverse action** if it amounted to a material change in the secretary's working conditions. *Washington v. Illinois Dep't of Revenue*, 420 F.3d 658 (7th Cir. 2005).

♦ A personnel clerk in a finance accounting unit of the Department of Defense filed discrimination complaints against two supervisors, and the department settled the claims. A year later, she applied for a similar position with the Department of Justice (DOJ). Her supervisors gave her negative references, calling her a bad employee. The hiring official at the DOJ admitted that the **negative references** might have been enough to keep him from hiring the clerk, but stated that he decided not to hire her because he thought her fingernails were too long for the typing she would have to do. When she sued under Title VII for retaliation, a Colorado federal jury awarded her $25,000 even though it found she would not have been offered the new job anyway. The court vacated the award, but the Tenth Circuit reinstated it. Here, the harshness of the references seriously impaired her ability to obtain employment at the DOJ in the future and could be considered adverse employment action. *Hillig v. Rumsfeld*, 381 F.3d 1028 (10th Cir. 2004).

♦ A white Internal Revenue Service (IRS) manager (chief of the quality management branch in Indianapolis) supervised a black woman who filed charges of race and sex discrimination against the IRS. During the investigation, the manager stated that he was skeptical about the charges. His superiors instructed him to investigate the employee, and he found an alleged ethics violation, issuing the employee a reprimand. She then filed discrimination charges against him. The IRS determined that he did not discriminate against her, but removed the reprimand from her file. He then filed a Title VII retaliation lawsuit against the IRS, claiming that because of his opposition to the employee's discrimination claim, several of his supervisors, who were black, subjected him to humiliation. An Indiana federal court ruled for the IRS, and the Seventh Circuit affirmed. **The Title VII anti-retaliation provision does not protect an employee who participates in an investigation on the employer's side.** Also, while the employee was being "humiliated," he also received performance-related bonuses and coveted assignments, as well as a promotion. *Twisdale v. Snow*, 325 F.3d 950 (7th Cir. 2003).

VII. AFFIRMATIVE ACTION

Affirmative action plans generally will be upheld if they have been instituted to remedy some prior discrimination. The employers, however, must not set quotas or hire strictly minorities in their attempts to rectify past wrongs. A prospective employee's minority status may only be used as one factor in the hiring process.

A. Affirmative Action Programs

1. Hiring Decisions

♦ A federal highway division, part of the U.S. Department of Transportation, awarded a prime contract to a Colorado contractor. The contractor hired a Hispanic subcontractor and received additional compensation for hiring a small business controlled by "socially and economically disadvantaged individuals." A non-minority subcontractor sued, claiming that the federal race-based presumptions violated its right to equal protection. The U.S. Supreme Court, affirming the principles laid out in *City of Richmond v. J.A. Croson Co.*, 488 U.S. 469 (1989), held that **the Fifth and Fourteenth Amendments require** that all racial classifications be narrowly tailored measures that further compelling government interests**. The Court rejected the government's plea for a less rigorous standard, ruling that only strict scrutiny would submit racial classifications to a sufficiently detailed examination. It remanded the case for a determination as to whether the use of the subcontractor compensation clauses (which provided for increased compensation for minorities) could be properly described as compelling. *Adarand Constructors, Inc. v. Pena*, 515 U.S. 200, 115 S.Ct. 2097, 132 L.Ed.2d 158 (1995).

♦ In 1972, a federal court determined that the Alabama Department of Public Safety had systematically excluded blacks from employment as state troopers in violation of the Fourteenth Amendment, and issued a **hiring quota** order. By the early 1980s, there still were no blacks promoted to corporal. The court determined that the test used for promotions had an adverse impact on blacks and ordered the department to promote at least 50% blacks to corporal if qualified black candidates were available. It also ordered the department to submit a realistic schedule for the development of promotional procedures for all ranks above entry level. The United States appealed the order, asserting that it violated the Equal Protection Clause of the Fourteenth Amendment. The U.S. Supreme Court held that **the one-black-for-one-white promotion requirement was permissible under the Fourteenth Amendment**. There was a compelling governmental interest in eradicating the department's pervasive and continuing discriminatory exclusion of blacks. Further, the order provided for promotions only when openings were available. Also, the requirement could be waived if no qualified black troopers were available. Finally, the requirement was only a temporary measure. The requirement did not impose an unacceptable burden on whites and was constitutional. *U.S. v. Paradise*, 480 U.S. 149, 107 S.Ct. 1053, 94 L.Ed.2d 203 (1987).

♦ The owner of a construction company, whose parents were born in Spain, brought a civil rights action against the New York State Department of Economic Development claiming that the state's definition of "Hispanic" for purposes of awarding contracts to minority-owned businesses violated the Equal Protection Clause. Under the definition, "Hispanic" excluded people of Spanish or Portuguese descent who did not also come from Latin America. The case reached the Second Circuit, which ruled in favor of the state. **New York could rationally conclude that Hispanics of Latin American origin were in greater need of remedial legislation than Hispanics who came from Spain or Portugal.** Also, the owner could not show that the racial classifications of New York's program warranted strict scrutiny analysis where he was unable to show anti-Spanish animus. *Jana-Rock Construction, Inc. v. New York State Dep't of Economic Development*, 438 F.3d 195 (2d Cir. 2006).

♦ A Florida county fire department with a history of discriminating against women implemented an affirmative action plan with a long-term hiring goal of 36% women. Several male applicants who were unsuccessful in their bids to become firefighters sued the county under Title VII and the Equal Protection Clause, asserting that the county's goal of 36% women was unreasonably high and improperly based on the number of women in the county rather than the number of women in the county who might wish to become firefighters. A federal court ruled in favor of the county, and the Eleventh Circuit Court of Appeals affirmed. Here, **the male applicants had presented no evidence that they would have been treated differently if the affirmative action number had been significantly lower**. Thus, they could not show a constitutional violation. However, the court cautioned the county that its plan needed to be evaluated to determine whether its goals were appropriate and legally permissible if it wanted to avoid future litigation. *Danskine v. Miami-Dade County Fire Dep't*, 253 F.3d 1288 (11th Cir. 2001).

- The Third Circuit held that a Pennsylvania city violated 42 U.S.C. §§ 1981 and 1983 when it utilized an oral exam designed to "minimize" any adverse impact a written exam had on African-American police applicants. **The policy allowed the city to eliminate applicants who had scored well on the written exam**, and the court found that it was used to discriminate against white applicants. The court noted that 1) the written exam was not culturally biased and was a powerful predictor of job performance; 2) the city refused to explain why any of the white officers failed the oral exam; 3) the city kept evidence of each applicant's race throughout the hiring process; and 4) while many white applicants who scored well on the written exam failed, very few African-American applicants who scored poorly on the same exam failed. *Hopp v. City of Pittsburgh*, 194 F.3d 434 (3d Cir. 1999).

- Three white Illinois correctional officers applied for a lieutenant position at a county boot camp for young criminals. At one point, the boot camp consisted of 68% black inmates while only 6% of the security staff was black with no male black supervisors. The county hired a black male for the lieutenant position, and the three white correctional officers sued department of corrections (DOC) officials for equal protection violations. The DOC officials did not deny race was a factor in the appointment but rather presented expert evidence that highlighted the penological necessity for the appointment. The district court ruled for the white correctional officers on liability, but denied the claims for damages, injunctive relief, and attorneys' fees. The Seventh Circuit affirmed. The preference given to the black male did not constitute an equal protection violation. Expert evidence indicated that **the boot camp would not succeed in its mission of pacification and reformation with such a white staff without the black male being appointed to the supervisory position**. At this time, the racial preference was constitutional. *Wittmer v. Peters*, 87 F.3d 916 (7th Cir. 1996).

2. Promotions

- A California county transportation agency voluntarily adopted an affirmative action plan. The plan allowed the agency to consider, as one factor, the sex of an applicant in making promotions. The long-term goal of the plan was to achieve a workforce whose composition reflected the proportion of women and minorities in the area labor force. When a road dispatcher position opened up, the agency promoted one of the qualified female applicants. A male employee who was passed over sued the agency in a federal court, which found that the woman had been selected because of her sex. It invalidated the agency's plan. The court of appeals reversed. The U.S. Supreme Court upheld the affirmative action plan. The agency had appropriately taken the woman's sex into account as one factor in determining that she be promoted. The agency plan was flexible and presented a case-by-case approach to effecting a gradual improvement in the representation of women and minorities in the agency. Thus, the plan was fully consistent with Title VII. **Even though the male candidate had shown a *prima facie* case of discrimination, the agency had shown a nondiscriminatory rationale for its decision, namely the affirmative action plan.** An employer need not point to its own prior discriminatory practices to justify its adoption of such a plan. It need only point to a conspicuous imbalance in traditionally segregated areas of employment. Since the plan had taken into account distinctions in qualifications to provide guidance, the agency had not merely engaged in blind hiring by the numbers. *Johnson v. Transportation Agency, Santa Clara County*, 480 U.S. 616, 107 S.Ct. 1442, 94 L.Ed.2d 615 (1987).

- Seven white male police officers for the Massachusetts Bay Transportation Authority were passed over for promotions in favor of minority or female candidates. They sued for discrimination and lost. The Supreme Judicial Court held that **the affirmative action rule used by the agency was narrowly tailored to redress past discriminatory practices**. The rule expired in 2000 and the promoted candidates were qualified for the job, even though they scored lower on the exams. The state's compelling interest in remedying discrimination justified the application of the rule on a limited basis. *Bracket v. Civil Service Comm'n*, 850 N.E.2d 533 (Mass. 2006).

- For a single year, the Chicago Police Department standardized the scoring for its promotional exams for the position of sergeant. This was done to remedy past discrimination against Hispanic and African-American officers. Non-minority officers filed a lawsuit challenging the affirmative action plan. The case reached the Seventh Circuit, which held that **the promotions made pursuant to the exam did not violate the Equal Protection Clause**. The standardized scores were both necessary to maintain the police department's effectiveness and narrowly tailored to meet that purpose. A number of high ranking police officials confirmed the need for diversity at the sergeant rank, and the results of the exam were only used for a five-year period. No race-conscious promotions were made after that time. *Petit v. City of Chicago*, 352 F.3d 1111 (7th Cir. 2003).

- Two employees of the Michigan Department of Treasury – one black, one white – applied for a promotion. The department's interviewers established model answers to their questions, but they still had to evaluate fairly subjective criteria for much of the promotion process. They ended up scoring the white employee about half what they scored the black employee. When the black employee was awarded the promotion, the white employee sued for reverse race discrimination under Title VII and Michigan's Civil Rights Act. A federal court ruled for the department, and the Sixth Circuit affirmed. The fact that the interviewers gave the two men vastly different scores did not mean that they manipulated the process to ensure that the black candidate was promoted. **Subjective factors can be used in the promotion process** as long as each candidate is evaluated using the same criteria. *Sutherland v. Michigan Dep't of Treasury*, 344 F.3d 603 (6th Cir. 2003).

* The Chicago Police Department decided to institute **a one-time affirmative action plan with respect to promotions to the position of detective**. It placed candidates into three groups – whites, blacks and Hispanics – and used a different cut-off score for each group. Out of 64 promotions from the written exam, the department promoted the top 42 from the eligibility list regardless of race. The other 22 promotions were made out of rank order and went to the 18 highest-scoring black officers and the four highest-scoring Hispanic officers. A number of white police officers sued under Title VII for reverse discrimination. The Seventh Circuit Court of Appeals ruled for the department. Here, the affirmative action plan was narrowly tailored to remedy real past discrimination. It was used for only one promotion period, and had a minimal impact on white officers. *Majeske v. City of Chicago*, 218 F.3d 816 (7th Cir. 2000).

* A police union brought two civil contempt actions against the city of Miami for reverse race discrimination in its 1992 promotion policies. A federal court found that the city had discriminated on the basis of race in its "special certification" of several minority promotion candidates, resulting in the unlawful promotion of one black sergeant and one black lieutenant. The court held the city in contempt of a consent decree that had been entered into by the city and the United States in 1977, which called for the city to establish promotional goals for protected minority groups. The court then ordered broad "make whole" relief to all adversely affected officers (35 officers who were passed over by the two improperly promoted black officers). The Eleventh Circuit vacated the lower court's award, finding that **it was excessive because it assumed that each of the 35 officers would have been promoted but for the illegal actions of the city**. Instead, the court should have taken the value of the two promotions and awarded that amount to the 35 officers on a *pro rata* basis. *U.S. v. City of Miami*, 195 F.3d 1292 (11th Cir. 1999).

3. Employment Terminations

* The U.S. Supreme Court ruled on the validity of an **affirmative action (or "affirmative retention") plan** implemented by the Jackson, Michigan, board of education, which called for the layoff of non-minority teachers with greater seniority than some minority teachers. The district court ruled that the importance of providing minority teachers as "role models" for minority students as a remedy for past "societal discrimination" justified the layoff provision. The Sixth Circuit affirmed the district court's decision and the non-minority teachers appealed to the U.S. Supreme Court. The Court reversed the lower court decisions and held that the non-minority teachers had been unfairly

discriminated against in violation of the Equal Protection Clause.

The Court rejected the school board's argument that race-based layoffs were necessary to remedy the effects of societal discrimination. Clear and convincing evidence must be presented that the government entity in question has engaged in past racial discrimination. The Court also rejected the "role model" justification for retaining minority teachers on the ground that such a theory would allow racially based layoffs long after they were needed to cure past discrimination. The Court held that even if the Jackson school board had sufficient justification for engaging in remedial or "benign" racial discrimination, the layoff of white teachers was too drastic and intrusive a remedy. **While hiring goals and promotion policies favorable to minorities are acceptable under the Equal Protection Clause, the actual laying off of a certain race of employees is unconstitutional.** The lower court rulings were reversed. *Wygant v. Jackson Board of Educ.*, 476 U.S. 267, 106 S.Ct. 1842, 90 L.Ed.2d 260 (1986).

♦ Following his election in 2002, the new Orleans Parish District Attorney (DA) **tried to hire a staff reflective of the racial composition of New Orleans. As a result, a great many white administrative staffers were fired.** The office staff went from 77 whites and 56 blacks to 27 whites and 130 blacks within the first 72 days the DA was in office. The fired staffers sued for race discrimination under Title VII, 42 U.S.C. § 1981 and state law. A federal jury and the Fifth Circuit ruled in favor of 34 white staffers (and one Hispanic), finding that they were illegally fired because of their race. The cultural-diversity report created by the DA's transition team was the equivalent of an affirmative action plan even though it wasn't specifically labeled as such. And the DA improperly fired the employees based on that cultural-diversity report. The court of appeals upheld the damage awards (of between $250 and $13,500) for the 35 plaintiffs. *DeCorte v. Jordan*, 497 F.3d 433 (5th Cir. 2007).

B. Procedural Issues

♦ Under a 1991 affirmative action plan, the city of New Orleans hired one black firefighter for every white one. As a result, a number of white firefighters were hired after lower-scoring black applicants. They didn't discover the existence of the plan until a lawsuit was filed by another group of white applicants in 1996, at which time the fire superintendent testified that the city had used an affirmative action plan in 1991. When they sued a year later, the Fifth Circuit held that **their action was timely** and that the firefighters were entitled to back pay because of the delay in their hiring. *Bourdais v. New Orleans*, 485 F.3d 294 (5th Cir. 2007).

♦ In compliance with affirmative action provisions in the collective bargaining agreement (CBA) between the Chicago firefighter's union and the city of Chicago, minority firefighters were promoted over non-minority firefighters who had scored higher on a promotional exam. The firefighters' union filed a grievance with the city, asking that all non-minority eligible firefighters be promoted before the affirmative action measures took place. The city denied the grievance. Although the union requested arbitration, it was never pursued and the grievances were never resolved. The eligible, non-minority firefighters sued the city for violating the city personnel rules, breach of an implied employment contract, and the taking of a property interest without due process. After the court granted the city pretrial judgment, the firefighters appealed to the Appellate Court of Illinois.

By challenging the method in which the city promoted firefighters, the non-minority firefighters were actually questioning the city's compliance with the CBA. In such situations, the firefighters were required to at least attempt to exhaust the arbitration and grievance procedures provided in the CBA before filing a lawsuit, except in certain situations where the union wrongfully refused to process the grievance. **Because the firefighters had not exhausted their administrative remedies or proved that the union was derelict in processing their grievances, they lacked standing to bring a lawsuit.** Further, any property interest that the firefighters had in a promotion was defined by the CBA and thus any due process rights were governed by the CBA. The court affirmed the lower court's judgment. *Mahoney v. City of Chicago*, 687 N.E.2d 132 (Ill. App. Ct. 1997).

♦ A union representing Ohio city police officers intervened in a class action lawsuit filed by black officers against the city for discriminatory hiring and promotional practices. The union challenged the consent decree, which resulted in a stipulated settlement agreement. In reaching the settlement agreement, the union withdrew its objections to the promotion of several minority officers who had failed to pass the promotional examination. Although the union was not among the signatories of the consent decree, it participated in all aspects of the settlement negotiations. Six white police officers then challenged the settlement agreement and consent decree, alleging race discrimination. The court dismissed the case, and the Sixth Circuit affirmed. The officers lacked standing to challenge the previously litigated settlement and decree. *Martin v. Wilks*, 490 U.S. 755 (1989), which held that the white firefighters who had not participated in the consent decree could bring independent race discrimination claims, was not applicable where the nonparties' interests had been adequately represented. **Because the officers' union had vigorously litigated the issue of the effect of mandatory promotions of minority police officers, the white officers were precluded from challenging the prior litigation.** *Rafferty v. City of Youngstown*, 54 F.3d 278 (6th Cir. 1995).

C. Termination and Modification of Programs

♦ In 1977, the city of Miami and the United States entered into a consent decree that implemented an affirmative action plan for the hiring and promotion of blacks, Hispanics and women within the city of Miami Fire Department. In 1989, the district court refused to dissolve the decree, concluding that the under-representation of favored groups in the promotional ranks of the department was the result of past discriminatory practices. It ordered that promotions be made according to an alternating promotion procedure. The union appealed to the Eleventh Circuit. **The court of appeals reversed and remanded to the** district court with instructions to grant the union's motion to dissolve the 1977 consent decree provisions relating to promotions. The city's expert testimony lacked appropriate value as a matter of law, and the court erred in accepting it. The expert failed to look at the number of employees of a given race or sex eligible for promotion, and failed to evaluate passing promotional exam scores on the basis of race or gender. Additionally, the expert's analysis did not take into account the number of qualified minorities and women interested in promotion at each rank. Finally, his opinion was premised on erroneous data in determining the relevant labor market. *U.S. v. City of Miami*, 115 F.3d 870 (11th Cir. 1997).

♦ The city of New Orleans entered into a consent decree with a class of African-American police officers to remedy racial imbalances in the police department. A one-time affirmative action program created supernumerary positions to be filled by African-American officers. When the supernumerary sergeant positions became filled, the city created new regular sergeant positions, transferred several supernumerary sergeants to the new positions, then filled the open supernumerary sergeant positions with African-American officers.

Several Caucasian officers were passed over for promotion, and the police association sued, alleging Equal Protection and Due Process Clause violations. The district court ruled against the city. The Fifth Circuit Court of Appeals affirmed. Although the city contended that the promotions and transfers were made to give a better reflection of the racial composition of the city, this alone does not justify a racial classification. **The city presented no evidence of specific past discrimination but merely offered the decree itself as a finding of past discrimination.** However, if the decree was not meeting its purpose of remedying racial imbalances in the police department, then the city should have petitioned the court to modify the decree prior to the promotions. Because modification was the only proper course, and the city failed to pursue it, the decree could not be used to justify actions aside from those mandated by its own terms. *Police Ass'n of New Orleans v. City of New Orleans*, 100 F.3d 1159 (5th Cir. 1996).

♦ A 1974 consent order required a race-conscious promotion policy until black sergeants comprised at least 20% of the total number of sergeants employed by the Charlotte, North Carolina police department. The city achieved this goal in 1987. However, it still adhered to an internal policy that required that a specific number of promotions to sergeant be given to black officers. In 1991, three black officers were promoted ahead of three more highly-ranked white officers. The white officers sued, alleging that the race-based promotion policy violated the Equal Protection Clause. The Fourth Circuit ruled that **the city promotion policy was neither necessary to achieve a compelling state interest nor narrowly tailored to achieve a diverse work force.** The city lacked sufficient subjective evidence that racial diversity was necessary for an effective police force. *Hayes v. North State Law Enforcement Officers Ass'n*, 10 F.3d 207 (4th Cir. 1993).

- Omaha, Nebraska entered into a consent decree requiring that its overall work force eventually contain at least 9.5% black officers. A group of white officers moved to dissolve the decree after the 9.5% goal had been met for over one year. Although black officers comprised 9.5% of the total work force of the police department, not every rank had this percentage. A federal court held that the goals had not been achieved and refused to dissolve the consent decree. The Eighth Circuit reversed. The goal of the consent decree was achieved when 9.5% of the overall police force was represented by black officers. **The police force did not need to have 9.5% black representation at each rank.** The court dissolved the consent decree. *Brotherhood of Midwest Guardians v. City of Omaha*, 9 F.3d 677 (8th Cir. 1993).

- A Maryland police department entered into a consent decree in 1974. The decree required that 13% of all state troopers be African-American in five years. Five years later, amid allegations of cronyism and written examinations, only 9.5% of all troopers were African-American. The department entered into a new consent decree, which required that most ranks be filled with at least 22% African-Americans. The Maryland Troopers Association intervened to oppose the new consent decree, and the Fourth Circuit ruled in their favor. It noted that the attorney general's report found instances of cronyism, not racism. **Even if the cronyism was racially motivated, independent efforts by the department were made to combat this perceived unfairness.** Although the percentage of African-American troopers did not exactly match the percentage of eligible African-Americans in the community, the percentage was steadily rising in both the lower and upper ranks of the department. *Maryland Troopers Ass'n v. Evans*, 993 F.2d 1072 (4th Cir. 1993).

VIII. PROCEDURAL MATTERS

A. Generally

- The U.S. Supreme Court held that even though a restaurant employee signed a mandatory arbitration agreement with respect to all employment disputes, the Equal Employment Opportunity Commission (EEOC) could sue the restaurant on the employee's behalf. Because the EEOC was not a party to the agreement, it was not bound by the arbitration requirement. *EEOC v. Waffle House, Inc.*, 534 U.S. 279, 122 S.Ct. 754, 151 L.Ed.2d 755 (2002).

- Five months after a Virginia college denied tenure to a Polish professor, he faxed a letter to an EEOC field office claiming he had been subjected to national origin, gender and religious discrimination. He then filed charges with the state and, 313 days after the denial of tenure, he filed a verified "Form 5 Charge of Discrimination." When he sued under Title VII, the college sought to dismiss the case on the grounds that he had failed to comply with the 300-day statute of limitations. A federal court found that the faxed letter was not a "charge" of discrimination within the meaning of Title VII, and that the verification could not relate back to the letter. The Fourth Circuit agreed, but the U.S. Supreme Court reversed, noting that **the faxed letter to the EEOC could qualify as a "charge" under Title VII,** and that the verification could relate back to the letter. Nothing in Title VII required the charge to be verified at the time it was made. The Court remanded the case. *Edelman v. Lynchburg College*, 535 U.S. 106, 122 S.Ct. 1145, 152 L.Ed.2d 188 (2002).

♦ A Massachusetts city created a second deputy police superintendent position and developed an evaluation process to fill both positions. A captain who had earlier settled a failure-to-promote claim and agreed not to apply for the next deputy superintendent position applied for the new position. When he was not selected, he sued instead of appealing to the civil service commission. Although he was initially awarded $68,000 in damages, the Massachusetts Court of Appeals reversed. The employee failed to exhaust his administrative remedies with the civil service commission, which he was required to do even though the process for selecting a deputy superintendent was new. Also, he was not entitled to the $68,000 salary differential because he failed to show that he would have gotten the job over the other two applicants. *Staveley v. City of Lowell*, 882 N.E.2d 362 (Mass. App. Ct. 2008).

♦ A New Jersey Sheriff's Officer failed to disclose an expunged conviction on his application for the job. His attorney had told him the expungement meant that the conviction never happened. He later learned that he had hepatitis C and alleged that other officers began to harass him because of his illness. Eventually he quit and sued for discrimination. The sheriff's office sought to have the case dismissed, claiming that his 1974 arrest and conviction barred his lawsuit. The trial court agreed, but an appeals court and the New Jersey Supreme Court disagreed. No state law barred a person with an expunged conviction from applying to law enforcement, and the sheriff's office did not have a policy on the matter. If the sheriff's office could show that it would have fired him upon learning of the expungement, it could avoid front pay damages. *Cicchetti v. Morris County Sheriff's Office*, 947 A.2d 626 (N.J. 2008).

♦ A specialist with the Oregon Department of Agriculture had problems with her supervisor and was laid off during a budget crisis. Another female employee who also experienced difficulty with the supervisor had her position eliminated too. The specialist sued under federal anti-discrimination laws and also alleged a violation of the Equal Protection Clause. A jury ruled in her favor on the equal protection claim, but the Ninth Circuit vacated the award. It ruled that **the employee could not sue as a "class of one"** under the Equal Protection Clause, noting that the government has far broader powers as an employer than it does as a regulator. *Engquist v. Oregon Dep't of Agriculture*, 478 F.3d 985 (9th Cir. 2007).

♦ A Missouri firefighter was fired for sleeping through a fire call, among other violations. The fire district's board put together a proposed agreement under which the firefighter would receive a one-year suspension instead of termination if he agreed to waive any claim against the district for discrimination. It sent him the proposed agreement five days in advance of a meeting between the board, the union and the firefighter. At the meeting, he alleged that board members pressured him to sign the agreement. He did so, but later sued for discrimination under Title VII. A federal court ruled against him, and the Eighth Circuit affirmed. Even though the firefighter was undoubtedly under stress, he could not prove duress. In other words, **he failed to show that he was prevented from exercising his free will when he signed the waiver**. *Clark v. Riverview Fire Protection Dist.*, 354 F.3d 752 (8th Cir. 2004).

B. Continuing Violation Doctrine

♦ Ten maintenance workers at O'Hare International Airport filed a lawsuit for racial harassment under Title VII and 42 U.S.C. § 1981. They claimed that their supervisor had insulted and harassed them for more than 20 years. However, a federal court and the Seventh Circuit ruled against them, noting that they had waited too long to sue. Even though the Supreme Court has held that employees can sometimes sue for harassment outside the limitations period under the continuing violation doctrine, **the employees here waited until after their supervisor retired, which prevented the city from being able to defend itself properly**. If what they said about their supervisor was true, they had an ample basis to sue 15 or even 20 years earlier. By unreasonably delaying, they waived their rights to pursue their claims. *Pruitt v. City of Chicago*, 472 F.3d 925 (7th Cir. 2006).

♦ An African-American foreman for the Massachusetts Bay Transportation Authority complained to his supervisors after harassment by co-workers, including shooting bottle rockets at him, dropping firecrackers near him and painting "fag bait" on his locker. His supervisors then called him racially derogatory names, disciplined him unfairly and changed promotion rules to his detriment. When he sued, a jury awarded him $500,000 in compensatory damages and $1 million in punitive damages, which the court reduced to $500,000. On appeal, the Massachusetts Supreme Judicial Court ordered a new trial on the issue of damages because the jury had been improperly instructed on the continuing violation doctrine, and there was a chance they might find he should have filed his charges earlier. *Clifton v. Massachusetts Bay Transportation Authority*, 839 N.E.2d 314 (Mass. 2005).

♦ A postal service employee told her station manager, her union president and a workplace intervention specialist that she was being sexually harassed. She also contacted the EEOC, which sent her forms to formalize her complaint. She instead chose to continue working. She began outpatient psychiatric treatment and went on Federal Employees Compensation Act leave as a result of depression. More than 45 days later, she filed a formal complaint with the EEOC. In the lawsuit that followed, a North Dakota federal court dismissed her claim, noting that federal employees must file a complaint with the EEOC within 45 days of the discrimination. The Eighth Circuit reversed and remanded the case, noting that because of *National Railroad Passenger Corp. v. Morgan*, 122 S.Ct. 2061 (2002), her claim may have been timely. *Morgan* states that harassment occurring outside the limitations period may be actionable where at least one of the harassing acts takes place within the limitations period. Here, **the postal service's continuing failure to take corrective action to remedy the harassment while she was on leave might subject it to liability** under the continuing violation doctrine. *Jensen v. Henderson*, 315 F.3d 854 (8th Cir. 2003).

♦ A lesbian employee in a county sheriff's department alleged that a captain and another officer harassed her for several years. When she made a formal written complaint, the sheriff transferred the harassers and offered her the opportunity to work in another area. She accepted the offer and, within two years of the last alleged act of harassment, filed a lawsuit against the sheriff under the state Law Against Discrimination. A trial court dismissed her claims as untimely, but the New Jersey Superior Court, Appellate Division, reversed in part. It noted that she could pursue her claims of a hostile work environment under the continuing violation doctrine where **at least one harassing act took place within the two-year statute of limitations,** and where the acts that constituted her claim were part of the same unlawful employment practice. She also was able to pursue her claims against the individual defendants who allegedly committed the harassment against her. *Caggiano v. Fontoura*, 804 A.2d 1193 (N.J. Super. Ct. App. Div. 2002).

♦ In 1969, a Florida city hired a Hispanic as a temporary employee and repeatedly refused to make him a permanent employee for the next 10 years. In 1979, it made him a permanent employee. He retired in 1993 and began collecting his pension, which would have been greater if he had been made a permanent employee earlier. He sued the city under Title VII on behalf of a class of Hispanic temporary employees, alleging that the city repeatedly failed to classify them as permanent employees while white employees were being elevated to permanent status. A federal court approved certification of the class, but the Eleventh Circuit held that the lawsuit had to be dismissed on statute of limitations grounds. Here, **the last act of discrimination occurred in 1979.** The employee could not avoid dismissal under the continuing violation doctrine, because that doctrine does not apply to discrete acts of discrimination occurring outside the 300-day limitations period. *City of Hialeah v. Rojas*, 311 F.3d 1096 (11th Cir. 2002).

CHAPTER TWO

Discipline, Suspension and Termination

	Page
I. EMPLOYEE DUE PROCESS RIGHTS	106
A. Hearing Rights	106
1. Notice and Opportunity to Respond	108
2. Evidentiary Issues	110
3. Impartial Decision Maker	113
B. Property and Liberty Interests	115
1. Probationary Employees	117
2. Transfers	119
3. Reputation Interests	121
4. Property Interests	123
C. Employment Handbooks and Policies	126
1. Procedures	126
2. Employment Status	128
D. Statutes and Ordinances	129
1. Procedures	129
2. Employment Status	132
E. Collective Bargaining Agreements	133
1. Procedures	134
2. Investigatory Interviews	136
II. EMPLOYMENT ABANDONMENT AND RESIGNATION	138
A. Abandonment	138
B. Resignation	140
1. Voluntary Resignation	140
2. Withdrawal of Resignation	142
III. EMPLOYEE MISCONDUCT	143
A. Official Misconduct	143
1. Ethics Codes	143
2. Neglect of Duty	145
B. Criminal Violations	147
C. Violations of Employer Rules and Policies	149
1. Rules and Policies	149
2. Refusal to Follow Orders	153
D. Off-Duty Misconduct	156
IV. LAYOFFS FOR FINANCIAL REASONS	159
V. RETALIATION	162
A. Whistleblower Protection Acts	162
1. Retaliatory Actions	162

2. Employment Termination 166
B. Wrongful Discharge..170

VI. NATIONAL SECURITY..173

I. EMPLOYEE DUE PROCESS RIGHTS

Due process refers to substantive fairness as well as the specific procedural protections to which an employee may be entitled by contract or law. The procedural rights granted by the Due Process Clause of the Fifth and Fourteenth Amendments include notice and an opportunity to be heard.

Due process attaches when employees have a property or liberty interest in their employment. Property rights are created by contracts, statutes and ordinances or similar claims of entitlement. Common employment contracts include written employment policies or handbooks and collective bargaining agreements.

Liberty interests most often refer to an employee's good name. In other words, where firing an employee involves a stigma upon the employee's character, then a liberty interest attaches and the employee is entitled to due process.

A. Hearing Rights

Public employers generally must provide notice and an opportunity to be heard before firing employees. If the employer provides some sort of post-termination due process, then the pre-termination due process need only be a check against mistaken decisions.

♦ Ohio law protected all civil service employees from dismissal except for "misfeasance, malfeasance, or nonfeasance in office." Employees who were terminated for cause were entitled to an order of removal stating the reasons for termination. Unfavorable orders could be appealed to a state administrative board, whose determinations were subject to state court review. A security guard hired by a school board stated on his job application that he had never been convicted of a felony. Upon discovering that he had in fact been convicted of grand larceny, the school board dismissed him for dishonesty in filling out the job application. He was not afforded an opportunity to respond to the dishonesty charge or to challenge the dismissal until nine months later. In a second case, a school bus mechanic was fired because he had failed an eye examination. The mechanic appealed his dismissal because he had not been afforded a pre-termination hearing. A federal court rejected both of the employees' claims, and they appealed to the U.S. Court of Appeals, Sixth Circuit, which reversed the decisions.

The U.S. Supreme Court consolidated the appeals by the school districts. The Court held that **the employees possessed a property right in their** employment and were entitled to a pre-termination opportunity to respond to the dismissal charges against them. The pre-termination hearing, stated the Court, need not resolve the propriety of the discharge, but should be a check against mistaken decisions; essentially, it should be a determination of whether there were reasonable grounds to believe that the charges against the employee were true and supported the proposed action. The Court upheld that portion of the lower court decisions which found that the delay in the guard's administrative proceedings did not constitute a separate constitutional violation. The Due Process Clause required a hearing "at a meaningful time," and here the delay stemmed in part from the thoroughness of the procedures afforded the guard. On the matter of the right to a pre-termination hearing, however, both cases were remanded for further proceedings, consistent with the Court's decision. *Cleveland Board of Educ. v. Loudermill,* 470 U.S. 532, 105 S.Ct. 1487, 84 L.Ed.2d 494 (1985).

* A police officer employed by a Pennsylvania state university was arrested in a drug raid and charged with several felony counts related to marijuana possession and distribution. The university's human resources director immediately suspended the officer without pay. Although the criminal charges were dismissed, university officials demoted the officer. He sued university officials for failing to provide him with notice and an opportunity to be heard before his suspension without pay. The court granted pretrial judgment to the officials, but the Third Circuit reversed. The U.S. Supreme Court then stated that the court of appeals had improperly held that a suspended public employee must always receive a paid suspension under *Cleveland Board of Educ. v. Loudermill,* above. **The university did not violate due process by refusing to pay a suspended employee charged with a felony pending a hearing.** The Court noted that the officer here faced only a temporary suspension without pay, and not employment termination, as was the case in *Loudermill*. It reversed and remanded the court of appeals' judgment for consideration of the officer's arguments concerning a post-suspension hearing. *Gilbert v. Homar,* 520 U.S. 924, 117 S.Ct. 1807, 138 L.Ed.2d 120 (1997).

* Federal employees who were subjected to adverse actions by their employer agency made false statements to federal investigators regarding alleged misconduct. In addition to the misconduct charges, the agency also included the false statements as a ground for adverse action. The Merit Systems Protection Board and a federal appeals court found that no penalty could be imposed based on a false denial of the misconduct charges. The appellate court held that the Fifth Amendment Due Process Clause prohibits a federal agency from charging an employee with falsification based on the employee's denial of another charge. On appeal, the U.S. Supreme Court reversed. It noted that **neither the Due Process Clause nor the Civil Service Reform Act precluded the government from sanctioning an employee for making false statements to it about alleged misconduct**. Even though due process requires notice and an opportunity to be heard, it does not include the right to make false statements with respect to charged conduct. *LaChance v. Erickson,* 522 U.S. 262, 118 S.Ct. 753, 139 L.Ed.2d 695 (1998).

1. Notice and Opportunity to Respond

The notice required generally need not be a formal written statement; however, the employee must be told of the proposed termination and must also be given an opportunity to respond to the charges alleged.

* A California city employee was notified that he was being laid off. He wrote his manager, requesting a pre-termination hearing. His manager gave his letter to the city's HR director, who informed the employee that he wasn't entitled to a pre-termination hearing under his union contract because he was being laid off and not fired for cause. However, she met with the employee informally for a few minutes. After the layoff, the employee sued. A federal court held that he should have been granted a limited pre-termination hearing and ordered a full post-termination hearing in its place. The Ninth Circuit affirmed. **Because the employee had a property interest in continued employment, he should have been granted a pre-termination hearing even though his union contract didn't call for one.** *Levine v. City of Alameda*, 525 F.3d 903 (9th Cir. 2008).

* The board of trustees of a Kansas county hospital hired a hospital administrator. Six years later, it fired her. She sued under 42 U.S.C. § 1983, asserting a violation of her due process rights as well as breach of her employment contract. She claimed she was entitled to notice and a hearing before the board could fire her. A federal court and the Tenth Circuit disagreed. There were two statutes potentially addressing her rights. One authorized the board to appoint an administrator, set compensation and remove the administrator, but did not grant a property right to continued employment. The other allowed the board to contract for the management of the hospital and seemed to grant a property right. However, the court of appeals noted that the first statute was the appropriate one to apply because the second statute addressed the management of the hospital, and the administrator was not hired to manage the hospital. Thus, **she was an at-will employee and not entitled to due process before her termination.** *Alderfer v. Board of Trustees of Edwards County Hospital and Healthcare Center*, 261 Fed.Appx. 147 (10th Cir. 2008).

* A Rhode Island animal control supervisor found five baby raccoons in his father's attic and brought them to work, where they became an attraction. Staff at the shelter allowed visitors into the raccoons' kennel, and the supervisor occasionally took the raccoons out into the community. Later, it was discovered that one of the raccoons had rabies. Although no people appeared to have contracted the disease, 56 people received rabies shots. The supervisor was fired, and his union filed a grievance. The arbitrator found that the city had just cause to fire the supervisor, but that he did not receive due process in the form of a pre-termination hearing. The arbitrator ordered the supervisor to be reinstated to another position. The city challenged that decision and the Rhode Island Supreme Court agreed with the city that the arbitrator exceeded his authority by ordering the employee reinstated to another job. **The failure to

provide a pre-termination hearing did not nullify the just cause for the firing. The city did not have to rehire the supervisor. *City of East Providence v. United Steelworkers of America, Local 15509*, 925 A.2d 246 (R.I. 2007).

• A housing authority employee's excessive absenteeism as well as insubordination resulted in a 15-day suspension. The employee continued to abuse sick leave and was fired. He filed grievances over the suspension and termination, then signed a last chance agreement. The agreement specified that he waived his rights under the collective bargaining agreement as well as any federal, state or local law. He then missed work again to appear in family court and was fired a second time. He sued for due process violations and the Rhode Island Supreme Court held that **he was not entitled to a hearing either before or after his termination because of the last chance agreement**. *Monahan v. Girouard*, 911 A.2d 666 (R.I. 2006).

• The chief of police of a Pennsylvania township ordered an officer to end his extramarital affair with another woman. The officer failed to do so. The chief then sent him a *Loudermill* notice informing him that he could be disciplined for disobeying the chief's order and offering him a chance to provide any information that might cause the chief to reconsider. The officer's union attorney sought more investigatory details, but the township declined to provide them because the investigation was ongoing. It fired the officer, who then filed a grievance. An arbitrator and the Pennsylvania Commonwealth Court ruled that **the notice complied with the officer's due process rights**. He received a post-termination opportunity to address the issues involved. The discharge was upheld. *Delaware County Lodge No. 27, Fraternal Order of Police v. Township of Tinicum*, 908 A.2d 362 (Pa. Commw. Ct. 2006).

• Two Illinois police officers were fired after missing work for four days in a row – a violation of the absent without permission policy from their collective bargaining agreements that allowed for immediate termination under police department rules. One officer was allowed to write a memo explaining why he failed to call in, and the other was allowed to meet with his captain to explain his absence. Both terminations were upheld. The officers then sued, claiming that their pre-termination due process rights were violated. The Seventh Circuit Court of Appeals ruled against them, noting that because of the extensive post-termination grievance procedures available, **they only had to receive minimal pre-termination due process**. Here, they were both notified of the terminations and given the opportunity to respond before the terminations became final. This was adequate due process. *Hudson v. City of Chicago*, 374 F.3d 554 (7th Cir. 2004).

• The chief of a Missouri fire protection district was notified by the three-member fire protection board that the district suffered from a morale problem. After an investigation, the board sent the chief a letter detailing his substandard performance and announcing its decision to terminate him. The board conducted a pre-termination hearing, but its attorney refused to let the board members speak to the chief. Also, the board members refused to let the chief's attorney speak for him. When he was fired four days later, he sued the district in federal court under the Due Process Clause of the Fourteenth Amendment. The court ruled for the district, and the U.S. Court of Appeals, Eighth Circuit, affirmed. Here, the chief waived his right to sue in court by failing to file an administrative appeal first. The chief could not raise as a defense the fact that he was unaware the district was a state agency under the Missouri Administrative Procedures Act. He could have found that out easily. And **even though the pre-termination procedures were barely adequate constitutionally, the statute provided extensive post-termination protections**, including the right to call and examine witnesses, introduce documents and exhibits, and object to the introduction of evidence. The post-termination safeguards were constitutionally adequate under *Loudermill*. As a result, the chief was not entitled to relief. *Krentz v. Robertson Fire Protection Dist.*, 228 F.3d 897 (8th Cir. 2000).

2. Evidentiary Issues

♦ A postal employee with three prior but minor disciplinary actions against her received a fourth while the first three were in the grievance process. In light of the prior actions, she was fired. She appealed to the Merit Systems Protection Board, where an administrative law judge (ALJ) independently reviewed the disciplinary actions despite the pending grievances. The ALJ found that the three prior disciplinary actions were not clearly erroneous, and that the termination was reasonable in light of those actions. The board upheld the ALJ's findings, but the Federal Circuit reversed, holding that prior disciplinary actions subject to pending grievances may not be used to support a penalty's reasonableness. The case reached the U.S. Supreme Court, which reversed the court of appeals. Here, **the board could independently review the prior disciplinary actions despite the fact that they were subject to pending grievances**. However, because the first disciplinary action had been resolved in the employee's favor, the case had to be remanded for a determination of whether the termination was still reasonable. *U.S. Postal Service v. Gregory*, 534 U.S. 1, 122 S.Ct. 431, 151 L.Ed.2d 323 (2001).

♦ A California corrections officer was fired for failing a drug test. The officer appealed to the state personnel board, claiming the positive drug test had been caused by his ingestion of Mexican diet medication that he had legally obtained in Mexico, and he was unaware that taking the medication could result in a positive test for amphetamines. The board upheld the termination, but a state court ruled for the officer. The state court of appeal affirmed. Here, there was **insufficient evidence to support a conclusion that the officer had legally adequate notice**, for due process purposes, that his foreign prescription could result in his testing positive for amphetamines. Also, the prescribed weight-loss medication the officer was taking was not itself an amphetamine. Rather, the body metabolized it into an amphetamine. *Valenzuela v. California State Personnel Board*, 153 Cal.App.4th 1179, 63 Cal.Rptr.3d 529 (Cal. Ct. App. 2007).

- A West Virginia State Police officer was found passed out in his cruiser, which was still running. He was given an intoxilyzer test, which showed a blood alcohol level of .169%. After he was convicted of driving under the influence, he was fired, even though his conviction had been overturned (because the intoxilyzer test was administered before *Miranda* warnings were given). He challenged his discharge and lost. The Supreme Court of Appeals noted that the circumstantial evidence supported the administrative finding that the officer drove while intoxicated. **The higher "beyond a reasonable doubt" standard of criminal law did not apply** to the administrative hearing over his firing. *Montgomery v. West Virginia State Police*, 600 S.E.2d 223 (W.Va. 2004).

- After receiving an excellent rating and a new contract, an Oklahoma elementary school principal was sent a written notice of suspension, citing employee reports that she brought liquor to school, that employees smelled alcohol on her breath, that she left school with other teachers to smoke cigarettes and that she used vulgar language. At her pre-termination hearing, she sought to cross-examine the 13 witnesses who had made the accusations in their affidavits. The board refused to let her question them, then voted to uphold the termination. She sued in federal court under the Fourteenth Amendment's Due Process Clause, and the case reached the Tenth Circuit. The court of appeals held that **she should have been allowed to cross-examine the witnesses at her pre-termination hearing**. Also, two board members, who allegedly stated before the hearing that they wanted to get rid of her, were not entitled to qualified immunity. However, the court held that the school district also should have been allowed to present evidence that it would have fired the principal even if it had not violated her due process rights. The court remanded the case for further proceedings. *McClure v. Independent School Dist. No. 16*, 228 F.3d 1205 (10th Cir. 2000).

- A New Jersey sheriff's department brought five charges against a corrections officer, including conduct unbecoming an officer, sexual harassment and verbal abuse. An internal decision maker sustained those charges after a hearing on the matter but dismissed the two others – insubordination and refusing to cooperate in an investigation. The officer, who was suspended for five days and agreed to forfeit five more vacation days, appealed to the state merit system board. At a hearing, the sheriff's department sought unsuccessfully to raise the two charges that previously had been dismissed. The merit system board adopted the administrative law judge's (ALJ's) recommendations and dismissed all the charges against the officer. It ordered the department to pay the officer back pay and restore his benefits for the time suspended. A New Jersey court affirmed the board's order, holding that **the ALJ properly refused to allow the sheriff's department to raise the two charges that had been previously dismissed**. No part of New Jersey's civil service law authorizes a public employer to prosecute charges before the merit system board that the employing agency itself dismissed after participating in the required internal disciplinary proceedings. *Hammond v. Monmouth County Sheriff's Dep't*, 721 A.2d 743 (N.J. Super. Ct. App. Div. 1999).

- An off-duty Nebraska police officer was traveling with his wife when he had an encounter with another driver where he drove recklessly and allegedly shot out the other vehicle's window. There were no indications that the officer's service weapon had been fired. However, the other vehicle had a bullet in it that matched two other bullets in the officer's weapon. At a review hearing before the personnel board, along with the physical evidence, the testimony of a polygraph examiner was admitted to show that the officer was deceptive regarding the details of the incident. The officer was fired for misconduct. A state court affirmed the board's decision to discharge the officer, and the Nebraska Supreme Court upheld that decision. It agreed with the officer that **the board had improperly admitted the polygraph testimony because polygraph results are inadmissible in administrative hearings**. However, the physical evidence, exclusive of the polygraph evidence, supported the board's decision. There was sufficient admissible, relevant evidence that the officer drove recklessly and fired a shot at another vehicle. *Mathes v. City of Omaha*, 576 N.W.2d 181 (Neb. 1998).

- A Chicopee, Massachusetts firefighter was stopped by a Holyoke, Massachusetts police officer and arrested for operating a motor vehicle without a license and possession of a controlled substance. During the booking process, the firefighter was belligerent. At a later hearing before the civil service commission, he was fired for conduct unbecoming a firefighter because of his possession of a controlled substance, his belligerence, and his prior criminal record. In the criminal case, the evidence against the firefighter was found to be inadmissible and the charges were dropped. The firefighter then appealed the civil service commission's termination decision to a state court, which vacated the decision. The commission appealed to the Supreme Judicial Court of Massachusetts, which focused on whether evidence that was properly suppressed in the criminal proceedings could be considered by the commission in its decision to discharge the firefighter. Here, the arresting officer and the firefighter were employed by different cities, so there was no argument that the firefighter's city was attempting to profit from its own wrongdoing and use the evidence to terminate his employment. Further, **no reasonable argument could be made that the arresting officer stopped the firefighter in the hopes of acquiring evidence in order to fire him**. The court reversed the lower court's judgment and affirmed the commission's decision to discharge the firefighter. *Kelly v. Civil Service Comm'n*, 691 N.E.2d 557 (Mass. 1998).

- An Illinois police officer was indicted on the charge of official misconduct for allegedly soliciting sexual favors from a prostitute in exchange for not issuing her a traffic citation. He was suspended without pay pending termination. The officer was personally served with written notice of the charges against him and the time and place of a pre-termination hearing. He chose not to attend but answered the charges in writing. After he was discharged, he filed a grievance against the city. An arbitrator affirmed the officer's termination. When the officer was acquitted of the criminal charge, he asked to be reinstated with back pay. His request was denied. He sued the city in federal court, alleging violations of his due process rights under 42 U.S.C.

§ 1983. The court held that because **the officer was personally served with specific written notice of the charges against him and given a chance to tell his side of the story**, he was given adequate due process. Here, by choosing to respond in writing instead of personally appearing to give his version of events, the officer waived his right to such a hearing. The court dismissed the case. *Meek v. Springfield Police Dep't*, 990 F.Supp. 598 (C.D. Ill. 1998).

♦ Two Buffalo, New York, police officers observed two men in the back seat of a parked car. The officers searched the car and found marijuana between the front seats. One of the car occupants was a state trooper. He said that the marijuana was his girlfriend's and asked the officers to give him a break. The officers issued him a summons for unlawful possession of marijuana. The Buffalo City Court suppressed the evidence because it was the result of an illegal search and seizure. However, the hearing officer admitted the evidence in the trooper's disciplinary proceeding, and the officer was discharged. A state appellate division court reversed the termination because it was based on evidence obtained by an illegal search and seizure. The Court of Appeals of New York noted that **the deterrent effect of the exclusionary rule has to be measured against the adverse impact on the truth-finding process should the evidence be excluded**. Here, the adverse impact that would result from the exclusion outweighed the potential deterrent effect on illegal police behavior. The termination was upheld. *Boyd v. Constantine*, 597 N.Y.S.2d 605 (N.Y. 1993).

3. Impartial Decision Maker

♦ An Illinois fire inspector was diagnosed with cancer. With the mayor's approval, two of his co-workers solicited donations from businesses to help with his medical expenses. After he was treated and returned to work, the fire chief discharged him for using money from businesses in his district to pay for his cancer treatment. **Contrary to village procedures, members of the village board presided over both his pre-termination and post-termination hearings.** He filed a lawsuit under 42 U.S.C. § 1983, asserting due process violations because the board members were biased against him. The Seventh Circuit agreed with him that the board's actions were questionable. However, he had an adequate remedy under the Illinois Administrative Review Act and thus could not assert a federal due process claim. *Michalowicz v. Village of Bedford Park*, 528 F.3d 530 (7th Cir. 2008).

♦ After sheriff's deputies reported that a massage therapist exposed her breasts and proposed a sexual act, a county board of supervisors revoked the license of the massage clinic's owner. When the owner appealed, the county followed its practice of selecting a hearing officer unilaterally and on an *ad hoc* basis. The owner objected to that practice, asserting that **the hearing would be unfair because there was a financial incentive for the hearing officer to rule in favor of the county.** (Since the county was paying the hearing officer's fee, and since the hearing officer's future employment would be determined by how satisfied the county was, the hearing officer was much more likely to rule in favor of the county.) The hearing officer recommended revoking the owner's license, and the board upheld the revocation. The California Supreme Court held that the license revocation had to be set aside. Here, the process used by the county was fundamentally unfair to the other party. The county had to use another means of selecting hearing officers. *Haas v. San Bernardino County*, 119 Cal.Rptr.2d 341 (Cal. 2002).

♦ A Utah police officer was accused of using excessive force. This charge was investigated by a lieutenant against whom the officer had previously brought charges of police misconduct. After the investigation, the police chief, who was angry about the misconduct charges brought against the lieutenant, fired the officer for dishonesty in the investigation. The officer appealed to the civil service commission, which conducted a post-termination hearing. Excluding the officer's evidence of the chief's and the lieutenant's retaliatory motives, the commission affirmed the chief's decision. The Utah Court of Appeals found that the **excluded evidence of the chief's and the lieutenant's intention, bias, and motives prevented the officer from effectively challenging the credibility of two primary witnesses**. Because the excluded evidence prevented the commission from properly reviewing the chief's decision, the officer was denied a fair hearing. Further, even if the officer had lied during the excessive force investigation, the commission had abused its discretion because the punishment of discharge was inappropriate to the charged misconduct. The court reversed the commission's decision and reinstated the officer. *Lucas v. Murray City Civil Service Comm'n*, 949 P.2d 746 (Utah App. 1997).

♦ A white Tennessee police lieutenant stopped a speeding vehicle, instructed the two African-American male occupants to get out, and sprayed them with pepper gas when they refused. As it turned out, the two occupants were undercover police officers. The lieutenant was the only officer, among several at the scene, to be charged with violating departmental regulations. The city's African-American mayor told police officials to fire the lieutenant because he was getting pressure from the black community. After the lieutenant was fired, the Civil Service Commission remanded the matter to the police department for another hearing, where the charges were sustained but the discipline was reduced to an eight-day suspension. The lieutenant then sued the city under 42 U.S.C. § 1983, alleging violations of the Due Process and Equal Protection Clauses of the Fourteenth Amendment.

Although the lieutenant had been afforded a pre-termination hearing, the court found that the hearing had violated his procedural due process rights. When the outcome of a municipal employee's pre-termination hearing has been pre-determined regardless of the proof presented, the concerns and goals of the pre-termination hearing have not been met. In particular, the hearing no longer provides a meaningful opportunity to invoke the decision maker's discretion or avoid the possibility of a mistaken decision. Here, the lieutenant's pre-termination hearing was a sham because the outcome was pre-determined. Additionally, the city had violated the lieutenant's equal protection rights. The lieutenant had presented credible, direct evidence of racial discrimination establishing that the mayor wanted him fired because of pressure from the black community. *Wagner v. City of Memphis,* 971 F.Supp. 308 (W.D. Tenn. 1997).

• An Alabama city personnel director, who could be fired only for cause, failed to explain certain payroll discrepancies at an executive session of the city council. His immediate supervisor initiated termination proceedings, and the mayor concurred. A pre-termination hearing was conducted, and the supervisor served as the hearing officer. When the supervisor testified, the mayor served as the hearing officer. Objections were made to the supervisor and mayor serving as hearing officers because they, as well as one council member, testified as material witnesses. Nevertheless, the personnel director was fired. A post-termination hearing, a review board, the city council and a trial court all upheld the termination. The Supreme Court of Alabama ruled that the personnel director was denied due process. **Due process requires an unbiased and impartial decision maker.** A person serving as a hearing officer in a case in which he or she testifies as a material witness offends due process. The post-termination hearing did not and could not remedy the absence of due process in the pre-termination hearing. *Stallworth v. City of Evergreen, Alabama,* 680 So.2d 229 (Ala. 1996).

B. Property and Liberty Interests

The Due Process Clause of the Fourteenth Amendment provides that no state shall "deprive any person of life, liberty or property, without due process of law." In order to establish that a termination or suspension violates an employee's constitutional rights, the employee must first establish that he or she has a liberty or property interest in continued employment.

As *Board of Regents v. Roth* and *Perry v. Sindermann,* below, illustrate, a property interest must be more than a mere expectation of continued employment. An employee must show a legitimate claim of entitlement to it or, as in *Sindermann,* a common understanding between employer and employee.

• The Wisconsin state university system hired an assistant professor under a one-year contract. As the year drew to a close, the university notified the professor that his contract would not be renewed. The notice conformed to university rules, which did not require any reason for non-retention or any hearing for the teacher. Wisconsin tenure law required teachers to have four years of service before becoming "permanent" employees. The teacher sued the state college board in a federal district court, alleging that the failure of university officials to give any reason for non-retention violated his procedural due process rights. The court held for the teacher on his due process claim, and the U.S. Court of Appeals, Seventh Circuit, affirmed.

In dismissing the teacher's due process claims, the U.S. Supreme Court stated that no liberty interest was implicated because in declining to rehire the teacher, the university had not made any charge against him such as incompetence or immorality. Such a charge would have made it difficult for the teacher to gain employment elsewhere and thus would have deprived him of liberty. **As no reason was given for the non-renewal of his contract, the teacher's liberty interest in future employment was not impaired,** and he was not entitled to a hearing on these grounds. Also, because the teacher had not acquired tenure, he possessed no property interest in continued employment at the university. The teacher had a property interest in employment during the term of his one-year contract, but upon expiration the interest ceased to exist. Thus, the university did not violate his property interest in reemployment. The Court reversed and remanded the case. *Board of Regents v. Roth,* 408 U.S. 564, 92 S.Ct. 2701, 33 L.Ed.2d 548 (1972).

♦ A Texas junior college employed a professor for four years under a series of one-year contracts. At the end of his fourth year, he was not rehired. He was not given a reason for his non-renewal, and the college did not offer him a hearing to challenge its decision. He sued the college in a federal district court, asserting that his due process rights had been violated. The court ruled for the college, and the professor appealed to the U.S. Court of Appeals, Fifth Circuit, where he prevailed. The U.S. Supreme Court then ruled that although the professor was not tenured, he still might have a due process right to a hearing. **If the professor could show that a common understanding existed that essentially made him a tenured professor, then he had a property interest sufficient to require a hearing.** The Court affirmed the court of appeals' decision and remanded the case to the district court to determine if such a mutual understanding of continued employment existed between the college and the professor. *Perry v. Sindermann,* 408 U.S. 593, 92 S.Ct. 2717, 33 L.Ed.2d 570 (1972).

♦ A policeman in a North Carolina city was dismissed by the city manager upon the recommendation of the police chief. A city ordinance allowed for the termination of a permanent employee, which the officer was, if he failed to perform work up to the standard of his classification. Upon being discharged, the officer sued city officials in a federal district court, asserting that he had a constitutional right to a pre-termination hearing. He also argued that he had been deprived of property and liberty interests by his dismissal. The court ruled against the officer and the U.S. Court of Appeals, Fourth Circuit, affirmed. The officer then appealed to the U.S. Supreme Court. The Court held that the district court was correct when it concluded that the officer "held his position at the will and pleasure of the city." Also, **no liberty interest had been violated because no stigma attached through any public communication.** The reasons for his dismissal had been kept private. And since he was an at-will employee, he had no property interest to be protected. The court affirmed the lower court decisions and held that no pre-termination hearing had been necessary. *Bishop v. Wood,* 426 U.S. 341, 96 S.Ct. 2074, 48 L.Ed.2d 684 (1976).

♦ An Oregon Department of Agriculture employee was denied a promotion and ultimately discharged after a supervisor eliminated her job during a department reorganization. She sued the department, claiming the actions were illegal under the Equal Protection Clause, not because they were based on any protected status she had but because the actions were arbitrary and irrational. A jury awarded her $175,000 in compensatory damages and $250,000 in punitive damages. The court of appeals reversed, and the U.S. Supreme Court affirmed, holding that **the "class of one" theory of equal protection does not apply in the public employment context**. The government has greater leeway when acting as an employer than it does when acting as a regulator. Granting "class of one" status to public employees would be contrary to the at-will concept of public employment. *Engquist v. Oregon Dep't of Agriculture*, 128 S.Ct. 2146 (U.S. 2008).

1. Probationary Employees

Public employers typically require new employees to undergo a probationary period to ensure that the employee can meet job expectations. During a probationary period, the employee is generally not entitled to the full protection enjoyed by permanent or tenured employees.

* An applicant for a position at a state psychiatric center disclosed on his application that he had been convicted of a crime, but he disclosed only one of his eight convictions. Two months after he began his employment, and **while he was still in his probationary period, the center discovered the full extent of his criminal record and terminated his employment** for falsifying the employment application. He brought an Article 78 proceeding to challenge his termination. The case reached the New York Supreme Court, Appellate Division, which held that he was properly fired. The termination did not violate Corrections Law Section 752 (prohibiting unfair discrimination against previously convicted persons) because it was based on his failure to disclose his criminal record completely and truthfully. *Smith v. Kingsboro Psychiatric Center (KPC)*, 35 A.D.3d 751, 828 N.Y.S.2d 419 (N.Y. App. Div. 2006).

* A Maryland county hired an employee to run a program created by the employee (while he was still an independent contractor) to comprehensively treat prison inmates. The employee signed a one-year contract that required him to work as a probationary employee for six months. Four months later, he was fired for insubordination and job performance issues. He sued, claiming the county acted in bad faith by refusing to allow him to appeal through the county's internal grievance process. A Maryland federal court ruled against him. **Because of his at-will probationary status, he was not entitled to the protections of a permanent employee.** *Burkett v. Wicomico County*, No. 05-896, 2006 WL 827381 (D. Md. 3/24/06).

* The Idaho health department took over the operation of a hospital-based emergency medical services communications center and offered to transfer certain positions to state employment. Three employees who accepted the offer and began working as probationary state employees did so with the benefit of only draft copies of their job descriptions. A month later, they were told that they were going to be fired if they did not resign. The day after their terminations, the state filled out evaluations for them and cited "unsatisfactory performance" as

the reason for the discharge. The employees sued the state, asserting that they had **a right to a pre-termination evaluation**. The Supreme Court of Idaho disagreed. Idaho law requires state employers to provide probationary employees with performance evaluations "no later than thirty (30) days after the expiration of the probationary period." The employees here had helped design the newly created positions and had helped to create the standard upon which they were to be evaluated. *Clark v. State of Idaho*, 5 P.3d 988 (Idaho 2000).

♦ A Wisconsin police officer was promoted to sergeant. He was given a memo from the chief that he would receive a permanent appointment to the sergeant position after completing a one-year probationary period. Before the year was up, the chief's successor demoted him back to officer, and he sought a "just cause" hearing under a state statute. The city fire and police commission refused to grant him one, and he sought review in state court. The Wisconsin Court of Appeals found that **the promotion could not be taken away without just cause**. The statute stated that "[n]o subordinate may be ... reduced in rank ... based on charges filed by the chief ... unless the board determines whether there is just cause ... to sustain the charges." Here, the officer was a "subordinate," and the police department sought to "reduce" his rank based on "charges ... by the chief." While the use of probationary terms for law enforcement officers is an excellent means of examining candidates, **Wisconsin law recognizes only newly hired police officers as probationary employees**. The officer in this case satisfied his probationary period after he was initially hired. Having cleared that hurdle, any promotion he received could not be taken away without "just cause." *Antisdel v. City of Oak Creek Police & Fire Comm'n*, 600 N.W.2d 1 (Wis. Ct. App. 1999).

♦ A Missouri probationary firefighter was hired by a city and discharged 21 days later for alleged falsification of his employment application. The city asserted that he had failed to disclose past criminal convictions. The firefighter filed suit against the city in state court, alleging that he was in fact discharged (in violation of state statute) because he was a convicted felon. The court dismissed the claim, and the firefighter appealed to the Missouri Court of Appeals. Although a probationary employee is an at-will employee, who generally does not have a property interest in a public job, **the state statute governing disqualification or disability prevents disqualification from employment because of a criminal conviction**. Specifically, the statute provides that no person shall suffer any legal disqualification or disability because of a finding of guilt, or conviction of a crime, or the sentence of his conviction unless one of the enumerated exceptions applies. In the instant case, none of the exceptions applied, so the employee could not be discharged solely on the basis of his felony conviction. As a result, he was entitled to judicial review of the discharge to determine if the reason for the discharge was prohibited by the statute. *Hardy v. City of Berkeley*, 936 S.W.2d 879 (Mo. Ct. App. 1997).

♦ A Los Angeles city probationary police officer arrested a chronic drug abuser. During the arrest and booking procedure, the officer gave the arrestee his business card and told her to call him if she needed help. The arrestee filed a complaint against the officer, alleging that he had rented a motel room under a fictitious name and that they had consensual sex together. The officer admitted renting the motel room under a fictitious name in order to talk and to avoid discrediting the department but contended that he left when she made sexual advances. The department initiated an investigation and, because of the officer's previously unblemished record, his supervisors imposed only a 22-day suspension. The chief overturned the suspension and fired the officer. The California Court of Appeal held that sufficient evidence existed to support the chief's discharge decision. **California law did not require that a probationary police officer be given a pre-termination hearing.** The law also did not require the department to produce substantial evidence to support the reasons for the discharge. Such a holding would improperly give probationary employees nearly the same protection as tenured police officers. *Riveros v. City of Los Angeles*, 49 Cal.Rptr.2d 238 (Cal. Ct. App. 1996).

2. Transfers

♦ Three sergeants who received Like-Work-Like-Pay promotions to the rank of lieutenant, then were reverted to the rank of sergeant after three months, sued San Francisco under 42 U.S.C. § 1983, claiming their promotions gave them a property interest in continued employment as lieutenants, and that their transfers back to sergeant violated their due process and equal protection rights. A federal court ruled for the city, and the Ninth Circuit affirmed. **The temporary promotions did not create a property interest in continued employment at the rank of lieutenant.** And the reversions to sergeant, to make room for the appointment of applicants who demonstrated better qualifications by achieving higher scores on the new eligibility list test, were rationally related to the government's interest in delivering quality services and therefore did not violate the sergeants' equal protection rights. *Fewer v. City and County of San Francisco*, 240 Fed.Appx. 185 (9th Cir. 2007).

♦ A District of Columbia lottery employee was transferred from his job as an auditor to a new position in the security division. The next day, he was informed that a reduction in force would eliminate his new position. He sued under the First and Fifth Amendments, claiming he was transferred in retaliation for reports he'd made as an auditor, criticizing a contractor, and that he'd been denied due process in his termination because he did not receive notice and a hearing. A federal appeals court noted that under *Garcetti v. Ceballos*, 547 U.S. 410 (2006), he was not entitled to First Amendment protection because his speech occurred in the course of his official duties. However, **he had a protected property interest in his job at the time he was transferred to the doomed new position** and thus should have received due process (notice and a hearing). The transfer constructively removed him from his position. *Thompson v. District of Columbia*, 530 F.3d 914 (D.C. Cir. 2008).

♦ A high-level employee of an Illinois state agency was reassigned to another position while an internal investigation was conducted into his handling of "comp time" for employees he managed. He lost his office, agency car and supervisory responsibilities, but kept his same salary and job classification. When he sued, claiming he had been demoted without due process, the Seventh Circuit Court of Appeals held that he was not deprived of due process. Since he had kept his same salary and job classification, **his reassignment did not amount to a demotion such that he was entitled to due process**. Further, the reassignment did not amount to a constructive discharge. *Atterberry v. Sherman*, 453 F.3d 823 (7th Cir. 2006).

♦ A police sergeant in San Diego had some physical restrictions regarding her ability and willingness to wear a gun belt and body armor. She was transferred from her position at a police station to a sergeant's position at a detention facility. Another officer fell asleep several times on the job for no apparent reason. When he refused to undergo a physical exam, the sheriff's department placed him on restricted duty, which prevented him from working overtime outside his station. Both officers tried to appeal their respective transfers, but the civil service commission rejected the requests. A California trial court upheld the commission's decision, and the Court of Appeal affirmed. The officers were not entitled to a "just cause" hearing over their transfers because the transfers did not amount to removal from their positions for disciplinary reasons. Rather, **the officers were transferred for safety reasons**. *Dobbins v. County of San Diego Civil Service Comm'n*, 75 Cal.App.4th 125, 89 Cal.Rptr.2d 39 (Cal. Ct. App. 1999).

♦ Two Washington state correctional officers were charged with gross misconduct for failing to properly secure firearms. They denied the charges, claiming that they were set up by co-workers. Their supervisor temporarily demoted and reassigned them. After a hearing where all parties were represented by counsel, the examiner affirmed the supervisor's decision to demote them. So did the personnel appeals board. Because they were both members of the emergency response team and therefore unpopular with prisoners, the officers resigned, fearing for their safety in their new assignment. They sued their employer and supervisor for constructive discharge and tortious interference with employment. Because the officers were not constructively discharged for refusing to commit an illegal act, exercising a legal right or privilege, or whistleblowing, the Supreme Court of Washington found that **they failed to establish a claim of wrongful discharge**. It rejected the officers' argument that since they were set up by co-workers, this was a violation of public policy. Although personal vendettas of fellow officers is unworthy conduct, it did not constitute a wrongful discharge or contravene public policy because their firing was essentially a matter of private concern. Their tortious interference claim also failed because the personnel appeals board had determined that they committed gross misconduct. *Reninger v. State Dep't of Corrections*, 951 P.2d 782 (Wash. 1998).

♦ Two Wisconsin police officers who worked for a city's Tactical Enforcement Unit voiced concerns about a new departmental policy prohibiting all members of the unit from conducting any follow-up investigations or assisting the detective bureau without the deputy inspector's direct authorization. They communicated these concerns to several co-workers, including officials of their union. Ultimately, the deputy inspector was pressured by both the media and local politicians to rescind the policy. The two officers were then transferred to street duty. The transfers were unusual in that transfers normally occurred for one of three reasons: promotion, on request, or discipline. Neither officer had requested a transfer, and street duty was not a promotion. Despite their qualifications, they also were not selected for open positions in the unit. They sued under 42 U.S.C. § 1983, alleging retaliation for exercising their right to free speech under the First Amendment and that the transfers violated their due process rights.

Regarding the due process claim, the Seventh Circuit found that the officers had neither a property nor liberty interest in their assignments. Although the court previously has found liberty deprivations in cases where an employee was fired for a publicly announced reason that impugned his moral character and where an employee was demoted to a position far beneath the one he had, neither applied in this case. **No contractual or statutory provision indicated that the officers had a property interest in particular job assignments.** Therefore, the due process claim failed. The court noted, however, that it would not go so far as to say that there can never be a property interest in a job assignment. *Gustafson v. Jones*, 117 F.3d 1015 (7th Cir. 1997).

3. Reputation Interests

• An environmental control director for a Virginia county was fired for insubordination and performance failure after county commissioners found a number of cost overruns at the landfill he supervised. The next day, the commissioners held an open meeting. They presented their annual audit of the county's finances, and without naming the landfill supervisor, noted that he "had authorized work in excess of the contract without entering change orders as required." They sought a state investigation. The local media immediately linked the fired director to the investigation. After the state declined to prosecute the matter and the media reported that the director had been cleared of any wrongdoing, the director sued the county under 42 U.S.C. § 1983, asserting that he had been deprived of a liberty interest in his reputation without due process. A federal court ruled against him. Here, **the county commissioners never connected his termination to the landfill investigation and never named him as a target of the investigation.** Also, the implications in the media were akin to allegations of mismanagement and did not stigmatize the director's reputation to the point where constitutional issues were raised. *Etter v. Spencer*, 548 F.Supp.2d 248 (W.D. Va. 2008).

• A doctor who worked as a medical director for the city and county of San Francisco never took a civil service exam for the position, which was not posted, and his name did not appear on any eligibility list. He signed a form indicating that he was "exempt-permanent," but he apparently didn't understand that he was an at-will employee. The city removed him from his position for non-disciplinary reasons and he sued, asserting that he should have received a pre-termination hearing before he was released. He claimed that he was stigmatized by the firing such that his due process liberty interests were violated. A trial court ruled in his favor, but the California Court of Appeal reversed. Even if the doctor performed supervisory duties which were more characteristic of someone in a non-exempt position, he never went through the civil service process. Further, **his discharge did not give rise to a liberty interest because no stigmatizing charges were publicly disseminated** upon his release. *Kreutzer v. City and County of San Francisco*, 82 Cal.Rptr.3d 644 (Cal. Ct. App. 2008).

♦ A probationary police officer in Virginia was placed on administrative duty because, according to the acting chief, he had pushed up the odometer on his police cruiser by 10,000 miles so he could get a new car sooner. He was then notified by letter that he was being fired for destroying city property. He sued the city, claiming the letter contained false charges and was placed in his personnel file, which might become available to prospective employers, thereby depriving him of his Fourteenth Amendment liberty interests without granting him a name-clearing hearing. After a federal court dismissed his suit, the Fourth Circuit ruled that he was entitled to amend his complaint. **The city's charge against him implied dishonesty and could place a stigma on his reputation.** Further, although state law restricted government employers from disseminating personnel files, the city admittedly disclosed them to prospective employers who inquired as to why employees left. *Sciolino v. City of Newport News*, 480 F.3d 642 (4th Cir. 2007).

♦ A Minnesota councilwoman criticized the city's only police officer, essentially calling him a liar and a cheat at an open council meeting. He filed a grievance and, at a closed-door council meeting, read a prepared statement responding to the accusations. Afterwards, the county went into open session and voted to obtain police services from the county, eliminating his job. Rather than seek a post-termination public hearing to clear his name, he sued for violations of his due process property and liberty rights. A jury awarded him $125,000 on his liberty interest claim, but the Eighth Circuit reversed. Here, **the officer was given adequate pre-termination due process to clear his name**, and he wasn't deprived of post-termination due process because he never asked for it. *Winskowski v. City of Stephen*, 442 F.3d 1107 (8th Cir. 2006).

♦ An 11-year-old Massachusetts boy told his principal that his art teacher had karate-chopped his arm a few times. Although there were holes in the boy's story and the teacher denied it, the school superintendent decided to go ahead with the teacher's termination. He sent a copy of the termination letter (noting that the teacher hit a student) to the state commissioner of education, which oversees teaching certification. The teacher sued the principal, the superintendent and the town under 42 U.S.C. § 1983 for depriving her of her liberty interest in her reputation. A federal court and the First Circuit ruled against her. **The letter to the commissioner was essentially a form of internal communication that did not amount to a "public disclosure."** *Burton v. Town of Littleton*, 426 F.3d 9 (1st Cir. 2005).

♦ A probationary police officer in Philadelphia was arrested and charged with statutory sexual assault of a 13-year-old girl. The city fired the officer. He was then acquitted of the charges and sought reinstatement with the police department. When the police department refused to rehire him, he sued it, claiming he was entitled to a name-clearing hearing because he had a constitutionally protected liberty interest in his reputation. The case reached the Third Circuit Court of Appeals, which noted that his interests were genuine and weighty. However, the city's failure to provide him with a name-clearing hearing did not deprive him of his Fourteenth Amendment liberty interest rights. **He had ample opportunity to refute the allegations against him in the criminal trial.** The city did not have to rehire him. *Graham v. City of Philadelphia*, 402 F.3d 139 (3d Cir. 2005).

♦ A member of a school district advisory board in New York City was fired after a fellow board member **accused her of practicing "voodoo"** on a school board official whose political opinions she opposed. She appealed to the Board of Education, which found that the investigation had been incomplete and the investigators illogical. It ordered her reinstatement to the advisory board. She then sued under 42 U.S.C. § 1983, alleging First Amendment violations – specifically, retaliation for engaging in protected expression. A federal court dismissed her lawsuit, but the Second Circuit reinstated it. She had to be given a chance to prove that the chancellor who fired her deprived her of a liberty interest in her reputation without providing her a proper hearing, and that he retaliated against her because of her protected speech. *Velez v. Levy*, 401 F.3d 75 (2d Cir. 2005).

♦ Three female jail detainees accused a lieutenant of exchanging sexual favors for reduced jail time and lower fines. After an investigation, the county prosecutor decided not to press charges, but the prosecutor and the city's mayor persuaded the police chief to fire the lieutenant. A local newspaper then reported that the lieutenant had been investigated for sexual misconduct with female inmates and that the prosecutor's office had recommended the officer's termination. The lieutenant sued the city and various officials under 42 U.S.C. § 1983 for **violating his procedural due process rights by firing him without giving him an opportunity to contest the allegations at a hearing**. During the trial, two of the three jail detainees recanted their allegations, and the city conceded that the allegations were false. The Arkansas federal court ruled that the city should have given the lieutenant a hearing before firing him. The Eighth Circuit affirmed. Here, the lieutenant successfully showed that he was deprived of a liberty interest in his good name. He should have been provided with an opportunity to clear his name before being fired. *Speer v. City of Wynne*, 276 F.3d 980 (8th Cir. 2002).

4. Property Interests

♦ The police chief of an Illinois village was the son of the village president. When the village board voted to remove him from the job because he allegedly gave beer to underage boys, used a local brickyard for a firing range and rode a motorcycle without a valid license, he sued under 42 U.S.C. § 1983, asserting that it violated his due process rights under the Fourteenth Amendment. He claimed he had a property right in his job because of a statute that sets out procedures for removing a police chief. He also argued that under a village ordinance only his mother could fire him. The Seventh Circuit found no due process violation, noting that **just because a statute lays out procedures for termination, that does not mean it provides a substantive property right** protected by the Fourteenth Amendment. He might be able to sue in state court. *Miyler v. Village of East Galesburg*, 512 F.3d 896 (7th Cir. 2008).

♦ A Wisconsin university employee held a permanent "back-up" position in the provost's office and a temporary appointed position as a vice chancellor. When allegations of an affair with a student arose, he was asked to resign from his vice chancellor position. For seven months he received paid vacation leave, sick leave and annual reserve leave. He sought to return to work and sued for a violation of his due process rights when he was not allowed to return. The Seventh Circuit ruled that he could not prove a due process violation. **He never specifically asked to be placed in his back-up job, and he was not fired** so as to entitle him to automatic placement in that position. Further, he suffered no economic loss because he was compensated for the time he was on leave. *Barrows v. Wiley*, 478 F.3d 776 (7th Cir. 2007).

♦ A Dallas assistant police chief who had been an executive-rank officer with the city for 15 years was promoted to chief. Five years later, the city manager fired him because his continued presence would be "disruptive." However, the city manager acknowledged that the firing was not "for cause." Citing the Dallas City Charter, the former chief sued under 42 U.S.C. § 1983, **asserting that he had a Fourteenth Amendment property right in continued employment as an assistant chief**. The city charter specified that any chief selected from the ranks who was removed for unfitness, "and not for any cause justifying dismissal," be returned to the rank and grade held prior to the promotion. The Fifth Circuit held that the former chief's lawsuit required a trial. There was a question of fact as to whether the former chief rose from within the "ranks of the police department" so as to be entitled to return to the assistant chief position. *Bolton v. City of Dallas*, 472 F.3d 261 (5th Cir. 2006).

♦ A New Mexico state employee's job required her to perform computer work, which exacerbated her migraine headaches and caused her to accumulate numerous absences. She applied for other positions, but two directors determined that she could not do any computer work, and they refused to transfer her. Eventually, they fired her and did not provide a post-termination hearing. She sued the state and the directors for violating her due process rights, and the Tenth Circuit Court of Appeals ruled in her favor. A state regulation provided for the termination of employees who could not perform their jobs, where other suitable positions were not available and where the employees could not be accommodated in their jobs. However, this regulation placed limitations on the government and created a property interest in employment for non-probationary employees. Here, **the employee's due process rights were** violated by the lack of a post-termination hearing. *Brown v. New Mexico State Personnel Office*, 399 F.3d 1248 (10th Cir. 2005).

♦ In 1993, two employees were offered one-year contracts with the Arizona State Schools for the Deaf and Blind as management personnel. Under an older state law, they had become permanent employees after their probationary periods ended. However, under a new law, the superintendent had the authority to decide whether to renew management and supervisory contracts. The employees' contracts were renewed each year until April 2002, after which the employees sued under 42 U.S.C. § 1983 for deprivation of their Fourteenth Amendment property interest in continued employment. They also asserted a claim for wrongful termination under state law. The case reached the Arizona Supreme Court, which held that the legislature had validly changed the terms of employment, and that **the employees did not have a contractual right to continued employment**. *Proksa v. Arizona State Schools for the Deaf and the Blind*, 74 P.3d 939 (Ariz. 2003).

♦ The wife of an Arkansas city street superintendent criticized city council members at a public meeting. Five weeks later, the street superintendent was fired without written notice. He sued the city under the First and Fourteenth Amendments, but a federal court ruled against him. The Eighth Circuit affirmed, finding no connection between the wife's comments at the meeting and his firing. Further, the employee could not show that he had a property interest in continued employment by virtue of the employee handbook. **Even though the handbook stated that written notice of termination would be provided, it also stated that the city was an at-will employer**, and that the city could fire employees at any time. As a result, the employee did not have a property interest in continued employment and his Fourteenth Amendment claim could not succeed. *Thompson v. Adams*, 268 F.3d 609 (8th Cir. 2001).

♦ A warden employed by the Virginia Department of Corrections was excluded from the protection of the state's grievance procedure after the Virginia Personnel Act was enacted. He received a memo from a female subordinate accusing him of propositioning her, of sending her unwarranted derogatory notes, and of improperly lowering her performance rating. After an investigation, he was fired. At the pre-termination hearing, he was not allowed to confront or examine any witnesses. After two appeals, during which he was again not allowed to examine any witnesses, the secretary of public safety rehired the warden at a lower-paying position. The warden sued, alleging deprivations of his property interest in continued employment and in rights secured by state grievance procedures. The Fourth Circuit ruled that the official who decided to discharge the warden and the official who upheld the discharge were not immune from liability. They had disregarded longstanding law in attempting to retroactively apply the personnel act to eliminate the warden's preexisting substantive right to employment. **Because the warden had been deprived of his livelihood, he was entitled to at least one opportunity for a full hearing**, which included the right to call witnesses and produce evidence on his own behalf and to challenge the factual basis for the state's decision.

However, the warden did not have a clearly established property right to post-termination procedure provided by the Virginia Personnel Act. *Garraghty v. Comwlth. of Virginia*, 52 F.3d 1274 (4th Cir. 1995).

C. Employment Handbooks and Policies

Employment handbooks and policies often define specific employee rights and employer obligations, such as disciplinary procedures. Although many handbooks contain disclaimers indicating that the handbook does not constitute an employment contract, some courts have found that the handbook may limit the employer's ability to fire an employee by defining specific conduct for which employment may be terminated.

The employee's employment status then changes from "at-will" (where she may be fired or quit at any time) to "just cause" or "for cause" (where she may only be fired for certain specified types of conduct).

1. Procedures

♦ A Maryland city had an employee handbook that was broken into sections. Section 17 dealt with discipline of employees who had been with the city more than 90 days. At the end of the section, a disclaimer appeared, reserving to the city the right to waive or change its policy. However, the disclaimer was preceded by four asterisks, which also followed two of the enumerated disciplinary measures. After an employee was fired, he sued for breach of contract, claiming the city violated its handbook when it fired him. The Fourth Circuit refused to dismiss the case. Here, **the disclaimer language did not clearly apply to the entire handbook**. It could be interpreted as applying only to the two disciplinary measures for employees who had been with the city for more than 90 days. *Whittington v. City of Crisfield*, 204 Fed.Appx. 183 (4th Cir. 2006).

♦ An airport maintenance employee for a South Dakota city received the city's personnel policy, which stated that he could quit or be fired at any time for any or no reason. The policy also dictated behaviors that were encouraged and expected. He signed the policy, which was then placed in his personnel file. After receiving a notice that he was being fired for violating certain behaviors in the policy, he was allowed to meet with city officials to discuss why he should not be fired. He met with the officials but was fired anyway. He then sued for wrongful termination, claiming he should have been afforded post-termination due process. The case reached the South Dakota Supreme Court, which noted that **the personnel policy did not create an implied contract that required the city to follow certain procedures**. Nor did it alter the employee's at-will status. The employee was properly fired. *Aberle v. City of Aberdeen*, 718 N.W.2d 615 (S.D. 2006).

♦ Two transit authority employees (a mechanic and a driver) were terminated after testing positive for drugs. An arbitrator ordered the employees reinstated because they had not been impaired on the job, and because the transit authority had not followed its progressive disciplinary procedures by firing them. The public employee labor relations board vacated the arbitrator's decision, and the case reached the Supreme Court of New Hampshire. The court noted that even though the transit authority had not adopted a zero-tolerance drug policy until after the two employees were discharged, it did have **an anti-drug policy in place that subjected workers to discipline up to termination**. The arbitrator's reinstatement award also was unenforceable because there was a strong public policy against allowing employees who test positive for drugs to remain in safety-sensitive positions. However, the public policy that prevented reinstatement did not compel automatic termination, and the case had to be remanded for a determination of the appropriate remedy. *In re Amalgamated Transit Union, Local 717*, 741 A.2d 66 (N.H. 1999).

- A county employee was given a written notice that she was to be terminated as of 11:59 a.m. that day. The notice did not give a reason for the termination, and no hearing was scheduled. She sued, claiming that the handbook created an implied contract that the county had breached by terminating her without notice and a hearing. The handbook stated that employees could be dismissed for "any reasonable cause." It also said that employees would be given written notification of the grounds for dismissal and that a hearing would be scheduled with the administrator. Under the heading "Dismissal," the handbook stated that certain actions were grounds for immediate termination. A state trial court dismissed her lawsuit, but the Appellate Court of Illinois reversed and remanded the case, holding that the handbook was sufficiently clear to lead the employee to believe that she would be fired only for reasonable cause, and that she would **receive written notice of the reason for the discharge as well as a hearing**. *Wood v. Wabash County*, 722 N.E.2d 1176 (Ill. App. Ct. 1999).

- An Oregon county employee became a "permanent" employee who could be disciplined only for cause. However, county personnel policies also included a disclaimer, which stated that "under no circumstances shall these policies be construed to act as any type of employment contract with any employee of the County." The employee was later fired for unsatisfactory job performance, and he sued the county in federal court, alleging that he had a constitutionally protected property interest in his job. The court agreed, and after a jury found that his due process rights were violated, the employee was awarded damages. The county appealed to the U.S. Court of Appeals, Ninth Circuit.

Although he was a permanent employee under county personnel policies, the employee held his job "during the pleasure of the appointing officer." **The court found that he was an at-will employee who had no property interest in his job, and therefore was not entitled to due process before being fired.** The court rejected the employee's contention that the policy regarding discipline of permanent employees created a property interest in the job given the disclaimer contained therein. Such a disclaimer can retain an employee's at-will status, even when the personnel policy provides for termination for specific reasons and an appeals process. Even though the policy distinguished probationary employees from permanent employees, at-will status was not erased; the disclaimer contained the expression "under no circumstances," which indicated an intent to retain at-will status for county employees. The discipline policy was merely a non-binding framework for disciplining an at-will employee. *Lawson v. Umatilla County*, 139 F.3d 690 (9th Cir. 1998).

2. Employment Status

♦ Tenured professors at a Colorado state college teamed with their union to sue the board of trustees, alleging that changes to the employee handbook breached their employment contract and denied them procedural due process. Under the old handbook, nontenured faculty would be laid off before tenured faculty in the event of a reduction in force. Under the new handbook, that provision was not included. Nor was a provision requiring the college to make efforts to relocate dismissed faculty within the college. There were also limitations put on the hearing procedures in the event of a reduction in force. A trial court dismissed the lawsuit because the mere possibility of a future layoff did not constitute an actual controversy. The court of appeals then held that **to the extent certain tenure provisions in the old handbook afforded the professors vested rights, the board of trustees did not have the authority to unilaterally modify those provisions.** Also, the procedure set forth in the new handbook giving the college president the power to both initiate and resolve a dismissal violated the professors' procedural due process rights. *Saxe v. Board of Trustees of Metropolitan State College of Denver*, 179 P.3d 67 (Colo. Ct. App. 2007).

♦ A food services administrator at a school district in Mississippi worked as an at-will employee for 10 years. His contract was renewed on a probationary basis in 1999, with a requirement that he follow a nine-step improvement plan. He was supposed to be given a hearing on October 1 to determine whether his contract would be renewed for the following year, but the hearing never occurred. Instead, he was fired in March of 2000 for failing to follow school board policies and for mismanaging school board property and funds. He sued the school district for wrongful termination, but the state court of appeals ruled against him. It found that he did not qualify for the employment handbook exception to the at-will doctrine because **a disclaimer in the handbook made clear that he was an at-will employee.** *Griffin v. Kemper County School Dist.*, 909 So.2d 1139 (Miss. Ct. App. 2005).

♦ An office manager for a township in Pennsylvania was fired without notice or a hearing because of behavior problems. She sued under 42 U.S.C. § 1983, asserting that the township's personnel handbook, which promised to impose discipline only for "just cause," gave her a property right to her job. She also claimed that there was not just cause for the firing. The Third Circuit Court of Appeals ruled against her, noting that despite the existence of the personnel handbook, Pennsylvania law mandated that a public employee is subject to summary removal. Without express legislative authority, a local government cannot employ workers on anything but an at-will basis. Thus, **despite the handbook, the township could not confer "just cause" status on the** employee, and she could be fired for no reason, without notice or a hearing. *Elmore v. Cleary*, 399 F.3d 279 (3d Cir. 2005).

• A computer network administrator agreed to work for a Michigan county as an at-will, nonunion employee and received a letter to that effect. When he believed his supervisor had a conflict of interest because of an ownership interest in a private company providing services to several cities, he began monitoring the supervisor's e-mails. He was fired when his e-mail monitoring was discovered. He sued the county for wrongful discharge, and also asserted a whistleblower claim. A jury found for the county on the whistleblower claim, but awarded him $80,000 for wrongful discharge. The Sixth Circuit reversed, noting that he was not wrongfully discharged because as an at-will employee, he could be fired at any time for any reason or no reason at all. Even though personnel policies provided a list of 23 offenses that could result in discipline, that **list did not turn his employment into "for cause" rather than at-will employment.** *Mannix v. County of Monroe*, 348 F.3d 526 (6th Cir. 2003).

• A Texas city conferred "just cause" status upon certain at-will employees by ordinance through its employment manual. A "just cause" employee had termination procedures brought against him. After a pre-termination hearing, the employee was discharged. The employee left before the conclusion of his post-termination hearing and a final decision was never issued. He sued the city for breach of his employment contract. The case reached the Texas Supreme Court, which noted that **the city had modified the employment terms of its at-will employees by conferring "just cause" status on them**. At the same time, an employee's remedies were limited to administrative review as the exclusive remedy. Since the employee continued working for the city after it promulgated the manual, he accepted both his new "just cause" status and administrative review as his exclusive remedy for challenging adverse employment decisions. Although the employee could have sought judicial review of the city's administrative decision and forced the city to render a post-termination hearing decision, he could not have a jury decide whether there was just cause to fire him. He also could not bring an independent claim for breach of contract. *City of Odessa, Texas v. Barton*, 967 S.W.2d 834 (Tex. 1998).

D. Statutes and Ordinances

Many states have statutes or local ordinances, such as civil service laws, which set forth the procedures for discipline, suspension or termination of employees. Additionally, these laws may designate an employee's employment status as "just cause," which limits the employer's ability to fire the employee.

1. Procedures

• An employee of a U.S. Forest Service private contractor that operated a Kentucky National Recreation Area made a joke at a Forest Service manager's expense, then refused to apologize for it when asked to do so by her superior. She was fired two days later. She sued the Forest Service manager in state court, alleging that he interfered with her employment contract. The U.S. Attorney, on behalf of the Attorney General, certified that the manager was acting in the course and scope of his employment, then denied the allegations and sought to remove the case to federal court and to substitute the U.S. as the defendant under the Westfall Act (28 U.S.C. § 2679(b)(1)). The case reached the U.S. Supreme Court, which held that Westfall Act certification was proper because **the act was designed to immunize covered federal employees not just from liability but from being sued as well.** And the Attorney General could deny the allegations and still have the case removed to federal court, with the U.S. substituted as the defendant. *Osborn v. Haley*, 549 U.S. 225, 127 S.Ct. 881, 166 L.Ed.2d 819 (U.S. 2007).

♦ Two corrections employees in Colorado filed administrative appeals after a reduction in force eliminated their jobs, forcing one to transfer to a new position and the other to transfer to a new location. While their appeals were pending, the prison director sent an e-mail to Department of Correction (DOC) wardens advising them that displaced staff seeking positions at their facilities "MUST drop their cases against us." Ultimately, an administrative law judge ordered the DOC to refrain from retaliating against one of the two. The other's case was still pending at the time they sued the DOC under 42 U.S.C. § 1983, alleging that DOC officials violated the Due Process and Equal Protection Clauses by engaging in a policy of blacklisting employees who maintained administrative appeals of personnel actions. They claimed that they were not promoted because of their appeals. A federal court dismissed the action and the Tenth Circuit affirmed. **The employees did not lose their jobs, and they had no due process or equal protection rights to a promotion.** *Teigen v. Renfrow*, 511 F.3d 1072 (10th Cir. 2007).

♦ On her first day in office, a newly elected town administrator fired the police chief. She claimed she could do so without cause. He disagreed and sued for wrongful discharge, seeking a temporary restraining order to prevent his removal from the job. A trial court agreed with him that he could not be fired without cause, and the case reached the Rhode Island Supreme Court. Here, the town's charter provided that a town administrator **could discharge an employee "for the good of the services."** Previously, the supreme court determined that this language meant "for cause." Since the administrator did not have cause to fire the police chief, the court upheld the order in favor of the chief. *Kells v. Town of Lincoln*, 874 A.2d 204 (R.I. 2005).

♦ A Utah prison official and former career service employee allegedly violated department policies and was placed on administrative leave. After an investigation, he was fired for cause and notified that he could appeal the decision within five working days. Instead, he and his attorney sent a series of letters denying the charge and seeking reinstatement. He also asserted that he had the right to be reassigned to another career service position following his termination. When he sued, the Tenth Circuit Court of Appeals ruled against him, noting that he had made no showing that he in fact desired to be reassigned to a career service position. He merely asserted that he should retain that right.

Sec. I   EMPLOYEE DUE PROCESS RIGHTS   131

This was not a sufficiently imminent injury to justify court intervention. *Morgan v. McCotter*, 365 F.3d 882 (10th Cir. 2004).

♦   When a tax assessor died in office, the mayor appointed her assistant to fill the vacancy. The appointment, made by letter, was for the 64 days remaining in the term and for the next full four-year term. The mayor sent the letter to the city council, but the council never formally approved the appointment. Neither the council nor the mayor said anything when the tax assessor continued in the position for a second full term. After the mayor stepped down midway through that second term, his replacement fired the tax assessor, who then sued for reinstatement. A trial court found that the assessor's continued service, coupled with the mayor's and city council's silence, was essentially a reappointment giving rise to tenure. The New Jersey Supreme Court reversed, noting that state law specifically delegated to the mayor and city council separate functions in appointing officials, such as the tax assessor. The mayor had the authority to appoint the official, but the city council had to provide formal "advice and consent" to the appointment. **By its continued silence, the city council failed to meet its statutory obligation to affirmatively approve the tax assessor's appointment, and the new mayor was legally entitled to discharge him.** *Casamasino v. City of Jersey City*, 730 A.2d 287 (N.J. 1999).

♦   A California county civil service commission reversed a termination order against two deputy sheriffs, reinstated their employment and awarded them back pay. The deputies then requested interest on the back pay. When the commission refused, the deputies sued. A trial court held that administrative agencies were prohibited from awarding interest unless the interest was expressly authorized by law. The California Court of Appeal reversed. Here, a civil service commission determined that **the sheriff's department acted wrongfully in ordering the deputies' termination and in withholding their pay,** and the wrongful action took place before the administrative procedure was even started. Accordingly, the court found that the law permitted the deputies to receive interest on the withheld benefits. *San Diego County Deputy Sheriffs Ass'n v. San Diego County Sheriffs Dep't*, 80 Cal.Rptr.2d 712 (Cal. Ct. App. 1998).

♦   An Illinois firefighter injured his ankle while playing basketball. He and three others, including his superior officer, falsely reported that the injury had occurred in the weight room because they feared that their basketball privileges would be revoked if they told the truth. The fire chief initiated an investigation, during which one of the firefighters confessed that they had lied. The chief sent the superior officer a notice of disciplinary charges and conducted a hearing. The officer was allowed to explain the reasons for his behavior, but no witnesses were called to testify. After he was fired, the officer appealed to the Board of Fire and Police Commissioners. He admitted that he had lied but denied pressuring the other firefighters to do so. The board affirmed the termination, and the officer sued.

The Supreme Court of Illinois noted that the essential requirements of due process are notice and an opportunity to respond. Because the officer availed himself of a pre-termination hearing where he admitted lying, and because he was given a prompt, post-termination evidentiary hearing, the ordinance was not unconstitutional as applied to him. Even though the municipal code failed to expressly include discharge in its definition of major disciplinary action, other provisions of the ordinance, taken collectively, demonstrated that **employees who were subject to discharge were to be accorded the same procedural rights as those conferred on employees subject to major discipline.** The ordinance was therefore not unconstitutional on its face. The officer was not denied due process of law and was not entitled to reinstatement. *Villegas v. Board of Fire & Police Comm'rs,* 656 N.E.2d 1074 (Ill. 1995).

2. Employment Status

♦ A probationary police officer in New York was fired for making false and misleading statements to members of the Internal Affairs Bureau concerning a crime he was allegedly involved in prior to his employment as a police officer. He sued for bad faith dismissal, claiming that the dismissal was procedurally improper because it was based on pre-hiring conduct; therefore, exclusive authority over his termination should have rested with the Department of Citywide Administrative Services. The Supreme Court, Appellate Division, disagreed. It was not the pre-hiring conduct that caused the termination, but rather the post-hiring conduct of lying to the Internal Affairs officers. **The probationary officer failed to show that he was fired in bad faith.** *Duncan v. Kelly,* 43 A.D.3d 297, 841 N.Y.S.2d 237 (N.Y. App. Div. 2007).

♦ A Kentucky utilities commission hired a superintendent under a three-year contract. However, the state had previously passed a "Home Rule Statute" that gave local mayors the power to appoint and remove all city employees except as protected by statute, ordinance or contract. When the mayor tried to fire him for personnel problems and his inability to get along with the public, he sued under 42 U.S.C. § 1983 and state law, alleging due process violations and breach of contract. A federal court ruled against him, and the Sixth Circuit affirmed. Here, **the commission never had the authority to enter into an employment contract with the superintendent** because of the Home Rule Statute. Thus, the superintendent was an at-will employee with no property rights. The mayor had the power to fire him. *Williams v. London Utility Comm'n,* 375 F.3d 424 (6th Cir. 2004).

♦ A classified employee with the Louisiana Department of Health and Hospitals was convicted of aggravated battery. He was fired from his job (working with residents of a state facility for the developmentally disabled) under a state law that made termination automatic upon a felony conviction. He and the union appealed the discharge and also sued to have the statute declared unconstitutional. The Supreme Court of Louisiana found that the statute violated the state constitution because **the legislature did not have the power to mandate termination for classified executive branch employees.** That power rested with the Civil Service Commission, which had not yet ruled on whether the termination was justified. However, if the employee had been unclassified (with no property right to continued employment), he could have been fired under the statute. *AFSCME, Council 17 v. State of Louisiana*, 789 So.2d 1263 (La. 2001).

♦ A man worked for a Texas city as an at-will employee for 22 years and rose to the rank of "Laborer II." During the term of his employment, he received at least three written reprimands. Further, from 1993 through 1995, he took 70 days of sick leave. In June of 1995, the employee decided to take a sick day to go fishing. When his supervisor caught him, the city fired him, provided him with a statement of reasons for the discharge, and informed him of his right to appeal. The employee sued the city and several officials under 42 U.S.C. § 1983, alleging that the defendants terminated his employment in violation of his right to due process and equal protection under the Fourteenth Amendment and the Texas Constitution. A federal court noted that with respect to the due process claim, **the employee could not prove that he had a property right in his job because the city never modified the nature of his employment from at-will to for cause**. With respect to the employee's equal protection claim, the city had a legitimate interest in disciplining its employees for violating its policies, and the employee failed to show that either the purpose or effect of those policy provisions was to arbitrarily discriminate against him. The court ruled for the city and officials on the federal claims, and remanded the claim under the Texas Constitution to a state trial court. *Miller v. City of Nederland By and Through Wimer*, 977 F.Supp. 432 (E.D. Tex. 1997).

♦ A Wyoming non-probationary police officer was suspended for 40 hours without pay based upon the police chief's review of an internal affairs investigation regarding her unsatisfactory job performance. The police chief provided her written notification of the suspension, which included informing her that she was not entitled to a hearing on the suspension. She requested a hearing before the city police civil service commission, but the commission denied the request. She then filed for judicial review. The Supreme Court of Wyoming first determined that the officer had a property interest in her continued employment. Second, the 40-hour suspension triggered due process protections because it was not a *de minimis* deprivation. Third, **the officer would be entitled to both a pre-deprivation hearing and a post-deprivation hearing**. Prior to the suspension, the officer had to be afforded written notice of the charges against her and an opportunity to respond either in person or in writing. Alternatively, a post-deprivation hearing would require a full evidentiary hearing and examination of witnesses before the commission. The court remanded the case for further proceedings. *Mondt v. Cheyenne Police Dep't*, 924 P.2d 70 (Wyo. 1996).

E. Collective Bargaining Agreements

In some instances, collective bargaining agreements may define the specific procedural protections afforded employees. Occasionally, conflict arises between collective bargaining agreements and civil service laws in terms of the applicable substantive and procedural rights.

1. Procedures

♦   A Connecticut corrections officer was arrested at her home following a complaint that she had threatened to shoot a co-worker who refused to answer questions about posting union-related material. Police searched her home for her registered gun and in the process found marijuana and a pill bottle. To avoid a conviction, the officer agreed to participate in a pretrial rehabilitation program. After she was fired, she and her union appealed, arguing that the arbitrator should not have used her participation in the rehabilitation program against her. The Connecticut Court of Appeals ruled that **the arbitrator could consider her participation in the rehabilitation program to infer her culpability**. She was properly fired. *AFSCME, Council 4, Local 1565 v. Dep't of Correction*, 945 A.2d 494 (Conn. App. Ct. 2008).

♦   A Pennsylvania teacher's aide locked herself in a restroom and had to be rescued by police. A friend had given her a Fentanyl patch, which she had placed on her back. She then had a bad reaction to it. The school district fired her, and her union filed a grievance, asserting that her behavior did not rise to the level of "immorality" so as to allow her discharge under the collective bargaining agreement. An arbitrator agreed, and the school district appealed. A court vacated the award, but the Supreme Court of Pennsylvania reversed, noting that generally speaking, judicial review of grievance arbitration awards under state law was subject to the two-pronged "essence test." **If the issue is within the proper subject of collective bargaining and the arbitrator's interpretation can rationally be derived from the agreement, then courts must uphold the award.** *Westmoreland Intermediate Unit #7 v. WIU #7 Classroom Assistants Educ. Support Personnel Ass'n PSEA/NEA*, 939 A.2d 855 (Pa. 2007).

♦   The union representing detectives in a Pennsylvania county reached an impasse with the county while bargaining over a new collective bargaining agreement. The parties proceeded to interest arbitration, and the arbitration board included a "just cause" clause in the award. It stated that no member of the detective bargaining unit could be discharged, demoted, suspended, reprimanded or otherwise disciplined without a sufficient just cause basis. The county appealed, claiming that the "just cause" provision infringed upon the District Attorney's power to supervise its employees. The Commonwealth Court agreed that the "just cause" provision was beyond the powers of the arbitration board, and that the District Attorney retained the right to discipline the detectives. **The bargaining agreement could not infringe that right.** *Westmoreland County v. Westmoreland County Detectives*, 937 A.2d 618 (Pa. Commw. Ct. 2007).

♦   A nonunion District of Columbia firefighter and emergency services technician was fired for insubordination based on noncompliance with the department's substance abuse policy. He admitted to being dependent on the codeine in Tylenol. The Office of Employee Appeals (OEA) upheld the discharge, and the employee sued. He claimed that he should have been granted a *de novo* evidentiary hearing at the OEA because he was not bound by the collective bargaining agreement as he would have been were he a union member. The District of Columbia Court of Appeals ruled against him. **Because the union bargained for all employees, whether union or not, he was bound by the same conditions as all other employees in the bargaining unit.** *Davidson v. Office of Employee Appeals*, 886 A.2d 70 (D.C. 2005).

◆ A city police commission unilaterally revised the police department's disciplinary procedures. Prior to the change, an officer facing sanctions could appear before a disciplinary hearing board. After the change, the officer would only be entitled to a hearing before the chief. The police union filed a grievance seeking to compel arbitration on the matter. The state public employee relations board held that the grievance was arbitrable, but the Supreme Court of New Hampshire reversed. It noted that **the collective bargaining agreement granted the commission the right to revise rules and regulations,** as well as policies and working conditions, to improve the efficiency of the department. The agreement also provided that any such change or revision would not be subject to the grievance procedure. Accordingly, the union was not entitled to arbitrate the commission's unilateral change. *In re City of Manchester*, 743 A.2d 821 (N.H. 1999).

◆ A Washington city suspended an officer for two-and-one-half days after he caused an accident during a high-speed chase. On the same day the officer appealed the suspension to the city's civil service commission, his union also filed a grievance with the city. The civil service commission found that the officer had broken several traffic laws and police department regulations, and increased the officer's suspension to 10 days. However, in the grievance hearing, the arbitrator ordered the city to decrease the suspension to a written reprimand based on findings that although the officer had violated department regulations, the city did not have just cause under the collective bargaining agreement to suspend him. The Washington Supreme Court found that the civil service commission used a different, narrower standard to review the suspension than the arbitrator. Because the two bodies were not reviewing the same issue, **the commission's decision was not determinative of whether the city had the authority to suspend the officer under the bargaining agreement**. Thus, the officer could arbitrate his grievance. *Civil Service Comm'n v. City of Kelso*, 969 P.2d 474 (Wash. 1999).

◆ Because the superintendent for a New Hampshire school district had substantial control over the hiring and firing of teachers, his warning that one teacher would not continue to be rehired in the future unless his performance improved was disciplinary action covered by the parties' collective bargaining agreement. **The teacher was therefore entitled to arbitration over his grievance that the warning was issued without just cause.** The teacher had received an evaluation from his principal recommending "with reservations" that he be renominated for the next year. If the teacher did not improve his interpersonal skills to an acceptable standard, the principal recommended that he not continue to be renominated. The New Hampshire Supreme Court noted that because the principal did not have the authority to nominate teachers, he had no authority to impose termination as a penalty. The superintendent, however, did have that authority by virtue of his power to refuse to renominate the teacher the following year. As such, the superintendent's letter constituted a disciplinary action subject to arbitration. *In re Lincoln-Woodstock Cooperative School Dist.*, 731 A.2d 992 (N.H. 1999).

♦ A Montana firefighter was suspended with pay after he allegedly misappropriated several items. The department sent him a notice that there would be a termination hearing the next day. The hearing was twice postponed, once pending discussion of additional violations and again upon the firefighter's request. When the city manager unilaterally discharged the firefighter pursuant to the city's termination procedures, the firefighter objected, alleging that the discharge violated a state law requiring firefighters' termination hearings to be held before the city council or commission. After his objections were overruled, the firefighter sought court review of the department's decision. The Supreme Court of Montana held that the department improperly attempted to supersede the statutory duty of the city council to hold a hearing before firing a suspended firefighter. **The collective bargaining agreement provided that "the employer may suspend an employee with pay pending the final decision as to the appropriate discipline** by the appropriate authority." Because the appropriate authority was the city council, the unilateral discharge by the city manager violated state law. The court reinstated the firefighter to his former position. *Phillips v. City of Livingston,* 885 P.2d 528 (Mont. 1994).

2. Investigatory Interviews

In *NLRB v. Weingarten,* 420 U.S. 251 (1975), the Supreme Court held that a union employee has a right to union representation at an investigatory interview that the employee reasonably believes will result in discipline.

♦ The New York City Transit Authority interviewed a car inspector after he allegedly used a racial slur. It refused to allow a union representative to accompany the employee. When the union filed an unfair labor practice charge against the Transit Authority, the Public Employment Relations Board (PERB) upheld the charge, finding a violation of the employee's *Weingarten* right. The Court of Appeals of New York reversed, noting that **New York public employees did not have the same rights as private sector employees**. Under the state's Taylor Law, a violation of an employee's *Weingarten* right results not in an improper practice proceeding before the PERB, but rather in the exclusion from a disciplinary hearing of statements made at the interview and evidence obtained as a result. The employee did not have the right to union representation at the meeting. *New York City Transit Authority v. New York State PERB,* 8 N.Y.3d 226, 864 N.E.2d 56 (N.Y. 2007).

♦ A New Hampshire town conducted an investigatory interview of a police officer after a citizen complained about a traffic ticket he had been issued. He asserted that the officer had been harassing him and his family. An investigation revealed that the officer improperly used the State Police On-Line Technology Systems to issue the ticket. The town refused to let the officer's attorney be present at the interview, and the officer refused union representation. Five days later, the union made the attorney a union representative. After the officer was fired, the union filed an unfair labor practice charge against the town. The case reached the Supreme Court of New Hampshire, which ruled that **the town did not violate the officer's *Weingarten* rights by denying the attorney access to the interview**. The attorney was not a union rep at that time. *In re Exeter Police Ass'n*, 904 A.2d 614 (N.H. 2006).

♦ When an Illinois sheriff learned of rumors of misconduct regarding a sergeant, he ordered her to speak with him so he could find out what happened on the day of the alleged misconduct. The sergeant told the sheriff that she would not speak with him outside the presence of a union representative. The merit commission eventually fired her for insubordination, but the Illinois Appellate Court found that the sheriff's order that she speak with him without a union representative was an unlawful order because she had a right to such representation. The sheriff appealed to the Supreme Court of Illinois. While **there was a question regarding the right to union representation during an investigatory interview where the employee reasonably feared the investigation would result in discipline**, the supreme court did not address that question because it found that the sergeant's collective bargaining agreement (CBA) specifically waived such a right. The applicable CBA granted the sergeant a right to union representation during an interrogation, but not during an informal inquiry. The court rejected the sergeant's contention that the sheriff's order amounted to an interrogation and upheld the termination. *Ehlers v. Jackson County Sheriff's Merit Comm'n*, 697 N.E.2d 717 (Ill. 1998).

♦ A Massachusetts correctional officer reported an incident concerning a co-worker's conduct to her superior. During the investigation, the officer was interviewed in the presence of her union representative. After questioning her, the investigator asked if she wished to add anything. She consulted with her union rep outside the interview room, then the union rep attempted to question the officer in the investigator's presence to elicit additional information. The investigator did not allow the questioning but stated that the union rep could provide a summation of the officer's position, which he did. The union then filed a charge with the Labor Relations Commission, alleging that the state had engaged in a prohibited practice by precluding the questioning. The commission dismissed the case. The Supreme Judicial Court of Massachusetts held that **the department did not violate the officer's rights by precluding the union rep from questioning her in the presence of the investigator**. The union rep was neither relegated to the role of a passive observer nor precluded from assisting the employee or clarifying the facts. The union rep had assisted the officer by his presence and his summation. No law established a right to have a union rep question an employee directly in an investigatory interview conducted by the employer. Therefore, the commission's dismissal was affirmed. *Massachusetts Correction Officers Federated Union v. Labor Relations Comm'n*, 675 N.E.2d 379 (Mass. 1997).

II. EMPLOYMENT ABANDONMENT AND RESIGNATION

A public employee's prolonged absence from work without authorization may result in the employee losing his or her position. In particular, the employer may deem the absence job abandonment or resignation.

A. Abandonment

Some states have statutes or regulations that set forth the consequences for prolonged unauthorized absences from work. Generally, the statutes designate a specific time period, such as three days or one week, in which an employee may be absent before the employer may deem the position abandoned.

• After two co-workers complained about him to a supervisor, a Pittsburgh employee asked for a new job, but was refused. He became upset to the point of tears, felt chest pains and began sweating. When he couldn't reach his supervisor, he called the city's employee assistance program to obtain help. He then took time off work but called in daily to report his status. He eventually took FMLA leave and received short-term disability (STD) benefits. The city fired him five months later for failing to provide proper medical documentation and because the insurer refused to extend his STD benefits. An arbitrator ordered his reinstatement and the Pennsylvania Commonwealth Court upheld that determination. **The employee did not engage in misconduct disruptive of core city functions by being absent for several months because of job-related stress.** Thus, the city did not have just cause to fire him. *City of Pittsburgh v. Brentley*, 925 A.2d 188 (Pa. Commw. Ct. 2007).

• A Massachusetts firefighter notified the department that he was ill and then stayed away from work for two weeks. A deputy chief called him at home to remind him of department protocol governing work absences, which included meeting with the department's physician the next day. He failed to do so. Nor did he request that his accrued sick leave be applied to his absence. When he was fired for taking an unauthorized absence for 14 days without providing notice or obtaining approval to use accrued time off to cover the absence, he sued the city for wrongful discharge. The Massachusetts Court of Appeals ruled against him. **Fire departments would be put in a difficult position if employees could decide not to work on a given day without providing notice**, simply relying on an unspoken assumption that accrued time off would be used to cover the absence. *Sisca v. City of Fall River*, 838 N.E.2d 609 (Mass. App. Ct. 2005).

• A Louisiana civil service employee was temporarily assigned to the second shift (3:00 p.m. to 11:00 p.m.) to alleviate a critical personnel shortage. She claimed she was ill and did not report to her new assignment. When she later reported at her usual time of 8:00 a.m., she claimed she could not work the second shift because of child care problems. Her supervisors directed her to punch out and return at 3:00 p.m. However, she did not punch out until 1:15 p.m., and then left a note stating she would not be able to return for the second shift. She did not return to work. Although she intermittently telephoned the department, she gave no reason for her absence. After she was fired for abandoning her job, she appealed to the Civil Service Commission, which affirmed the discharge. The Supreme Court of Louisiana found that the commission's decision was not arbitrary or capricious. **The employee had refused to accept her job assignment and, without adequate explanation, did not return to work.** The commission hearing addressed all of her complaints and found that her objection to the new position did not relieve her of the obligation to follow orders that are not manifestly illegal or immoral. *Bannister v. Dep't of Streets*, 666 So.2d 641 (La. 1996).

♦ A Florida park ranger, who worked for the state Department of Environmental Protection, was transferred to another park located in north Florida but decided she would rather give up her job than move. Although she had been notified of her new assignment, she did not report to her new position. Eventually, she requested leave without pay status for "personal" reasons. Her new supervisor responded that her job was "indispensable" and requested more information. Her leave request was subsequently denied, and she was directed to report for work. She was notified that if she failed to appear for work she would be dismissed for abandonment of her job. She stated that she was financially unable to move and did not report to work. After she was dismissed, the Public Employees Relations Commission issued a final order finding that the ranger had decided to give up her state job. She appealed the order to the District Court of Appeal of Florida, First District, which affirmed the commission's order. Here, the ranger was able to work, did not have approved leave of any kind, was able to move, and **intentionally failed to report to work despite being previously warned that her failure to report would be considered job abandonment**. *Springfield v. Dep't of Environmental Protection*, 648 So.2d 802 (Fla. Dist. Ct. App. 1994).

♦ After 28 years with the Department of Health and Rehabilitative Services, a Florida public assistance specialist severely injured his back while working. As a result, he was out of work for one year and received workers' compensation benefits. When he was able to return to his job, he often lost time from work due to back pain. At a counseling session, his supervisor informed him that if he had back problems he should wait until he saw the doctor before calling in to explain his status. The specialist called the office to report his absence one day but did not call in to explain the absence until seven days later, at which time he was informed that his unexplained absence was considered a voluntary abandonment of his position. When the specialist received notice of separation, he filed an administrative appeal, which he lost. The specialist appealed to the Court of Appeal of Florida, which reversed the decision to dismiss the specialist, noting that **a state employee need only show that he had a reasonable basis for his failure to seek authorization**, which he had done by indicating that his supervisor had not expected him to call in until he saw his doctor. *Tomlinson v. Dep't of Health & Rehabilitative Services*, 558 So.2d 62 (Fla. Dist. Ct. App. 1990).

B. Resignation

Employees may voluntarily resign from their positions, and sometimes do so in order to avoid being fired or other adverse consequences. If an employee voluntarily resigns, however, he or she may not be entitled to withdraw the resignation and be reinstated.

1. Voluntary Resignation

♦ A wage and hour compliance specialist with the Department of Labor learned that he was being reassigned to work under a former supervisor. He alleged that the former supervisor had harassed him, calling him a "mad dog foaming at the mouth" and even sabotaging the specialist's work. He expressed his concerns to a district director, who assured him that she had told the supervisor to treat the specialist in a professional manner. Nevertheless, the specialist took an "early out" retirement rather than return to the supervisor's chain of command. He then claimed that he was involuntarily removed from his position. The case reached the U.S. Court of Appeals, Federal Circuit, which ruled against him. **His subjective fear of future harassment was not sufficient to show that he had no reasonable alternative but to resign.** *Wyche v. Dep't of Labor*, 180 Fed.Appx. 965 (Fed. Cir. 2006).

♦ After a New York sanitation worker tested positive for drugs for the third time, the county accepted his resignation pursuant to a last chance agreement that he had signed at a prior disciplinary proceeding. **The last chance agreement provided for automatic resignation upon any subsequent positive test.** When the sanitation worker challenged his automatic resignation, claiming a problem with the chain of custody of his sample, the Supreme Court, Appellate Division, ruled for the county. Here, the sanitation worker, in lieu of termination at the earlier disciplinary proceeding, knowingly relinquished his right to appeal or otherwise challenge the test results or testing procedures. His automatic resignation stood. *Presti v. Farrell*, 23 A.D.3d 211, 806 N.Y.S.2d 5 (N.Y. App. Div. 2005).

♦ When a city bus driver tested positive for marijuana, he was fired. After a grievance hearing, he was reinstated with a 60-day suspension provided that he enroll in the city's employee assistance program for drug rehabilitation and take drug tests every two weeks for six months. At the end of his treatment, the city's physician released him to return to work on the condition that he not drive a bus. The city notified him that it was reassigning him to a security guard position at the same rate of pay and hours. However, **he failed to return to work and was fired** again after a pre-termination hearing. He sued the city for violating his due process rights under the Fourteenth Amendment. A New Mexico federal court ruled for the city, and the Tenth Circuit affirmed. The employee was not denied due process by the city's decision to reassign him. Further, his refusal to report to work amounted to a voluntary resignation. *Garcia v. City of Albuquerque*, 232 F.3d 760 (10th Cir. 2000).

- A Washington city engineer received a memo from his supervisor requesting his resignation. The memo alleged various problems with communication, supervisory skills and related skills, and requested the engineer's resignation in lieu of other action. Although the engineer disagreed with the allegations, he sent a handwritten letter of resignation to the city manager. He stated that he resigned because he believed he had no choice, then sued alleging that he was constructively discharged. A court ruled for the city, and the Court of Appeals of Washington affirmed. It held that the engineer voluntarily resigned. The court stated that a resignation is presumed to be voluntary, and that the claimant bears the burden of rebutting the presumption. Further, **a resignation is not rendered involuntary simply because the employee submitted it to avoid termination for cause**, nor is it relevant that the employee subjectively believes he or she had no choice but to resign. Here, the engineer had a choice to dispute the allegations rather than resign. *Molsness v. City of Walla Walla, Washington*, 928 P.2d 1108 (Wash. Ct. App. 1996).

- A female West Virginia correctional officer for a county jail became the subject of sexual advances by an inmate, disputed her assignment to a "constant watch" of the inmate, and needed to shower or change but could not because of a lack of female facilities. She repeatedly requested that her supervisors provide a relief officer to finish her shift. At one point, she indicated she would be forced to "walk out" without a relief officer, even though she had no desire to quit. The chief correctional officer told her to leave her resignation on his desk, which she did not do. When a relief officer arrived, she spoke to him to verify his presence and then went home. When she arrived at work the next day, the sheriff told her that if she wanted her job back she would have to go through the civil service commission. He claimed she had quit. The county civil service commission ordered reinstatement with full pay. The sheriff appealed to the Supreme Court of Appeals of West Virginia, which held that the officer did not quit. The testimony tended to support the officer's position. **The chief correctional officer did not believe she had quit because he received no resignation letter from her.** *In re Queen*, 473 S.E.2d 483 (W.Va. 1996).

- A routine traffic stop in Los Angeles resulted in the recovery of a weapon that had been reported stolen from a Mississippi police department. The weapon had been traded to a pawnbroker by a narcotics officer. The chief of police informed the narcotics officer of the ongoing criminal investigation, but the officer could not recall where he got the weapon, stating that he probably obtained it through a confiscation. The officer feared the stigma of termination and voluntarily resigned. After no criminal charges were brought, the officer unsuccessfully sought reinstatement. He then filed suit alleging denial of due process and constructive discharge. The case eventually reached the Supreme Court of Mississippi, which ruled that **there was no due process issue because hearings were unavailable to employees who voluntarily resigned**. Also, no constructive discharge occurred because the chief did not make conditions so intolerable that he reasonably would feel compelled to resign. Humiliation or embarrassment resulting from a criminal investigation failed to satisfy this standard. *Bulloch v. City of Pascagoula*, 574 So.2d 637 (Miss. 1990).

2. Withdrawal of Resignation

• A Kentucky Department of Corrections employee was promoted to Offender Records Specialist at a correctional facility. She found the position to be less than ideal and submitted a resignation, stating that she would be resigning her position "with the Department of Corrections as Offender Information Supervisor." It also stated that she had enjoyed her time with the department, but was looking forward to new avenues for her career. She claimed that the resignation was just for the new position, but the department claimed it was a resignation from state employment entirely. When she sought to rescind her resignation, the warden refused to do so. The Court of Appeals of Kentucky eventually ruled that substantial evidence supported the administrative finding that she had resigned from public employment. Further, the warden had informed his superior of the resignation and sought permission to fill the job. **This was an acceptance of the resignation, permitting the warden to refuse to allow the resignation to be withdrawn.** *Comwlth., Justice and Public Safety Cabinet, Dep't of Corrections v. Searcy*, 2007 WL 1113542 (Ky. Ct. App. 4/6/07).

• A District of Columbia Water and Sewer Authority (WASA) employee tendered his resignation. Several days after the resignation took effect, he attempted to rescind it. WASA refused to reinstate him. Over 16 months later, he filed an administrative appeal, alleging that he had resigned because of workplace harassment and mistreatment, and that WASA abused its authority in refusing to give him his job back. He sought reinstatement with seniority and back pay. The District of Columbia Court of Appeals ruled against him, noting that **he should have initiated the grievance process within 15 days of WASA's refusal to reinstate him**. *Watson v. District of Columbia Water and Sewer Authority*, 923 A.2d 903 (D.C. 2007).

• A New York state university employee, after being informed that his position was being eliminated and that he would be reinstated at a lower grade, offered a letter of resignation. The university's HR manager accepted it. Two days later he sought to withdraw his resignation. The HR manager refused his request on the grounds that she had already accepted the resignation. He later challenged the decision to deny his withdrawal request and the case reached the New York Supreme Court, Appellate Division. The court noted that **the HR manager now listed the employee's work performance deficiencies as the reason for denying withdrawal**. As a result, there was a fact issue to be resolved. If the real reason was that she'd already accepted the resignation, that could be considered an abuse of discretion allowing for the employee's reinstatement. The court remanded the case for further proceedings. *Martinez v. State Univ. of New York-College at Oswego*, 787 N.Y.S.2d 409 (N.Y. App. Div. 2004).

III. EMPLOYEE MISCONDUCT

This section considers specific forms of misconduct that have led to the discipline or discharge of public employees. In these cases, courts engage in a factual analysis to determine whether the evidence sufficiently justifies the specific adverse employment action taken.

A. Official Misconduct

Official misconduct often arises when a public employee violates an ethics code or neglects his or her duty to the public. Ethics codes usually proscribe particular types of conduct for public employees, such as receiving gifts.

• A New Hampshire police chief took some ammunition from the police station and gave it to a garage owner who fixed his car. When confronted with his actions, he initially denied taking the ammunition, then later admitted doing so, but maintained that the ammunition was old, unfit for police work and worth only about $45. He was then fired. His challenge to the termination eventually reached the New Hampshire Supreme Court, which ultimately upheld the discharge. Even though he was not charged with a crime, the town had "substantial cause" to fire him. **Taking the ammunition without authorization and then lying about it showed egregiously poor judgment,** casting doubt on his ability to perform a job demanding integrity. *Yoder v. Town of Middleton*, 876 A.2d 216 (N.H. 2005).

• An employee claimed that his supervisor harassed him because he was Lebanese and a man. He claimed that she humiliated him in front of others on a constant basis, and that she incited another employee to file a baseless claim of sexual harassment against him for "staring" at the other employee. He lost his temper one day and orally threatened the supervisor. After he was fired for insubordination and threatening behavior, he sued for sex and national origin discrimination under Title VII, but the Seventh Circuit Court of Appeals ruled against him. **Even though his threats were not accompanied by a violent gesture, they frightened the supervisor and co-workers, and thus justified the discharge.** *Merheb v. Illinois State Toll Highway Authority*, 267 F.3d 710 (7th Cir. 2001).

1. Ethics Codes

• A union rep in Michigan assisted two fellow county employees in an investigation of misconduct. She told one of the employees to deny that he had written derogatory remarks on a newspaper photograph of a supervisor so that the union would have more time to "put things together." When a forensic document analysis showed that the employee wrote the remarks, he was fired. At his unemployment compensation hearing, she admitted telling the employee to lie. She was then fired. Her union sued the county for violating public policy. The Michigan Court of Appeals ruled in favor of the county, noting that she did not have an absolute privilege to speak without consequences at the unemployment hearing. **The county did not violate public policy by firing her for telling her co-worker to lie.** *Michigan AFSCME Council 25 v. Livingston County Road Comm'n*, 2007 WL 3357398 (Mich. Ct. App. 11/13/07).

• The chief pharmacist at a VA hospital in Maine requested free samples of Lipitor from a drug company rep. After an employee reported the pharmacist to the head of HR, security escorted the pharmacist from the premises. At an investigatory interview, **the pharmacist admitted taking the samples, but claimed there was an unofficial policy allowing this.** The U.S. Attorney's office declined to pursue criminal charges, but the pharmacist refused to be interviewed any further because his attorney felt he was still susceptible to prosecution. The VA suspended him for 45 days and demoted him for refusing to cooperate in the investigation. He sued and lost. The First Circuit held that the 45-day suspension and the demotion with its corresponding reduction in pay grade were reasonable disciplinary measures. Also, the pharmacist had been adequately represented by counsel and was deemed to be aware of his immunity from criminal prosecution if he participated in the investigation. *Sher v. U.S. Dep't of Veterans Affairs*, 488 F.3d 489 (1st Cir. 2007).

• A judicial clerk for a New Jersey judge told him she had been called back for a second interview with a Long Island law firm. He told her she needed to make sure he didn't give her any black marks, then allegedly hugged and kissed her. As a result, he was suspended for two months without pay. He appealed, asserting that the kiss never occurred. However, the Supreme Court of New Jersey found the law clerk's evidence more credible and upheld the suspension. *In re Subryan*, 900 A.2d 809 (N.J. 2006).

• An Illinois police officer was suspended without pay after it was discovered that he had made nearly $53,000 in false overtime claims. Six years later, the public safety board of commissioners finally got around to terminating him. After obtaining his pension benefits, **he sued the town to recoup the six years of pay he was denied while he was on suspension.** A federal court and the Seventh Circuit ruled against him, noting that he was not in the same situation as a public employee who is reinstated after a long, unpaid suspension. There was no due process or equal protection violation by the town in refusing to pay him. *Stachowski v. Town of Cicero*, 425 F.3d 1075 (7th Cir. 2005).

• A special agent with a Florida alcohol and tobacco agency was dismissed for using abusive and vulgar language. She sued, asserting that the agency had condoned the use of such language in the workplace by refusing to discipline other employees who had used similar language. The Florida District Court of Appeal noted that there was substantial evidence that the agent had made inappropriate comments to a trainee and that those comments had not been condoned by the agency. Thus, **her behavior justified a one-week suspension.** However, she also presented evidence that the agency condoned the other behavior at issue and that no other employees had been disciplined or warned about the use of bad language as she had been. Thus, she should not have been fired. The agent was entitled to reinstatement and back pay, as well as reasonable attorneys' fees and costs. *Dep't of Business and Professional Regulation v. Doyle*, 750 So.2d 746 (Fla. Dist. Ct. App. 2000).

• A Tennessee town secretary issued a building permit to a citizen and, at the same time, borrowed $600 from him. Over the next three years, she continued to borrow money in exchange for sexual favors. When town officials discovered her conduct, they fired her for immoral conduct, citing the employee handbook. She collected unemployment compensation. When the benefits expired, she sued for wrongful discharge and sex discrimination, asserting that men were treated differently. The Tennessee Court of Appeals noted that although the men who had not been fired had committed misconduct (assault, sexual harassment and lying), **their misconduct was not as serious as having an extramarital affair or accepting money for sexual favors**. Further, the handbook allowed the termination of any employee who acted in a manner that could discredit the town government. Also, the secretary had agreed to forgo certain termination procedures in the handbook in exchange for unemployment benefits. *Seiber v. Town of Oliver Springs*, 2000 WL 555233 (Tenn. Ct. App. 2000).

• A Florida probation officer displayed rude and contemptuous behavior in a courtroom when a judge who was conducting other proceedings refused to sign a rush warrant on an offender whose probation was about to expire. The department of corrections suspended the officer for five days. She appealed to the Public Employees Relations Commission and then to the Court of Appeal, alleging that two supervisory employees had been less severely disciplined for more severe infractions. They had assaulted co-workers in the prison where they were assigned. One had received a written reprimand, and the other had been suspended for one day. The court found that **the probation officer was not similarly situated to the two supervisors because her misconduct had occurred in a public courtroom before a judge**. Whether their misconduct was more egregious did not matter. Because no comparison could be made between the two types of misconduct, the employee's suspension was upheld. *Rawls v. Public Employees Relations Comm'n*, 743 So.2d 592 (Fla. Dist. Ct. App. 1999).

2. Neglect of Duty

• A Mississippi corrections officer at a maximum security unit was fired after a deputy warden observed her sitting down in the prison yard with both eyes closed. The deputy warden watched her for about five seconds, then asked her why she was sitting with her eyes closed. She claimed her eyes were never closed and that she was sitting because of a fall she took three days earlier. When she challenged her termination, the Court of Appeals of Mississippi upheld it. There had been testimony that prisoners in the yard were aware that the officer was not paying attention to them. This presented a danger both to the officer and to other prisoners. **Her inattentiveness to her duties made her termination justifiable.** *Cox v. Mississippi Dep't of Corrections*, 969 So.2d 900 (Miss. Ct. App. 2007).

♦ After an audit, the Department of Agriculture learned that the executive director of the U.S. Farm Services Agency in Arkansas had engaged in improper dealings and that fraudulent reports had been submitted by people in the office. It fired the executive director as well as the program manager, who was not implicated in any wrongdoing. She sued, alleging a violation of her due process rights and that her discharge was arbitrary and capricious. The Eighth Circuit ruled against her, finding that she had no property right in continued employment and that the discharge had not been arbitrary. **She mismanaged the programs she oversaw, which contributed to the fraud against the government.** She was not merely a scapegoat. *U.S. v. Massey*, 380 F.3d 437 (8th Cir. 2004).

♦ An advocate in an Arizona county's victim witness program was discharged from her job for neglect of duty, dishonesty, willful disobedience, discourteous treatment of the public and misuse of county property, among other charges. The advocate admitted that she failed to make contact with victims, that she left early one day and that she did not report to juvenile court on a day when she was supposed to. She also conceded that she referred to a juvenile defendant in a case as "a little bitch" in the presence of an adult victim. Nevertheless, she appealed her dismissal to the county employee merit commission, which revoked the dismissal and ordered her reinstatement with back pay. On appeal, the Court of Appeals of Arizona noted that **undisputed evidence established that the advocate neglected three of her duties at the juvenile court, and violated the employer's policy prohibiting profanity in public.** Since those charges warranted taking action, the county attorney did not act arbitrarily or without reasonable cause in firing her, and the merit commission erred in revoking the action taken. The court reversed and remanded the case for a determination of whether the discharge or a less severe sanction was appropriate. *Pima County v. Pima County Merit System Comm'n*, 944 P.2d 508 (Ariz. Ct. App. 1997).

♦ An Illinois police officer went home on break and parked his squad car in his garage. He considered himself on duty during the break, but admitted to parking the squad car in his garage to avoid being bothered by citizens. He damaged the car while backing out of his garage. The police chief suspended him for five days for neglecting his duty and for damaging the squad car. The officer appealed to a city commission, which affirmed the suspension and added 10 more days. He filed a complaint for administrative review in a state court. The court focused on the damage to the squad car and found that the suspension did not fit the "crime." It reversed the board's decision. The Appellate Court of Illinois reversed, finding that the district court had focused on the wrong issue. First, the police officer had clearly violated the department's rules of conduct. Second, **the focus should have been on the neglect of the officer's duty to serve the public by hiding**, rather than the minimal squad car damage. The officer violated the Rules of Conduct and the 15-day suspension was not arbitrary or unreasonable. *Nessel v. Board of Fire and Police Comm'rs of Northlake, Illinois*, 664 N.E.2d 207 (Ill. App. Ct. 1996).

♦ A Las Vegas police officer allegedly advised two suspected prostitutes of techniques for avoiding arrest. He then entered their motel room, browsed through pornographic magazines, and slid his hand down one woman's panties. The prostitutes later agreed to engage in a sting operation against the officer. Upon his return, the scantily clad prostitutes helped him remove his clothes and then signaled to several officers waiting outside the room. The officer was found naked, attempting to hide behind the door. The department and the Civil Service Board discharged him for giving assistance to suspects, neglect of duty, conduct unbecoming an employee, and consorting with persons of ill repute. The district court reversed and ordered a lesser penalty, based in part on the prostitutes' unavailability to testify at the board hearing, ruling that neither the momentary perusal of the pornographic magazine nor the fondling incident arose to neglect of duty. The Supreme Court of Nevada reversed, ruling that the board did not abuse its discretion in sustaining the department's decision. **The officer's conduct could reasonably be construed to support the neglect of duty and improper assistance charges.** Moreover, the penalty was not disproportionate with other disciplinary measures imposed for comparable conduct. Because the discharge was supported by substantial evidence, the district court had abused its discretion when it substituted its judgment for that of the board. The district court ruling was reversed, and the dismissal was reinstated. *Las Vegas Metropolitan Police Dep't v. Berni*, 899 P.2d 1106 (Nev. 1995).

B. Criminal Violations

An employee may also be subject to discipline, suspension, or termination from employment upon violation of a criminal law. A criminal conviction may not be necessary in order to impose some consequences on the employee.

♦ A New York police officer had an off-duty relationship with a 16-year-old girl that resulted in his misdemeanor conviction for endangering the welfare of a child. He was acquitted of the felony charges against him. After his conviction, he was fired, and he sued, claiming that he was entitled to a pre-termination hearing. A state court agreed, but the New York Court of Appeals reversed. It found that **the officer's conduct conclusively established a lack of moral integrity**, an offense for which summary dismissal was appropriate. A pre-termination hearing was not necessary. *Feola v. Carroll*, 890 N.E.2d 219 (N.Y. 2008).

♦ A Pennsylvania youth counselor for delinquent students was arrested for perjury in a grand jury investigation unrelated to his work. The development center he worked for suspended him for 60 days, then fired him. He appealed to the state civil service commission and the case reached the Pennsylvania Supreme Court. The court held that **the arrest, by itself, was not sufficient to justify the discharge**. Here, needing just cause to fire the counselor, the center should have shown through an investigation how the arrest actually compromised his ability to do his job. *Woods v. State Civil Service Comm'n*, 912 A.2d 803 (Pa. 2007).

♦ A New Jersey toll collector, stuck in traffic on his way home from work, fired a paintgun at a slow-moving van. After he was fired, his union filed a grievance and an arbitrator ordered his reinstatement 11 months later. But he received no back pay and had to undergo physical and psychological fitness exams before he could return to work. The turnpike authority challenged the arbitrator's decision, and the New Jersey Supreme Court upheld the reinstatement. The court noted that the reinstatement did not violate public policy because **the law did not require someone convicted of disorderly conduct to forfeit his job.** Also, the arbitrator's award was reasonable; the collector lost nearly a year's wages and had to undergo fitness-for-duty exams. *New Jersey Turnpike Authority v. Local 196*, 920 A.2d 88 (N.J. 2007).

♦ A task force in Wisconsin learned that some Madison firefighters were involved in illegal drug activity. One firefighter admitted using cocaine and marijuana before recanting his admission. Disciplinary charges were filed against him, and he was eventually fired for violating five departmental rules, including one requiring him to observe "laws and ordinances," another requiring him to "speak the truth at all times" and a third requiring him to conduct himself so as not to bring "disrepute" to the department. He sued and the Court of Appeals upheld the termination. **The rules put him on notice that he could be fired for off-duty drug use.** *Gentilli v. Board of Police and Fire Commissioners*, 717 N.W.2d 853 (Wis. Ct. App. 2006).

♦ New Jersey authorized private companies to run many local motor vehicle agencies. An employee at one of the companies was convicted of "official misconduct" for conspiring with his boss at a local department of motor vehicles to issue fake licenses and registrations. He appealed the conviction, **arguing that he could not be convicted of official misconduct because he was not a public employee.** The Supreme Court of New Jersey upheld the conviction, noting that the employee and his boss were carrying out a governmental function for the state, and that the law was intended to prevent the perversion of government authority. *State of New Jersey v. Perez*, 883 A.2d 367 (N.J. 2005).

♦ An Internal Revenue Service (IRS) employee in Arizona told her ex-husband she was going to call the agency and request an audit if her husband failed to return tax exemption forms that would entitle the employee to a child care credit for their daughter. The ex-husband then called the IRS to report the threat, and the IRS fired the employee for violating the 1998 IRS Reform and Restructuring Act. She challenged the firing, and the U.S. Court of Appeals, Federal Circuit, ruled against her. Even though the employee was incapable of affecting the audit, she still misused her position by making **a prohibited threat to audit for personal gain.** *James v. Tablerion*, 363 F.3d 1352 (Fed. Cir. 2004).

♦ Two Michigan deputies were charged with granting inmates preferential treatment in exchange for gifts and favors. A third deputy was charged with padding the department's overtime. At a preliminary hearing, the trial court concluded that the prosecution failed to link the inmates' gifts to the deputies' favors and dismissed the charges. The court of appeals affirmed on the ground that deputy sheriffs did not hold public office. The court of appeals concluded instead that the deputies were public employees and, as such, were not capable of engaging in the crime of misconduct in office. The Michigan Supreme Court held to the contrary, noting that a **"deputy sheriff is a public official for purposes of misconduct in office charges** when the allegations supporting the charges arise from the performance of that deputy's official duties." *People v. Coutu*, 589 N.W.2d 458 (Mich. 1999).

* The Bureau of Alcohol, Tobacco and Firearms issued a letter stating that law enforcement officers previously convicted of a misdemeanor crime of domestic violence who continue to possess firearms would be violating the Omnibus Consolidated Appropriations Act of 1997 and might therefore be subject to criminal penalties. As a result, a Georgia deputy sheriff who had pled "no contest" to misdemeanor battery in a domestic violence case was fired. He appealed to the county personnel board and then sued, asserting that the statute was unconstitutional. A federal court determined that limiting the ability of a domestic violence misdemeanant to possess a firearm was reasonably related to Congress' purpose of protecting public safety by keeping firearms out of the hands of potentially dangerous or irresponsible persons. Although the ultimate effect of the facially neutral statute might be to **bar certain domestic violence misdemeanants of a career that requires the ability to possess a firearm legally**, the classification was rational and not discriminatory. *National Ass'n of Government Employees, Inc. v. Barrett*, 968 F.Supp. 1564 (N.D. Ga. 1997).

C. Violations of Employer Rules and Policies

Many employers establish specific rules and policies, which employees must abide by in order to avoid disciplinary action or employment termination. Included in the category of employer rules and policies are orders given by superior officials, which employees also must follow to avoid discipline.

1. Rules and Policies

* An investigator at a Louisiana prison had surgery for prostate cancer, during which radioactive seeds were implanted in his body. A common side effect of that treatment is fatigue. A few weeks later, he fell asleep on the job. Rather than resign, he accepted a demotion to prison guard so he could keep his medical insurance. He then appealed to the civil service commission, which upheld the decision to demote him. The Louisiana Court of Appeal affirmed, explaining that **sleeping on the job in a prison "inherently impairs the efficiency of the public service"** and actually would have allowed for termination. *Shortess v. Dep't of Public Safety & Corrections*, 991 So.2d 1067 (La. Ct. App. 2008).

* A Missouri city employee with a history of violent outbursts told an HR coordinator that a park naturalist had made sexual comments towards him at about the same time the naturalist informed her supervisor that the employee

had blown up at her when they were discussing park policy. The city investigated and was unable to confirm any harassment by the naturalist. It suspended and then fired the employee, who sued for retaliation under state law. A federal court and the Eighth Circuit ruled for the city, noting that **even if the employee had a reasonable belief he was opposing sexual harassment, he was still legitimately fired for violating workplace rules.** The city reasonably believed he'd made false allegations and verbally abused the naturalist. *Richey v. City of Independence,* 540 F.3d 779 (8th Cir. 2008).

♦ A Chicago police officer was fired for violating department rules prohibiting other employment while on paid medical leave. The officer, while on paid medical leave for injuries sustained in a car accident, also worked as a security guard for the Chicago Board of Education at an elementary school. She asserted that she should not be fired because **she was unaware her employment with the board of education violated department rules.** After an administrative review, she was suspended for five years. The Appellate Court of Illinois then held that the police board had a sufficient basis for firing the officer. It did not matter that other officers who committed offenses she deemed more serious were not fired. No completely related case existed as a basis for comparison. *Siwek v. Police Board of City of Chicago,* 374 Ill.App.3d 735, 872 N.E.2d 87 (Ill. App. Ct. 2007).

♦ A Pennsylvania Department of Transportation senior highway maintenance manager sent his male subordinates off-color e-mails despite an agency policy against such behavior. After an investigation and a pre-termination hearing, he was fired. Ten months later, the civil service commission determined that **although the e-mails were inappropriate, they were not sexually suggestive or pornographic.** Thus, the commission reinstated and demoted him, noting that his behavior reflected poorly on his role as senior manager. Both he and the department appealed, and the Pennsylvania Commonwealth Court upheld the action taken. His conduct justified the demotion, and he was not entitled to back pay or seniority for the 10 months he was off the job. *Webb v. State Civil Service Comm'n,* 934 A.2d 178 (Pa. Commw. Ct. 2007).

♦ An airport worker's supervisors discovered discrepancies between his badge swipes and his time sheets, and were unable to locate him at work one day. After he served a suspension, he left work early without telling his supervisor. The airport fired him and he filed a grievance, claiming a violation of the collective bargaining agreement. An arbitrator ruled that even though his misconduct was a serious breach of trust, the airport did not have "just cause" to fire him, and it changed the termination to a 30-day suspension. The Commonwealth Court of Pennsylvania ruled that the airport in fact had just cause to fire the worker. **He misused his security badge,** and firing him was core to the airport's public mission of maintaining a secure facility. *Allegheny County Airport Authority v. Construction General Laborers and Material Handlers Union,* 874 A.2d 1250 (Pa. Commw. Ct. 2005).

- An employee with an Indiana city had an exemplary record for her first nine years on the job. However, her behavior then began to change. She breached client confidentiality, provoked fights at work, habitually returned late from lunch and wore a head covering to work in violation of the agency's dress code. She was suspended, demoted and fired, after which she sued for age and gender discrimination. A federal court and the Seventh Circuit ruled against her. She was not able to show that people outside her protected class were treated better than she was. **Her insubordination seemed to be a reaction to major changes in the agency** and justified the discipline taken against her. *Jordan v. City of Gary*, 396 F.3d 825 (7th Cir. 2005).

- A school bus driver in New York worked for 13 years without a single blemish on her record. Then a co-worker reported her for erratic driving. She confronted the co-worker, used threatening and obscene language and stated that she was going to "get a hit out on" him. The school district filed disciplinary charges against her, and a hearing officer recommended termination. The school board adopted the hearing officer's findings and recommendation. A trial court held that termination was too harsh given the driver's previous employment record, but the Supreme Court, Appellate Division, reversed. Here, the termination was not so shocking to the court's sense of fairness that it had to be set aside. **The safety issues raised by the dangerous driving and the threats justified the firing.** *Bottari v. Sarasota Springs City School Dist.*, 771 N.Y.S.2d 261 (N.Y. App. Div. 2004).

- A nurse at a veteran's center in Pittsburgh was fired for making three medication errors in one year. She was ordered reinstated when the evidence supported only one medication error. Before she was officially reinstated, the state required her to pass a physical exam. During that exam, she informed the nurse that she suffered back pain from an old injury. The center's director of nursing then required her to provide medical documentation of her ability to do the job without restrictions. She refused, and the center rescinded the reinstatement offer. She appealed from an order of the Civil Service Commission upholding the termination, and the Commonwealth Court of Pennsylvania affirmed the ruling against her. **An employer may condition an employee's return to work on a medical exam after an absence if the job in question is physically demanding.** The court also noted that the employee failed to tell the center whether she intended to return to work. *Florian v. State Civil Service Comm'n*, 832 A.2d 1171 (Pa. Commw. Ct. 2003).

- A Colorado Department of Corrections employee told investigators that one of her supervisors had sexually harassed her. Subsequently, she recanted that assertion and stated that he did not harass her. The department fired her on the grounds that her conduct violated its administrative regulations. She appealed to the state personnel board and then to the Colorado Court of Appeals, asserting that the statements she made in the proceeding involving her supervisor were privileged and thus improperly relied upon for her termination. The court of appeals disagreed. Here, **the employee violated regulations that required her to "demonstrate the highest standards of personal integrity"** and "cooperate fully with the office of the Inspector General." To allow her false statements to be privileged would frustrate public policy. As a result, the employee's firing was justified. *Hoffler v. State of Colorado*, 7 P.3d 989 (Colo. Ct. App. 1999).

♦ A former purchasing director of a New Jersey state university sued after he was fired for extensive misconduct. He claimed that he had been discharged in retaliation for filing discrimination complaints with the university's affirmative action office. After he brought suit, the university learned that he had been convicted of taking bribes while serving as purchasing director for a Pennsylvania transportation agency. The university sought pretrial judgment under New Jersey law, which disqualifies anyone with a past criminal conviction from holding public employment in the state, but the trial court denied the university's motion. The appeals court reversed. Here, **the director had lied on his job application about ever having a criminal conviction**. Even though the university could not ordinarily defeat a wrongful discharge claim simply by showing a misrepresentation on a job application, because the director was absolutely disqualified under state law from holding the position, the university was prohibited from hiring him and would have been required, in any event, to discharge him once it became aware of his conviction. *Cedeno v. Montclair State Univ.*, 725 A.2d 38 (N.J. Super. Ct. App. Div. 1999).

♦ Massachusetts law prohibited police officers and firefighters from smoking either on or off the job. A town's police chief received complaints that an officer was smoking excessively in her cruiser. The officer admitted to smoking and stated that she was having difficulty in trying to quit. The chief suspended her without pay for five days and recommended that she be fired. After she was fired, she appealed to the civil service commission, which held that she should be restored to her position upon demonstrating that she no longer used tobacco. The Supreme Judicial Court of Massachusetts noted that **the purpose of the no-smoking law was to prevent police officers and firefighters from increasing their risk of hypertension and heart disease** – conditions that those employees are already at high risk of developing. The court upheld the decision to fire the officer. *Town of Plymouth v. Civil Service Comm'n*, 686 N.E.2d 188 (Mass. 1997).

♦ A Maryland police officer damaged a county fuel pump when she drove away with the nozzle still in the car. Among the documents placed in her file was a report that documented the damage to county property. On that form, her supervisor wrote "counselled" under the section on steps taken to prevent reoccurrence, even though it was the second such incident. The police officer also received an internal investigation notification form. Later, she received a second such form from a lieutenant investigating the incident. The police officer was found to have violated department rules, and the acting chief imposed a $400 fine. After her appeal to an administrative hearing board, she was found guilty. The board recommended disciplinary action of a $150 fine, which the acting chief imposed. A state court reversed the board's decision, and the county appealed to the Court of Special Appeals of Maryland.

The officer alleged a violation of the Double Jeopardy Clause of the

U.S. Constitution, which prevents individuals from being subject to multiple punishments and prosecutions. She argued that the first punishment entailed the counseling and placement of the documents in her file, and the second punishment was the chief's $150 fine. The multiple prosecution argument rested on the two forms with their respective punishments. The court of appeals held that **the county did not institute multiple punishments or prosecutions**. The counseling and placement of documents in her file was not punishment but was merely a remedial administrative action. Thus, no violation of the Double Jeopardy Clause existed. The court reversed the circuit court decision. *Montgomery County v. Krieger*, 678 A.2d 621 (Md. Ct. Spec. App. 1996).

2. Refusal to Follow Orders

♦ A Missouri police officer's employment record showed a number of performance problems, including difficulty resolving conflicts with other employees. He also ranked in the bottom one-third for traffic stops and was formally advised about the possible misuse of sick time. After several more incidents, the chief called a meeting, at which several other officers called the officer a "back-stabber" and directed other insults at him. A few weeks later, the city council voted to suspend him. Unbeknownst to the council, he had hired an attorney to defend him against charges that he was spreading rumors about the department. **The day after the city learned that he had hired an attorney, he was fired for refusing to attend a meeting with the chief** (on the advice of his attorney, who could not attend the meeting with him). He sued the city, alleging a First Amendment violation, and lost. The Eighth Circuit held that the city had documented his performance problems before he hired the attorney, and the fact that he was fired the day after the city learned of that association did not make the discharge retaliatory. *Morris v. City of Chillicothe*, 512 F.3d 1013 (8th Cir. 2008).

♦ A Louisiana police officer, who was third in command of the department, began sick leave for a work-related adjustment disorder, as diagnosed by his psychiatrist. The police chief ordered him to submit to an independent medical examination by a psychiatrist, and to bring his medical records with him. The officer failed to comply with the order and was fired for insubordination. He challenged the termination, claiming that he didn't show up for the psychiatric examination because his records hadn't yet arrived at the doctor's office. However, the doctor testified that he could have conducted the exam first and reviewed the records later. Further, **because the officer was third in command, his failure to follow orders impaired his ability to supervise the 80% of the force under his authority**. The officer was properly fired. *Almerico v. Harahan Municipal Fire and Police Civil Service Board*, 973 So.2d 799 (La. Ct. App. 2007).

♦ When a sergeant and a captain with the department of corrections for a New York county refused to assist in the internal investigation of a corrections officer suspected of smuggling contraband to inmates, charges were brought against them. Although the charges were ultimately dropped, the sergeant and captain sued the county under 42 U.S.C. § 1983, asserting that they were deprived of their right to equal protection. They asserted that they were treated differently than other similarly situated corrections officers because of a malicious intent to injure them. The Second Circuit Court of Appeals ruled against them, noting that **the department had a legitimate interest in having them participate in the investigation.** Also, the motivation for the charges was to secure their compliance with departmental objectives, not malice. *Bizzarro v. Miranda*, 394 F.3d 82 (2d Cir. 2005).

• Two civilian Navy employees **refused to be vaccinated for anthrax** when their ship was headed for a port in Korea. They asserted that they were entitled to medical waivers (one because he had asbestosis as a result of exposure to Agent Orange in Vietnam, and the other because he suffered headaches and body pains after receiving the first two doses of the anthrax series). The employees were transferred off the ship, then removed from the Navy in administrative proceedings. The case reached the Federal Circuit Court of Appeals, which upheld the employees' removal for insubordination. Removal was within the discretion of the administrative law judge and was neither an unauthorized nor an excessive penalty. *Mazares v. Dep't of the Navy*, 302 F.3d 1382 (Fed. Cir. 2002).

• An Iowa firefighter with a poor disciplinary record was ordered by her supervisor to come into his office to review a performance evaluation. She refused because the supervisor had allegedly made previous unwelcome sexual overtures while they were alone in his office. She was fired for refusing to obey his order, and the civil service commission affirmed the discharge. The Court of Appeals of Iowa held that not every refusal to obey a supervisor's order amounts to misconduct. First, because there was evidence showing that the firefighter had been subjected to unwelcome sexual touching in a previous private meeting in her supervisor's office, the court found her refusal to obey his order reasonable. While it was true that the firefighter's employment history was tainted by numerous incidents of misconduct, her history did not preclude her from objecting to inappropriate sexual behavior. Second, even if the firefighter's allegations against her supervisor were untrue, the court held that **her "misconduct" did not warrant discharge because it was not detrimental to the public interest** and did not bring into question her ability to perform her job as a firefighter. *Clay v. City of Cedar Rapids*, 577 N.W.2d 862 (Iowa Ct. App. 1998).

• Allegations of sexual assault were brought against an Illinois police officer. In order to determine whether he was fit for duty and whether he should be referred for counseling, the officer was ordered by his supervisor to undergo a psychological exam. Even though the psychological exam was not considered part of the disciplinary process, the officer refused because he believed the request was wrong. The police board fired the officer based on his refusal to obey a direct order and because of his prior disciplinary record of nine sustained charges of misconduct. The Appellate Court of Illinois found that the officer's refusal was not justified by his mistaken belief that he should not have to take a psychological exam. **An officer does not have the prerogative of actively disobeying an order from a supervisor** while he subjectively determines whether the order is lawful or reasonable. The officer was properly fired. *Haynes v. Police Board of Chicago*, 688 N.E.2d 794 (Ill. App. Ct. 1997).

* Shortly before verdicts were returned in the federal cases against the officers involved in the Rodney King beating, a California police sergeant was required to implement the police department's civil unrest response plan. He complained about the plan's stand-by procedures, alleging violations of the labor association's Memorandum of Understanding. He also advised officers to claim 24 hours of overtime while on stand-by. The sergeant himself did not remain on stand-by or participate in devising and implementing the new plan as the department required. The department then transferred the sergeant to another division. He sued the department, claiming that the stand-by policy violated Fair Labor Standards Act (FLSA) overtime provisions. The court found an FLSA overtime violation but denied the sergeant's retaliation claim. The sergeant appealed to the Ninth Circuit, which held that the reasons for the transfer were legitimate and non-retaliatory. **The transfer took place because of the sergeant's lack of cooperation with the stand-by procedures, willful disobeyance of orders, and willingness to create dissent during a critical time.** The sergeant's complaints about the stand-by policy and overtime advice were held to be insignificant reasons for the transfer. The court of appeals affirmed the district court decision. *Knickerbocker v. City of Stockton*, 81 F.3d 907 (9th Cir. 1996).

* A blind social worker employed by the North Carolina Department of Human Resources was ordered to teach certain lifetime skills to a blind client infected with AIDS. The services requested by the client would require the use of sharp objects. After learning that AIDS patients suffering blindness are in the most contagious stages of the disease, she expressed safety concerns to her supervisor. Although the supervisor knew that the social worker instructed by touch, she issued a memorandum confirming the order to serve the client. The social worker's requests for proper training about how to prevent the spread of AIDS were denied. She was fired for insubordination. The Court of Appeals of North Carolina held that the department unreasonably required the untrained, blind social worker to give hands-on instruction involving sharp instruments to the AIDS patient. Moreover, **because there was good cause for the social worker's refusal to treat the patient, the department had improperly found that this action amounted to insubordination**. Without assurance that a sighted employee would perform the hands-on training, the social worker's refusal was not a punishable offense. The court overturned the discharge and awarded attorneys' fees to the social worker. *Mendenhall v. North Carolina Dep't of Human Resources*, 459 S.E.2d 820 (N.C. Ct. App. 1995).

* An employee of a state mental retardation center had to retrieve a resident who created a disturbance and ran off. The resident was injured, and the employee and his supervisor refused to submit to a polygraph examination. After they were fired, they sued. The Mississippi Supreme Court held that the

request for the exam was reasonable. It noted that the center had a duty to investigate any injury to a resident, and that employees had a duty to cooperate. **The court agreed with a number of decisions that have upheld dismissal of public employees based on a refusal to take a polygraph exam.** The employees had signed pre-employment statements authorizing polygraph exams. They also were advised of the limited scope of the exam, and were granted a guarantee that the results would not be used in later criminal proceedings. The dismissals were upheld. *Jackson v. Hudspeth Mental Retardation Center*, 573 So.2d 750 (Miss. 1990).

D. Off-Duty Misconduct

Public employees may be disciplined or discharged for their conduct while off duty. A public employee's behavior that negatively reflects on the officer and department, thereby reducing the effectiveness of the department, may result in disciplinary action.

• While in uniform and on her way to work, **a black Alabama corrections officer showed up at another county's jail, where her son was incarcerated. She was disrespectful to the sheriff there.** He wrote a letter to her boss complaining of her behavior. She was suspended for 15 days, with five days deferred pending six months of good behavior. When she appealed, the county personnel board extended the suspension to 15 days with no deferred days. She sued under 42 U.S.C. §§ 1981 and 1983, alleging race discrimination. A federal court and the Eleventh Circuit ruled against her. The two white officers who allegedly received preferential treatment were not similarly situated. One acted inappropriately in a private residence, and the other directed his inappropriate behavior toward a civilian and not a high-ranking officer of a neighboring county. *McCann v. Tillman*, 526 F.3d 1370 (11th Cir. 2008).

• A Louisiana police sergeant was fired after he was arrested for driving while intoxicated (DWI) and careless operation of a motor vehicle. His blood alcohol level registered .152%, but he claimed it was because he had taken Nyquil. He later admitted to drinking whisky as well as Nyquil. After his termination, he was acquitted of driving while intoxicated. He then challenged the termination, claiming he had been coerced into admitting he drank whisky in order to retain his retirement benefits and that his acquittal required his reinstatement. The Court of Appeal ruled against him. Here, **he had committed other misconduct besides the DWI**, including asking the arresting officers not to process his arrest as a DWI and making false statements. The sergeant was properly fired. *Bailey v. Dep't of Public Safety and Corrections*, 951 So.2d 234 (La. Ct. App. 2006).

• A deputy court administrator in New Jersey was pulled over for speeding. She refused to put down her cell phone, resisted being handcuffed and kicked out a side window of the police car. She later tested at 0.10 and 0.11 on the breathalyzer. After she was fired, she appealed to the merit systems appeal board, which reduced her discipline to a six-month unpaid suspension. An appellate court upheld that determination. **The employee had a spotless record prior to her arrest** and she suffered a panic attack during the arrest, which permitted the lesser punishment for conduct unbecoming a public employee. *Thurber v. City of Burlington*, 903 A.2d. 1079 (N.J. Super. Ct. App. Div. 2006).

♦ An air traffic controller in Missouri claimed that she was subjected to a hostile work environment. She also claimed that she was fired in retaliation for her complaints. The Federal Aviation Administration maintained that the reason for the firing was the deteriorating atmosphere in the workplace caused by her complaining. She got a job at a bank, then sued under Title VII. A jury awarded her damages, including back pay, and she then sought front pay in lieu of reinstatement. Meanwhile she was fired from her bank job for processing a false loan application. The Eighth Circuit held that **the after-acquired evidence doctrine applied to the employee's post-termination misconduct**. Thus, the employee might be denied front pay if her post-termination misconduct would render her ineligible for reinstatement. The court remanded the case. *Sellers v. Mineta*, 358 F.3d 1058 (8th Cir. 2004).

♦ A New York police officer cooperated with internal affairs investigators over the cover-up of a hit-and-run accident involving the brother of a state trooper. About a year later, while assigned to protect the lieutenant governor, he was found passed out or asleep (and possibly intoxicated) behind the wheel of an official car. He claimed that in retaliation for his cooperation in the earlier investigation, co-workers conducted an excessive and prolonged investigation into his off-duty misconduct. He sued, asserting violations of the First, Fourth and Fourteenth Amendments, and arguing that he should have been afforded the courtesy of the "blue wall of silence" by his fellow officers. A jury awarded him compensatory damages of $1.5 million. However, the Second Circuit reversed, finding no constitutional violations. **He had no right to be treated in such a way as to protect him from the consequences of his misconduct.** *Diesel v. Town of Lewisboro*, 232 F.3d 92 (2d Cir. 2000).

♦ A "Morale, Welfare and Recreation" (MWR) manager at a Marine Corps camp in North Carolina had an affair with the wife of a Marine major who was assigned overseas. When the affair was discovered, the manager was fired. He appealed to the Merit Systems Protection Board, which upheld the discharge. On further appeal, the Federal Circuit affirmed. Even though the manager's **off-duty misconduct** was private in nature and did not affect his official responsibilities, it **impaired the efficiency of the Marines' operations**. Further, because trust in MWR managers was essential, and because his misconduct undermined that trust, the Navy was justified in firing him. *Brown v. Dep't of Navy*, 229 F.3d 1356 (Fed. Cir. 2000).

♦ A Montana county deputy sheriff, while off duty, was at a bar with a friend who refused to leave after repeated requests. When other deputies arrested the friend, the deputy became verbally abusive. After the deputies left, he began breaking things at the bar and locked himself in. Eventually, he came out and was brought to the county jail, where he damaged the jail surveillance camera. The deputy was charged with a criminal offense, and the county terminated his employment based on his conduct that night. After his termination, he moved to dismiss his criminal charge, claiming that his prosecution violated the Double Jeopardy Clause of the U.S. Constitution because the same conduct underlying the criminal prosecution formed the basis for his employment termination. The district court dismissed the charge on this basis, and the state appealed to the Supreme Court of Montana, which held that **a public employee may be both terminated from employment and criminally prosecuted without violation of the Double Jeopardy Clause**. Employment termination served the legitimate non-punitive, remedial purpose of protecting public safety and property, and of promoting public confidence and trust in law enforcement. *State of Montana v. Schnittgen*, 922 P.2d 500 (Mont. 1996).

♦ A psychologist employed by the Nevada Department of Prisons formed a corporation with the aim of establishing a brothel, saloon and dance hall, all legal activities within the state. He then hired inmates through a hobby craft program to type mailing labels and stuff envelopes with flyers advertising his venture and offering coupons to the brothel. Although he did not seek explicit approval from his supervisor, he allegedly discussed his plans with a supervisory employee and followed established procedures in obtaining inmate labor. After these activities were reported in local newspapers, the department fired the psychologist for his alleged violations of several administrative rules and regulations. On appeal, a hearing officer found only two violations and remanded the matter for imposition of a less severe discipline. The Supreme Court of Nevada noted that a hearing officer's view of the facts are entitled to deference and should not be disturbed if they are supported by substantial evidence. **Although the psychologist's venture had little social value, it was legal in the state and did not permanently affect his ability to do his job.** Consequently, the court upheld the hearing officer's ruling and remanded the matter to the department for imposition of progressive discipline, ranging from suspension to demotion. *Knapp v. State, Dep't of Prisons*, 892 P.2d 575 (Nev. 1995).

♦ A police officer employed by an Arkansas city police department attended a Halloween party at the Fraternal Order of Police (FOP) Lodge dressed in black face, wearing bib overalls and a black, curly wig, and carrying a watermelon. Although the party was not an official police function, many off-duty police officers attended. Several African-American police officers objected and ultimately resigned from the FOP. In response, the department conducted several prejudice reduction workshops and discharged the officer for violating two department rules prohibiting derisive behavior and conduct that could result in the justified criticism of the officer or the department. On appeal to the Civil Service Commission, the officer testified that he wore the costume "to have a good time." The commission upheld the discharge, and the officer sued the city, alleging First Amendment and due process violations. A federal court ruled for the city, and the U.S. Court of Appeals, Eighth Circuit, affirmed. The officer's costume was not intended to convey a "particularized message" and was therefore not protected speech under the First Amendment. Because **the regulations under which the officer was disciplined were rationally related to the department's legitimate interest in maintaining discipline,** *esprit de corps,* **and uniformity within its ranks**, the court held that they were not unconstitutionally vague and overbroad. *Tindle v. Caudell*, 56 F.3d 966 (8th Cir. 1995).

IV. LAYOFFS FOR FINANCIAL REASONS

Employees who become subject to layoff for financial reasons may be entitled to certain protections described in state laws or contained in an applicable collective bargaining agreement. However, laid off employees may not be entitled to the same notice and due process protections that are afforded to employees who are discharged for cause.

♦   A New York building department aide worked full time for a town for over four years until it restructured its building department. To keep down costs and increase efficiency, the town eliminated her position and created two part-time positions. She sought reinstatement to her old job, as well as back pay and benefits, but the Supreme Court, Appellate Division, ruled against her. First, she failed to prove that she worked in a noncompetitive class position for five continuous years. Second, even if she had been in a protected position, **the town could eliminate her position for purposes of economy or efficiency**. Although the town may not have saved money by its actions, it did increase its efficiency by being open 16 more hours per week, by not closing over the lunch hour, and by allowing her benefits to go to a full-time building inspector it was able to hire by eliminating her position. *Lamb v. Town of Esopus*, 35 A.D.3d 1004, 827 N.Y.S.2d 307 (N.Y. App. Div. 2006).

♦   A materials manager and a solid waste supervisor with the city of Albuquerque informed city council members about wasteful spending and inefficiency in the solid waste department's vehicle maintenance division. **A newly elected mayor then ordered all department heads to reduce their budgets.** As a result of that directive, the two employees were transferred out of their division. They kept their job titles, salaries and benefits. Nevertheless, they sued for retaliation under the First Amendment, claiming their transfers had been substantially motivated by their complaints on a matter of public concern. The Tenth Circuit Court of Appeals ruled against them. Here, the appointed official who transferred the employees apparently did not even know about the complaints they had made to the city council. *Maestas v. Segura*, 416 F.3d 1182 (10th Cir. 2005).

♦   The District of Columbia closed a prison complex because federal law required it. At the same time, because of congressional appropriations and the surplus of corrections officers from the closing prison, the mayor approved a series of reductions in force among corrections officers. The layoffs occurred shortly after more inmates were transferred to the existing penal facility. The officers' union sued the mayor and the Department of Corrections under 42

U.S.C. § 1983, claiming deliberate indifference to the officers' safety in violation of the officers' substantive due process rights. The U.S. Court of Appeals, D.C. Circuit, ruled that the defendants' actions were not so egregious or outrageous that they shocked the conscience. Also, they never intended to injure the officers; they merely made a personnel and program decision in response to a congressional dictate. *Fraternal Order of Police v. Williams*, 375 F.3d 1141 (D.C. Cir. 2004).

♦ Six years after they were laid off, former county engineers in Massachusetts learned that the county violated their rights to a hearing before a retirement board when it discharged them. They sued in state court for back pay, claiming the county failed to follow the procedural requirements of a state statute in effect at the time. While the lawsuit was pending, the state legislature repealed the statute, and the trial court dismissed the case. The Appeals Court of Massachusetts affirmed. The new statute did not include a "savings clause," which would have protected the engineers' interest in the pending lawsuit. **Even if the engineers had been given notice and a hearing, the retirement board probably would have upheld the county's reason for laying them off** – to avoid a substantial budget crisis. *Dupont v. Commissioners of Essex County*, 704 N.E.2d 530 (Mass. App. Ct. 1999).

♦ A town council in Indiana held a public hearing to discuss the upcoming year's budget. At the hearing, a council member proposed that the number of deputies in the town's police department be reduced by two. The budget was adopted by a unanimous vote of the council, effectively terminating the employment of the two least senior-officers as of the end of the year. The two officers sued, asserting that the council had illegally terminated their positions by failing to give them notice and a hearing as required by Indiana law. They also asserted that the council had not acted in good faith when it eliminated their positions. After the court ruled for the council, the Court of Appeals of Indiana affirmed. The council was exempt from the notice and hearing procedures because the statute did not apply when a town was exercising its authority to eliminate positions under the economic exception. Here, the officers were being dismissed for economic reasons, which did not amount to disciplinary action against them. **Since the actions were position-directed and not person-directed, the officers were not entitled to the procedures available for "for cause" dismissals.** Also, there was no showing of bad faith. *Pfifer v. Town of Edinburgh*, 684 N.E.2d 578 (Ind. Ct. App. 1997).

♦ A New York City superintendent engineer employed by the U.S. Postal Service (USPS) was informed that he would be affected by a nationwide restructuring to eliminate positions. He also was notified that he would not be laid off or receive a reduction in pay or grade but could be reassigned to a new geographical location. Later, the USPS offered supervisory employees not yet reassigned the opportunity to voluntarily participate in an incentive program where they could receive cash payments for accepting bargaining unit positions in lieu of reassignment. The engineer applied for the incentive program by the specified date and accepted an offer of employment. After the Merit Systems

Protection Board (MSPB) issued decisions holding that the restructuring had resulted in an appealable reduction-in-force (RIF) action, the engineer filed an appeal, asserting that the decision to accept the other position had been involuntary. The U.S. Court of Appeals, Federal Circuit, found that the engineer had voluntarily accepted the incentive program. Thus, he had no appealable RIF action. The decision to accept the incentive program offer occurred prior to any action by the USPS. The USPS never informed him he would not be selected for reassignment to a position at his previous grade level or retained in another executive and administrative schedule position. The court also noted that **there was no obligation to notify the engineer of his RIF rights because he received no notice of reassignment or release from the USPS prior to acceptance of the offer.** *Torain v. U.S. Postal Service*, 83 F.3d 1420 (Fed. Cir. 1996).

♦ The Virginia governor ordered his cabinet secretaries to abolish "duplicative" or "unnecessary" positions in their respective agencies. Three employees had their positions abolished as a result, and a fourth was temporarily ordered to report directly to his agency head. The fact that an employee reported directly to an agency head automatically changed the employee's classification and exempted that employee from the protections afforded by the Virginia Personnel Act (VPA), including the right to file grievances for various employment decisions. The employees sued, claiming a property interest in their former classifications and positions. The Fourth Circuit Court of Appeals noted that the Virginia code did not grant state employees a "legitimate claim of entitlement" to continued employment at a particular classification. Thus, regardless of how the employees were classified, the VPA provided no remedy. Virginia granted the governor broad discretion over personnel matters and the employees' reclassification was therefore lawful. Also, the classified employees were not entitled to pre-termination due process. **No property right exists when employees are dismissed for non-grievable circumstances** such as "reduction in work force" and "job abolition." *Mandel v. Allen*, 81 F.3d 478 (4th Cir. 1996).

♦ The Board of Tax Appeals of Ohio discharged a certified fiscal officer after it abolished his position in a staff reorganization. Following the reorganization, and citing efficiency concerns, the executive director hired a new unclassified employee to perform all fiscal duties. The discharged fiscal officer sued the board, alleging that the abolishment of his position was in bad faith. The Court of Appeals of Ohio noted that state law authorized abolishment of positions for "efficient operation of the appointing authority, for reasons of economy, or for lack of work." However, **an employee whose position has been abolished has the right to any available vacancy within the employee's classification**. Here, the board had transferred the officer's job duties to a new employee in order to subvert the civil service system. The board should have allowed the officer to fill the new "more efficient" position. Consequently, the abolishment of the officer's position was in bad faith. The court ordered the board to reinstate the officer. *Swepston v. Board of Tax Appeals of Ohio*, 626 N.E.2d 1006 (Ohio Ct. App. 1993).

V. RETALIATION

Public employers are prohibited from dismissing employees in retaliation for the good-faith exercise of rights protected by state and federal laws, including the filing of claims for workers' compensation benefits and complaints of discrimination. For cases dealing with retaliation for filing discrimination charges, please refer to Chapter Five, Retaliatory Discrimination.

A. Whistleblower Protection Acts

The Whistleblower Protection Act, which prohibits adverse employment action against employees who report violations of law, protects federal employees from retaliatory discharge. Many states also have enacted similar legislation to protect employees from good-faith reports concerning violations of law.

1. Retaliatory Actions

♦ The head of a nonprofit organization that administered the city of St. Louis' women and minority business enterprise program made comments to the newspaper that criticized the way the program was run. Four months later, a new mayor decided to move the program to the St. Louis Airport's disadvantaged business enterprise office, and the employee lost his job. He sued the city for First Amendment and whistleblower retaliation, claiming that he should have been rehired to a comparable job. However, the Eighth Circuit ruled against him because he never applied for a new job. Nor did he show that a comparable job had opened up. Further, **even if certain officials told him he would be rehired, they were not responsible for hiring personnel for the airport program.** *Green v. City of St. Louis*, 507 F.3d 662 (8th Cir. 2007).

♦ An accountant in the Detroit Police Department wrote a letter to the deputy chief, detailing what he believed was mismanagement in the department's Fiscal Operations Division. When the deputy chief did not respond, the accountant sent another letter to the chief and sent a copy to the mayor. Seven months later he was allegedly called in to a meeting with the deputy chief, who **told him his letter to the chief and the mayor was the last straw and that he'd better start looking for a job**. His duties were also reduced, according to his testimony. He sued under the Michigan Whistleblowers Protection Act and a jury awarded him $600,000. The city appealed, and the Court of Appeals of Michigan upheld the award. The jury had sufficient evidence to find for the accountant, and the award was not excessive under the whistleblower statute. *Heckmann v. City of Detroit*, 2007 WL 1989518 (Mich. Ct. App. 7/10/07).

♦ A Missouri firefighter told the chief that he and other firefighters had been having sex at the fire station. After talking with his attorney, he signed a disciplinary agreement that allowed him to keep his job. The agreement provided that he would be suspended for six months and demoted, and that he would not sue the union or the fire department. After he returned to work, he complained to his superiors that he was threatened by co-workers upset with his statements. He then sued for First Amendment violations and sex discrimination. A Missouri federal court ruled against him, and the Eighth Circuit affirmed. Here, **the waiver of his right to sue was binding**. It was not signed under duress even though his alternative was to be fired. *Littrell v. City of Kansas City*, 459 F.3d 918 (8th Cir. 2006).

♦ A Newark police officer claimed that the city retaliated against him because he gave information to federal investigators about a police director who was then convicted of embezzlement. He sued the city more than two years after he was denied a promotion and transferred to a position under the command of a hostile supervisor. He claimed violations of his First Amendment rights under 42 U.S.C. § 1983 and his whistleblower rights under state law. The case reached the Third Circuit, which held that **even though the continuing violation doctrine applied to Section 1983 cases, it did not apply where the retaliatory actions were discrete**, as opposed to a series of related acts that added together amount to retaliatory harassment. Here, the acts taken against him were largely discrete. Therefore, he was bound by the two-year statute of limitations and had waited too long to sue. *O'Connor v. City of Newark*, 440 F.3d 125 (3d Cir. 2006).

♦ An assistant U.S. attorney in Cleveland ran the environmental crimes task force and prosecuted a businessman for illegally dumping hazardous waste at an airport. While prosecuting that case, the attorney determined that the National Aeronautics and Space Administration was illegally dumping waste on its landfill next to the airport. He investigated the dumping and then, after suffering adverse action, filed a whistleblower lawsuit against the government, claiming that the Department of Justice retaliated against him for conducting the investigation. The case reached the Sixth Circuit, which ruled against the attorney. It stated that **he was not a whistleblower because his job required him to conduct the investigation into possible illegal dumping**. Thus, he was not doing anything outside the scope of his regular duties, and was not "risking his personal job security" by conducting the investigation. His whistleblower claim failed. *Sasse v. U.S. Dep't of Labor*, 409 F.3d 773 (6th Cir. 2005).

♦ A police officer filed a discrimination complaint on behalf of a fellow officer, then experienced retaliation and filed another complaint, eventually retiring and suing the city under Massachusetts' whistleblower law. After a jury awarded him $90,000 in damages as well as $41,000 in interest, the city claimed that he failed to provide the requisite notice under the whistleblower statute. The First Circuit ruled against the city, noting that it waited too long and therefore was deemed to have waived the defense. *Bennett v. City of Holyoke*, 362 F.3d 1 (1st Cir. 2004).

♦ An outspoken New Jersey firefighter and self-proclaimed advocate of fire safety challenged a number of departmental policies and was a vocal opponent of the town manager's proposal to close two fire stations and replace the fire code official with a civilian. After several disciplinary actions were taken against him because of charges by the chief and the town manager, he sued the township and various officials for retaliation under the First Amendment. A jury awarded him $382,000 in compensatory damages, and $150,000 in punitive damages, but the Third Circuit reversed in part. Although a jury could reasonably attribute retaliatory motives to the town manager's actions against the firefighter, those actions could not result in liability for the township because the town manager was not the final policymaker on employment decisions. Also, there was no evidence that the town manager acted out of either recklessness or callousness. As a result, the punitive damages award was struck down, and the award of compensatory damages had to be reassessed to determine how much should be paid by the town manager. *Brennan v. Norton*, 350 F.3d 399 (3d Cir. 2003).

♦ An employee at a correctional center in North Carolina reported to prison officials that her supervisor made inappropriate sexual comments and gestures to her. She claimed that the prison officials then retaliated against her by increasing her workload and giving her poor performance evaluations. Rather than proceeding administratively under the State Personnel Act, the employee sued under the Whistleblower Act. Using the Title VII retaliation standard, a state court ruled in favor of the prison. The North Carolina Court of Appeals affirmed. Here, the employee was assigned more work because one co-worker was on long-term sick leave and another co-worker had been transferred to another facility. The remaining staff, including the employee, had to pick up their workload as a result. Also, the employee received "below good" evaluations from more than one supervisor for missing work, being tardy and poor co-worker relations. Thus, she failed to overcome the prison's **legitimate, non-retaliatory reasons for the actions taken against her**. *Wells v. North Carolina Dep't of Corrections*, 567 S.E.2d 803 (N.C. Ct. App. 2002).

♦ A probationary drug agent with the Puerto Rico Department of Justice became suspicious of corruption in the Special Investigations Bureau where he was assigned, and reported three different incidents to his supervisor. However, during an internal investigation, it was revealed that he also jeopardized agents' lives during a surveillance and made other mistakes in undercover operations. The department maintained his probationary status for three years. He filed a lawsuit under 42 U.S.C. § 1983, **asserting that his continued probationary status was retaliation for his whistleblowing activities**. A federal court and the First Circuit ruled against him, finding no First Amendment violation. Even if the agent's supervisors were unhappy with his whistleblowing activities, they had legitimate reasons for their actions. His poor performance on surveillance and undercover operations justified the extension of his probationary period. *Guilloty Perez v. Pierluisi*, 339 F.3d 43 (1st Cir. 2003).

♦ A food service instructor at a Pennsylvania prison discovered that inmates were stealing thousands of pounds of meat and selling it to other inmates, who operated an illegal sandwich-making enterprise. When he reported the activity to the prison's deputy superintendent, he was ostracized by some of the staff and harassed by inmates. The prison then reassigned him to the food service line in the dining hall, a less desirable post with no supervisory duties. The prison did so to reduce friction between staff and inmates and not for any retaliatory reason. Nevertheless, the reassignment prevented him from earning extra pay or being considered for promotion. He sued the Department of Corrections for lost back wages under the state whistleblower act, but a trial court dismissed his action, finding that the department had no retaliatory motive when it reassigned him. The Pennsylvania Supreme Court reinstated his lawsuit. **It did not matter that the department did not have a retaliatory motive** because the statute required only that the department take action as a result of the report of wrongdoing. Here, despite its good intentions, the department admitted it would not have reassigned the employee except for the report of meat theft. Thus, the employee could sue for lost back wages. *O'Rourke v. Comwlth. of Pennsylvania Dep't of Corrections*, 778 A.2d 1194 (Pa. 2001).

* A psychologist at a federal prison in Florida wrote a memo to the associate warden seeking to formalize an agreement with the base hospital for use of its facilities in the event there was a suicidal inmate. Alternatively, he wanted to create a suicide watch room at the prison. He later called an official to notify him that directives requiring confidentiality of counseling information might have been violated when his department's telephone log was copied during an investigation of his conduct by prison officials. **He was later reassigned to a new facility and claimed that it was done in retaliation for his whistleblowing activities.** The Federal Circuit Court of Appeals held that the psychologist could not show that he reasonably believed that a law, rule or regulation was being violated such that his disclosures would be protected by the Whistleblower Protection Act. With respect to the memo, he failed to show that the informal agreement in place presented a substantial safety risk. As for his phone call, the telephone log was not intended to contain confidential information, and he failed to show that confidential information was copied from it. The reassignment was upheld. *Herman v. Dep't of Justice*, 193 F.3d 1375 (Fed. Cir. 1999).

* A Tennessee Valley Authority (TVA) nuclear power plant engineer attended to the plant's conformance with fire safety regulations issued by the Nuclear Regulatory Commission (NRC). When the TVA switched from the use of "staff augmentees" in its nuclear engineering program to "managed task contracts," nearly 1,000 staff augmentees, including the engineer, were not given contract renewals. Two weeks after the expiration of the engineer's contract, the NRC announced a surprise inspection of the plant to investigate safety regulation compliance. In preparation for the inspection, plant officials recommended the formation of a review team to investigate apparent noncompliance with the safety regulations. One official stated that "he did not want any contractors working on problems which they had discovered." The engineer filed a complaint with the U.S. Secretary of Labor, alleging that the official statement constituted direct evidence of retaliatory discrimination in violation of the whistleblower provision of the Energy Reorganization Act. The secretary denied the claim, and the engineer appealed to the Sixth Circuit.

The court of appeals affirmed, ruling that **the official's decision not to hire** the engineer because he had discovered the problem was the result of a legitimate and pragmatic policy determination. The goal of hiring a review team whose members brought a new and fresh perspective to detected problems was part of a policy untainted by unlawful discrimination. The engineer failed to introduce evidence that belied this explanation. The court held that the engineer failed to state a *prima facie* case of retaliatory discrimination and dismissed the case. *Bartlik v. U.S. Dep't of Labor*, 73 F.3d 100 (6th Cir. 1996).

2. Employment Termination

♦ A Michigan city employee who worked as a crane/shovel operator believed that dirt being removed from a former dumping ground was toxic. He initially refused to move the dirt despite being shown documentation that it was safe. After he agreed to move it, his superiors tested it for toxins. He took sick leave, complaining to the state's occupational health agency that toxins in the dirt may have made him ill. After an extended sick leave, he returned to work and attended a seminar with people from other cities as well as some private sector employees. During a break, he told an instructor that a supervisor once asked a co-worker to punch a hole in a building wall so he could declare the building ready for emergency demolition. This implied that the city was involved in illegal demolitions. He was fired, then sued for protection under the state's whistleblower act. A federal court ruled against him, noting that **he failed to prove his discharge was related to his complaint of toxins in the soil. Instead, he was fired for his inappropriate comment at the seminar.** *Hester v. City of Flint*, 2008 WL 2397632 (E.D. Mich. 6/11/08).

♦ An Idaho fire rescue receptionist complained that two co-workers' constant talking amounted to a waste of manpower and amounted to office mismanagement. **She claimed that two lieutenants told her to keep a log of the wasted time, and then began keeping a secret diary.** One of the co-workers found it while covering for her on a lunch break. When she refused to apologize for the diary, the chief fired her for disrupting employee relations. She sued under the state's whistleblower law, and a court granted pretrial judgment to the county. The Idaho Supreme Court reversed, finding issues of fact that required a trial. Even though she did not present the diary to her superiors prior to her termination, she may have kept the diary with the intent to do so. *Curlee v. Kootenai County Fire & Rescue*, 2008 WL 4595239 (Idaho 10/16/08).

♦ A North Carolina public employee worked as a finance officer for a regional health services agency. After she was fired, she claimed that the reason for the termination was retaliation for whistleblowing activity, which came about when she told a superior that a fellow employee had been fired illegally, and that if he sued the agency, she would testify truthfully. The agency claimed **the termination was for breaching her confidentiality obligations with respect to patient information**, in violation of HIPAA, state and local privacy laws. When she sued the agency, she lost. The North Carolina Court of Appeals noted that she never testified or cooperated in any governmental investigation into the fellow employee's termination. She merely stated an intent to do so. Further, the agency offered a legitimate reason for her firing – her breach of confidentiality with respect to patient medical information. *Holt v. Albemarle Regional Health Services Board*, 655 S.E.2d 729 (N.C. Ct. App. 2008).

♦ A deputy city administrator in Michigan sent newspaper articles to city officials regarding the person they intended to hire as city administrator, but failed to explain why he sent the articles. The articles discussed allegations of legal problems. When the city hired the candidate, the candidate fired the deputy administrator, who then sued for wrongful termination under the state's Whistleblowers' Protection Act. The Michigan Court of Appeals ruled for the city, noting that **the deputy administrator was not entitled to whistleblower protection because he did not make a "report" under the law**. He merely gave newspaper articles to city officials without explaining why he was doing so. *DeMaagd v. City of Southfield*, No. 267291, 2006 WL 2312086 (Mich. Ct. App. 8/10/06).

♦ A supervisor of tax appraisers in the District of Columbia Office of Tax and Revenue (OTR) disagreed with his boss about how to handle an informal practice known as the "five-o'clock" rule. Under the rule, a property owner could withdraw an appeal to a tax appraisal by 5:00 p.m. on the day of the hearing (so as to avoid the risk of an increased assessment). As a result of the disagreement, he refused an order to call a property owner's attorney and made a report to the OTR's inspector general. When his boss fired him, he sued under the District of Columbia's Whistleblower's Protection Act. He asked the court to enjoin the OTR from carrying out the termination until the whistleblower claim was resolved. The court refused to do so, and the District of Columbia Court of Appeals upheld that decision. Since the supervisor helped create the rule, he could not reasonably have believed that his boss's order pursuant to the rule was illegal. *Zirkle v. District of Columbia*, 830 A.2d 1250 (D.C. App. 2003).

♦ A University of Texas employee alleged that she was fired for using a telephone hotline, set up by the state workers' compensation act, to report a violation of the act by the university. After the university notified her that she was being fired, she initiated a first-level appeal (by notifying her immediate supervisor). After this was denied, she initiated a second-level appeal (a letter to the personnel manager), which also was denied. Rather than initiate a third-level appeal (a written statement explaining why the termination decision was unacceptable), she sued under the state's Whistleblower's and Workers' Compensation Acts. The Texas Court of Appeals dismissed her claims, finding that **the university had sovereign immunity on the workers' compensation act claim**, and that the employee failed to remain in the appeals process under the Whistleblower Act for the required 60 days. *Univ. of Texas Medical Branch at Galveston v. Savoy*, 86 S.W.3d 782 (Tex. Ct. App. 2002).

♦ The head radiologist at a Florida VA clinic discovered that a radiology technician under his supervision was not properly certified. He notified a human resources officer and voiced concerns about the technician's certification for the next three years. After he reported that the technician failed to follow instructions during two different procedures, the technician's union intervened. During a subsequent investigation, the patients involved in the procedures contradicted the radiologist's version of the events. The radiologist was fired for abusive and threatening behavior several months later. He challenged his discharge before the Merit Systems Protection Board (MSPB), then sued the VA under the Whistleblower Protection Act, asserting that the VA took the technician's side because it was afraid of his union. The Federal Circuit Court of Appeals ruled in favor of the VA. It upheld the MSPB's ruling that **the radiologist would have been fired even if he had not engaged in whistleblowing activities.** *Yunus v. Dep't of Veterans Affairs*, 242 F.3d 1367 (Fed. Cir. 2001).

♦ A lawyer with the South Carolina Department of Corrections filed an affidavit with the department's personnel administrator questioning the circumstances surrounding how a manager for the prison records division was hired. Although the manager had scored the highest on a written exam, she had been allowed to consult reference materials while taking the test. The lawyer was fired a month later for having bad work habits and a poor attitude. He sued, asserting that his termination violated the state's whistleblower act, and a state court dismissed the case. The state supreme court affirmed, noting that **the lawyer had failed to identify in his affidavit any prison policy, practice or rule that the manager or state officials broke** in the process. This was a necessary element of such a claim and, thus, his whistleblower claim failed. Further, he could not show that he had been fired in violation of public policy because he was not asked to violate the law and his firing itself did not violate the law. *Lawson v. South Carolina Dep't of Corrections*, 532 S.E.2d 259 (S.C. 2000).

♦ A county investigator was ordered by his superiors to provide testimony to the attorney general's office in a case involving the chief investigator and one of his lieutenants. They were alleged to have used their positions to purchase three vehicles leased to the county's narcotics task force. The investigator's testimony apparently supported the allegations. However, state officials later declined to bring criminal charges. The county prosecutor then brought administrative charges against the two investigators but resigned shortly thereafter. A new prosecutor took over but, in the meantime, the chief investigator also resigned. The charges against him were then dropped. After the lieutenant pled guilty to neglect of duty, the new prosecutor reinstated him. Subsequently, the investigator who had testified was fired. He sued under the state's whistleblower protection act, and the Supreme Court of New Jersey found that he was entitled to the act's protections. **The act was not limited to situations involving employer misconduct.** It also applied where an employee communicated information regarding co-employee misconduct to employers or public bodies. The case was remanded for a determination as to whether the reasons given for the investigator's firing were a pretext for retaliation under the act. *DeLisa v. County of Bergen*, 755 A.2d 578 (N.J. 2000).

- A branch director of the Ohio Bureau of Workers' Compensation wrote a report to her supervisor regarding the statewide director's attempt to authorize successive payments of more than $16,000 to a claimant who was not entitled to them. She also wrote to the assistant for the bureau's top administrator about an overpayment issued as part of a collective bargaining settlement. She was then fired for poor performance. She appealed to the state personnel board, claiming that she had been retaliated against for attempting to block improper expenditures of state funds. The personnel board upheld the termination, as did the Ohio Court of Appeals. Substantial evidence supported the firing, including her failure to meet stated goals and increasing backlogs. The branch director also had developed an adversarial relationship with employees in her office, particularly union representatives, and she spent a lot of time defending complaints against her. These problems predated the whistleblower actions. So, **while her report to internal security regarding the statewide director involved protected action, the personnel board could reasonably find that it was not the basis for her termination.** *Wade v. Ohio Bureau of Workers' Compensation*, No. 98AP-997, 1999 WL 378409 (Ohio Ct. App. 1999) (Unpublished).

- A school district in Washington had a whistleblower policy that required employees to submit a written report to their supervisor or a district designee, identifying in detail incidents believed to be improper. The policy also stated that an employee would not be eligible for whistleblower protection if he or she failed to make a good-faith attempt to follow the reporting procedures. When a maintenance manager was asked to move furniture at his supervisor's home during lunch, **he did not follow the district's whistleblowing policy, but rather asked a co-worker, who had not been present, to report it.** After his department was eliminated in a district-wide reorganization, the manager claimed that the district fired him in retaliation for reporting supervisory misconduct. The Washington Court of Appeals rejected the manager's argument that because he had authorized the co-worker to use his name, the co-worker was acting as his agent. Further, a letter that the manager wrote to his supervisor regarding employees' compensation requests also did not amount to whistleblowing. The employee did not report any legal misconduct or abuse of authority. *Dewey v. Tacoma School Dist.*, 974 P.2d 847 (Wash. Ct. App. 1999).

- A highly regarded U.S. Border Patrol agent observed a Mexican drug smuggler crossing the border into Arizona. After losing radio contact with his partner, he fired several warning shots into the air and gave chase. His partner shot and killed the smuggler with an unauthorized weapon given to him by the agent and then suggested that they bury the body and not report the incident. The agent refused and, after waiting 15 hours, reported the shooting, as well as his own misconduct. The partner was tried and acquitted of murder, causing extensive negative publicity for the border patrol. After the border patrol fired the agent for his violation of agency regulations, the Merit Systems Protection Board upheld that decision, ruling that although the dismissal was partially based on the agent's protected disclosure, the border patrol would have taken the same action had it been alerted to the misconduct by some other means. The agent appealed to the U.S. Court of Appeals, Federal Circuit, alleging violations of the federal Whistleblower Protection Act (WPA). The court noted that **the WPA requires only that an agency demonstrate by clear and convincing evidence that it would have taken the same personnel action even absent the protected disclosure**. The dismissal was affirmed. *Watson v. Dep't of Justice*, 64 F.3d 1524 (Fed. Cir. 1995).

B. Wrongful Discharge

Some states allow claims for wrongful discharge based on adverse employment actions that violate public policy. The public policy exception to at-will employment often rests on issues of public safety or interest as well as First Amendment rights (see Chapter Three).

* A South Carolina police dispatcher and office worker received six written reprimands for violating the dress code, tardiness, performing poor work, leaving work without permission, and using abusive language. After she was fired, she sued for wrongful discharge, claiming that the employee handbook gave her certain grievance rights that the city did not follow. The Supreme Court of South Carolina ruled for the city. Even though the dispatcher should have been allowed to present evidence of grievance proceedings that occurred after her final termination date, the error in refusing to do so was harmless. **The city had ample reason to fire the dispatcher**, even if she could have proven the handbook created a contract that altered her at-will employment. *Conner v. City of Forest Acres*, 363 S.C. 460, 611 S.E.2d 905 (S.C. 2005).

* A male human resources employee of the Puerto Rico Highway Authority obtained confidential information about employees' salaries and became convinced that women were being paid more than men. He asked for a raise, citing the confidential information. Instead, the authority notified him that he was subject to termination for misusing the confidential information for personal purposes. After he was fired, he sued, claiming wrongful termination. A federal court and the First Circuit ruled against him. He received notice and an opportunity to be heard in accordance with his due process rights. And he **failed to show that the true reason for the discharge was his political affiliation**. *Cepero-Rivera v. Fagundo*, 414 F.3d 124 (1st Cir. 2005).

* A police officer investigated a burglary complaint at an apartment complex and got into an altercation with the sister of the alleged victim. He sought to arrest her, but was instructed by his supervisor not to do so. Later, however, he obtained warrants against her and her sister. After his superiors ordered him to take no further action in the matter as a police officer, he appeared in uniform and on duty before a magistrate judge and obtained an arrest warrant against his supervisor for obstruction of justice. He was then fired for disobeying an order and abuse of his position. He filed a wrongful discharge suit against the city, and the case reached the Supreme Court of Virginia, which noted that **the officer had no cause of action for wrongful discharge in violation of the state's public policy**. The obstruction of justice statute did not state a public policy, and allowing the officer to use it would permit wrongful discharge suits by virtually

any officer who thought personnel decisions obstructed the officer's enforcement of the law. *City of Virginia Beach v. Harris*, 523 S.E.2d 239 (Va. 2000).

• A therapist at a Tennessee hospital noticed that a new employee failed to properly clean medical equipment, drank alcohol while on call, reported late to work, and falsified her time cards. After supervisors ignored his complaints, the therapist asked for and received a transfer to a lower-paying job in another department. Subsequently, the employee brought a harassment grievance against the therapist. The therapist resigned seven months after that and sued the hospital under 42 U.S.C. § 1983, alleging constructive discharge in retaliation for the exercise of his free speech rights. A federal court ruled for the hospital, and the Sixth Circuit affirmed. Even if there was a First Amendment violation, the therapist could not establish that he had been subject to an adverse employment action as a result. Because the therapist waited seven months to resign after his last conflict, **he could not establish that the resignation was anything but voluntary.** *Coffey v. Chattanooga-Hamilton County Hospital Authority*, 194 F.3d 1311 (6th Cir. 1999).

• The chief of a Wisconsin city police department assigned a police captain to conduct an internal investigation in response to a citizen complaint. The captain uncovered evidence that the chief had intimidated and harassed certain witnesses and victims. The captain agreed to keep the alleged victims' identities confidential to avoid retaliation by the chief. He then failed to honor the chief's request to turn over the materials until he had opportunity to consult the district attorney about his pledge of confidentiality. The chief ultimately recovered the materials and filed a personnel complaint with the City Police and Fire Commission, seeking to terminate the captain's employment. After a two-day hearing, the commission suspended the captain without pay for 32 days, and a Wisconsin trial court affirmed the disciplinary measures. The captain then filed a wrongful discipline lawsuit in a Wisconsin trial court. The trial court dismissed the claim. The Supreme Court of Wisconsin agreed with the dismissal, noting that where the legislature has created a statutory remedy for wrongful discharge and wrongful discipline, that remedy is exclusive. Because the legislature already had enacted a statutory mechanism that protected police officers from being wrongfully disciplined, **they could not state a cause of action for wrongful discharge or wrongful discipline** by invoking the public policy exception to the employment-at-will doctrine. *Larson v. City of Tomah*, 532 N.W.2d 726 (Wis. 1995).

• A Montana landfill employee contacted the federal Occupational Safety and Health Administration (OSHA) and reported that his employer did not provide shelter, bathroom facilities, or any means of emergency communication. OSHA informed the landfill that failure to provide emergency communication to workers might be a violation of the Occupational Safety and Health Act. It then requested that the landfill investigate the conditions, make the necessary corrections, and advise OSHA in writing of the results. The landfill did not respond to OSHA and fired the employee. The employee filed a wrongful discharge lawsuit against the landfill in a Montana trial court, alleging that he had been fired in retaliation for reporting public policy violations. The trial court granted pretrial judgment to the landfill, ruling that because the employee's report did not result in an OSHA citation or investigation, he could not base his claim upon a violation of public policy. The employee appealed to the Supreme Court of Montana.

The supreme court reversed, noting that Montana law defines public policy as a policy, in effect at the time of the discharge, concerning the public health, safety, or welfare established by constitutional provision, statute, or administrative rule. Regardless of whether the employee's report actually resulted in a citation or investigation, a cognizable retaliation claim existed where the employee made the report in good faith. Although the report did not result in an OSHA citation, the landfill had failed to show that his report of working alone without emergency communication was baseless. Consequently, the supreme court held that **whether the discharge came in retaliation for a good-faith reporting of what he reasonably perceived to be a violation of public policy** raised a genuine issue of material fact with respect to the wrongful discharge claim. The trial court ruling was reversed, and the case was remanded. *Motarie v. Northern Montana Joint Refuse Disposal Dist.*, 907 P.2d 154 (Mont. 1995).

♦ An unclassified chief deputy clerk employed by the Municipal Court of the City of Cleveland, Ohio performed clerical, non-policy-making duties. She requested a leave of absence to become a candidate for the Cleveland City Council. Her supervisor refused the request and terminated her employment a month later. The clerk filed a tortious wrongful discharge lawsuit against her supervisor in an Ohio trial court, seeking reinstatement, back pay, punitive damages, and attorneys' fees. The trial court held for the clerk, but the court of appeals reversed. The clerk appealed to the Supreme Court of Ohio, which held that the state constitution does not guarantee unclassified public employees a right to seek partisan-elected office while holding public employment. **A public policy exception to the presumption of employment at will could be based on the Ohio and U.S. Constitutions, legislation, administrative rules, and the common law.** However, such an exception should be recognized only where "the public policy alleged to have been violated is of equally serious import as the violation of a statute." Because the clerk's at-will status as a public employee was prescribed by statute, not the common law, and her dismissal did not violate a constitutional right, there was no clear public policy against her dismissal. Consequently, the wrongful discharge claim was dismissed. The holding of the appellate court was affirmed. *Painter v. Graley*, 639 N.E.2d 51 (Ohio 1994).

♦ A New Jersey shop teacher who had not acquired tenure complained to the school principal about safety and air quality conditions in his metal shop. After submitting numerous complaints and being transferred to teach plastic shop, he complained to the superintendent of schools. The principal obtained an air quality test, which determined that the teacher's classroom was safe. He then recommended that the teacher not be rehired, thus depriving him of tenure. The teacher filed a lawsuit against the board of education, alleging retaliatory discharge in violation of the state Conscientious Employee Protection Act, and seeking punitive damages. A trial court awarded the teacher compensatory damages of $60,000 as well as punitive damages. The Supreme Court of New Jersey held that the record supported a finding that the board's action constituted retaliatory discharge. **The teacher had reasonably believed that his workplace was unsafe and his complaints were protected by public policy.** The board of education was liable to the teacher. *Abbamont v. Piscataway Board of Educ.*, 138 N.J. 405, 650 A.2d 958 (N.J. 1994).

VI. NATIONAL SECURITY

When national security is at stake, the federal government has fewer restraints when it comes to discharging employees. However, the government employer may not use national security as a pretext for eliminating all employees whose lifestyles do not meet with their employer's approval.

- The Navy hired a veteran's-preference civilian employee to work at its refit facility on the Trident submarine. All employee positions at the facility are classified as sensitive. While waiting for a security clearance, the employee performed only limited duties. His security clearance was denied after he had been at the facility for more than a year because the Navy discovered that he had several felony convictions. He was dismissed for cause after administrative proceedings were held, and he appealed. He argued that because he had been removed for cause and not for national security reasons, he had not been afforded sufficient procedural protections. The Ninth Circuit Court of Appeals agreed, and the Navy appealed to the U.S. Supreme Court. The Court held that the employee received sufficient procedural due process. It stated that the employee had been dismissed for cause because he did not have the necessary security clearance. **The decision not to issue a security clearance was not reviewable in this case, where national security granted broad discretion to the Navy to determine who should have access to classified information.** The Court held that since a security clearance was a requirement for employment at the facility, the clearance-denied employee had been dismissed for just cause. The Court reversed the court of appeals' decision. *Dep't of the Navy v. Egan*, 484 U.S. 518, 108 S.Ct. 818, 98 L.Ed.2d 918 (1988).

- The National Security Agency (NSA) terminated the employment of a cryptographic technician for engaging in homosexual relationships with foreign nationals. After a hearing, the employee's security clearance was revoked. Because this was a condition to NSA employment, his termination became final. The employee then requested a hearing before the Secretary of Defense, claiming that the 1959 NSA Act did not authorize termination without a hearing before the defense secretary. The secretary's response was that the removal was for cause under the NSA's regulations and did not require the secretary's authority. The employee sued the secretary, claiming that the act did not delegate authority to remove employees to the NSA's director. The case reached the U.S. Supreme Court.

The Court noted that the NSA Act authorized the defense secretary or his designee to establish positions and make necessary appointments to carry out the function of the agency. The authority to appoint also implied a power to remove. The act was not the exclusive means to remove NSA employees for national security reasons. The alternative selected by the NSA director was a correct procedure for removal because of permissive language in the act. **The secretary had broad discretion to terminate employees consistent with national security**, just as discretion was present in the selection of NSA employees. The termination procedure selected by the NSA director provided a hearing equivalent to that provided under the NSA Act. *Carlucci v. Doe,* 488 U.S. 93, 109 S.Ct. 407, 102 L.Ed.2d 395 (1988).

On remand, the court of appeals stated that the NSA neither violated nor misapplied its regulations. The case turned on whether the employee was terminated for cause, in which case Chapter 370 of the NSA regulations would apply, or terminated for national security reasons, in which case Chapter 371 would apply. The court stated that **the employee was terminated for cause, not for national security reasons**, as indicated by the fact that the NSA took 15 months to fire the employee after first giving notice. The court also stated that since a federal employee has no right to a security clearance, the employee could not argue that the NSA deprived him of a property interest without due process. The employee was denied no protectable liberty interest since the NSA's actions were not stigmatizing. *Doe v. Cheney,* 885 F.2d 898 (D.C. Cir. 1989).

* A Washington, D.C., man was hired as a clerk by the Central Intelligence Agency (CIA) and was later promoted to an undercover position. Over a six-year period, he was consistently rated "strong or outstanding" on fitness reports. Only at the end of this time did he disclose his homosexuality. He was placed on administrative leave and then discharged pursuant to the National Security Act. The clerk filed suit in federal court alleging that his termination violated the Administrative Procedure Act (APA) and his constitutional right to equal protection. The district court held that the clerk's termination violated the procedural rights due him under the APA, but the U.S. Court of Appeals, District of Columbia Circuit, reversed. On appeal, the U.S. Supreme Court held that **decisions made pursuant to the National Security Act could not be reviewed under the APA**, but "colorable constitutional claims" could be reviewed. *Webster v. Doe,* 486 U.S. 592, 108 S.Ct. 2047, 100 L.Ed.2d 632 (1988).

On remand, the district court held that the clerk had been deprived of a constitutionally protected property interest, and the CIA appealed to the U.S. Court of Appeals, District of Columbia Circuit. The court of appeals stated that given the CIA director's broad discretion involving termination decisions, **the clerk did not have a constitutionally protected property interest in his employment**. Nor did assurances made in the CIA handbook, or statements made by other employees, endow the clerk with an "agency fostered" property interest. Next, a single assertion by a security officer that the employee's homosexuality violated CIA regulations was not sufficient to establish a violation of the Equal Protection Clause. Finally, even if the CIA intentionally excluded homosexuals, the clerk's termination was not the result of such a policy. Rather, his nondisclosure of his homosexual activity implicated legitimate concerns about his trustworthiness. The holding of the district court with respect to the clerk's property claim was reversed. *Doe v. Gates,* 981 F.2d 1316 (D.C. Cir. 1993).

♦ An African-American civilian employee of the U.S. Navy's Military Sealift Command in the Philippines obtained a Nuclear Weapons Personnel Reliability Program (PRP) certification (equivalent to security clearance for purposes of this case) as a condition of employment. However, his PRP certification was revoked after several alleged disciplinary problems, including run-ins with Philippine and military police, verbal and physical altercations with other mariners, unfavorable performance reviews, and displays of disrespect toward superiors. He refused to accept assignment to another ship, which did not require PRP certification, and was discharged. The employee filed a Title VII race discrimination lawsuit against the Navy. The Ninth Circuit Court of Appeals noted that the U.S. Supreme Court ruling *Dep't of the Navy v. Egan* precludes judicial review of security clearance decisions made by the executive or his delegee. **Consideration of the employee's Title VII lawsuit would improperly require the court to perform some review of the merits of the security clearance decision.** Even when the court faced independent evidence of discriminatory motive, it still would be necessary to weigh the validity of the defendant's alleged reasons when deciding if they were pretextual. The court ruled in favor of the Navy. *Brazil v. U.S. Dep't of Navy*, 66 F.3d 193 (9th Cir. 1995).

CHAPTER THREE

Freedom of Expression and Privacy

	Page
I. FREEDOM OF SPEECH	177
A. Supreme Court Cases	178
B. The *Garcetti v. Ceballos* Issue	181
C. Protected Speech	183
1. Matters of Public Concern	184
2. Speaker's Interest Outweighs Government's Interest	186
3. Speech Reporting Criminal Activity	190
4. Prior Restraint	192
D. Unprotected Speech	193
1. Government's Interest Outweighs Speaker's Interest	194
2. Speech of a Personal Nature	199
3. Qualified Immunity and Other Defenses	204
E. Freedom of Association	207
F. Defamation	210
II. UNION AND POLITICAL ACTIVITY	214
A. Union Activities	215
B. Political Activities	218
1. Managerial and Discretionary Positions	219
2. Participation in the Political Process	224
3. Running for Public Office	227
4. Retaliation Against Same Party Members	229
C. Loyalty Oaths	230
III. PERSONAL APPEARANCE AND DRESS CODES	233
IV. RELIGIOUS FREEDOM	238
V. PRIVACY	242

I. FREEDOM OF SPEECH

The First Amendment to the U.S. Constitution guarantees freedom of speech and prevents the government from abridging that freedom without a good reason. However, certain kinds of speech are entitled to more protections than others. For example, the U.S. Supreme Court has held that obscenity is not protected by the First Amendment. Nor is defamation.

A. Supreme Court Cases

Pickering v. Board of Educ., 391 U.S. 563, 88 S.Ct. 1731, 20 L.Ed.2d 811 (1968), sets forth a balancing test to determine whether an employee's interest as a citizen in commenting upon matters of public concern outweighs the interest of the government in preventing that speech. If, for example, the government's interest in promoting efficiency in the workplace outweighs the employee's right to speak on a matter of public concern, then the speech will not be protected by the First Amendment.

The Court held in *Connick v. Myers*, 461 U.S. 138, 103 S.Ct. 1684, 75 L.Ed.2d 708 (1983), that a public employee's speech upon matters of purely personal interest is not afforded constitutional protection.

Under *Rankin v. McPherson*, 483 U.S. 378, 107 S.Ct. 2891, 97 L.Ed.2d 315 (1987), whether an employee's speech addresses a matter of public concern must be determined by the content, form, and context of a given statement as revealed by the entire record. Whether speech is protected is a question of law to be determined by the court.

- An Illinois school district fired a high school teacher for sending a letter to the editor of the local newspaper. The letter criticized the board and district superintendent for their handling of school funding methods. The letter particularly criticized the board's handling of a bond issue and allocation of funding between school educational and athletic programs. The teacher also charged the superintendent with attempting to stifle opposing views on the subject. The board held a hearing at which it charged the teacher with publishing a defamatory letter. The board then fired the teacher for making false statements. An Illinois court affirmed the board's action, finding substantial evidence that publication of the letter was detrimental to the district's interest. The Illinois Supreme Court affirmed the dismissal, ruling that the teacher's speech was unprotected by the First Amendment because his teaching position required him to refrain from statements about school operations.

    The U.S. Supreme Court disagreed that public employment subjected the teacher to deprivation of his constitutional rights. The **state interest in regulating employee speech was to be balanced with individual rights**. The Court outlined a general analysis for evaluating public employee speech, ruling that employees are entitled to constitutional protection to comment on matters of public concern. The public interest in free speech and debate on matters of public concern was so great that it barred public officials from recovering damages for defamatory statements unless they were made with reckless disregard for their truth. Because there was no evidence presented that the letter damaged any board member's professional reputation, **the teacher's comments were not detrimental to the school system** but only constituted a difference of opinion. Since there was no proof of reckless disregard for the truth by the teacher and the matter concerned the public interest, the board could not constitutionally fire him. The Court reversed and remanded the case. *Pickering v. Board of Educ.*, 391 U.S. 563, 88 S.Ct. 1731, 20 L.Ed.2d 811 (1968).

- An untenured teacher was not rehired after a number of incidents that led the school board to conclude that he lacked tactfulness in handling professional matters. After the board decided not to reemploy the teacher, he asked for and received a list of the reasons for the board's decision. The board gave general reasons for its failure to rehire the teacher and noted that he had made an obscene gesture and had given an on-air opinion about school dress codes at a local radio station. The teacher sued for reinstatement on the grounds that his discussion with the radio station was protected by the First Amendment and that to refuse reemployment was a violation of his free speech rights. An Ohio federal court and the Sixth Circuit agreed.

The U.S. Supreme Court reversed the lower court decisions, holding that apart from the actions for which the teacher might claim First Amendment protection, the board could have chosen not to rehire him on the basis of several other incidents. The radio station incident, while clearly implicating a protected right, was not the substantial reason for non-renewal. The board could have reached the same decision had the teacher not engaged in constitutionally protected conduct. **A marginal employee should not be able to prevent dismissal by engaging in constitutionally protected activity** and then hiding under a constitutional shield as protection from all other actions that were not constitutionally protected. The lower courts had to determine whether the board's decision could have been reached absent the constitutionally protected activity of phoning the radio station and, if so, whether remedial action to correct the constitutional violation would be necessary. *Mt. Healthy City School Dist. v. Doyle*, 429 U.S. 274, 97 S.Ct. 568, 50 L.Ed.2d 471 (1977).

- When the district attorney of New Orleans proposed to transfer an assistant district attorney (DA) to a different section, the assistant DA opposed the transfer. She expressed her views on the matter to several superiors. Shortly thereafter, she prepared and distributed a questionnaire to other assistant DAs in the office concerning the office's transfer policy, morale, the level of confidence in superiors, and whether the employees felt pressured to work for political campaigns, among other things. The district attorney then fired her for refusing the transfer and for insubordination in distributing the questionnaire. The assistant sued, alleging that she had been discharged in violation of her First Amendment rights. The district court agreed, and she was reinstated with back pay and attorneys' fees. The U.S. Court of Appeals, Fifth Circuit, affirmed.

The U.S. Supreme Court stated that in order to determine a public employee's rights of free speech, the balancing test of *Pickering v. Board of Educ.*, above, must be utilized. The interests of the employee as a citizen in commenting upon matters of public concern must outweigh the interest of the state, as employer, in promoting efficiency in the workplace. When **a public employee speaks not as a citizen upon matters of public concern, but as an employee upon matters of only personal interest**, a federal court is not the appropriate forum in which to review the wisdom of a personnel decision taken by a public agency in reaction to that speech. Here, except for the assistant's question regarding pressure to work in political campaigns, the questions were not matters of public concern. The state also need not prove substantial disruption of the office in order to justify dismissal when the First Amendment right is limited. Here, the district attorney's action was reasonable if he thought that the speech in question would disrupt the office, undermine his authority and destroy working relationships in the office. *Connick v. Myers,* 461 U.S. 138, 103 S.Ct. 1684, 75 L.Ed.2d 708 (1983).

♦   A nurse at an Illinois public hospital allegedly gave a negative report about the obstetrics department to a cross-trainee. She also criticized her supervisors, saying that they were "ruining the hospital." When the hospital fired the nurse, she sued, alleging that the discharge was in response to her criticism of the hospital's cross-training and staffing policies in violation of her First Amendment rights. The district court held for the supervisor and the hospital. The Seventh Circuit reversed, holding that the employee was discharged for engaging in speech protected by the First Amendment. The supervisor and the hospital appealed to the U.S. Supreme Court, which noted that **government action based on protected speech may violate the First Amendment even if the public employer honestly believes the speech is not protected**. However, the Court expressly declined to adopt a specific test to determine when to adopt procedural safeguards protecting employee speech. Instead, it looked to the facts as the employer reasonably found them to be. Here, there was a material issue of fact about the supervisor's actual motivation. The case had to be remanded to determine whether the nurse was fired because of her criticisms, and whether that speech was protected. *Waters v. Churchill,* 511 U.S. 661, 114 S.Ct. 1878, 128 L.Ed.2d 686 (1994).

♦   A data entry employee in a Texas county constable's office was discharged for a remark to a co-worker, after hearing of an attempt on President Reagan's life, "If they go for him again, I hope they get him." The statement was overheard by another employee who reported it to the constable. The employee sued, alleging that the constable had violated her First Amendment rights by firing her. The case reached the U.S. Supreme Court, which stated that **the content, form, and context of the employee's statement supported the conclusion that her speech was on a matter of public concern**. Although a statement that amounted to a threat to kill the President would not be protected by the First Amendment, the employee's speech, in this instance, could not be characterized as a threat. The Court also stated that the employee's relatively low position in the office and the lack of evidence that her statement interfered with the efficient functioning of the office undermined the argument that the state had an interest outweighing the employee's First Amendment rights. *Rankin v. McPherson,* 483 U.S. 378, 107 S.Ct. 2891, 97 L.Ed.2d 315 (1987).

♦   An amendment to the Ethics in Government Act broadly prohibited most federal employees from accepting any compensation for making speeches or writing articles. Two unions and several career civil servants below grade GS-16 sued to challenge the constitutionality of the act. The U.S. Supreme Court noted that although congressional directives are generally deemed valid, **the widespread impact of the honorarium ban improperly chilled potential speech before it happened**. Here, the blanket restriction on remuneration for any type of employee expression – even if the subject matter was not related to the individual's official duties – was overbroad. Because the act was not reasonably necessary to protect the alleged government interest, it was unconstitutional as applied to executive branch employees below grade GS-16. However, the act reasonably applied to members of Congress, judges and high-ranking officials in the executive branch. *U.S. v. National Treasury Employees Union*, 513 U.S. 454, 115 S.Ct. 1003, 130 L.Ed.2d 964 (1995).

B. The *Garcetti v. Ceballos* Issue

After the Supreme Court decided *Garcetti v. Ceballos*, below, courts began to look at whether an employee's speech is made pursuant to the employee's official duties. If so, the speech is not protected by the First Amendment.

• A deputy district attorney in California examined a search warrant affidavit presented by a defense attorney and determined that it contained serious misrepresentations. He recommended dismissing the case and, at a subsequent meeting, a heated discussion ensued. The district attorney's office decided to proceed with the prosecution, and the deputy district attorney was reassigned, then transferred to another courthouse and denied a promotion. He sued under 42 U.S.C. § 1983, claiming First Amendment violations. The case reached the U.S. Supreme Court, which held that **public employees who make statements pursuant to their official duties are not speaking as citizens for First Amendment purposes**. Thus, they are not insulated from employer discipline when they do so. Here, it was part of the deputy district attorney's job to advise his supervisors about the affidavit. If his supervisors thought his speech was inflammatory or misguided, they had the authority to take corrective action against him. *Garcetti v. Ceballos*, 547 U.S. 410, 126 S.Ct. 1951, 164 L.Ed.2d 689 (U.S. 2006).

• A computer analyst with the Texas Lottery Commission sent two e-mails to state legislators accusing the commission of racially based employment policies and financially fraudulent practices. He was fired two days later and sued under the First Amendment, claiming illegal retaliation. His supervisor claimed he was fired for insubordination for refusing to answer questions about the e-mails. He asserted that he had asked if the questions could be put in written form so he could provide written responses. The case reached the Fifth Circuit, which held that his speech was protected as a matter of law. **Unlike the employee in *Garcetti*, his speech (the e-mails) was not part of his job duties.** Thus, he was speaking on a matter of public concern and not as an employee. However, a jury would have to decide if he was fired for insubordination or in retaliation for his protected speech. *Charles v. Grief*, 522 F.3d 508 (5th Cir. 2008).

• A New Jersey police officer was involved in an investigation into another officer's alleged corruption. Eventually he testified in the case against the other officer. He claimed that he was then targeted for retaliation by his supervisor and the police chief. He resigned rather than take a demotion, and he sued under the First Amendment. A federal court denied the supervisor and the chief immunity, and the Third Circuit affirmed that decision. It held that the First

Amendment protected the officer's testimony even after *Garcetti*. **While testifying in a trial, the officer was speaking as a citizen on matters of public concern.** It did not matter if he was acting pursuant to his official duties during parts of the investigation. *Reilly v. City of Atlantic City*, 532 F.3d 216 (3d Cir. 2008).

♦ A New York police officer served as his precinct's training and safety officer. His duties included investigating health problems in the precinct. He conducted an investigation into employee illnesses and the toxicity of leaks in the precinct's underground fuel tanks. After he issued a report, the city began an environmental evaluation and found contaminants above OSHA and EPA standards. He claimed that he was then transferred to a less desirable precinct, given less desirable assignments and disciplined for trivial reasons. He sued for retaliation under the First Amendment, then amended his complaint to allege that he was retaliated against for filing the lawsuit. A federal court and the Second Circuit ruled against him. Under *Garcetti*, **his health report was not protected speech because it was part of his job.** And his lawsuit-related retaliation claim failed because it amounted to an airing of personal grievances rather than the advancement of a public purpose. *Ruotolo v. City of New York*, 514 F.3d 184 (2d Cir. 2008).

♦ An Illinois state trooper was assigned to manage a firing range used by both the state police and the public. He was responsible for all aspects of managing the range, including making sure it was safe at all times. After he began to experience joint aches, headaches and fatigue, he requested a blood test, which came back positive for lead. He expressed his concerns to his superiors about the lead levels at the range and requested that it be shut down so that the toxic lead could be cleaned out. The range was shut down, but he claimed that he was then improperly disciplined and that his supervisors made false statements about him to co-workers. He sued for retaliation under the First Amendment, but lost when the district court held that his speech was not protected under *Garcetti*. **His responsibilities included keeping the range safe, so his speech on lead levels was part of his official duties.** *Bivens v. Trent*, 2008 WL 1805760 (S.D. Ill. 4/18/08).

♦ A Missouri public works director was required to attend city council meetings to report about public works issues. He attended a training seminar that included a session on the state's "Sunshine Law." Afterwards, he became convinced the city council was violating the law by holding non-public sessions and passing city ordinances without public discussion. He raised his concerns at a number of meetings. Later, the mayor told him that open meetings were none of his business. A month after he told the mayor that he was going to meet with the assistant attorney general to discuss the issue, he was fired. He sued under 42 U.S.C. § 1983, claiming violations of his First Amendment rights. The city sought pretrial judgment, and the mayor sought qualified immunity, but a federal court and the Eighth Circuit refused to grant it. Here, the director was speaking as a citizen and not an employee when he criticized the closed-door meetings. **Even though he attended a seminar on the Sunshine Law, his job** was not to ensure its compliance. Thus, *Garcetti v. Ceballos* did not apply to deprive him of First Amendment protection. His lawsuit could continue. *Lindsey v. City of Orrick, Missouri*, 491 F.3d 892 (8th Cir. 2007).

• An Illinois police detective began working with federal agencies on a task force to combat his city's problem with gangs and drugs. He believed that some task force members leaked information about an impending raid so that several targeted suspects were able to evade arrest. When he reported the misconduct, he was told to keep quiet about the circumstances surrounding the raid. A short time later, he was removed from the task force and the investigation. He sued under 42 U.S.C. § 1983, alleging retaliation for engaging in First Amendment activity. A federal court and the Seventh Circuit ruled against him. **The detective was not speaking outside his capacity as an investigator** and task force member when he complained of the leak. Therefore, he was not speaking as a citizen entitled to First Amendment protection. *Sigsworth v. City of Aurora, Illinois*, 487 F.3d 506 (7th Cir. 2007).

• An Ohio police officer in charge of the canine handling program wrote a memo to his chief protesting the cost-containing decision to cut back on the number of hours that would be reimbursed for training police dogs. A month later, the officer was fired for insubordination and failing to report for duty after he refused to show up to assist with a drug search. He sued for wrongful discharge, asserting he was fired for exercising his First Amendment right to comment on a matter of public concern. The Sixth Circuit ruled against him, noting that under *Garcetti*, he was not protected under the First Amendment because **his memo was written in the course of his official duties**. Thus, he was not speaking out as a citizen. *Haynes v. City of Circleville, Ohio*, 474 F.3d 357 (6th Cir. 2007).

• A lab technician/detention officer for an Oklahoma county suspected that a particular drug test she conducted had yielded a false-positive result. The county did not have a confirmation procedure in place, and her supervisor repeatedly denied her request to implement one. She therefore arranged for a confirmation test by an outside hospital, which confirmed the false positive. The county then adopted a confirmation policy. However, she claimed her lab tech job was made more difficult and she was transferred back to a detention officer position on an evening shift. She told her supervisor she couldn't work the evening shift because she had to care for her children, and was fired when she didn't show up for the new job. She sued under the First Amendment and lost. The Tenth Circuit held that **her speech on the need for a formal confirmation policy was made pursuant to her official employment responsibilities**. Thus, she was not speaking as a citizen on matters of public concern. *Green v. Board of County Commissioners*, 472 F.3d 794 (10th Cir. 2006).

C. Protected Speech

When speech touches on a matter of public concern, as opposed to a purely private matter, it is afforded protection by the First Amendment. However, the employee's speech still must be balanced against governmental interests to determine if the speaker's rights outweigh those of the government.

1. Matters of Public Concern

♦ An Oregon police chief reported the city attorney to the state bar association after the attorney pressured her to dismiss criminal charges against his private clients. Afterwards, the city attorney criticized the chief on his Web site and at city council meetings. The chief eventually had an outburst that required her to see a psychologist. Then she took a few weeks' leave and filed for workers' compensation. While on leave, she was fired. She sued for wrongful termination, and the Oregon Court of Appeals allowed the case to proceed to trial. Here, she presented a viable First Amendment retaliation claim by making a preliminary showing that **the city had a policy of allowing its attorney to retaliate against anyone who spoke out against him**. *Dew v. City of Scappoose*, 145 P.3d 198 (Or. Ct. App. 2006).

♦ The Defense Logistics Agency (DLA) had a policy allowing employees to post information of general interest on various "notice bulletin boards." However, they could not post items of a religious nature or promoting outside businesses like real estate or Mary Kay. One ad was posted for the Combined Federal Campaign (CFC), a charitable fundraising organization for federal employees. In response, an Ohio employee sought to post a flyer warning co-workers that supporting the CFC might mean money going to support abortion, sexual promiscuity and homosexual agendas. When the DLA rejected his request to post the flyer, he sued. A federal court ruled in his favor, noting that the bulletin board was a non-public forum. Accordingly, the DLA could restrict employee access only if the restrictions were reasonable and not viewpoint discrimination. Here, **the DLA policy amounted to viewpoint discrimination**. *Lister v. Defense Logistics Agency*, 482 F.Supp.2d 1003 (S.D. Ohio 2007).

♦ A Hispanic New York police officer wrote a letter to his chief complaining about bigotry against Spanish-speaking officers. He later filed a hostile work environment lawsuit against the department, which settled. He also deliberately decreased the number of tickets he issued each month (allegedly to avoid antagonizing co-workers by creating more work for them). When he was passed over for a promotion because of his resulting low productivity numbers, he sued for First Amendment violations. The Second Circuit ruled against him, noting that **even though his letter and lawsuit were protected speech, the department had a legitimate reason for passing over him** – his deliberately low productivity scores. *Cotarelo v. Village of Sleepy Hollow Police Dep't*, 460 F.3d 247 (2d Cir. 2006).

♦ An auditor with the District of Columbia lottery board repeatedly told superiors that two of the board's contractors were engaged in fraudulent activities. They rejected his reports, and he ignored their repeated requests to stop his investigations. A few months after he accused the contractors of taking computer equipment without paying for it, he received an unsatisfactory performance evaluation and was transferred to a new position. The next day, the board announced that it was eliminating that position. After he lost his job, he sued under the First Amendment. **The board gave conflicting reasons for why it fired the employee – claiming it was a reduction in force and also asserting that his speech disrupted its operations.** As a result, the auditor was entitled to a trial. *Thompson v. District of Columbia*, 428 F.3d 283 (D.C. Cir. 2005).

* A New York music teacher helped a custodian file a gender discrimination lawsuit against the school district where they worked. Afterwards, she sued the district herself, claiming that she was removed from teaching orchestra because of her involvement with the custodian's lawsuit. The parties settled that lawsuit. Two years later, she sued the district again, claiming that the district was still retaliating against her by rejecting her for several band and orchestra teaching positions. The Second Circuit held that she could pursue this second lawsuit under the First Amendment because it was based on retaliation for her first lawsuit. **Her speech was on a matter of public concern because it involved gender discrimination as well as her potential testimony** in court or other administrative procedures. However, she would still have to show that the school district's actions were "adverse" and also that they were taken because she engaged in protected speech. *Konits v. Valley Stream Cent. High School*, 394 F.3d 121 (2d Cir. 2005).

* Two environmental inspectors for a Texas county sent in regular reports concerning septic system compliance with state and county health codes. They were fired after septic system designers, installers and builders complained that they were too strict in enforcing environmental standards. When they sued the county and various commissioners, the case reached the Fifth Circuit. The court of appeals held that the routine reports involved "public" speech and were more than just routine communication. In one fax, one of the inspectors stated that members of the county government were purposefully ignoring health violations to appease installers and builders of septic tanks. **The inspectors' speech involved exposing official misconduct.** The case would have to proceed to trial for a determination of whether the inspectors' speech outweighed the county's need for departmental efficiency and coordination. *Wallace v. County of Comal*, 400 F.3d 284 (5th Cir. 2005).

* An African-American convention center director in New Mexico sent e-mails to her supervisor protesting what she believed to be harsh treatment of minority customers and contractors who did business with the center. She also criticized her supervisor's handling of an African-American subordinate. Shortly thereafter, the mayor fired her for failing to keep the convention center clean. She sued under 42 U.S.C. §§1981 and 1983, claiming discrimination and wrongful termination in violation of her First Amendment rights. A jury awarded her $1.3 million and the Tenth Circuit Court of Appeals affirmed. A jury could reasonably find that she was fired in retaliation for her speech. Several city employees testified that conditions at the center were exemplary and that the supervisor and mayor were very close. **Even though some of the director's speech addressed her private dispute with her supervisor, much**

of it addressed a matter of public concern – race discrimination. *Hardeman v. City of Albuquerque*, 377 F.3d 1106 (10th Cir. 2004).

• A Pennsylvania city's director or emergency medical services (EMS) made statements to the press, in which he indicated that the city's EMS program was inadequately equipped and understaffed. He claimed the program was missing 500 calls a year as a result. In a second newspaper article, he warned that the combination of low pay and high demands was driving EMS paramedics into other fields, and stated that he believed a crisis was coming. A month later, he was fired. He sued the city under 42 U.S.C. § 1983, asserting that the termination was in retaliation for protected speech. The city argued that the speech was not protected because it was not on a matter of public concern. A federal court ruled in favor of the director, noting that **his statements were designed to raise awareness of potential threats to the public health and safety of the community**. *Lloyd v. City of Bethlehem*, No. 02-0830, 2002 WL 31341093 (E.D. Pa. 2002).

• An Illinois health inspector noted that a produce market was committing health violations because it was selling packaged food without a license. However, her superiors, including the mayor, took no action to stop the market from operating. The market closed in the fall, but reopened in the spring and even added another location. When the inspector again noted that it was committing health violations, her superiors allegedly told her to have no further involvement with the market. After a local newspaper reported the market's failure to obtain the proper health permits, the inspector spoke with the manager of the mall where the second market was located and told him that the market was in violation of its permit. She was then suspended for five days, after which she sued the mayor and another official for violating her First Amendment rights. A federal court granted the defendants pretrial judgment, but the Seventh Circuit reversed and remanded the case. It noted that **her speech was on a matter of public concern even though it contradicted the city's policy decision** not to take action against the market. There was also a question of fact as to whether the inspector had violated a superior's order to avoid involvement with the market. *Myers v. Hasara*, 226 F.3d 821 (7th Cir. 2000).

2. Speaker's Interest Outweighs Government's Interest

• A Missouri city employee bought a parcel of land for residential development and sought to have the zoning changed to allow it. The city initially approved the zoning request, then rescinded its approval. A lawsuit resulted and the employee received the zoning change as well as $20,000 in damages and attorneys' fees. However, he was then denied a promotion to a superintendent position. He sued the city and various officials for retaliation in violation of the First Amendment, **claiming he was denied the promotion because of his lawsuit**. A federal court granted pretrial judgment to the city and officials, but the Eighth Circuit reversed. It found issues of fact that required a trial. *Gunter v. Morrison*, 497 F.3d 868 (8th Cir. 2007).

- An Oklahoma public defender office changed its policy regarding the way in which requests for expert testimony were approved. A public defender believed that the policy would adversely affect clients' rights and yield grounds for appeal. When she told her boss about her concerns, he fired her. She sued him and the office under the First Amendment, alleging that she was fired for raising a matter of public concern. Both defendants sought to have the case dismissed on grounds of immunity, but the Tenth Circuit refused to do so. Clearly, the public defender's speech went beyond internal office procedure. It **related directly to the right of a criminal defendant to effective assistance of counsel.** Further, her speech outweighed her boss's interest in maintaining efficient operations because he conceded that her speech did not disrupt the office. *McFall v. Bednar*, 407 F.3d 1081 (10th Cir. 2005).

- A Texas police officer witnessed an arrest at which excessive force was allegedly used. He reported the incident to Internal Affairs. The chief ordered an investigation and issued a memo advising officers not to discuss the case. However, when a reporter approached the officer and asked about the incident, the officer defended two other officers who had observed the arrest and criticized the officer who had used excessive force. He also criticized the Internal Affairs investigation. The chief then demoted him from sergeant to patrol officer and fired him after a 90-day disciplinary probation period. The officer sued for retaliation under the First Amendment, and a federal court granted pretrial judgment to the city. The Fifth Circuit reversed, finding that the officer's statements had involved a matter of public concern. **For the city to prevail at trial, it would have to show that its interest in efficient operations outweighed the officer's interest in speaking out.** *Markos v. City of Atlanta, Texas*, 364 F.3d 567 (5th Cir. 2004).

- A probationary court administrator in Oregon supported the promotion of a court clerk who had won a Title VII retaliation suit against the city in the past. However, her supervisor was reluctant to promote the clerk, allegedly because of the prior discrimination claim. Eventually, the supervisor agreed to the promotion, but then extended the administrator's probationary period and fired her a month later. She sued the city, and a federal court granted pretrial judgment against her. The Ninth Circuit reversed, finding issues of fact as to whether the supervisor violated the First Amendment by firing the administrator. A jury would have to determine whether the city's interest in efficient government outweighed the administrator's right to speak out on a matter of public concern. The city might also be able to show that it had legitimate non-retaliatory reasons for firing the administrator. *Thomas v. City of Beaverton*, 379 F.3d 802 (9th Cir. 2004).

- An African-American high school teacher in North Carolina with excellent evaluations was promoted to assistant principal at a predominantly white elementary school because an "African-American presence" was needed there. However, the more she voiced her concerns about discriminatory treatment of African-American students, the more negative her evaluations became. After three years, she was reassigned to her high school teaching position. She sued the district superintendent and others for violating her First Amendment rights, but a federal court granted pretrial judgment to the defendants. The Fourth Circuit Court of Appeals reversed, finding that **her complaints about discriminatory discipline against African-American students involved a matter of public concern**, and that a trial was required to determine whether her protected speech outweighed the school district's interest in efficient operations. *Love-Lane v. Martin*, 355 F.3d 766 (4th Cir. 2004).

♦ Tensions arose between the newly elected Democratic mayor of an Indiana city and a department manager who had been appointed by the former Republican mayor. The manager agreed to take a non-supervisory position in the sanitation department and to stay low-key with respect to the union. While the employee was working at a demolition site, a waste management company driver asked him where to place a trash bin that was being delivered. The employee, apparently frustrated that such a simple task could not be properly handled by the city, responded with: "The city administration does not know what it is doing from one day to the next." A city resident overheard this remark and passed it on to the mayor, who fired the employee for insubordination. The city's board of public works conducted a post-termination hearing and concluded that the employee should be suspended for 45 days without pay and placed on a six-month probation. The employee sued under the First and Fourteenth Amendments, and the Seventh Circuit ruled in his favor. Here, **his comments were on a matter of public concern even though they did not contain "shocking revelations or insightful analysis"** as to why the administration was incompetent. And the mayor's interest in preventing office disruption did not outweigh the employee's interest in making the statement. Finally, the post-termination hearing did not satisfy the employee's procedural due process rights. *Wainscott v. Henry*, 315 F.3d 844 (7th Cir. 2003).

♦ Two nurses at a New York county jail (employed by a private contractor) wrote letters to public officials criticizing the jail's mental health services. They were later fired, and sued county officials for violating their First Amendment rights. In their lawsuit, they called the jail's administrator as a witness. He testified about matters of prison administration, problems with the mental health services and the county executive's role in firing the nurses. The next day, the administrator was informed that he was being investigated for failing to pay for blood tests he and his wife received through the jail. Apparently, the sheriff never sent him the bill. Two weeks later, on the same day the nurses settled their claim for $1.2 million, the sheriff suspended the administrator, firing him the following week. The administrator then sued the county, the sheriff and two other officials for wrongful discharge under the First Amendment and 42 U.S.C. § 1983. A federal court refused to grant the defendants qualified immunity, and the Second Circuit affirmed. **The administrator had a clearly established right to testify at trial about mismanagement at the jail.** And the sheriff's need to maintain smooth jail operations was outweighed by the administrator's (and the public's) interest in the testimony he provided. *Catletti v. Rampe*, 334 F.3d 225 (2d Cir. 2003).

♦ A firefighter shift captain reported to the chief that hundreds of files of hard-core pornography existed on the fire station's computers. The pornography had been downloaded from the Internet despite a policy prohibiting firefighters from displaying nude pictures and videotapes. There was not a specific policy prohibiting the use of computers to view pornographic Web sites. The chief turned the matter over to the local police chief, who conducted an investigation but ultimately filed no charges. Meanwhile, the shift captain was reprimanded after a male co-worker reported that he had made sexually inappropriate remarks in front of a female firefighter. He received a second reprimand for forcing open a locked door (the key was missing) to get a list of replacement firefighters after a firefighter called in sick. He was finally fired for meeting with his staff to determine what problems they had with his leadership. This was interpreted by management as creating a hostile work environment. When he sued fire department officials for violating his First Amendment rights, an Idaho federal court refused to grant the defendants immunity. The Ninth Circuit Court of Appeals affirmed. Here, the shift captain's speech involved a matter of public concern, and the interest served by allowing him to express himself outweighed the department's interest in promoting workplace efficiency and avoiding workplace disruption. Thus, **if he was fired for his whistleblowing activities, he was wrongfully terminated**. The court remanded the case for trial. *Hufford v. McEnaney*, 249 F.3d 1142 (9th Cir. 2001).

♦ A firefighters' union in California supported an incumbent mayor's opponent. After the incumbent's reelection, the city council voted for significant cuts in fire service and the dismissal of firefighters. At the council's request, an outside accounting firm traced payroll problems to the firefighters' informal practice of receiving overtime for working unscheduled shifts regardless of whether they had worked their scheduled shifts. Even though the practice was allowed under the union contract, the fire chief launched his own investigation into the matter. Meanwhile, a fire broke out in a residential area, resulting in the death of a child. A firefighter who also served as the union's public information officer **told the local paper that the tragedy was the direct result of the mayor and city council placing politics above people's safety**. The firefighter was fired a month later and sued, claiming he had been retaliated against for exercising his First Amendment rights. The district court ruled for the city, but the Ninth Circuit reversed. In light of the slashed budget and layoffs, the statement conveyed far more than an accusation against the city council for having caused the child's death. Further, the firefighter's interest in making the statement outweighed the department's interest in promoting the efficiency of public service. Finally, the firefighter's right to issue the release was clearly established such that fire department officials were not entitled to immunity. *Gilbrook v. City of Westminster*, 177 F.3d 839 (9th Cir. 1999).

♦ North Carolina passed a law establishing a statewide permit program for carrying a concealed weapon and required persons seeking the permit to first complete an approved course in the safety and use of concealed handguns. A sergeant qualified as a course instructor and scheduled his first class during his off-duty hours. Following department procedure, he submitted an application for permission to engage in off-duty employment. The chief, a vocal opponent of the new law, denied the application and, after the sergeant filed a grievance, he took away the sergeant's supervisory status. When the sergeant conducted the class, he was suspended for two weeks, put on probation for a year and told he would be fired if he engaged in secondary employment without permission.

The Fourth Circuit Court of Appeals held that: 1) **the proper use and manner of carrying a concealed handgun was clearly a matter of public concern**, 2) because the speech would be made while the sergeant was off-duty and in a location unrelated to the city, there was no indication that the speech would interfere with the chief's ability to run the department, and 3) the termination threat was clearly intended to chill the sergeant's right to engage in protected speech. The sergeant's complaint sufficiently alleged that his interest in engaging in the speech outweighed the city's interest in providing effective services to the public. The chief and other city officials were not entitled to immunity. *Edwards v. City of Goldsboro*, 178 F.3d 231 (4th Cir. 1999).

3. Speech Reporting Criminal Activity

♦ A police officer learned from a colleague that a number of officers in the department's major crimes unit were drinking on duty, stealing money and planting evidence. He reported the information to his supervisor, and his colleague reported the information to the chief. The task force officers involved in the misconduct were eventually fired, but the officer and his colleague became the target of a series of retaliatory actions that grew progressively more threatening. For example, the officer had his locker wired shut; he had his uniforms dumped in the trash; he was denied backup on a police call; and he received death threats. The officer finally sued the city, alleging that it had violated his First Amendment right to inform his superiors of misconduct in the police department. A California federal court dismissed the case, but the Ninth Circuit Court of Appeals reversed the dismissal. It noted that the officer had raised **genuine issues of fact over whether city policymakers tacitly approved a custom or policy of suppressing whistleblowers**. It did not matter that the officer could not identify all the individuals who had targeted him for retaliation. Further, it was for the jury to decide whether the city had acted appropriately to stop the retaliation. The case would have to proceed to trial. *Blair v. City of Pomona*, 223 F.3d 1074 (9th Cir. 2000).

♦ Three female employees of the Houston Police Department complained of discrimination and a hostile working environment. The head of the Identification Department where they worked was forced to resign, and his son took over the position. The women then sued various police department employees alleging that the son sought to avenge his father's termination by retaliating against them. The case reached the U.S. Court of Appeals, Fifth Circuit, after a Texas federal court found that the individual defendants were not entitled to qualified immunity. The Fifth Circuit reviewed the women's claim that their First Amendment rights under 42 U.S.C. § 1983 were violated after they filed a grievance alerting police officials to internal tampering with criminal files. Here, **although the women were motivated by personal** concerns over their careers in filing the grievance, the grievance involved matters of public concern – tampering of individual criminal histories – and was therefore protected speech. However, for their Section 1983 claim to go to trial, the women also had to show that the city took adverse action against them.

The only triable issue regarding adverse action was whether the department had actually demoted two of the women after the grievance was filed. One was stripped of her managerial title, and the other was stripped of her cadet training position. The defendants were not entitled to qualified immunity for taking this action because they should have known that they could not retaliate against the women for exercising their First Amendment rights. The Fifth Circuit also found that one of the women raised a triable issue of fact over whether her department head intentionally inflicted emotional distress by assigning the woman to work with someone who had been romantically involved with her and who had sexually abused her daughter during the relationship. *Benningfield v. City of Houston*, 157 F.3d 369 (5th Cir. 1998).

• A security director for the District of Columbia Lottery and Charitable Games Control Board determined that money was missing from a safe. He reported the theft to the police. The police report placed a relative of the deputy director's under scrutiny because the relative was responsible for the money. When the deputy director became the acting director, approximately three months later, she fired the security director, sending him a letter indicating that he had no right to appeal. The security director filed a complaint under 42 U.S.C. § 1983, claiming his firing violated his First Amendment right to free speech and due process. A federal court found that the report was not a matter of public concern, but the U.S. Court of Appeals, D.C. Circuit, held that **the report qualified as a public concern because of its "potential interest" to the public**. The court vacated the district court ruling and remanded for the application of the rest of the *Pickering* test (whether the employee's interest in making the report outweighed the employer's interest in efficiency of the office). *Fox v. District of Columbia*, 83 F.3d 1491 (D.C. Cir. 1996).

• A Georgia deputy cooperated with the state bureau of investigation regarding an allegation of corruption in the sheriff's department. The deputy gave information to investigators believing it would be confidential. However, the sheriff and other employees in the department found out about the cooperation. The sheriff was indicted but was reelected, and the charges eventually were dismissed. Upon returning to office, the sheriff did not renew the deputy's commission. The deputy sued the sheriff alleging retaliation for exercising his right to free speech. The Eleventh Circuit Court of Appeals ruled that **the corruption investigation cooperation constituted protected speech under the First Amendment**, thereby removing the sheriff from the protection of qualified immunity. Corruption in a police department is an issue of public concern not outweighed by the sheriff's interest in efficient management of the department. *Cooper v. Smith*, 89 F.3d 761 (11th Cir. 1996).

4. Prior Restraint

• Conflicts arose between a New York suburban police chief and the town board over how the police department should be run. They escalated to the point where the board threatened to abolish the department. The chief then filed several lawsuits claiming that the town retaliated against him for speaking out on the issues. A federal court entered pretrial judgment for the town, but the U.S. Court of Appeals, Second Circuit, reversed. Because the chief had made comments about crime rates, police staffing, equipment shortages and related budgetary matters, the Second Circuit held that, under the First Amendment, his speech involved matters of public concern. The court then held that the chief suffered an adverse employment action (termination) as a result of the decision to abolish the department. Statements the town supervisor made in a radio interview that, as a result of the lawsuits, she would pursue abolition of the department raised a material question of fact as to whether the decision was retaliatory. Moreover, **the town supervisor's public threat to discipline the chief if he "talk[ed] to the press without getting permission"** raised a question as to whether the town had engaged in prior restraint. The Second Circuit remanded the case for trial on these issues. *Morris v. Lindau*, 196 F.3d 102 (2d Cir. 1999).

• A Milwaukee police chief issued a directive stating that if a departmental employee made a verbal or written complaint about another department member, the employees involved were not to discuss the matter with anyone, including their union. While the chief was on vacation, his top aides put out two more directives prohibiting employees from talking to their lawyers, but allowing them to contact the Equal Employment Opportunity Commission (EEOC) if the matter involved an EEOC issue. The union sued the chief under Section 1983, asserting that the directives violated its members' free speech and association rights, and seeking a preliminary injunction to keep the directives from being enforced. The chief then issued a fourth directive, stating that no union representatives could be contacted unless the matter involved criminal or disciplinary charges. After a Wisconsin federal court denied the preliminary injunction, the Seventh Circuit held that the district court had improperly considered only the first directive when it denied the injunction. In cases of prior restraint, **the government must show that "the interests of both potential audiences and a vast group of present and future employees in a broad range of present and future expression are outweighed** by that expression's 'necessary impact' on the actual operation" of the government. The court remanded the case. *Milwaukee Police Ass'n and Julie Horter v. Jones*, 192 F.3d 742 (7th Cir. 1999).

• Two New York City executive orders restricted contact between the media and employees of the city's child welfare agencies. The orders required referral of all potential media contacts, inquiries and requests for information to the media relations office prior to communication with the media. One employee was suspended for failure to obtain approval prior to talking with a news reporter. She sued, arguing that the media contacts policy was unconstitutional as a prior restraint of speech in violation of the First and Fourteenth Amendments. Another employee, whose request to speak was denied, intervened in the suit. The court held that **the portions of the executive orders requiring prior approval before city employees could discuss any agency policy or activity with the media violated the First Amendment.** The executive orders were likely to induce excessive caution in the speaker, causing the filtering of any speech with which an employee suspects his or her supervisor will disagree. They also substantially increased the likelihood that the agency would discipline an employee speaking without approval. The city failed to demonstrate that employee speech posed a significant threat to the efficient operation of the child welfare agencies. Also, the pre-clearance procedure was overly inclusive because it required review of all contacts. The city failed to demonstrate a real harm and failed to show why enforcement of the state confidentiality laws would not suffice to protect the information. As a result, the interests of the employees and the public at large outweighed the city's interests. *Harman v. City of New York*, 945 F.Supp. 750 (S.D.N.Y. 1996).

♦ An assistant fire chief employed by an Ohio city fire department was concerned with certain departmental issues and wished to speak publicly regarding those concerns. Initially, he was informed by his superiors that he could not speak publicly at all. After a couple of years, he was granted permission to speak as a citizen but not as an assistant fire chief. The chief and the safety service director continually refused his requests to speak as an assistant fire chief based on **a fire department rule that prohibited all speech on departmental issues without prior approval from the chief or the director.** Over a year later, in an allegedly unrelated matter, the assistant fire chief was charged with insubordination for failing to obey direct orders from the chief. The assistant chief was given a detailed notice and a hearing at which he was represented by counsel and was permitted to actively participate. However, he retired before any disciplinary action was taken against him. The employee sued, alleging First Amendment and procedural due process violations as well as constructive discharge. The district court held that **the fire department rule was a prior restraint on speech protected by the First Amendment and was therefore facially unconstitutional.** The court also held that although the content of the assistant chief's speech may have been unacceptable to the chief and others because they disagreed with his opinions, the city had failed to demonstrate any overriding interests that necessitated silencing the assistant chief. Thus, the fire department rules also were unconstitutional as applied to the assistant chief. Finally, the court held that genuine issues of material fact existed with respect to the assistant chief's claims for constructive discharge and retaliation. *Spain v. City of Mansfield*, 915 F.Supp. 919 (N.D. Ohio 1996).

D. Unprotected Speech

Speech can be unprotected when it does not address a matter of public concern, or when it is outweighed by the government's interest in running an efficient and effective department.

♦ A Texas police chief conducted an investigation into city council meeting improprieties rather than have an external agency handle it as the city manager recommended. Later, he reported the city's chief building inspector to another city's police department because the building inspector had misrepresented himself as a police officer. The city manager objected to his report because she already had suspended the building inspector and considered the matter closed. During a heated exchange over the suspension, the chief called the city manager "Hitler." The city manager recommended that the chief be fired for insubordination, and the city council adopted her recommendation. The chief then sued under the First Amendment, **alleging that the real reason for the firing had been his investigation into city council wrongdoing**. A federal court and the Fifth Circuit rejected his claim. Even though city employees "gossiped" about the chief's investigation, there was insufficient evidence that city council members (who worked in the private sector) knew about it. Also, the investigation did not amount to "speech" under the First Amendment. *Tharling v. City of Port Lavaca*, 329 F.3d 422 (5th Cir. 2003).

1. Government's Interest Outweighs Speaker's Interest

♦ A San Diego police officer **made a video in his off-duty time** that showed him stripping and then masturbating. He sold the video online. When his superiors learned of the video, they fired him. He sued, alleging a violation of his First Amendment rights, but a California federal court dismissed his lawsuit. The Ninth Circuit Court of Appeals reversed, noting that the officer's "speech" fell within the protected category of "citizen comment on matters of public concern," even though it contained no political content. The Supreme Court reversed the Ninth Circuit, stating that the officer's "speech" did not touch on a matter of public concern and thus was not subject to the *Pickering* balancing test. Further, the officer's activities, although outside the workplace, exploited his employer's image and were detrimental to the mission and functioning of the police department – not to mention against regulations. As a result, the officer's speech was not protected. *City of San Diego v. Roe*, 543 U.S. 77, 125 S.Ct. 521, 160 L.Ed.2d 410 (2004).

♦ An Arizona police officer created sexually explicit CDs of himself and his wife, which he sold over the Internet. He was careful to avoid any connection between the CDs and his police job. However, news of the CDs leaked out, causing unflattering media reports and disrupting the police department's operations and recruiting efforts. After the department fired him, he sued under the First Amendment, claiming he had a constitutional right to run his sex-oriented business. A federal court and the Ninth Circuit ruled for the department. The court of appeals noted that even though this case wasn't exactly like *City of San Diego v. Roe*, 543 U.S. 77 (2004), because this officer was trying to hide his connection with the department rather than flaunt it, he was still properly fired. **Although he may have had the constitutional right to run his sex-oriented business, he had no constitutional right to be a police officer at the same time.** The city's interests outweighed his. *Dibble v. City of Chandler*, 515 F.3d 918 (9th Cir. 2008).

- A public university in Texas permitted adjunct professors access to its e-mail system only if they were teaching at least one class during a given semester. The e-mail system also limited user accounts to 20 megabytes of memory, after which the users were restricted from sending further e-mails. An adjunct professor formed a group to advocate on behalf of his fellow adjuncts and challenged the university's e-mail restrictions. He also claimed that the university retaliated against him for bringing the lawsuit. A federal court and the Fifth Circuit ruled against him. Here, **the university's policy did not violate the First Amendment because the restrictions were not content-based**. Also, the university could cut the teaching load for its adjuncts as a way to pay less in benefits. And it cut the load for almost all adjuncts, not just the professor suing it. *Faculty Rights Coalition v. Shahrokhi*, 204 Fed.Appx. 416 (5th Cir. 2006).

- A California social worker who helped residents transition off welfare was an evangelical Christian and objected to his employer's policy preventing him from discussing religion with clients and displaying religious items where clients could see them. He put a Spanish-language Bible on his desk and hung a sign on his wall that read "Happy Birthday, Jesus." After he was reprimanded, he sued. A federal court and the Ninth Circuit ruled that **he did not have a First Amendment right to violate the "no religion" policy**. The restriction on his speech rights was reasonable under the *Pickering* balancing test. *Berry v. Dep't of Social Services*, 447 F.3d 642 (9th Cir. 2006).

- The executive director of the Arkansas Local Police and Fire Retirement System met with the governor's staff to discuss a bill that would add two new positions to the five-member board of trustees. She told them the board opposed the expansion, even though that was merely her position and even though she had been told in the past not to get involved with board appointments. When the staff told a legislator what she had said, he informed the board of her comments and she was fired. She sued under the First Amendment, but the Eighth Circuit held that the board and the legislator were not liable. The legislator was entitled to qualified immunity for his statements to the board, and the board was not liable under the *Pickering* balancing test. **The government's interest in effectively managing the retirement system outweighed her interest in speaking out on substantive policy.** *Hinshaw v. Smith*, 436 F.3d 997 (8th Cir. 2006).

- A white police officer and two white firefighters in New York rode on a float in a parade in their community wearing black face and afros. That night, amateur video of the "racist float" aired on a local newscast. Extensive press coverage followed. Eventually, a newspaper reported that police and fire department employees had been involved. After the three employees were fired, they sued for violations of their free speech rights. A federal court ruled in their favor, but the Second Circuit Court of Appeals reversed. **It wasn't so much the content of the speech but the notoriety which caused the disruption to the city** and affected its image adversely. The city's concern for the negative impact of their speech outweighed whatever First Amendment protections they had in commenting on the racial makeup of their neighborhood. *Locurto v. Guiliani*, 447 F.3d 159 (2d Cir. 2006).

• A White House chef filed an EEO complaint alleging that he was passed over for promotion because he was engaged to a black woman. He later spoke to a newspaper and radio station about the Clintons' food preferences, the staff's refusal to heed the President's food allergies, his lateness for dinner and the poor service the staff was providing. He also threatened another employee and filed a number of lawsuits against his co-workers. When the executive chef was asked to resign, the entire kitchen staff was dismissed so the new executive chef could hire his own staff. He rehired everyone except the chef, who did not impress him. The chef sued, but the Federal Circuit Court of Appeals held that he could not show discrimination, and that his First Amendment claim could not succeed. **Even if the chef's remarks were on a matter of public concern, his right to make them was outweighed by the disruption they caused** and by the White House staff's need to keep private matters private. *Haddon v. Executive Residence at the White House*, 313 F.3d 1352 (Fed. Cir. 2002).

• A fire marshal in Nevada learned that two of the five inspector positions (one male, one female) in his unit were going to be eliminated. He met with the fire chief, who believed the move was part of a deal the deputy city manager had struck with the union. The fire marshal then met with a female captain and a female engineer with another unit. He discussed with them the rumor that the city and the union were trying to get rid of women over 40. They then sent memos to the deputy city manager, telling him about the conversations. Subsequently, the fire marshal was suspended for 10 days for violating fire department rules by spreading untrue rumors. Almost two years later, the fire marshal's position was reclassified to a lower-paying position. He sued the city for violating his First Amendment rights, but a federal court ruled against him. The Ninth Circuit affirmed, finding that even though he had spoken out on a matter of public concern (discrimination), **the city's interest in maintaining smooth operations outweighed his interest in speaking privately** with the captain and engineer about rumors that he failed to verify, and which were in fact untrue. *Skaarup v. City of North Las Vegas*, 320 F.3d 1040 (9th Cir. 2003).

• An Arkansas housing authority employee had a souring relationship with the authority's executive director, which only got worse after she offered testimony in a lawsuit alleging fraud and wrongful eviction of a housing authority tenant. After the director fired her, the employee was reinstated. She circulated a petition critical of the director to housing authority tenants, and was accused by the director of making obscene gestures and mouthing an obscenity at her. After the director resigned, a tenant called the police to complain about the employee's continuing harassment. The authority then fired the employee, who sued for wrongful discharge. A federal court ruled against her, and the Eighth Circuit affirmed. Here, the petition was not protected free speech because it was not on a matter of public concern. And even if it was, **the authority's interest in limiting disruption to its services outweighed her interest in circulating the petition.** Also, there was no due process violation because 1) the employee received a post-termination hearing; 2) the reasons given for the firing – insubordination and tenant complaints – were not sufficiently stigmatizing to implicate a liberty interest; and 3) there was no evidence that the authority made the reasons for the firing public. *Allen v. City of Pocahontas*, 340 F.3d 551 (8th Cir. 2003).

• The interim executive director for a county housing authority in Illinois began changing the housing authority's operations and wrote memos to board members complaining about the chairman's conduct and asking them to rein him in. Eighteen days later, the board removed him from his position and fired him for insubordination. He sued the authority under 42 U.S.C. § 1983, asserting that he had been discharged in violation of the First and Fourteenth Amendments. The Seventh Circuit Court of Appeals affirmed the lower court ruling in favor of the authority. Here, the interim executive director was either a policymaking official who could be fired for his political views, or he was **a rank-and-file employee whose right to speak out and act on matters of public concern was outweighed** by the authority's need to prevent his speech and actions from disrupting its operations, and who was properly fired for insubordination. Moreover, since he was an at-will employee, he had no constitutionally protected property right in continued employment. Thus, his Fourteenth Amendment due process claim could not succeed. He was not entitled to a hearing before his discharge. *Garcia v. Kankakee County Housing Authority*, 279 F.3d 532 (7th Cir. 2002).

• After a Georgia fire captain became president of the local union, he prepared and distributed a questionnaire to candidates for the county board of commissioners. The questionnaire asked the candidates to respond to questions about employment and staffing, including grievance procedures, vacation policies, promotion guidelines and pension benefits. When his chief saw the questionnaire, he threatened to discipline the captain for sending out any more questionnaires or for engaging in any similar action. He noted that it was the captain's responsibility to maintain public confidence in the ability of the emergency management agency to carry out its public safety mission. Subsequently, the national union's president wrote the chief a letter expressing concern over the chief's threat. The chief then placed the captain on probation and later demoted him to private. The ex-captain sued under the First Amendment, and the Eleventh Circuit held that **the county's interest in the efficiency of its public services outweighed his interest in distributing a questionnaire** that addressed predominantly employee-related grievances. As a result, the demotion did not violate the captain's First Amendment rights. *Anderson v. Burke County*, 239 F.3d 1216 (11th Cir. 2001).

• An employee of the Wichita Federal Public Defender's Office met a man at a gun show who told the employee that he intended to use biological weapons against the government. The employee contacted the Federal Bureau of Investigation (FBI). His supervisors at the public defender's office commended him for informing the FBI of the potential threat but prohibited him from further contact with the FBI because the man was a potential client. When the employee continued to work with the FBI, he was fired. He sued under the First Amendment, asserting that his termination was unconstitutional. The case reached the Tenth Circuit Court of Appeals, which upheld the firing. **The public** defender's interest in regulating the employee's conduct outweighed the employee's interest in cooperating with the FBI. *Rupp v. Phillips,* 15 Fed.Appx. 694 (10th Cir. 2001).

• A Wisconsin firefighter also served as the pastor for his church, where he preached about the evils of homosexuality. He was reprimanded on numerous occasions for tardiness and was disciplined at least twice for insubordination. In 1996, a female division chief was videotaped hitting and yelling at a recruit during a training session. The female fire chief conducted an investigation and determined that the division chief's behavior had been reasonable under the circumstances. She extended the division chief's probation and ordered her to attend a leadership class. The firefighter then distributed a pamphlet that referred to homosexuality as a "filthy scourge" and blamed gays for disease and child molestation. After being suspended and warned that further conduct would result in his termination, the firefighter **issued a press release accusing the chief of playing favorites with other female workers because she was a homosexual,** and attacking her "radical lesbian agenda." The chief fired him and he sued under the First Amendment. The Seventh Circuit ruled against him. Even though his speech was on a matter of public concern, the chief was justified in firing him because leaving him unpunished would disrupt the department's operations, undermine the chief's authority and incite disharmony within the ranks. *Greer v. Amesqua,* 212 F.3d 358 (7th Cir. 2000).

• After an education association's collective bargaining agreement expired, teachers began wearing buttons that asked for a quick settlement. When the school superintendent told the teachers not to wear the buttons in front of students on school grounds, the association sued. At issue was a school board "conflict of interest" policy that prohibited employees from: 1) actively campaigning on school property, 2) displaying campaign materials on election day, and 3) engaging in activity with students (during performance of their duties) designed to further a voting issue. The case reached the Superior Court of New Jersey, Appellate Division, which noted that the first two parts of the policy were unconstitutional because they were overbroad. However, the third part was constitutional. **Teachers could be prevented from wearing the buttons in their classrooms and on school grounds in front of students.** Because teachers are authority figures, and students are their captive audience, teachers could be restricted to educating students in the classroom. *Green Township Educ. Ass'n v. Rowe,* 746 A.2d 499 (N.J. Super. Ct. App. Div. 2000).

• The Fourth Circuit Court of Appeals upheld one of the first state laws restricting state employees' use of the Internet during working hours. The plaintiffs in the case were six Virginia state university professors concerned about their ability to conduct research on sex-related topics without restrictions. The challenged regulation **required state employees to obtain supervisory approval before using state-owned or state-leased computers to download sexually explicit material off the Internet.** Here, the court found that the challenged restriction regulated the speech of state employees only in their capacity as employees, not as citizens speaking on a matter of public concern.

Because the employees were still free to access materials on their own computers, they were not restricted from engaging in speech protected by the Constitution. *Urofsky v. Gilmore*, 216 F.3d 401 (4th Cir. 2000).

♦ An Indiana police officer was also the president of the local Fraternal Order of Police. After a private citizen was shot and killed by a fellow police officer pursuant to an arrest, a great deal of racial tension arose in the community. The officer, although not working the case and not authorized by the police department to make any statements regarding the status of the investigation, nevertheless released two statements to the local media. Both statements contained premature conclusions that made it seem that the outcome of the investigation was predetermined, and that the grand jury was simply a formality to sanction the result. The city board of public works fired the officer for misconduct.

The Court of Appeals of Indiana rejected the officer's contention that his statements were constitutionally protected and that he could not be fired. Although the officer's speech involved a matter of public concern, **his interest in expressing himself did not outweigh the government's interest in achieving effective and efficient public service**. His conduct interfered with an ongoing investigation, and this interference threatened to undermine the authority of the police department and the prosecutor's office. The disruptive nature of his conduct sufficiently outweighed whatever First Amendment value his speech may have had. *Davidson v. City of Elkhart, Indiana*, 696 N.E.2d 58 (Ind. Ct. App. 1998).

2. Speech of a Personal Nature

♦ A Pennsylvania probation officer wrote a letter to the judge who ran her department complaining about the stressful conditions in the office and accusing one of her supervisors of calling their clients "scum." She essentially gave the judge an ultimatum: to keep either her or the supervisors. The judge fired her and she sued under 42 U.S.C. § 1983, claiming First Amendment protections. The case reached the Third Circuit, which ruled against her, noting that **even though her letter brushed gently against a matter of public concern, that did not convert what was really a personal grievance into protected speech**. Her firing did not violate the First Amendment. *Miller v. Clinton County*, 544 F.3d 542 (3d Cir. 2008).

♦ A county courts manager in Kentucky sent an e-mail to several judges explaining that, due to staff shortages, they would not be able to work on an updated orientation video for jurors, and that the Louisville and Kentucky Bar Associations wanted the money they had forwarded for funding the project returned. Shortly thereafter, the manager was fired. The chief judge stated that the reason was her mismanagement of the jury pool office staff. When she sued under the First Amendment, a federal court and the Sixth Circuit ruled against her. **Her e-mail did not involve a matter of public concern, but rather centered on an internal matter regarding staffing and lost funding.** *Miller v. Administrative Office of the Courts*, 448 F.3d 887 (6th Cir. 2006).

♦ An Indiana police chief decided to cut the number of crime prevention officers, reassigning a number of them to active patrol duty. After the meeting describing the plan, a sergeant protested, asserting that community organizations would not allow the changes to be made. She then received a memo disapproving of her attitude, and also was assigned to patrol duties. When she sued the city and the chief for violating her First Amendment rights, the Seventh Circuit ruled against her. Here, she made her statements while on duty, in uniform and engaged in discussion with her superiors. **Because she was speaking in her capacity as a public employee contributing to the formation and execution of official policy, her speech was not protected.** *Mills v. City of Evansville, Indiana*, 452 F.3d 646 (7th Cir. 2006).

♦ Two Florida deputies, while off duty, appeared in pornographic photos and videos that were sold on a pay-per-view Internet site. Even though they were partially disguised, they were identifiable, and a citizen complained. After an administrative hearing, the sheriff fired them for violating department rules regarding off-duty conduct. They sued under the First Amendment. A federal court dismissed their lawsuit and the Eleventh Circuit affirmed. **Their paid participation in Internet pornography did not qualify as a matter of public concern** for which they were entitled to First Amendment protection. Further, the deputies failed to seek prior written approval before engaging in their commercial enterprise. *Theater v. Palm Beach County Sheriff's Office*, 449 F.3d 1342 (11th Cir. 2006).

♦ When a Maine police chief spotted a dog running loose on the streets, he called an animal control officer, who cornered the dog in its owner's garage. Even though the dog was arguably no longer at large, the animal control officer issued the owner a summons. The owner then called the town manager to complain, and the town manager asked the police chief to have the summons dismissed. The chief told the town manager he was uncomfortable doing so, but he did agree to relay the request to the district attorney. A year later, the town manager fired the chief after a suspension and an investigation into unrelated matters. The chief sued, alleging First Amendment and whistleblower violations, but a federal court and the First Circuit disagreed with him. Here, **his speech was on internal working conditions**. Also, he never reported to anyone his belief that the town manager's request was illegal. *Tripp v. Cole*, 425 F.3d 5 (1st Cir. 2005).

♦ Several current and former employees of the Illinois Department of Human Services sued after being suspended or fired for speaking out on what they alleged were matters of public concern. A federal court and the Seventh Circuit Court of Appeals ruled against them, deciding that the speech did not involve matters of public concern so as to be protected by the First Amendment. One was a complaint about a transfer that was a purely personal workplace grievance. One was a complaint that air vents and window screens were dirty that was also an internal workplace grievance. And another was an employee's repeated refusal to meet with police outside the presence of his attorney, which was a purely private matter. *Carreon v. Illinois Dep't of Human Services*, 395 F.3d 786 (7th Cir. 2005).

* A North Carolina police sergeant **testified at a co-worker's grievance hearing** and was then issued an oral reprimand for failing to support the department's administration. Believing the reprimand was in retaliation for his testimony, he filed a grievance and a lawsuit against the police chief, who then demoted him. When he sued the chief and the city under the First Amendment, a federal court granted pretrial judgment to the defendants. The Fourth Circuit Court of Appeals affirmed. Here, his testimony at the grievance hearing did not involve a matter of public concern. And even though the First Amendment grants the right "to petition the Government for a redress of grievances," making the lawsuit a matter of public concern, the officer still lost. He was unable to show that he had a "clearly protected" First Amendment right that was violated by the chief's actions. Further, the chief maintained that the demotion was in response to the officer's failure to properly update his investigation reports. *Kirby v. City of Elizabeth City*, 388 F.3d 440 (4th Cir. 2004).

* A police officer engaged in a bit of horseplay with two other officers and found herself handcuffed to a fence as a result. She radioed for help and later filed an administrative complaint against the officers. She was not disciplined for her part in the horseplay, but the other two officers were. When she complained that their discipline was too lenient, the department conducted an investigation and discovered that **she had falsified her job application by concealing her criminal record**. She was fired, and she sued the city in an Illinois federal court, alleging that she was terminated in retaliation for exercising her First Amendment rights. A jury ruled in her favor, but the Seventh Circuit Court of Appeals reversed. Here, the department had a legitimate reason for firing her – her fraud – and her speech was not protected under the First Amendment anyway. It did not address a matter of public concern, but rather involved private personnel matters. *Durgins v. City of East St. Louis, Illinois*, 272 F.3d 841 (7th Cir. 2001).

* A Texas police officer began wearing a religious pin while working in a plainclothes assignment. After he was transferred to a uniformed position, he was told that he could no longer wear the pin. Police department regulations stated that buttons, badges, medals and other similar items could not be worn on the uniform shirt unless approved by the chief in writing on an individual basis. The chief gave the officer a number of options – wearing the pin under his shirt or collar, transferring to a non-uniformed position, and wearing a ring or bracelet. The officer rejected all offers and was fired for insubordination. He sued the city under the First Amendment and lost. The Fifth Circuit Court of Appeals upheld the ruling in favor of the city. Here, **the officer was not speaking out on a matter of public concern, but rather on a purely private matter**. The symbolic conveyance of religious beliefs was intensely personal. Further, wearing the pin with the uniform ran the risk that people would perceive the city to be endorsing his religious message. *Daniels v. City of Arlington*, 246 F.3d 500 (5th Cir. 2001).

* An Indiana county health department employee made a number of negative comments about the personnel and policies of his employer. At one point, a

local developer wrote to one of his supervisors to complain about his "negative attitude and his personal antagonism toward the policies of the Local and State Health Departments with regard to septic systems and water supply" in the county. The next day, the employee refused to carry out a directive to return some boxes to storage. He was suspended without pay. While the department contemplated further disciplinary action, he resigned, then sued the department under the First Amendment. He alleged that the department retaliated against him for publicly criticizing the department's operations. A federal court ruled against him, and the Seventh Circuit Court of Appeals affirmed. **The employee failed to prove that he had spoken out on a matter of public concern** such that he was entitled to the First Amendment's protections. The developer's letter indicated only that he had a negative attitude and was antagonistic. It did not reveal what specific policies were discussed, or even the gist of the comments. *Michael v. St. Joseph County*, 259 F.3d 842 (7th Cir. 2001).

♦ A Florida state employee, who was legally blind, requested special computer equipment and "pink lights" for her work space. During this time she also testified at a grievance hearing on behalf of her former supervisor, who had been charged with insubordination. The charge was overturned, but the supervisor was later fired and, at another hearing, the employee testified on her former supervisor's behalf again. When the employee did not receive the accommodations she requested, she sued under the Americans with Disabilities Act, the Rehabilitation Act and 42 U.S.C. § 1983, asserting that the refusal to accommodate was in retaliation for her exercising her free speech rights. The Eleventh Circuit held that the defendants were entitled to qualified immunity. **The employee had not been speaking on a matter of public concern; thus, she was not entitled to First Amendment protection.** Here, she did not relate her concerns about state policies to the public or testify about fraud or corruption in a state department. She was merely trying to help her former supervisor challenge misconduct charges and win reinstatement. *Maggio v. Sipple*, 211 F.3d 1346 (11th Cir. 2000).

♦ A child abuse investigator for the state of Massachusetts also served as a city council member for four years. When she lost her bid for reelection, she attended a party for outgoing council members and made a **racist joke** that was reported in the press, resulting in numerous complaints from members of the community and from the department's clients. One department employee was refused entrance into a client's home because of the comment. The department fired the investigator, and she sued, claiming that her discharge infringed upon her First Amendment right to free speech. The Massachusetts Supreme Court disagreed. It stated that **her speech had not been on a matter of public concern**, so it was not protected. Further, although the First Amendment can extend to speech outside the workplace, even if her speech had been protected, the department's interest in maintaining the efficient operation and delivery of public services outweighed her interest in making the joke. Her firing did not violate the First Amendment. *Pereira v. Commissioner of Social Services*, 733 N.E.2d 112 (Mass. 2000).

• Two long-time police officers for a Texas town worked as internal affairs investigators. They suspected another officer of wrongdoing, but their police chief stopped the investigation after he learned that one of the investigators was going to present the case to the grand jury. Believing the chief to be covering up for the officer, the investigators filed a grievance against the chief and then transferred out of internal affairs. They were fired after their replacement told the chief that they had left an enormous backlog in their wake. The investigators sued, claiming that the chief had retaliated against them for exercising their First Amendment rights. The Fifth Circuit ruled for the town. **Speech regarding police misconduct is a matter of public concern, but the speech here also involved matters of private concern** – the investigators' grievance over the chief's handling of their investigation. The balance fell on the side of a private interest because although the content of the speech was predominantly public, the context and form in which it was made were private – a grievance addressing only the investigators' frustration with the way their termination was handled and the failure to provide due process. *Teague v. City of Flower Mound*, 179 F.3d 377 (5th Cir. 1999).

• Several Kansas police officers complained internally and publicly about sexual harassment and discrimination in the department. They then filed a lawsuit in federal court, seeking damages under 42 U.S.C. § 1983. Specifically, they claimed that they had been subjected to sexual harassment by a supervisor who had made unwelcome homosexual advances, denying them equal protection of the law. The officers also claimed that the city violated their First Amendment rights by retaliating against them after they complained about the harassment and discrimination. A federal court granted pretrial judgment for the city on the First Amendment claim. **Because the officers' speech concerned personal grievances as opposed to matters of public concern, the speech was not entitled to First Amendment protection.** Here, the officers' speech lacked the element of societal importance. Instead, it addressed the officers' own personal grievances and nothing else. Although the officers lost their First Amendment claim, the court allowed them to go forward with their claim that the city violated their equal protection rights. *Carney v. City of Shawnee, Kansas*, 24 F.Supp.2d 1185 (D. Kan. 1998).

• A secretary for the New York State Power Authority was required to attend a company-endorsed "values program" encouraging excellence, innovation, integrity and teamwork. Promotional "values buttons" were distributed to employees to wear at work as a sign of support for the program. The secretary placed two values buttons over her breasts and one over her pelvic area and asked, "How do you like my values?" The Authority fired her for inappropriate behavior. She sued under the First Amendment. A federal court held that the secretary's express disapproval of the values program, coupled with her after-the-fact attempt to link the program with government waste of taxpayer money, did not establish that her criticisms were matters of public concern. Although the state cannot dictate expressive behavior, **public employers may formulate requirements that are part and parcel of an employee's job**. Here, the Authority's values program permissibly encouraged employees to do a good job. Since the secretary's speech was not a matter of public concern and she was not forced to wear a values button, her First Amendment rights were not violated. *Harris v. Beedle*, 845 F.Supp. 1030 (S.D.N.Y. 1994).

3. Qualified Immunity and Other Defenses

♦ A New Mexico school district's director of bilingual education feared that the school board might be planning to eliminate the bilingual program. She wrote the board president an e-mail, spoke at an Indian Education Committee meeting, wrote a column for the local paper and sent an e-mail to the paper's editor, thanking him for publishing the column, stating that teaching Navajo was a "lonely battle when the powers-that-be knock the job." That e-mail was published too. Around that time, her performance began to slip. She missed deadlines for certain funding applications, then had her directorship responsibilities taken away and was put on a performance improvement plan. After further problems, she was fired. She sued for retaliation under the First Amendment and lost. Here, **many months had passed since she engaged in her protected speech. And the district documented the instances of poor performance.** *Deschenie v. Board of Educ.*, 473 F.3d 1271 (10th Cir. 2007).

♦ Employees in a Georgia county purchasing department met with a county commissioner to discuss irregularities in the department's bidding and contracting process. They also discussed general work environment concerns. After the meeting, their supervisor allegedly singled them out unfavorably, stripping them of duties and excluding them from meetings, as well as requiring them to publicly display their time sheets. They quit, then sued their former supervisor for First Amendment retaliation, claiming they had been constructively discharged. A federal court granted the supervisor qualified immunity, but the Eleventh Circuit reversed in part, holding that the supervisor's conduct could amount to an adverse action that constituted retaliation, and that the employees' meeting with the commissioner about irregularities was protected speech. Further, **the supervisor had fair warning that the employees' speech was protected and that his actions could constitute constructive discharge.** The case required a trial. *Akins v. Fulton County*, 420 F.3d 1293 (11th Cir. 2005).

♦ Three high-level administrators for a California school district met with several school board members to complain about a deputy superintendent's personnel evaluation practices and to charge him with spending Title I money to pay for consultants and other personnel in violation of federal guidelines on how the funds should be spent. One of the board members told the deputy superintendent about the administrators' statements. Shortly thereafter, the deputy superintendent tried to reassign one of the administrators, but he failed to give her timely notice, and she kept her job. More than a year later, after an outside evaluation into the school district's operations, the deputy superintendent demoted two of the administrators and reassigned the other. He based his actions on the outside evaluation of the district's operations. The administrators sued the district under the First Amendment, claiming that the adverse action had been taken in retaliation for their statements to the school board members. A federal court ruled for the school district, and the Ninth Circuit affirmed. Even though the deputy superintendent was not protected by qualified immunity, **the administrators failed to show that their constitutionally protected conduct was a motivating factor in the decision to demote and reassign them**. They failed to prove more than that the deputy superintendent knew about their statements to the board members. *Keyser v. Sacramento City Unified School Dist.*, 265 F.3d 741 (9th Cir. 2001).

* An Oklahoma road equipment operator was questioned by the FBI and the county district attorney's office during a grand jury investigation into alleged misappropriation of county funds on road and construction projects. He cooperated with the criminal investigation and kept in contact with the investigators for 18 months. He told a few co-workers about it but did not tell his supervisors. Subsequently, the operator used profanity and racial slurs toward a supervisor, refusing to follow a work order. He also used profanity during an investigation of the incident by a project manager. As a result, the county commissioner fired him and issued a policy statement to other county employees that the use of profanity against supervisors would no longer be tolerated. The operator sued in federal court, claiming that the county violated his First Amendment rights to cooperate with a criminal investigation. The district court found that his participation in the investigation involved protected speech but that **none of the officials involved in the operator's termination had any knowledge of the operator's cooperation with the FBI** until he filed his lawsuit. The Tenth Circuit affirmed. *Henry v. Oklahoma County Board of County Commissioners* 182 F.3d 931 (10th Cir. 1999) (unpublished).

* A 10-year commissioned officer for the Texas Public Safety Department, who took the Texas Rangers' written exam, received one of the highest scores and appeared before the oral interview board. The chief of the Rangers, a member of the interviewing board, asked to see her written scores and then directed the rest of the board to give two other female applicants higher scores on their interviews. The chief stated that he didn't want the officer to be selected because she was too independent and too opinionated. He told other senior officers that he blackballed her because she was a "women's libber." When she sued, the Fifth Circuit Court of Appeals held that the First Amendment could not protect her because **there was no evidence that she engaged in First Amendment activity. That is, she never actually spoke out about her ideals**; nor did she present any evidence that she was a member of a feminist organization or supported a feminist group. As such, the chief's bad motive alone was insufficient to establish a First Amendment violation. *Steadman v. Texas Rangers*, 179 F.3d 360 (5th Cir. 1999).

* A caseworker for the Missouri Sex Offender Program continually voiced concern about his supervisor's handling of various matters and eventually filed a formal grievance against her. Specifically, he alleged that she was retaliating against him for his criticisms. The director of the program and the caseworker's supervisor both investigated and responded to the caseworker's grievances. The director discharged the caseworker for work performance that was not

satisfactory and because his continued employment would risk morale problems and jeopardize the program's reputation with the Department of Corrections. The caseworker sued, alleging that his discharge violated his First Amendment rights. The district court ruled for the supervisors. The U.S. Court of Appeals, Eighth Circuit, noted that **the caseworker's criticisms adversely affected the efficiency of the program's operation**. His continued presence would constitute a "risk to staff morale, the program's reputation and to the inmates with whom he had contact." Consequently, his free speech rights were not "clearly established," and the supervisors were entitled to **qualified immunity** with respect to the First Amendment wrongful discharge claim. *Grantham v. Trickey*, 21 F.3d 289 (8th Cir. 1994).

♦ A North Carolina housing authority mechanic was responsible for maintaining the boiler system in a public housing complex. After boiler problems resulted in the death of two residents from carbon monoxide poisoning, the mechanic gave a newspaper interview recounting how he repeatedly pointed out boiler problems to the housing authority, which ignored his warnings. An independent investigation into the deaths found that housing authority employees, at all levels, were accountable for the deaths. The housing director resigned and when the new director came into office, he fired the mechanic because of his failure to perform proper boiler maintenance and because of a negative job attitude, but specifically **denied that the firing was in retaliation for the mechanic's whistleblowing activities**. The mechanic sued the housing authority for violations of his First Amendment rights. A federal court ruled against him, noting that even assuming his speech was on a matter of public concern and that his interest in the speech outweighed the housing authority's interest in an efficient workplace, **he failed to show that his speech was a motivating or substantial factor in the decision to fire him**. It was the new director's prerogative to make a "clean sweep" to correct problems. *Mutschler v. Housing Authority of Raleigh, North Carolina*, 985 F.Supp. 612 (E.D.N.C. 1998).

♦ A New York corrections officer witnessed an inmate being subdued by the jail staff and indicated in her incident report that she believed excessive force had been used. A subsequent investigation of the incident led to some officers being disciplined. After the officer submitted her report, the undersheriff and other employees collected information documenting alleged rule infractions committed by the officer. In a meeting with the undersheriff and other officers, she was confronted with the infractions. When she responded with "no comment," she was immediately fired. She filed suit in federal court under 42 U.S.C. § 1983, alleging that she had been fired in violation of her free speech rights because of the incident report. The jury returned a verdict in the officer's favor. The Second Circuit Court of Appeals affirmed. It rejected the **dual motivation defense, which applies where the same decision would have been made without considering the protected speech**. The jury reasonably found that the employee would not have been fired on the same day she actually was absent the protected speech. *Sagendorf-Teal v. County of Rensselaer, New York*, 100 F.3d 270 (2d Cir. 1996).

E. Freedom of Association

The First Amendment provides for "the right of the people peaceably to assemble" and has been interpreted by the U.S. Supreme Court to guarantee freedom of association. However, that right is not absolute.

• Three Connecticut corrections officers joined the local chapter of the Outlaws Motorcycle Club, a reputedly violent organization. During an investigation, two of the officers claimed they had since quit and the third claimed he had never been a member. The officers were fired for engaging in unprofessional behavior, on or off duty, that could reflect negatively on the Department of Corrections (DOC). They sued, alleging a violation of their First Amendment rights, arguing that their association with club members was unrelated to their employment. A federal court and the Second Circuit ruled against them. **Even though the officers' membership was unrelated to their jobs and occurred off duty, there was still a nexus between that association and the DOC's operations.** And the fact that law enforcement agencies believed the Outlaws were a criminal enterprise made the terminations acceptable. *Piscottano v. Murphy*, 511 F.3d 247 (2d Cir. 2007).

• A probationary Transportation Security Administration (TSA) employee posted union notices on the employee bulletin board at the California airport where he worked. He claimed he was disciplined as a result and filed a grievance. He was then fired. When he and the union sued under the First Amendment, alleging speech and associational rights, a federal court dismissed the lawsuit because of the post-9/11 law: the Civil Service Reform Act, which gave the TSA "comprehensive" authority to govern federal personnel matters. However, the Ninth Circuit Court of Appeals reversed. It noted that Congress did not clearly state in the act its intent to deny federal employees the ability to redress constitutional violations. The court remanded the case for further proceedings. *American Federation of Government Employees Local 1 v. Stone*, 502 F.3d 1027 (9th Cir. 2007).

• A deputy clerk in a Tennessee county's court system became romantically involved with a lawyer in the private sector who happened to be married to another court employee. She was fired because her relationship was causing tension in the workplace. She sued the county under 42 U.S.C. § 1983, claiming that the county had retaliated against her for exercising her First Amendment right to intimate association. A federal court and the Sixth Circuit Court of Appeals ruled against her. Even though the county did not have an anti-nepotism policy, it could fire her because **her relationship with a man married to another court system employee had an unacceptably disruptive effect on the workplace.** *Beecham v. Henderson County*, 422 F.3d 372 (6th Cir. 2005).

• An Indiana probation officer bought a car for her fiancé at a dealership that employed one of her probationers. She was then fired for violating the county court's code of conduct, which prohibits probation officers from doing business with any company that employs probationers under their supervision. She sued, claiming the code of conduct violated her First Amendment right to intimate association. A federal court and the Seventh Circuit ruled against her. Here, **the code only minimally interfered with her right of intimate association**, and it had a rational relationship to the county's legitimate interest in making sure that probation officers conduct themselves in a manner that avoids the appearance of impropriety. *Montgomery v. Stefaniak*, 410 F.3d 933 (7th Cir. 2005).

* A publicly run provider of electricity in Tennessee had **an exogamy rule, which required that when two permanent-status employees married, one of them had to quit**. When two employees decided to get married, they were informed that one of them would have to quit, but that whichever one did could continue on in a temporary capacity until he or she found a new job. The employees married and returned to work without deciding which one would leave. The husband was then called in to his supervisor's office, where he indicated that he did not agree with the policy. He was fired and sued under the First Amendment, alleging that the policy violated his constitutional right to marry (freedom of association). He also asserted that he was fired in retaliation for speaking out against the policy. A federal court granted pretrial judgment to the provider, and the Sixth Circuit affirmed in part. Here, the policy did not significantly restrict his ability to marry. However, there was a question of fact as to whether he had been fired for speaking out against the policy. That issue required a trial. *Vaughn v. Lawrenceburg Power System*, 269 F.3d 703 (6th Cir. 2001).

* Kansas City passed an ordinance prohibiting certain supervisory employees from belonging to the same labor organization as the employees they supervised. The city then refused to recognize a local bargaining unit of supervisory-level firefighters because the unit was affiliated with the International Association of Firefighters (IAFF), as was the local unit that represented non-supervisory firefighters. A Missouri federal court held that the ordinance was unconstitutional, and the Eighth Circuit affirmed. The ordinance violated the firefighters' First Amendment right to freedom of association because **the city failed to show that the local units' association with the IAFF would interfere with the management-level firefighters' duties**. Thus, its infringement of their associational rights was not reasonable. *IAFF, Local 3808 v. Kansas City*, 220 F.3d 969 (8th Cir. 2000).

* An Illinois guard at a prison with a 60% minority population was associated with the Ku Klux Klan. During non-working hours, the guard distributed literature to the public, sponsored a Klan rally at his home, and appeared on television to promote the rally. The Illinois Department of Corrections (DOC) investigated this matter and found that the guard had attempted to recruit co-workers to attend rallies, distributed literature, used racially motivated language such as "white power," and gave co-workers Klan hand signals. The guard was fired for engaging in conduct that was unbecoming to or impaired the operations of the DOC. He sued the DOC for violating his First Amendment right of freedom of association. A federal court found that the guard's message and associated activity involved a matter of public concern. However, it then

balanced the First Amendment right to expression against the DOC's interest in an effective and disciplined prison. Since the prison had a 60% minority population, most of whom were gang members, **the guard's association with the Klan could be viewed as being disruptive to racial harmony and prison security**. The court held that the guard's right to association with the Klan did not outweigh the DOC's interest in maintaining security and racial harmony in the Illinois prison system. The court ruled for the DOC. *Weicherding v. Riegel*, 981 F.Supp. 1143 (C.D. Ill. 1997).

- Two Wisconsin firefighters were members of the Chief Officers Association. Although not a union, the association did look after its members' interests. Annual membership dues were $206. The firefighters lost interest with the association and subsequently became delinquent in paying their dues. They eventually quit the association. Soon after, their supervisor evaluated them as "below average" in the category of "professional qualities." Although these evaluations were sent to the chief of the fire department, they generally were not used by the department in determining promotions, pay increases, demotions, discipline or discharge. The firefighters sued the city for retaliation and violation of their First Amendment rights not to associate. The case reached the Seventh Circuit Court of Appeals, which noted that a public employee is protected by the First Amendment when the issue is of public concern. Here, **the firefighters' disillusionment with the association had nothing to do with matters of public concern** such as politics, social issues or religious goals, but with the private issue of whether their salaries would be increased. The fact that their supervisor gave them a poor rating in one category of a performance review did not constitute an infringement of their First Amendment rights. *Balton v. City of Milwaukee*, 133 F.3d 1036 (7th Cir. 1998).

- A Missouri woman was elected to a county ambulance district board of directors, which adopted, over her objection, **a resolution limiting her participation as a member of the board because her husband had worked as an emergency medical technician and supervisor for the district** for the past two years. The board sought to prevent the misappropriation of information for personal gain and the appearance of impropriety, as well as to promote the free flow of ideas among members of the board. The resolution, however, restricted her participation in discussion and voting on a variety of employment matters without regard to whether her husband was associated with the matters. The woman sued in federal court for injunctive relief, alleging a violation of her rights under the First and Fourteenth Amendments and under the free speech clause of the Missouri Constitution. The district court denied her request, but the Eighth Circuit reversed, finding that the resolution impinged on her First Amendment associational rights and her Fourteenth Amendment equal protection rights. Here, the restraint on her participation even where discussions did not directly relate to her husband did not rationally relate to the board's asserted interests, thereby implicating her associational rights. Also, the resolution violated her equal protection rights because it created a standard specific to her that treated her differently from other board members. *Peeper v. Callaway County Ambulance Dist.*, 122 F.3d 619 (8th Cir. 1997).

♦   A Mississippi police officer came under investigation because of his friendship with a murder suspect. He was suspended during the internal investigation, and later he was fired. He sued, alleging that he was fired because he exercised his freedom of association rights under the First Amendment. The court determined that **the First Amendment does not contain a generalized right of social association, although a right of intimate association exists**. The right of intimate association protects against unjustified government interference with an individual's right to enter into and maintain certain intimate human relationships, such as marriage and the bearing and rearing of children. Here, the officer and suspect were only friends. Thus, they lacked the requisite affinity to create a constitutionally protected associational right under the First Amendment. The court entered pretrial judgment against the officer. *Tillman v. City of West Point, Mississippi,* 953 F.Supp. 145 (N.D. Miss. 1996).

F. Defamation

Distinguishable from a public employee's comments upon matters of public concern, defamatory statements generally find no constitutional protection. To recover for defamation, an employee must show that the statement was false and that it was published to third parties.

♦   Two Baltimore police officers were part of a "flex squad" that came under scrutiny after a woman claimed she had been raped by a member of the unit. Two other officers investigating the rape allegedly made false statements in an affidavit for a warrant to search the two officers' lockers. The affidavit claimed that the officers kept illegal drugs in their lockers, and that one of the officers stole cell phones and planted drugs on suspects. After those false statements were leaked to the press, the victim officers sued the other two officers for defamation. The lawsuit was dismissed, but the Maryland Court of Appeals reversed, holding that **the two defendant officers were not entitled to absolute immunity for making allegedly false statements in the affidavit**. Their statements were not the equivalent of statements made in a judicial proceeding because of the ex parte (one-sided) nature of the warrant proceedings. The case would continue, with the defendant officers entitled to only qualified immunity. *Smith v. Danielczyk,* 928 A.2d 795 (Md. 2007).

♦   A Connecticut university police officer applied for jobs with two cities and gave her consent for the departments to obtain job references from the university. When contacted about her qualifications, her supervisors indicated that she took too much time off work, that she had been seen dancing at a nightclub while on medical leave, that she had poor leadership skills and that she wasn't ready for a job with a regular police department yet. One city nevertheless hired her as a probationary employee. When she had trouble performing for the new police department, she was fired. She sued the university police department for defamation, claiming that the negative job references adversely affected her. The Connecticut Supreme Court held that **the department had a qualified privilege to provide the negative job references**. Here, the statements made about the officer were not given in bad faith. And more than 20 states have similar laws protecting such references. *Miron v. Univ. of New Haven Police Dep't*, 931 A.2d 847 (Conn. 2007).

- A New York city's mayor fired the head of the public works department. A newspaper article discussed how the employee's staff had been accused of using drugs but added that the charges had not been substantiated. The mayor then met with community leaders to discuss the termination and said he heard that the employee ran a cabaret without a license, took an unauthorized payment for city-owned property, never paid a cell phone bill and struck a co-worker. The employee was not told about the meeting, but insisted that the rumors were false. He later sued for "stigma-plus" defamation and due process violations, **alleging that the mayor's comments stigmatized his reputation and damaged his ability to find future employment**. The Second Circuit held that the mayor made stigmatizing statements and did not give the employee an adequate opportunity to clear his name. The employee was entitled to a new trial on damages for the due process violations. *Patterson v. City of Utica*, 370 F.3d 322 (2d Cir. 2004).

- A school bus driver in Minnesota was selected for a random drug test and was required to provide a urine sample of at least 45 milliliters. Although the test came back negative, the superintendent sent the driver a letter informing him that he was suspended for failing to provide an adequate sample. She directed him to submit to another test. He refused, and filed a lawsuit for defamation and violation of the state's Government Data Practices Act. A federal court ruled for the school district and the Eighth Circuit affirmed. Here, **the superintendent did not "publish" the letter (the allegedly defamatory statement) to third parties**. Rather, the bus driver self-published the letter, voluntarily showing it to people in the community to demonstrate the injustice he felt had been done to him. There was also insufficient evidence that the Government Data Practices Act had been violated. *Anderson v. Independent School Dist.*, 357 F.3d 806 (8th Cir. 2004).

- After rumors began circulating about the administration of a Missouri city, the mayor issued a press release that accused the city administrator of defrauding the city's health insurance program and contract-bidding process. A month later, the mayor broke a 3-3 tie of the board of aldermen and voted to fire the city administrator. The administrator requested and received a public hearing at which he and his attorney spoke. Subsequently, the administrator sued for defamation and violation of his due process liberty interests. A federal court ruled for the city, and the Eighth Circuit affirmed. First, there was no defamation because **the mayor's statement was protected as a non-actionable "opinion,"** which was privileged under the law of defamation. Second, there was no due process violation because the administrator received a public hearing at which he was allowed to speak. This was sufficient process to allow him to clear his name for the purposes of his liberty interests. His lawsuit against the city failed. *Hammer v. City of Osage Beach*, 318 F.3d 832 (8th Cir. 2003).

♦ A Glenn County, California, police officer applied for a job in Washington and signed a release authorizing the Glenn County Sheriff to furnish the Washington police department with information about his work record, reputation and financial and credit status and excused Glenn County from liability resulting from providing this information. The day before the officer was to begin work, **the sheriff spoke with the Washington police department and allegedly made several defamatory statements about the officer**. After the job offer was revoked, the officer sued the sheriff and the county. A California federal court granted pretrial judgment to both defendants, and the officer appealed. The Ninth Circuit reversed, finding that the release violated Section 1668 of the California Civil Code by shielding the sheriff from liability for intentional torts. Accordingly, the release was not enforceable. *McQuirk v. Donnelley*, 189 F.3d 793 (9th Cir. 1999).

♦ An Illinois police officer applied for positions with the U.S. Drug Enforcement Agency (DEA) and the Bureau of Alcohol, Tobacco, and Firearms (BATF). In the course of background checks, the police chief was interviewed regarding the officer's employment with the city. The police chief told the prospective employers that the officer was called "Code Red," which was the departmental code word for a person acting crazy, that he was unstable, and that he would not be rehired. Neither the DEA nor the BATF offered the officer a job. The officer sued the police chief for defamation. The court dismissed on the basis of qualified immunity, and the officer appealed to the Appellate Court of Illinois. Qualified immunity protects discretionary acts unique to a particular public office and made in furtherance of a governmental policy. The police chief here was not required by any official mandate to provide employment information, but decided to provide the prospective employers with statements. More importantly, **the decision that caused the officer's injury was not the decision to provide information but the statements actually provided**. Since these decisions were not unique to his position as police chief, the chief was not exercising his official discretion. Because the police chief's statements were not discretionary and were not policy determinations, he was not entitled to qualified immunity. The court reversed and remanded the case. *Stratman v. Brent*, 683 N.E.2d 951 (Ill. App. Ct. 1997).

♦ A South Carolina dispatcher alleged that the assistant chief of police had sexually harassed her, but she failed a polygraph test. The assistant chief denied the allegations, but still agreed to take a polygraph test conditioned upon a particular place or operator, or advance notice to verify the operator's qualifications and reputation. In response to this request, the city administrator declared, in the presence of other police officers, that he had no choice but to conclude the assistant chief had sexually harassed the dispatcher and had lied about it. The assistant chief was suspended, and the city administrator indicated that he would recommend termination. The next day, a newspaper printed an article about the suspension. The assistant chief retired and sued for defamation, intentional infliction of emotional distress, and constructive wrongful termination. A jury found for the assistant chief and awarded actual and punitive damages. The Supreme Court of South Carolina found that **the city**

administrator's conduct rose to the level of constitutional actual malice. The investigation revealed no justification for the city administrator to conclude that the assistant chief had sexually harassed the dispatcher. Also, there was no justification for defaming him in front of other officers. Moreover, the city administrator had expressed serious reservations about the dispatcher's allegations. Thus, the statements were made with reckless disregard for the truth, constituting actual malice. The damage awards were upheld. *Miller v. City of West Columbia, South Carolina*, 471 S.E.2d 683 (S.C. 1996).

* A Washington state trooper issued a citation to a speeder, who contested it. Later, the speeder returned to the same area and approached a car the trooper had stopped. The speeder asked the other driver if he felt he deserved the ticket. The other driver admitted speeding and refused to join a protest of the tickets. The trooper, who had been in his patrol car, approached the speeder and sternly requested that he leave. The trooper, corroborated by the driver and passenger of the stopped car, stated that he never touched or threatened to shoot or kill the speeder. The speeder, however, sent a letter to the Governor's Office for Constituent Affairs alleging that the trooper pushed him, unclipped his pistol, and threatened to "blow his head off." An internal investigation revealed that the allegations were unfounded. The trooper sued the speeder for defamation, and a jury found for the trooper. The court of appeals affirmed, and the Supreme Court of Washington granted review.

  The speeder argued that an absolute privilege, rather than a qualified privilege, should apply to citizens who complain of police conduct. The supreme court rejected this argument, finding that prior cases have drawn no constitutional distinctions based on the status of a public official. In particular, courts have applied a qualified privilege in cases involving police officers, implicitly recognizing the police officers' legitimate interests in protecting their reputations. As a result, a defamatory statement made with actual malice or reckless disregard for its truth would be actionable. The court also rejected the speeder's argument that the First Amendment's right to petition the government for redress of grievances protected his speech. The lower court decisions were affirmed. *Richmond v. Thompson*, 922 P.2d 1343 (Wash. 1996).

* A police officer resigned his position with a Montana city and thereafter obtained a deputy sheriff position with a state county. He again resigned and applied for a similar position with a third city police department. As part of his application, the officer signed a form authorizing previous employers to release his employment records. The prospective employer requested information about the officer's employment history from the first city's police chief and was notified that he "lacked appropriate personal habits, did not have good attendance habits, did not satisfactorily follow instructions, did not handle stress well, and was not suitable for reemployment." The applicant was not hired, and he filed a libel action against the city and police chief based on the chief's allegedly defamatory statements. A trial court ruled for the chief and city, and the Supreme Court of Montana affirmed. **Communications made by public employers within the scope of their employment are privileged.** Because the chief was acting in his official capacity when he responded to the request for

information, the exchange was a privileged communication that could not form the basis of a defamation action. *Wolf v. Williamson*, 889 P.2d 1177 (Mont. 1995).

♦ A prison warden employed by the Virginia Department of Corrections discovered a memo from a subordinate in an envelope on his desk. The memo accused him of propositioning the subordinate on several occasions, of sending her unwarranted derogatory notes, and of improperly lowering her performance rating. The warden reported the memo to his superiors and requested a full investigation. Based on the investigation, he was discharged and later hired by the department at a lower-paying position. The warden then filed a defamation lawsuit against the subordinate. A trial court awarded him $152,597 in compensatory damages (later reduced) and $100,000 in punitive damages. The subordinate appealed. The Supreme Court of Virginia rejected the subordinate's argument that her speech was constitutionally protected opinion, ruling that the memo contained factual statements that could form the basis of a defamation action. **The trial court's findings that the allegations in the memo were false and that the disciplinary notes were not retaliatory were supported by substantial evidence.** Also, the reduction of damages was proper because a larger award could result in the subordinate's financial ruin. The trial court's ruling was affirmed. *Williams v. Garraghty*, 455 S.E.2d 209 (Va. 1995).

♦ A Michigan police sergeant was informed that a citizen had contacted relatives about his intent to commit suicide. The citizen was intoxicated and on drugs, and his family reported hearing small caliber weapons fire in the house. Despite requests for police assistance, the sergeant never dispatched any officers to the scene. The citizen was found dead in his home the next morning from a self-inflicted gunshot wound. A disciplinary proceeding against the sergeant, which was shown to media representatives, resulted in his demotion, suspension and probation. The sergeant sued the city, alleging defamation, invasion of privacy, and violations of public policy. A trial court dismissed the claims, and the sergeant appealed. The Court of Appeals of Michigan held that **truth was an absolute defense**, and that the defamation and false light claims had been properly dismissed. The department could not be held liable for the characterization of truthful information by the media. Moreover, the material disclosed by the city concerned a subject about which the public had a legitimate interest, and the trial court had properly dismissed the sergeant's claim that the city had invaded his privacy by publicly disclosing private facts. *Porter v. City of Royal Oak*, 542 N.W.2d 905 (Mich. Ct. App. 1995).

II. UNION AND POLITICAL ACTIVITY

The extent to which public employees may engage in the free exercise of speech regarding union or political activities varies depending upon the governmental entity for which the employees work, the context of the speech, and the importance of such speech.

A. Union Activities

Although limitations exist on a public employee's right to engage in political activities, it is well established that public employees have a First Amendment right to form unions and to engage in union activities. Although labor relations are discussed, for the most part, in other chapters, free speech issues often arise in the union context.

* A New York corrections officer served as the president of the local union. The county paid his salary and benefits while he was on paid leave; the union reimbursed the county. As part of the leave agreement, he was not supposed to represent the local union in grievances, administrative proceedings or other labor matters against the county. When he criticized, at a county legislative open meeting, an unnamed undersheriff for disciplining corrections officers in what he believed was an unlawful manner, his union leave was revoked. He returned to his job as a corrections officer and sued under the First Amendment. A federal court granted pretrial judgment to the county on the grounds that he did not suffer an adverse action, but the Second Circuit reversed. **A jury would have to decide whether the leave revocation was an adverse action**, substantially altering his responsibilities and duties. Also, he clearly spoke out on a matter of public concern. *Hoyt v. Andreucci*, 433 F.3d 320 (2d Cir. 2006).

* Five Department of Corrections (DOC) officers in a New York county refused to work "forced overtime," citing fatigue. They submitted doctors' notes to verify their exhaustion. However, the DOC's chief of operations had been told that officers who normally volunteered for overtime would not do so because of stalemated talks over a new collective bargaining agreement. He believed that the officers had engaged in an unlawful "job action." After the officers were fired, an arbitrator determined that they had not disobeyed any rules and that the county failed to tie them to the work stoppage. Upon their reinstatement, two of the officers sued, asserting that their constitutional right to freedom of association had been violated. A jury awarded each officer $35,000, but the Second Circuit vacated the awards. **The officers' union membership alone was not a motivating factor in their discipline.** Even though the DOC may have been mistaken about their involvement in the work stoppage, that did not transform the disciplinary decision into something motivated by anti-union animus. *Cobb v. Pozzi*, 363 F.3d 89 (2d Cir. 2004).

* A New Mexico school board required a teacher to submit to a performance improvement plan. The plan required her to try to get along better with her co-workers and to exercise professionalism in conducting her affairs. **She claimed that the plan was put in place in retaliation for her helping fellow union members file complaints and grievances against the district**, but the school's principal maintained that it resulted from the complaints of four unnamed teachers. She filed a grievance, but the school board's personnel director told her that her complaint was not a grievable matter. She resigned when the school superintendent denied the grievance. A federal court dismissed her lawsuit for retaliation under the First Amendment, and the Tenth Circuit

affirmed. Although adverse acts short of dismissal may be actionable under the First Amendment, trivial acts generally will not support a retaliation claim. Here, the acts alleged were too trivial to support her lawsuit. *Lybrook v. Farmington Municipal Schools Board of Educ.*, 232 F.3d 1334 (10th Cir. 2000).

• During contract negotiations between a city and a police union, relations between the chief and the union became strained. **The chief allegedly told one officer that because of his union activities, he no longer had a career in the department.** When that officer and several others applied for promotions to sergeant, the chief and several interviewing members of the promotion panel rated them low because of their union activities. The city's new mayor then refused to make any promotions during the effective period of the promotion lists. The officers sued in a Pennsylvania federal court, alleging retaliation for the exercise of their First Amendment rights. The court dismissed their lawsuit, holding that even if their rankings were lowered in retaliation for their protected activity, they could not recover because they could not show that they would have been promoted absent the retaliation. The Third Circuit reversed and remanded the case. The officers had raised a question of fact as to whether the chief's retaliatory actions were sufficient to deter a person of ordinary firmness from exercising his First Amendment rights. Some relief might be proper, and the burden was now on the city to show that the officers would not have been promoted. *Suppan v. Dadonna*, 203 F.3d 228 (3d Cir. 2000).

• A minority faction of the union representing New York City transit workers believed that union leaders were in collusion with management and not furthering the transit workers' interests. Two union officials headed the minority faction and circulated a petition calling for the recall of certain union leaders who negotiated a dispute over a pension plan. As union officers, they participated in a "release time" program that allowed them to conduct union business while still being paid by the authority. When they failed to sign in immediately after arriving at the union office, allegedly violating the release time program's policy, the union's new labor relations director suspended them. They sued the director and the transit authority under 42 U.S.C. § 1983, claiming retaliaton for exercising their First Amendment rights. The district court ruled for the authority on the retaliation issue but refused to grant the labor relations director immunity for the suspension. The Second Circuit agreed with the lower court on the retaliation issue but held that the director was entitled to immunity. Although **the officers enjoyed a constitutional right to be free from retaliation for their dissenting activities,** that right was not clearly established at the time they were suspended, so the labor relations director was entitled to qualified immunity. *Clue v. Johnson*, 179 F.3d 57 (2d Cir. 1999).

• Several state union employees attended a three-day seminar sponsored by the Michigan Democratic Party on election campaign strategies. The employees primarily used union officer leave or administrative leave buy-back to participate in the seminar. Under union officer leave, the union reimburses the employer for the gross total cost of the employee's wages and the employer's share of the insurance premiums and retirement. The administrative leave buy-back allows the employer to submit a bill to the union for net salary during the period of absence; however, the insurance premiums and fringe benefits are paid by the employer. When the state civil service commission issued a rule prohibiting the use of union leaves of absence for partisan political activities, civil service employees and their unions challenged the rule. The Supreme Court of Michigan noted that the state's political freedom act prohibits partisan political activity during work hours when the state employee is being compensated by the employer. However, where the union reimburses the state for the employees' wages and fringe benefits, the state may not prohibit those employees from participating in partisan political activities. **The state could not prohibit employees from participating in partisan political activities while on union leave** unless such activities were shown to adversely affect job performance. Therefore, the rule prohibiting union leaves was invalid. *Michigan State AFL-CIO v. Michigan Civil Service Comm'n*, 566 N.W.2d 258 (Mich. 1997).

* A West Virginia city owned, operated, and managed a park consisting of a 150-acre public resort. A hotel and restaurant employees union began conducting an organizational campaign at the park – distributing leaflets and talking with employees as well as patrons. The park commission claimed that the organizers' activities obstructed the traffic flow and intimidated employees and patrons. After several requests that union representatives not engage in certain activities and not conduct specific activities in certain areas of the park, the park commission filed suit in state court seeking injunctive relief restricting the union's activities. The court issued a preliminary injunction, and the union appealed to the Supreme Court of Appeals of West Virginia, which found that the lower court did not use the appropriate standard for issuing an injunction under the First Amendment. **Injunctions are remedies imposed for violations (or threatened violations) of a legislative or judicial decree** and carry greater risks of censorship and discriminatory application than do general ordinances. Also, an injunction focuses on one person's or group's communicative activities. The case was reversed and remanded. *Wheeling Park Comm'n v. Hotel Union*, 479 S.E.2d 876 (W.Va. 1996).

* A Mississippi firefighter was hired for a 12-month probationary period. The chief discharged him eight hours before the end of the probationary period for having a poor attitude. The firefighter sued, alleging that the termination was in retaliation for his association with union members and thus a violation of the First Amendment. At trial, firefighters in his unit, his supervisors, and the assistant chief testified that he was a very good firefighter and had an excellent attitude. Further, no other firefighter had ever been discharged for having a poor attitude. Others testified that the chief had told them that the firefighter "hung out with the wrong crowd," that unions caused turmoil, and that the firefighter's extracurricular activity was going to get him in trouble. The district court held that the termination violated the firefighter's First Amendment rights, awarded him $30,558 in lost wages, and ordered reinstatement. The U.S. Court of Appeals, Fifth Circuit, affirmed, noting that freedom of association claims are not subject to the threshold public concern requirement. **Association with union members almost invariably implicates matters of public concern** and

an independent inquiry to this effect is unnecessary. Further, employers cannot intimidate public employees from joining a union and cannot retaliate against those who do. Therefore, the chief and the city had violated clearly established law and were not entitled to qualified immunity. *Boddie v. City of Columbus, Mississippi*, 989 F.2d 745 (5th Cir. 1993).

♦ The National Treasury Employees Union was engaged in a campaign to replace the American Federation of Government Employees as the bargaining representative of Social Security Administration (SSA) employees. To further its efforts, the union sought to distribute literature at SSA headquarters, which required a permit. The SSA had commonly granted permits to other organizations but refused to issue a permit to the union. Union members nevertheless began distributing literature on the headquarters' walkways. While at the SSA's facilities, several physical confrontations between rival union members resulted. The union members filed suit, alleging that the SSA's refusal to grant them a permit violated their First Amendment rights.

The district court noted that organized labor literature was a form of speech, which was protected by the First Amendment. **Generally, distribution of literature and other expressive activities can be conducted on public property.** Here, the walkways were not public property because they were almost exclusively used by SSA employees. However, the SSA's nonrestrictive regulations, which governed speech on the walkways, its history of granting other organizations permission to distribute literature, and the virtual impossibility of alternative, less disruptive forms of expression led the court to conclude that the SSA had created public forums by designation. Thus, the denial of a permit to the union violated its First Amendment rights. *National Treasury Employees Union v. King*, 798 F.Supp. 780 (D.D.C. 1992).

♦ A city charter contained a provision that forbade any city official from "recognizing" a collective bargaining agent or representative of city employees. On numerous occasions, in private meetings with city officials, representatives from the Fraternal Order of Police (FOP) were told that they would be met with as individuals, but not as FOP representatives. The representatives were never denied a right to speak at city council meetings or at any other meetings that were open to the public. FOP sued, alleging that the charter provision and its application violated its freedom of speech and equal protection rights. The Fourth Circuit noted that **the First Amendment guarantees free speech, but does not guarantee a right to collective bargaining.** The city could legally recognize a particular union, and the provision was not per se unlawful. Further, FOP had no right to privately address city officials, and thus had no right that was burdened. *Fraternal Order of Police v. Mayor and City Council of Ocean City Maryland*, 916 F.2d 919 (4th Cir. 1990).

B. Political Activities

Employees can be terminated for their political beliefs if they are employed in managerial or discretionary positions, or positions that require loyalty to certain elected officials.

♦ A lawyer and an accounting firm in Puerto Rico entered into a contract with a city. The contract was signed by the mayor. When a new mayor from another party was elected, he refused to pay them for their services and they sued. They claimed First Amendment violations. A federal court dismissed their case, but the First Circuit reversed. **The only reason for the nonpayment appeared to be political affiliation**, so unless the city had some legitimate policy-making interest in not paying the independent contractors, it would be liable for violating the First Amendment. The court remanded the case. *Ramirez v. Arlequin*, 447 F.3d 19 (1st Cir. 2006).

1. Managerial and Discretionary Positions

♦ The governor of Illinois instituted a hiring freeze for every agency under his control. Exceptions were granted through the governor's personnel office with a majority going to those employees affiliated with the Republican Party. Five state employees sued, alleging discrimination with respect to promotions, transfers and recalls because they had not been supporters of the state's Republican Party. The U.S. Court of Appeals, Seventh Circuit, noted that only those employment decisions that have the effect of a dismissal violate the First Amendment. The U.S. Supreme Court determined that employees who did not compromise their beliefs tended to lose increases in pay and job satisfaction attendant to promotions, transfers and recalls. These were significant penalties imposed in retaliation for the exercise of rights guaranteed by the First Amendment. Therefore, promotions, transfers and recalls based on political affiliation were an impermissible infringement on the First Amendment rights of public employees. The Court established the constitutional principle "that **party membership is not a permissible factor in the dispensation of government jobs, except those jobs for the performance of which party affiliation is an appropriate requirement.**" *Rutan v. Republican Party of Illinois*, 497 U.S. 62, 110 S.Ct. 2729, 111 L.Ed.2d 52 (1990).

♦ A group of Republicans who were non-civil service employees of an Illinois sheriff's office brought a class action suit alleging that they were discharged, or threatened with discharge, because they were not affiliated with or sponsored by the Democratic party. Finding that the group had failed to show irreparable injury, the district court denied their motion for a preliminary injunction and ultimately dismissed their lawsuit for failure to state a claim upon which relief could be granted. The U.S. Court of Appeals, Seventh Circuit, reversed, and the U.S. Supreme Court granted review. The Court stated that the practice of patronage dismissals violates the First and Fourteenth Amendments. Patronage dismissals severely restrict political belief and association and **the government may not force a public employee to relinquish his right to political association as the price of holding a public job**. Though First Amendment rights are not absolute, they may be curtailed only by interests of vital importance, the burden of proving the existence of which rests on the government. The inefficiency of wholesale replacement of public employees on a change of administration belies the argument that employees not of the same political persuasion will not be motivated to work effectively. *Elrod v. Burns,* 427 U.S. 347, 96 S.Ct. 2673, 49 L.Ed.2d 547 (1976).

♦ A hearing officer in an Illinois village adjudicated citations issued under village ordinances, handling such matters as parking, zoning, and regulation of property and pets. He backed the loser in a mayoral election, then was replaced by the mayor and sued for wrongful termination under the First Amendment. A federal court and the Seventh Circuit ruled against him, noting that political affiliation was a legitimate qualification for the job. Hearing officers had discretion over how to enforce some of the regulations they were charged with handling. This impacted the mayors because **the way a hearing officer enforced such issues as neat neighborhoods affected whether a mayor might be re-elected.** *Walsh v. Heilmann,* 472 F.3d 504 (7th Cir. 2006).

♦ The chief of the sign shop for the Illinois Department of Transportation (DOT) had a job description that stated he was afforded broad latitude in accomplishing his duties, and that he formulated and implemented policies. He supervised five employees directly and 20 employees indirectly. He also controlled inventory and a $3.7 million annual budget. After his termination, he sued under the First Amendment, claiming he'd been improperly fired because of his political affiliation. A federal court granted pretrial judgment to the DOT, but the Seventh Circuit reversed. **Just because the job description said the chief was responsible for formulating policy did not mean he was a policy maker** for First Amendment purposes. The job description raised questions about the judgment and discretion the chief of the highway sign shop exercised. The case required a trial. *Moss v. Martin,* 473 F.3d 694 (7th Cir. 2007).

♦ An assistant deputy sheriff for field training supported the sheriff in an upcoming election. However, the sheriff's opponent won the election and two months later fired the assistant deputy sheriff. A lawsuit resulted, claiming a First Amendment violation, but a Massachusetts federal court and the First Circuit ruled in favor of the new sheriff. The court of appeals held that the assistant deputy sheriff could be discharged for supporting the incumbent once there was a new sheriff in town. **Political affiliation was an appropriate requirement for the job of assistant deputy sheriff.** He was a top-level official who advised the sheriff on policy, implemented the sheriff's policy and acted as an internal spokesperson for department policy. This was a policymaking or confidential position. *Hadfield v. McDonough,* 407 F.3d 11 (1st Cir. 2005).

♦ A Utah city treasurer supported the losing mayoral candidate in an election. Afterwards, the new mayor sent her a letter informing her that because she failed to offer her support during the election, it would be in the city's best interests to have another treasurer appointed. The treasurer stepped down, then sued the city and mayor under the First and Fourteenth Amendments. A federal court ruled against her, and the Tenth Circuit affirmed. Here, as a political appointee, the treasurer did not have a property interest in continued employment, so she was not entitled to Fourteenth Amendment due process protections. As for the First Amendment claim, the mayor had a right to expect the treasurer to be loyal to her. The treasurer had significant authority for setting the city's monetary policies, for hiring staff, and for handling citizen complaints about their bills. **She worked under the broad policy guidance of the mayor in a job that required political allegiance.** *Snyder v. City of Moab*, 354 F.3d 1179 (10th Cir. 2003).

* A Pennsylvania city manager supported certain city council candidates for election. When the opposition candidates won the election, the city council voted to dismiss him from his job. He sued, alleging retaliation for exercising his First Amendment rights. A federal court ruled for the city, and the Third Circuit affirmed. Here, the city manager ran day-to-day operations, oversaw all city departments, and managed all city employees. His position required confidentiality and a close working relationship with city council members to effectively implement their policies. **Political affiliation was a reasonable requirement for the city manager job**, and the city council members had good reason to doubt whether they could rely on him to follow and implement their policies. *Curinga v. City of Clairton*, 357 F.3d 305 (3d Cir. 2004).

* The chairperson of Milwaukee's Board of Zoning Appeals served for 13 years until the city elected a new mayor, who indicated that he would not renew the chairperson's appointment. However, when the city council stated that it would not approve a replacement (keeping the chairperson in place indefinitely), the mayor reappointed him. Seven years later, the mayor finally chose not to reappoint the chairperson. In the lawsuit that followed under 42 U.S.C. § 1983, the chairperson alleged that the mayor violated his First Amendment rights by refusing to reappoint him for political reasons. A Wisconsin federal court dismissed the chairperson's lawsuit, and the Seventh Circuit affirmed. Because political affiliation is an appropriate criterion for public employment when the **effective operation of government would be compromised by requiring a public official to retain a potential political enemy** in a position of responsibility, the mayor did not violate the First Amendment by refusing to reappoint the chairperson. Because board members had considerable discretion to implement the broad goals of city zoning policy, political affiliation was a proper criterion for the job. *Pleva v. Norquist*, 195 F.3d 905 (7th Cir. 1999).

* A Virginia temporary employee, who belonged to the Democratic Party, worked full time for a county and received life and health insurance benefits even though he was not entitled to them. When the Republican Party gained control of the county's governing board, the employee's benefits were taken away in an attempt to achieve uniformity in the county's employment policies. The employee sued, asserting that his benefits had been taken away because of his political affiliation. A federal jury ruled for the employee, and the district court reinstated his benefits and awarded him $15,000 in damages. The Fourth Circuit reversed. It first noted that **the employee's position was a non-policymaking and non-confidential one protected from adverse action because of political affiliation**. However, the employee failed to show that his

political affiliation motivated the decision to deny him benefits. Here, county policy dictated that temporary employees should not receive health insurance, and state law provided that temporary employees should not receive life insurance. Accordingly, the decision to deny benefits was not improper. *Cooper v. Lee County Board of Supervisors*, 188 F.3d 501 (4th Cir. 1999).

• The First Amendment rights of a police captain of the Harford County, Maryland, Sheriff's Office were not violated when he was terminated after the sheriff he supported for reelection lost to the challenger. The U.S. Court of Appeals, Fourth Circuit, explained that sheriffs are "responsible for implementing a political agenda that has been approved by the voters through the sheriff's election." In these circumstances, party affiliation can be used to determine whether a sheriff's deputy or other high-ranking official can effectively perform the duties of the office. Here, **the sheriff could properly rely on the captain's political affiliation as grounds for termination**. In a department of 230 people, the captain was the fifth highest-ranking officer. Further, after the election, the sheriff learned that none of the other members of the upper-level staff wanted to work with the captain and that many lower-level deputies had expressed concerns about his police and command acumen. *Mills v. Meadows*, 187 F.3d 630 (4th Cir. 1999) (Unpublished).

• A Texas county assistant district attorney supported a losing candidate for the position of criminal district attorney (DA). After her candidate was defeated, the employee received a letter from the new DA informing her that her position would be eliminated. She sued the new DA and other officials under 42 U.S.C. § 1983, alleging that her First Amendment rights were violated because she was fired in retaliation for her political affiliation. The court noted that although the First Amendment generally prohibits an employer from terminating an employee because of her political affiliation, there is an exception where an employee's private political belief would interfere with the discharge of her public duties. Here, the employee, in addition to being an assistant district attorney, was also in charge of the Appellate and Hot Check Divisions. Both these areas accorded her complete discretion and made her answerable only to the DA. She was also responsible for the implementation of other policies within the office. Her position required a close working relationship with the DA. **Because of the political and discretionary nature of the position, the employee was not entitled to First Amendment protections.** The court ruled for the defendants. *Cudd v. Aldrich*, 982 F.Supp. 463 (S.D. Tex. 1997).

• A California assistant district attorney (DA) was fired when he decided to run for election against his boss. The assistant DA was an at-will employee who was one of the most senior attorneys in the office and had the title of head attorney. As head attorney, he had a higher salary, was assigned the high profile cases, and created and implemented several programs in the district attorney's office. The assistant DA sued the city and county for violating his First Amendment rights, but the U.S. Court of Appeals, Ninth Circuit, ruled that he could be fired for purely political reasons without violating the First Amendment. **Taking into consideration the assistant DA's seniority and** position within the office, he was a policymaker. *Fazio v. City and County of San Francisco*, 125 F.3d 1328 (9th Cir. 1997).

• A Republican county manager in Washington was dismissed by the newly elected Democratic county executive. The manager's position included responsibilities such as governing elections, performing quasi-judicial functions on challenges to voter registration, and formulating and implementing policy. The manager sued under 42 U.S.C § 1983, alleging that her discharge for political reasons violated her First and Fourteenth Amendment rights. The district court held that the political patronage dismissal was justified. **Political affiliation was an appropriate requirement** because of the manager's level of discretion, authority, and scope of duties. The court rejected the manager's argument that the position's requirement of non-partisanship foreclosed a political patronage dismissal. *Soelter v. King County*, 931 F.Supp. 741 (W.D. Wash. 1996).

• A newly elected Democrat attorney general in Indiana discharged a number of employees, almost all of whom were white, male Republicans over the age of 40. She allegedly fired one such assistant because "his contributions to the operations of the office did not fit [her] expectations." The assistant sued the attorney general, alleging that he had been unlawfully discharged based on his political party affiliation and his age in violation of the First Amendment and the ADEA. The Seventh Circuit noted that **the attorney general's assistants officially acted on behalf of the state, and the position inherently necessitated meaningful input into governmental decisionmaking in politically sensitive areas**. Consequently, political loyalty was an appropriate job requirement. The court also dismissed the age discrimination claim because an assistant attorney general was not an "employee" under either Title VII or the ADEA. *Americanos v. Carter*, 74 F.3d 138 (7th Cir. 1996).

• An Ohio Department of Transportation administrative assistant took a temporary leave of absence. Another employee was temporarily promoted to that position. The promotion was rescinded three days later, but the position became a permanent vacancy when the former administrative assistant decided not to return from his leave of absence. The employee unsuccessfully sought the position and then sued the department and its officials, alleging that another person was appointed to the job as a political patronage maneuver in violation of the First Amendment. The U.S. Court of Appeals, Sixth Circuit, noted that **party affiliation need not be an essential requirement (just an appropriate requirement) for the job to justify discharge based on political affiliation**. Even though the employee performed mainly administrative tasks at a local office, he controlled local lines of communication to the director. Thus, the administrative assistant position had a political dimension, and party affiliation was an appropriate requirement for the position. Consequently, the employee's discharge did not violate the First Amendment. *Rice v. Ohio Dep't of Transportation*, 14 F.3d 1133 (6th Cir. 1994).

♦ A democratic challenger upset the Republican incumbent governor of West Virginia. The democratically controlled legislature passed legislation that broadened the group of employees who could be discharged for their political affiliation. The new governor and other state officials required that all county maintenance superintendents be transferred to subordinate positions but at the same pay. The superintendents sought reinstatement, alleging that the transfers were impermissible because they were politically motivated. The district court held that the superintendents' involuntary transfers violated the First Amendment and that the state officials were not entitled to qualified immunity. The Fourth Circuit Court of Appeals noted that the more highly ranked an employee was, the less First Amendment protection he or she received. **Because of the employees' lower-level policymaking authority and limited contact with the public, party affiliation was not an "appropriate requirement" for the effective performance of the job.** Accordingly, the new statute, as applied to the superintendents, was unconstitutional. However, since all the superintendents continued work at different positions but for the same salary, their First Amendment rights were not violated. *Akers v. Caperton*, 998 F.2d 220 (4th Cir. 1993).

2. Participation in the Political Process

♦ A group of Utah public employee unions challenged the state's Voluntary Contributions Act (VCA), which prohibited any state or local public employer from withholding voluntary political contributions from its employees' paychecks. The Attorney General argued that the governmental payroll systems were the property of the state intended for non-speech purposes, and that the law was reasonable in light of the payroll system's primary purpose: processing paychecks. A federal court disagreed and applied the strict scrutiny test, holding that the VCA was not narrowly tailored to a compelling state interest. On appeal, the Tenth Circuit used a modified test to find that **the VCA violated the First Amendment by restricting the method of making political contributions** in a manner that was not closely drawn to match a sufficiently important governmental interest. *Utah Educ. Ass'n v. Shurtleff*, 512 F.3d 1254 (10th Cir. 2008).

♦ A recreational director for a Tennessee city, after supporting the incumbent mayor, was fired after the mayor lost her bid for reelection. He sued under the First Amendment, claiming he was improperly fired because of political affiliation. After a pretrial disposition, the case reached the Sixth Circuit, which noted that there were issues of fact to be resolved, necessitating a remand. Here, the city charter and the city's handbook stated that political affiliation was not a job requirement. On the other hand, the handbook allowed the mayor to delegate policymaking authority to subordinates. The new mayor claimed that the director was a policymaker because he managed his own department, made the budget for it, handled employment decisions and generally acted as the city's "alter ego." However, **those assertions did not show how the director's inherent duties required political affiliation.** A trial was required. *Lane v. City of LaFollette*, 490 F.3d 410 (6th Cir. 2007).

- The director of environmental education for the New Jersey Meadowlands Commission lost her job when a new administration took office. She sued under 42 U.S.C. § 1983, claiming a violation of her First Amendment rights. A federal court granted pretrial judgment to the commission, but the Third Circuit reinstated her lawsuit. First, there was a question as to whether her job was a policymaking one. Although she was a supervisor, she allegedly had no power to hire or fire and merely offered information to her superiors, who implemented policy. Second, **the fact that she was not a member of a political party did not mean she wasn't entitled to political affiliation protection** under the First Amendment. Third, there was a question as to whether her superiors knew of her political silence. And finally, the commission offered inconsistent explanations for her firing, at one point citing poor performance even though her division received an award for excellence while she was in charge. Also, 18 Democratic-affiliated employees were hired after she and 11 unaffiliated or Republican employees were fired. *Galli v. New Jersey Meadowlands Comm'n*, 490 F.3d 265 (3d Cir. 2007).

- The head of road repairs for an Arkansas county sued under 42 U.S.C. § 1983 after he was fired, asserting that the reason for his termination was his failure to support the county's chief executive officer (CEO) in the previous election. A federal court and the Eighth Circuit ruled against him. First, he failed to show that politics was a motivating factor in his termination. The county's CEO told him that the reason for his discharge was his lack of leadership and the fact that his workers were not doing their jobs. Second, even if politics had been a motivating factor, **political loyalty was a proper requirement for the road foreman job**. The court of appeals found no First Amendment violation. *Langley v. Hot Spring County, Arkansas*, 393 F.3d 814 (8th Cir. 2005).

- A county road manager and a county administrator in Mississippi campaigned against the president of the county board of supervisors in an election, but their candidate lost. Afterward, the board voted 3-2 to not renew their contracts, with the president casting the deciding vote. They sued the county under the First Amendment, asserting that while they owed allegiance to the board as a whole, they did not have to demonstrate political loyalty to the board president. The case reached the Fifth Circuit Court of Appeals, which ruled against them. It held that they could not choose political favorites or enemies among the board members. The court also noted that **their jobs were of a policy-making nature such that they could be terminated for disloyalty**. The road manager position was the second highest non-elected management position in the county, and the way the roads were managed greatly influenced how the public viewed their elected supervisors. The county manager position required working closely with the board to set policy and ensure that its orders were executed. The two positions allowed the employees to strongly influence public opinion about the board. No First Amendment protection was available to them. *Gentry v. Lowndes County, Mississippi*, 337 F.3d 481 (5th Cir. 2003).

♦ Two dispatchers in a Virginia county sheriff's department supported the sheriff's opponent in an election. A month after the opponent lost, the sheriff notified the dispatchers that they would not be reappointed when their terms expired at the end of the year. He cited confidentiality concerns as a result of information leaked about a murder investigation. The dispatchers sued the sheriff under 42 U.S.C. § 1983, claiming the sheriff violated their First Amendment rights. A federal court held that the sheriff was not entitled to qualified immunity, and he appealed. The Fourth Circuit reversed, noting that even if the dispatchers were fired for supporting the sheriff's opponent in the election, **the law was not clearly established that their interest in commenting on a matter of public concern outweighed the sheriff's interest** in maintaining a loyal and efficient sheriff's department. The sheriff was entitled to qualified immunity. The court also noted that the dispatchers here, while not deputies, did have access to confidential information, making it less clear that the decision to fire them for their political affiliation (if true) violated the First Amendment. *Pike v. Osborne*, 301 F.3d 182 (4th Cir. 2002).

♦ During city elections, a Kansas police chief placed a local television ad warning voters that some candidates for city office were convicted felons. A few months later, he placed a sign on his front lawn regarding city recall elections that stated, "Vote no on recall." The chief was eventually fired for his activities and sued the city, alleging that his termination was in retaliation for exercising his First Amendment rights. The U.S. Court of Appeals, Tenth Circuit, found **no evidence that the chief's conduct created disruption within the city**. The city merely made speculative allegations that the chief's speech caused or would cause disruption. It failed to demonstrate that the chief's speech contributed to any specific disruption within the city administration or the police department, or jeopardized the efficient provision of law enforcement services. *Cragg v. City of Osawatomie, Kansas*, 143 F.3d 1343 (10th Cir. 1998).

♦ Two employees of a Pennsylvania county social services agency helped their union on a volunteer basis by distributing non-political leaflets, such as information about contract negotiations, to their co-workers. Following a union request, the employees also distributed pamphlets explaining the union's opposition to members of the Republican Party running for local office. Because **state civil service law expressly prohibits any person in classified service from promoting or opposing candidates in a partisan election**, the civil service commission ordered that they be suspended for 30 days.

On review, the Commonwealth Court of Pennsylvania held that the suspension was supported by substantial evidence. Violations of the statute need not be intentional, so the employees' argument that they did not know what was in the pamphlets was meritless. This was particularly true because the employees knew about the prohibition against distributing political pamphlets at work and had some obligation to examine the pamphlets before distributing them. Nor were the employees' due process rights violated just because the civil service law authorizes the commission to act as prosecutor and judge in cases involving civil service employees. Procedures had been enacted to ensure that the prosecutorial and adjudicative functions were isolated from each other.

Accordingly, the employees' due process rights had been met. *Hetman v. State Civil Service Comm'n*, 714 A.2d 532 (Pa. Commw. Ct. 1998).

• Several corrections officers for New York City's Department of Corrections (DOC) campaigned for George Pataki. After Pataki was elected governor, the DOC investigated whether two corrections officers used their positions to organize up to 600 corrections officers to assist in the campaign. One officer provided no information and was transferred to another facility to keep him from tainting others who might otherwise cooperate. Four other officers who had also worked on the campaign were transferred to different work sites pending the conclusion of the investigation. However, six other officers who had worked on the campaign were not transferred. The investigative team eventually concluded that no officers had been threatened or coerced into working on the campaign. The transferred officers sued, alleging retaliation for exercise of their First Amendment rights under 42 U.S.C. §§ 1983 and 1985. The district court ruled against the officers, finding that they had failed to establish their claim under Section 1983. **They failed to show the existence of a New York City policy or custom to transfer employees on the basis of their political beliefs or association.** The court also dismissed the Section 1985 claim. *Soto v. Schembri*, 960 F.Supp. 751 (S.D.N.Y. 1997).

• Supervisory police officers employed by a Florida county police department allegedly discouraged several subordinates from supporting an opponent of the incumbent sheriff. The subordinates were later transferred to positions that did not involve demotions in pay or rank, but caused scheduling hardships or loss of supervisory responsibilities. The subordinates sued, alleging retaliation for their political support of the sheriff's opponent in violation of the First Amendment. The court denied the supervisory officers' requests for qualified immunity, and they appealed. The Eleventh Circuit reversed. Because no bright-line standard put reasonable public employers on notice of constitutional violations with respect to restrictions on employee speech, such employers were entitled to immunity except where adverse action was clearly unlawful. Although employees generally may not be demoted because of their political speech, **the transfers in the present case were not violations of clearly established law at the time they occurred**. Because the supervisory employees' actions were not clearly unlawful, they were entitled to qualified immunity. *Rogers v. Miller*, 57 F.3d 986 (11th Cir. 1995).

3. Running for Public Office

The Hatch Act, 5 U.S.C. §§ 7321-27, prohibits all employees of the executive branch or any individual employed by the government of the District of Columbia from using the employee's **official authority or influence** for the purpose of interfering with or affecting the outcome of an election.

However, an employee may take an active part in political management or in political campaigns. Further, the employee retains the right to vote as the employee chooses and to express an opinion on political matters.

The act also prohibits federal employees from engaging in political activity while on duty, in any room or building occupied in the discharge of official duties by a government employee or office holder, while wearing a uniform or official insignia identifying their office or position, or using any vehicle owned or leased by the U.S. Government.

Employees who have been determined by the Merit Systems Protection Board to have violated on two occasions certain of these provisions will be removed from their positions and will no longer be entitled to federal employment. Before its amendment in 1993, the Hatch Act prohibited employees from actively participating in political campaigns or their management.

The constitutionality of the Hatch Act has been brought before the U.S. Supreme Court twice and upheld on both occasions. In *U.S. Civil Service Commission v. National Ass'n of Letter Carriers*, 413 U.S. 548, 93 S.Ct. 2880, 37 L.Ed.2d 796 (1973), the Court held that the prohibition against employees assuming an active role in political campaigning or management was neither overbroad nor unconstitutionally vague.

In *United Public Workers of America v. Mitchell*, 330 U.S. 75, 67 S.Ct. 556, 91 L.Ed 754 (1947), the Court stated that it was within Congress' power to regulate the political conduct of federal employees. **The Hatch Act does not apply to most state and local employees, but many states regulate the political activities of their employees by statute, regulation or departmental rules.**

- Prior to the 2000 presidential election, the postal workers union issued posters comparing George W. Bush's and Al Gore's positions on issues of importance to its membership. The posters did not recommend either candidate, but suggested that the Democratic ticket was more favorable to workers' interests. The posters were displayed on dedicated union bulletin boards. The postal service challenged the poster display as violative of the Hatch Act, which prohibits federal employees from taking an active part in political campaigns. It sought to have the posters removed. A New York federal court ruled in favor of the union, finding that the Hatch Act was not intended to curtail normal and traditional methods of communication between the union and its members, and that such communication was constitutionally protected speech. The Second Circuit Court of Appeals reversed, noting that the Hatch Act prohibition against political activity encompassed the hanging of partisan posters on bulletin boards in post offices. Even though the Hatch Act did not prevent employees of politically sensitive agencies from voting or expressing their opinions, it did prevent them from actively participating in a political campaign. *Burrus v. Vegliante*, 336 F.3d 82 (2d Cir. 2003).

- An Illinois deputy announced his intent to run against the sheriff in the next election. If elected, he promised to delegate more authority to deputy sheriffs. Following his announcement, the sheriff placed him on unpaid leave of absence until the election. He lost the election, returned to his job, and filed suit under 42 U.S.C. § 1983. He alleged that the unpaid leave violated the First

Amendment because he had not discussed politics while on duty. He sought lost wages. A federal court granted pretrial judgment to the sheriff, and the deputy appealed to the Seventh Circuit. The deputy contended that the amended regulations, which placed him on unpaid leave during his campaign, violated his First Amendment rights. The court of appeals disagreed, noting that the deputy's declaration of candidacy would foster political enmity and prevent him from serving the current sheriff loyally. Consequently, **the sheriff could place him on leave without proving that the candidacy actually disrupted efficient operation of the sheriff's office**. Thus, the deputy was permissibly placed on unpaid leave, and he was not entitled to recover lost wages. The lower court decision was affirmed. *Wilbur v. Mahan,* 3 F.3d 214 (7th Cir. 1993).

♦ Two West Virginia deputy sheriffs from different counties sought Democratic nominations for public office. Neither deputy resigned their civil service deputy sheriff positions. A lawsuit was brought seeking the removal of the deputies from the official ballots, claiming that the deputies violated the state law prohibiting deputy sheriffs from engaging in partisan politics. The Supreme Court of Appeals of West Virginia noted that while the state has the power to regulate partisan political activities of deputy sheriffs, the West Virginia Constitution confers a fundamental right to run for public office. The deputies could not be denied their right to engage in politics, and the voters had the right to expect that their electoral choice would be honored. Accordingly, **removal from the deputy position rather than removal from the ballot was the appropriate remedy**. *State of West Virginia v. Lincoln County Comm'n,* 474 S.E.2d 919 (W.Va. 1996).

4. Retaliation Against Same Party Members

♦ A city assembly clerk in Puerto Rico was the lone supporter of a candidate for the assembly. Everyone else in the office supported another candidate from the same party. Prior to the election, the office became the unofficial campaign headquarters for the other candidate, leaving the clerk with little to do. Two weeks after the election, the clerk's contract was not renewed. He sued under the First Amendment, and a jury awarded him $60,000 in compensatory damages, $250,000 for harassment, and $300,000 in punitive damages against the assembly's president, who made the decision not to renew the contract. The court reduced the latter two awards. The First Circuit affirmed the ruling for the clerk, noting that the evidence permitted the inference that **the contract non-renewal was in retaliation for the clerk's political affiliation**. However, the lower court should have given the clerk the option of a new trial on the damages issue before reducing the award. *Bisbal-Ramos v. City of Mayaguez,* 467 F.3d 16 (1st Cir. 2006).

♦ A newly appointed Ohio Republican county auditor replaced his bitter enemy, who was associated with a different faction of the Republican Party. The two factions had a longstanding, rancorous rivalry that appeared to have no ideological content. However, the newly appointed auditor fired several employees based on a "fiduciary" or confidential relationship with the former auditor. All the fired employees also had actively campaigned for the previous auditor. The employees filed a Section 1983 suit in federal court, arguing that they were fired solely because of their political affiliation with the other faction. The U.S. Court of Appeals, Sixth Circuit, held that **the First Amendment protected non-ideological factions within the same party from adverse employment actions**. *McCloud v. Testa,* 97 F.3d 1536 (6th Cir. 1996).

♦ A supervisor employed by the Hudson County Improvement Authority in New Jersey was repeatedly reprimanded for failing to properly perform his duties, smoking in working areas, and threatening his co-workers. He took a leave of absence to support the mayor in his struggle for control of the Democratic party leadership. The director of the center supported the mayor's Democratic opponent, who ultimately prevailed. The supervisor continued to engage in prohibited behavior and continued to harass employees based on their political affiliation. The director eventually discharged the supervisor for insubordination. The supervisor filed a 42 U.S.C. § 1983 claim against the county in a U.S. district court, alleging political patronage discharge in violation of the First Amendment and violations of the Due Process Clause. The court held for the county on both claims, and the supervisor appealed to the Third Circuit.

The court of appeals rejected the county's argument that the First Amendment prohibits politically motivated discharges only with respect to members of different political parties. The dangers inherent in vigorous intra-party conflicts are equivalent to the dangers presented by inter-party conflict. However, the court held that **the supervisor produced insufficient evidence to substantiate the claim that his political affiliation with the mayor was a substantial or motivating factor in his discharge**. The court also held that because the supervisor was an at-will employee and had not been deprived of pursuing a career, he lacked the protected property or liberty interests necessary to state a due process claim. The trial court ruling in favor of the county was affirmed. *Robertson v. Fiore*, 62 F.3d 596 (3d Cir. 1995).

C. Loyalty Oaths

♦ An Arkansas statute required every teacher employed by a state-supported school or college to file an annual affidavit listing every organization to which he or she had belonged in the past five years. A teacher who had worked for an Arkansas school system for 25 years and who was a member of the NAACP was told he would have to file such an affidavit before the start of the next school year. After he failed to do so, his contract for the next year was not renewed. He sued the school district. The court upheld the statute, finding that the information requested by the school district was relevant. The U.S. Supreme Court noted that the state certainly had a right to investigate teachers, since education of youth was a vital public interest. It stated that the requirement of the affidavit was reasonably related to that interest. However, **requiring teachers to name all their associations was an interference of teacher free speech and association rights**. The Court ruled that because fundamental rights were involved, governmental screening of teachers had to be narrowly tailored to the state's ends. Because the statute went beyond what was necessary to meet the state's inquiry into the fitness of its teachers, it was unconstitutional. *Shelton v. Tucker,* 364 U.S. 479, 81 S.Ct. 247, 5 L.Ed.2d 231 (1960).

♦ A Florida law required all state employees to submit a written oath, certifying that they had never lent counsel, advised, aided or supported the Communist Party. Failure to submit such an oath resulted in the employee's immediate termination. A teacher who had taught in the same Florida school district for nine years was dismissed when he refused to sign the oath. The teacher sought a declaration that the statute was unconstitutional and an injunction to prevent its enforcement. Eventually, the U.S. Supreme Court struck the statute down as a violation of the Fourteenth Amendment's Due Process Clause. **The statute was too vague to pass constitutional standards.** It compelled state employees to take the oath or face immediate dismissal. Because the statute lacked objective standards, no employee could truthfully take the oath. Statutes that made persons of average intelligence guess at their possible meanings and applications violated the Due Process Clause. *Cramp v. Board of Public Instruction of Orange County,* 368 U.S. 278, 82 S.Ct. 275, 7 L.Ed.2d 285 (1961).

♦ Faculty members at the University of Washington sued to declare two state laws unconstitutional. One required all state employees to take loyalty oaths, and the other required all teachers to take an oath as a condition of employment. Both oaths dealt with employee loyalty to the U.S. Constitution and government. Another law applied to all public employees and defined a "subversive person" as one who conspired to overthrow the government, and named the Communist Party as a subversive organization. Persons designated as subversives or Communist Party members were ineligible for public employment. The U.S. Supreme Court held that the statutes were vague and overbroad, and violated the Due Process Clause. The statutes were too vague to provide sufficient notice of what conduct was prohibited. This violated the teachers' due process rights. **The university could not require its teachers to take an oath that applied to some vague behavior in the future.** *Baggett v. Bullitt,* 377 U.S. 360, 84 S.Ct. 1316, 12 L.Ed.2d 377 (1963).

♦ An Arizona teacher who was a Quaker refused to take an oath required of all public employees under Arizona law. The oath swore that the employees would support both the Arizona and the U.S. Constitutions as well as state laws. The legislation also stated that anyone who took the oath and supported the Communist party or the violent overthrow of government would be discharged from employment and charged with perjury. The teacher sued for declaratory relief in the Arizona courts, having decided she could not take the oath in good conscience because she did not know what it meant. The case reached the U.S. Supreme Court, which held that political groups may have both legal and illegal aims and that there should not be a blanket prohibition on all groups that might have both legal and illegal goals. Such a prohibition would threaten legitimate political expression and association. Mere association with a group cannot be prohibited without a showing of "specific intent" to carry out the group's illegal purpose. **The Arizona statute was constitutionally deficient because it was** not confined to those employees with a "specific intent" to do something illegal. The statute infringed employee rights to free association by not punishing specific behavior that yielded a clear and present danger to government. The statute was struck down as unconstitutional. *Elfbrandt v. Russell*, 384 U.S. 11, 86 S.Ct. 1238, 16 L.Ed.2d 321 (1965).

♦ A teacher was offered a position with the University of Maryland. However, he refused to take a loyalty oath required by the university for its employees. He sued to challenge the oath's constitutionality. The U.S. Supreme Court decided that the oath's constitutionality had to be considered in conjunction with the state statute allowing the university board of regents to establish the oath. In addition, free speech rights were implicated because the First Amendment protects controversial as well as conventional speech. The Court held that the authorizing statute was unconstitutionally vague and overbroad. It falsely assumed that someone belonging to a subversive group also supported the violent overthrow of the government. The statute also put continuous surveillance on teachers by imposing a perjury threat. Such a concept was hostile to academic freedom, limiting the free flow of ideas in places of learning. The Court ruled that the line between permissible and impermissible conduct must be clearly drawn. **Because the statute failed to clearly define prohibited behavior, it was unconstitutional.** *Whitehill v. Elkins*, 389 U.S. 54, 88 S.Ct. 184, 19 L.Ed.2d 228 (1967).

♦ Two Jehovah's Witnesses applied for positions with the California Community College District. As part of state-mandated preemployment procedures, the district required the applicants to sign an oath swearing "true faith and allegiance" and to "support and defend" the United States and California Constitutions. The applicants refused to take the oath due to their religious beliefs, and the district rejected their applications. The applicants filed suit against the district under the Religious Freedom Restoration Act of 1993 (RFRA), challenging the validity of the loyalty oath as a condition precedent for employment. A California federal court held that the RFRA applied retroactively, that the applicants had timely filed their claim within the state's catch-all three-year statute of limitations, and that the community college district was not qualifiedly immune from suit. Next, the court held that **requiring the applicants to take an oath that violated their religious tenets placed an undue burden on their right to free exercise of religion.** The district failed to assert that the loyalty oath furthered a compelling government interest or was the least restrictive means of achieving that interest. Although employee loyalty was a compelling interest, the evidence failed to establish that a loyalty oath effectively achieved this goal. An alternative oath directed to an applicant's actions rather than his or her beliefs would be equally effective and less restrictive. Because the loyalty oath could not be justified under the compelling interest test articulated in the RFRA, the court enjoined the district from administering the loyalty oath to the applicants. *Bessard v. California Community Colleges*, 867 F.Supp. 1454 (E.D. Cal. 1994).

It should be noted, however, that the Supreme Court held that the RFRA was unconstitutional (as applied to state actions) in *City of Boerne, Texas v. Flores*, 521 U.S. 507, 117 S.Ct. 2157, 138 L.Ed.2d 624 (1997).

III. PERSONAL APPEARANCE AND DRESS CODES

In general, the government may regulate the appearance of its employees provided that the regulation is rationally related to a governmental purpose and is not arbitrary.

• A New York county police department had a regulation that established **hair-grooming standards** for male members of the police force. The regulations were directed at the style and length of hair, sideburns, mustaches, beards and goatees. The local patrolmen's benevolent association sued the county under 42 U.S.C. § 1983, claiming that the regulation violated the patrolmen's rights to freedom of expression under the First Amendment and their due process and equal protection rights under the Fourteenth Amendment. The district court and court of appeals held for the association, and the U.S. Supreme Court granted review. It noted that the association sought the protection of the Fourteenth Amendment, not for members of the citizens at large, but for employees of the police department. The Court stated that this was highly significant because **the state had a wider latitude in imposing restrictive regulations on its employees than it did in regulating its citizens at large**. The association would have to have shown no rational connection between the regulation and the promotion of safety of persons and property. Since the desire to make police officers readily recognizable to the public and to foster the *esprit de corps* that uniform garb and appearance may inculcate within the police force was sufficiently related to the department's goals, the Court held that the regulation was not unconstitutional. *Kelley v. Johnson*, 425 U.S. 238, 96 S.Ct. 1440, 47 L.Ed.2d 708 (1976).

• A Kentucky library employee had previously done volunteer work with the library, often wearing religious T-shirts, but was told when she was hired that she could no longer do so. A year after she was hired, the library director amended the dress code policy to include a ban on wearing religious jewelry as well. The employee refused to remove a cross necklace, or even to wear it under her shirt, and was told to go home. Eventually she was fired for insubordination. She sued the library and various officials, claiming a violation of her free speech and free exercise of religion rights. The library officials sought and were granted qualified immunity. Although wearing a cross necklace was protected under the First Amendment, and the library made no showing that the employee's necklace was disruptive, the officials were entitled to immunity because the employee's right to wear the necklace was not clearly established at the time she was fired. **The officials believed, in good faith, that allowing her to wear the necklace violated the Establishment Clause.** *Draper v. Logan County Public Library*, 403 F.Supp.2d 608 (W.D. Ky. 2005).

• Three maintenance workers at a Kentucky state park were fired after they refused to comply with the park department's dress code. Specifically, they refused to tuck in their shirts because doing so was uncomfortable and because they thought the rule was arbitrary and unreasonable. They sued under the First Amendment, claiming they had the right to express themselves by the way they dressed. The Sixth Circuit disagreed. **Untucked shirts are not speech on a matter of public concern.** *Roberts v. Ward*, 468 F.3d 963 (6th Cir. 2006).

♦   A group of Connecticut police officers had spider-web tattoos on their elbows. When the police chief learned that the tattoos were viewed by some as racist symbols, he wrote a memo ordering all officers to cover tattoos that were "deemed as offensive and/or presenting an unprofessional appearance." The officers sued under the First and Fourteenth Amendments, but a federal court and the Second Circuit ruled against them. **The officers had conceded that their tattoos did not have symbolic meaning as political, social or religious expression**, and the government could restrict their freedom of expression as reasonably necessary to promote efficiency. Also, the officers' due process and equal protection rights were not violated by the order requiring them to cover up the tattoos while on duty. *Inturri v. City of Hartford*, 165 Fed.Appx. 66 (2d Cir. 2006).

♦   A carpenter for a county hospital district in Texas volunteered to organize a bargaining unit. He and other pro-union employees decided to wear "Union Yes" buttons during their work shifts even though they knew the buttons violated the hospital's dress code. A supervisor made the carpenter remove the button, but he put it back on after calling a union representative. He was then suspended for three days and received only a 3% raise instead of the usual 4%. He sued the hospital under 42 U.S.C. § 1983, and a federal court ruled in his favor. The Fifth Circuit Court of Appeals reversed. The hospital's uniform non-adornment policy was a content and viewpoint neutral restriction which applied only to employees' conduct on the job. It served to prevent employees from wearing buttons that were either pro- or anti-union, or that took any position on abortion, gay marriage or countless other issues. Therefore, **the hospital district did not violate the employee's First Amendment rights by disciplining him for refusing to remove the button**. *Communication Workers of America v. Ector County Hospital Dist.*, 467 F.3d 427 (5th Cir. 2006).

♦   A van driver for a New York county's "Meals on Wheels" program only wore dresses because of deeply held cultural values. When the county instituted a dress code that required all drivers to wear pants, she sought an exception. Her supervisor denied her request. When she wore a skirt anyway, the county suspended her from the driver position, then transferred her to another department where she earned the same pay and could wear a skirt. She sued the county for violating her rights under the First and Fourteenth Amendments. A federal court ruled in favor of the county, and the Second Circuit affirmed. Here, the employee was not entitled to First Amendment protection because the court could not find a "particularized" message in her desire to wear skirts. The court next stated that even though the employee had a liberty interest in her personal appearance that was protected by the Fourteenth Amendment, it was not a fundamental right. Because the county had a rational basis for requiring its drivers to wear pants (for safety reasons), **the county's legitimate dress code outweighed her liberty interest in wearing a skirt**. *Zalewska v. County of Sullivan*, 316 F.3d 314 (2d Cir. 2003).

♦ A correctional officer employed by the Ohio Department of Rehabilitation and Correction (ODRC) began practicing Native American Spirituality. He believed that growing one's hair at the base of the neck was essential to obtaining spiritual knowledge and wisdom. The ODRC, however, had instituted an employee grooming policy that required male uniformed personnel to keep their hair "collar length or shorter in the back." The prison warden notified the officer that he would have to cut his hair or face employment termination. The officer filed suit against the ODRC and warden in the U.S. District Court for the Southern District of Ohio, seeking injunctive relief under 42 U.S.C. § 1983, the Religious Freedom Restoration Act and Ohio law. Although he made a *prima facie* showing that the policy substantially burdened his sincerely held religious belief, the court held that the government demonstrated a compelling state interest and chose the least restrictive means to further that interest. **The grooming policy furthered compelling state interests of safety, discipline, and *esprit de corps*.** In particular, grooming policies served to protect the legitimate authority of the prison staff and to physically protect them and others because the uniforms highlight and broadcast the solidarity, discipline, unity, and similarity of uniformed prison employees. Also, the ODRC demonstrated that the grooming policy was the least restrictive means of furthering that compelling interest. Differences between the standards for men and women did not prevent the policy from being the least restrictive means to achieve the compelling interest in safety furthered by uniformity. Accordingly, the court held for the defendants. *Blanken v. Ohio Dep't of Rehabilitation & Correction*, 944 F.Supp. 1359 (S.D. Ohio 1996).

♦ The New York City Police Department (NYPD) restricted members of the Latino Officers Association to marching in uniform in a parade behind the banner of the Hispanic Society, a separate and distinct organization with views to which the members of the Association did not subscribe, or to marching behind the banner of the Association but not in uniform. The Association and its president sued for a temporary restraining order to allow its members to march in uniform behind the Association banner. Although the court agreed with the department that the wearing of a police uniform in a parade was not a constitutional right, the police department in this case was permitting officers to march in uniform but only if they marched behind the banner of one particular organization. By conditioning the wearing of police uniforms in the parade on marching behind the banner of the Hispanic Society, **the police department infringed on the officers' right to free expression in violation of the First Amendment**. Because a violation of the First Amendment constituted irreparable harm and a likelihood of success on the merits existed, the court issued a preliminary injunction enjoining the police department from conditioning the wearing of a police uniform in the parade on marching behind the banner of the Hispanic Society. On further appeal, the Second Circuit affirmed. Wearing the official uniform of the NYPD in a public parade had a unique expressive quality, the court stated, that would be lost with merely handing out fliers or carrying a banner. *Latino Officers Ass'n, New York, Inc. v. City of New York*, 196 F.3d 458 (2d Cir. 1999).

♦ A retired Arizona police officer received a retired officer's badge and kept a uniform with an official police department shirt containing the official department insignia on shoulder patches. He wore the badge and uniform at a gun show where he operated a booth handing out political literature. When two active police officers advised him to remove the items because their unauthorized use violated a city ordinance, he refused. The officers then **charged him with wearing an official badge or insignia without authorization and impersonating a police officer**. After being found guilty of violating the ordinance, the retired officer appealed to the Court of Appeals of Arizona, alleging, among several arguments, that the ordinance violated his First Amendment right of free speech. The court affirmed, finding the ordinance content-neutral and constitutional. It prohibited the unauthorized wearing of an official insignia without regard to a particular expressive activity or political viewpoint. The city also had a legitimate governmental interest in regulating the use of its official insignia. The unauthorized use of the insignia jeopardized the appearance of political neutrality and impartiality of the police department and city. *State of Arizona v. McLamb*, 932 P.2d 266 (Ariz. Ct. App. 1996).

♦ An armed services veteran employed by a Pennsylvania corrections institute challenged the implementation of a regulation that mandated display of a flag patch on the right sleeve of the uniform shirt, where the star field was oriented toward the rear. He believed that the display desecrated and debased the flag and that displaying the flag with the star field to the rear signified cowardice and retreat. Consequently, he refused to comply with the flag patch regulation and filed a First Amendment claim under 42 U.S.C. § 1983. The district court held for the state, and the Third Circuit Court of Appeals affirmed, holding that the employee failed to show a reasonable likelihood of success on the merits because he did not make the necessary threshold showing that he was coerced to engage in expressive conduct in violation of the First Amendment. The state regulation did not amount to compelled expression because **the employee could not show that observers would likely understand the wearing of the patch to be communicative or to be telling them anything about his beliefs**. Nor did his refusal to comply amount to a symbolic protest protected by the First Amendment. *Troster v. Pennsylvania State Dep't of Corrections*, 65 F.3d 1086 (3d Cir. 1995).

♦ A Native American correctional officer for the New York Department of Corrections practiced the Mohawk Longhouse religion. The officer stopped cutting his hair because hair length symbolized spirituality. A departmental policy provided that the hair of male correction officers not extend beyond a prescribed length. The officer refused verbal and written orders to cut his hair and was discharged. He challenged the dismissal unsuccessfully in arbitration and then in a state court. The court entered judgment for the employee. The New York Supreme Court, Appellate Division, held that the department failed to establish any state interest that outweighed the officer's right to practice his religion. **The alleged need for short hair to foster** *esprit de corps* **and discipline was belied by the department's permissive policy toward beards and mustaches.** Further, female employees were permitted to have hair of any length if it was tied or pinned up. Similar measures would effectively address the department's alleged concern that the Native American officer's long hair would be seized by inmates. Finally, the department failed to demonstrate that the officer's long hair had caused problems during his 14 months of employment. The lower court decision was affirmed. *Rourke v. New York State Dep't of Correctional Services*, 615 N.Y.S.2d 470 (N.Y. App. Div. 1994).

♦ Twelve Georgia African-American firefighters suffered from pseudofolliculitis barbae (PFB), a bacterial disorder causing their faces to become infected if they shaved them. In order to accommodate these individuals, the city allowed qualified firefighters to wear very short "shadow" beards. However, six years later, the city again amended the policy to require that firefighters be clean shaven. Those who failed to comply were temporarily reassigned and then fired. The 12 firefighters filed a class action lawsuit alleging that the new policy was discriminatory and violated Title VII and the Rehabilitation Act. The Eleventh Circuit Court of Appeals determined that even if discriminatory, **the department's no-beard policy was necessary to adhere to an important business goal of worker safety** because an imperfect seal of their respirators might expose the firefighters to outside contaminants. An absence of unfortunate incidents over the six-year period during which the shadow beards were permitted did not itself establish that they could be worn safely. *Fitzpatrick v. City of Atlanta*, 2 F.3d 1112 (11th Cir. 1993).

♦ The District of Columbia **Fire Department regulations required that male firefighters be clean shaven and have short hair**. Although handlebar mustaches, goatees and beards were strictly prohibited, employees suffering from PFB were allowed to wear neatly trimmed one-quarter inch beards. A firefighter grew a handlebar mustache and beard in direct contravention of the regulations. After the department fired him, he filed a complaint with the District of Columbia EEO Director, alleging that the grooming regulations violated the D.C. Human Rights Act. At the hearing, the firefighter demonstrated that he could obtain a proper seal between his face and his self-contained breathing apparatus despite the presence of the beard and mustache. The EEO director held for the firefighter, the superior court reversed, and the firefighter appealed to the District of Columbia Court of Appeals.

Regulations promulgated pursuant to the Human Rights Act prohibited discriminatory employment practices based on an employee's "personal appearance." Personal appearance was defined as "the style of personal grooming including, but not limited to, hair style or beards." The court rejected the department's argument that the prohibition on facial hair was necessary to insure firefighter safety, noting that PFB-afflicted firefighters had suffered no reported incidents resulting from improperly secured face masks. Further, the entire safety justification was belied by the bearded firefighters' ability to obtain a proper seal. Also, the regulation was not uniformly applied, did not foster *esprit de corps* and, in fact, largely undermined department morale. Because substantial evidence supported the director's conclusion, the court held that **the department's facial hair regulation was discriminatory as applied to the firefighter**. *Kennedy v. District of Columbia*, 654 A.2d 847 (D.C. 1994).

♦ Four Massachusetts police forces merged into a single entity pursuant to state statute. The colonel of the largest of the four police units was appointed as the executive and administrative head, and was given broad powers to formulate rules and regulations for the unified force. One regulation prohibited officers from wearing mustaches except for undercover assignments or for health reasons. A similar regulation previously had been in effect for the largest of the four pre-merger units. Six officers sued for an injunction to prevent the no mustache policy from going into effect. They alleged that such a policy would violate their First and Fourteenth Amendment rights. The district court denied relief, and the officers appealed. The First Circuit Court of Appeals determined that the officers were not entitled to injunctive relief because they were unlikely to succeed on the merits of the case at trial. **Since there was a need for similarity in appearance and a sense of** *esprit de corps***, the rules proscribing mustaches were not irrational.** Further, these goals fostering police unity were especially important in light of the recency of the departmental mergers. The holding of the district court was affirmed. *Weaver v. Henderson*, 984 F.2d 11 (1st Cir. 1993).

♦ An Ohio woman employed by the city of Cincinnati was promoted to the position of meter reader. The dress code required that she wear a uniform that included navy blue trousers. During her first day of field training, the woman showed up in a navy blue skirt. She was sent home to change into the uniform trousers. However, she requested permission to continue wearing the skirt because wearing men's apparel was prohibited by her religion. The city denied her request. It cited safety concerns including protection from exposure to the elements commonly confronted on the job. She repeatedly refused to wear trousers and was demoted. The Court of Appeals of Ohio stated that **the employment action was arbitrary and unreasonable. The job could be done while wearing a skirt,** and the employer's safety rationale was arbitrary and did not "promote a reasonable public interest." The court ordered the employee reinstated to the position of meter reader. *City of Cincinnati v. Dixon*, 604 N.E.2d 193 (Ohio Ct. App. 1992).

IV. RELIGIOUS FREEDOM

Public employees wishing to engage in the free expression of their religion may find protection in the Free Exercise Clause of the First Amendment.

♦ In *Employment Division, Dep't of Human Resources of Oregon v. Smith*, two Native American employees were fired and denied unemployment benefits after they admitted ingesting peyote as a sacrament during a religious ceremony of the Native American Church. The employees filed suit disputing the denial of the unemployment benefits and questioning the constitutionality of a controlled substance law as applied to their use of peyote in religious observances. The Court held that **the Free Exercise Clause in the First Amendment did not forbid the state of Oregon from banning sacramental peyote use** through its general criminal prohibition on the ingestion of the drug.

Sec. IV RELIGIOUS FREEDOM 239

The Court abandoned the compelling governmental interest test, holding that neutral laws of general applicability that burden the exercise of religion require no special justification to satisfy the Free Exercise Clause. *Employment Division, Dep't of Human Resources of Oregon v. Smith*, 485 U.S. 660, 108 S.Ct. 1444, 99 L.Ed.2d 753 (1988).

* A Utah corrections officer claimed that she was harassed by her supervisor. She was allowed to transfer to another position even though the department was unable to substantiate her claim. Four months later, she was reprimanded for telling her supervisor's Latter Day Saints stake president about the alleged harassment. She filed charges with the EEOC, but dropped them in exchange for the department's promise to keep the supervisor out of her chain of command. Shortly thereafter, the department decided to audit her job and discovered that she had misrepresented her educational degrees on her application. She did not have BAs, but rather an equivalency degree. Upon her termination, she sued for retaliation and a violation of her free exercise rights. The Tenth Circuit ruled against her. The department reasonably believed she had made a false claim. Also, **her conversation with the supervisor's clergy was not protected under the Free Exercise Clause**. *Kosan v. Utah Dep't of Corrections*, 290 Fed.Appx. 145 (10th Cir. 2008).

* Without consulting her superior, an evangelical Christian guidance counselor in Wisconsin discarded literature instructing students in the use of condoms. She ordered literature advocating abstinence to replace the discarded condom literature. She also prayed with several students who had come to her for guidance. When the school district decided not to renew her contract – which would have given her lifetime tenure, so that she could not have been fired without just cause – she sued, alleging a violation of her free exercise rights. A federal court and the Seventh Circuit ruled against her. Here, **it was not her beliefs that caused the nonrenewal, but rather her conduct**. *Grossman v. South Shore Public School Dist.*, 507 F.3d 1097 (7th Cir. 2007).

* A Philadelphia firefighter with pseudofolliculitis barbae was also a practicing Muslim required by the tenets of his religion to grow a beard. When he sought an exemption from the fire department's clean-shaven rule, submitting notes from his doctor and Imam, the department suspended him without pay. He sued under the state's Religious Freedom Protection Act, **claiming that the clean-shaven rule substantially burdened the free exercise of his religion**, and that with the new respirators, a clean-shaven face was no longer necessary for safety reasons. The Pennsylvania Court of Common Pleas ruled issued a preliminary injunction to keep the firefighter employed while his case went through the trial process. *DeVeaux v. City of Philadelphia*, No. 3103, 2005 WL 1869666 (Pa. Ct. of Common Pleas 7/14/05). However, the firefighter lost his case on the merits two months later.

* The contract between a New York board of education and a teachers' union allowed teachers to take up to three paid days of leave for religious observance. When two teachers filed a written request for such leave, the board directed the

teachers to use their personal leave instead. The union brought a lawsuit to compel the board to comply with the provision, but a trial court found that the provision violated the Establishment Clause. The New York Supreme Court, Appellate Division, reversed. This provision did not designate particular religious holidays. It imposed no requirements over which religious holidays could be invoked. Thus, it did not prefer particular religions over others. **The religious observance provision did not violate the Establishment Clause.** *Maine-Endwell Teachers' Ass'n v. Board of Educ.*, 771 N.Y.S.2d 246 (N.Y. App. Div. 2004).

♦ A Jewish police officer with the position of deputy inspector was denied a promotion to inspector on two occasions. He sued the county for religious discrimination under Title VII, then was twice more denied the promotion and involuntarily transferred to an executive officer position, which he considered a demotion. He also alleged that he was retaliated against for speaking out at a county meeting some years earlier about the department's religious bias. A New York federal court granted pretrial judgment to the county, but the Second Circuit Court of Appeals reversed. In addition to the officer's testimony regarding anti-Semitism, the court cited to testimony by a rabbi who served as the department chaplain. According to the rabbi, **every police commissioner in the past 20 years had acknowledged that anti-Semitism was a problem**, but none had taken any concrete action to remedy it. The court then noted that despite the passage of time between when the officer spoke out about the department's anti-Semitism and the failure to promote, there was sufficient evidence for a jury to consider whether the refusal to promote was taken in retaliation for the officer's exercise of his First Amendment rights. *Mandell v. County of Suffolk*, 316 F.3d 368 (2d Cir. 2003).

♦ A Texas public school teacher sent her children to a private religious school. The district superintendent asked her if she would move her children into public schools so that she could be considered for the assistant principal position. She expressed interest in the position, but refused to remove her children from the religious school. When the superintendent told her that he did not recommend her for the position because her children attended private school, she sued him and the district under 42 U.S.C. § 1983. A federal court granted pretrial judgment to the superintendent on qualified immunity grounds, but the Fifth Circuit reversed. It held that **public school employees have a clearly established constitutional right to send their children to private schools**. *Barrow v. Greenville Independent School Dist.*, 332 F.3d 844 (5th Cir. 2003).

♦ A nurse consultant with the Connecticut Department of Health lectured a patient in the end stages of AIDS, telling him that God did not like "the homosexual lifestyle." The patient filed a complaint against her, and she was suspended for two weeks without pay. She was also restricted from making home visits to patients. She sued the department for violating her First Amendment religious freedom rights. Another Connecticut state employee worked as a sign-language interpreter and shared her religious views with a client who had been sexually abused. She also was disciplined for her religious activity, receiving a letter of reprimand. She also sued the state for violating her Free Exercise Clause rights. The cases reached the U.S. Court of Appeals, Second Circuit, which ruled that no constitutional violation occurred. **Allowing the employees to use religious speech in front of clients was disruptive to the delivery of services the state was providing.** In addition, there was an Establishment Clause issue with respect to state employees propounding religious beliefs. The disciplinary actions were upheld. *Knight v. Connecticut Dep't of Health*, 275 F.3d 156 (2d Cir. 2001).

♦ The warden at a Minnesota corrections facility required employees to attend a training session on gays and lesbians in the workplace. An employee objected to the mandatory session, believing that it would raise deviant sexual behavior to a level of social acceptability. The warden then issued a memo stating that the program was part of the facility's commitment to creating an environment where people were treated with respect and was not designed to tell them what to believe. When the employee and two other co-workers attended the session, they protested by reading their Bibles, copying scripture and participating in only a limited fashion. Prison officials issued the employees written reprimands, making them ineligible for promotions for the next two years. The employees then sued under the First Amendment, claiming that they were unfairly targeted for reading their Bibles while other employees who weren't paying attention were not disciplined. A federal court dismissed their lawsuit, but the Eighth Circuit Court of Appeals reversed, finding that there were issues of fact as to **whether the prison officials had disciplined the employees for insubordination or for expressing their religious opposition to the training**. *Altman v. Minnesota Dep't of Corrections*, 251 F.3d 1199 (8th Cir. 2001).

♦ A South Carolina notary public applicant and atheist had stricken through the portion of the oath on the application that read "so help me God." His application was returned by the secretary of state along with a letter explaining that the application was being returned because it did not comply with the South Carolina Constitution and statutes applicable to notaries. He then sent his application to the governor, whose staff returned the application because it no longer met the statutory requirement that a notary application be signed by one-half of the members of the applicant's county legislative delegation. The applicant sued to have two portions of the state constitution declared in violation of the federal constitution (the challenged provisions prohibited public office holding by persons who denied the existence of a Supreme Being). The Supreme Court of South Carolina held that **the state constitution's "Supreme Being" provisions violated both the First Amendment and the Religious Test Clause of the U.S. Constitution**. *Silverman v. Campbell*, 486 S.E.2d 1 (S.C. 1997).

♦ A Seventh Day Adventist employed by the New York Department of Correctional Services was occasionally required to work on his Sabbath, which ran from sundown Friday until sundown Saturday. When he decided that he could no longer work on his Sabbath and requested accommodations from a supervisor, he was allowed to "swap shifts" with other officers, but his supervisor refused to take further affirmative steps to guarantee particular days off. After the employee failed to show up for work on his Sabbath on several occasions, the department suspended him without pay. The employee sued the department and his supervisors, alleging Title VII religious discrimination and First Amendment claims. The district court denied the defendants' motions for pretrial judgment based on qualified immunity, and they appealed.

In addressing the employee's religious accommodation claim under the Free Exercise Clause of the First Amendment, the Second Circuit Court of Appeals held that the type of accommodation made by the department here – allowing the employee to voluntarily swap shifts with other employees – satisfied the requirements of Title VII. Because the extent of a state employee's right to have his religion accommodated under the Free Exercise Clause was not clear, at least given that the workplace was governed by a collective bargaining agreement, the court of appeals held that **the department had not violated clearly established constitutional rights of the employee by refusing to take further steps to accommodate his religion.** Consequently, the supervisors and the department were entitled to partial pretrial judgment based on qualified immunity. *Genas v. State of New York Correctional Services*, 75 F.3d 825 (2d Cir. 1996).

♦ The assistant chief of police for the Los Angeles Police Department (LAPD) also served as an elder for his church. One council member questioned whether the assistant chief's views interfered with his ability to perform his official duties without bias and whether he had improperly consulted with religious elders on issues of public policy. The police commissioner requested an investigation to ensure that the assistant chief's personal beliefs had not created any adverse impact on any job-related matters. No violations could be substantiated, and the investigation was terminated. The assistant chief sued the city, the city council and several of the investigating parties, alleging that the investigation had violated his state and federal constitutional rights. **The Ninth Circuit rejected the assistant chief's allegation that the investigation had interfered with his freedom to worship as he chose.** Because the city had investigated his on-duty activities (not his private religious activities) and no disciplinary action had been taken, the investigation had not substantially burdened his religious free exercise rights. Nor had it resulted in an excessive government entanglement with religion so as to violate the Establishment Clause. Also, the relatively short duration of the investigation precluded a finding of ongoing government interference with the assistant chief's religious beliefs. *Vernon v. City of Los Angeles*, 27 F.3d 1385 (9th Cir. 1994).

V. PRIVACY

Generally, the right to privacy protects individuals from intrusions into their personal lives. Several state constitutions provide constitutionally protected rights to privacy. Also, state privacy laws and the federal Privacy Act provide some privacy protections.

Sec. V   PRIVACY   243

- The U.S. Forest Service issued a report detailing the agency's response to a fire in Idaho, during which two firefighters were killed. The report contained the names of 22 Forest Service employees. After the deaths, the Agriculture Department's Office of Inspector General and OSHA were critical of the Forest Service, and OSHA issued the Forest Service multiple citations for unsafe working conditions. Subsequently, the Forest Service Employees for Environmental Ethics (FSEEE) filed a Freedom of Information Act request for the report, and the Forest Service issued the report with the employee names redacted. The FSEEE sued to get an unredacted copy, and an Oregon federal court denied its request. The Ninth Circuit affirmed, finding that **the employees' privacy interests outweighed any contribution their identities would make to the public's understanding of what happened**. The employees named held low- and mid-level jobs, and they weren't accused of official misconduct. *Forest Service Employees for Environmental Ethics v. U.S. Forest Service*, 524 F.3d 1021 (9th Cir. 2008).

- An Arizona county manager used county funds to buy sniper rifles and other equipment without authorization. A newspaper filed a public records request for all the e-mails the administrator sent or received over a two-month period. The county released 706 e-mails, but it withheld others the administrator considered personal or confidential. When the newspaper threatened to sue, the administrator sought an injunction to block their release. The case reached the Arizona Supreme Court, which held that the definition of "public records" does not include documents of a purely private or personal nature. Instead, **public records are only those documents that have a "substantial nexus with a government agency's activities."** The court remanded the case to the trial court to conduct an "in-camera" (private) inspection of the e-mails claimed to be personal. *Griffis v. Pinal County*, 156 P.3d 418 (Ariz. 2007).

- A Massachusetts state college became concerned about security when a former client under criminal investigation gained unauthorized access to an office after normal business hours. The public safety director installed a hidden camera in the receptionist area of the office and programmed it to run 24 hours a day, seven days a week. Subsequently, the office receptionist went to the rear of the office, behind a partition, to apply sunburn medication to her neck and chest. She also occasionally changed back there. When she learned about the hidden camera, she sued the college under 42 U.S.C. § 1983 for violating her Fourth Amendment privacy rights. The case reached the Supreme Judicial Court of Massachusetts, which ruled that **she had no reasonable expectation of privacy because the office was open to the public** and was not limited to her exclusive use. *Nelson v. Salem State College*, 845 N.E.2d 338 (Mass. 2006).

- A Connecticut teacher was placed on leave after his students accused him of using foul language, making sexual remarks and breaching school security. He remained on leave for three years because he refused to sign a release allowing a psychiatrist or school board representative to review his past medical records. The release contained no time or subject-matter restrictions, so it would have included his treatment for alcoholism 13 years earlier. When he sued, claiming due process violations, the Second Circuit ruled that he could proceed with his substantive due process claim. If he could prove that the school board intended to injure him by insisting on a needlessly broad medical release as a condition of his reinstatement, it would have violated his **due process privacy rights in his medical records**. However, if the school board acted out of incompetence or confusion, it would not be liable. *O'Connor v. Pierson*, 426 F.3d 187 (2d Cir. 2005).

♦   A New York City Health Department employee was subjected to discipline for also holding a job with the city's transit authority. At an internal disciplinary hearing, his Social Security number, address and work schedule were disclosed. He sued for violations of his privacy rights, but the U.S. Court of Appeals, Second Circuit, ruled against him. It held that he had no right of action under the Privacy Act or the Freedom of Information Act, and he was not entitled to protection under 42 U.S.C. § 1983 for constitutional rights violations. **The disclosure of information was related to his employment**, indicative of a potential conflict of interest and not highly personal. *Pennyfeather v. Tessler*, 431 F.3d 54 (2d Cir. 2005).

♦   An applicant for a job as a part-time security officer with a Montana airport agreed to a criminal background check as part of the application process. The background check went back 10 years and found nothing. However, during the officer's probationary period, another security officer requested a separate, unauthorized background check that went back more than 10 years. This check revealed an arrest from 30 years before. The officer was fired before the end of his probationary period, and he sued the airport for violating his right to privacy under the state constitution. The Montana Supreme Court ruled that there was no constitutional violation because **he had no reasonable expectation of privacy with respect to his arrest record**. *Barr v. Great Falls Int'l Airport*, 107 P.3d 471 (Mont. 2005).

♦   As part of an investigation into whether two City of Clearwater employees were operating a private business on city time, a Florida newspaper sought to compel the release of all e-mails the two employees sent and received. The Florida Supreme Court held that the employees' personal e-mails were not public records. Even though the employees sent and received the e-mails on city-owned computers, the e-mails were not sent or received in connection with official city business and "with the intent to perpetuate, communicate, or formalize knowledge of some type" so as to be public records under state law. As a result, **the newspaper could not obtain the employees' personal e-mails**. *State of Florida, Times Publishing Co. v. City of Clearwater*, 863 So.2d 149 (Fla. 2003).

♦   *The Philadelphia Inquirer* asked a federal court to order the Pennsylvania State Police to disclose more than 50 internal affairs documents involving investigations into sexual harassment by state troopers. The court ordered the records unsealed, but also ordered that the names of those troopers who had been cleared of wrongdoing be redacted. Further, the names of victims, witnesses and confidential informants had to be blacked out. *Haber v. Evans*, 268 F.Supp.2d 507 (E.D. Pa. 2003).

• A maintenance worker at a postal service facility in Washington, D.C. missed several weeks of work while suffering from an AIDS-related illness. His supervisor sent him a letter warning of possible discipline if he did not submit a medical certificate explaining the nature of the illness. The letter also informed him that he might qualify for Family and Medical Leave Act (FMLA) leave so as to avoid discipline for being absent without leave. The worker completed the FMLA medical certification form, and his doctor stated that he had an AIDS-related infection. The worker, concerned about revealing his HIV status, submitted the form to an administrative assistant at the postal service rather than his supervisor. When he returned to work, he discovered that his HIV status had become common knowledge. He sued under the Rehabilitation and Privacy Acts, and a federal court granted pretrial judgment to the postal service. The U.S. Court of Appeals, D.C. Circuit, reversed. Here, **if the worker's supervisor found out about the worker's HIV status from the FMLA form and told co-workers about it, there would be Privacy Act liability**. Also, the submission of the FMLA form was in response to the postal service's inquiry about his medical condition within the meaning of the Americans with Disabilities Act's medical examination confidentiality provision and was not a voluntary disclosure of the worker's condition. Thus, his Rehabilitation Act claim also should have been allowed to proceed. *Doe v. U.S. Postal Service*, 317 F.3d 339 (D.C. Cir. 2003).

• The operators of two controversial Web sites that were highly critical of the police sought a list of full names of all law enforcement officers and attorneys employed by local police agencies in Washington, along with job titles and pay scales for each position. One county, citing exemptions under the Public Disclosure Act, refused to provide more than the pay scales for each rank. A lawsuit resulted, and a court ruled that the county had to provide the officers' last names and ranks. The Washington Court of Appeals held that **the full names and ranks of all police officers had to be disclosed**. Because the county regularly released officers' names (including undercover officers' names) to legitimate news media, it could not make an exception for the operators of the Web sites. Nor could it assert that there was a safety issue that overrode the public's right to know. Finally, no Washington case has held that public employees' names are subject to the personal privacy exemption of the Act. *King County v. Sheehan*, 57 P.3d 307 (Wash. Ct. App. 2002).

• An employee of the Los Angeles Police Relief Association (LAPRA) enrolled officers in the program, paid claims and processed retirement benefits – responsibilities that brought her into daily contact with the officers' confidential files. She later became romantically involved with a convicted felon, who was serving a 15-year sentence for burglary. When she told her superior that she intended to marry the inmate, the superior expressed concern. A month later, the LAPRA board decided that the employee would have to resign if she intended to maintain her relationship with the inmate. When the employee refused to resign, she was fired. She sued the LAPRA for violating her right to privacy under the California Constitution. A state court ruled against her, and the court of appeal affirmed. Here, **she had a right of privacy to marry who she wished**, and the board's decision to fire her was a serious invasion of that right. However, the LAPRA had a legitimate interest in preventing the improper disclosure of confidential information to criminals. Its decision to fire her was a rational means of pursuing that interest. As a result, her invasion of privacy claim could not succeed. *Ortiz v. Los Angeles Police Relief Ass'n*, 120 Cal.Rptr.2d 670 (Cal. Ct. App. 2002).

♦ A city in Ohio passed an ordinance authorizing the use of a digital recording system in its police and fire departments. The system was installed in the police department to record all incoming and outgoing calls, but in accordance with the Ohio wiretap statute, one pay phone and the chief's line were excluded from the monitoring device. A number of officers sued after one of them overheard the chief playing a recording in his office of a personal phone call the officer had made on a non-emergency line. The district court refused to grant the chief qualified immunity, and he appealed.

In reversing, the U.S. Court of Appeals, Sixth Circuit, held that the law was not clearly established at the time the system was installed that doing so and tapping police phone lines would violate the Fourth Amendment. The officers claimed that they had a reasonable expectation of privacy in their personal phone calls because of a city policy allowing them to use department non-emergency phones for personal calls. But **Ohio law allowed interception of telephone lines into and out of a police department so long as the line was limited to administrative use** and at least one other phone was available for private conversations. The Sixth Circuit agreed with the chief that a reasonable person in his position could perceive that he could implement the recording system within the confines of the Ohio statute because no federal or state law existed at the time to guide him as to the statute's constitutionality. The court did find, however, that the chief would not be protected for any "calculated monitoring" of officers' conversations (including the alleged installation of intercoms disguised as carbon monoxide detectors and monitoring officers' conversations from his home via a modem). *Blake v. Wright*, 179 F.3d 1003 (6th Cir. 1999).

♦ **A Kansas police officer was involved in a gun battle in which a private citizen was killed.** The police department's internal policy on media relations prohibited the release of the names of officers involved in critical incidents, such as shootings. Despite this policy, his name was released to the media, and the officer and his family received threats of revenge. The officer sued the city for negligence under the Kansas Tort Claims Act (KTCA). After the court ruled for the city, the officer appealed to the Supreme Court of Kansas.

The court found that the police department had violated its established policy regarding the release of an officer's name. The KTCA, however, provided that a governmental entity could not be liable for a failure to enforce any written personnel policy that protected persons' health or safety unless a duty of care, independent of such policy, was owed to the specific individual injured. **The city had no duty not to release the officer's name** independent of the policy. Almost every police officer is exposed to the risk of becoming involved in a shootout with a private citizen. Once involved in such an incident, an officer is further exposed to the risk of retaliation by the family or friends of the shooting victim. Refusal to release the identity of the officer to the media may or may not reduce the risk of retaliation because the media might obtain that information through other channels. Accordingly, no separate duty not to disclose the officer's name arose. The lower court's judgment was affirmed. *Fettke v. City of Wichita*, 957 P.2d 409 (Kan. 1998).

* A Georgia man worked for the state board of pardons and paroles. The board investigated claims that he had harassed a co-worker and engaged in other misconduct and found that he had. When a local television station requested copies of the investigatory report, the board released it. The employee sued the board, alleging that the release of the report violated his rights under 42 U.S.C. § 1983 and the state Tort Claims Act. After the case was dismissed, the employee appealed to the Georgia Court of Appeals, which affirmed, finding that the board had released the report in accordance with state law. That law provides that all public records of an agency, except those prohibited by a court order or specifically exempted, must be open for public inspection. The court rejected the employee's argument that the report automatically was a part of his personnel file, and was therefore exempt from disclosure. **Because the report was prepared and maintained in the course and operation of the state board, it was a public record.** Also, the report was not protected from disclosure because it related to the employee's conduct as a public official. The employee did not have a legitimate expectation of privacy in public records that addressed his misconduct as a public official. Even if he had a privacy interest, it was outweighed by the public's need for disclosure. *Fincher v. State of Georgia*, 497 S.E.2d 632 (Ga. Ct. App. 1998).

* The Director of Rabies Control for a Tennessee county secretly tape recorded conversations among four of his employees by placing a recorder in their common office. The employees sued him and his wife after he listened to the tapes with his wife, and after he dictated letters to his wife (based on the recordings) in an attempt to get two of the employees fired. The employees claimed violations of the federal wiretapping statute. The court awarded damages against the director and his wife, and the Sixth Circuit Court of Appeals affirmed, finding that the director had violated the statute. **The employees had a reasonable expectation of privacy that the director had violated by secretly taping them.** However, his wife did not violate the statute by simply listening to the tapes. Further, the award of damages had to be reversed. The district court had discretion to decline imposing damages for violations of the statute. *Dorris v. Absher*, 179 F.3d 420 (6th Cir. 1999).

* The Department of Housing and Urban Development (HUD) and the Department of Defense (DOD) required several employees to complete questionnaires concerning illegal drug use and financial history. HUD employees in public trust positions were required to complete the questionnaire

because of their access to a computer database, which controlled federal funds. DOD employees with access to classified information or in a position designated as "critical sensitive" also were required to complete questionnaires based on national security interests. In separate actions, the HUD employees were granted pretrial judgment and the DOD questionnaires were restricted. The U.S. Court of Appeals, D.C. Circuit, consolidated the appeals and **declined to determine whether a constitutional right to avoid disclosure of personal information existed**. It held that assuming the right exists, the government had not violated it on the facts of these cases. The agencies' interests in protecting the integrity of the computer database and national security outweighed the employees' interests. The decisions of the lower courts were reversed. *American Federation of Government Employees, AFL-CIO v. Dep't of Housing & Urban Development,* 118 F.3d 786 (D.C. Cir. 1997).

♦ Two Maine employees at a mental health institute were disciplined as the result of a patient death. They filed grievances, and an arbitrator concluded that the discipline imposed against them was without just cause. The arbitrator ordered all reference to the discipline removed from their personnel files. During this time, a request for copies of all of the disciplinary actions taken as a result of the patient's death was made to the Department of Mental Health and Mental Retardation by a legislative committee. The employees sought to prevent disclosure of the arbitrator's decisions. The Supreme Judicial Court of Maine ruled against them, finding that the arbitration decisions were subject to disclosure under the state Freedom of Access Act. Under the Act, **an exception to the confidentiality rule allows disclosure of the final written decision relating to disciplinary action**. The employees argued that the exception should not apply when discipline was ultimately found to have been unjustified. The court disagreed. The public's interest in improper discipline is no less important than its interest in proper discipline. *Doe v. Dep't of Mental Health, Mental Retardation, and Substance Abuse Services,* 699 A.2d 422 (Me. 1997).

♦ A California county jail experienced a series of thefts in which inmates' funds were stolen from the release office in the booking section of the jail. A video camera with no audio capabilities was placed in the release office without a warrant. The release office did not have a lock on the door and it was accessible to employees, supervised inmates cleaning the room, and occasionally outside agency personnel who used the phone. The county deputy sheriffs' association and three deputy sheriffs filed suit in state superior court. Among several claims, they alleged an unconstitutional search and seizure in violation of the Fourth Amendment. The court ruled against them, stating that they had no reasonable expectation of privacy from video surveillance within the release room. They appealed to the California Court of Appeal, which affirmed. **In the context of a prison or jail, privacy expectations are diminished due to the institutional security concern.** Deputy sheriffs working in a jail also have a diminished privacy expectation because of the nature of their employment. Here, the plaintiffs lacked a reasonable expectation of privacy when balanced against institutional security. The office was a logical place for the camera because the object of the investigation was to find missing inmate money that disappeared from that office. *Sacramento County Deputy Sheriffs' Ass'n v. Sacramento County*, 59 Cal.Rptr.2d 834 (Cal. Ct. App. 1996).

* An Iowa woman worked as a cook for a county hospital, where she received below-standard performance evaluations and was placed on probation several times. One criticism was that she failed to inform her supervisor before scheduling days off. She subsequently scheduled a cancer biopsy at the hospital and, without notifying her supervisor, arranged for other employees to cover any shifts she might miss. Although she executed a form requesting confidentiality, her supervisor's routine review of the day's list of patients revealed her name. The supervisor checked the work schedule where she discovered that coverage had been arranged without prior authorization in violation of hospital policy. The cook was fired. After a "name-clearing" hearing, the dismissal was affirmed. The cook sued, alleging a state law invasion of privacy claim.

The district court granted the defendants pretrial judgment on the state law invasion of privacy claim. The first element, an "intrusion on seclusion," was met by the supervisor intentionally seeking information concerning the identity of the patient despite her specific request for confidentiality. However, the claim failed on the second element that required the intrusion to be "highly offensive to a reasonable person." **Because of the supervisor's status at the hospital and the limited nature of her inquiry, the intrusion and disclosure were not "highly offensive."** Rather, the employees of the hospital reasonably came within the "curtain of seclusion." The court also found that the cook's privacy claim of unreasonable publicity failed for lack of any publicity. *Hanson v. Hancock County Memorial Hospital*, 938 F.Supp. 1419 (N.D. Iowa 1996).

* An Ohio police officer was accused of sexual harassment and bragging to women while on duty that he had an open marriage and swinging lifestyle. The police department conducted an internal affairs investigation, interviewing several people including the officer and his wife. The investigator asked the officer's wife if her husband had dated anyone because there were rumors circulating that she and her husband were swingers and had an open marriage. Several female co-workers were also interviewed; two mentioned references to an open marriage or swinging. The allegations were not substantiated, and the files were destroyed. The officer and his wife then sued, alleging that their marital privacy and rights to free association were invaded by the investigation. The district court granted pretrial judgment to the city, but not to the individual officials. The officials appealed to the Sixth Circuit.

The court of appeals reversed, finding that the officials should have been granted qualified immunity. Although general rights to privacy and free association exist, those rights were not so clearly established that the officials would have realized their actions were violating the law. **The investigation was not unreasonable because the claims involved misconduct while on duty,** and the questions pertained to claims that the officer had harassed and been extensively involved with the individuals interviewed. Questioning the officer's wife also was reasonably related to the allegations of sexual misconduct; if she had confirmed their open relationship it would have supported the allegations of the officer's bragging. Because a reasonable investigator would not have known that he or she was intruding on a privacy or associational right, the individual officials should have been granted qualified immunity. *Hughes v. City of North Olmsted*, 93 F.3d 238 (6th Cir. 1996).

♦ An HIV-positive employee of the Southeastern Pennsylvania Transportation Authority began taking Retrovir, a prescription drug used solely to treat HIV. After being assured that no one would link his name with the drug, he filled his prescription through the authority's health insurance. The director of benefits highlighted the names of several employees who were taking Retrovir and asked the head of the medical department about the drug. The head of the medical department informed him that it was AIDS-related and then told the employee that his name had been highlighted on an "AIDS list." The employee filed a 42 U.S.C. § 1983 action against the authority and the director for violations of his right to privacy. A jury held for the employee and awarded substantial damages. The authority appealed to the U.S. Court of Appeals, Third Circuit, which held that **an individual using prescription drugs has a right to expect that such information will customarily remain private**. However, the authority's need for access to employee prescription records, for the purpose of monitoring the plans by those with a need to know, outweighed the employee's interest in keeping his prescription drug purchases confidential. Although a potential for harm to the employee existed, he had not suffered any tangible adverse employment action. The authority's minimal intrusion, although an impingement on privacy, was not a constitutional violation. The lower court decision was reversed. *Doe v. Southeastern Pennsylvania Transportation Authority*, 72 F.3d 1133 (3d Cir. 1995).

CHAPTER FOUR

Governmental Immunity and Tort Liability

	Page
I. SOVEREIGN IMMUNITY	252
A. Generally	252
B. Insurance as Waiver	256
II. GOVERNMENTAL EMPLOYEE IMMUNITY	258
A. Absolute Immunity	258
B. Qualified Immunity	262
1. Supreme Court Cases	262
2. Emergency Calls	264
3. Improper Office Behavior	265
4. Police Misconduct	267
5. Other Employee Misconduct	270
C. Constitutional Violations	271
1. First Amendment Speech Rights	271
2. Fourteenth Amendment Rights	273
3. Fourth Amendment Rights	276
4. Eighth Amendment Rights	278
5. Fifth Amendment Rights	279
D. Special Duty to Protect	279
1. Supreme Court Case	279
2. Police Officers	280
3. Other Public Employees	281
III. GOVERNMENTAL AND EMPLOYEE LIABILITY	283
A. Generally	284
1. Suicides	284
2. Domestic Disputes	285
3. The Firefighter's Rule	287
4. Vicarious Liability	288
5. Other Liability Cases	291
B. 42 U.S.C. § 1983	293
1. Supreme Court Cases	293
2. Police Officers' Actions	295
3. Firefighters' and Other Employees' Actions	300
C. The Federal Tort Claims Act	303
D. State Tort Claims Acts	305

I. SOVEREIGN IMMUNITY

The doctrine of sovereign immunity prevents suits against the government unless the government agrees to be sued. Most states, as well as the federal government, have assented to tort suits by citizens through Tort Claims Acts (see below). Other instances also exist where sovereign immunity does not attach or it has been deemed waived.

A. Generally

♦ The U.S. Supreme Court upheld states' sovereign right to be immune from private lawsuits for monetary damages under the Fair Labor Standards Act (FLSA). The Court held that **Congress lacked the power to subject non-consenting states to private suits for damages in state courts.** Because the state of Maine did not consent to be sued by state employees for overtime under the FLSA, it was entitled to sovereign immunity in a lawsuit filed by probation officers in state court seeking back pay for those overtime hours. The decision came three years after the Supreme Court held in *Seminole Tribe of Florida v. Florida*, 517 U.S. 44, 116 S.Ct 1114, 134 L.Ed.2d 252 (1996), that Congress could not force states to be sued in federal court for money damages without their explicit consent. *Alden v. Maine*, 527 U.S. 706, 119 S.Ct. 2240, 144 L.Ed.2d 636 (1999).

♦ A New York mathematical physicist sought employment at a laboratory operated by the University of California pursuant to a contract with the federal government. He sued the regents of the university in federal court claiming a breach of contract because the university agreed to employ him but wrongfully refused to hire him when he could not obtain the required security clearance from the Department of Energy (DOE). The district court concluded that the Eleventh Amendment, which provides for state immunity from lawsuits, barred him from maintaining his breach of contract action. However, the U.S. Court of Appeals, Ninth Circuit, reversed. On appeal, the physicist contended that the Eleventh Amendment did not apply because any award of damages would be paid by the DOE, and therefore have no impact on the treasury of the state of California. The U.S. Supreme Court rejected this argument, finding that an entity's potential legal liability, rather than its ability to require a third party to reimburse it, or to discharge the liability in the first instance, was the relevant inquiry when determining the immunity issue. **The Eleventh Amendment protects a state from the risk of adverse judgments even though the state may be indemnified by a third party.** The judgment of the court of appeals was reversed. *Regents of the Univ. of California v. John Doe*, 519 U.S. 425, 117 S.Ct. 900, 137 L.Ed.2d 55 (1997).

♦ An Oklahoma woman refused to exit her vehicle following a police chase despite two orders from a reserve deputy sheriff to do so. The deputy pulled her from the car and spun her to the ground, causing injuries to her knees. She sued the county under 42 U.S.C. § 1983, asserting that the county was liable because of the sheriff's inadequate hiring and training policies. A Texas federal jury ruled in her favor, and the Fifth Circuit affirmed with respect to the hiring claim alone. However, the U.S. Supreme Court vacated and remanded the case. It noted that the county could not be held liable for negligent hiring because the woman failed to show that the sheriff's decision to hire the deputy reflected a conscious disregard of an obvious risk that excessive force was likely to follow. *Board of County Commissioners of Bryan County v. Brown*, 520 U.S. 397, 117 S.Ct. 1382, 137 L.Ed.2d 626 (1997).

On remand, the Fifth Circuit upheld the jury's verdict that **the county was liable as a result of the sheriff's failure to train the reserve deputy**. Here, it should have been obvious to the sheriff that the highly predictable consequence of failing to train the reserve deputy would be his unconstitutional use of excessive force. *Brown v. Bryan County*, 219 F.3d 450 (5th Cir. 2000).

• Two workers injured while working for a commuter railroad operated by the Port Authority Trans-Hudson Corporation sued it under the Federal Employers' Liability Act. The case reached the U.S. Supreme Court, which noted that bi-state entities created by compact were not subject to the unilateral control of a single state. Thus, **the port authority was not entitled to Eleventh Amendment immunity**. *Hess v. Port Authority Trans-Hudson Corp.*, 513 U.S. 30, 115 S.Ct. 394, 130 L.Ed.2d 245 (1994).

• The Federal Savings and Loan Insurance Corporation (FSLIC) became the receiver for a failed California-chartered thrift institution and fired a senior thrift officer pursuant to its policy of firing the management of failed thrifts. The officer filed a *Bivens* action (a cause of action for damages against federal agents for deprivation of a federal constitutional right) against the FSLIC, alleging that he was denied his right to continued employment without due process of law. A federal court held for the officer and awarded damages. The Ninth Circuit affirmed, and the FSLIC appealed. The U.S. Supreme Court reversed, ruling that allowing a *Bivens* action against federal agencies would potentially subject the federal government to enormous financial burdens. Further, **permitting *Bivens* actions against federal agencies would circumvent the qualified immunity defense** and encourage claimants to bypass actions against federal officers in favor of suits against federal agencies. As a result, the *Bivens* remedy's deterrent effect against individual federal officers would be lost. Thus, although the FSLIC effectively waived sovereign immunity, the officer could not collect damages pursuant to a *Bivens* remedy. *FDIC v. Meyer*, 510 U.S. 471, 114 S.Ct. 996, 127 L.Ed.2d 308 (1994).

• A professor at Kennesaw State University was accused of sexual harassment by a student. He was later exonerated when the student admitted lying about the accusation. The professor claimed that the university improperly kept a record of the accusation in his file and denied him a promotion because of the accusation. He also claimed colleagues continued to harass him about the matter. He sued the university in state court, alleging violations of the Georgia Tort Claims Act and 42 U.S.C. § 1983, which provides remedies when a state official acting under color of state law deprives someone of his or her constitutional or federal statutory rights. The board of regents removed the case to federal court, then sought to have it dismissed on grounds of Eleventh Amendment immunity. The question of whether the university was entitled to Eleventh Amendment immunity reached the U.S. Supreme Court, which ruled that the university had waived its immunity. **By voluntarily removing the case to federal court, the university could no longer claim immunity under the Eleventh Amendment.** *Lapides v. Board of Regents of Univ. System of Georgia*, 535 U.S. 613, 122 S.Ct. 1640, 152 L.Ed.2d 806 (2002).

• A psychologist ran a $5 million study funded by the National Institute of Drug Abuse to evaluate treatment regimens for pregnant drug addicts. She worked for a private, nonprofit medical research institute affiliated with Cook County Hospital in Chicago until the institute fired her. She then brought a *qui tam* action (under Section 3729 of the False Claims Act) against the county, alleging that the county and the institute had submitted false statements to the federal government regarding the funding and how it was being administered. She claimed she was fired for reporting the fraud. The case reached the U.S. Supreme Court, which held that cities and counties are "persons" subject to *qui tam* actions. Thus, the psychologist could continue her lawsuit against the county. *Cook County v. U.S. ex rel. Chandler*, 538 U.S. 119, 123 S.Ct. 1239, 155 L.Ed.2d 247 (2003).

• A Pennsylvania emergency medical technician (EMT) responded to an emergency call at a housing complex for elderly persons owned and operated by the county housing authority. While lifting a garage door to gain access to the facility, the EMT was struck in the head by a falling piece of metal and sustained injuries. He sued the housing authority for negligence. After a jury was unable to reach a verdict, the trial court ruled in favor of the housing authority. The EMT appealed to the Pennsylvania Commonwealth Court, which affirmed the lower court ruling. Here, **the EMT failed to show that the housing authority had actual or constructive notice of the alleged defect**, as was required to apply the real estate exception to the housing authority's governmental immunity. Further, the EMT failed to prove that the metal piece that hit him was part of the garage door, so as to allow liability against the county under *res ipsa loquitur* (circumstantial proof of negligence). *Gurnari v. Luzerne County Housing Authority*, 911 A.2d 236 (Pa. Commw. Ct. 2006).

• A Florida county employee claimed that his female supervisor sexually harassed him and repeatedly refused to promote him. He sued under the Florida Civil Rights Act, and a jury awarded him $230,000 in compensatory damages and $20,000 in back pay. The trial judge added $291,000 in attorneys' fees and $18,000 in costs, but then **reduced the entire award to $100,000 because of a state law that limited waivers of sovereign immunity**. The employee appealed, claiming that the cap on damages should only apply to the award of compensatory damages. The District Court of Appeal disagreed. According to the statute, "the total amount of recovery" against the state could not exceed the $100,000 limitation in the sovereign immunity provisions. *Gallagher v. Manatee County*, 927 So.2d 914 (Fla. Dist. Ct. App. 2006).

- An administrative aide for the New York City Police Department brought a sexual harassment lawsuit under state and federal law. She was awarded $400,000 in compensatory damages and $1 million in punitive damages. The New York Court of Appeals was then asked whether Section 8-502 of the state Human Rights Law allowed for the recovery of punitive damages against the city. The court said no. Even though the law provided for punitive damages against both public and private employers, **it did not expressly waive the city's sovereign immunity**. The aide was not entitled to punitive damages. *Krohn v. New York City Police Dep't*, 778 N.Y.S.2d 746, 811 N.E.2d 8 (N.Y. 2004).

- A day-care licensor for the Wyoming Department of Family Services used paid sick leave on a number of occasions. She sought more leave and was informed that she had used up her Family and Medical Leave Act (FMLA) leave, meaning she would have to work another 12 months to qualify for more time. A month later, the department suspended her for 10 days for improperly using e-mail. When she failed to return to work, she was fired. She sued for money damages under the FMLA, and a federal court ruled against her. The Tenth Circuit affirmed, noting that the state was immune to her lawsuit. Even though the Supreme Court has held that a history of sex discrimination in the workplace justified eliminating **immunity** under the FMLA for cases involving family members with serious health conditions, the self-care provision was not premised on stereotypes about women's roles as caregivers. *Brockman v. Wyoming DFS*, 342 F.3d 1159 (10th Cir. 2003).

- An education services technician at a high school in Arizona used a wheelchair to get around. When school officials directed her to tie a flagpole to her wheelchair to make herself more visible to students in the classroom, she objected, believing the order to be discriminatory. Because of her continued refusal to put a flagpole on her wheelchair, she was fired. She sued the school district for money damages in a federal court under Title I of the Americans with Disabilities Act (ADA) and the Rehabilitation Act. The district asserted that it was entitled to Eleventh Amendment immunity as an arm of the state, but the court ruled against it. The Ninth Circuit Court of Appeals affirmed. Here, even though the district received money from the state, that money was directly tied to the operating expenses of the district. Since any judgment against the district would not be satisfied out of state funds, **the district was not entitled to immunity**. *Savage v. Glendale Union High School Dist.*, 343 F.3d 1036 (9th Cir. 2003).

- A Texas corrections officer reported an incident of alleged inmate abuse and drafted a witness statement regarding the incident. Shortly thereafter, she was accused of having sexual relations with an inmate. She was arrested and, a month later, she was fired. After being acquitted by a jury on the criminal charges, she sued the state under the Texas Whistleblower Act, asserting that the real reason for her discharge had been the report she made of the incident. The state removed the case to federal court, then sought to dismiss it on immunity grounds. The court ruled in the state's favor, and the Fifth Circuit Court of Appeals affirmed. Even though the Supreme Court had ruled that a state's removal of a case to federal court waives its sovereign immunity, the officer failed to make that argument before the district court. She first raised the issue on appeal. As a result, **the state could claim immunity**. Further, the evidence indicated that the officer had sex with the inmate and that she would have been fired regardless of whether she reported the incident of inmate abuse. *Martinez v. Texas Dep't of Criminal Justice*, 300 F.3d 567 (5th Cir. 2002).

• The director of a New York residential youth facility was warned that he was close to losing his job because of his failure to implement certain policies at the facility. He took a sick leave for job-related stress that was designated as FMLA leave and, while he was gone, state officials conducted a search of the facility and found it unkempt and disorganized. They notified him that he was going to be fired when his FMLA leave expired. Because he held tenured status, his firing meant that he was demoted to a lower-paying position. He sued the state under the FMLA, and the Second Circuit Court of Appeals held that **Congress exceeded its authority under the Fourteenth Amendment by eliminating the states' sovereign immunity under the law**. *Hale v. Mann*, 219 F.3d 61 (2d Cir. 2000).

• An Illinois postal worker suffered continual harassment at work, even from her supervisors. She filed two complaints with the EEOC, and received compensatory damages of $50,000. She asserted that she was entitled to both compensatory and punitive damages. The Seventh Circuit held that **the postal service was a "governmental agency" that was exempt from punitive damages under Title VII**. The presence of the "sue and be sued" provision in the postal service's charter did not mean that the postal service was no longer a governmental agency. *Baker v. Runyon*, 114 F.3d 668 (7th Cir. 1997).

B. Insurance as Waiver

• An employee of a tree-cutting company in Georgia stepped into an open manhole while clearing brush. The manhole was located on an easement held by a city and the power company. The employee sued the county, whose employees mowed the grass above the manhole, asserting that they must have knocked the manhole cover off, and that the county had waived its sovereign immunity because it had insurance covering motor vehicles – in this case, a tractor. However, the Georgia Court of Appeals ruled against him, finding that **he was not entitled to the insurance waiver to immunity because he failed to prove that county employees knocked the manhole cover off**. *Dunn v. Telfair County*, 653 S.E.2d 537 (Ga. Ct. App. 2007).

• A Missouri public employee who was fired after 23 years sued for breach of contract and wrongful discharge, claiming retaliation for whistleblowing activities (i.e., reporting violations of various municipal codes, policies and state laws). The city sought to dismiss his lawsuit, claiming that he failed to exhaust his administrative remedies, and asserting sovereign immunity. After a court granted the dismissal, the Missouri Supreme Court held that the employee was not required to exhaust his administrative remedies. Also, **the employee was asserting that the city had procured liability insurance to handle**

employment-related actions brought against it. If this was the case, the employee might be entitled to recover from the city for wrongful discharge. Also, the breach of contract claim was not barred by sovereign immunity. The lower court should not have dismissed the lawsuit. *Kunzie v. City of Olivette*, 184 S.W.3d 570 (Mo. 2006).

• A Missouri police officer, who suffered numerous injuries during his 13 years on the job, and who filed for workers' compensation at least twice, was fired because there were no light-duty positions available, and because he could not bend, squat or run – duties required of all department officers. He sued the city for wrongful discharge (retaliation) under the state's workers' compensation act, but the Eighth Circuit held that the city had sovereign immunity despite purchasing insurance through the state's risk management fund. Sovereign immunity was waived only to the extent of insurance coverage, and **the insurance here did not cover deliberate acts like retaliatory discharge**. Also, the city was not liable under the ADA because the officer was not qualified to perform the particular job of police officer. *Epps v. City of Pine Lawn*, 353 F.3d 588 (8th Cir. 2003).

• A teacher confined to a wheelchair sued her school district for failing to make certain accommodations that she had requested. The school district sought to have the lawsuit dismissed on the grounds that it was entitled to sovereign immunity under the state constitution. A trial court refused to grant the school district constitutional immunity, and the Arkansas Supreme Court affirmed. It noted that **school districts – like counties, cities and towns – are not, strictly speaking, part of the state**. As a result, they are entitled only to statutory immunity. That is, they can be sued for damages to the extent they are covered by liability insurance. The teacher's lawsuit could proceed. *Dermott Special School Dist. v. Johnson*, 32 S.W.3d 477 (Ark. 2000).

• A Maryland police officer pulled over a woman on suspicion of driving while intoxicated. He told her he would not arrest her and offered to drive her home. Instead, he raped her. When she sued him (and the county) for violating her civil rights, the county offered to defend him. A jury awarded her over $1 million in her lawsuit against the officer, but the court held that the county was not liable. She then sued the county a second time, seeking to recover the judgment she had been awarded against the officer. A trial court ruled in favor of the county, and the Maryland Court of Special Appeals affirmed. The county's liability insurance policy provided that **the county would be liable only where an employee committed wrongful acts within the scope of his employment**. Here, the rape did not occur within the scope of the officer's employment because he was not hired to perform such an act, and the rape did not, even in part, further the county's purposes. Moreover, in addition to the policy's exclusion, state law barred the county from paying the judgment for the rape. The county did not have to pay the jury's award to the victim. *Wolfe v. Anne Arundel County*, 761 A.2d 935 (Md. Ct. Spec. App. 2000).

II. GOVERNMENTAL EMPLOYEE IMMUNITY

Government employees may be entitled to protection from liability based on absolute or qualified immunity. Absolute immunity generally applies only to certain individuals in the judicial and executive branches of government. Qualified immunity, however, applies to most public employees as long as the employee does not violate a clearly established law or constitutional right of which a reasonable person would have known. An employee also may lose his or her immunity protection in circumstances where a special duty to protect has been created.

A. Absolute Immunity

The U.S. Supreme Court, in *Harlow v. Fitzgerald*, defined the scope of absolute immunity, finding that only policymaking public employees are entitled to absolute immunity as a defense. Subsequent cases further refined the application of absolute immunity to particular positions.

• A management analyst with the U.S. Department of the Air Force appeared before a joint congressional committee and testified about cost overruns, which embarrassed his superiors. The department then conducted a reorganization and reduction in force to promote economic efficiency of the armed forces, and the analyst's position was eliminated. He sued two White House aides in a federal district court, asserting that he had been unlawfully discharged in retaliation for his public statements. The White House aides asked the court to dismiss the suit, claiming that they were entitled to absolute immunity, but the court refused. Their appeal reached the U.S. Supreme Court.

The Supreme Court stated that **absolute immunity exists for the President, legislators, and judges in their judicial functions, and for certain officials in the executive branch.** However, for most executive officials, the Court recognized only qualified immunity. These officials required some protection to shield them from undue interference with their duties, but they also could be held liable for constitutional violations of citizens' rights. In order to be entitled to absolute immunity, a Presidential aide would first have to show that his job included functions so sensitive that absolute immunity was essential. Because they had not shown that their jobs were of such a sensitive nature, the aides were not entitled to absolute immunity. However, they were entitled to qualified immunity provided that their actions did not violate clearly established statutory or constitutional rights of which a reasonable person would have known. The Court remanded the case for a determination as to whether the aides' conduct fell within the immune category. *Harlow v. Fitzgerald,* 457 U.S. 800, 102 S.Ct. 2727, 73 L.Ed.2d 396 (1982).

• In 1970, the attorney general of the United States authorized a warrantless wiretap for the purpose of gathering intelligence about activities of a radical group that had made tentative plans to threaten the nation's security. After the wiretap, the U.S. Supreme Court ruled that warrantless wiretaps were not constitutional in cases involving domestic threats. After this ruling, the man who had been wiretapped sued the attorney general in a federal district court, asserting that the surveillance he had been subjected to violated the Fourth Amendment. The attorney general sought to dismiss the lawsuit on immunity grounds, and the man who had been wiretapped sought a declaration that the attorney general was not immune. The district court ruled against the attorney general, who then appealed to the Third Circuit. The court of appeals held that he was not entitled to absolute immunity. The U.S. Supreme Court held that even though he was a cabinet officer, **the attorney general was not absolutely immune from a suit for damages**. However, the Court held that he was entitled to qualified immunity for his authorization of the wiretap because his action was not a violation of clearly established law. Even though the Court had held warrantless wiretaps to be illegal and unconstitutional, it had not done so until after the attorney general had authorized the wiretap. *Mitchell v. Forsyth*, 472 U.S. 511, 105 S.Ct. 2806, 86 L.Ed.2d 411 (1985).

♦ Police in Rhode Island conducted a court-authorized wiretap of a house and determined that marijuana had been used there. Accordingly, an officer drew up felony complaints against several persons, charging them with possession of marijuana. He presented the complaints to a state judge who signed the warrants, and the officer arrested the suspects. However, the charges were dropped when the grand jury did not return an indictment. The arrestees then sued the officer in a federal district court, asserting violations of their constitutional rights. The case reached the U.S. Supreme Court, which ruled that **the officer was not entitled to absolute immunity just because he submitted the warrants to a neutral magistrate**. He could only assert qualified immunity as a defense. This required a finding that he knew probable cause existed or that he reasonably believed probable cause existed before seeking the warrants. His act in applying for the arrest warrants was not automatically reasonable because he believed certain facts were true and relied on the judge's determination of whether to issue them. The Court remanded the case for a determination on that issue. *Malley v. Briggs*, 475 U.S. 335, 106 S.Ct. 1092, 89 L.Ed.2d 271 (1986).

♦ After a Massachusetts city passed an ordinance eliminating a department, an employee sued the city, the mayor and the vice president of the city council under 42 U.S.C. § 1983, claiming that the action was discriminatory and in violation of the First Amendment (retaliating against her for filing a complaint against another employee). A jury returned a verdict in favor of the defendants on the issue of race discrimination but found in favor of the employee on the First Amendment issue. Citing absolute legislative immunity, the defendants appealed to the Fourth Circuit, which stated that the mayor's and the vice president's actions were not legislative because they relied on facts relating to a particular individual in the decision-making process. The U.S. Supreme Court reversed. Noting that federal, state and regional legislators have long been absolutely immune from civil liability for their legislative activities, the Supreme Court held that **local legislators also are absolutely immune from suit under Section 1983 for their legislative activities**. Absolute immunity attaches to all actions taken within the sphere of legitimate legislative activity.

The ordinance reflected a discretionary, policymaking decision implicating the budgetary priorities of the city and the services it provided. *Bogan v. Scott-Harris*, 523 U.S. 44, 118 S.Ct. 966, 140 L.Ed.2d 79 (1998).

♦ A prosecuting attorney in Washington began a criminal proceeding against an individual based on the alleged theft of computer equipment from a school. She filed three documents in court, two of which were unsworn pleadings. The third was an affidavit setting forth certain facts. Based on the affidavit, the court found probable cause and ordered an arrest warrant to be issued. However, the affidavit contained two inaccurate factual statements. After the charges against the individual were dismissed, he sued under 42 U.S.C. § 1983, alleging that the prosecutor had violated his constitutional right to be free from unreasonable seizures. A federal court denied her request for absolute immunity. The Ninth Circuit and the U.S. Supreme Court affirmed. Section 1983 may create a damages remedy against a prosecutor for making false statements of fact in an affidavit supporting an arrest warrant, because such conduct is not protected by absolute prosecutorial immunity. **Absolute immunity applies when a criminal prosecutor is performing the traditional functions of an advocate.** However, when she is functioning as a complaining witness by personally attesting to the truth of the facts set forth in an affidavit, she is not functioning as an advocate. Accordingly, she is protected only by qualified immunity. *Kalina v. Fletcher*, 522 U.S. 118, 118 S.Ct. 502, 139 L.Ed.2d 471 (1997).

♦ A New York police officer was disciplined twice in a four-month period. He claimed a violation of his due process rights and brought a 42 U.S.C. § 1983 lawsuit against the chief and a sergeant, alleging that they offered false testimony at his disciplinary hearing before an arbitrator, who struck most of the charges against him. A federal court ruled for the defendants, and the Second Circuit affirmed. Here, **the chief was entitled to absolute immunity for his witness testimony at arbitration**. The chief testified under oath, responded to questions on direct and cross-examination, and could have been prosecuted for perjury the same as if he gave false testimony in a trial court proceeding. Also, the sergeant's allegedly false charges did not deprive the officer of any property or liberty interest protected by due process. *Rolon v. Henneman*, 517 F.3d 140 (2d Cir. 2008).

♦ Two nonresident firefighters of a Rhode Island town showed up for the town's annual meeting, but were told they could not speak at the meeting or videotape it. That privilege was reserved for the media. One of the firefighters was ejected from the meeting for being disruptive, and the other was allegedly threatened with removal as well. They sued the fire district's chief and the district's moderator for restricting their behavior at the meeting. A federal magistrate judge held that **the rules restricting their behavior were legislative acts entitling the defendants to absolute immunity**. Also, the rule preventing nonresidents from speaking was reasonable, and the rule prohibiting videotaping did not violate the firefighters' First Amendment rights. The court accepted the magistrate's recommendation and report, and it ruled in favor of the defendants. *Carlow v. Mruk*, 425 F.Supp.2d 225 (D.R.I. 2006).

* The attorney general and assistant attorney general of Georgia conducted an investigation into the alleged misconduct of a county sheriff and his deputy. The investigation stemmed from allegations that the deputy planted drugs on criminal suspects and then falsely arrested them. After a grand jury indicted the deputy on one count, the attorney general had the deputy arrested. However, the attorney general dropped the case after the deputy was released on bond. The deputy then sued in federal court under 42 U.S.C. § 1983, seeking damages for abuse of process, false imprisonment and conspiracy. A federal court found that the attorney general and his assistant were not entitled to immunity. The U.S. Court of Appeals, Eleventh Circuit, reversed. **The attorney general and his assistant were entitled to absolute prosecutorial immunity because they had not stepped outside their prosecutorial roles.** *Mastroianni v. Bowers*, 173 F.3d 1363 (11th Cir. 1999).

* An Alabama city established a public safety director position to consolidate supervision and control of the city's police, fire and emergency medical divisions. The mayor offered the new position to the police chief, who accepted on the condition that the city would hold the police chief position open such that he could return to the police chief position at any time. If the director position were abolished, the director would automatically be reinstated as police chief. Six years later, when the city council voted to abolish the position, the director requested a pre-termination hearing and sued in federal court under 42 U.S.C. § 1983 after no hearing was granted. Citing *Bogan v. Scott-Harris*, 523 U.S. 44, above, the court noted that **local lawmakers have absolute immunity from Section 1983 liability for their legislative activity**. Motive or intent is not relevant to the immunity determination. Here, the city council voted to abolish a position created by ordinance, and its actions could be considered legislative, even if its motivation was solely to get rid of the director. *Lumpkin v. City of Lafayatte, Alabama*, 24 F.Supp.2d 1259 (M.D. Ala. 1998).

* A member of a Virginia county board of supervisors confronted two other members with abusive language. The full board decided to formally censure the abusive member for one year and remove him from all standing committees. The abusive member sued, alleging, among other things, that the board violated his First Amendment rights. The defendant board members asserted legislative immunity and moved to dismiss the lawsuit, which the court granted. The U.S. Court of Appeals, Fourth Circuit, affirmed. While the abusive member was arguably disciplined for speaking out, the legislative body's disciplinary action was protected by absolute legislative immunity. Disciplinary action taken by a county board against one of its members is legislative in nature. Moreover, **absolute immunity protects legislative speech and voting as well as the exercise of self-disciplinary power**. *Whitener v. McWatters*, 112 F.3d 740 (4th Cir. 1997).

* A Massachusetts couple obtained monetary judgments in a tort action against the state. However, they failed in their attempts to get paid. They learned that the assistant attorney general had recommended that payment not be authorized while he explored possible avenues of appeal or settlement. When

the assistant attorney general and his supervisor took no action, the couple filed a civil rights suit against the two attorneys and the state, seeking redress for the nonpayment of the judgments. The attorneys and the state sought to dismiss the case. The Supreme Judicial Court of Massachusetts held that absolute immunity protected the attorneys' actions from civil rights claims based on state and federal law. Similar to criminal prosecutors who receive absolute immunity for activities closely related to the judicial phase of a criminal proceeding or involving the skills or judgment of an advocate, **the court extended absolute immunity to government attorneys in the conduct of civil litigation.** *Dinsdale v. Comwlth.*, 675 N.E.2d 374 (Mass. 1997).

B. Qualified Immunity

Public employees are entitled to qualified immunity for their actions if they can show that a reasonable person in their position would believe his or her acts were justified. Where negligence arises out of the performance of discretionary duties, and not ministerial duties, immunity applies.

1. Supreme Court Cases

♦ A Puerto Rico police officer was fired after testifying in a criminal case about false evidence allegedly offered by two other agents. The officer appealed to an administrative commission, which reinstated him. He then sued his supervisor in a federal district court under 42 U.S.C. § 1983, contending that his due process rights had been violated, and that his reputation in the community had been damaged. The district court dismissed the case because the supervisor was entitled to qualified immunity for acts done in good faith within the scope of his official duties, and because the officer had failed to state in his pleading that the supervisor had acted in bad faith. The officer appealed unsuccessfully to the U.S. Court of Appeals, First Circuit. The U.S. Supreme Court held that the qualified immunity defense depends on facts that are "peculiarly within the knowledge and control" of the public official making the defense. The official must act sincerely and with a belief that he is doing the right thing by his action. Since the officer could not know if his supervisor was so acting, the Court determined that **the burden was on the supervisor to plead that "his conduct was justified by an objectively reasonable belief that it was lawful."** The Court reversed the appellate court's decision. *Gomez v. Toledo*, 446 U.S. 635, 100 S.Ct. 1920, 64 L.Ed.2d 572 (1980).

♦ A Federal Bureau of Investigation (FBI) agent conducted a warrantless search, with other law enforcement officers, of a Minnesota family's home. He was seeking a suspected bank robber, but the suspect was not there. The family then sued the FBI agent, who moved for pretrial judgment on qualified immunity grounds. The court granted pretrial judgment, but the Eighth Circuit reversed. It held that unresolved factual questions existed regarding probable cause, and further held that the right to be protected from warrantless searches was clearly established. The agent further appealed to the U.S. Supreme Court, which held that the agent was entitled to pretrial judgment on qualified immunity grounds if he could establish that a reasonable officer would have believed the search comported with the Fourth Amendment. Further, the Court ruled that the right that the agent had violated was not a clearly established right if probable cause and exigent circumstances existed. It was not inappropriate to give qualified immunity to government officials who had acted reasonably. **Even if the agent violated the Fourth Amendment, the search was not necessarily unlawful if a reasonable officer could have believed that the search was lawful.** The Court vacated the court of appeals' decision and remanded the case for a determination as to whether the agent's actions had been reasonable. *Anderson v. Creighton*, 483 U.S. 635, 107 S.Ct. 3034, 97 L.Ed.2d 523 (1987).

♦ The newly elected auditor general of Pennsylvania discharged a group of employees in her office, claiming they had "bought" their jobs through payments to a former employee. The employees sued the auditor general, seeking monetary damages under 42 U.S.C. § 1983. A federal district court dismissed the Section 1983 claims under *Will v. Michigan Dep't of State Police*, 491 U.S. 58, 109 S.Ct. 2304, 105 L.Ed.2d 45 (1989), in which the Supreme Court held that state officials "acting in their official capacities" are outside the class of "persons" subject to liability under Section 1983. The court of appeals reversed, holding that since the employees sought damages from the auditor general in her personal capacity, they could maintain an action under Section 1983. The auditor then appealed to the U.S. Supreme Court. The Supreme Court held for the employees. The Court stated that the holding in *Will* did not mean that officials who act in their official capacity are immune to suit under Section 1983. The phrase "acting in their official capacity" is best understood as a reference to the capacity in which the state officer is sued, not the capacity in which the officer inflicts the injury. **State officials sued in their personal capacities are "persons" within the meaning of Section 1983.** Unlike official capacity defendants – who are not "persons" because they assume the identity of the government that employs them – officers sued in their personal capacity fit comfortably into the statutory term "person." *Hafer v. Melo*, 502 U.S. 21, 112 S.Ct. 358, 116 L.Ed.2d 301 (1991).

♦ A Tennessee prisoner filed suit in federal district court against two prison guards, alleging violation of his constitutional rights under 42 U.S.C. § 1983. The guards asserted qualified immunity and moved to dismiss the case. The district court denied the motion, holding that because they worked for a private company rather than the government the law did not grant them immunity. The Sixth Circuit and the U.S. Supreme Court affirmed. **Private prison guards, unlike those who work directly for the government, do not enjoy Section 1983 immunity.** Immunity does not apply to private entities. Mere performance of a governmental function does not support immunity for a private person, especially one who performs a job without supervision or direction. The Court left open the question of whether privately employed prison guards could be liable under Section 1983. *Richardson v. McKnight*, 521 U.S. 399, 117 S.Ct. 2100, 138 L.Ed.2d 540 (1997).

2. Emergency Calls

♦ The family of a New Jersey woman who was abducted and murdered by a former boyfriend sued the city for wrongful death, claiming that a series of missteps by a 911 operator caused the police to look for the wrong car in the wrong location, missing any opportunity they would have had to save her life. A court found the city immune under the state's tort claims act, but the Superior Court, Appellate Division, reversed and remanded the case. **The 911 operator's failure to follow official police department policies was a negligent ministerial act rather than a discretionary act for which the city would be entitled to immunity.** However, the city might still be able to defeat the suit under the 911 statute, which limits liability to where 911 operators act with wanton and willful disregard for the safety of people or property. *Massachi v. AHL Services, Inc.*, 935 A.2d 769 (N.J. Super. Ct. App. Div. 2007).

♦ A motorist, whose vehicle was struck by an airport police vehicle that was responding to an emergency call on airport property, sued the officer and the airport for negligence and vicarious liability. A jury found that the officer was 25% negligent and the motorist was 75% negligent. It also found that the motorist's damages were $25,000. The trial court allocated damages in accordance with fault, but ordered only the airport to pay. The airport appealed to the Supreme Court of Missouri, which held that even though the officer was entitled to official immunity because he was exercising discretion in an emergency situation, the airport was not entitled to immunity and was vicariously liable for the motorist's injuries. **Official immunity that is personal to the officer does not preclude a finding of negligence or shield a government employer from liability.** *Davis v. Lambert-St. Louis Int'l Airport*, 193 S.W.3d 760 (Mo. 2006).

♦ Three emergency medical technicians (EMTs) for the city of El Paso responded to a call for assistance and determined that a man needed to be taken to a hospital. As their ambulance neared an intersection, one of the EMTs loosened the restraint that ran across the man's chest so that another EMT could check his blood pressure and vital signs. The ambulance entered the intersection on a red light without its siren on and struck another car, and the man fell off the stretcher. His family sued. The trial court refused to grant qualified immunity to the EMTs, and the city appealed. The court of appeals noted that **a governmental employee is generally entitled to official immunity from suit if his or her actions involve the performance of discretionary duties**, provided the employee acts in good faith. Here, even though transporting a patient to the hospital required the exercise of significant discretion, the EMTs were not entitled to qualified immunity because they did not act in good faith. The EMT who drove the ambulance went through a red light in a controlled intersection without putting on the ambulance's emergency siren. Nor was there any evidence that a reasonably prudent EMT would have believed that loosening a passenger's restraint as the ambulance went through an intersection was justified in light of the clear risk of harm to the passenger being transported. *City of El Paso v. Higginbotham*, 993 S.W.2d 819 (Tex. Ct. App. 1999).

♦ While responding to an emergency call, a paramedic for a Minnesota city noticed a pedestrian crossing the street in front of him. With his siren activated and his lights flashing, the paramedic slowed down and switched lanes to get away from her, but when she saw his vehicle, she froze and was struck as the paramedic hit the brakes. The pedestrian filed suit, and a state court ruled for the city and the paramedic. The Minnesota Supreme Court upheld that decision, noting that it had previously held that police officers acting conscientiously should not be subject to liability for split-second decisions made in hot pursuit of a fleeing suspect. **Paramedics responding to medical emergencies in emergency vehicles are entitled to the same considerations.** The court rejected the pedestrian's argument that because the statute did not explicitly exempt the paramedic from yielding to the right-of-way of a pedestrian in a crosswalk, he acted outside the law and therefore with malice. The proper standard was not whether the paramedic complied with the traffic statute, but whether he unreasonably put the pedestrian's safety at risk. That was not the case because the paramedic had his sirens on and lights flashing, and he was driving cautiously as he approached the crosswalk. *Kari v. City of Maplewood*, 582 N.W.2d 921 (Minn. 1998).

♦ A Rhode Island police officer arrived at the scene of a drive-by shooting, observed the victim bleeding from a gunshot wound and immediately called for rescue personnel. Also on the scene were the victim's brothers, although the officer did not know their identities. When one brother attempted to drive the victim to the hospital, the officer advised him not to do so because the rescue squad was on its way. A struggle ensued. Although the rescue squad arrived and treated the victim, he died due to a loss of blood. His estate sued the city, alleging that the police were negligent in preventing the victim from getting necessary medical treatment. Finding that the officer was immune from liability because he was rendering emergency assistance, the court ruled for the city. The estate appealed.

The Rhode Island Supreme Court disagreed with the estate that the officer was grossly negligent in thwarting the brothers' attempt to get medical assistance. Because the officer had arrived at the scene unaware of the circumstances surrounding the shooting or of the identity of the men purporting to be the victim's brothers, it was reasonable and appropriate for him to secure the scene and safeguard the victim before the arrival of rescue personnel. **Although the officer did not render affirmative medical assistance, his emergency assistance fell within the state immunity law.** The estate had not shown that there was gross, willful, or wanton negligence so as to overcome his immunity. The court affirmed the lower court's judgment. *Brandon v. City of Providence*, 708 A.2d 893 (R.I. 1998).

3. Improper Office Behavior

♦ An assistant principal at a middle school in South Carolina made sexual advances to a teacher. When she rebuffed him, he refused to have the air conditioning and heating unit in her classroom repaired. He also moved her class to the cafeteria stage, claiming that her classroom was being used as a computer lab. When she sued the assistant principal for the "tort of outrage" under state law, a jury awarded her $400,000. The assistant principal appealed, alleging that he was entitled to governmental immunity. The South Carolina Supreme Court held that the assistant principal was not entitled to immunity because **he was not acting within the scope of his employment when he retaliated against the teacher for rejecting his sexual advances.** None of his actions furthered the school's legitimate interests. The court upheld the award against him. *Frazier v. Badger*, 603 S.E.2d 587 (S.C. 2004).

• An African-American woman, employed as an appeals referee by the Florida Department of Labor (DOL), alleged that she was harassed by her supervisor, who **followed her with a bullwhip** and exclaimed, "this is my sexual fantasy for you." He also made other sexually suggestive comments and took other actions. She informed the chief supervisor of the incident, and the chief supervisor removed the whip from the office. Afterward, she alleged that the supervisor continued to make sexual remarks about her in front of the chief supervisor and that they both subjected her to angry stares. She eventually transferred to another office with the same pay, rank, and benefits where the chief supervisor worked. She claimed that the chief supervisor subjected her to harsh and constant criticism as well as increased visits. She sued both supervisors and the DOL for sexual harassment and race discrimination. The supervisors moved for pretrial judgment on the basis of qualified immunity. When their motions were denied, they appealed to the Eleventh Circuit.

The court of appeals held that unless the referee could show a violation of a clearly established right, the supervisors would be entitled to immunity. It rejected the referee's argument that the chief supervisor actively participated in and impliedly authorized the harassment against her. Other than allegations of angry stares, frequent trips to the referee's new office and criticisms, nothing indicated that the chief supervisor personally participated in sexual harassment or race discrimination. **Because the chief supervisor had taken some action after receiving the complaints, his response was not so obvious, flagrant and rampant to take away qualified immunity.** However, the alleged conduct of the second supervisor, specifically the incident with the bullwhip, was so clearly and obviously in violation of existing federal law that he lost his qualified immunity. *Braddy v. Florida Dep't of Labor and Employment Security*, 133 F.3d 797 (11th Cir. 1998).

• A group of New York state employees held at-will jobs at the discretion of the attorney general (AG). They worked in a highly specialized office that exercised traditional prosecutorial discretion in its choice of cases. When the newly elected AG came into office, they lost their jobs. They sued the AG and other state officials under 42 U.S.C. § 1983 for violation of their First Amendment right of association. The AG moved for dismissal on the grounds that the employees were political employees who were not protected under the First Amendment and that the AG was entitled to qualified immunity. The court ruled for the AG, and the U.S. Court of Appeals, Second Circuit, affirmed. Here, the office was highly specialized, prosecuting complex, high profile, fraudulent schemes in the Medicare system, and had access to highly confidential information relating to pending investigations or prosecutions. The employees fell within the First Amendment's political appointment exception, and **the AG's decision to fire them was not a violation of clearly established law**. *Danahy v. Buscaglia*, 134 F.3d 1185 (2d Cir. 1998).

• A 13-year-old Florida boy was placed in a foster home in Georgia where other young children also lived. Before being placed in the home, the boy was caught masturbating in front of other boys in a group home. When asked if the boy had any incidents of prior sexual misconduct, the caseworker did not inform the foster parents of the masturbation incident. While living in the foster home, the boy allegedly sexually abused a five-year-old. The foster parents sued the caseworker and the Florida Department of Human Resources under 42 U.S.C. § 1983 and the Georgia Tort Claims Act. The case reached the Court of Appeals of Georgia, which found that **a reasonable social worker under the same circumstances would have placed the boy into the foster home without necessarily telling the foster parents about the masturbation incident**, and therefore the caseworker and the department were entitled to qualified immunity. There was no evidence that the caseworker improperly withheld information about the boy's past and there were no previous incidents of sexual assault. There was no showing of "deliberate indifference" that would sustain a claim under Section 1983 or state law. *Sherin v. Florida Dep't of Human Resources*, 494 S.E.2d 518 (Ga. Ct. App. 1997).

4. Police Misconduct

• While Vice President Gore was speaking at a newly created national park, an animal rights protester removed a banner from under his jacket and attempted to put it up on a fence separating the vice president from the public. Two military police officers moved to intercept him. They grabbed the banner, took him by the arms, and half-walked, half-dragged him away. They took him to a nearby military van and allegedly shoved him inside. After being driven to a military police station, he was held for a short time, then released. He sued the arresting officer for violating his Fourth Amendment rights by using excessive force to remove him from the area. A California federal court granted the officer pretrial judgment, holding that he had qualified immunity. The Ninth Circuit reversed, and the case reached the U.S. Supreme Court. The Court reinstated the district court's grant of immunity to the officer. **Even if he acted with excessive force, he reasonably believed he was acting within the bounds of the law.** He did not know the full extent of the threat the protester posed, and his actions were not so severe as to injure the protester. *Saucier v. Katz*, 533 U.S. 194, 121 S.Ct. 2151, 150 L.Ed.2d 272 (2001).

• After unsuccessful attempting to pacify a Somali man who was wielding a machete and a tire iron, including using a taser on him several times, Minneapolis police officers shot and killed the man as he approached them in a threatening manner. His estate sued the city and the officers for wrongful death, as well as negligence. The estate asserted that the city failed to train its officers properly on how to approach individuals with mental illnesses, and that it failed to provide someone who could speak Somalian. A federal court granted the defendants qualified immunity, and the Eighth Circuit affirmed. Here, the officers did not use excessive force in shooting the man. Also, **what caused the man's death was not any failure by the city, but rather the man's dangerous behavior**. *Hassan v. City of Minneapolis*, 489 F.3d 914 (8th Cir. 2007).

♦ A North Dakota sheriff repeatedly made perverse comments to his only female deputy, though he never actually touched her or requested sexual favors. When she eventually complained, an attorney who was unfamiliar with sexual harassment law found that the sheriff's comments were inappropriate but not unwelcome. Later she quit and sued under 42 U.S.C. § 1983, alleging a violation of her rights under the Equal Protection Clause. The sheriff claimed he was entitled to qualified immunity, but the Eighth Circuit disagreed. It held that **the right to be free of behavior like his was clearly established** at the time he made his vulgar comments. *Wright v. Rolette County*, 417 F.3d 879 (8th Cir. 2005).

♦ An Ohio state trooper pulled over a car with a faulty headlight. The car contained two resident aliens. He confiscated their green cards and held them for four days before verifying that the aliens were legally in the country. In the lawsuit that resulted, the aliens alleged that the trooper violated their Fourth and Fourteenth Amendment rights. The trooper sought qualified immunity, but the Sixth Circuit ruled against him. Here, if the trooper selectively enforced a neutral traffic regulation in a way that discriminated against the aliens because of their Hispanic appearance, he would have violated their Fourteenth Amendment equal protection rights. Also, keeping the green cards for four days was an unreasonable seizure under the Fourth Amendment. **Since both constitutional rights were clearly established at the time, the trooper was not entitled to qualified immunity.** The lawsuit was remanded for a determination of the facts. *Farm Labor Organizing Committee v. Ohio State Highway Patrol*, 308 F.3d 523 (6th Cir. 2002).

♦ An informant for a Mississippi police department asked a detective to lend him a gun because he feared a second man. The detective lent the informant a gun. Later, the informant encountered the second man and shot him in the face, blinding him. The victim sued the detective and the city under 42 U.S.C. § 1983, claiming that his Fourteenth Amendment due process rights were violated when the detective gave the informant the gun. A federal court ruled that the detective and city were entitled to qualified immunity, and the Fifth Circuit Court of Appeals affirmed. Here, the detective's conduct was at most negligent, and it was not unreasonable in light of clearly established law at the time. Even though the Supreme Court, in *DeShaney v. Winnebago County DSS*, 489 U.S. 189 (1989), held that states might be constitutionally liable for creating a danger that results in an individual's injury, the Supreme Court never explicitly held that states were liable. Thus, **the law was not clearly established at the time the detective lent the informant the gun**, and immunity was proper. *McClendon v. City of Columbia*, 305 F.3d 314 (5th Cir. 2002).

♦ Four former Texas police officers sued a city and their police chief for wrongful discharge, claiming that the chief had ridiculed them, made their working conditions intolerable and singled them out for harassment. A state court of appeals found that the chief was an "irascible individual" who engaged in constant yelling and name-calling. But **the chief acted in good faith by firing the officers because their terminations were directly attributable to their conduct.** As such, the chief was entitled to official immunity. Here, the first officer was fired because of the chief's belief that he was providing information to the subject of one of the department's investigations that could put the investigators and their families in jeopardy. The second officer was fired for using excessive force and then falsifying his report about it. The third officer was fired after he refused an order to issue a ticket to the driver of an automobile who was driving without a license. The fourth officer resigned after he was demoted to patrol for circulating a "no confidence" letter against the chief in a manner that violated department policy. The terminations were within the chief's scope of authority and were discretionary functions. *City of Hildalgo v. Prado*, 996 S.W.2d 364 (Tex. Ct. App. 1999).

♦ Seven Miami-Dade County police officers sued the county and the assistant director of police services, claiming that their former supervisor at the department's airport district, a Cuban lieutenant, forced them to be transferred out of, or blocked them from being transferred into, the airport because they were not Cuban. The court held that because the officers could not establish that the assistant director violated any clearly established law in the way he responded to their discrimination charges, he was entitled to qualified immunity. Here, **once the assistant director received reliable information about the problem, he authorized an investigation, which revealed that some of the claims might have merit.** He then relieved the lieutenant of his command. This was an adequate response to the claims of discrimination. The court rejected the officers' argument that the assistant director was required to be on notice of all operations, including transfers, that occurred within the eight districts under his supervision. *Buzzi v. Gomez*, 24 F.Supp.2d 1352 (S.D. Fla. 1998).

♦ A Chicago police officer worked in a multi-jurisdictional unit that required a security clearance and included overtime as well as use of an official vehicle. After receiving a grand jury subpoena, he invoked his Fifth Amendment privilege against self-incrimination. Shortly thereafter, the deputy superintendent transferred him to another division where he was assigned to uniform duty and his clearance was revoked. His rank and salary, however, remained the same. An arbitrator ordered his reinstatement in the intelligence division, but lacked jurisdiction to order reinstatement to the multi-jurisdictional unit. The officer sued under 42 U.S.C. § 1983, alleging that he was transferred in retaliation for asserting his constitutional right against self-incrimination. The district court granted the superintendent qualified immunity, and the Seventh Circuit affirmed. Here, **the superintendent's transfer of the officer did not amount to the sort of penalty that could be considered coercion to waive his Fifth Amendment rights.** The officer did not lose rank or pay, and the only concrete detriment was the loss of two incidental benefits that went with the task force position – an opportunity for overtime pay and a government car. *Chan v. Wodnicki*, 123 F.3d 1005 (7th Cir. 1997).

5. Other Employee Misconduct

♦ A Philadelphia airport employee responsible for ensuring that restaurants complied with various regulations insisted that the owner of an airport restaurant comply with a safety regulation. She was later fired, and she obtained evidence linking her termination to her refusal to budge on enforcing safety regulations at the airport. She filed a wrongful discharge lawsuit and sought to depose the mayor. The city fought the deposition, and a federal court held that she could not require the mayor to be deposed. **High-ranking government officials are entitled to limited immunity from being deposed**, and the employee here failed to show that the mayor's testimony would lead to any admissible evidence. *Robinson v. City of Philadelphia*, No. 04-3948, 2006 WL 1147250 (E.D. Pa. 4/26/06).

♦ A Florida city had a promotion process that required candidates to take a competitive, race-neutral, written exam from which a two-year eligibility list was created. The highest person on the list was promoted when a vacancy opened or a new position was created. Nine days before the expiration of an eligibility list, the fire rescue division chief proposed to the black fire chief that he create four new captain positions to be filled by the top four candidates on the list. The fire chief thought the idea was good, but decided to wait for a new eligibility list. The top four candidates sued the city and chief for violating their equal protection rights under the Fourteenth Amendment. They claimed that the chief decided not to create the new positions so he wouldn't have to put four white males in the job. The Eleventh Circuit ruled that the chief was entitled to qualified immunity. Even though a decision not to create new positions solely on the basis of race or gender violated the Equal Protection Clause (absent a valid affirmative action plan), **it was not clearly established at the time of the chief's decision that the failure to create new positions was unlawful**. *Williams v. City of Jacksonville*, 341 F.3d 1261 (11th Cir. 2003).

♦ The Second Circuit held that **two legislators were entitled to qualified immunity for opposing a public contractor's effort to renew a bid for work**. Here, the contractor provided security services to a Brooklyn public housing project and sought to renew the contract when it expired. Believing the contractor had ties to Rev. Louis Farrakhan's Nation of Islam, the legislators initiated an investigation into its eligibility to bid on a renewal contract. The U.S. Department of Housing and Urban Development concluded that the contractor had no official affiliation with either Farrakhan or the Nation of Islam, and the FBI informed the legislators that it did not consider the Nation of Islam to be a hate group. However, the legislators continued their efforts to prevent the contractor from getting the bid. When the effort to renew the contract failed, the contractor sued. Because the legislators here did not hold the ultimate decision-making authority over whether or not to award the contract, they were entitled to immunity. *X-Men Security v. Pataki*, 196 F.3d 56 (2d Cir. 1999).

• A Massachusetts woman was injured at a subway station as a result of pushing and jostling by a large group of city high school students on a field trip. The woman sued the city, alleging that it had provided too few supervisors and that the supervisors present had been negligent. The city moved for pretrial judgment on the grounds that the discretionary function exception to governmental tort liability barred the suit. The trial court granted the city's motion, and the woman appealed to the Appeals Court of Massachusetts. The appeals court held that the city was immune from liability for failure to provide a sufficient number of supervisors. However, **no immunity attached to the supervisors who had negligently supervised the students**. The immunity statute provided immunity for the exercise of discretionary duties that rise to the level of policymaking or planning. Although student supervision involves some exercise of discretion, it does not rise to the level of a policy or planning function as required by the statute. Rather, the decision not to intervene in the students' pushing and jostling was ministerial in nature. Thus, the supervisors were not entitled to immunity. The court reversed and remanded the case. *Alake v. City of Boston*, 666 N.E.2d 1022 (Mass. App. Ct. 1996).

• While a Virginia city was in a snow emergency, a snowplow operator collided with a bus. The operator of the snowplow was spreading salt at the time of the accident. Two passengers on the bus were injured and sued the city and the snowplow operator for their injuries. The employee contended that he was performing a governmental function requiring the exercise of judgment and was thus immune from liability. The trial court found for the employee, and the injured passengers appealed. The Supreme Court of Virginia held that **driving the plow involved discretionary actions** because the employee was required to decide whether and how to salt the road. This was more than the simple operation of the truck in routine traffic. Accordingly, the supreme court upheld the decision of the trial court and found that the employee was entitled to immunity. *Stanfield v. Peregoy*, 429 S.E.2d 11 (Va. 1993).

C. Constitutional Violations

1. First Amendment Speech Rights

• A Wyoming town attorney got into an inflammatory conversation with the town administrator, calling him a liar and a "whore" for the mayor and town council, as the administrator had once called himself in jest. The conversation was accidentally recorded because the town administrator inadvertently left his cell phone on and connected to a town clerk, who played the conversation over her speaker phone. A town council member eavesdropped on the conversation and reported it to the mayor, who then threatened to fire the attorney if he didn't resign. The attorney resigned with a severance package, then sued under the First and Fourteenth Amendments. A federal court denied the defendants immunity, but the Tenth Circuit ruled that they were entitled to it. The attorney's speech was made pursuant to his official duties, and **he had no reasonable expectation of privacy in his work-related quarrel**. *Hesse v. Town of Jackson, Wyoming*, 541 F.3d 1240 (10th Cir. 2008).

♦ An Ohio police officer contacted the FBI with concerns over the way the police department used the grand jury, as well as the department's policy of barring officers from speaking to the press. He was then suspended for mishandling a citizen complaint, and the chief recommended he be fired for insubordination. Instead, he was suspended for 30 days. When he sued for retaliation under the First Amendment, the chief claimed he was entitled to qualified immunity. The Sixth Circuit held that there were questions of fact as to **whether a reasonable person in the chief's position would have believed the officer's statements to the FBI were knowingly or recklessly false**. The case required a trial. *See v. City of Elyria*, 502 F.3d 484 (6th Cir. 2007).

♦ A supervisor at the Pennsylvania Office of Inspector General assigned a fraud investigator to a case involving the chief pharmacist at a state hospital. The investigator wanted to broaden the investigation into bribes of state officials by the pharmaceutical industry, but the supervisor told him to stay focused on his task. He admonished the investigator three times, then removed him from the lead investigator role but without a reduction in pay, benefits or job classification. When the investigator sued for retaliation under the First Amendment, the Third Circuit ruled that the supervisor was entitled to immunity. **His admonishments would not have deterred a reasonable person from speaking out on a matter of public concern**, and the investigator did not suffer an adverse action. *McKee v. Hart*, 436 F.3d 165 (3d Cir. 2006).

♦ An employee of the Texas Cosmetology Commission wrote a letter to a state representative accusing the commission of misusing state funds and cheating on numbers to make performance levels higher. The letter also addressed some private grievances. A month later she was fired. She sued the commission's executive director for wrongful termination, claiming **retaliation for the exercise of her First Amendment rights**, among other claims. The executive director sought immunity, but the Fifth Circuit held that she was not entitled to it. Here, the letter to the state representative discussed matters of public concern in addition to the private matters. *Modica v. Taylor*, 465 F.3d 174 (5th Cir. 2006).

♦ An Oklahoma police officer also served as the pastor of a church. For purely secular reasons, his chief sought to encourage his resignation. The chief arranged for the officer to be given day shift assignments on Sundays so that the officer would have to choose between his pastor work and his police job. The officer quit the department and sued under 42 U.S.C. § 1983, alleging a **violation of his free exercise of religion rights**. The chief claimed he was entitled to qualified immunity. A federal court and the Tenth Circuit Court of Appeals disagreed, finding issues of fact that required a trial. If the chief used the officer's religious beliefs to assist him in compelling the resignation, then he would be liable for damages. *Shrum v. City of Coweta, Oklahoma*, 449 F.3d 1132 (10th Cir. 2006).

♦ Three employees in a Georgia county's purchasing department met with a county commissioner to discuss irregularities in the department's bidding

Sec. II GOVERNMENTAL EMPLOYEE IMMUNITY   273

process. Afterwards, they claimed that the department's director made their working conditions so intolerable that one of them had to obtain a transfer and the other two were forced to quit. When they sued the director for retaliation under the First Amendment, asserting that they were entitled to protection as whistleblowers, he claimed that he was entitled to qualified immunity. He believed his actions did not amount to adverse action and that he was not on notice that he could be violating their First Amendment rights. A federal court agreed, but the U.S. Court of Appeals, Eleventh Circuit, reversed, finding issues of fact that required a trial. Further, **the director should have known that his actions could constitute retaliation.** *Akins v. Fulton County*, 420 F.3d 1293 (11th Cir. 2005).

- A school bus driver in Georgia held a team leader position and also was president of the United School Employees Association (USEA). She solicited co-workers to join the association, the mission of which was primarily to ensure child safety. After her supervisors tried to silence her, they had her transferred to another zone, where she would no longer be a team leader, and thus would no longer be guaranteed 40 hours per week. She sued for retaliation under the First Amendment, and the supervisors claimed they were entitled to qualified immunity. The Eleventh Circuit Court of Appeals disagreed. Here, **her speech was on a matter of public concern (child safety)** and she suffered an adverse action by no longer being guaranteed 40 hours per week. Further, the law was clearly established that a school district which allowed solicitations by groups like United Way and Girl Scouts could not bar her from soliciting members for the USEA. *Cook v. Gwinnett County School Dist.*, 414 F.3d 1313 (11th Cir. 2005).

2. Fourteenth Amendment Rights

- A Utah police officer and SWAT team member attended a seminar and while there had an affair with a fellow county SWAT team member. As a result, she lost her job with the SWAT team and was given an oral reprimand for having the affair. She sued the city for violating her Fourteenth Amendment substantive due process rights by reprimanding her for private, off-duty conduct. A federal court granted pretrial judgment to the city, and the Tenth Circuit affirmed. It noted that **a police officer does not have a fundamental right under the Constitution to engage in private, off-duty sexual relations.** The city's law enforcement code legitimately required officers to keep their private lives unsullied as an example to all, and to behave in a manner that did not bring discredit to the officers or the city. *Seegmiller v. Laverkin City*, 528 F.3d 762 (10th Cir. 2008).

- When the owners of a "doggie daycare" in Denver opened their business, an official with the city's licensing department told them they didn't need a kennel license. After a few weeks, the city changed its policy. A business license inspector showed up at the doggie daycare center, acting agitated and aggressive. He assaulted one of the owners and pushed the other. They sued the inspector and the city under 42 U.S.C. § 1983, alleging a violation of their substantive due process rights under the Fourteenth Amendment. A federal court and the Tenth Circuit ruled against them, noting that the inspector's conduct did not rise to the level of a constitutional violation for two reasons. **First, unlike police officers, he was not authorized to use force, and second, he did not abuse his authority to further the attack.** Instead, the attack was spontaneous. Their only remedy was in civil tort law. *Williams v. Berney*, 519 F.3d 1216 (10th Cir. 2008).

• An Alaska state trooper responded to a call about a car parked on a highway pull-out around 2:00 A.M. The man behind the wheel of the car tried to drive away despite being ordered to stop. He made suspicious movements and began to drive toward another patrol car after being pepper-sprayed. The trooper fired at the car, killing the driver, whose parents sued him for violating the driver's Fourteenth Amendment due process rights. A federal court denied the trooper qualified immunity, but the Ninth Circuit ruled that the lower court had used an improper standard to deny immunity. Instead, the lower court **should have granted immunity unless the parents could show that the trooper acted with the intent to harm their son for reasons unrelated to legitimate law enforcement objectives**. The court remanded the case for further proceedings. *Porter v. Osborn*, 546 F.3d 1131 (9th Cir. 2008).

• The wife of a Philadelphia police officer got restraining orders against him after he physically abused her for years. He violated the orders and threatened to kill her many times. Once, while police officers were present in the wife's home, he called to threaten her life several more times. The police stated that nothing could be done because he wasn't physically present. Four days later, the troubled officer shot his wife in the chest, then took his own life. She survived the shooting and sued the police department, as well as several officers, alleging due process violations under 42 U.S.C. § 1983. The officers sought qualified immunity, which the Third Circuit granted. **The wife did not have a procedural due process right to have the officers enforce the restraining orders against her husband.** They had the discretion to decide whether to arrest her husband. *Burella v. City of Philadelphia*, 501 F.3d 134 (3d Cir. 2007).

• While on the way to a fire, a Kansas firefighter moved into a lane of oncoming traffic and went through a red light because the vehicles in front of his truck were not responding to his siren and emergency lights. As he slowed and went through the intersection, his fire truck struck a car at approximately 24 miles per hour, killing the driver. The driver's estate sued him and the county for violating his Fourteenth Amendment due process rights. A federal court refused to grant qualified immunity to the defendants, but the Tenth Circuit reversed. The Supreme Court has established a clear rule, under which **government officials in a situation calling for "fast action" violate the Fourteenth Amendment only when they have an intent to harm**. Here, the firefighter clearly did not intend harm. *Perez v. Unified Government of Wyandotte County*, 432 F.3d 1163 (10th Cir. 2005).

• The assistant chief examiner of an Ohio city opposed the city commission's plan to diversify the fire department because she believed it directly contravened the civil service procedure for implementing new rules. The civil service board then placed her on paid administrative leave. A month later, she wrote a letter to the newspaper criticizing the commission's attempts to implement the diversity plan. The board **fired her without giving her a chance to appeal**, and she sued under the First and Fourteenth Amendments. When the board members sought immunity, the Sixth Circuit held that they were entitled to it on the free speech claim but not on the due process claim. The employee was a policy-maker who could be fired for expressing her views, but she was also a classified employee with property rights in her position. Thus, she was entitled to due process. *Silberstein v. City of Dayton*, 440 F.3d 306 (6th Cir. 2006).

- Pursuant to an Arkansas city policy regarding subpoenas for personnel files, an employee in the HR office **released the personnel files of two police officers to a criminal defense attorney** representing a man the officers had arrested on drug charges. The attorney gave the copies to the man, who made veiled threats against the officers. After jail officials seized and destroyed the files, the officers sued the city for violating their Fourteenth Amendment due process rights to privacy. A jury awarded them $225,000 each, but the Eighth Circuit reversed. At most, the city's actions amounted to gross negligence, not deliberate indifference to the risk of danger to the officers. Still, the city should provide notice to officers or redact sensitive personal information before releasing personnel files under subpoenas. *Hart v. City of Little Rock*, 432 F.3d 801 (8th Cir. 2005).

- A New York police officer with a history of drinking problems was never counseled by his supervisors. In fact, some of his supervisors drank with him off duty. After one stretch of drinking that lasted 12 hours, the officer ran a red light and killed three people, one of whom was pregnant. When their estates sued under the Fourteenth Amendment, a federal court refused to grant the individual supervisors qualified immunity. The Second Circuit reversed, noting that even though the supervisors may have violated the victims' constitutional rights to be free from a state-created danger, at the time of the accident **the law was not clearly established that they could be held liable for encouraging the officer's excessive drinking.** *Pena v. DePrisco*, 432 F.3d 98 (2d Cir. 2005).

- A Missouri county sheriff grabbed at several male employees' clothed crotch areas and made a number of vulgar comments to them. He also grabbed a female employee's breast and made offensive comments to her. In addition, he pointed his service revolver at his employees on numerous occasions, threatening to shoot them. When the employees sued him for violating their substantive due process rights under 42 U.S.C. § 1983, the sheriff sought to have the lawsuit dismissed on grounds of qualified immunity. The case reached the Eighth Circuit Court of Appeals, which noted that the men had no cause of action against the sheriff for his sexually harassing behavior. Even though it was offensive and inexcusable, it was not sufficient to violate the substantive due process rights of the employees. However, the female employee could maintain her action against the sheriff under Section 1983. Further, with respect to the pointing of a loaded gun at the employees, the Section 1983 lawsuit could continue because **no reasonable official in the sheriff's shoes could have thought it was within his duties to threaten employees with deadly force**. *Hawkins v. Holloway*, 316 F.3d 777 (8th Cir. 2003).

♦ A New Mexico police officer responded to an accident scene and was told by a man that his girlfriend had run him off the road. A citizen arrived and explored the scene with the officer. Suddenly, the man tried to grab the officer's gun. While wrestling for control of the weapon, the officer yelled to the citizen: "Hit him with your flashlight. Hit him. Get him off me." As the citizen approached the struggling pair, the man obtained possession of the gun, and the officer fled to the bushes. The man then shot the citizen in the chest, killing him. The citizen's personal representative filed suit under 42 U.S.C. § 1983, alleging that the officer violated the citizen's **Fourteenth Amendment right to substantive due process** by recklessly creating the dangerous situation that culminated in his death. A New Mexico federal court found that the officer was not entitled to qualified immunity because his conduct of placing the citizen in a position of danger and failing to take steps to protect him shocked the conscience and gave rise to a substantive due process claim. On appeal, the Tenth Circuit held that **the officer's conduct did not give rise to liability under Section 1983**. Here, the officer was confronted with a suddenly explosive law enforcement situation. He had no time for deliberation and was required to make an instantaneous decision. Though his acts may have been negligent, reckless or indifferent, they were not intentional. The district court's decision was reversed. *Radecki v. Barela*, 146 F.3d 1227 (10th Cir. 1998).

3. Fourth Amendment Rights

♦ A California city contracted with a company to provide pagers and text messaging services to some of its employees. The city's e-mail and Internet use policy allowed it to monitor employees' computers for inappropriate usage, but it did not incorporate text messaging into its formal policy. After a sergeant exceeded the text message limit several times (and paid for the overage each time), the chief decided to review the text messages to make sure they were business related. The chief asked the company to provide transcripts of the sergeant's text messages, and it did so. The sergeant, having been told by a superior that his messages would not be audited if he paid for the overages, sued the chief, the police department, the city and the company for violating his rights under the Storage Communication Act and the Fourth Amendment. The case reached the Ninth Circuit, which held that **the chief was protected by qualified immunity, but the lawsuit against the city, the police department and the company could continue**. The sergeant had a reasonable expectation of privacy in his text messages, and the chief violated that expectation by reading his messages without his consent. *Quon v. Arch Wireless Operating Co.*, 529 F.3d 892 (9th Cir. 2008).

♦ A Florida county sheriff's department sergeant struck an employee on the neck with a three-ring binder to let her know he was ready to discuss her performance issues, then berated her during the meeting until she fled the office in tears. She sued the sergeant and the sheriff under 42 U.S.C. § 1983, alleging that she was unlawfully seized under the Fourth Amendment. A federal court and the Eleventh Circuit ruled against her. Here, **the sergeant's actions, however troubling, did not involve a Fourth Amendment seizure.** This was simply a meeting between supervisor and employee, and the employee was never restrained from leaving the meeting. *Reyes v. Maschmeier*, 446 F.3d 1199 (11th Cir. 2006).

* Southwest Airlines allowed employees to play practical jokes on new employees who had completed their probationary periods. As a practical joke, an employee's supervisors called the Albuquerque Police Department and **convinced two officers to pretend to arrest her.** They placed handcuffs on her at the airport in front of passengers and employees. As they led her away, someone jumped out of an elevator and yelled, "Congratulations for being off probation." She started seeing a psychologist and was diagnosed with post-traumatic stress disorder, then sued the officers for violating her Fourth and Fourteenth Amendment rights. A federal court granted the officers qualified immunity, but the Tenth Circuit reversed. Seizing a private person without a legitimate basis was unlawful, even as a prank. *Fuerschbach v. Southwest Airlines*, 439 F.3d 1197 (10th Cir. 2006).

* Based on statements made by a probation officer and a fellow trooper, a Pennsylvania trooper arrested a man on the unconfirmed belief that an arrest warrant existed in another county. The trooper and his partner transferred the arrestee into the custody of officers from the other county. While en route to the prison, the officers were informed that the prison could not locate an outstanding warrant for the man's arrest. The officers, however, did not immediately release him. The man sued under 42 U.S.C. § 1983, alleging a violation of his right to be free from unlawful seizures under the Fourth and Fourteenth Amendments. The court entered pretrial judgment in favor of the troopers on the unlawful arrest claim. The Third Circuit noted that the arrest was unlawful. As a result, the arrest violated the man's Fourth Amendment right to be free from unlawful seizures. Qualified immunity did not protect the arresting trooper because **he never received a clear statement from a fellow law enforcement officer confirming the existence of probable cause for the man's arrest**. In contrast, the statements he made to his partner and the other officers were clear and unambiguously indicated the existence of an arrest warrant, thereby entitling them to qualified immunity. However, the officers who detained the man after learning there was no reason to hold him in custody would not enjoy qualified immunity beyond that point. The court reversed in part and affirmed in part. *Rogers v. Powell*, 120 F.3d 446 (3d Cir. 1997).

* At a demonstration marking the one-year anniversary of a lockout at an Illinois manufacturing plant, police officers sprayed pepper into the crowd in response to some type of surge against the police line. The demonstrators sued, alleging a violation of the Fourth Amendment because an unreasonable amount of force was used. The officers moved for pretrial judgment. Although no cases specifically state that the pepper-spraying of demonstrators violates the Fourth

Amendment, the court found that **enough widespread constitutional and judicial protection of First Amendment demonstrators existed to put the officers on notice that unnecessary force was prohibited**. The alleged excitability of the crowd did not undermine this status. Therefore, qualified immunity was inappropriate and pretrial judgment was denied. The court also denied pretrial judgment on the issue of excessive force. The severity of the crime (at the most, trespass) was negligible, no immediate threat to the safety of the officers or others existed, and the demonstrators were unarmed and not actively resisting arrest. Accordingly, the complaint alleged facts that could support a finding of excessive force that would constitute a seizure under the Fourth Amendment. *Lamb v. City of Decatur, Illinois*, 947 F.Supp. 1261 (C.D. Ill. 1996).

♦ An Oklahoma woman arrested for public intoxication and subjected to a visual strip search for contraband was able to sue the sheriff for violating her Fourth Amendment rights. The court also held that she could seek punitive damages. The court refused to grant the sheriff qualified immunity, considering **strip searches** to be the "most debasing indignities" to which the government could subject a citizen. Here, there were numerous alternative methods, short of the strip search, to ensure the security of the other detainees. *Draper v. Walsh*, 790 F.Supp. 1553 (W.D. Okla. 1991).

4. Eighth Amendment Rights

♦ A Georgia man suffered from manic depression and required prescription medication. After not taking his medication, he was arrested for speeding and having a suspended license. When he was admitted to the county jail, the dispatcher noticed that his pants were inside out and wet. During his eight-day incarceration, he stopped eating, stripped naked, began preaching and barked like a dog. The chief jailer was informed of his failure to eat and knew of his barking and preaching. Although her duties and the dispatcher's duties included regular walk-throughs of the jail, neither remembered seeing any sign that the inmate's health was deteriorating. The inmate died of malnutrition and dehydration. His estate sued the county and its officers under 42 U.S.C. § 1983. Both parties moved for pretrial judgment. The court denied qualified immunity to the chief jailer and dispatcher who were responsible for watching over and caring for the inmate during his detention.

Prior case law clearly established that **deliberate indifference to a prisoner's serious medical needs or providing an inmate with inadequate psychiatric care constituted cruel and unusual punishment**. Here, any reasonable officer would have made some effort to ensure that the inmate either ate or got some form of medical or psychiatric care. In particular, a reasonable officer would have: 1) checked on a prisoner after being told the prisoner had not eaten for three days, 2) considered requesting a psychiatric evaluation after hearing him bark and preach, and 3) noticed that a prisoner under his care was unconscious. The court also denied qualified immunity to the sheriff, but granted pretrial judgment to the city and remaining officers. *Duffey v. Bryant*, 950 F.Supp. 1168 (M.D. Ga. 1997).

Sec. II   GOVERNMENTAL EMPLOYEE IMMUNITY   279

5. Fifth Amendment Rights

• A Boston police officer was one of a number of officers called to a nightclub robbery, where an undercover black officer was mistakenly attacked by several white officers. After the beating occurred, the officer told Internal Affairs what he saw, but because his story conflicted with what other officers had said, he was called to testify at a grand jury investigation. When the department refused to give the officer immunity, he refused to testify, asserting his Fifth Amendment rights against self-incrimination. After his second refusal to testify, he was placed on paid administrative leave for 18 months, making him ineligible for extra duty. He then sued the department and the city under the First, Fifth and Fourteenth Amendments. A Massachusetts federal court granted the defendants immunity from suit on all but the Fifth Amendment claims. The First Circuit Court of Appeals then granted immunity to the defendants on that claim. Because of the discrepancies in the statements, **the department had a legitimate concern over whether the officer had made a false report**, and his refusal to testify made his administrative leave a reasonable measure. *Dwan v. City of Boston*, 329 F.3d 275 (1st Cir. 2003).

• Four Baltimore police officers were under investigation by a Maryland state attorney for alleged criminal behavior. The attorney required each officer to submit to a polygraph examination or face immediate suspension or discharge. All four officers took the polygraph but **they were not compelled to waive their Fifth Amendment rights nor were their statements ever used against them**. In fact, no charges were ever brought against them. The officers filed a civil rights suit alleging that the compelled polygraph examination violated their clearly established Fifth Amendment rights. The court denied the state attorney's motion to dismiss based on qualified immunity. The U.S. Court of Appeals, Fourth Circuit, reversed. Compelling a statement where there was neither a Fifth Amendment waiver nor subsequent use of the statement against the maker did not violate the Fifth Amendment. Here, the officers had been required to take the polygraph examination, but the state attorney never attempted to secure Fifth Amendment waivers nor did he use the results against the officers. Thus, the state attorney was entitled to qualified immunity. *Wiley v. Doory*, 14 F.3d 993 (4th Cir. 1994).

D. Special Duty to Protect

1. Supreme Court Case

• County officials in Wisconsin became aware that a young boy was probably being abused. However, they did not feel they had enough evidence to retain the boy in the custody of the juvenile court. Instead, they made recommendations to his divorced father to seek counseling and to enroll the boy in a preschool program. Over the next year, the boy was admitted to the emergency room on two separate occasions. His caseworker also noticed suspicious injuries on the boy's head when she visited the boy at home. Even though all this information was recorded and presumably made known to the county officials, they took no action. The boy was admitted to the emergency room again, this time in a coma. Emergency brain surgery revealed a series of traumatic injuries inflicted over a long period of time. The boy suffered severe brain damage. His father was convicted of child abuse. His mother then sued the county officials, claiming that they had deprived her son of his liberty interest in bodily integrity in violation of his Fourteenth Amendment rights.

The case reached the U.S. Supreme Court, which ruled that **a state's failure to protect an individual against private violence generally does not constitute a Fourteenth Amendment violation.** The county officials' knowledge of the danger to the boy and their willingness to protect him did not establish a "special relationship" so as to create an affirmative duty to protect him. The county officials did not create the danger to the boy, nor did they do anything to make him more vulnerable. Accordingly, the officials had not committed any constitutional violation. *DeShaney v. Winnebago County DSS*, 489 U.S. 189, 109 S.Ct. 998, 103 L.Ed.2d 249 (1989).

2. Police Officers

♦ During a drag race on the outskirts of Detroit, one of the racers lost control of his car. It veered into a crowd of spectators, killing a woman. Although police officers arrived at the scene before the race and had an opportunity to prevent it from beginning, they not only failed to stop the race, but according to testimony, they expressly allowed the race to proceed. They faced criminal charges for neglect of duty, a state-law civil lawsuit and a lawsuit under 42 U.S.C. § 1983 for violating the woman's substantive due process rights. After a Michigan federal court ruled for the defendants, the Sixth Circuit affirmed. Here, regardless of the abhorrent actions of the officers, **they did not have custody of the woman at the time of the accident, nor did they place her in any more danger than she voluntarily placed herself in** before they arrived. *Jones v. Reynolds*, 438 F.3d 685 (6th Cir. 2006).

♦ A Tennessee police officer was dispatched to the scene of a two-car accident. Upon arrival, the officer noticed that one of the drivers displayed signs of intoxication. The officer ordered the intoxicated driver to stand on the sidewalk. While the officer was taking down certain information, the driver got into his vehicle and drove off. The officer pursued the driver with emergency lights and sirens. Eventually, the driver ran a stop sign and struck another vehicle, injuring the vehicle's driver. The victim sued the officer and the police department for negligence. The court dismissed the victim's claim, and the Court of Appeals of Tennessee affirmed.

Here, **the officer did not have a special duty to protect the victim as a result of the state's drunk driving laws or the laws regarding warrantless arrests.** Further, the officer's actions did not amount to a "gross or reckless deviation" from the standard of care expected from him. Thus, he could not be held liable under the reckless misconduct exception to the public duty doctrine. *Gardner v. Insura Property and Casualty Insurance Co.*, 956 S.W.2d 1 (Tenn. Ct. App. 1997).

• A West Virginia woman had a longstanding domestic dispute with the father of her two daughters. She had numerous direct and indirect contacts with the city police department, and eventually obtained a temporary protective order. Subsequently, the man killed her, as well as two other people and then himself. The personal representatives of the decedents sued the city in a federal court, seeking damages under 42 U.S.C. § 1983 and state law. The city moved for pretrial judgment. The representatives alleged that the city had violated the substantive due process rights of the decedents by failing to adequately protect them from the ex-boyfriend's violent behavior. The court rejected this argument, finding that the representatives failed to establish a "special relationship" necessary to give rise to substantive due process rights. An affirmative duty to protect under Section 1983 arises when a custodial relationship such as incarceration or institutionalization exists, not upon promises and assurances. Absent a custodial relationship, **a police officer could only be held liable for injuries to a plaintiff under Section 1983 where the officer creates or enhances a danger faced by an individual**; however, creation of the danger requires affirmative misconduct, not merely a failure to protect. Because the decedents were not in the custody of the police department and the representatives failed to show that the police created or enhanced the danger faced by them, the court granted the city pretrial judgment. *Semple v. City of Moundsville*, 963 F.Supp. 1416 (N.D. W.Va. 1997).

• A Louisiana trooper responded to a one-car accident on an interstate highway, and stopped traffic on both lanes of the highway to facilitate towing away the damaged vehicle. However, a truck failed to stop in time and collided with the vehicle in front of it, severely injuring one driver and killing another. A negligence lawsuit was filed against the trooper, the state of Louisiana, and its insurer. The Supreme Court of Louisiana dismissed the suit. Although the trooper had an affirmative duty to see that motorists were not subjected to unreasonable risks of harm, **the scope of his duty was to choose a course of action that was reasonable under the circumstances as opposed to the "best" or even a "better" method**. Upon reviewing the testimony, the court found that the trooper's actions conformed with accepted traffic control procedures at the scene of an accident or emergency situation. Because he had not breached any duty to the plaintiffs, there could be no finding of liability. *Syrie v. Schilhab*, 693 So.2d 1173 (La. 1997).

3. Other Public Employees

• An Emergency Medical Technician (EMT) for the city of Detroit arrived at the home of a woman who was experiencing breathing problems. She informed him that her family had a history of hypertension, but that she had not been diagnosed with hypertension, nor was she on medication for that condition. The EMT allowed her to walk to the ambulance without taking her vital signs. Inside the ambulance, her condition deteriorated and the EMT gave her two injections (.5 cc each) of epinephrine, still without taking her vital signs, without contacting the hospital and despite protocols that provided for the administration of only .3 cc of epinephrine (and even then only after calling the hospital). They arrived at the hospital and waited nine minutes for a doctor. She had a heart attack and died, apparently from the epinephrine injections. When her estate sued, a federal court and the Sixth Circuit granted the city qualified immunity. Here, **the EMT's actions did not give rise to a special relationship with the woman** triggering an affirmative duty to provide adequate medical care. Nor did the EMT create the danger that resulted in the woman's death. *Baker v. City of Detroit*, 217 Fed.Appx. 491 (6th Cir. 2007).

♦ A Michigan corrections officer had a poor relationship with her supervisor. When a new prisoner with a history of violent felonies entered her unit, he stared at her, followed her when she made her rounds, came on to her and sought frivolous items and favors. She asked to have him transferred to another unit, but even though that was a common practice, the supervisor refused to transfer the prisoner. After the officer wrote the prisoner a major misconduct ticket for insolence, he assaulted her. She sued her supervisor and the warden, alleging a state-created danger and intentional infliction of emotional distress. A federal court noted that there was evidence the warden and supervisor knew of the danger presented by the prisoner. However, they were entitled to pretrial judgment on qualified immunity grounds because **a reasonable prison official might not have understood that the conduct at issue here violated established law.** Nevertheless, the court allowed the emotional distress claim to go forward. *McFaul v. Randall-Owens*, 2007 WL 3104801 (E.D. Mich. 10/22/07).

♦ Two Wisconsin children were adjudicated to be children in need of protection or services in separate juvenile court proceedings. They were placed in the temporary custody of the county department of social services for foster home placement. Both children were placed in the same foster home, and both claimed they had been sexually abused at the home. The children sued the county to recover for their injuries. The Supreme Court of Wisconsin held that the public officials were not entitled to qualified immunity. **The children had a clearly established constitutional right under the Due Process Clause of the U.S. Constitution to safe and secure placement in a foster home.** Further, the standard to be used in determining whether the children's rights were violated was the professional judgment standard, not the deliberate indifference standard. Because the state assumes responsibility for an individual's safety when it takes an individual into custody, and because the public officials were found to have adequate notice that a violation of that right could lead to liability, they were not entitled to qualified immunity. *Kara B. by Albert v. Dane County, Wisconsin*, 555 N.W.2d 630 (Wis. 1996).

♦ A Minnesota parolee placed on supervised release status was told to report directly to a halfway house and telephone his supervising agent within 24 hours. The parolee instead abducted, raped and murdered a woman. The supervising agent learned of the failure to report a few days later and immediately called for issuance of a fugitive warrant. Four days later, the parolee was apprehended and admitted committing the murder. The woman's trustees filed a wrongful death action against the state, county, their respective agents, and the halfway house.

The Supreme Court of Minnesota held that **the defendants were entitled to immunity and that the halfway house had no duty to control the parolee**. The state's decision to release the parolee was protected as a discretionary function. Regarding the halfway house, the court determined that no duty existed because it had no custody, special relationship, or ability to control the parolee. *Johnson v. State of Minnesota*, 553 N.W.2d 40 (Minn. 1996).

♦ The Florida Department of Health and Rehabilitative Services (HRS) granted a conditional daycare license to a woman despite documented sexual abuse by the woman's husband and his son. The HRS and the couple had orally agreed, as a condition of the license, that the husband would not visit the daycare facility. However, the husband regularly visited the facility. He was later convicted of sexual battery on several children at the daycare facility. Their parents filed a negligence suit against the HRS. The court dismissed the claims based on sovereign immunity, and the parents appealed to the District Court of Appeal of Florida.

The appellate court affirmed, finding that the HRS did not have a common law or statutory duty to the parents or children. The monitoring of specific permit conditions by inspection, such as the husband's compliance with the no-contact requirement, was similar to the inspection of buildings for compliance with the building permit laws. This is an enforcement activity of government not subject to liability. **The HRS did not have a duty to warn the prospective clients** because this was not a case of a dangerous condition existing on property controlled, maintained, or operated by the government. Finally, no statutory duty existed because there were no allegations of prior abuse to an individual child that could have created a custodial relationship between a particular minor and the HRS. *Brown v. Dep't of Health and Rehabilitative Services*, 690 So.2d 641 (Fla. Dist. Ct. App. 1997).

♦ A man charged with first-degree assault for an incident involving the shooting of a woman was released without bond by the jailer and the circuit clerk. He later assaulted another citizen who sued the county, the jailer and the circuit clerk in a Kentucky trial court, seeking to recover for the injuries. The case reached the Supreme Court of Kentucky, which determined that government officials in their individual capacity have no duty to prevent unforeseeable injuries to unidentifiable victims. Consequently, the jailer and the clerk were not individually responsible for the criminal acts of the inmate, who had been released from their custody for over two months. Also, **the lack of a special relationship between the victim and the public officials precluded liability** in their official capacities. The victim was not restrained by the state, and the violence was not perpetrated by the individual defendants. *Fryman v. Harrison*, 896 S.W.2d 908 (Ky. 1995).

III. GOVERNMENTAL AND EMPLOYEE LIABILITY

The government and public employees can be liable in tort to the same extent as private individuals. There are often limits put on government liability, and attorneys' fees are often provided to the successful party. However, a litigant generally must pursue various administrative remedies before attempting to use the courts.

A. Generally

1. Suicides

◆ An Ohio city employee applied for a promotion. However, before signing off on the final forms that would make the promotion active, his military reserve unit was called to Afghanistan. When he returned, he was placed in his old job and **was told the city had no obligation to hold the promotion for him because he never completed the application process**. The mayor learned of his plight through the media and directed city officials to promote him or pay him as if he'd been promoted. However, no one notified the employee of the efforts being made on his behalf, and before the necessary steps were taken, the employee killed himself. His estate sued the city. The Ohio Court of Appeals ruled for the city because the suicide could not have been foreseen. *Coats v. City of Columbus*, 2007 WL 549462 (Ohio Ct. App. 2/22/07).

◆ A Mississippi man, found lying in the middle of a public highway in an apparent suicide attempt, was taken to his home and released. Two days later, he barricaded himself in a room and threatened to kill himself. Police officers called to the scene refused to intervene. Three days later, he killed himself by setting fire to the home. His corpse was loaded into the bed of a truck where the carcasses of several dogs who had perished in the fire had been placed. His estate sued the city, a firefighter and the coroner. A federal court held that **although persons in custody have a right to protection against suicide, the man here was no longer in custody at the time he killed himself**. Further, the city did not have a duty to hold him for the sole purpose of providing medical care. Finally, the coroner who directed that the body be placed in the truck with the dogs, and the firefighter who placed the body there, were entitled to qualified immunity because the family had no clearly established constitutional right to have the body treated in a respectful manner. *Bynum v. City of Magee, Mississippi*, 507 F.Supp.2d 627 (S.D. Miss. 2007).

◆ An Indiana police lieutenant responded to a possible suicide. He told another officer to keep the man's counselor back until he and another officer checked inside the man's apartment. As he reached the apartment, the door opened and the man walked out with a shotgun. The lieutenant fired one shot, fatally wounding him. The man's widow filed suit in state court against the city, the lieutenant, and another officer under 42 U.S.C. § 1983 and state law. A jury returned a verdict in favor of the widow, and the lieutenant and city appealed. The Court of Appeals of Indiana found that **the jury could have found the city liable for its failure to train its officers in the area of suicide intervention**. First, the city knew that officers would confront individuals threatening suicide based on the lieutenant's testimony that he had been dispatched to 50 to 100 actual or threatened suicides and an expert's testimony that officers will regularly encounter suicide calls. Second, the jury could have concluded that the failure to have a policy on suicide intervention would likely result in officers making wrong choices. Third, the jury could have concluded that the wrong choice could cause the deprivation of citizens' constitutional rights. Accordingly, the jury verdict was affirmed. *Wallace v. Estate of Davies by Davies*, 676 N.E.2d 422 (Ind. Ct. App. 1997).

2. Domestic Disputes

• A 911 dispatcher used his job to access unauthorized information about his ex-girlfriend and her current boyfriend. His supervisor suspended him for a week but allowed him to continue working for another week before the suspension took effect. During that time, the dispatcher used the system to get the new boyfriend's vehicle and license plate registration. While on suspension, he called two co-workers, who gave him personal information about the new boyfriend. His ex-girlfriend reported his unauthorized use of the system, and the supervisor fired the employee, who called his co-workers to tell them he had nothing to live for anymore and that his ex-girlfriend and her new boyfriend were going to pay. The supervisor called the local police, but not the police departments where the ex-girlfriend or the new boyfriend lived. When the fired dispatcher killed his ex-girlfriend and her new boyfriend, the county, the supervisor and the co-workers were sued for wrongful death. A Pennsylvania federal court dismissed the case, but the Third Circuit reversed in part, noting that **if the allegations were true, the state created the danger by giving the dispatcher information he should not have had**. *Phillips v. County of Allegheny*, 515 F.3d 224 (3d Cir. 2008).

• A Colorado woman repeatedly called the police to inform them that her ex-husband had violated a restraining order by abducting their three young daughters. The police put her off several times, choosing not to track down the ex-husband and arrest him. Some hours later, the ex-husband drove to the police station with the bodies of the girls in his truck and shot at police until they killed him. The woman sued the city for violating her Fourteenth Amendment due process rights, but the U.S. Supreme Court ruled that **she did not have a constitutional right to have the police enforce the restraining order**. *Town of Castle Rock v. Gonzales*, 545 U.S. 748, 125 S.Ct. 2796, 162 L.Ed.2d 658 (2005).

• While responding to a request for assistance, two Michigan police officers encouraged an intoxicated man to leave his girlfriend's home. When the man walked outside, he was arrested after a loud and profane protest. The man alleged that as he was being forced into a police vehicle one of the officers struck and fractured his knee. The man was charged with trespassing, but the charge was dismissed in exchange for his signature on a release that discharged the city and its employees from all civil liability arising out of his arrest. Despite signing the release, the man sued the city and officers. The Court of Appeals of Michigan found **release-dismissal agreements** are not per se invalid, but stated that they must be strictly scrutinized on a case-by-case basis with the relevant factors established by the U.S. Supreme Court in *Town of Newton v. Rumery*, 480 U.S. 386 (1987). In determining a release-dismissal's enforceability, the court must conclude that: **1) the agreement was voluntary; 2) there was no evidence of prosecutorial misconduct; and 3) enforcement of the agreement will not adversely affect relevant public interests**. The burden of proving these elements rests upon the party seeking to invoke the agreement. The court remanded the case for trial. *Stamps v. City of Taylor*, 554 N.W.2d 603 (Mich. Ct. App. 1996).

♦ A Los Angeles resident received a telephone call from the brother of her estranged husband warning her that the latter was on his way to her house to kill her and any others present. The resident immediately dialed 911 but no car was sent. Fifteen minutes later, the estranged husband shot and killed the resident and four others. The resident's estate sued the county alleging that its failure to classify requests for assistance relating to domestic violence as emergencies violated the Equal Protection Clause. A dispatcher testified that it was the practice of the county not to classify domestic violence 911 calls as emergency procedure calls and that dispatchers were not instructed to treat such calls as emergencies. County officials testified that there was no written policy or procedure that precluded dispatchers from sending a patrol car to domestic violence scenes. The district court granted the county's motion for pretrial judgment, and the estate appealed.

The U.S. Court of Appeals, Ninth Circuit noted that **evidence that dispatchers had a practice of treating domestic violence calls differently from non-domestic violence calls, if proved, could establish the county's liability**. The district court had improperly concluded that no genuine issues of material fact existed on this issue. Next, although the estate failed to offer any evidence of discriminatory intent, it could prove an equal protection violation if the classification was held not to be rationally related to a legitimate government interest. Finally, because all dispatchers received an eight-hour course on how to handle domestic violence cases, the court affirmed the district court dismissal of the deliberate indifference claim. *Navarro v. Block*, 72 F.3d 712 (9th Cir. 1995).

♦ Two Maine police officers investigated a domestic violence report. They were informed that the alleged assailant was armed with two knives and had threatened to use them against any police officer who approached. Upon their arrival, the officers roused the apparently intoxicated assailant and read him his *Miranda* rights. He became upset, entered his home and returned carrying a steak knife in each hand. He then allegedly advanced, flailing his arms, and made a lunging motion toward the officers, who shot him. He was badly injured and filed a civil rights action against the officers, alleging unconstitutional excessive force. A federal court ruled for the officers and the city, and the assailant appealed. The First Circuit noted **the deferential standard accorded police officers where potential danger, emergency conditions or other exigent circumstances are present**. Because a reasonable jury could not find the present officers' conduct so deficient that no reasonable officer would have resorted to deadly force, their actions did not constitute unconstitutional excessive force. Although the officers may have done the wrong thing, they were not plainly incompetent nor were their actions clearly proscribed. Also, the town's failure to provide Mace to the officers was not deliberate indifference to the arrestee's constitutional rights. The holding of the district court was upheld. *Roy v. Inhabitants of City of Lewiston*, 42 F.3d 691 (1st Cir. 1994).

3. The Firefighter's Rule

The firefighter's rule generally provides that firefighters (and often police officers) cannot recover damages for injuries suffered in the scope of employment. For example, where a firefighter is injured because of a homeowner's negligence, he or she cannot recover if the injury was sustained while fighting a fire.

This sometimes means that firefighters and police officers cannot recover for the negligence of their co-workers either, unless the negligent acts cause injuries in situations that fall outside the special risks inherent in the duties the employees are hired to perform.

• Responding to a call of an altercation at a bar, a New Jersey police officer was attacked by one or more patrons and sustained head and neck injuries. He sued the bar owners for negligence for failing to provide adequate security as mandated by city ordinance. The bar owners sought to dismiss the lawsuit on the grounds that it was barred by the firefighter's rule – which prevents a police officer or firefighter from recovering for the negligence of a landowner or occupier who has been negligent in creating the hazard the officer or firefighter is responding to. The officer asserted that the firefighter's rule had been abrogated by a 1993 state statute. The case reached the Supreme Court of New Jersey, which held that the 1993 statute abrogated the firefighter's rule in its entirety, thus allowing **police officers, firefighters and other emergency workers to seek recovery from landowners or occupiers who negligently created the hazard they were exposed to**. *Ruiz v. Mero*, 917 A.2d 239 (N.J. 2007).

• An Ohio firefighter entered a porch located on the second floor of a residence while responding to a fire. He leaned over a decorative railing that gave way and fell to the ground, suffering extensive injuries. The fire department determined that the railing on the porch had not been properly secured to the roof of the house. The firefighter filed a negligence lawsuit against the homeowner, seeking damages for constructing and maintaining the railing in a defective condition, for failing to warn the firefighter of the loose railing, and for violating the building code. The court granted pretrial judgment to the homeowner, and the court of appeals affirmed.

The firefighter appealed to the Supreme Court of Ohio, arguing that the **fireman's rule** should be limited so that a firefighter can recover against a negligent landowner where, as here, the dangerous condition that caused the injury was in no way associated with the emergency to which the firefighter responded. The supreme court disagreed, holding that an owner or occupier of private property could be liable to a firefighter or police officer who entered a premises and was injured in the performance of his or her official job duties only if: 1) the injury was caused by the owner's willful or wanton misconduct, 2) the injury was the result of a hidden trap on the premises, 3) the injury was caused by the owner's violation of a statute enacted for the benefit of firefighters or police officers, or 4) the owner or occupier was aware of the firefighter's or police officer's presence on the premises, but failed to warn them of a known, hidden danger. Here, **the record did not contain any evidence of willful or wanton misconduct or an affirmative act of negligence by the homeowner.** *Hack v. Gillespie*, 658 N.E.2d 1046 (Ohio 1996).

♦ In three unrelated incidents in New York, a volunteer firefighter and three police officers filed suit against a combination of state and private entities, seeking damages for injuries occurring on their premises. The first case involved a police officer who was injured when he slipped on a snow-covered metal plate as he was approaching a picketer who was packing snowballs, presumably to throw at departing Greyhound buses. The second case involved a volunteer firefighter who was paralyzed when a canopy roof collapsed on him during a blaze, allegedly as a result of negligent construction by the contractor. The final case involved two police officers who were injured while rushing down a flight of wet, recently mopped stairs in response to a radio call for assistance from another officer.

The New York Court of Appeals noted that **the firefighter rule precludes firefighters and police officers from recovering damages for injuries caused by "negligence in the very situations that create the occasion for their services."** In *Cooper v. City of New York*, 81 N.Y.2d 584, 601 N.Y.S.2d 432, 619 N.E.2d 369 (N.Y. 1993), the court held that the rule must be applied to bar common law negligence claims where the injury sustained is related to dangers that police officers and firefighters are expected to assume as part of their duties. The necessary connection between a plaintiff's injury and the special hazards associated with police and fire duties is present where the performance of the police officer's or firefighter's duties increased the risk of injury happening, and did not merely furnish the occasion for the injury. The negligence claims in all three cases had been properly dismissed. The injuries were risks that the firefighters and officers were compensated to confront. *Zanghi v. Niagara Frontier Transportation Comm'n*, 626 N.Y.S.2d 23 (N.Y. 1995).

4. Vicarious Liability

♦ A 13-year-old Georgia boy fatally shot himself after a police officer gave the boy his police service weapon. The officer was coaching the boy's soccer team at the time. The boy's family sued the officer's current and former employers, alleging that their negligence caused their son's death. The case reached the Georgia Court of Appeals, which held that a trial was required. The officer had a history of inattentiveness and disregard for safety rules, and his former employer may have misrepresented his record in a favorable light. Also, even though he was off duty at the time of the accident, he used his police officer status to recruit players and was in uniform at the time of the death. **Both** cities might be vicariously liable for the officer's negligence. *Govea v. City of Norcross*, 608 S.E.2d 677 (Ga. Ct. App. 2004).

♦ A correctional officer at a county jail in Illinois arranged to allow certain inmates to attack a pretrial detainee who had been charged with attempted first-degree murder of his infant son. The detainee sued the officer, who had pled guilty to a charge of official misconduct, and obtained an award from the officer of $400,000. He then sued the county, seeking to have it pay the award. A federal court ruled that the officer had been acting in the course of his employment and that the county was thus liable for the award, but the Seventh Circuit reversed. **The officer was not serving the county by instigating the attack on the detainee**, who had not even been convicted of a crime. The county did not have to pay the judgment against the officer. *Copeland v. County of Macon*, 403 F.3d 929 (7th Cir. 2005).

♦ An Indiana city hired a police officer who had a history of using unnecessary force while employed by other police departments. The routine psychological exam also revealed that the officer could be overly aggressive. However, the public safety board was not informed of these facts. While off duty, the officer stopped a motorist outside the city limits. The officer was not in uniform and was driving an unmarked car. He kicked and shoved the motorist, and slammed a truck door on the motorist's arm. The motorist sued the city for, among other things, negligence in the way it hired, retained and trained the officer. A jury returned a verdict for the motorist, and the city appealed. The Indiana Court of Appeals reversed. Evidence showed that department policy prohibited officers from making traffic stops outside city boundaries, out-of-uniform and in unmarked cars. Consequently, without even reaching the issue of negligent hiring, the court held that **the conduct occurred outside the officer's scope of employment and that the city could not be liable**. *City of Fort Wayne v. Moore*, 706 N.E.2d 604 (Ind. Ct. App. 1999).

♦ A former client of a North Dakota county social service agency sued a social worker and the county for sexual abuse. The social worker confessed judgment for $250,000. In return, the former client agreed to release the social worker from liability, forgo collection and seek collection from the county. The county moved for pretrial judgment on the issue of vicarious liability. The court granted pretrial judgment to the county, and the client appealed to the North Dakota Supreme Court. In general, political subdivisions are subject to vicarious liability for acts of their employees committed within the scope of employment. An act is within the scope of employment if it takes place during working hours and furthers the interest of the employer. Here, the social worker sexually abused the woman during business hours at business-related locations, making the county potentially liable for the abuse. However, **since the client released the social worker from any liability, the settlement agreement released the county from vicarious liability**. The client could not agree to release the social worker from liability without also releasing the county from liability. *Nelson v. Gillette*, 571 N.W.2d 332 (N.D. 1997).

♦ A shift supervisor and several Wyoming town police officers agreed to pull a practical joke on an acquaintance employed at a local 7-Eleven store. One officer wearing a mask and a trench coat entered the store carrying the town's M-16 automatic rifle, loaded with blanks, with a large plastic garbage bag at the end of the barrel to catch any residue from the blanks. The officer allegedly discharged the weapon after he told the employee to get on the ground but before the employee recognized him. The officers were disciplined, and the employee sued the town and three of the officers in federal court, alleging Fourth Amendment and due process violations as well as negligence, assault and emotional distress claims. The court ruled for the officers and the town on the constitutional claims, and a jury found that the officers had not committed assault or extreme and outrageous conduct.

The Tenth Circuit Court of Appeals affirmed. The employee had failed to establish that the staged robbery in any way implemented or executed an official policy or that an official policy was the moving force behind the alleged constitutional violation. Next, **because the acts of the individual officers in performing the staged robbery were not duties that the town had requested or authorized, they did not fall within the officers' scope of duties**. The court also held that the individual officers were not acting "under color of state law" and that the constitutional claims against them had been properly dismissed. Finally, the jury had properly ruled in favor of the defendants on the assault claim after finding that the employee had recognized the officer as his friend. *Haines v. Fisher*, 82 F.3d 1503 (10th Cir. 1996).

♦ A California fire marshal entered a local business under color of state authority to conduct a fire inspection. He then committed arson by setting off incendiary devices that ultimately destroyed the premises. The owner sued the city, alleging that it was liable for the ensuing loss under *respondeat superior* principles and for negligently supervising the marshal. The trial court dismissed the case, and the California Court of Appeal, Second District, affirmed. **An employer could not be held vicariously liable for the criminal acts of an employee committed in furtherance of the employee's personal purposes.** Because the fire marshal's actions were sufficiently "startling and unusual" as to be outside those risks that should fairly be imposed upon the city, the court declined to impose *respondeat superior* liability. The court also rejected the owner's negligent supervision claim, ruling that its recognition would essentially swallow the rule proscribing *respondeat superior* liability and eliminate the protection now afforded public employers. *Thorn v. City of Glendale*, 35 Cal.Rptr.2d 1 (Cal. Ct. App. 1994).

♦ An inmate at an Illinois jail repeatedly complained about illness and his inability to control his bowel movements. Two other inmates advised several paramedics that he was too ill to come to the regular treatment room. However, the paramedics refused to treat the inmate in his cell, and he died the following morning due to complications arising from a distended bowel and a large fecal mass in his abdomen. His representative sued the county and the sheriff on *respondeat superior* principles, alleging that they had negligently failed to provide adequate medical care. After the lawsuit was dismissed, the Supreme

Court of Illinois held that no employment relationship existed between the sheriff and the county for purposes of vicarious liability. The sheriff was a county officer with statutorily prescribed duties independent of any governing body. Although other factors such as the right to discharge should be considered, the decisive element was the employer's right to control the employee. Because the sheriff was a public officer (not an employee) and was not under the county's control, **the county could not be held vicariously liable for his alleged negligence**. The court affirmed the dismissal of the lawsuit. *Moy v. County of Cook*, 640 N.E.2d 926 (Ill. 1994).

5. Other Liability Cases

♦ While passing through a door at a county jail, an African-American deputy sheriff in New York was struck in the ribs, sprayed with shaving cream and squirted in his eyes with mace. One of his attackers – a fellow deputy sheriff – said "Now you are a white man with an afro." The African-American deputy sheriff did not report the incident, but he sued the county, the sheriff and the deputy who led the attack. The county and the sheriff avoided liability, but the deputy was ordered to pay $100,000 in compensatory damages for intentional infliction of emotional distress. *Patterson v. Balsamico*, 440 F.3d 104 (2d Cir. 2006).

♦ A Pennsylvania corrections officer and his wife contracted an antibiotic-resistant staph infection from an inmate the officer was guarding. He sued the county, claiming that it violated the First Amendment by failing to disclose that there was a communicable disease in the workplace. A federal court ruled against him. Here, even though the county suspected that the inmate population was plagued by the staph infection, it did not know of any employees who were infected. Further, the officer did not have a right to know about everything that was not going well in the workplace. *Kaucher v. County of Bucks*, No. CIV.A. 03-1212, 2005 WL 283628 (E.D. Pa. 2/7/05).

♦ A paraplegic arrested at a bar in Kansas asked police officers if he could empty his urine bag before being transported to the police station. The officers refused his request. He suffered injuries when he was transported to the station in a police van that was not equipped to transport wheelchairs. He fell to the floor after releasing a strap that was putting pressure on his urine bag. He injured his shoulder and back and got a bladder infection. When he sued police officials under Title II of the Americans with Disabilities Act (ADA) and the Rehabilitation Act, he won a judgment of more than $1 million in compensatory damages and $1.2 million in punitive damages. The court vacated the punitive damages award, but the Eighth Circuit reversed. The U.S. Supreme Court then held that punitive damages were not available. Since the remedies under Title II of the ADA and the Rehabilitation Act are the same as the remedies under Title VI, and since punitive damages are not available under Title VI, **punitive damages are not available under Title II of the ADA or the Rehabilitation Act**. *Barnes v. Gorman*, 536 U.S. 181, 122 S.Ct. 2097, 153 L.Ed.2d 230 (2002).

♦ While housed in a New York City halfway house run by a private company for the Bureau of Prisons, an inmate with a heart condition was forced to walk up five flights of stairs to his room. He normally was allowed to use the elevator, but on this occasion was not allowed to do so. He suffered a heart attack and sued the company for $4 million under *Bivens v. Six Unknown Named Agents of Federal Bureau of Narcotics*, 403 U.S. 388 (1971). A *Bivens* action allows an individual, in certain circumstances, to sue a federal official for damages resulting from a constitutional violation. The inmate claimed that the company failed to provide him with his medication after he ran out several days before the heart attack. The case reached the U.S. Supreme Court, which held that the inmate could not use a *Bivens* action to sue the private company. ***Bivens* was designed to deter individual federal officers (not private companies) from committing unconstitutional acts.** Here, the inmate could have brought a negligence action against the company or sued the Bureau of Prisons for injunctive relief. *Correctional Services Corp. v. Malesko*, 534 U.S. 61, 122 S.Ct. 515, 151 L.Ed.2d 456 (2001).

♦ An Illinois sheriff was sued by two former employees for sexual harassment and retaliation, among other claims. The employees sued him in his official capacity and entered into a consent decree for $250,000 each. However, they agreed that the judgment would be paid out of the sheriff's office budget. The employees then tried to recover the judgment from the county (which funded the sheriff's office). The county resisted on the grounds that the sheriff was not a county employee, and that **the sheriff had not been acting within the scope of his employment when he harassed and retaliated against the employees**. The case reached the Supreme Court of Illinois, which held that under the Tort Immunity Act, the county sheriff was a "local public entity." Because the county funded the sheriff's office, and because the sheriff had been sued in his official capacity, the county was required to provide funds to the sheriff's office to pay the settlement judgment. *Carver v. Sheriff of La Salle County*, 787 N.E.2d 127 (Ill. 2003).

♦ A Connecticut teacher had her competency questioned by her principal after an incident in which the teacher let a student board a bus for home when he was supposed to be attending an after-school program. When another teacher reported that she was acting in a strange manner, the principal and a school psychologist met with her in her classroom and expressed concerns about her health. Three days later, the principal placed the teacher on a paid leave of absence, called her daughter to tell her that her mother was acting differently, and called the police to escort the teacher to her car. She resigned at the end of the school year and sued for intentional infliction of emotional distress and tortious interference with contract. The Connecticut Supreme Court ruled in favor of the school board and the principal, finding that **their conduct had not been "extreme and outrageous" as was necessary for an emotional distress claim**. Also, since the teacher had resigned, she could not show that the defendants had interfered with her contract. *Appleton v. Stonington Board of Educ.*, 254 Conn. 205, 757 A.2d 1059 (Conn. 2000).

Sec. III GOVERNMENTAL AND EMPLOYEE LIABILITY 293

♦ A New York man was the victim of a hit-and-run accident. A few minutes after the accident, a park employee found the injured man and went to get help. Before an ambulance arrived, four off-duty police officers stopped to investigate. Two officers felt for but found no pulse in the victim's neck, one officer called police headquarters and described the scene as an apparent dead on arrival, and the other officer took over crowd control. Believing the victim dead, none of the officers attempted any kind of first aid or checked to see if his airway was obstructed. The ambulance technicians arrived and concluded that he was dead. However, a review of the victim's autopsy report revealed that he did not die from his impact-related injuries but because he choked on his tongue, and had an officer checked and cleared the obstructed air passage he could have been resuscitated. The victim's estate and survivors filed suit under 42 U.S.C. § 1983. The court found that although the officers might have been liable under state law for negligence, negligence did not transform into a Section 1983 claim simply because the defendant was a state actor. Further, it would be against sound public policy if every accident scene to which a police officer responded could potentially frame federal lawsuits. **Because no basis existed to find a constitutional right to first aid, the court ruled for the defendants.** *Mueller v. County of Westchester, New York*, 943 F.Supp. 357 (S.D.N.Y. 1996).

B. 42 U.S.C. § 1983

1. Supreme Court Cases

♦ A handgun, purported to have been destroyed in a police department's property room, turned up in the possession of a felon. This prompted an investigation and the eventual dismissal of the police chief by the city manager. The chief was not given any reason for the discharge and was only given a written notice that the dismissal was made according to the city charter. He then sued the city, the city manager and the city council members in a Missouri federal court under 42 U.S.C. § 1983, alleging that he had been discharged in violation of his due process rights. The U.S. Supreme Court held that Section 1983 actions against municipalities were not barred by immunity. It further held that the city's officers could not assert that they had acted in good faith as a defense to a Section 1983 action. **A city has no discretion to violate the Constitution.** When it does, it cannot claim that it was exercising its own judgment or discretion and in that way avoid liability. Since it was the liability of the city itself that was at issue, there was little, if any, injustice in subjecting the city's officials to liability. *Owen v. City of Independence,* 445 U.S. 622, 100 S.Ct. 1398, 63 L.Ed.2d 673 (1980).

♦ An architect worked for the city of St. Louis, rising to a management-level city planning position in one of its agencies. The agency had a policy of requiring advance approval before taking on private clients. Some time after this policy went into effect, the architect accepted outside employment without prior approval and was suspended. He successfully challenged the suspension. He was then transferred and subsequently laid off. **He sued the city under 42 U.S.C. § 1983, alleging that he had been penalized for exercising his**

First Amendment rights. A federal court found the city liable, and the U.S. Court of Appeals affirmed. The case then came before the U.S. Supreme Court. The Court held that the court of appeals had applied the wrong legal standard for determining when isolated decisions by municipal supervisors or employees could expose the city to Section 1983 liability. The architect would have had to show the existence of an unconstitutional policy promulgated by officials having such authority. Here, there was no policy permitting retaliatory transfers or layoffs. Further, there was insufficient evidence to show that supervisors were authorized to establish employment policies of the city with respect to transfers and layoffs. Therefore, the Supreme Court reversed the appellate court's decision against the city and remanded the case. *City of St. Louis v. Praprotnik*, 485 U.S. 112, 108 S.Ct. 915, 99 L.Ed.2d 107 (1988).

♦ An employee in a Texas city's sanitation department died of asphyxia after entering a manhole to unstop a sewer line. His widow sued the city under 42 U.S.C. § 1983 alleging that her husband had a right under the Fourteenth Amendment's Due Process Clause to be free from unreasonable risk of harm and to be protected from the city's alleged custom and policy of deliberate indifference toward its employees' safety. She argued that the city violated that right by failing to properly train its employees and by providing inadequate equipment. The U.S. Supreme Court held that **a city's failure to train or warn its employees about known hazards in the workplace does not violate the Due Process Clause**. Section 1983 cannot provide a remedy for a municipal employee based on such a failure. In addition, the Court stated that an abuse of governmental power is not a necessary element of a Section 1983 claim. Section 1983 requires only that a plaintiff's harm be caused by a constitutional violation and that the city be responsible for that violation. The Due Process Clause cannot be used to guarantee minimum levels of safety and security in the workplace. *Collins v. City of Harker Heights*, 503 U.S. 115, 112 S.Ct. 1061, 117 L.Ed.2d 261 (1992).

♦ The U.S. Supreme Court held that an Alabama county could not be held liable for a sheriff's actions in wrongfully convicting a man of murder. The man filed a 42 U.S.C. § 1983 suit against the county. Because states are not subject to Section 1983 liability, and because Alabama sheriffs are policymakers for the state, not for the county, **the county was not liable for the sheriff's actions**. *McMillian v. Monroe County, Alabama*, 520 U.S. 781, 117 S.Ct. 1734, 138 L.Ed.2d 1 (1997).

♦ A litigious and outspoken prisoner in the District of Columbia's correction system was transferred to Florida because of overcrowding. His belongings were transferred separately, and he did not receive them until several months later. He sued a D.C. correctional officer under 42 U.S.C. § 1983, alleging that the diversion of his property was in retaliation for exercising his First Amendment rights. The U.S. Court of Appeals, D.C. Circuit, held that in an unconstitutional-motive case against a public official, a plaintiff must establish motive by clear and convincing evidence. The U.S. Supreme Court disagreed, finding that nothing in the text of Section 1983, any other federal law or the

Federal Rules of Civil Procedure required imposing a **clear and convincing burden of proof** upon plaintiffs in such cases. *Crawford-El v. Britton*, 523 U.S. 574, 118 S.Ct. 1584, 140 L.Ed.2d 759 (1998).

♦ A motorcyclist and his 16-year-old passenger were speeding down a California road. A deputy sheriff began a high-speed pursuit of the motorcycle and when the motorcycle tipped over, he struck and killed the passenger. The passenger's estate sued the deputy, the sheriff's department and the county in a federal court under 42 U.S.C. § 1983, alleging a deprivation of the passenger's Fourteenth Amendment substantive due process right to life. The case reached the U.S. Supreme Court, which held that **high-speed chases with no intent to harm suspects physically or to worsen their legal plight do not give rise to liability under the Fourteenth Amendment**. *County of Sacramento v. Lewis*, 523 U.S. 833, 118 S.Ct. 1708, 140 L.Ed.2d 1043 (1998).

♦ A Tennessee statute allowed police officers to use deadly force to apprehend fleeing felons. When a police officer shot and killed a suspect who was trying to climb a fence to elude capture, his father sued the city under 42 U.S.C. § 1983, alleging that the statute was unconstitutional. The case reached the U.S. Supreme Court, which held that the statute violated the Fourth Amendment's requirement that searches and seizures be reasonable. *Tennessee v. Garner*, 471 U.S. 1, 105 S.Ct. 1694, 85 L.Ed.2d 1 (1985).

♦ The U.S. Supreme Court held that a Georgia county deputy did not violate the Fourth Amendment rights of a speeding motorist when he rammed into the back of the motorist's car to get him to stop, even though **ramming the car resulted in paralyzing injuries** to the motorist. The deputy's actions were reasonable when weighed against the risk of harm to the public caused by the motorist's reckless driving. *Scott v. Harris*, 550 U.S. 372, 127 S.Ct. 1769, 167 L.Ed.2d 686 (U.S. 2007).

2. Police Officers' Actions

♦ A Connecticut police officer in charge of an underage alcohol sales sting program convinced three young women that he needed not only clothed photos of them for the operation, but also nude or semi-nude photos. He later **talked one of the women into posing topless for a child pornography sting operation**. After the facts came out and the officer was fired, the woman sued the city and the chief under 42 U.S.C. § 1983, alleging other claims as well. A federal court largely ruled in favor of the defendants, finding the city and chief not liable for failure to properly train the officer. Nor was the chief liable under Section 1983 for deliberate indifference to the rights of others through grossly negligent supervision. However, the city might have to indemnify the officer for the damage caused by the first set of photos. A trial was required on that issue. *Wilson v. City of Norwich*, 507 F.Supp.2d 199 (D. Conn. 2007).

♦ Responding to a domestic violence call, officers confronted the husband, who was outside his house in his pajamas. When he refused to comply with their orders to approach them, they ordered their police canine to attack him and sprayed him in the face with pepper spray. He suffered several bite wounds. After pleading guilty to resisting arrest, he sued the city under 42 U.S.C. § 1983, alleging excessive force was used. The case reached the Ninth Circuit, which overruled *Vera Cruz v. City of Escondido*, 139 F.3d 659 (9th Cir. 1997), and held that "deadly force" means not just "force reasonably likely to kill" but also **"force reasonably likely to result in serious bodily injury."** Also, despite the guilty plea, the arrestee could bring a Section 1983 action. The arrestee's lawsuit was allowed to proceed. *Smith v. City of Hemet*, 394 F.3d 689 (9th Cir. 2005).

♦ A rookie with eight days of experience responded with his partner to a call about a restaurant fight. The two officers saw a man run out of the restaurant with a gun and enter a car. The rookie stepped out from the cover of the police car just before another armed man ran from the restaurant. The armed man yelled, "Freeze!" and the two officers yelled, "Drop it!" The two officers then shot and killed the second armed man, who turned out to be an off-duty police officer. After a jury found that **the rookie violated the off-duty officer's Fourth Amendment rights**, the off-duty officer's mother sued the city of Providence under 42 U.S.C. § 1983. A Rhode Island federal court granted pretrial judgment on the claim of negligent failure to train, but the First Circuit reversed, finding an issue of fact that required a trial. Here, a jury could find that the rookie was not properly trained regarding interactions with off-duty cops, and that by stepping out from cover he increased his vulnerability and the likelihood that deadly force would have to be used. *Young v. City of Providence*, 404 F.3d 4 (1st Cir. 2005).

♦ A Georgia man was arrested for DUI and mistakenly missed his court appearance. A bench warrant was issued and entered into the statewide criminal information database. Eventually, he learned of the missed court date, went to court and pled no contest. His guilty plea was reported to the database, but the sheriff's office failed to remove the warrant. Subsequently, a police officer from a neighboring county pulled him over for a malfunctioning taillight and arrested him after a check of his driver's license revealed the outstanding warrant. He sued his county under 42 U.S.C. § 1983, claiming that its unofficial practice of failing to remove expired warrants from the database resulted in the deprivation of his constitutional rights. The Eleventh Circuit held that the county could not be liable for the failure of the sheriff's office. Under the Georgia Constitution, the sheriff's office is independent and separate from the county; only the state has control over the sheriff's authority. As a result, **the county could not be held liable under Section 1983 because it did not have control over the sheriff's actions.** *Grech v. Clayton County*, 335 F.3d 1326 (11th Cir. 2003).

♦ The family of a man with bipolar disorder applied for involuntary commitment for him when his condition deteriorated. A crisis intervention worker determined that involuntary commitment was proper and arranged for the police department to pick him up. Officers brought the man to the hospital, but he escaped. When his family tracked him down, officers were sent to his apartment to pick him up again. However, a violent confrontation ensued, and one of the officers shot and killed him. His family sued the police department and the county for violating his rights under the Americans with Disabilities Act (ADA), the Rehabilitation Act and 42 U.S.C. § 1983. A Pennsylvania federal court found that the family stated an actionable claim for substantive due process violations under Section 1983. Also, they stated a claim under the ADA and the Rehabilitation Act because the statutes protected individuals with disabilities from the denial of benefits "of the services, programs or activities of a public entity." Since these terms seem to include all core functions of government, **there was potential liability for failing to properly train police officers for peaceful encounters with disabled persons**. The court refused to dismiss the case. *Schorr v. Borough of Lemoyne*, 243 F.Supp.2d 232 (M.D. Pa. 2003).

♦ A Pennsylvania police officer saw a car parked in a lot near a beer distributor, which had been the target of several burglaries. He called for backup. Both officers approached the car and discovered two young men who had been drinking (a 17-year-old and an 18-year-old). They also found condoms in the car. After arresting them, one of the officers allegedly lectured them that the Bible counseled against homosexual activity, then warned the 18-year-old that if he did not tell his grandfather about his homosexuality, the officer would do so. When the 18-year-old was released from custody, he committed suicide. His mother sued the city and the officers under 42 U.S.C. § 1983, asserting that they violated her son's constitutional privacy rights by threatening to tell his family about his homosexuality. The Third Circuit denied qualified immunity to the officers. **The officer who threatened to tell the 18-year-old's grandfather about his homosexuality knew or should have known that his conduct violated clearly established law.** Because the man was an adult, the officer should not have interfered with his family situation. The lawsuit could proceed. *Sterling v. Borough of Minersville*, 232 F.3d 190 (3d Cir. 2000).

♦ A Texas woman lived with a multimillionaire for three years until his physical abuse of her escalated. After she moved out, he harassed her and vandalized her property, then contacted two burglary detectives and had them threaten to arrest her for stealing items from his apartment. The detectives also moonlighted for a private investigator with a criminal record. Eventually, the woman filed a formal complaint with the police department, which investigated and found no wrongdoing. Subsequently, the woman was shot four times in a murder attempt and became a paraplegic. The private investigator and three other men were convicted of attempted murder. The woman sued the city under Section 1983 after learning that an informant had warned a police officer that the murder was being planned. The Fifth Circuit Court of Appeals ruled in favor of the city. Here, **she failed to prove that the detectives were involved in the murder attempt, or that the city was deliberately indifferent** to the likelihood that her constitutional rights would be violated. As a result, the city was not liable under Section 1983. *Piotrowski v. City of Houston*, 237 F.3d 567 (5th Cir. 2001).

♦ After a murder at a Starbucks in Washington, D.C., an informant approached police and said that he had heard someone talking about the incident while buying cocaine at a housing complex in his neighborhood. Four police officers staged an undercover drug purchase at the house where the informant had purchased the cocaine. They gave him $80 and dropped him off at the house. He was robbed and killed by unknown assailants. His mother sued the officers and the District of Columbia for recklessly failing to provide adequate protection for her son. The case reached the D.C. Court of Appeals, which ruled that the officers could be found liable for punitive damages for recklessly placing the informant in a situation they knew was potentially life threatening. However, the District of Columbia – while liable for compensatory damages for the informant's wrongful death – could not be held liable for punitive damages where **it did not have in place a policy or custom of deliberate indifference to informants**. *Butera v. District of Columbia*, 235 F.3d 637 (D.C. Cir. 2001).

♦ A St. Louis police officer stopped a vehicle that was missing its rear license plate and discovered that there was an outstanding arrest warrant for a female with the same last name as the driver. Also, one of the aliases used by the fugitive matched the driver's first name. The driver explained that the fugitive was her sister, but the officer arrested her anyway. At the station, a second officer processed the woman, who again asserted that she was not the individual named in the warrant. The woman asked to be fingerprinted so that she could prove her identity, and the second officer did so. Shortly thereafter, a fingerprint technician discovered that the woman's prints did not match those of the person wanted on the warrant and sent an e-mail to the second officer informing her of that fact. The officer claimed never to have received it. The arrested woman spent six days in jail until her parole officer (she had a prior record, too) discovered that she was there. After her release, the woman sued the second officer under 42 U.S.C. § 1983, **asserting that the officer had acted with deliberate indifference to the information verifying that the detention was unlawful**. A jury awarded her $10,000, and the Eighth Circuit affirmed. The evidence indicated that the officer had ignored the message verifying the woman's identity. *Kennell v. Gates*, 215 F.3d 825 (8th Cir. 2000).

♦ A female officer assigned to an elite unit of the Houston Police Department endured daily sexual harassment but did not follow the department's formal complaint policy. However, she did discuss the harassment during an interview with Internal Affairs. As a result, the harassers were transferred from the unit and suspended without pay. The officer claimed that her co-workers then harassed her for breaking the department's code of silence. She asked to be transferred to a less prestigious position and sued the city under 42 U.S.C. § 1983. A jury found that **the city was liable to the officer for $10,000 for the sexual harassment and for $100,000 for the retaliation**. In affirming the awards, the Fifth Circuit held that that the city knew or should have known about the harassment but failed to remedy it. *Sharp v. City of Houston*, 164 F.3d 923 (5th Cir. 1999).

♦ A New York man was involved in an automobile accident. His wife was trapped inside the vehicle and suffered serious injuries. During the rescue, the man was directed to step away from the accident by rescue personnel. However, he repeatedly went back to the site to instruct the rescuers on how to free his wife. At one point, he approached and detained a firefighter who was carrying the jaws of life to the vehicle. When he refused to step away from the car, a deputy arrested him for obstruction of governmental process and disorderly conduct. The man was eventually acquitted, and sued the sheriff's department and the deputy in his individual and official capacity under Section 1983 for false arrest and false imprisonment in a New York federal court. An action brought under Section 1983 requires that a person or entity, under color of state law, violate a person's constitutional rights. **Official immunity is a defense to a false arrest and imprisonment case if, at the time of the arrest, probable cause existed.** Here, the man admitted that he had failed to obey the deputy after being told to step away from the accident site. He also admitted that he detained the firefighter and that his conduct was disorderly. Taking all these factors into consideration, the district court found that there was probable cause for the arrest. The deputy's actions in arresting the man were not clearly unreasonable under the circumstances, and he was entitled to official immunity. *Decker v. Campus*, 981 F.Supp. 851 (S.D.N.Y. 1997).

♦   A New Jersey police officer took field notes at the scene of a robbery in which he recorded the widely discrepant recollections of eyewitnesses. The officer's investigation report described the perpetrator as a light-skinned black male with a thin mustache, tightly but compactly muscled. The report, however, listed the perpetrator as being shorter than any of the eyewitness estimates found in his field notes. A short black male who weighed 140 pounds and wore a mustache was arrested, prosecuted, and acquitted. He then sued under 42 U.S.C. § 1983 and state law.

The man argued that the township police officers were not adequately trained and that the township and police chief failed to promulgate any policies or training on the preservation of field notes. The district court disagreed, finding that the evidence did not indicate that the training received by the police officers was inadequate. The manual of rules and regulations issued by the police department provided that **no employee could knowingly falsify any official report or enter or cause to be entered any inaccurate, false, or improper information** on records of the department, and that no employee could withhold any information concerning criminal activity. In addition, the reports filed by a police officer were checked for internal consistency, even though such reports were not compared to field notes on which they were based. Because the man did not show that the township's training on field notes was inadequate or contrary to accepted practice, the failure-to-train claim failed. The court ruled in favor of the defendants on the Section 1983 claims. *Robinson v. Winslow Township*, 973 F.Supp. 461 (D.N.J. 1997).

♦   A mildly retarded North Carolina man was observed by a police officer picking up a $5 bill dropped by a woman in a bus station ticket line. The officer believed the man saw the woman drop the money. He ordered the man to return it to her. According to the officer and a ticket window attendant, the man responded by simply waving the money in the face of the tearful woman. The woman did not accept the money, allegedly thinking it to be a crude proposition. The man then fled with the money, the officer gave chase and a struggle ensued. The officer threw his weight against the man's right leg and wrenched his knee, tearing the anterior cruciate ligament. The man filed a Section 1983 lawsuit against the officer and the city in a federal court, alleging the use of unconstitutionally **excessive force**, unlawful detention, and due process violations. The case reached the Fourth Circuit, which examined whether the totality of the circumstances justified the officer's use of force. Here, **the officer had inflicted a serious injury on a smaller and more passive retarded man over a lost $5 bill**. A jury could reasonably conclude that no reasonable officer could believe this conduct to be lawful. A trial was required on that issue. However, because evidence supported the arrest for misdemeanor larceny and because the man was in custody for only 15 minutes, his unreasonable detention and due process claims were dismissed. *Rowland v. Perry*, 41 F.3d 167 (4th Cir. 1994).

3. Firefighters' and Other Employees' Actions

♦ After he was fired by a Massachusetts city, a black police officer sued for race discrimination. A settlement agreement was reached, under which he would receive $81,000 and be reinstated upon passing a physical and retraining. His physical exam revealed a slightly abnormal liver function, and the city's doctor informed the city attorney that he might have Hepatitis C. The attorney required the officer to get a liver biopsy, which came back negative. She refused to reinstate the officer and instead forwarded the biopsy results to the city doctor for review. When the officer sued the city and attorney under 42 U.S.C. § 1983 for conspiring to impede his reinstatement, a federal court ordered the attorney to pay him $10,000 in punitive damages. The First Circuit upheld the award. The evidence showed that **the city attorney deliberately stalled the officer's reinstatement**. *Powell v. Alexander*, 391 F.3d 1 (1st Cir. 2004).

♦ A corrections officer in Massachusetts saw a co-worker playing cards with an inmate in violation of jail rules and reported the incident upon the orders of a supervisor. Afterwards, he faced numerous instances of harassment by his colleagues, including having his tires slashed and his car defaced with feces. He made 30 complaints to the Sheriff's Investigative Division, which largely ignored them. Eventually, he quit, then sued the county under 42 U.S.C. § 1983, alleging First Amendment violations. A jury awarded him $500,000 and the First Circuit upheld the award. It noted that **sheriff's department officials had a regular practice or custom of allowing retaliation against employees who violated the code of silence**. *Baron v. Suffolk County Sheriff's Dep't*, 402 F.3d 225 (1st Cir. 2005).

♦ A Nevada kindergarten teacher sent a letter to her state senators criticizing a new school program. She was then fired, and she sued under the First Amendment. She received $135,000 and was reinstated to her job. However, she later received written summaries of meetings discussing her job performance (considered progressive discipline). She again sued, this time for retaliation under 42 U.S.C. § 1983. A jury awarded her $75,000 and the Ninth Circuit upheld the award. Here, the school board had delegated employee matters to the district superintendent, making him the final decision-maker, and making the district liable for retaliatory actions taken against the teacher. Under *Monell v. Dep't of Social Services*, 436 U.S. 658 (1978), a municipal employer is liable under Section 1983 for the actions of its official, if the official is the "final policymaker" with regard to the employment matter in dispute. *Lytle v. Carl*, 382 F.3d 978 (9th Cir. 2004).

• An Illinois corrections officer was suspended for failing to prevent a prisoner's suicide. Her termination hearing was delayed several times. The state personnel review board, after 633 days, decided that she should have been suspended for only 60 days. She then sought back pay from the sheriff for 573 days. He paid her for only 106 days, determining that she was not entitled to back pay for delays caused by continuances she requested or did not oppose. She then sued under 42 U.S.C. § 1983. The case reached the Seventh Circuit, which ruled that another hearing was required to determine how much back pay she was entitled to. To avoid back pay for the full 573 days, the sheriff would have to show that her requests for continuances were not justified. As for the Section 1983 claim, the officer was not entitled to a pre-deprivation hearing on the back pay issue. The post-deprivation hearing was sufficient to provide her an adequate remedy. *Ellis v. Sheahan*, 412 F.3d 754 (7th Cir. 2005).

• A Georgia county director of administrative services criticized a proposed contract between the board of county commissioners and a private corporation. Shortly thereafter, three members of the board voted to eliminate several county jobs, including the director's. She sued the county, asserting that the vote to eliminate her job came in retaliation for her speech criticizing the board. A jury found in her favor. The jury found that only one of the board members was motivated by the director's protected speech, but that he influenced the other two members to vote to eliminate the position. On appeal, the Eleventh Circuit Court of Appeals held that **the county could not be liable under 42 U.S.C. § 1983 for the single board member's retaliatory action**. His motivations could not be deemed to be an official county policy. The director was not entitled to get her job back. *Matthews v. Columbia County*, 294 F.3d 1294 (11th Cir. 2002).

• A veterinarian's assistant worked at an animal hospital owned by a veterinarian, who also served as a city alderman. She began a relationship with the veterinarian. He then exercised increasing control over her life, threatening her on several occasions and allegedly using the police to track her down when she left town. Eventually, the veterinarian was arrested on conspiracy charges. The assistant sued the city under 42 U.S.C. § 1983, claiming that the veterinarian used his authority as an alderman to sexually harass her. A Tennessee federal court ruled in favor of the city, and the Sixth Circuit Court of Appeals affirmed. **Even though the veterinarian had allegedly used his position to harass her, he was not acting under color of state law when he did so.** He was not furthering the interests of the city, and the police officers testified that they did not view him as having any authority. Thus, the city was not liable for his abusive behavior. *Waters v. City of Morristown*, 242 F.3d 353 (6th Cir. 2001).

♦ A clerk with a county district attorney's office used her position to access a confidential database for the purpose of locating her husband's ex-wife (so he could serve her with a notice of an upcoming custody hearing). As a result, the ex-wife and her children had to leave the battered women's shelter where she had been staying while hiding from another man. For safety reasons, the shelter refused to let people stay there when their ex-spouses knew their whereabouts. The ex-wife sued the clerk and the county under 42 U.S.C. § 1983, claiming that the county failed to properly train and supervise the clerk, and that the clerk was acting under color of state law when she accessed the database. A California federal court ruled for the county and held that the clerk was not acting under color of state law. The Ninth Circuit affirmed in part, agreeing that the county was not liable, but finding that **the clerk had been acting under color of state law when she improperly accessed the database.** *McDade v. West*, 223 F.3d 1135 (9th Cir. 2000).

♦ An employee of the Wyoming Boys' School suspected the school's superintendent of drinking on the job. He reported the incident to a state official, which resulted in the superintendent's paid suspension. The superintendent voluntarily checked himself into a treatment program. The director of the state's Department of Family Services then fired the superintendent. She also sent out a bulletin to a state law enforcement agency indicating that the superintendent had checked himself out of the treatment program, was suicidal, and might try to go after state employees. However, he remained in treatment at that time. He later sued the department and the director under the Americans with Disabilities Act (ADA), the Family and Medical Leave Act (FMLA), 42 U.S.C. § 1983 and state law. The Tenth Circuit affirmed the lower court's rulings in favor of the defendants. **The allegedly defamatory bulletin concerning the superintendent's potential for violence following his termination did not occur "in the course of" his termination.** Thus, the bulletin did not deprive him of a liberty interest that would allow recovery under Section 1983. His other claims likewise failed. As an at-will employee, he could not show that he could only be terminated for cause. Further, his drinking on the job was not protected by the ADA, and the FMLA granted him no more rights than an employee who remained at work. *Renaud v. Wyoming Dep't of Family Services*, 203 F.3d 723 (10th Cir. 2000).

♦ A volunteer fire department discharged a firefighter after he told the department that some of its members lacked necessary training and qualifications. The firefighter sued the department in a Maryland federal court for violation of his First Amendment rights under 42 U.S.C. § 1983. The court noted that volunteer fire companies had the authority to enter buildings where a fire was in progress and order persons to leave. Also, members had the powers of deputy sheriffs while at fires and on their way to and from fires. Accordingly, **the department was a state actor under Section 1983 and could be sued for violating the firefighter's First Amendment rights.** The court denied the department's motion for pretrial judgment. *Goldstein v. Chestnut Ridge Volunteer Fire Co.*, 984 F.Supp. 367 (D. Md. 1997).

♦ A discharged employee of the Chicago Housing Authority filed a successful lawsuit against the authority under 42 U.S.C. § 1983 for deprivation of his liberty and property interests without due process. He was awarded damages, reinstatement, and back pay. Approximately two and one-half years later, the authority still refused to reinstate him until the appeals process was completed, and the employee still had failed to find alternate employment. The employee submitted an amended calculation of back pay and interest to an Illinois federal court. The authority challenged the amended back pay request, arguing that the employee failed to mitigate his damages. The court held that where a plaintiff is genuinely unable to find work or is forced to lower his sights and accept an inferior position, the defendant will be responsible for the difference (however great) between what the employee would have been earning and what he actually earned during the period prior to his reinstatement. Here, **although the authority demonstrated that the employee did not make a good-faith effort to find alternate employment**, it failed to show that further efforts on the employee's part might have succeeded. As a result, the court awarded additional back pay and interest. *Coleman v. Lane*, 949 F.Supp. 604 (N.D. Ill. 1996).

C. The Federal Tort Claims Act

The Federal Tort Claims Act (FTCA) provides a limited waiver of sovereign immunity, allowing individuals to sue the federal government in certain circumstances. However, where a federal employee commits a tortious act outside the scope of his or her employment, the government cannot be held liable.

♦ An airline passenger at a Tennessee airport **fell when taking off her shoes before going through airport security**, allegedly because the Transportation Security Administration (TSA) negligently failed to provide a chair. She sued the TSA in a federal court under the Federal Tort Claims Act. The court granted the TSA pretrial judgment, and the passenger appealed. The Sixth Circuit affirmed, finding no evidence that the passenger's fall was foreseeable so as to give rise under Tennessee law to a duty on the part of the TSA to provide a chair for people removing their shoes. Among the thousands of people going through airport security before the incident, there were no reported instances of similar incidents. *Barnes v. U.S.*, 485 F.3d 341 (6th Cir. 2007).

♦ A Navy engineer assigned to a ship in Hawaii rear-ended a car as he was leaving the base after work. The woman whom he hit exhausted her no-fault benefits as required by Hawaii law, then sued the engineer in state court for negligence. The U.S. Attorney for the District of Hawaii certified that the engineer was acting in the scope of his employment at the time of the accident and removed the case to federal court. The U.S. Attorney then substituted the United States as the defendant. The court ruled that the engineer was acting in the scope of his employment. As a result, the Federal Tort Claims Act governed the case, which had to be dismissed because the plaintiff failed to exhaust her administrative remedies under the act. The Ninth Circuit reversed, finding that **the engineer was acting outside the scope of his employment when the** accident occurred. Thus, the engineer had to be reinstated as the defendant. *Clamor v. U.S.*, 240 F.3d 1215 (9th Cir. 2001).

• A supervisor employed by the U.S. Department of Agriculture, Food and Safety Inspection Service informed several subordinates that their work was sub-par and that they needed to carry out their duties more diligently. The supervisor allegedly posted a picture depicting one of the subordinates as a "Mama Pig" and the others as "suckling piglets." The subordinates sued the supervisor for defamation. The attorney general substituted the United States as party-defendant, but the court refused to accept the substitution because the supervisor's conduct did not fall within the scope of his employment. The supervisor appealed to the Eighth Circuit, which held that the district court had erroneously refused to substitute the United States. Even if the supervisor had posted the picture, he could have been acting within the scope of his employment. The picture could have been a disciplinary measure or a means of communicating his official disapproval of the subordinates' performance. The court of appeals reversed and remanded the case. If the supervisor either did not post the picture, or posted it for disciplinary reasons, he was acting within the scope of his employment and the case could then be dismissed because **the FTCA precluded lawsuits against the United States for defamation**. *Heuton v. Anderson*, 75 F.3d 357 (8th Cir. 1996).

• A federal prison inmate filed a claim under the FTCA alleging that the United States was liable for a sexual assault committed by a federal corrections officer employed by the Bureau of Prisons in Kentucky. Allegedly, while the prisoner was being transported to a doctor's office, the officer stopped the government car, removed the prisoner's handcuffs and told her that his apartment was nearby. She indicated that she did not wish to go to his apartment, but the officer stated that if she did not go with him, he would claim that she had tried to escape. While at his apartment, he sexually assaulted her. She sued the federal government. The district court granted the government's motion to dismiss the case, and the inmate appealed to the U.S. Court of Appeals, Sixth Circuit. In order to succeed on a tort claim against the United States, the plaintiff must show that the act occurred during the course of employment. Here, **the sexual assault by the officer obviously was far from what he was employed to do**, his apartment was clearly outside the space limit of his employment, and he was not serving any purpose of the Bureau of Prisons. Therefore, the court affirmed the decision of the trial court and determined that the employee acted outside the scope of his employment. No claim under the FTCA could be based on his conduct. *Flechsig v. U.S.*, 991 F.2d 300 (6th Cir. 1993).

• A U.S. Navy officer was assigned to active duty on the *USS Iowa*. While sailing, the *Iowa's* crew was engaged in firing exercises from 16-inch gun turrets. The officer was participating in an exercise when a series of explosions occurred, causing his death and the deaths of 46 other sailors. The officer's parents filed suit in a Virginia federal court under the FTCA. The court granted the government's motion to dismiss, and the parents appealed to the U.S. Court of Appeals, Fourth Circuit. The FTCA abrogated the United States' sovereign immunity in certain actions for its tortious conduct. However, **the U.S. Supreme Court has determined that the U.S. government is immune from tort suits filed by military personnel**. The court noted three reasons for granting immunity. First, the nature of the relationship between the government and members of the armed services requires a uniform federal remedy that does not vary based upon the site of the incident. Second, litigants may not use the FTCA for remedial recovery when Congress has provided an adequate and uniform compensation system for injuries or death of those in the armed services. Third, federal courts should avoid involvement in the military or unnecessary infringement in the military's relationship with its members because this relationship is grounded upon the need for discipline and compliance with orders, and should not be second-guessed. The court affirmed the dismissal. *Blakey v. U.S.S. Iowa*, 991 F.2d 148 (4th Cir. 1993).

* A Virginia middle school cross country runner was struck by an automobile while he was running in a national park owned by the U.S. government. The U.S. government had authority to designate speed limits and otherwise install road signs. The government had not posted signs, which warned motorists that the roads were used by pedestrians. The student's father filed a lawsuit under the FTCA seeking compensation for his son's injuries. The district court noted that the FTCA subjects the U.S. government to certain tort claims but is subject to several exceptions. The government contended that **the decision not to post signs warning drivers of pedestrians involved a policy judgment and thus fell under the discretionary function exception to the FTCA**. The district court agreed. The government need not deliberately consider a given policy judgment in order for it to fall under the discretionary function exception. Consequently, whether the government actually considered placing the signs on the roadway was irrelevant. Further, no established safety policy required posting signs on the roadway. Thus, the posting of road signs was a discretionary function, and the father's negligence action failed under the FTCA. *Alderman by Alderman v. U.S.*, 825 F.Supp. 742 (W.D. Va. 1993).

D. State Tort Claims Acts

* While responding to an automobile accident in his own vehicle, a Kansas volunteer firefighter was struck and killed by a police officer who was speeding to the scene. His estate sued the county under the state tort claims act and also alleged a violation of his constitutional due process rights under 42 U.S.C. § 1983. A federal court ruled for the county on the due process claim, and the Tenth Circuit affirmed. **The estate's sole remedy was under the state tort claims act.** *Moore v. Board of County Commissioners of County of Leavenworth*, 507 F.3d 1257 (10th Cir. 2007).

* On a dark and rainy night, a Maine man, intending to commit suicide, drove to the parking lot behind the police station and began screaming and smashing windows with a hammer. When an officer yelled at him to stop, he raised the hammer. She shot him until he fell to the ground. Two more officers arrived on the scene and ordered him to stay down and show them his hands. Instead, he

rolled toward them. They spotted a metallic object, thought it was a gun, and fired when he failed to respond to their orders. He survived the shooting, then sued the officers under 42 U.S.C. § 1983 and the Maine Tort Claims Act (MTCA). The case reached the First Circuit, which held that the officers were entitled to qualified immunity. **They did not use excessive force in violation of the Fourth Amendment or the MTCA when they fired upon him, even though he was lying on the ground.** Even if other means of subduing him were available, their actions were not unreasonable. *Berube v. Conley*, 506 F.3d 79 (1st Cir. 2007).

◆ Without conducting a background or criminal-records check, the city of Boston hired a man to supervise a summer program involving neighborhood youths. It later hired a 16-year-old as part of the program and assigned her to work with the supervisor. A week after she began the program, the supervisor told her she needed to sign additional job-related paperwork that he had left at his apartment. When she went with him at the end of the day, he raped her and told her she would lose her job if she told anybody. He raped her again a few days later. She then told a friend, and the city eventually found out about the rapes. It fired the supervisor. The 16-year-old sued the city for sexual harassment and negligent hiring, claiming that had the city conducted either a background or criminal-records check, it would have discovered that the supervisor had served time for rape. A Massachusetts trial court refused to dismiss the case. Here, even without a criminal background check, **the supervisor's résumé should have put the city on notice to conduct a reasonable inquiry because of the lengthy gap in his employment history** (while he was in prison). Further, workers' compensation did not bar recovery by the 16-year-old because her injury did not arise out of and in the course of her employment. Her injury occurred outside the workplace, during personal time, in the supervisor's apartment. *Brimage v. City of Boston*, No. CIV.A. 97-1912, 2001 WL 69488 (Mass. Super. 2001).

◆ While investigating a burglary, a Texas police officer was dispatched to assist another officer on a theft in progress. The officer proceeded on an emergency basis using his siren, lights, and air horn. He tried to make a left turn crossing three lanes, but a large truck blocked his view and his car collided with an oncoming car, injuring the occupants. The occupants sued the officer and the city for personal injuries and property damage, alleging negligence and gross negligence. The officer and the city moved for pretrial judgment on the basis of immunity. The trial court denied their motion. The Supreme Court of Texas affirmed, finding that the officer had failed to set forth sufficient evidence to establish that he had acted in good faith. Under Texas law, **a governmental employee has official immunity for the performance of discretionary duties within the scope of the employee's authority**, provided that the employee acts in good faith. Good faith depends on how a reasonably prudent officer would have assessed both the need to which an officer responds and the risks of the officer's course of action, based on the officer's perception of the facts at the time of the event. Although the officer in this case presented evidence about the nature of the dispatch call, the circumstances that made it necessary for him to quickly reach the scene, and the viability of the alternative routes he could have taken, the evidence did not address the degree, likelihood, and obviousness of the risks created by his actions. Thus, the evidence did not conclusively establish that the officer acted in good faith. *Wadewitz v. Montgomery*, 951 S.W.2d 464 (Tex. 1997).

• An Illinois woman applied for a village firefighter position, aware that she was required to pass a physical agility test before being considered. She signed an agreement releasing the village from liability for any injury that might occur during the test. While performing the test, she fell from a station approximately eight feet off the ground. She sued the village, alleging that its fire department conducted the agility test in a negligent manner. The court granted the village pretrial judgment, and the Appellate Court of Illinois affirmed, finding that the state Tort Immunity Act immunized the administrators of the physical agility test because they had been performing discretionary acts. More importantly, the special duty doctrine exception to immunity was inapplicable because no special relationship had arisen between the village and the woman. The woman was not compelled in any way to take the physical agility test. Rather, she voluntarily took the test even though she could have refused. **The village could not be held liable simply because its employees set up the test and instructed the woman on how to take it.** *White v. Village of Homewood, Illinois*, 673 N.E.2d 1092 (Ill. App. Ct. 1996).

• A seventh-grade Tennessee middle school student asked her physical education instructor if she could be dismissed from class a few minutes early because of an injury. When she entered the girls' locker room, a group of students accosted her and one challenged her to a fight. The student claimed that she was then assaulted and thrown into a shower. The instructor intervened about 15 minutes later, but the student already had received injuries requiring hospitalization. She suffered psychological injuries and was diagnosed as having posttraumatic stress disorder. She transferred to another school while remaining under the care of a psychiatrist. Five of the students accused of assault were expelled for the rest of the school year, and the victimized student sued under the state Governmental Tort Liability Act. The Court of Appeals of Tennessee determined that the state governmental liability act exempted the government from liability. **There was no evidence that the physical education instructor had been aware of the fight nor did a record of problems in the girls' locker room exist.** The assault could not have been anticipated and was unforeseeable. Also, a decision to assign a single teacher to the class did not create potential liability. The trial court had properly dismissed the lawsuit. *Chudasama v. Metropolitan Government of Nashville and Davidson County*, 914 S.W.2d 922 (Tenn. Ct. App. 1995).

• A New Jersey police officer began pursuing a motorcyclist who had fled after being pulled over for speeding. Although department policy forbade officers from leaving their patrol zones unless instructed to do so by a supervisor, the officer chased the motorcyclist outside his zone toward one of the most congested intersections in the county. The township shift commander ordered the officer to terminate the chase if there was a risk of danger to himself or others. After activating his siren and warning lights and slowing down to look for traffic, the officer entered the intersection through a red light and collided with another vehicle. The other driver was severely injured. The driver filed a negligence lawsuit against the officer and the township. A trial court ruled that the defendants were immune from liability under the state tort claims act. The Supreme Court of New Jersey held that, **absent willful misconduct, the tort claims act grants absolute immunity to officers and municipalities with respect to injuries caused by officers in pursuit of escaping persons.** Here, the officer's violation of internal department policy and his failure to abide by the commander's order arguably established willful misconduct that required a trial. The court then held that the officer would be entitled to immunity under federal law unless his conduct "shocked the conscience." *Fielder v. Stonack,* 661 A.2d 231 (N.J. 1995).

♦ A volunteer for an Oregon city was killed while topping trees for the city during an Arbor Day cleanup. After his death, his estate sued the city for wrongful death. A jury found that the volunteer and the city were each 50% negligent in causing the death, and awarded over $270,000 to the volunteer's wife and daughters. The case was appealed to the Oregon Court of Appeals, which held that the daughters had received a substantial remedy under the state's workers' compensation law and that they were thus not entitled to recovery in the wrongful death action. On further appeal, the Oregon Supreme Court affirmed. It noted that the state constitution (which guarantees every person a remedy for personal injury) did not bar application of the state tort claims act, which granted immunity to public bodies for injuries that are covered by workers' compensation. Here, **since the volunteer would have been barred from suing the city if he survived, his estate also was barred from suing.** Workers' compensation was the only remedy available to the volunteer's daughters. *Storm v. McClung,* 47 P.3d 476 (Or. 2002).

♦ A California police officer assisted a man with self-inflicted stab wounds and became covered with the man's blood. After being committed for psychiatric evaluation, the man stated that he was dying from AIDS. The officer was assured by the county medical center that the man would be tested for AIDS. However, the man was released without being tested. Months later, the man was again located and tested positive for AIDS. The officer sued the medical center, alleging that its failure to immediately test the man caused him injuries. The case reached the Court of Appeal of California, which noted that government institutions are generally immune from tort liability. However, public entities are liable for the ordinary negligence of their employees when they act within the scope of their employment unless the employees are immune from liability. Since the medical center employees had agreed to obtain the blood sample, the medical center was not immune from liability. Although the California Tort Claims Act grants immunity to those who negligently provide medical examinations, **immunity does not apply to laboratory analyses of potentially toxic substances.** *Smith v. County of Kern,* 25 Cal.Rptr.2d 716 (Cal. Ct. App. 1993).

- A county sheriff and a West Virginia state trooper arrested a suspect for brandishing a weapon and discharging a firearm. While the sheriff was placing the firearm in the trunk, it accidentally discharged. Shell fragments hit the trooper, and he injured his shoulder. The trooper filed a negligence suit against the sheriff and the county commission in a West Virginia circuit court. The circuit court denied the defendants' pretrial judgment motion, and they appealed to the Supreme Court of Appeals of West Virginia. The court noted that the sheriff, as an employee of a political subdivision, was immune from suit unless: **1) his act was outside the scope of his employment, 2) his act was in bad faith or reckless, or 3) he was liable under another statute**. Since none of these exceptions applied in the present case, the sheriff was immune and the suit against him dismissed. However, the commission could be held liable if the sheriff's actions were negligent. *Beckley v. Crabtree*, 428 S.E.2d 317 (W.Va. 1993).

CHAPTER FIVE

Searches and Seizures

                                                    Page

I. SEARCHES OF HOMES, OFFICES AND PERSONS 311
   A. Applicable Standard of Reasonableness 312
   B. Expectations of Privacy 317

II. BLOOD AND DRUG TESTING 321
   A. Balancing Public and Individual Rights 321
      1. Assertions of Overbroad Policies 322
      2. Safety-Sensitive Positions 325
      3. Random Testing 330
      4. Direct Observation 333
      5. Post-Accident Testing 336
   B. Standards for Reasonable Suspicion 337
      1. Police Officers and Firefighters 338
      2. Corrections Officers and Court Employees 340
      3. Transportation Employees 342
   C. Testing and Unemployment Benefits 344
   D. Adequacy of Testing Procedures 346

I. SEARCHES OF HOMES, OFFICES AND PERSONS

The Fourth Amendment to the U.S. Constitution guarantees the "right of the people to be secure in their persons, houses, papers, and effects, against unreasonable searches and seizures. ..."

Searches and seizures are generally supposed to be performed only where officials have a warrant based upon probable cause describing with particularity the things or persons to be seized. In the context of public employment, searches and seizures implicate the Fourth Amendment only if the employee has a reasonable expectation of privacy in a place to be searched.

In cases involving work-related misconduct, searches taking place in government offices do not resemble searches of a private home, where Fourth Amendment protections are in full effect. It is true, however, that under certain circumstances government employees may have reasonable privacy expectations at work.

The courts suspend the general requirement of a search warrant supported by probable cause for cases involving searches of public offices and utilize a reduced standard of "reasonableness."

A. Applicable Standard of Reasonableness

A leading case on the standard for public employer searches is *New Jersey v. T.L.O.*, 469 U.S. 325, 105 S.Ct. 733, 83 L.Ed.2d 720 (1985), a school case that established a two-part inquiry into whether the action by the public official was justified at its inception, and whether the search itself was reasonable in scope and circumstances.

* In the *T.L.O.* case, a New Jersey high school teacher found two students smoking in the lavatory and brought them to an assistant vice principal's office. One of the students admitted smoking in the lavatory, while the other denied being a smoker. The assistant vice principal then asked her to come to an inner private office, where he opened her purse and found a pack of cigarettes. In removing the cigarettes, he discovered rolling papers and decided to thoroughly search the purse. He also found marijuana, a pipe, empty plastic bags, a number of one-dollar bills and a list of "people who owe me money." The student appealed the adjudication of delinquency, contending that the search of her purse had violated her constitutional rights under the Fourth Amendment. The state supreme court ruled that the search had been unreasonable.

The prosecution appealed the case to the U.S. Supreme Court, which noted that **school officials should not be held to the probable cause standard to which law enforcement officers are held**. The legality of student searches by teachers and other school officials should depend simply upon the reasonableness of the search under all the circumstances. Ordinarily, the search of a student by a school official is justified at its inception where there are reasonable grounds for suspecting that the search will turn up evidence that the student has violated or will violate the law or rules of the school. A search is permissible in scope when the measures adopted are reasonably related to the objectives of the search and not excessively intrusive in light of the student's age and sex, in view of the suspected violation. In this case, the search was not unreasonable under the Fourth Amendment. The Supreme Court reversed the New Jersey Supreme Court's decision. *New Jersey v. T.L.O.*, 469 U.S. 325, 105 S.Ct. 733, 83 L.Ed.2d 720 (1985).

* After a physician/psychiatrist at a California state hospital had occupied the same office for 17 years, hospital officials became concerned about possible improprieties in his management policies. The hospital's executive director asked the employee to take paid administrative leave during an investigation. A hospital administrator then searched the employee's office under a hospital policy of conducting routine inventory of state property in the offices of terminated employees. However, when the search was conducted, the employee remained on administrative leave and had not yet been fired. The search involved several entries into the office and seizure of items from the employee's desk and file cabinets, including personal items such as photos and a valentine's card. The investigators put the remainder of the employee's personal property in storage and placed it at the employee's disposal. The employer used the seized items in a proceeding before a state personnel hearing officer to impeach the employee's credibility.

Sec. I   SEARCHES OF HOMES, OFFICES AND PERSONS   313

The employee sued the hospital administrators in a federal court for violating his Fourth Amendment rights. The court granted the administrator's motion for pretrial judgment, ruling that the search was proper. However, the U.S. Court of Appeals, Ninth Circuit, reversed and remanded, ruling that the employee had a reasonable expectation of privacy in his office. The U.S. Supreme Court granted review and noted that the employee had occupied the same office by himself for 17 years. Thus, he had a reasonable expectation of privacy in his desk and file cabinets.

However, **the employee's reasonable expectation of privacy was to be balanced against the public employer's interest in supervision, control and efficient operation of the workplace**. The Court refused to impose a search warrant requirement for public employers, because such a requirement would frustrate the governmental purpose behind the search. The warrant requirement should be imposed only with respect to searches that were not work related. Obtaining a warrant would disrupt the daily work routine of government business and would require officials to become familiar with probable cause standards. The governmental interest in efficiency outweighed the employee's privacy expectation. The reasonableness standard established in *New Jersey v. T.L.O.* was the appropriate standard for work-related non-investigatory intrusions of work-related misconduct. The reasonableness of such a search involved inquiry into whether the action was justified at its inception and reasonably related in scope to the circumstances that justified the interference in the first place. Generally, a search could be justified at its inception when there were reasonable grounds for suspecting that it would turn up evidence that a public employee was guilty of work-related misconduct, known as **"individualized suspicion."** Thus, pretrial judgment was inappropriate. The court reversed and remanded the case to the court of appeals to resolve factual disputes about the reasonableness of the search. *O'Connor v. Ortega*, 480 U.S. 709, 107 S.Ct. 1492, 94 L.Ed.2d 714 (1987).

♦   As part of a random search necessitated by an increase in the number of inmates testing positive for illegal drug usage, a sergeant at a Louisiana correctional facility was asked to submit to a general search, under which he would have to remove his clothing down to his underwear. General searches were conducted in a private place by a member of the same sex. Department regulations stated that general searches could be conducted without cause. The sergeant refused to submit to the search and was fired. His administrative appeal was denied. The Court of Appeal of Louisiana noted that the general search was not a strip search or partial strip search, which would require the existence of reasonable suspicion. Further, **the manner by which he was asked to submit to the search was random and reasonable** even though it was not done by a "blind" system. *Anderson v. Dep't of Public Safety and Corrections*, 985 So.2d 160 (La. Ct. App. 2008).

♦   An Omaha police officer arrested a man who accused him of stealing $106 during the arrest. Internal Affairs investigators looking into the complaint asked the officer about a $120 casino wager he made the day after the arrest. He told the investigators he withdrew cash from an ATM before his visits to the casino.

The police department then ordered him to produce his bank records for the day of the arrest and the day after. The officer complied, but no record of a withdrawal appeared. After the arrestee's polygraph showed truthful responses and the officer's polygraph showed deception, a pre-termination hearing was held, the officer was fired, and then a post-termination hearing was conducted. The officer sued, but the Eighth Circuit ruled against him. **The request for the bank records for the two days in question was reasonable** in scope and did not violate the Fourth Amendment. Also, the officer received adequate due process, bringing his attorney to both hearings. *Westbrook v. City of Omaha*, 231 Fed.Appx. 519 (8th Cir. 2007).

♦   A Michigan state police post commander needed to search troopers' lockers for missing radios that had to be reprogrammed by a certain date to avoid having to reschedule the programming at a considerable cost. He conferred with the troopers' union representative, who prepared and obtained an administrative search warrant. Later, the union sued the state police, asserting that its members' constitutional rights had been violated. The case reached the Michigan Court of Appeals, which ruled against the union, noting that the dispute was a matter of contract interpretation for an arbitrator and not a constitutional question requiring a court's attention. The collective bargaining agreement set forth the situations under which a union would agree to a search, and **any dispute arising from an administrative search warrant had to be resolved by an arbitrator.** *Michigan State Police Troopers Ass'n v. Michigan Dep't of State Police*, No. 237648, 2003 WL 22514650 (Mich. Ct. App. 2003).

♦   A female corrections officer at an Ohio correctional facility was strip-searched by two male co-workers and a female highway patrol officer without reasonable suspicion that she was carrying contraband. She sued the officers under 42 U.S.C. § 1983, alleging that the search violated the Fourth Amendment as well as the terms of an earlier settlement agreement that required reasonable suspicion for all strip searches and a witness of the employee's choosing. A federal court held that the defendants were entitled to qualified immunity, and the Sixth Circuit Court of Appeals affirmed. The court stated that **if the strip search was unconstitutional, that fact was not clearly established at the time the search was conducted in 1999.** As a result, the defendants were entitled to immunity. *Virgili v. Gilbert*, 272 F.3d 391 (6th Cir. 2001).

♦   An Ohio county sheriff's office installed an electronic recording system that not only taped incoming and outgoing calls, but also inadvertently recorded the dispatchers' private conversations. The office assumed that the dispatchers could avoid being taped by switching off their headsets while conducting personal conversations. However, two dispatchers later discovered a rear console microphone that was recording every conversation in the office and that sheriff's department officials apparently were unaware existed. The dispatchers sued under the Fourth Amendment and the federal Omnibus Crime Control and Safe Streets Act. Two months later, the sheriff's office replaced the recording system altogether. The case eventually reached the U.S. Court of Appeals, Sixth Circuit, which held that **the unintentional eavesdropping was not an** unreasonable search in violation of the Fourth Amendment. Further, the office, as a law enforcement agency, was exempt from the federal act's prohibition on electronic interception of communications. *First v. Stark County Board of Commissioners*, 234 F.3d 1268 (6th Cir. 2000) (Unpublished).

• An electronic engineer with a division of the Central Intelligence Agency had his own office and a computer with Internet access. The division had established an Internet and e-mail policy, which informed employees that accessing unlawful material was prohibited, that computers were to be used for official government business only, and that the division would periodically audit, inspect and monitor users' Internet access. When the division learned that the engineer had accessed a large number of unauthorized sex sites, it conducted a remote search of the engineer's computer and copied certain files. Some of the images the engineer had downloaded were pornographic pictures of minors. The division then authorized an employee to enter the engineer's office, remove the original hard drive, and replace it with a copy. After the engineer was convicted of receiving and possessing child pornography, he challenged the convictions in a Virginia federal court, asserting that the searches violated the Fourth Amendment. The case reached the Fourth Circuit, which held that **the engineer had no reasonable expectation of privacy in using the Internet to access pornography** because of the division's Internet policy. Thus, the remote search was not unconstitutional. Further, the warrantless entry into the engineer's office to retrieve the hard drive was not unreasonable. Thus, the search results did not have to be suppressed under the Fourth Amendment. *U.S. v. Simons*, 206 F.3d 392 (4th Cir. 2000).

• A child protective investigator in Illinois investigated instances of child neglect, abuse and sexual abuse. Her duties included photographing evidence for use in court proceedings. Because her office had limited storage facilities, she bought a file cabinet and a storage unit in which she locked evidentiary photographs, equipment, files and documents. A co-worker anonymously informed a detective in the Cook County Sheriff's Department that she worked in the investigator's office and that the investigator had pornographic pictures of children in her file cabinet. The next day, the investigator's supervisors entered her office (police officers waited outside), unlocked the storage unit and pried open the investigator's file cabinet and desk. They then called the detective who had received the tip into the office where he told them that the photographs were evidence and not pornography. When the investigator, who had not been in the office, found out about the search, she sued the supervisors and police under 42 U.S.C. § 1983 for violating her right to be free from unreasonable searches and seizures under the Fourth Amendment. After a federal court dismissed the case, the investigator appealed to the Seventh Circuit.

The investigator argued on appeal that the reasonableness test from *O'Connor v. Ortega* was not applicable because the search was not a workplace search but a criminal investigation. The Supreme Court has held that **a warrant or probable cause standard does not apply when a government employer searches an employee's office, desk or file cabinet to retrieve government property while investigating work-related misconduct**. Here, although the cabinets were purchased by the investigator, she used them primarily for the storage of work-related materials. Accordingly, she did not have a reasonable expectation of privacy in the file cabinet or storage unit. Further, her desk also likely had work-related materials in it. Under *Ortega,* a workplace search is reasonable if it is justified at its inception and reasonably related in scope to the circumstances that prompted the search. Here, the search met both prongs of the test. Although the tip was anonymous, it showed sufficient signs of reliability and made specific allegations of misconduct. Further, it stated where the pictures could be found. The court also determined that the search was reasonable in scope. The search did not extend to places where the pictures would not reasonably have been found. Moreover, the presence of several police officers did not transform the search into a criminal search requiring probable cause and a warrant. The court affirmed the dismissal of the case. *Gossmeyer v. McDonald,* 128 F.3d 481 (7th Cir. 1997).

♦ A Massachusetts university police officer harassed, threatened and stalked his former girlfriend. After a phone message that she believed came from the officer, she contacted the police because she believed he had killed one of her former boyfriends. Concerned about the officer's potential dangerousness, a police captain contacted a psychologist, who advised him that the caller might be homicidal or suicidal and should be evaluated by a mental health professional. Arrangements were made at a psychiatric hospital for an evaluation. Although the officer agreed to accompany officers to the hospital, he refused to voluntarily admit himself and was admitted involuntarily pursuant to state statute. After he was released, he continued to call his former girlfriend, which led to his discharge for conduct unbecoming an officer. He appealed, **alleging that his involuntary admission to the hospital violated his Fourth Amendment right to be free from unreasonable searches and seizures**. The court of appeals noted that under Massachusetts' involuntary hospitalization statute, a police officer may commit an individual to a hospital in an emergency situation if he or she believes that person would create a likelihood of serious harm by reason of mental illness. In this context, Fourth Amendment standards require a showing of probable cause. Here, there was undisputed evidence, including the officer's threat and his history of harassment, that failure to hospitalize him would create a danger of serious physical harm. The discharge was upheld. *Ahern v. O'Donnell,* 109 F.3d 809 (1st Cir. 1997).

♦ A mason inspector employed by the city of Chicago was reimbursed for the mileage logged on his car. Suspecting mileage misrepresentation, the Office of the Inspector General (OIG) investigated the inspector, compiled a case summary, and shredded the notes, despite the fact that they exculpated him from any misconduct. Several OIG employees forcibly placed the inspector in a room without windows, stationed a guard outside the room, and escorted him when he used the restroom facilities. He was then interrogated and told to sign a written statement admitting to the alleged misconduct. The inspector signed the statement after being assured that he would not lose his job if he cooperated. When he was fired, he sued the city and various OIG officials in a federal court, alleging constitutional violations. The court noted that **the inspector's seizure** was neither justified at its inception nor was the scope of the intrusion reasonably related to the seizure that did take place. Although the OIG officials knew that the allegations of misconduct were false well before the date of the seizure, they unreasonably tried to coerce a confession in violation of the Fourteenth Amendment. The individual officials were not entitled to qualified immunity because the seizure and forced confession were objectively unreasonable. Because the Inspector General had final policymaking authority, the city of Chicago could be held liable under 42 U.S.C. § 1983. *Angara v. City of Chicago*, 897 F.Supp. 355 (N.D. Ill. 1995), 947 F.Supp. 1252 (1996).

B. Expectations of Privacy

♦ Several New York police officers noticed a camera in a locker room (which had been placed there due to vandalism) and objected to its presence. They claimed that they were then retaliated against, receiving assignments usually reserved for junior members of the department. They sued under 42 U.S.C. § 1983, claiming a violation of their First and Fourth Amendment rights. A federal court first held that the placement of the camera in the locker room did not constitute a search under the Fourth Amendment. **The officers had no reasonable expectation of privacy in that area of the locker room, which was apart from the area where the showers and bathrooms were.** Further, there was no evidence any recordings were ever made. The First Amendment claim also failed because the officers never raised an issue of public concern. *DeVittorio v. Hall*, 589 F.Supp.2d 247 (S.D.N.Y. 2008).

♦ An Oklahoma city employee brought his personal computer to work so he wouldn't have to share a computer with a co-worker. He networked his computer to the city computer and failed to password-protect his computer, turn it off or take other steps to prevent third-party use. When his co-worker had difficulty opening files on the city's computer, she asked a police officer who was a former computer salesman to look at her machine. He suspected the problem might be that the employee's personal computer was open to the same files. When he checked the employee's machine, he found child pornography. The employee, after pleading guilty, sought to suppress the evidence found on his computer. The Tenth Circuit Court of Appeals held that **he did not have a reasonable expectation of privacy in his computer because he took no measures to prevent others from using it.** *U.S. v. Barrows*, 481 F.3d 1246 (10th Cir. 2007).

♦ After receiving confidential information that an officer was using cocaine, the Pennsylvania State Police ordered the officer to submit a hair sample for analysis. The officer let a sergeant and a beautician cut hair from his head, neck and shoulder blade. When the test results came back negative for illegal drugs, the officer sued, alleging that his Fourth Amendment rights had been violated. The Third Circuit disagreed, noting that **the cutting of hair is like the taking of fingerprints or voice and handwriting samples: none are within the protection of the Fourth Amendment.** Because the hair was not inside the officer's body, but rather exposed to public view, he did not have a reasonable expectation of privacy in preventing the removal of small samples. *Coddington v. Evanko*, 112 Fed.Appx. 835 (3d Cir. 2004).

♦   A Commerce Department employee alleged that the department's inspector general sexually harassed her and later used profanity during a phone call with her. She contacted the Equal Employment Opportunity Commission, which began an investigation of her claims. She later asserted that the department's acting general counsel and assistant general counsel retaliated against her, and she kept detailed notes and related documents on everything that happened. When she gave the documents to one of the department's head attorneys for safekeeping, the general counsel and assistant general counsel reviewed them. She sued the two officials for violating her Fourth Amendment right to be free from unreasonable searches, but a federal court dismissed her action, finding that she first had to exhaust her administrative remedies under the Civil Service Reform Act (CSRA). The U.S. Court of Appeals, D.C. Circuit, reversed, noting that **the CSRA does not cover warrantless searches**. As a result, she could pursue her Fourth Amendment lawsuit against her co-workers. If she had a legitimate expectation of privacy in the places searched – the head attorney's safe and locked cabinet – the officials would have violated the Fourth Amendment. *Stewart v. Evans*, 275 F.3d 1126 (D.C. Cir. 2002).

♦   The box office manager at the University of Alaska worked in a 12-by-12 room with an open ticket window and an open door to an inside hallway. When the university became suspicious that she was stealing cash from ticket receipts, it reviewed cash audits, which revealed substantial shortages. Campus police then installed a camera in a ceiling vent without obtaining a warrant and captured images of her taking money. After she was convicted of theft, she asserted that the video evidence against her should have been suppressed because she had a reasonable expectation of privacy that was violated by the lack of a warrant. The Alaska Supreme Court disagreed, holding that **even if she had an expectation of privacy, that expectation was outweighed by the university's need to use video surveillance to enforce the law**. The conviction was upheld. *Cowles v. State of Alaska*, 23 P.3d 1168 (Alaska 2001).

♦   An Ohio city employee placed a number of personal items (including bottles of beer, *Playboy* magazines, his wedding album and his marriage license) in several lockers and a storage box at work, some of which were marked as his and some of which were unmarked. After his supervisor had trouble locating him one day, a decision was made to inspect the lockers in the locker room. The search was made the following day when he was at home. Although a message was left on his answering machine prior to the search, the search began before he retrieved the message. His supervisors first opened lockers that did not have names on them, but when they found the personal items listed above, they decided to open lockers with names on them. As a result of the searches, the employee was disciplined for possessing alcohol on city property and insubordination (for keeping inappropriate magazines at work), among other offenses. He sued, alleging that he had a reasonable expectation of privacy in his marked lockers and his marked storage box. Both sides moved for pretrial judgment on the issue of the employee's expectation of privacy. An Ohio federal court held that the searches were unlawful because **the employee had a reasonable expectation of privacy in his marked lockers and his storage box**. No searches had been conducted in the five years he had been employed by the city, and, prior to searching, the supervisors had no basis for believing the lockers contained contraband or that the employee had committed wrongdoing. However, to succeed on his lawsuit, he would still have to show that the supervisors were acting under an official policy. *Stein v. City of Toledo*, 1999 U.S. Dist. Lexis 4523 (N.D. Ohio 1999).

♦ A New York police officer kept a personal diary in which he expressed hostility and extreme dissatisfaction with his job and his co-workers. Someone gave the diary to a police lieutenant, who then gave it to the police chief. The chief met with the officer and told him that he had the diary, but he refused to return it immediately. The chief stated that he was concerned about the officer's emotional problems, which included his dislike of his supervisors in the department and his general unhappiness, particularly because the officer carried a weapon. As a result, the chief gave the book to the police psychiatrist for evaluation. The officer sued the chief and the city in a federal court, alleging that the chief's retention of his diary violated his Fourteenth Amendment right to due process.

Although the officer had a property interest in his diary, the police chief's retention of the diary did not violate due process. No possible pre-deprivation hearing could have been afforded before the chief unexpectedly gained possession of the diary, and the officer had not requested a hearing. Moreover, the chief had a responsibility to city residents to evaluate the diary in order to determine whether the officer was mentally competent to continue as a police officer. He also had a responsibility to his department to determine whether the officer's attitude and treatment of other members of the department were undermining department morale and effectiveness. Retaining the diary to allow the police psychiatrist to investigate its troubling contents was reasonable. The officer's interest in having his diary immediately returned did not outweigh the city's compelling interest in immediately assessing the fitness of one of its officers. The court ruled against the officer. *Verri v. Nanna*, 972 F.Supp. 773 (S.D.N.Y. 1997).

♦ A Florida department of corrections employee was searched, along with other employees and prisoners entering the prison, using an Ionscan test. The procedure involves vacuuming the subject for dust particles, which are then analyzed by the Ionscan machine, which can detect the presence of narcotics or explosive residues. The employee tested positive for the presence of cocaine particles. He was then required to submit to a strip and body cavity search. Department of Corrections (DOC) employees also searched the employee's apartment on prison property. A narcotics search dog alerted the DOC employees to the apartment refrigerator, but no drugs were found. That afternoon, the employee was asked to submit to a urine test, which indicated a positive result for cocaine. The DOC discharged the employee, and he appealed the final order of the Public Employees Relations Commission to the District

Court of Appeal of Florida, Fourth District. The employee argued that the Ionscan test was a drug test under the state statute and therefore it required reasonable suspicion. The court rejected this argument, finding that the statute, read as a whole, protected employees from unwarranted intrusive drug testing that required samples of bodily fluids and tissues. **The Ionscan provided a less intrusive means of searching** than the "shakedown" method upheld in a previous Florida case. The court noted that a prison entrance is similar to a border and enables officials to conveniently stop and inspect for contraband before it is dispersed inside. A DOC rule also required employees to submit to a search or inspection of their persons, personal property or vehicle while entering, departing or otherwise on the premises of the institution. Accordingly, the Ionscan test was not unreasonable. Furthermore, the court concluded that a positive Ionscan test result constituted good reason to conduct further reasonable search procedures and could constitute reasonable suspicion. *Mitchell v. Dep't of Corrections*, 675 So.2d 162 (Fla. Dist. Ct. App. 1996).

♦ An Illinois university police officer was accused of gambling while on duty, in violation of the orders of the chief of police. During an investigation of the accusation, a hidden video camera was installed to observe the officer. University officials observed the officer playing poker in the office, and he was discharged. An Illinois circuit court upheld the discharge, and the officer appealed to the Appellate Court of Illinois. On appeal, the officer argued that the videotape should not have been allowed into evidence since no search warrant had been obtained. The officer argued that he had a reasonable expectation of privacy in the police department office and so a warrantless search violated his Fourth Amendment right against unreasonable search and seizure. The court stated that the Fourth Amendment prohibits only unreasonable intrusions. The issue was whether the officer exhibited an expectation of privacy and whether society was ready to recognize that expectation as reasonable. **Although the officer exhibited an intention to keep his activities private, the court did not believe that expectation was reasonable. The office under surveillance was used by all officers and was not a private office.** The search was not unreasonable, and the discharge was affirmed. *Thornton v. Univ. Civil Service Merit Board,* 507 N.E.2d 1262 (Ill. App. Ct. 1987).

♦ The estranged wife of a California state employee called the employee's supervisor to report that her husband was bringing home things that she thought were state property. A security officer was assigned to investigate the report. With the aid of the local sheriff's office, the security officer and the wife then broke into the husband's home. The wife led the officer through the house, identifying things taken from the husband's employer. The officer seized the items. At a criminal hearing, the search of the house was held to be illegal, the evidence was suppressed, and the criminal charges were dismissed. The state began disciplinary proceedings against the employee, utilizing the evidence gained in the illegal search. A court upheld the dismissal. The employee appealed to the California Court of Appeal, **arguing that illegally seized evidence should not have been allowed in the disciplinary hearings**. The court agreed, holding that there was no justification for admitting the evidence here. The deterrent effect of the exclusionary rule would be undermined by allowing its use. Also, since the illegality of the search already had been determined at the criminal trial, the state would not be allowed to deny its illegality in the disciplinary proceedings. *Dyson v. California State Personnel Board,* 262 Cal.Rptr. 112 (Cal. Ct. App. 1989).

II. BLOOD AND DRUG TESTING

It is undisputed that compulsory urinalysis or blood testing of public sector employees qualifies as a "search and seizure" within the meaning of the Fourth Amendment. This is true whether or not the urinalysis procedures involve direct visual inspection of urination.

In Shoemaker v. Handel, *795 F.2d 1136 (3d Cir. 1986), an early case on the subject of the "reasonableness" of mandatory drug testing, the U.S. Court of Appeals, Third Circuit, upheld the random drug testing by urinalysis of jockeys, trainers, groomers and race officials under the administrative search exception. Courts generally followed the* Shoemaker *decision only in employment areas involving security and public safety.*

More recently, in two cases decided on the same day, Skinner v. Railway Labor Executives' Ass'n *and* National Treasury Employees Union v. Von Raab *(see summaries below), the U.S. Supreme Court set out some general principles for determining the legitimacy of drug testing programs.*

Individualized suspicion of a particular employee is not necessary under the Constitution, nor does a drug problem need to be documented at a particular workplace. Rather, when the testing serves a special need beyond the scope of normal law enforcement, it is necessary to balance government interests against the individual's privacy expectations.

The Supreme Court has recognized at least three interests it feels are sufficiently compelling to justify a search of all employees: 1) maintaining workplace integrity; 2) enhancing public safety; and 3) protecting truly sensitive information.

A. Balancing Public and Individual Rights

◆ Railway labor organizations sued the U.S. Secretary of Transportation in a federal court for an order that would prevent enforcement of regulations under the Federal Railroad Safety Act of 1970. The regulations required testing after major train accidents and permitted railroads to administer breath or urine tests after serious incidents and where supervisors had reasonable suspicion from observing individual behavior. The court concluded that the public and governmental interest in safety outweighed the labor organization members' interest in privacy. The Ninth Circuit Court of Appeals held that the testing was unconstitutional. It reversed the district court decision, ruling that government action was not sufficient to implicate the Fourth Amendment for the permissive tests, and that the required tests failed to use particularized suspicion to confine the tests to actual detection of currently impaired employees.

The Supreme Court ruled that **private railroads acting with the government's encouragement in taking blood and urine samples were performing searches and seizures under the Fourth Amendment.** The appeals court had failed to balance the interests among the employers, employees and the public. The public interest was strong enough to constitute a "special need" beyond normal law enforcement and justified departure from the usual warrant and probable cause requirements. Obtaining a warrant was likely to frustrate the government effort to reveal drug use, and privacy interests were minimal. The Court reversed the appeals court and affirmed the district court's decision for the secretary. *Skinner v. Railway Labor Executives' Ass'n,* 489 U.S. 602, 109 S.Ct. 1402, 103 L.Ed.2d 639 (1989).

* U.S. Customs Service employees contested the service's right to implement a drug testing program for employees seeking transfer or promotion to some positions. Employees seeking jobs requiring direct involvement in drug interdiction and enforcement, use of firearms, or handling of classified material were to be tested under the program. The employees' union sued the customs service in a federal court, claiming that the testing program violated the Fourth Amendment. The court ruled in the employees' favor, but the Fifth Circuit vacated the lower court's order prohibiting enforcement of the testing program. The union appealed to the U.S. Supreme Court, which followed the *Skinner* case, above, in finding that the taking of urine constituted a search or seizure under the Constitution. The customs service testing program served a special government need beyond normal law enforcement. The program was designed to deter drug use among persons eligible for sensitive positions. **The special need to keep drug abusers from these positions justified departure from the usual warrant and probable cause requirements.** The government's need to conduct searches without reasonable suspicion outweighed the privacy interest for employees engaged in drug interdiction and for employees required to carry firearms. However, the record was insufficient to assess the government's reasonable interest in testing employees required to handle classified material. Accordingly, the Court affirmed the appeals court decision in part and remanded the case for a determination of the necessity to test employees who handled classified material. *National Treasury Employees Union v. Von Raab,* 489 U.S. 656, 109 S.Ct. 1384, 103 L.Ed.2d 685 (1989).

1. Assertions of Overbroad Policies

* The Georgia Legislature enacted a statute requiring certain candidates for state office to certify that they had taken a urinalysis drug test and that the result was negative. Anyone who declined to take the test, or who tested positive, was barred from holding office. Testing could, at the option of the candidate, be performed at an approved medical testing laboratory or at the office of the candidate's physician. The test was designed to reveal the presence or absence

of five illegal drugs. Libertarian Party candidates challenged the statute in a federal court, alleging violations of their constitutional rights. The court held for the state, and the Eleventh Circuit affirmed. The U.S. Supreme Court granted review. To be reasonable under the Fourth Amendment, a search ordinarily must be based on individualized suspicion of wrongdoing. However, exceptions based on "special needs" are sometimes warranted. Here, the Court found that **there was no special need to justify the drug testing**. The state did not assert any evidence of a drug problem among its elected officials; those officials do not perform high-risk, safety-sensitive tasks; and the certification would not immediately aid an interdiction effort. Therefore, the Court reversed the lower courts' judgments. *Chandler v. Miller*, 520 U.S. 305, 117 S.Ct. 1295, 137 L.Ed.2d 513 (1997).

♦ For three years an Ohio sewer district contracted out its operations to a private company. A maintenance worker with the district passed a drug test and went to work for the contractor, then reapplied with the district when the contract expired. This time he tested positive for drugs and was discharged. He sued the district, challenging the drug test as unconstitutionally unreasonable. While his lawsuit was pending, he applied for two other district positions he was qualified for and passed the drug tests, but was not hired when the district reassigned two internal employees to the positions. An Ohio federal court ruled that the failed drug test was proper. He was already subject to random drug testing to maintain his commercial driver's license, and he had nearly two months' notice prior to the test he challenged as unreasonable. **Since he was technically not a public employee when he failed the pre-hire test, the test was reasonable.** *Fontaine v. Clermont County Board of Commissioners*, 2007 WL 2627338 (S.D. Ohio 9/6/07).

♦ Two federal criminal investigators were authorized to carry firearms and thus were subject to random drug urinalysis testing under the agency's Drug Free Workplace Plan. After testing negative, they brought a *Bivens* action against agency officials for violating their Fourth Amendment rights, asserting that the otherwise valid "special needs" drug test was made impermissible by the officials' use of the warrantless drug tests to gather evidence for criminal proceedings against them. [A *Bivens* action is a lawsuit for money damages against a federal official in his or her individual capacity for violation of the plaintiff's constitutional rights. The special needs exception to the warrant requirement involves a special governmental interest beyond the normal needs of law enforcement.] A federal court held that **the officials' use of the random drug testing procedure to obtain evidence for a criminal investigation violated the employees' Fourth Amendment rights**. However, the officials were entitled to immunity because the rights violated were not clearly established at the time of the violation. *Freeman v. Fallin*, 422 F.Supp.2d 53 (D.D.C. 2006).

♦ A New Mexico city had regulations that required drug testing of employees who held city operating permits. Employees who had to have such permits were those who were required to have commercial driver's licenses because they operated heavy vehicles. A city mechanic was subjected to a drug test under the regulations, despite the fact that he had not recently operated or worked on heavy vehicles. He was fired after he failed the test. The mechanic sued the city in a state trial court, alleging violations of his constitutional rights, among other claims. After a judgment was entered in the city's favor, the mechanic appealed to the Court of Appeals of New Mexico.

Although drug testing constitutes a search under the Fourth Amendment, suspicionless drug testing is allowed in certain circumstances concerning public safety. Moreover, federal regulations require drug testing of drivers of heavy vehicles. Authority also exists for suspicionless drug testing of vehicle mechanics because of safety issues. However, those issues did not apply here, since the justification for the drug test was not the mechanic's work on heavy vehicles, but his driving of such a vehicle. The court held that **the drug testing was unconstitutional because the mechanic had not worked on heavy vehicles for nine months and was not likely to be transferred to such an assignment in the future**. The city failed to show the need to test every city mechanic who might be qualified to work on heavy vehicles. The Constitution required more than mere speculation that the mechanic might be required to drive a heavy vehicle in the future. *Jaramillo v. City of Albuquerque,* 958 P.2d 1244 (N.M. Ct. App. 1998).

♦ A California city instituted a drug testing program that required all individuals conditionally offered new positions with the city and current employees approved for promotion to a new position to undergo urinalysis as part of a pre-placement medical examination. The program applied to all positions, without regard to whether the city had any basis for suspecting that a particular applicant currently abused drugs or alcohol. A taxpayer sued to enjoin further expenditure of public funds for the drug testing program. The court found that the city could not lawfully impose a drug testing requirement for all city positions in either the pre-employment or pre-promotion context, and concluded that the drug testing program was valid only for certain job categories. The court of appeal affirmed in part.

The Supreme Court of California concluded that the across-the-board drug testing program was invalid as applied to current employees conditionally approved for a promotion, but was valid as applied to job applicants. Pre-promotional drug testing for every promotion without regard to the nature of the position, is unconstitutional. Instead, the reasonableness of such testing turns upon the nature and duties of the position in question. Therefore, **the city's program imposing a drug testing requirement upon every current employee offered a promotion was unconstitutional**. In the pre-employment context, however, an employer has a significantly greater interest in conducting suspicionless drug testing. Furthermore, the imposition of a urinalysis drug testing requirement as part of a lawful pre-employment medical examination involves a lesser intrusion on reasonable expectations of privacy. As a result, the city's pre-employment drug testing program was constitutional. The lower court decision was reversed. *Loder v. City of Glendale, California,* 927 P.2d 1200 (Cal. 1997).

♦ The U.S. Department of Treasury **required public trust Internal Revenue Service employees to respond to a questionnaire disclosing information about their past illegal drug use**. Failure to answer the questionnaire subjected employees to removal or other adverse employment action. The department did not give its employees criminal use immunity for potentially incriminating responses. The National Treasury Employees Union challenged the use of the questionnaire in a Texas federal court, alleging that it violated its members' Fifth Amendment privilege and their constitutional right to privacy. The court held for the union and enjoined further questions about the employees' past illegal drug use. The department appealed to the Fifth Circuit, which stated that the union failed to show that at least one of the represented employees had sustained, or was in immediate danger of sustaining, some direct injury because of the drug-related questioning. Because the alleged injury was hypothetical, the union did not have standing to assert the Fifth Amendment claim. Next, none of the employees had a reasonable expectation of privacy. Given the importance the government attached to a drug-free society, its employees had a diminished expectation of privacy in their past drug and alcohol abuse being kept secret. Since the information collected in the questionnaire would not be disclosed to the public, it made only a minimal intrusion on the privacy of the employees. The union did not have standing to assert either constitutional claim. The court reversed the district court's decision. *National Treasury Employees Union v. Dep't of Treasury*, 25 F.3d 237 (5th Cir. 1994).

♦ A police officer was hired by the Honolulu police department and submitted to a pre-employment physical and urinalysis drug test. After the officer served for roughly two years, the department instituted an additional drug testing plan. The officer refused to be tested and was forced to surrender her badge and gun while reassigned to a desk job. The officer's challenge of the plan eventually reached the Hawaii Supreme Court. The court noted that **urinalysis was the only effective, and also the least restrictive, method of achieving the state's interest in attempting to ensure the public's safety**. The testing procedures in this case were narrowly tailored for this purpose and included safeguards for accuracy and against overdisclosure or use in a criminal trial. Additionally, random testing was allowed in order to ensure against off-duty drug use. This was found to be necessary to protect the integrity of the department and because the officer could be called upon at any time. The court upheld the plan. *McCloskey v. Honolulu Police Dep't*, 799 P.2d 953 (Haw. 1990).

2. Safety-Sensitive Positions

♦ Police and fire department unions in Anchorage sued the city, alleging that the city's suspicionless substance abuse testing policy was unconstitutional. The policy subjected police and fire department employees in safety-sensitive positions to suspicionless substance abuse testing in certain situations – upon job application, promotion, demotion, or transfer, and after a traffic accident – and at random. The case reached the Supreme Court of Alaska, which upheld the policy except for the random testing provision, which it decided violated the Alaska Constitution's prohibition against unreasonable searches and seizures.

The other situations fell within the "special needs" exception to the warrant and probable cause requirement. The degree of intrusion of such searches was not significant given the reasonable expectation of a loss of privacy that police officers and firefighters had by working in a heavily regulated field. Therefore, on application, promotion, demotion, transfer and after a traffic accident, the policy was justified. However, the city could not justify avoiding warrants or probable cause with respect to the more intrusive random searches. *Anchorage Police Dep't Employees Ass'n v. Municipality of Anchorage*, 24 P.3d 547 (Alaska 2001).

♦ An Indiana city adopted a policy of unannounced, random drug testing for employees who worked in "safety-sensitive" positions. A driver with the Streets and Sanitation Division who had previously tested positive for marijuana (and was suspended, then reinstated) refused to take the test and was fired. He sued under the Fourth Amendment, claiming that since he did not have a commercial driver's license and had never been in an accident, he could not be forced to take the test. The Seventh Circuit ruled for the city. Even though the collective bargaining agreement referred only to the federal transportation standards of safety sensitive, **the driver held a "safety-sensitive" position because he operated large vehicles and equipment** in the city around pedestrians and other vehicles. Thus, the random test served special governmental needs. Further, the driver had a diminished expectation of privacy because he had been tested before. *Krieg v. Seybold*, 481 F.3d 512 (7th Cir. 2007).

♦ The collective bargaining representative for police officers employed by the New Jersey Transit Corporation sought to prevent the police chief from continuing to implement and enforce a medical examination program that was compulsory for all transit police officers. The policy required all police officers to submit to a medical exam once a year to determine physical capability to perform the job. It also required the disclosure of medical history and blood and urine testing. A trial court dismissed the complaint, finding that the policy did not violate the state or federal constitutions, and appeal was taken to the Superior Court of New Jersey, Appellate Division. The appellate court held that **the physical examination was constitutional as an administrative search of a pervasively regulated industry** pursuant to a substantial government interest. Public safety justifications overrode the privacy concerns of the officers involved, and all results were kept confidential. The policy was constitutional. *New Jersey Transit PBA Local 304 v. New Jersey Transit Corp.*, 895 A.2d 472 (N.J. Super. Ct. App. Div. 2006).

♦ The Fresno Irrigation District implemented a new drug-free workplace program and **classified the position of construction and maintenance worker as safety sensitive**. This required those employees to undergo random drug testing. Before the testing was actually implemented, the district gave any employee who had a substance abuse problem a grace period of six months in which to obtain counseling and treatment without the risk of termination. After the grace period expired, any employee who tested positive for any amount of an illegal drug would be terminated.

In a random test administered soon after the grace period ended, an employee tested positive for drugs. After he was fired, he sued the district for violating his federal and state constitutional rights to privacy. A state trial judge found that the classification of his position as safety sensitive was improper and that the district violated his constitutional rights when it required him to undergo random testing. A jury then awarded the employee $240,000 in damages, and the district appealed. The California Court of Appeal reversed, noting that the employee's expectation of privacy was diminished by the six months' advance notice the district had provided to all employees. In addition, the drug test was conducted in as minimally intrusive a manner as possible, without direct monitoring. **Further, the district had an obligation to maintain a safe workplace that outweighed the employee's privacy interests.** The employee worked as part of a crew that climbed in and out of 10-foot trenches and crawled through water pipes in the trenches to replace damaged pipes. The employee operated power tools and heavy equipment in close proximity to his co-workers. He also stood watch while a co-worker was lowered into a trench. Among other things, the potential for injury from a collapsing pipe, gas fumes and from water and debris that had collected in the pipe was so severe, even the employee's expert witness called the job "extremely dangerous." *Smith v. Fresno Irrigation Dist.*, 84 Cal.Rptr.2d 775 (Cal. Ct. App. 1999).

♦ A Louisiana firefighter failed a random drug test when he tested positive for cocaine and marijuana in his urine. The department dismissed him pursuant to an internal policy calling for immediate termination from employment. The firefighter received both a disciplinary letter and a pre-termination notice regarding the dismissal. He admitted he had been using drugs, but stated that no disciplinary actions had ever been taken against him prior to this incident. The firefighter challenged his dismissal, but the Civil Service Commission ruled against him. He appealed to the Court of Appeal of Louisiana, arguing that the immediate termination policy was an attempt to supersede the civil service rule mandating that the appointing authority give deference and consideration to 11 enumerated factors. Therefore, he argued, the policy violated the law, and the disciplinary action taken against him was annullable. The court rejected this argument and held that **the mere presence of illegal drugs in the firefighter's system was sufficient to prove impairment that warranted dismissal. The firefighter position was a safety-sensitive position**, and the threat of such impairment represented an unacceptable risk to co-workers and to the general public. Moreover, the civil service rule allowed the appointing authority to take discretionary action that it deemed appropriate after giving deference and consideration to the 11 enumerated factors. More importantly, the rule specifically allowed consideration of the separate needs of a sensitive position. Thus, the firefighter had been appropriately dismissed. *Montegue v. City of New Orleans Fire Dep't*, 675 So.2d 810 (La. Ct. App. 1996).

♦ A New Mexico city ordinance stated that "safety-sensitive" employees, including firefighters, could be dismissed if they tested positive for drugs. After suffering personal and emotional problems, a firefighter referred himself to the city's Employee Health Center for an evaluation, where he was required to submit to a reasonable suspicion drug test. He allegedly diluted his first urine sample with tap water, and his second sample tested positive for marijuana. The fire chief conducted a pre-termination hearing and discharged the firefighter based on his positive drug test. The firefighter also received a post-termination grievance hearing, at which he was allowed to present evidence and to confront and examine adverse witnesses. After the Personnel Board upheld the discharge recommendation, the firefighter filed a 42 U.S.C. § 1983 lawsuit against the city, alleging Fourth Amendment and due process violations. The court granted pretrial judgment to the city, and the firefighter appealed.

The Tenth Circuit held that **the city had properly required the firefighter to submit to a reasonable suspicion drug test** and affirmed the lower court's holding on the Fourth Amendment claim. This holding was proper in light of the firefighter's employment in a safety-sensitive position, his self-referral to the health center, his warning to supervisors that he might become violent if provoked, and the city's knowledge that he had lost his temper while in uniform and had engaged in a public altercation with his girlfriend. The firefighter also had received due process. The city had provided the firefighter with pre-termination notice and a hearing. Also he had participated in the city's post-termination grievance process. The district court ruling was affirmed. *Saavedra v. City of Albuquerque*, 73 F.3d 1525 (10th Cir. 1996).

♦ The U.S. Secretary of Transportation announced a drug testing program for some transportation department employees. The testing was for unlawful drug use only and divided employees and applicants into seven categories depending on safety and security matters. Employees in positions having a direct impact on public health, safety or national security could be required to submit to random testing. Employees in this category include air traffic controllers, mechanics, inspectors and engineers involved in air, rail, highway and water transportation. The testing involved two separate tests, and employees who tested positive could insist on being retested. Employees with positive results would be assigned to non-safety or non-security duties but generally could not be removed from federal employment unless they tested positive a second time. A federal court upheld the program, and the employees' labor organization appealed to the U.S. Court of Appeals, District of Columbia Circuit.

The appeals court noted that **federal employee drug testing did not require a probable cause standard where the program tested only those employees whose jobs were directly related to public health and safety, protection of life and property, law enforcement or national security**. Here, over 94% of employees subject to random testing worked for the Federal Aviation Administration, and most were air traffic controllers. The government interest in protecting public safety was more compelling than employee privacy interests. The deterrent effect of random urinalysis was a reasonable means for detecting and preventing drug-related injuries. The district court had properly granted pretrial judgment to the transportation department. *American Federation of Government Employees v. Skinner,* 885 F.2d 884 (D.C. Cir. 1989).

♦ The Veterans Administration (VA) promulgated a drug testing plan for its employees. The plan provided for six different categories of drug testing:

random testing, reasonable suspicion testing, post-accident testing, follow-up testing, applicant testing, and voluntary testing. Several groups of employees sued the VA seeking to enjoin implementation of the plan. A federal court granted a preliminary injunction with respect to random, post-accident, and reasonable suspicion testing. The court then ruled on each category except voluntary and applicant testing. It stated that random testing was valid only when the government had an interest that outweighed the employees' interest and where there was a nexus between the duties in question and the nature of the feared violation. **"Safety-sensitive" positions, such as health care workers, police, guards, and firefighters, were therefore legitimately subject to random testing, while positions such as electrician, pipefitter, and welder were not.** The reasonable suspicion testing was valid only with respect to safety-sensitive positions because the VA's testing criteria were not confined to on-duty drug use. Further, the plan did not sufficiently limit the types of employee behavior that could give rise to drug testing. Post-accident testing was also invalid because it left the decision to initiate testing within the discretion of a supervisor. Finally, follow-up testing was legitimate because it was accomplished by a process of random selection. *American Federation of Government Employees v. Derwinski*, 777 F.Supp. 1493 (N.D. Cal. 1991).

♦ The federal Department of Transportation (DOT) implemented a plan that required extensive drug testing of employees involved in what the DOT felt were safety-sensitive positions. The plan required testing in many situations, including pre-employment, post-employment, random testing, and testing for reasonable cause. Two labor unions challenged the appropriateness and constitutionality of the plan. A California federal court ruled for the DOT, and the unions appealed. The Ninth Circuit Court of Appeals upheld the plan even though the DOT was unable to show a specific drug use problem among the employees to be tested. In fact, the employees pointed to the safety record as an argument against the need for the plan. The DOT argued that the plan protected against the potential for catastrophic harm to the public's safety. The court found this reasonable. The court also upheld the constitutionality of random testing. It balanced the employees' interest in privacy against the DOT's interest in public safety. Here, the **potential safety concerns led to diminished privacy expectations** even absent other regulations of the employees' functions. *I.B.E.W., Local 1245 v. Skinner*, 913 F.2d 1454 (9th Cir. 1990).

♦ A Michigan man applied for a county position involving the operation of riding lawnmowers on highway medians, the driving of a variety of trucks, and the use of saws, wood chippers and front end loaders. The applicant underwent a pre-employment drug test after signing a questionnaire indicating that he had not taken prescription medication within the last month. He also signed a medical examination form, which stated that he was "not taking any medication at the present time." The applicant began working as a provisional employee but was discharged after he tested positive for opiates and cocaine. He filed suit against the county in a Michigan trial court, alleging that the drug test violated his constitutional rights. The case reached the Supreme Court of Michigan, which noted that **several courts have held pre-employment drug tests to be** warranted for positions involving the operation of heavy machinery or motor vehicles, during which a momentary lapse of attention could have disastrous results. Here, the court held that the applicant's specialized duties involving the operation of lawnmowers and mechanical equipment on or near public roadways could not be analogized to "vehicle use by the general public." The risks inherent in the job outweighed the applicant's privacy rights. *Middlebrooks v. Wayne County*, 521 N.W.2d 774 (Mich. 1994).

3. Random Testing

♦ City street and sanitation department employees sued the city alleging that its random drug testing policy violated the Fourth Amendment. They also claimed that the firing of an employee for refusing to take the random test violated his due process rights. An Indiana federal court ruled that **the employees were bound by the union's consent to random drug testing** even if they were not required to possess commercial driver's licenses. The employees were aware of the current bargaining agreement permitting the random testing. Also, the employee who was fired had no due process property interest in his job because he was an at-will employee. Further, he chose not to attend a board of public works meeting at which his termination was to be discussed. The policy was constitutional, and the employee was properly fired. *Krieg v. Seybold*, 427 F.Supp.2d 842 (N.D. Ind. 2006).

♦ The Michigan Civil Service Commission adopted a drug and alcohol testing program for probation and parole officers; corrections or community health department employees who had regular unsupervised access to prisoners; psychologists, nurses, occupational therapists and social workers who provided health care services to prisoners; and employees who provided health care to the mentally ill and developmentally disabled in state hospitals and veterans' homes. A union challenged the program under the Fourth Amendment and lost. The Sixth Circuit upheld the drug and alcohol testing program because **the state had a special public safety need** that outweighed the employees' constitutionally protected right to be free of unreasonable searches. It did not matter that there was no evidence of an existing drug abuse problem. The testing was random, only 15% of the affected work force was tested each year, and employees could close and lock the bathroom door while the specimen collector stayed outside. *Int'l Union v. Winters*, 385 F.3d 1003 (6th Cir. 2004).

♦ An Arizona city instituted a comprehensive drug testing program for its firefighters that included reasonable suspicion testing after an accident, return-to-duty testing and random testing. A firefighter sued challenging the random testing practice as a violation of the Fourth Amendment. The Arizona Supreme Court struck down the practice, noting that Fourth Amendment searches require some showing of "individualized suspicion." Here, there was no evidence of even a single instance of drug use, or that firefighters had consented to the practice, and there was no evidence that the other components of the drug testing program failed to deter drug use. Unlike *National Treasury Employees Union v. Von Raab*, 489 U.S. 656 (1989), where the U.S. Supreme Court held that customs agents could be randomly tested, the firefighters here were not involved with drug interdiction, did not carry firearms, and did not have to use deadly force in the regular course of their duties. **The random testing practice was an unreasonable search.** *Petersen v. City of Mesa*, 83 P.3d 35 (Ariz. 2004).

• An employee of a New Jersey city's department of public works who held a commercial driver's license was ordered to submit to a random drug test but was unable to produce a sample, allegedly because of direct observation. The city rejected his offer to take another drug test the following day. He was suspended without pay and eventually fired for insubordination, and this decision was affirmed by the merit system board. The employee appealed to the New Jersey Superior Court, Appellate Division, which found that **given the safety-sensitive position of the employee, random drug testing did not violate the Fourth Amendment**. Instead, the main issue of focus was the manner in which the drug testing was conducted. The city did not precede the testing with the adoption and dissemination of a detailed, written testing policy or give notice as required by the regulations. Furthermore, the city failed to have a licensed medical professional or a properly trained technician at the testing site. Finally, the city failed to follow the strict rules regarding direct observation. Because the drug testing was done without the benefit of an acceptable and complying protocol, it was constitutionally defective. The decision of the merit system board was reversed. *Reames v. Dep't of Public Works*, 707 A.2d 1377 (N.J. Super. Ct. App. Div. 1998).

• Under the authority of the Omnibus Transportation Employee Testing Act of 1991, the Federal Highway Administration promulgated rules governing drug and alcohol testing of drivers who hold a commercial driver's license (CDL). A Massachusetts town, pursuant to the act, created a controlled substance and alcohol use testing policy for the town's drivers holding CDLs. The policy included random testing of employees who drove town-owned commercial vehicles. Although the vehicles were mainly used for transportation within the town limits, they occasionally traveled out of state for various purposes. Several public works department employees sued the town, challenging the validity of the policy, including a 42 U.S.C. § 1983 claim that the policy violated the Fourth Amendment. A federal court held that the Section 1983 claim failed because the policy did not violate the Fourth Amendment. Although the intrusion upon the security and privacy of the employees was substantial, a governmental interest in drug and alcohol testing outweighed their individual interests. **Deterrence of drug and alcohol use by commercial drivers was the primary objective of the random drug testing provisions.** And random testing was the most effective deterrent to drug and alcohol use. Therefore, the random drug testing provisions did not violate the Fourth Amendment. The court also found that the act preempted the other claims. *Keaveney v. Town of Brookline*, 937 F.Supp. 975 (D. Mass. 1996).

• A New York county police department authorized a random drug testing program for the 100 members of the special narcotics enforcement unit. Each month 10 of the 100 members were tested at random. Selection of a member in one month did not result in the removal of that member from the selection process for subsequent months. The county police benevolent association sued to prohibit the department from implementing the drug testing program, which it alleged would be impermissibly intrusive. A trial court dismissed the case, but the appellate division reversed, holding that the plan was "unreasonably intrusive." The Court of Appeals of New York reversed the appellate division and upheld the random drug testing program. The association admitted that **a compelling state interest would be achieved by a random drug testing plan** and that police officers might have a diminished expectation of privacy. Here, there were sufficient procedural safeguards to ensure that the officers were not subject to "unregulated discretion." Nor was an individual officer's maximum exposure to drug tests (12 times per year) sufficiently intrusive to warrant invalidation of the program. Also, the officers were part of an elite corps of volunteer officers subject to extraordinary scrutiny. *Delaraba v. Nassau County Police Dep't*, 610 N.Y.S.2d 928 (N.Y. 1994).

♦   The Department of Health and Human Services developed a "Drug Free Workplace Plan," whereby certain employees would be randomly tested for drugs. Two unions representing non-passenger motor vehicle carriers sought an injunction prohibiting this drug testing procedure in a federal district court. Both the department and the unions moved for pretrial judgment. The U.S. District Court, District of Columbia, stated that the justification of random drug tests required individualized suspicion or that the government's interest outweighed the individual's privacy rights. Here, **there were neither safety concerns for passengers nor security concerns for the U.S. government**. Thus, there was not a legitimate government interest that outweighed the union workers' privacy interests. The district court granted the union's motion for pretrial judgment and an injunction against the random drug test. *American Federation of Government Employees v. Sullivan*, 787 F.Supp. 255 (D.D.C. 1992).

♦   The police commissioner of Boston issued a rule authorizing drug testing of police officers on both a reasonable suspicion and random basis. A police officer sued, claiming that the random urinalysis portion of the rule violated article 14 of the Massachusetts Declaration of Rights. A superior court judge ruled that the random urinalysis provision of the rule did not violate article 14. The Supreme Judicial Court of Massachusetts granted direct appellate review. The court stated that even though claims brought under the Fourth Amendment were generally foreclosed by *National Treasury Employees Union v. Von Raab*, constitutional claims based on article 14 were still viable. The court held that the rule violated article 14 and was unconstitutional. The court stated that **the commissioner had not demonstrated that conditions warranted random drug tests**. There was no indication of a drug problem in the Boston police department. The government needed to show a concrete, substantial governmental interest that would be served by imposing random urinalysis on unconsenting citizens. This it failed to do. *Guiney v. Police Commissioner of Boston*, 582 N.E.2d 523 (Mass. 1991).

♦   An executive order required the head of each executive federal agency to establish a program to test for the use of illegal drugs by employees in sensitive positions. The Department of Justice (DOJ) implemented a plan that subjected five categories of DOJ employees to random drug testing. Possible penalties ranged from reprimand to dismissal, and always resulted in removal from any sensitive position. A group of DOJ employees challenged the rule as unreasonable under the Fourth Amendment since there was "no nexus between fitness for duty, security and integrity on the one hand, and compulsory random urinalysis drug testing on the other, where no drug problem is believed to exist." A federal district court enjoined the implementation of the tests on this basis, and the DOJ appealed to the U.S. Court of Appeals, D.C. Circuit.

The court of appeals stated that, in this case, **maintaining the integrity of the work force was an insufficient interest to support the random testing**. There was no nexus between the nature of the employees' duties and any feared drug violation, whereas in *Von Raab* the tested employees were those involved in drug interdiction. Federal employment alone does not justify such a test. The Court of appeals also stated that the public safety rationale adopted in *Von Raab* and *Skinner* focused on the immediacy of the threat. No such immediacy was apparent here. The court also held that the government's interest in protecting sensitive information was sufficient to support the testing, but only with respect to those DOJ employees with access to top-secret national security information. The court of appeals affirmed the injunction with respect to the remaining employees. *Harmon v. Thornburgh,* 878 F.2d 484 (D.C. Cir. 1989).

♦ The New York Correctional Department issued a departmental directive that required two additional random drug tests to be conducted during an employee's 18-month probationary term. The departmental statistics showed that a steady percentage of officers tested positive for drug use from 1986 to 1988 despite advance warning of the test. The Corrections Officers Benevolent Association of the City of New York brought suit alleging that the two additional random drug tests were unconstitutional. A trial court dismissed the case, and the Appellate Division affirmed, finding that **the random tests were supported by a substantial governmental interest and did not constitute unreasonable searches and seizures or a violation of the right to privacy**. Since the petitioners already were required to submit to drug tests, they had a lower expectation of privacy with respect to the two additional tests. The union then appealed to the Court of Appeals of New York, which upheld the random drug tests as constitutional. The state's interest in keeping its prison guards drug free was high. Further, other methods adopted by the correction department failed to adequately address the growing drug problem among the prison guards. *Seelig v. Koehler,* 556 N.E.2d 125 (N.Y. 1990).

4. Direct Observation

♦ A corrections officer at a medium-security facility in St. Louis was subject to random drug testing and, if the test was positive, dismissal. The city contracted with a health services company for assistance with the drug testing process. When the employee was selected for a drug test, a female employee of the health services company stood to his back outside the stall while he provided the urine specimen. It tested positive for marijuana, and he was fired.

After a civil service commission upheld the firing, the officer sued the city for violating his Fourth Amendment rights. A Missouri federal court held that the search was reasonable and that the city's need to conduct it outweighed his privacy rights. The Eighth Circuit affirmed. **The employee's privacy rights were not violated by the presence of a female monitor.** Since the manner of the collection was not so intrusive as to constitute an unreasonable search, there was no Fourth Amendment violation. *Booker v. City of St. Louis*, 309 F.3d 464 (8th Cir. 2002).

♦ Pursuant to a collective bargaining agreement (CBA) between a Delaware city and the firefighters' union, the firefighters agreed to random drug testing. A private company conducted the testing, requiring the firefighters to produce a urine sample under the direct observation of authorized monitors. Although the monitors were directed only to observe the collection process and not focus on the firefighters' genitals, **the firefighters alleged that the monitors looked at their genitals as they produced samples.** The union filed a grievance with the city, protesting the direct observation method, which the city denied. The union sued the city in the U.S. District Court for the District of Delaware, alleging a violation of the Fourth Amendment. The court found that the direct observation method did not violate the firefighters' Fourth Amendment rights. The firefighters appealed to the U.S. Court of Appeals, Third Circuit, which focused on whether the direct observation method was unreasonable by considering the nature of the firefighters' privacy interests, the character of the search, and the governmental concern. Here, the firefighters held a diminished expectation of privacy because they were in a highly regulated industry and had previously agreed to random drug testing in their CBA. **Although direct observation significantly intruded on the firefighters' privacy, given the reality of exposed urinals in public restrooms, there was not significant intrusion upon the male firefighters' privacy.** Even though the female firefighters' privacy was significantly intruded upon, the company had taken steps to minimize the intrusion, and the testing procedure was appropriate. Finally, the direct observation method served the government's compelling interest in preserving the integrity of its drug tests, which outweighed the firefighters' expectations of privacy. The lower court's judgment was affirmed. *Wilcher v. City of Wilmington*, 139 F.3d 366 (3d Cir. 1998).

♦ A female correctional officer employed by the California Department of Corrections signed an agreement requiring her to submit to one year of random drug testing after she admitted smoking marijuana. The agreement was subject to the guidelines set forth in the collective bargaining agreement (CBA). During CBA negotiations, the union had objected to visual observation during drug testing and had never expressly agreed to it. The employee tested negative on five occasions. Each time, a female monitor was assigned to observe her while she was urinating. In a preliminary action filed by the officer, the U.S. District Court for the Northern District of California granted her request for a temporary restraining order preventing further visual observations. The court then considered the officer's claims against the department, in which she alleged that the visual observation violated her state and federal constitutional rights.

The court noted that given the doctrinal trends evident in cases such as *Piroglu v. Coleman*, below, it was likely that most federal courts would eventually find that the Fourth Amendment prohibits direct observations absent a reasonable suspicion of an intent to tamper with the sample. However, because the officer's privacy right was not clearly established, the individual defendants were entitled to pretrial judgment based on qualified immunity on the Fourth Amendment claim. Nevertheless, because **there were less intrusive means to prevent sample tampering – preventing access to water, requiring positive identification of subjects, requiring the removal of outer garments, and measuring the temperature of the sample** – and because the alternative means would cause substantially less harm to the plaintiff's privacy interests than direct observations, the court held that the drug tests violated her right to privacy under the California Constitution. *Hansen v. California Dep't of Corrections*, 920 F.Supp. 1480 (N.D. Cal. 1996).

* A probationary emergency medical technician (EMT) for the District of Columbia Fire Department was notified prior to the four-week mandatory training course that she was subject to an unscheduled drug test. Near the end of the training course, she was ordered to urinate into a bottle, allegedly in the presence of two female observers. The employee alleged that they watched her urinate into the bottle. The district alleged that the observers watched the employee but did not observe the passage of urine into the bottle. Because the first specimen felt cold, the observers ordered the employee to produce a second sample. The second sample tested positive for cocaine. Based on this positive result, the employee was discharged for failure to successfully complete her probationary period. The employee sued the department, alleging violations of her Fourth and Fifth Amendment rights. The district court granted pretrial judgment to the department, and the employee appealed to the U.S. Court of Appeals, District of Columbia Circuit.

The court of appeals remanded the employee's Fourth Amendment claim, stating that the department's visual observation of the employee's act of urination may have been an unreasonable search and seizure. **If the observation was unobstructed and complete and without reasonable suspicion that the employee had tampered with her urine sample, the collection was unreasonable under the Fourth Amendment.** Conversely, it was reasonable if the department did not have the employee in plain sight during the collection of the first sample. However, even if the department violated the employee's Fourth Amendment rights, her remedy was one for damages, not reinstatement. Next, the court held that the department's strong interest in testing trainees without a warrant outweighed the employee's privacy rights. Further, the advance notice and the uniform nature of the drug test sufficiently decreased the employee's expectation of privacy, even absent authorizing regulations. Finally, since probationary employees had no property interest in their employment, the court dismissed the employee's Fifth Amendment claim. *Piroglu v. Coleman*, 25 F.3d 1098 (D.C. Cir. 1994).

* A Mississippi hospital instituted a mandatory drug testing program. All employees were given advance notice of the test and were required to give

written permission for the procedure. The hospital's testing procedure required the subjects to completely disrobe behind a privacy screen, put on a hospital gown and provide a specimen in an enclosed room. The subjects were not observed while providing the specimen. A scrub technician refused to disrobe, but stated that she would allow a staff member to observe her while she provided a specimen. The testing staff was not authorized to deviate from the established procedure and refused to make accommodation. The scrub technician was fired for failing to participate in the test. She sued the hospital, claiming that the test constituted an unreasonable search and seizure in violation of the Fourth Amendment.

The U.S. Supreme Court has established requirements to limit the intrusiveness of a testing procedure. They are: 1) that the testing be conducted in a medical environment; 2) that the collection be done by medical personnel; 3) that the procedures be similar to those required for regular physical examinations; and 4) that there is no requirement that the test monitor observe the employee while producing the sample. The procedures used by the hospital met all of these requirements. **Although the alternative requested by the scrub technician was more intrusive than the procedures used by the hospital, the hospital was justified in refusing this accommodation.** The court ruled for the hospital. *Kemp v. Clairborne County Hospital,* 763 F.Supp. 1362 (S.D. Miss. 1991).

5. Post-Accident Testing

♦ A firefighter employed by the White Plains, New York, Fire Department was involved in an accident while driving his car off duty. A police officer arrived on the scene and observed that the firefighter was "incoherent and smelled of alcohol." He was then charged with driving while intoxicated and was asked to submit to a urinalysis. The firefighter refused. When the fire chief heard of the accident, he ordered the firefighter to participate in a urinalysis or be suspended. The urinalysis revealed that he had smoked marijuana. As a result, the firefighter was discharged following an administrative hearing. He appealed to the New York Supreme Court, Appellate Division, contending that the urinalysis was an illegal search because no reasonable suspicion existed that he had used illegal drugs. The appellate division disagreed, holding that **the important government interest in protecting the public outweighed the firefighter's minimal privacy interests. Further, the serious car accident was deemed a "triggering event."** As an employee in a safety-sensitive position, his involvement in such a "triggering event" required that the fire chief test him for drugs, and no individualized suspicion was needed. Thus, given the accident, the officer's observation that the firefighter smelled of alcohol at the scene of the accident, and his initial refusal to submit to a urinalysis, the fire chief reasonably suspected that the firefighter used drugs. The termination was upheld. *Longo v. Dolce,* 600 N.Y.S.2d 962 (N.Y. App. Div. 1993).

♦ A bus driver for the Greater Cleveland Regional Transit Authority (CRTA) rear-ended an automobile. CRTA's drug testing policy mandates post-accident testing, and the employee tested positive for marijuana. The employee agreed to be suspended for 30 days and to submit to future testing. Following his reinstatement, the employee again tested positive in a routine scheduled physical. He was then fired. The employee filed a lawsuit in a federal district court alleging numerous violations of his rights. The issue was later determined to be whether the drug testing procedures violated the employee's right to privacy. CRTA moved for pretrial judgment. The court explained that although drug testing constitutes a search for Fourth Amendment privacy purposes, **a warrant is not needed when: 1) there is little discretion involved in invoking a test; 2) it is used for administrative purposes only, and 3) a warrant requirement would add little to the protection of privacy interests**. An important factor in weighing the government's interest is the possibility for disastrous consequences that could result from a momentary lapse of attention. Here, there was medical testimony that the use of marijuana might have "residual impairment effects" on a driver. Further, the employee was aware of the upcoming test, and the testing procedures minimized the intrusion to the employee's privacy. The policy did not violate the employee's privacy rights. CRTA was granted pretrial judgment. *Holloman v. Greater Cleveland Regional Transit Authority,* 741 F.Supp. 677 (N.D. Ohio 1990).

♦ Two New Orleans police officers stopped an off-duty firefighter after they observed him disobeying traffic laws. The firefighter became combative and cursed the officers when he was asked to exit his vehicle. His superior was called to the scene and apprised of the firefighter's reckless driving and belligerent attitude. Based on this information, the fire chief ordered the firefighter to take a drug test. After the sample tested positive for cocaine, he was notified of the charges against him and then discharged following a pre-termination hearing. The firefighter appealed his discharge to the City Civil Service Commission. The commission dismissed the appeal, and the firefighter appealed to the Court of Appeal of Louisiana.

The court of appeal held that **the department had reasonable suspicion to test the firefighter for substance abuse. Information from law enforcement officials was inherently reliable.** Here, the officers had stopped the firefighter for traffic violations, observed his belligerent attitude and then determined that he was "on something." Next, the court held that the firefighter had received sufficient notice and an adequate pre-termination hearing during which he was able to respond to the charges. Consequently, he had been afforded due process. Finally, the court determined that testimony from several witnesses established an unbroken chain of custody. The firefighter failed to produce evidence that his sample was tampered with, lost or not the one tested. The court upheld the commission's discharge based on the positive drug test. *George v. Dep't of Fire,* 637 So.2d 1097 (La. Ct. App. 1994).

B. Standards for Reasonable Suspicion

♦ A Kentucky county allowed reasonable suspicion drug testing where a supervisor's direct observation of an employee led the supervisor to believe the employee was under the influence of drugs or alcohol. An employee was arrested for drug possession and his supervisor found out about it. He was suspended for 5 days and ordered to take a drug test, but refused to do so. In lieu of termination, he agreed to participate in an employee assistance program (EAP), then tested positive for illegal narcotics. He resigned, then sued under 42 U.S.C. § 1983, claiming the drug testing and mandatory participation in the EAP violated his Fourth Amendment rights. A federal court and the Sixth Circuit ruled against him. **Even though learning of the arrest was not direct observation of the employee, it constituted reasonable cause to justify the drug test** and his participation in the EAP. *Relford v. Lexington-Fayette Urban County Government*, 390 F.3d 452 (6th Cir. 2004).

1. Police Officers and Firefighters

◆ Two Louisiana police officers also worked security at a nightclub. A fellow nightclub employee told one of the officers that his roommate had a large amount of marijuana in their apartment. The officer notified his superiors, who obtained a search warrant for the apartment. The second officer who worked at the club allegedly helped lure the roommate back to the apartment, where drugs and steroids were found. In the aftermath of the raid, the officers were subjected to reasonable suspicion drug testing, during which the second officer and another police officer tested positive for steroids. They were fired. The second officer appealed, claiming that reasonable suspicion did not exist for the drug test. The Louisiana Court of Appeal agreed. **The procedure manual listed the ways reasonable suspicion could exist, and they all involved either suspicious behavior, possession of drugs or a reliable tip, none of which were present here.** Thus, the second officer should not have been tested and was entitled to reinstatement. *Richard v. Lafayette Fire and Police Civil Service Board*, 983 So.2d 195 (La. Ct. App. 2008).

◆ During a drug investigation, a narcotics detective patted down a suspected dealer and observed what he believed were several packets of heroin. He arrested the suspect. When they arrived back at the station, the suspect told him the packets had fallen from the suspect's pants and another officer had picked them up, telling the suspect not to mention that to anyone. As a result of that information, the New Orleans Police Department obtained a warrant to search the officer's home and car, where they found cocaine residue on a cellophane wrapper in the glove compartment. The officer was ordered to undergo a reasonable suspicion drug test, which came back positive for cocaine. He was suspended, then fired. He sued, **claiming that the cocaine residue found in his car was not sufficiently suspicious to require him to take a drug test**. The Louisiana Court of Appeal disagreed. Since the standard necessary was only "reasonable suspicion," the department had sufficient justification for ordering the drug test. The termination was upheld. *Razor v. New Orleans Dep't of Police*, 926 So.2d 1 (La. Ct. App. 2006).

◆ **A Maryland police officer, as a condition of being hired, signed a drug testing waiver in which he agreed that he could be tested at any time for drugs.** Several years later, the officer went to the hospital complaining of a tightness in his chest. He was released and finished his shift, but upon seeing the department's doctor, was placed on disability for three days and told to return for a follow-up visit. Before returning for the second visit, the chief of police received a tip that the officer was using drugs. He ordered the department's doctor to obtain a urine sample from the officer, and told the doctor that he did not need to inform the officer that his urine was going to be tested for drugs. When the results came back positive, the officer was suspended and later fired. He sued, claiming that the department had violated his Fourth Amendment rights by subjecting him to an unconstitutional drug testing policy. A federal court held that the city's drug testing policy was constitutional and that it had a right to conduct random drug searches. Moreover, based on the tip, the chief had a reasonable individualized suspicion that the officer was using drugs. Finally, **the test was not unconstitutional just because the officer wasn't told that his sample was going to be tested for drugs**. *Carroll v. City of Westminster*, 52 F.Supp.2d 546 (D. Md. 1999).

- A New Jersey police officer was observed sitting in his car with a passenger, holding a vial of cocaine, and exchanging money with a passerby. When narcotics squad officers arrived at the scene, the officer threw one of the vials to the sidewalk, and his passenger dropped two others on the car floor. The officer was the only one with money in his hand at this time. Pursuant to department drug screening guidelines, the head of the narcotics squad ordered the officer to submit to a drug test. The officer refused after telling the vice president of his union that he doubted that he could pass the test. The department denied the officer's request for an attorney. In a related criminal proceeding, the officer was acquitted. The department fired the officer for insubordination pursuant to a disciplinary proceeding at which the union vice president was required to testify regarding his conversation with the officer. The appellate division affirmed the dismissal.

  The Supreme Court of New Jersey determined that individualized reasonable suspicion, not probable cause, was required to justify a drug test. **Given the officer's possession of the vial of cocaine and the subsequent exchange of money, the department reasonably suspected that the officer used drugs.** Next, the court determined that the drug test did not violate the officer's Fifth Amendment right against self-incrimination. The officer had not been confused by the "perceived inconsistency between the *Miranda* warnings and the direction to take the drug test." Rather, he refused to take the test because he was afraid he would not pass it. Finally, the union vice president was not an attorney bound by the attorney-client privilege and could therefore be compelled to disclose the incriminating conversation. The dismissal was affirmed. *Rawlings v. Police Dep't of Jersey City*, 627 A.2d 602 (N.J. 1993).

- An officer with the Los Angeles Police Department (LAPD) was being investigated by the Internal Affairs Division (IAD). While off duty, he was seen at two different times with another officer from the same station. One afternoon, the officers were seen at two apartments known to be the sites of narcotics and drug sales. The officer under investigation was seen entering both buildings. Later that month, the two officers were seen drinking beer in a park. The officer being investigated returned to one of the apartment buildings alone. The IAD took the officer into custody, searched his car, and found some tinfoil (often used as packaging for cocaine). The IAD captain then ordered the other officer to provide a urine sample while under observation. He refused to comply with this order and was suspended for insubordination. After a grievance proceeding, the arbitrator found that the requested urinalysis was not authorized. The LAPD reinstated the officer with full benefits and back pay. The officer then filed suit against the LAPD seeking damages for alleged violations of his Fourth Amendment rights. A district court found for the officer and awarded him $154,747. The department appealed to the U.S. Court of Appeals, Ninth Circuit.

Subject to certain exceptions, a drug test is reasonable only where a warrant has issued upon probable cause or where there is individualized suspicion. Here, **the officer was arbitrarily singled out because of his association with the officer under investigation by the IAD**. The government had no compelling interest beyond law enforcement to justify the drug test. Further, the drug tests were not randomly administered pursuant to a department-wide policy. Thus, suspending the officer for refusing to submit to the drug test was a violation of the officer's Fourth Amendment rights. The district court decision was affirmed. *Jackson v. Gates,* 975 F.2d 648 (9th Cir. 1992).

2. Corrections Officers and Court Employees

♦ The Colorado Department of Corrections (DOC) maintained a formal policy of random drug testing of employees; however, the DOC's actual practice was to conduct tests solely on the basis of reasonable suspicion. Based upon information received from anonymous sources concerning two correctional officers' off-duty use of illegal drugs, the warden of a correctional facility requested that they submit to urinalysis. The officers tested positive for marijuana, admitted using marijuana, and were fired. On appeal, an administrative law judge (ALJ) determined that the DOC lacked reasonable suspicion to test the officers. Therefore, the testing had violated the DOC's established policy and the officers' Fourth Amendment rights. The ALJ concluded, however, that there was no basis for exclusion of the evidence or the officers' admissions despite the unlawful test request. The State Personnel Board ordered reinstatement, and the DOC appealed.

The Colorado Court of Appeals noted that **the officers were not tested pursuant to the DOC's formal policy of random drug testing, and the allegations of the officers' drug use did not rise to the level of reasonable suspicion** as established by objective and credible evidence; therefore, the test request was unlawful. However, the court vacated the order reinstating the officers and remanded the case for a determination of whether the evidence should be excluded from the civil proceedings against them. *Ahart v. Dep't of Corrections,* 943 P.2d 7 (Colo. Ct. App. 1996).

♦ The Federal Bureau of Prisons initiated a drug testing program pursuant to a 1986 executive order that required all employees in sensitive positions to be tested. The program provided for drug testing on reasonable suspicion of all employees and random drug tests for employees within correctional institutions. The American Federation of Government Employees sought to enjoin the use of the program in a U.S. district court. The district court partially enjoined certain reasonable suspicion drug tests and extensively restricted the scope of the random drug testing program. The bureau appealed to the U.S. Court of Appeals, Ninth Circuit. **The bureau contended that its employees within correctional institutions should be subject to random drug testing and that all bureau employees should be subject to reasonable suspicion drug testing.** The court of appeals agreed, noting the connection between correctional employee drug use and the smuggling of drugs into federal prisons. Given this connection and the correctional employees' reduced expectations of privacy, random drug testing of these employees was constitutional. The court also determined that all bureau employees would be subject to reasonable suspicion drug tests. The district court order was reversed in part. *American Federation of Government Employees v. Roberts,* 9 F.3d 1464 (9th Cir. 1993).

* Four officers employed by a New Jersey county were assigned to perform guard duty on the eighth floor of the county jail. The officers and an occasional nurse or workman were the only ones with access to a bathroom adjoining the sub-control room. A confidential informant reported an odor of marijuana in the bathroom to supervisory authorities. The warden ordered all four officers to submit to a drug test. After a positive result, one of the officers was fired. A New Jersey Department of Personnel policy provided that urine samples would be ordered if there was "individualized reasonable suspicion" to believe that an employee might be under the influence of an illegal drug, and employees who tested positive for drugs would be fired. On appeal by the officer, an administrative law judge concluded that the county did not have "individualized reasonable suspicion," but the Merit Systems Protection Board reversed and held for the county. The Superior Court of New Jersey, Appellate Division, noted that public agencies are required to abide by their own policies and procedures regarding the drug testing of employees. **Reasonable suspicion may be established by evidence that points to the guilt of at least one discrete group of officers.** The word "individualized" did not require that the reasonable suspicion be focused exclusively on the officer himself. Because the odor of marijuana in the eighth-floor bathroom was strong evidence that at least one of the correctional officers had been using illegal drugs, the officer was properly required to submit to a drug test, and was properly fired. *Drake v. County of Essex,* 646 A.2d 1126 (N.J. Super. Ct. App. Div. 1994).

* The Oregon Department of Corrections promulgated rules allowing for the search of an employee when there was reasonable suspicion that he or she possessed unauthorized property or contraband. Only the security manager or officer in charge had authority to instigate a search. At all times the employees had the right to a certain degree of privacy, but refusal to submit to the search could result in disciplinary action. Employees challenged the policy, and the Supreme Court of Oregon noted that although no statute expressly authorized searches of employees, **the department's duty to "govern, manage and administer" implicitly granted the department authority to search its employees.** Here, the department's authority to search the employees was reasonably related to its duty to provide a secure prison environment. Also, the

individualized suspicion requirement and other provisions in the rules were sufficient checks on the executives' discretion. Thus, sufficient statutory authority existed, and the rules were sufficiently systematic to be constitutional. *AFSCME Local 2623 v. Dep't of Corrections*, 843 P.2d 409 (Or. 1992).

* An Indiana court security deputy was responsible for disarming persons entering the courthouse and was required to carry a gun while on duty. The deputy had a history of tardiness and absences, and had received a verbal warning, a letter of reprimand and a suspension without pay for these reasons. During the spring of 1990, he underwent treatment for alcohol and drug abuse. He reported drinking a pint of whiskey daily and snorting three grams of cocaine per week. The deputy subsequently terminated the treatment, but his wife reported that he continued to use drugs and alcohol. In May 1990, the sheriff observed that the deputy had already missed 64 hours of work due to reported illness and ordered him to undergo a urinalysis. There was no formal drug testing policy, and the deputy was the first ever to be ordered to submit to a drug test. The deputy refused to submit to the test and was fired for insubordination. He challenged the legality of the drug test, and a trial court upheld the termination. The deputy appealed to the Court of Appeals of Indiana.

The court of appeals noted that persons required to carry a firearm on duty had a diminished expectation of privacy. The government had a compelling interest in preventing courthouse violence and the attendant loss of confidence in the system. The likelihood of such results would be increased if the deputy was under the influence of drugs. However, **since there was no established drug testing procedure in the present case, individualized suspicion that the deputy used drugs was a prerequisite to a lawful urinalysis**. The court deemed the deputy's past drug use, coupled with his present record of excessive absences, justified a reasonable inference that he was currently using drugs. Therefore, the deputy's refusal to submit to the drug test was insubordination, and the termination was warranted. *Miller v. Vanderburgh County*, 610 N.E.2d 858 (Ind. Ct. App. 1993).

3. Transportation Employees

* A state transportation department employee failed a random on-duty drug test and agreed to submit to random follow-up testing as a condition of his continued employment. He also agreed to remain drug and alcohol free. During an off-duty follow-up test, he registered positive for methamphetamines and was fired. The state personnel board upheld the termination. A state trial court set aside the termination, noting that off-duty testing intruded upon employees' constitutionally protected privacy rights, and that the state failed to use the least intrusive means of testing. The California Court of Appeal affirmed. It noted that because the department had a written policy providing that employees would be tested when they were on duty, **the employee had a reasonable expectation of privacy with respect to off-duty drug testing**. The court also issued an injunction to prevent the department from conducting any future off-duty drug tests. *Edgerton v. State Personnel Board*, 100 Cal.Rptr.2d 491 (Cal. Ct. App. 2000).

• A bus driver employed by the Southeastern Pennsylvania Transportation Authority (SEPTA) was ordered by several supervisors to submit to a body fluids drug test. The driver tested positive and was discharged. His union pursued three levels of grievance proceedings on his behalf, and it was determined that the tests requested were based on reasonable suspicion and that he had been properly discharged. The union did not submit the matter for arbitration. The driver filed a 42 U.S.C. § 1983 lawsuit against SEPTA and the union, alleging Fourth Amendment violations. The district court dismissed the case, and the driver appealed to the Third Circuit, arguing that SEPTA violated the suspicion-based testing policy codified in the collective bargaining agreement. The court of appeals disagreed, ruling that **whether reasonable suspicion existed in a given case was an issue involving interpretation of the collective bargaining agreement**. Courts must defer to the parties' interpretation pursuant to the grievance hearing unless the employee can show that the union breached its duty of fair representation. Because the question of reasonable suspicion was resolved in SEPTA's favor at all stages of the grievance process, and the driver had never alleged that the union breached its duty of fair representation, the proposed search was reasonable and the driver's complaints were not sufficient to support the Fourth Amendment claim. The district court ruling was affirmed. *Dykes v. Southeastern Pennsylvania Transportation Authority,* 68 F.3d 1564 (3d Cir. 1995).

• A city bus driver with 10 years of service was placed on physical layoff status following a work-related accident. Upon his scheduled return, he was subjected to a surprise drug test and tested positive for marijuana. City policy provided for drug testing as a prerequisite to obtaining a city operator's permit and as a condition of employment. The city acknowledged that the employee had an operator's permit but asserted that he was tested as a "new hire" because he had acquired a new position. The employee sued the city in a New Mexico federal court, claiming that he was denied procedural due process and that the mandatory drug test violated his Fourth Amendment right to be free from unreasonable searches and seizures. The court held for the city.

The U.S. Court of Appeals, Tenth Circuit, held that the city had unfairly implemented its policy. Neither of the provisions of the substance abuse policy had expressly applied to the driver at the time he returned to work. He already had a city operator's license and was not an applicant seeking employment with the city for the first time. Moreover, the drug test, given without advance warning, was among the most intrusive possible and contravened all reasonable expectations of privacy. **Given the unusually intrusive nature of the testing, and given that a positive test inevitably led to termination, the city's drug test constituted an unreasonable search in violation of the Fourth Amendment.** However, the court rejected the employee's due process claim, holding that the city's decision to treat positive drug tests as "just cause" for immediate discharge of safety-sensitive employees was constitutional. *Rutherford v. City of Albuquerque,* 77 F.3d 1258 (10th Cir. 1996).

• The New York City Transit Authority (TA) utilized urine-testing procedures to test for the use of marijuana. The policy was to take urine from TA employees in four circumstances: following an extended absence or suspension; as part of a periodic physical examination; as part of a physical examination for promotion; and when directed by a superior or manager following an incident that occurred while on duty. The employees and applicants who tested positive for marijuana and also denied drug use sued under the Fourth Amendment. Drug testing of employees in safety-sensitive positions, as well as applicants for such positions, does not violate the Fourth Amendment. However, the court noted, **when safety-sensitive work was not involved, the balance of private and government interests mandates a higher standard than mere reasonableness to satisfy the Fourth Amendment. It must be individualized suspicion.** The TA argued that its testing satisfied a reasonable suspicion standard based upon nationwide statistics for drug use and evidence that there were drug users on the TA work force. The court ruled, however, that these statistics were insufficient to impute a reasonable suspicion of marijuana use to all workers and applicants. The testing of non-safety employees for the reasons the TA advanced was insufficient to meet the reasonableness requirement. *Burka v. New York City Transit Authority,* 739 F.Supp. 814 (S.D.N.Y. 1990).

The employees then sought monetary and injunctive relief for violations of the Fourth Amendment. The court found that violations of the search and seizure clause entitled victims to only monetary relief. A due process violation would occur only when an employee could prove that the hearing would have produced a different result absent the use of the drug test result. Because of their own intervention, employees who later admitted drug use would not be able to prove a due process violation. However, any employee who tested positive but did not later admit to drug use did experience a violation of the Due Process Clause. Those employees were to have all records of the test or any hearing expunged. They were also to receive monetary damages. *Burka v. New York City Transit Authority,* 747 F.Supp. 214 (S.D.N.Y. 1990).

C. Testing and Unemployment Benefits

♦ A process operator employed in a "safety-sensitive" position by the Philadelphia Gas Works was randomly selected to provide a urine sample for drug testing on two occasions over the course of several months. He tested positive for illegal drugs on both occasions and was twice allowed to enroll in a drug treatment program in lieu of disciplinary action. He was ultimately required to take a return-to-work drug test after being released from treatment. Because his sample registered well above the normal temperature range (indicating tampering), the doctor required that he submit a second sample. The first sample tested negative, but the second sample tested positive for cocaine. The operator also allegedly submitted to a third drug test at the treatment center later that same day, which tested negative. After he was discharged pursuant to the employer's drug and alcohol policy, a hearing officer denied his application for unemployment compensation benefits.

The Unemployment Compensation Review Board reversed, and the employer appealed to the Commonwealth Court of Pennsylvania. The commonwealth court reversed, ruling that **the operator had been properly** discharged for his willful violations of the drug policy. In reversing the review board's decision, the court noted that the doctor had properly documented the chain of custody, retested the temperature of the sample with two different thermometers, took the operator's temperature to determine whether a fever had caused the high urine temperature, and requested a second sample. Because the board had based its decision on a credibility determination that was not supported by substantial evidence, the commonwealth court reversed the order granting benefits to the operator. *Philadelphia Gas Works v. Unemployment Compensation Board*, 654 A.2d 153 (Pa. Commw. Ct. 1995).

♦ A corrections officer employed by the Alabama State Department of Corrections was discharged after testing positive for marijuana use. An examiner for the Department of Industrial Relations denied the officer's claim for unemployment compensation benefits. An appeals referee affirmed, and the officer appealed. At trial, the officer contended that an inmate had "doctored" the coffee that he had consumed prior to the drug test. Before the drug test results were available, another inmate allegedly informed the officer that the first inmate had told him that the officer had tested positive for marijuana. The trial court reversed, ruling that the officer was entitled to unemployment compensation benefits. The Court of Civil Appeals of Alabama affirmed, ruling that a trial court's findings are presumed correct and should not be disturbed unless clearly erroneous. **Because the department failed to contradict the officer's version of the facts, the trial court had properly granted unemployment compensation benefits.** *State Dep't of Corrections v. Harris*, 656 So.2d 894 (Ala. Civ. App. 1995).

♦ An Air Force mechanic based in Utah had received several promotions, was given "secret" security clearance, and had generally maintained an unblemished record. After the Air Force Office of Special Investigations initiated an investigation, several co-workers implicated the mechanic for the illegal use of drugs. The mechanic admitted using drugs on one occasion but alleged that it was an isolated incident. He later voluntarily submitted to urinalysis and was then fired in spite of testing negative. The administrative law judge held that the mechanic's termination was not for "just cause" and that he should receive unemployment benefits. The Industrial Commission's Board of Review reversed the administrative law judge. The mechanic appealed to the Utah Court of Appeals, which affirmed. To sustain a "just cause" termination, the Air Force had to demonstrate that the mechanic possessed the necessary culpability and had knowledge of the potential penalties for the act. Culpability would be established if the incident was more than an isolated occurrence or if there was an expectation that it would be repeated. The court held that **because the mechanic took no steps toward drug treatment, or other steps that would reduce the possibility of future drug use, the mechanic was culpable.** Further, he testified that he had knowledge that dismissal was a potential penalty. Thus, just cause was established, and the mechanic was not entitled to unemployment compensation. *Wagstaff v. Dep't of Employment Security*, 826 P.2d 1069 (Utah App. 1992).

♦ Two supervisors in a Florida sheriff's department noted adverse changes in a dispatcher and suspected drug abuse. Later, the department received an affidavit from a person who claimed that he had seen the dispatcher snorting cocaine in her apartment. The sheriff ordered the dispatcher to submit to a urinalysis test. She was immediately suspended. After she refused to be tested and consulted an attorney, the sheriff sent her a letter inviting her to furnish him with a reason why she should not be discharged. She did not respond, and her employment was terminated. An appeals referee found the discharge unwarranted since the sheriff's department had no testing policy in place and had not made testing a condition of continued employment. The referee held that the dispatcher was entitled to unemployment compensation since the refusal to submit to this test was not misconduct. The Florida Unemployment Appeals Commission reversed the referee's award, stating that the dispatcher's refusal to submit to the sheriff's order was misconduct. The dispatcher appealed to the District Court of Appeal of Florida, which affirmed. Drug testing based on a reasonable suspicion that an employee is using drugs is legitimate. In this case, the suspicion was reasonable. **Since the test was legitimate, failure to submit to the test, after being warned that such a refusal could result in dismissal, constituted a deliberate disregard of the employer's interests. As such, it was misconduct.** Unemployment benefits were denied. *Fowler v. Unemployment Appeals Comm'n,* 537 So.2d 162 (Fla. Dist. Ct. App. 1989).

D. Adequacy of Testing Procedures

♦ An Oregon bus driver was fired after she failed to produce sufficient urine for a drug test. However, an arbitrator concluded that **the test was flawed because she was not given three full hours to produce a sample** as required by Department of Transportation regulations. He ordered her reinstatement, but the transportation district refused to reinstate her to the position until she completed a substance abuse evaluation. Her union then filed an unfair labor practice charge against the district. The case reached the Oregon Court of Appeals, which held that the district committed an unfair labor practice by refusing to reinstate the driver. Because the testing procedures did not comply with the governing regulations, the district lacked sufficient cause to fire her and therefore could not demand that she complete the substance abuse evaluation before being rehired. *Amalgamated Transit Union Local 757 v. Tri-County Metropolitan Transportation Dist.,* 195 P.3d 389 (Or. Ct. App. 2008).

♦ A New Orleans firefighter submitted to a random drug test. His urine sample was outside the acceptable temperature range, so the examiner required him to give another sample and a doctor observed him as he urinated into the cup. The first sample was discarded, and the examiner failed to indicate on the collection form that the doctor had observed the second collection. These were requirements of the Substance Abuse and Mental Health Services Administration (SAMHSA) guidelines, which the examiner wrongly believed did not apply to city employees. When the sample tested positive for cocaine, the firefighter was discharged. He appealed, and a hearing examiner upheld the termination. The Court of Appeal of Louisiana affirmed the ruling, noting that the fire department established a valid chain of custody, and the examiner's failure to follow the SAMHSA guidelines did not invalidate the positive drug test. *Krupp v. Dep't of Fire*, 995 So.2d 686, (La. Ct. App. 2008).

• While test driving a large grass-cutting machine he was repairing, a public employee in Louisiana struck the wall of the shop and caused minor damage to the electrical conduit and fire alarm. His supervisor made a report of the accident and ordered a drug test, pursuant to standard procedures. The employee went to a medical center and provided a double urine specimen, which was sealed in his presence and mailed to a lab for analysis. When the first specimen tested positive for marijuana, the employee exercised his option to have the second specimen tested at an independent lab. That specimen also tested positive. After the employee was fired, he appealed unsuccessfully to the personnel board and then sought review in the Court of Appeal of Louisiana.

Before the court, the employee challenged the validity of the testing procedures, asserting that the employer did not adequately establish a chain of custody for the urine sample. The court noted that the employer had adequately proven that proper procedures had been followed. The technician who had taken the sample testified that the sample had been sent by courier to the lab, and the manager of the lab testified as to the efforts taken to ensure an accurate analysis. **The chain of custody rule does not require that every person associated with the procedure be identified, only that safeguards be instituted to insure the integrity of the evidence.** Because the employer met its burden of proving the test was accurate, and because passive inhalation could not have caused the high levels of the marijuana metabolite in the sample, the court affirmed the decision in favor of the employer. *Cain v. Jefferson Parish Dep't of Fleet Management*, 701 So.2d 1059 (La. Ct. App. 1997).

• An Arkansas state police officer was fired after he tested positive for marijuana during a random drug screening pursuant to the department's Drug Free Workplace Policy. He appealed his discharge to the Arkansas State Police Commission (Commission). At the hearing, the testimony revealed that the department had failed to follow the departmental policy requirements that any positive results be submitted to the authorized medical review officer for confirmation, and that a positive test be reported only when both the initial and confirmatory tests have been completed and the positive result is not adequately explained to the satisfaction of the medical review officer after consultation with the employee or the employee's physician. Despite failing to have the results confirmed by a medical review officer, the Commission affirmed the officer's discharge. The officer unsuccessfully appealed to a state circuit court, and further appealed to the Supreme Court of Arkansas.

The supreme court reversed the officer's discharge, holding that the Commission's failure to follow its own procedures constituted an unlawful procedure because it prejudiced substantial rights of the officer. Not only did the officer have a right to standards of reasonableness under the Fourth Amendment and the Due Process Clause, but he also had a substantial interest in continued employment. Adherence to the procedures adopted by the department to ensure absolute confidence in the reliability of the results was essential to protect those substantial interests. Because the Commission had ignored its own requirements that the results be confirmed by a medical review officer, the fired police officer had been deprived of his rights. *Stueart v. Arkansas State Police Comm'n*, 945 S.W.2d 377 (Ark. 1997).

♦ A veteran New York City police officer with 17 years of experience was randomly selected for a urinalysis drug screening. His sample tested positive for cocaine, and he was charged for violation of department rules. At his pre-termination hearing, the director of the drug testing center detailed the steps used to guard against inaccuracies and chain of custody problems. Another officer testified that he had witnessed the officer fill the sample, seal it, and insert it into a tamper-evident envelope. The department denied his requests to cross-examine the toxicologists who actually did the testing or the laboratory technician who processed the sample. The hearing officer found the officer guilty as charged, and the department terminated his employment. On appeal by the officer, a New York trial court and the appellate division affirmed.

The Court of Appeals of New York then noted that **the Due Process Clause guarantees employees a limited right to cross-examine adverse witnesses in administrative proceedings**. Whether due process requires the production of a particular witness is dependent on the nature of the evidence, the potential utility of trial confrontation in the fact-finding process, and the burden of producing the witness. Here, the technician was unlikely to remember an individual sample, and his production would impose more than a minimal burden on the department. The officer was properly allowed to cross-examine the supervisor about every step of the drug testing procedure. Due process did not require production of all relevant witnesses in every case. The ruling was affirmed. *Gordon v. Brown*, 644 N.E.2d 1305 (N.Y. 1994).

♦ A Florida county corrections officer received numerous commendations and outstanding performance evaluations. During her biannual physical examination, which included a drug test, her urine sample tested positive for cocaine. Based on these results, the officer was discharged. She underwent a subsequent hair analysis test, which showed no evidence of cocaine use. She sought to introduce evidence of the test at a formal hearing before the Florida Criminal Justice Standards and Training Commission, alleging that her urinalysis test result contained a false-positive reading. The commission refused to admit the evidence, and the officer appealed to the District Court of Appeal of Florida, Third District. The court of appeal determined that the analysis of human hair is generally accepted in the scientific community. Specifically, it noted that **hair analysis can provide a more accurate history of drug use than conventional urinalysis**. Consequently, exclusion of the doctor's testimony regarding the possibility of a false-positive urinalysis result was an error. His testimony about the hair analysis test had to be allowed as evidence at the hearing to rebut the reliability of the urinalysis test. The holding of the commission was reversed. *Bass v. Florida Dep't of Law Enforcement*, 627 So.2d 1321 (Fla. Dist. Ct. App. 1993).

*   A Louisiana 17-year veteran policeman was ordered to submit a urine sample for a random drug screening. The sample tested positive for marijuana, but the results were not forwarded until nearly a month later. The officer's requests that a portion of the sample be made available to him for an independent test were repeatedly denied. The captain eventually informed the officer that his sample had deteriorated, even though the lab generally kept them frozen for at least a year following the test. The city fired the officer without allowing him to cross-examine the technician who tested his sample. The officer appealed to the Court of Appeal of Louisiana, alleging due process violations. The court determined that the officer was improperly denied the opportunity to cross-examine the technician who tested his sample, as well as access to the sample itself. Because **he was denied access to the only individual who could discern his sample from at least 700 others tested that day** and because he was never allowed to have his urine sample independently tested, he was denied due process. Consequently, the holding of the commission was reversed, and the officer was restored to his position. *Sciortino v. Dep't of Police*, 643 So.2d 841 (La. Ct. App. 1994).

*   An Alabama firefighter was discharged after he tested positive for marijuana. The county personnel board affirmed the dismissal, and the firefighter appealed to an Alabama circuit court. At trial, employees of the clinic who collected the urine sample testified to the procedures and safeguards used. The circuit court also affirmed, and the firefighter appealed to the Court of Civil Appeals of Alabama. The firefighter contended that the drug test was unreliable. The court of appeals disagreed, noting that **the evidence need not negate the most remote possibility of alteration**, but rather must prove to a reasonable probability that the item was the same as that which existed at the beginning of the chain. Here, given the intact bar-coded seals, the sealed tamper-proof bag, the protective box, and the identifying marks on both the custody form and the specimen bottle, and given that there were no signs of tampering, there was at least a reasonable probability that the item was the same. The ruling in favor of the city was affirmed. *Logan v. Personnel Board of Jefferson County*, 657 So.2d 1125 (Ala. Civ. App. 1995).

*   A Cleveland police chief decided to administer a drug test to a class of police academy cadets following reports that certain individuals were using illegal drugs. All the cadets were given containers and were ordered to urinate into them while their superior officers watched. The urine samples were sent to a company and were twice tested, each time by different procedures. The results revealed traces of marijuana in a group of the cadets' urine. When confronted, the cadets responded that they had not smoked recently and that they had only been exposed to secondhand smoke at parties. **The company later confirmed the results by retesting the urine samples using a more expensive and more reliable gas chromatography/mass spectrometry test.** The cadets who tested positive accepted the safety director's invitation to resign instead of waiting for termination. The cadets then sued the city and certain individuals, alleging constitutional violations resulting from the drug test. The district court held for the defendants, and the cadets appealed to the U.S. Court of Appeals, Sixth

Circuit. The cadets alleged that the testing methods used were unreliable and not administered pursuant to a procedure pre-approved by the city. Accordingly, they were entitled to retest their own urine samples. The court disagreed. The samples were repeatedly tested, and the cadets could not show that the procedure led to irrational results. *Feliciano v. City of Cleveland*, 988 F.2d 649 (6th Cir. 1993).

♦ A Cincinnati firefighter fell asleep in his car and failed to complete his inspection duties. He awoke 14 hours later and reported that he had no recollection of the previous night. He agreed to take a drug-screening test and, although he initially tested positive for cocaine, none was detected in one of two subsequent tests. The firefighter was dismissed from his position based on the results of these drug tests. He sued, alleging that the department utilized improper testing procedures. He sought reinstatement, back pay and lost benefits. The trial court held for the firefighter. The Court of Appeals of Ohio found that the trial court properly reversed the commission's decision. **The urinalysis did not conform with regulatory guidelines**, which require that the employee be tested in a hospital gown, in a private restroom, with the water in the sink turned off and with the water in the toilet colored with dye. Nor had the city established a legally sufficient chain of custody. The urine containers were not pre-labeled to show the employee's name, the date, or the time that the samples were collected. Additionally, the urine samples were not sealed in the firefighter's presence. Since the firefighter had been wrongfully discharged, he had been correctly reinstated with back pay and benefits. *Hall v. Johnson*, 629 N.E.2d 1066 (Ohio Ct. App. 1993).

CHAPTER SIX

Employee Benefits

	Page
I. PENSION BENEFITS	352
A. Eligibility	352
B. Statutory Amendments	354
C. Benefit Calculations	357
D. Misconduct Disqualification	361
II. DISABILITY AND WELFARE BENEFITS	364
A. Eligibility	364
B. Modification and Termination	368
C. Vacation and Sick Leave	372
III. EXEMPTIONS	376
A. Age Restrictions	376
B. Service Retirement	379
C. ERISA	379
IV. UNEMPLOYMENT AND WORKERS' COMPENSATION	380
A. Unemployment Compensation	380
B. Workers' Compensation	385
1. Arising From Employment	386
2. Exclusivity	391
3. Off-Duty Occurrences	393
4. Amount of Compensation	397
V. FAMILY AND MEDICAL LEAVE ACT OF 1993	400
A. Eligibility Issues	402
B. Documentation and Notice Issues	404
C. Intermittent Leave	406
D. Procedural Issues	407
1. Post-Leave Problems	407
2. Concurrent Paid Leave	408
3. Other Procedural Issues	409
VI. OTHER EMPLOYMENT BENEFITS CASES	411
A. Coordination of Benefits	411
B. Contribution Rates	413
C. Taxation	416

I. PENSION BENEFITS

A substantial amount of public employee pension litigation results from the determination of whether eligibility even exists, employee job transfers that involve entry into a new plan, amendments to plans by state and local lawmakers, and termination of participation rights due to misconduct. There also have been a number of cases involving discrimination in the provision of benefits or in premium costs. For cases involving discrimination generally, see Chapter One.

A. Eligibility

♦ A 911 dispatcher in Massachusetts got up from her desk. A police officer, in a poor attempt at horseplay, put her in a headlock and dragged her eight feet across the room before falling and taking her to the ground with him, causing her permanent wrist and elbow injuries. She sought accidental disability retirement benefits over and above workers' compensation. The Massachusetts Court of Appeals noted that **her injuries occurred as a result of horseplay** and not while she was performing the duties she was required to perform. This was not like a firefighter injured while rushing into a burning building or a police officer injured while chasing a fleeing felon. *Damiano v. Contributory Retirement Appeal Board*, 890 N.E.2d 173 (Mass. App. Ct. 2008).

♦ An undercover police officer performing electronic surveillance duties for a New York county fell from a telephone pole and injured his leg while repairing a court-ordered wiretap. He maintained that an inconsistency in the positioning of a peg on the pole caused him to fall during his descent. He applied for accidental disability retirement benefits. The comptroller denied them and the Supreme Court, Appellate Division, affirmed. The officer had used the same peg to climb up the pole and had climbed many similar poles during his employment. Thus, **his injury was not an accident within the meaning of the Retirement and Social Security Law.** *Engber v. New York State Comptroller*, 39 A.D.3d 1133, 835 N.Y.S.2d 495 (N.Y. App. Div. 2007).

♦ An Iowa teacher notified his school district that he planned to retire. He **asked for early retirement benefits but was turned down because he was over 65** at the time and the early retirement incentive plan was only available to teachers under that age. He sued under the Age Discrimination in Employment Act (ADEA) and won. The Eighth Circuit Court of Appeals noted that the plan defined "early" in terms of age rather than seniority or salary. Thus, two teachers with the same background, same number of accumulated sick days and same number of years with the district could receive entirely different retirement benefits based solely on age. The district's plan violated the ADEA. *Jankovitz v. Des Moines Independent Community School Dist.*, 421 F.3d 649 (8th Cir. 2005).

♦ A police sergeant in Rhode Island had hypertension, which he claimed was caused by job stress. He filed a request for injured-on-duty (IOD) status, but the city did not respond to the request within 15 days, as stipulated in the collective bargaining agreement. It did pay several months' medical expenses. Later, the retirement board found that the disability was not job related and denied him retirement benefits. The city then denied him IOD status and ordered him back to work. An arbitrator ruled that **the city's failure to respond within 15 days barred it from challenging the job relatedness of his claim**. The city appealed, and the Supreme Court of Rhode Island held that the arbitrator reasonably interpreted the bargaining agreement in favor of the sergeant. *City of Woonsocket v. Int'l Brotherhood of Police Officers*, 839 A.2d 516 (R.I. 2004).

♦ A Wisconsin county's employee retirement system provided that employees would be eligible for pension benefits after 10 years of creditable service so long as they were not terminated for "fault or delinquency." A local bargaining unit sued the county, claiming that it inappropriately took the position that any employee terminated for cause after 10 years of service was no longer entitled to pension benefits. The Wisconsin Supreme Court agreed, noting that a discharge for cause was not necessarily the same as a discharge for fault or delinquency. Under the system in place, a vested employee could be discharged for cause if he became unable to perform his duties as a result of a non-work-related disability. He would then be disqualified from receiving his pension. **This automatic disqualification violated employees' due process rights because they acquired a property interest in their pensions after 10 years on the job.** Before taking away their pensions, the county had to determine whether the discharges were for "fault or delinquency," rather than simply for cause. *Milwaukee Dist. Council 48 v. Milwaukee County*, 627 N.W.2d 866 (Wis. 2001).

♦ A county employee contracted cancer and took paid sick leave. With less than one day of sick leave left, she applied for and received disability retirement benefits. Over a year after her last day of work, she received a final compensation payment, including for the partial day of paid sick leave. After she died, her widower unsuccessfully sought a statutory death benefit. The North Carolina Supreme Court noted that a state statute allowed for payment of a death benefit to the beneficiary of a plan member who died within 180 days of the last day of the member's actual service. The last day of actual service was defined as the last day the member actually worked (in situations where employment was terminated) or the date on which an absent member's sick and annual leave expired (where employment was not terminated). Here, the employee's retirement terminated her employment. Thus, **her last day of actual service was the last day she actually worked**. Since over 180 days had passed between her last day of work and her death, the widower was not entitled to benefits. *Walker v. Board of Trustees of North Carolina Local Governmental Employees' Retirement System*, 499 S.E.2d 429 (N.C. 1998).

♦ A Florida public employee named his mother and two sisters as the beneficiaries of his retirement benefits in case of his death. However, his mother and sisters were not eligible for these benefits because they were not financially dependent upon him. He later married but made no effort to change beneficiaries. When he died of a heart attack, the employer would not grant the widow benefits because the employee had never changed beneficiaries. The employer stated that the widow would be awarded the benefits only if the mother and sisters would disclaim them, which they refused to do even though they were not qualified to receive them. The District Court of Appeal of Florida held that **designations of beneficiaries do not have to be strictly followed**. It was not logical to deny a widow death benefits on the ground that three unqualified beneficiaries refused to disclaim them. The court awarded benefits to the widow. *Eaves v. Florida Division of Retirement*, 704 So.2d 140 (Fla. Dist. Ct. App. 1997).

♦ A Utah firefighter and his wife of 43 years divorced. Less than six months later, the firefighter retired and began to receive retirement benefits. The family court entered an order awarding the former spouse one-half of the retirement benefits and all of the firefighter's spousal death benefits. Subsequently, the retirement board notified the former spouse that she would not be entitled to the death benefits unless the firefighter remarried by the time of his death. The board reached this conclusion because the statute granting spousal death benefits required that the retiree be married at the time of his or her death. The firefighter appealed to the Court of Appeals of Utah, which rejected the board's argument that the firefighter had to have a current spouse at the time of his death. The former spouse's interest in deferred compensation, such as pensions or death benefits, was a marital property claim. **There was no rational justification for conditioning the former spouse's right to death benefits on the marital status of the firefighter at the time of his death** because the death benefits were marital property, unaffected by his remarriage decision. The court reversed the decision of the board. *Epperson v. Utah State Retirement Board*, 949 P.2d 779 (Utah App. 1997).

B. Statutory Amendments

♦ Collective bargaining agreements between a Connecticut city and the firefighters' union permitted the city to make limited changes to the healthcare benefits plan it provided for retired firefighters, so long as the new benefits were not less than what the retired firefighters received under the old plan. The city could not modify the substantive right to health care. When the city sought to switch from the traditional but costly indemnity healthcare plan to a more fiscally conservative managed care plan for the retired firefighters, a lawsuit ensued. The case reached the Connecticut Supreme Court, which held that the city could modify the healthcare plan without violating the retired firefighters' rights under the bargaining agreements. Even though the bargaining agreements assured that retirees had a vested right to healthcare benefits, they did not guarantee specific benefits, and **the retirees could not show that under the new plan a given retiree would always be less well off than under the old plan**. *Poole v. Waterbury*, 831 A.2d 211 (Conn. 2003).

♦ A Missouri city passed an ordinance that required it to levy taxes to fund the police and fire departments' pension plan at an annual rate of 25 cents per

$100 of assessed value of all taxable real and personal property. Some years later, a group of firefighters sued the city under 42 U.S.C. § 1983, alleging that the city's failure to levy taxes at the rate provided for in the ordinance violated the Contract Clause and the Due Process Clause of the U.S. Constitution. A federal court dismissed the lawsuit, holding that the firefighters did not have standing to sue because they could not show that they experienced a direct injury as a result. They were merely beneficiaries. Here, **it was the pension fund, not the individual firefighters, that was potentially injured**. As a result, only the pension plan's trustees could bring an action against the city. Because the firefighters did not establish with sufficient particularity that the trustees failed to properly address their concerns, the lawsuit was dismissed. *Int'l Ass'n of Fire Fighters, Local 2665 v. City of Clayton*, 320 F.3d 849 (8th Cir. 2003).

* Six retired firefighters for the city of Lincoln, Nebraska, sought payments from a disability pension plan. Each had worked for the city for more than 20 years, and each had retired before the age of 55 because of injury or physical disability. A city ordinance set out different payment options for firefighters who retired because of disability than for those who retired voluntarily for other reasons. Pursuant to the ordinance, none of the six firefighters was offered a lump sum payment, and four firefighters had their reimbursement offset or reduced as a result of workers' compensation awards they had received.

The firefighters claimed the city violated their constitutionally protected contract rights by offsetting workers' compensation payments and denying them lump sum pension payments. They also claimed that the ordinance violated their equal protection rights by distinguishing between benefits for disabled and non-disabled firefighters. A state court dismissed the claims, and the Nebraska Supreme Court affirmed. The U.S. Constitution does not prohibit changes to state contracts, and it does not give a public employee the right to the best pension; it merely protects the firefighters from being made worse off than they were when their pension rights were created. Since **the ordinance did not cause the firefighters to receive less than the full measure of workers' compensation benefits they were entitled to**, and since they were not similarly situated to non-disabled retired firefighters, their claims failed. *Bauers v. City of Lincoln*, 586 N.W.2d 452 (Neb. 1998).

* In 1977, the state of Washington made several changes to its retirement system plan that covered police and firefighters. The changes resulted in a separate plan for employees hired after the changes became effective. The two plans were known as LEOFF I and LEOFF II. Subsequently, a firefighters' union sought to have the city of Seattle increase the service, duty disability and duty death retirement benefits for its LEOFF II members so that their benefits would be more in line with LEOFF I benefits. The case reached the Washington Court of Appeals, which found that a provision in LEOFF II excluded its members from participating in any pre-existing pension system. Further, despite the requirement under public sector employment laws that retirement benefits be mandatory bargaining subjects, the city could only bargain for proposals it was authorized by law to carry out. Here, **the state's retirement laws**

specifically prevented the city from carrying out the union's proposal. The LEOFF laws were created to establish a uniform, statewide retirement system to replace the various systems then in effect. *Int'l Ass'n of Fire Fighters, Local 27 v. City of Seattle*, 967 P.2d 1267 (Wash. Ct. App. 1998).

• The Maine public employee retirement system provides benefits for teachers and other employees based upon fixed contributions to the system. Retiring employees may qualify for a pension in one of several ways, including the reaching of the statutory retirement age with service requirements of a specified duration. The state legislature responded to a budget crisis in 1993 by increasing required member contributions, capping salary increases for inclusion in the calculation of benefits, delaying a cost-of-living adjustment, increasing the regular retirement age, increasing the penalty for early retirement and eliminating the use of sick or vacation pay for computing retirement benefits. The Maine Education Association and a group of public school teachers sued, and a federal court ruled that the amendments violated the Constitution's Contract Clause as to certain plan members who had satisfied the age and service requirements.

State officials appealed to the First Circuit, which held that a state legislature must clearly intend to bind itself in a contractual matter before a Contract Clause action may be brought. Absent a clear indication of intent to be bound, the presumption is that a law merely declares a policy to be pursued. Here, **the state of Maine had not unmistakably shown its intention to create enforceable private contract rights** with respect to the modification of employee retirement benefits prior to an employee's actual retirement. The amendments did not attempt to revoke retirement benefits earned by those teachers who already had retired; there was no Contract Clause violation. The court reversed the district court decision. *Parker v. Wakelin*, 123 F.3d 1 (1st Cir. 1997).

• The Illinois Constitution contains a pension protection clause that provides that membership in a public employee pension retirement system is an enforceable contractual right that cannot be diminished or impaired. The state legislature passed a statute that required the state and its officials to make certain levels of contributions to the public employees' pension system. When the state and its officials failed to make these required contributions, a group of participants sued the state and its officials to enforce the required contributions. After the case was dismissed, the Supreme Court of Illinois affirmed, stating that the pension protection clause and the statute did not give the participants an enforceable contractual right to control the funding of the pension system. The clause did not control funding or create any vested contractual relationships that allowed participants to enforce funding. **The clause created a contractual right to benefits, not a right to expect a particular level of funding.** *People ex rel. Sklodowski v. State of Illinois*, 695 N.E.2d 374 (Ill. 1998).

• The Rhode Island Legislature amended the state employees' retirement plan to no longer allow purchased pension credits, for prior service with the city or military service, to accelerate an employee's vesting date. The new plan required actual time in service to the city. Both the old and new plans contained a provision reserving the state's power to amend the pension plan. Prior to the amendments, a city employee joined the pension plan and purchased credits for his prior probationary period with the city and his military service. However, he was not vested at the time the amendments came into effect. The Rhode Island Retirement Board ruled that the purchased probationary credits, but not the military credits, could count toward his vesting time. When the employee sued, the U.S. Court of Appeals, First Circuit, held that the legislative amendments did not violate the Contract Clause, which prohibits states from passing any law impairing the obligation of contracts. **The explicit reservation of legislative power to amend or terminate the plan, except for vested employees, prevented any violation of the Contract Clause.** Accordingly, the employee's failure to vest prior to the amendments being enacted prevented impairment of any contractual obligations protected by the Contract Clause. *McGrath v. Rhode Island Retirement Board,* 88 F.3d 12 (1st Cir. 1996).

♦ A Maryland county legislature revised the county retirement plan for appointed and elected officials by reducing pension benefits retroactively to effect cost-saving changes in the plan. The county alleged that the reduction would restore actuarial soundness and eliminate pension benefits that were the product of self-dealing, deception, and outright misrepresentation of the costs. Several former appointed and elected officials sued, asserting violations of the Contract Clause and 42 U.S.C. § 1983. A Maryland federal court noted that the pension plan created a contractual duty toward persons with vested rights under the plan. Accordingly, **the reduction of benefits substantially impaired the officials' contract rights**. Moreover, the county failed to present sufficient evidence that the reduction was reasonable and necessary to serve an important public purpose. The purposes alleged by the county were not important enough. The county also failed to sufficiently show that it had adopted the least drastic means. The county violated the Contract Clause, but not Section 1983. *Andrews v. Anne Arundel County, Maryland,* 931 F.Supp. 1255 (D. Md. 1996).

C. Benefit Calculations

♦ The Massachusetts Turnpike Authority offered its employees an incentive program to reward them for taking fewer sick days. The "medical coverage" provision allowed a percentage of the value of accrued, unused sick leave to be placed in escrow to pay for health insurance premiums upon retirement. The "cash payment" provision paid employees a percentage of the value of accrued, unused sick leave upon retirement. Over the years, the program changed several times, and eventually the "medical coverage" provision was discontinued. When a 28-year employee retired, he was paid only 20% of his accrued, unused sick leave value and no health insurance premiums. **He sued to recover 50% of the cash value in accordance with one of the incentive offers**, and he also sought health insurance premiums for the time the program was in effect. The Massachusetts Court of Appeals ruled in his favor, noting that the authority never included a disclaimer in its materials that its offers did not constitute contracts with the employees. *LeMaitre v. Massachusetts Turnpike Authority,* 876 N.E.2d 888 (Mass. App. Ct. 2007).

♦ A number of city employees in Michigan utilized a loophole in the formula the city used to calculate retirement benefits. Because the city used bi-weekly pay periods, they were able to count back from a Friday payday 365 days to another Friday payday to achieve 27 pay periods in a year. They used their three highest-paid years for the purpose of calculating their final benefits and counted 27 pay periods for each of those three years. After they retired, the city faced an emergency financial crisis and only then discovered what they had done. A financial manager **directed retirement benefits to be recalculated, allowing only one year of 27 pay periods**. The retirees sued, alleging that their final average compensation based on three 27-pay period years was an accrued financial benefit that was shielded from diminishment or impairment under the state constitution. The Michigan Court of Appeals disagreed. The retirees were entitled only to benefits based on "annual" compensation. *Rutherford v. City of Flint*, 2007 WL 2743631 (Mich. Ct. App. 9/20/07).

♦ A New York physician provided services to a county nursing home and a jail from 1971 until 1999. He sought to include the years 1996 through 1999 in the calculation of his final average salary, but his request was denied because he had been an independent contractor for those years. The Supreme Court, Appellate Division, noted that there was substantial evidence to support the comptroller's decision. The county stopped withholding taxes from the doctor's paychecks, issued him 1099 forms instead of W-2 wage statements, and required him to turn in monthly vouchers and sign annual contracts. Further, he did not accrue sick or vacation leave during that time, nor was he eligible for workers' compensation or unemployment benefits. Thus, **he was an independent contractor for those years and was not entitled to have his salary adjusted upwards for benefit calculation purposes**. *Fernandez v. New York State and Local Retirement Systems*, 17 A.D.3d 921, 793 N.Y.S.2d 286 (N.Y. App. Div. 2005).

♦ A Massachusetts city employee retired and began receiving pension benefits from the county retirement system. She then took a job with a private agency that became a state agency and joined the state retirement system. Just before she retired from the agency, the state retirement board realized she should not have been enrolled in its system. It refunded her deductions of $10,000. The county retirement system then learned that she had made more working for the state than she would have if she continued working for the city. It voted to recoup the excess amount from her pension and began withholding benefits. She appealed, and the case reached the Massachusetts Court of Appeals. It ruled in favor of the county, noting that state law allowed the withholding and that **the employee did not lose any benefits to which she was rightfully entitled**. *Bristol County Retirement Board v. Contributory Retirement Appeal Board*, 841 N.E.2d 274 (Mass. App. Ct. 2006).

♦ Individuals classified as miscellaneous employees under three retirement plans for the city and county of San Francisco challenged the methodology used by the San Francisco Retirement Board to calculate their retirement benefits. The board computed retirement benefits by looking at years of service, age of employee and average final compensation. The employees claimed that the board improperly refused to include unused sick and vacation leave in the computation for retirement benefits. They asserted that the money they had been paid, upon their retirement, for unused vacation and sick leave should have been included in their average final compensation. The California Court of Appeal sided with the board and the trial court in holding that **the unused sick and vacation time did not need to be included in the average final compensation**. Monies paid out for unused sick or vacation time were paid only after the employee retired. Further, the board's longstanding interpretation of the plans was entitled to substantial deference. The court also referred to ordinances specifying that unused sick and vacation pay not be included in final computations. *Mason v. Retirement Board of City and County of San Francisco*, 4 Cal.Rptr.3d 619 (Cal. Ct. App. 2003).

* Some New York City managerial employees took early retirement between July 1, 1990 and June 30, 1992. Subsequently, a 3.5% retroactive salary increase was granted to municipal managerial employees by an executive order promulgated on August 13, 1992. The order expressly conditioned eligibility for the increase on active duty status as of June 30, 1992. A group of retired managerial employees sued the city in a state trial court seeking back pay and increased pensions pursuant to the order, alleging violations of the Age Discrimination in Employment Act (ADEA) and constitutional claims. The city's motion for pretrial judgment was granted, and the retirees appealed to the New York Supreme Court, Appellate Division.

The New York Constitution provides that "membership in any pension or retirement system of the state or of a civil division thereof shall be a contractual relationship, the benefits of which shall not be diminished or impaired." The court disagreed with the retirees' contention that the executive order impaired their contractual relationship with the city. The protection extended only to existing rights, which could not be infringed by subsequent legislation or executive action. Here, **the wage increase was not an existing contractual obligation of the city at the time the retirees took early retirement**. Further, the salary increase was based on each eligible individual's performance rating and not on an amount fixed by contract. The salary increase did not have a disparate impact upon the retirees and did not violate the ADEA. Any group of people who elected to take early retirement would be older because only senior employees (by virtue of age or length of service) qualify for early retirement. Their decision to take early retirement merely resulted in an exchange of the benefits of employment for those of early retirement, not discrimination. The lower court's judgment was affirmed. *Becker v. City of New York*, 671 N.Y.S.2d 88 (N.Y. App. Div. 1998).

* Under certain circumstances, a Utah police officer was required to work three additional hours in excess of the scheduled 40 hours per week. The three additional hours, known as gap time, were compensated at the officer's regular rate, and his employer made retirement contributions to the state retirement system based on that compensation. Several years later, the system refused gap time contributions, stating that any hours worked in excess of 40 per week would be considered overtime and thus ineligible for calculating retirement benefits.

The officer sought reconsideration before the state retirement board, but the board sustained the system's decision. The Utah Supreme Court noted that under the state's Public Safety Retirement Act (PSRA), "compensation" did not include overtime. The definition of overtime, as used in the PSRA, was hours worked in excess of an employee's regularly scheduled work period. Here, since the officer's regularly scheduled work period was 40 hours per week, **the three hours of gap time amounted to overtime under the PSRA and could not be used to calculate retirement benefits**. *O'Keefe v. Utah State Retirement Board,* 956 P.2d 279 (Utah 1998).

◆ Two Washington police officers from different cities received education pay in addition to their base salaries after they obtained bachelor's degrees. Both officers also contributed to the Law Enforcement Officers' and Firefighters' Retirement System Plan I. As part of their collective bargaining agreements, the education pay was included as "basic salary." However, the Department of Retirement Systems notified them that the education pay would not be included in their retirement calculations. They challenged this determination. The Court of Appeals of Washington found that education pay should not be included as "basic salary" in the "final average salary" calculations. The court gave the terms their ordinary meaning and determined that "basic" salaries are fundamental and attached to the position, whereas "special" salaries would be nonessential and based on attributes of an individual. Thus, the court concluded that **education pay constituted special salary and could be excluded because the police officers' positions did not require their level of education**. The education incentive pay merely rewarded their individual achievements. The court also distinguished positions requiring special training or risk and longevity pay. *Grabicki v. Dep't of Retirement Systems,* 916 P.2d 452 (Wash. Ct. App. 1996).

◆ Several Oregon public employees and unions in four separate cases challenged various state constitutional amendments affecting the Public Employees' Retirement System (PERS). The specific sections included Sections 10, 11 and 12. Section 10 prohibited employers from continuing to assume or pay the public employees' full 6% contribution to the retirement fund. Section 11 prevented public employers from continuing to guarantee any rate of interest or return on the monies in a retirement plan or system established by law. Section 12 forced public employers to stop using employees' accumulated, unused sick leave to increase retirement benefits.

The Oregon Supreme Court noted that the U.S. Constitution's Contract Clause prevents a state from passing any law impairing the obligation of contracts. The PERS pension plan constituted an offer for a unilateral contract that could be accepted by part performance of the employee. Pension rights vested upon acceptance of employment. Moreover, a state may undertake a binding contractual obligation with its employees including benefits that may accrue in the future for work not yet performed. As a result, the 6% pick-up, guaranteed rate of return, and sick leave credit were contractual obligations of the state. **Because the changes in Sections 10, 11 and 12 constituted alterations in the contract terms that substantially impaired the state's** contractual obligations, those sections violated the Contract Clause. *Oregon Police Officers' Ass'n v. State of Oregon*, 918 P.2d 765 (Or. 1996).

D. Misconduct Disqualification

♦ A New Jersey teacher received satisfactory performance evaluations for over 20 years. However, the school district then filed disciplinary charges against him, contending that he had sent notes containing inappropriate content to two female students. He was fired. Some years later, when he reached age 60, he filed for deferred retirement benefits, citing his many years of unblemished service. The teachers pension board determined that **he was ineligible for deferred retirement benefits because he had been removed for conduct unbecoming a teacher**. The Superior Court of New Jersey, Appellate Division, noted that a state statute plainly conditioned a member's eligibility for deferred retirement benefits on the absence of any for-cause removal. Retirement benefits were denied. *Mantone v. Board of Trustees of Teachers' Pension and Annuity Fund*, 2007 WL 1062412 (N.J. Super. Ct. App. Div. 4/11/07).

♦ A grand jury indicted the former governor of Rhode Island for racketeering, extortion and bribery while in office. The Retirement Board of the Employees' Retirement System sued to revoke the former governor's pension, and the Rhode Island Supreme Court agreed that the pension should be revoked pursuant to the Public Employee Pension Revocation and Reduction Act. The act authorizes the board to withhold benefits from any public official who violates the public trust. Here, however, **the governor's wife was an innocent spouse and therefore had an interest in the pension**. The court remanded the case for a determination of how much of the pension should be paid to her. Also, the court held that the governor's contributions to the pension fund should be returned to him without interest, less a pro rata deduction for the benefits to be paid to his wife. *Retirement Board of the Employees' Retirement System v. DiPrete*, 845 A.2d 270 (R.I. 2004).

♦ A police officer had a longtime friendship with a career criminal. After the officer's wife fell at their home and broke her ankle, the officer and the criminal conspired with one of the criminal's associates to defraud a homeowners' insurer. They claimed that the officer's wife injured herself at the associate's house as a result of his negligence. Their scheme netted them a $70,000 cash settlement from the insurer, which the parties split three ways. Subsequently, a federal grand jury indicted the officer on charges of conspiracy to commit insurance fraud. The officer – a 34-year veteran who had attained the rank of lieutenant – resigned a month later and then pled guilty to one count of mail fraud, a felony. The police retirement board began withholding pension benefits following his guilty plea and eventually issued a decision to deny him benefits. Eventually, the case reached the Illinois Supreme Court, which held that **the officer could be disqualified from receiving pension benefits because his felony conviction related to, or arose out of or in connection with, his service as a police officer**. Over a long period of time, the officer used his position to benefit the criminal in a variety of ways. This long-term relationship was what allowed him to defraud the insurer. *Devoney v. Retirement Board of Policemen's Annuity & Benefit Fund*, 769 N.E.2d 932 (Ill. 2002).

♦   As a result of prison riots at another facility, several inmates were transferred to a prison where a Pennsylvania corrections officer was assigned. He videotaped the inmates as they left the bus and entered the prison. Two years later, he testified to a federal grand jury that he had videotaped the last prisoners to leave the bus, even though he had heard that other officers might have assaulted prisoners who exited the bus later. He was indicted for perjury and pled guilty. When he later applied for retirement benefits, the state board and the commonwealth court denied them. He was not entitled to benefits because he pled guilty to perjury as part of a criminal investigation. **Perjury was a "crime relating to public office or employment."** *Gierschick v. State Employees' Retirement Board*, 733 A.2d 29 (Pa. Commw. Ct. 1999).

♦   A Massachusetts city police officer was convicted of federal crimes arising out of a scheme in which police officers stole and sold advance copies of police entrance and promotional examinations along with their answers. However, he was acquitted of providing his son an advance copy, even though his son had used a copy to obtain a perfect score and subsequent employment as a police officer. After he was fired, his wife sought a refund of his accumulated retirement deductions. The city retirement board denied the application on the ground that the officer had misappropriated city funds by supplying his son with a copy of the police entrance exam and answers. The board determined that the son was paid $157,050.55 for his services with the city police, and it charged the officer with misappropriation of funds in this amount. The Supreme Judicial Court of Massachusetts held that sufficient evidence supported the board's finding that the officer had provided his son with an advance copy of the police examination. His conduct constituted misappropriation of city funds. As a result, **the officer relinquished all rights to his retirement deductions because his misappropriation exceeded the value of his deductions.** *Doherty v. Retirement Board of Medford*, 680 N.E.2d 45 (Mass. 1997).

♦   A county utilities authority board member retired at age 52 with 31.5 years of service. Approximately two weeks later, he was indicted and eventually pled guilty to charges of accepting a bribe while a board member. After a hearing, the state division of retirement ruled that he had forfeited his retirement benefits under the Florida Retirement System by virtue of his guilty plea. He appealed to the District Court of Appeal of Florida, arguing that the forfeiture of his pension deprived him of vested property rights and violated both the state and federal constitutions. He argued that the forfeiture violated the constitutional prohibition against the impairment of contracts because he did not commit his crime until after his pension rights had vested. The court rejected this argument. **Conviction for bribery in connection with one's employment resulted in forfeiture of pension rights.** The forfeiture provision was a part of the pension contract between the board member and the state, and to the extent that his rights vested after 10 years of service, they vested subject to this provision. *Busbee v. State of Florida*, 685 So.2d 914 (Fla. Dist. Ct. App. 1996).

♦ Pennsylvania enacted the Public Employee Pension Forfeiture Act in 1978. The act provided for the mandatory disqualification and forfeiture of benefits upon "conviction or plea of guilty ... to any crime related to public office or public employment." In 1988, a state employee was promoted to a new position in which she continued to work until her voluntary resignation in 1991. She later pled guilty to "theft by deception" and "tampering with public records." The State Employees' Retirement Board then discontinued her pension benefits. The employee challenged the board's order, alleging that it was an unconstitutional impairment of a contractual obligation. The court noted that once a contractual obligation vests, it cannot be altered, amended or changed by unilateral action. However, **each time public employees are promoted or otherwise change job classifications, there is a termination and renewal of the contract** for purposes of the forfeiture act. Because the employee implicitly assented to the terms of the act when she was promoted, the termination of her benefits did not impair a vested contractual obligation. *Apgar v. State Employees' Retirement System*, 655 A.2d 185 (Pa. Commw. Ct. 1994).

♦ An off-duty Chicago police officer shot a youth following a traffic incident. The crime remained unsolved. The officer retired about six years later, and he began receiving his retirement annuity. When the officer's wife reported his involvement in the killing five years later, he was convicted of first-degree murder. The retirement board terminated his pension benefits. The Appellate Court of Illinois noted that the state Pension Code prohibited payments of benefits "to any person who is convicted of any felony arising out of or in connection with his service as a policeman." Here, the statute clearly contemplated situations where a police officer could commit a felony unrelated to his law enforcement duties. The legislature could have denied benefits for any felony conviction. **Because the officer's actions were not related to his police duties, his pension was reinstated.** *Cullen v. Retirement Board of Policeman's Annuity and Benefit Fund*, 649 N.E.2d 454 (Ill. App. Ct. 1995).

♦ After a New Jersey police officer testified in court in a manner contrary to his chief's advice, the chief assigned the officer to late-night foot patrol. The officer filed complaints, brought a civil suit and openly criticized the chief. The chief then stole the officer's police shotgun and suspended him for losing the weapon. An administrative law judge held that the chief's illegal behavior warranted partial forfeiture of his pension benefits. The board of trustees ordered total forfeiture, and an appellate court affirmed. The Supreme Court of New Jersey affirmed, noting that the chief had endangered the officer's life by assigning him to foot patrol. Each individual, daily decision to assign the officer to foot patrol was a separate offense. Therefore, the criminal conviction (for stealing the shotgun) was merely "the final act in a continuing series of multiple offenses." Even though much of the "continuing misconduct" was noncriminal, any misconduct deemed sufficiently serious by the court warranted pension forfeiture. **Since the noncriminal misconduct coupled with the criminal conviction violated the statutory requirement mandating honorable service, total forfeiture of pension benefits was warranted.** *Corvelli v. Board of Trustees*, 617 A.2d 1189 (N.J. 1992).

II. DISABILITY AND WELFARE BENEFITS

An injury must be incurred in the line of duty for a plan participant to qualify for public employee disability benefits. Where the disability is not the result of a work-related cause, benefits will not be awarded. Disability benefit payments may be terminated for misconduct or where the recipient is able to return to work.

A. Eligibility

♦ Kentucky created a disability pension plan that favored county and state "hazardous" workers who took disability retirement before they became eligible for a pension. A sheriff's department employee became eligible for normal or disability retirement at age 55. He continued to work until he became disabled at age 61, at which point the pension plan calculated his retirement pay as if he had retired without a disability. He sought to obtain the higher benefits available for employees who retired with a disability and sued under the ADEA when he was unsuccessful. The case reached the U.S. Supreme Court, which held that **Kentucky's disability retirement pension plan could favor younger workers because the plan did not discriminate against employees on the basis of age**. The plan had a clear non-age-related rationale for its disparity – to treat a disabled employee as if he became disabled after, rather than before, he became eligible for normal retirement. Age factored into the calculation only because the normal retirement rules permissibly included age as a consideration. *Kentucky Retirement Systems v. EEOC*, 128 S.Ct. 2361 (U.S. 2008).

♦ A former New Jersey housekeeper became an elevator operator at a county courthouse after suffering a heart attack. She lost the job when the county eliminated the position because of automation. When she applied for Social Security disability benefits, they were denied. After the Third Circuit Court of Appeals ruled that she was entitled to benefits, the case reached the U.S. Supreme Court, which held that she was not entitled to benefits. The Social Security Administration could find that she was not disabled because **she was able to perform her previous job as an elevator operator, even though that job no longer existed**. The agency did not have to investigate whether that work exists in significant numbers in the national economy before determining her eligibility for benefits. *Barnhart v. Thomas*, 540 U.S. 20, 124 S.Ct. 376, 157 L.Ed.2d 333 (2003).

♦ Various groups and public employees, along with the employees' same-sex domestic partners, sued the governor of Michigan seeking a judgment that the state's anti-gay marriage amendment to the state constitution only barred same-sex marriages. They claimed it did not preclude public employers from extending health insurance benefits to same-sex domestic partners. The case reached the Michigan Supreme Court, which held that **the marriage amendment prohibited public employers from providing health insurance benefits to their employees' qualified same-sex domestic partners**. By offering same-sex partners health insurance benefits, public employers were recognizing the partnerships in violation of the amendment. Therefore, such benefits could no longer be offered. *National Pride At Work, Inc. v. Governor of Michigan*, 748 N.W.2d 524 (Mich. 2008).

• An Illinois police officer on patrol in a transport vehicle was headed toward an airport to investigate complaints about speeders there. He was hit by a man driving a Buick and sustained injuries to his back and shoulder. He underwent surgery but was unable to return to work. After a hearing, the police pension board found him disabled from a non-duty injury. He appealed, and the Appellate Court of Illinois found that he was injured in the line of duty, entitling him to a higher level of pension benefits. **Even though the officer was driving a vehicle at the time of the accident (an ordinary risk), he was on routine patrol (acting in a capacity that involved a special risk) when he was injured.** *Jones v. Board of Trustees of the Police Pension Fund*, 894 N.E.2d 962 (Ill. App. Ct. 2008).

• New Jersey police and fire retirement funds allow participants to receive accidental disability retirement benefits for "mental-mental" disabilities (where an employee suffers from a strictly psychological trauma). However, to get these higher-than-ordinary disability retirement benefits, the disability must result from direct personal experience of a terrifying or horror-inducing event that involves actual or threatened death or serious injury, or a similarly serious threat to the physical integrity of the member or another person. A police officer who was verbally abused by his sergeant and ostracized by his co-workers after he was charged with domestic violence for breaking his girlfriend's nose was not entitled to the increased benefits. The New Jersey Supreme Court held that **he did not show a sufficient traumatic event to justify the increased benefits.** However, a police officer and a corrections officer who received death threats might be entitled to the increased benefits. *Patterson v. Board of Trustees, State Police Retirement System*, 942 A.2d 782 (N.J. 2008).

• A retired teacher in New York went to Canada and married his same-sex partner, then returned to New York and requested spousal medical and dental insurance coverage for his partner. The district denied health insurance to the partner, and the teacher filed a lawsuit. The New York Supreme Court (trial court) ruled in favor of the district, noting that under current state law, the teacher and his partner could not be considered spouses. Thus, spousal insurance benefits were not available to the same-sex couple, despite their marriage in Canada. On further appeal, the Supreme Court, Appellate Division, noted that the Department of Civil Service had since changed its policy to recognize same-sex marriages from other jurisdictions, thus mooting the case. *Funderburke v. New York State Dep't of Civil Service*, 854 N.Y.S.2d 466 (N.Y. App. Div. 2008).

• After an electrical inspector for a Tennessee town injured his back on the job for the third time, he consulted his family doctor without the town's authorization. He was referred to an orthopedic surgeon who operated on his back, again without the town's authorization. This allowed him to stop taking pain medication and resulted in only a 20% permanent disability. He then got in a car accident and saw a fourth orthopedic surgeon. (He saw two surgeons with the town's authorization for his first two injuries; neither recommended surgery.) The fourth surgeon said that the surgery had been reasonable, necessary and related to his work injuries. When the town refused to pay for the surgery, his insurer did so. He sued the town to force it to reimburse his insurer. The Tennessee Supreme Court required the town to do so even though the insurer had not intervened in the lawsuit because **the medical expenses were reasonable and necessary despite being unauthorized.** *Moore v. Town of Collierville*, 124 S.W.3d 93 (Tenn. 2003).

♦ An Anaheim police officer reported what he believed to be excessive force by colleagues in the gang unit. An internal affairs investigation cleared the colleagues, and the officer was then fired for conduct unbecoming a police officer, poor performance and misuse of sick time. He brought a whistleblower suit and won $63,000, but later filed for disability benefits, claiming he suffered from depression and anxiety as a result of anonymous death threats. The case reached the California Supreme Court, which ruled that to qualify for the benefits, the officer had to show more than that he was incapable of performing his duties for the city of Anaheim. He also had to show that he could not perform the usual duties of a patrol officer for other California cities covered by the Public Employees Retirement Law. *Nolan v. City of Anaheim*, 92 P.3d 350 (Cal. 2004).

♦ A senior New York court officer took lunch breaks that varied from 45 minutes to two hours, depending on the court's discretion. He was not prohibited from leaving the courthouse during his lunch period, and he was not paid for the time he spent on his lunch break. However, he remained on the premises and could have been summoned to assist in a work-related matter during his lunch break. **While he was eating his lunch in the courthouse locker room, a locker fell on him.** He applied for accidental disability retirement benefits. The New York Supreme Court, Appellate Division, held that he was not entitled to them because he was not on duty at the time of his injury. *Cossifos v. New York and Local Employees' Retirement System*, 713 N.Y.S.2d 568 (N.Y. App. Div. 2000).

♦ A number of retired engineers of the city of San Francisco brought suit to compel the city to provide them with the same city-funded dental benefits active employees had obtained through collective bargaining. The California Court of Appeal held that they were not entitled to the benefits because of changes that had been made to the city charter allowing collective bargaining for current employees. As a result, the bargaining agreement in place was not intended to apply to retired employees. **The city was not required to offer the retirees the same benefits it provided under its current bargaining agreement.** It was only required to provide the same benefits it had provided to employees before they gained the right to collectively bargain for health benefits. *Local 21, Int'l Federation of Professional & Technical Engineers v. City and County of San Francisco*, 90 Cal.Rptr.2d 186 (Cal. Ct. App. 1999).

♦ A police officer with 22 years of actual service and four years of creditable service from the Navy retired after being assured that he would continue to receive free health insurance for himself, his wife and his children. The city's collective bargaining agreement with the police union required the city to provide free health insurance coverage to retired employees. However, New Jersey law stated that only employees with 25 years of actual service were entitled to such coverage. When the city attempted to drop the retired officer's coverage 10 years later, a lawsuit ensued. The case reached the New Jersey Supreme Court, which held that the city could not discontinue coverage **because it had voluntarily paid for insurance coverage for 10 years, and the officer had relied on that action**. *Middletown Township Policemen's Benevolent Ass'n v. Township of Middletown*, 744 A.2d 649 (N.J. 2000).

♦ The Oregon Court of Appeals determined that a public health sciences university violated the state constitution's privileges and immunities clause (which requires governmental entities to make benefits available on equal terms to all Oregon citizens) by maintaining **a practice of denying health insurance coverage to the domestic partners of its homosexual employees**. The case arose after three university nurses were denied insurance coverage for their domestic partners. The university provided health insurance only to spouses, not unmarried partners. After the state employee benefits board upheld the denial of benefits, the nurses sued. The court of appeals stated that because homosexuals cannot marry under Oregon law, the university's health insurance benefits were made available on terms that, for gay and lesbian couples, were a legal impossibility. *Tanner v. Oregon Health Sciences Univ.*, 971 P.2d 435 (Or. Ct. App. 1998).

♦ An Iowa police officer was diagnosed with posttraumatic stress disorder and depression after he witnessed an accident where two people burned to death and after he had two confrontations with armed citizens. He applied for accidental disability benefits, claiming that he was totally and permanently incapacitated as a result of an injury incurred or aggravated by the actual performance of police duties. The state retirement system awarded him only ordinary disability benefits. He appealed. The Iowa Supreme Court found that the officer had established that **his mental injury was caused by workplace stress of greater magnitude than the ordinary day-to-day stress of police officers**. Therefore, he was entitled to accidental disability benefits. *City of Cedar Rapids v. Board of Trustees*, 572 N.W.2d 919 (Iowa 1998).

♦ The Supreme Court of Alaska held that a police chief who was fired (for failure to notify city officials of his whereabouts) after being hospitalized for depression was terminated "because of" his disability. It did not matter that the employer's action was not motivated by disability. **His disability was the actual cause of his termination** because it resulted in his unauthorized leave of absence. Accordingly, he was entitled to non-occupational disability benefits. However, a question of fact existed as to whether his disability was occupational or non-occupational. This question had to be resolved on remand. *Stalnaker v. M.L.D.*, 939 P.2d 407 (Alaska 1997).

♦ A Florida state law allows for early retirement benefits if a member of the state retirement system is totally and permanently disabled. A state employee was afflicted with several medical conditions including heart disease, diabetes, asthma, morbid obesity, degenerative arthritis and allergies. Her treating physicians indicated that her weight – over 300 pounds – contributed to her symptoms and ailments. When she applied for early retirement benefits, the State Retirement Commission denied her request based on its conclusion that she had not reached "maximum medical improvement." The employee appealed to the District Court of Appeal of Florida, which found that it was inappropriate to try to transplant concepts and definitions such as "maximum medical improvement" from workers' compensation law into the law governing the state retirement system. Therefore, it remanded for a determination of whether the employee was totally and permanently disabled as defined by the statute. Moreover, **the commission could not assume that she had the ability to lose enough weight to alleviate her conditions**. Rather, the commission should determine whether there was any reasonable probability that the employee, through good-faith efforts, could lose enough weight to alleviate her disabilities and provide "useful and efficient service." The court reversed the commission's decision. *Hassler v. State Retirement Comm'n*, 698 So.2d 897 (Fla. Dist. Ct. App. 1997).

♦ A Maryland firefighter began to suffer pain and stiffness in his joints and eventually was diagnosed with osteoarthritis. His condition began to interfere with his firefighter duties, causing him to be placed on light duty. The county requested that he file for disability retirement, but he preferred to continue working. The director of the Department of Fire and Rescue Services requested a disability retirement for the firefighter, and a temporary non-service-related disability retirement was granted. The firefighter pursued several appeals, arguing that his disability was permanent and service-related. On appeal to the Court of Special Appeals of Maryland, the firefighter contended that a service-related disability may result from a non-work-related condition. The court disagreed, concluding that the county retirement code required the worker's incapacity to be the natural and proximate result of a condition aggravated while in the actual performance of duty. **Suffering from a degenerative condition aggravated by work was not enough**; the aggravation itself must be the reason for the disability. The firefighter's condition was degenerative, and it was the condition, not the aggravation, that caused his disability. Therefore, service-related disability benefits were properly denied. *Ahalt v. Montgomery County, Maryland*, 686 A.2d 683 (Md. Ct. Spec. App. 1996).

B. Modification and Termination

♦ A U.S. Navy welder applied for disability retirement with the Office of Personnel Management (OPM). OPM determined that the welder's poor eyesight prevented him from performing his job and made him eligible for a disability annuity under 5 U.S.C. § 8337(a). Section 8337(d) provides that benefits for disabled federal employees will end if the employees are restored to an earning capacity fairly comparable to the current rate of pay of that position. After taking disability retirement, the welder had the opportunity to earn more money by working overtime on a part-time job. He contacted the Navy's Civilian Personnel Department, seeking information on how much he could earn without losing his benefits. **An employee gave him erroneous information from an old handbook. The welder relied on the information and took the overtime work, then lost his disability benefits** by going over the statutory limit. He sought review of the decision from the Merit Systems Protection Board (MSPB), which held that the OPM could not be prevented from enforcing a statutory requirement. The U.S. Court of Appeals, Federal Circuit, reversed the MSPB's decision, stating that the use of an out-of-date handbook was "affirmative misconduct" and could prevent the government from denying benefits. The U.S. Supreme Court reversed, holding that the government could deny benefits. *Office of Personnel Management v. Richmond*, 496 U.S. 414, 110 S.Ct. 2465, 110 L.Ed.2d 387 (1990).

• An Arkansas city council voted to eliminate retirees' healthcare coverage as a matter of economic necessity. However, the city had earlier agreed to pay retirees' healthcare premiums, and the collective bargaining agreement was still in effect. The retirees' union sued the city for violating the bargaining agreement and the Contract Clause of the U.S. Constitution. A federal court and the Eighth Circuit ruled for the union. **The decision to stop paying premiums while the bargaining agreement was still in effect violated the Contract Clause.** Had there been an unprecedented emergency like the Great Depression, the city could have taken an extraordinary measure like breaking the contract. However, the city failed to establish the economic necessity for doing so in this case. *AFSCME v. City of Benton*, 513 F.3d 874 (8th Cir. 2008).

• Pennsylvania law awards disability compensation to volunteer firefighters, based on a statewide average weekly wage, for injuries that occur in the line of duty. When a volunteer firefighter sustained a disabling injury, he was awarded disability compensation of $477.85 per week based on the statewide formula. However, he was also unable to perform his regular truck-driving job, and he claimed he should be paid his weekly earnings of $580 in addition to the statutory wage. The Pennsylvania Commonwealth Court disagreed. **Paying him both amounts would give him more than he had made before he was injured.** Also, the benefits he received were greater than what he would have gotten had he been injured while driving his truck. *Ballerino v. WCAB*, 938 A.2d 541 (Pa. Commw. Ct. 2007).

• A Massachusetts firefighter sustained injuries when she slipped on ice while responding to a fire. She went on medical leave. Nine months later at an independent medical exam, a neurologist determined she could perform light-duty work. Because her migraine medication caused dizziness, she was allowed to stay on leave for three more months. The town then set up another exam with another neurologist, who refused to look at her medical records or discuss her migraines. He rated her able to work in a moderate-duty capacity, and the fire chief ordered her to return to work. When she failed to do so, the town terminated her leave benefits. She filed a grievance with her union and sued the town under 42 U.S.C. § 1983 for violating her due process rights. The town settled the grievance by restoring her injured-on-duty status, but the lawsuit continued. The First Circuit ruled against the firefighter, noting that the ordered exam did not violate her due process rights. **She received notice of the exam and an opportunity to be heard regarding her continued leave.** And even if the exam was defective, the grievance cured the defects. *Mard v. Town of Amherst*, 350 F.3d 184 (1st Cir. 2003).

♦ A Chicago police officer suffered a knee injury in 1986 during training. After receiving physical therapy, her doctor determined that she could not return to work as a police officer. She was granted full-duty disability benefits by the police retirement board in 1993. In 1995, the board held a disability status review hearing. During the hearing, the board heard evidence that the officer completed a three-mile walkathon in less than an hour. The board also reviewed the report of a doctor who had examined the officer. The report contained inaccuracies, including mis-identification of the injured knee, but concluded that she was able to return to work as a police officer. This report contradicted the report of the officer's doctor. Based on the evidence presented, the board voted to remove the officer from the duty disability rolls fund. The Appellate Court of Illinois upheld that determination. **Her ability to complete a three-mile walk in a steady pace within an hour severely diminished her claim of disability.** *Jackson v. Retirement Board*, 688 N.E.2d 782 (Ill. App. Ct. 1997).

♦ A garbage collector for a New Hampshire city sustained work-related injuries and received annual disability pension benefits from the city's retirement system. Subsequently, he started his own trucking, lawn care and paving business. The city's retirement board, after receiving his annual earnings information and income tax return, determined that his disability pension benefits should be reduced by over $9,000. The employee disputed the reduction, arguing that the board should have subtracted from gross profits the cost of advertising, car and truck expenses, depreciation, office expenses and other legitimate business expenses he had reported on his federal income tax statement. The board upheld the reduction after a hearing, and the employee appealed. The Supreme Court of New Hampshire first held that **the employee's business constituted substantial gainful employment, a prerequisite to reducing disability benefits**. However, the retirement board should not have equated the term "pay" with gross profit. Rather, it should have subtracted from the employee's pay the valid business expenses he reported on his federal income tax statement. The court disagreed with the employee's argument that his benefits should not have been reduced at all because his business was for the primary purpose of rehabilitation. While the business arguably had a therapeutic component, its primary purpose was to earn additional income. The court remanded the case. *Appeal of Barry*, 700 A.2d 296 (N.H. 1997).

♦ Under a municipal law intended to protect firefighters injured in the line of duty, some injured New York firefighters, who had been out of work for an extended period of time, received full salary and leave credits. After medical exams found them fit to return to light-duty work, the city ordered them to do so. Citing incapacity, the firefighters sued the city in a state trial court, requesting a hearing before the date of their return to light-duty work as well as a preliminary injunction to stop the order until their grievance was resolved. The court held that although the law was intended to protect firefighters, it did not guarantee their right not to perform tasks within their diminished abilities. Here, the firefighters' return date had long since lapsed, and they exercised their right to refuse to return to work pending an administrative determination of their grievance. However, the court held that **the city had no obligation to hold hearings prior to the issuance of orders to return to light-duty work**. The firefighters would suffer no harm if the return date was not suspended, because the city continued to pay their salaries and only charged their absences against their available leave credits. Even if their claim of incapacity succeeded on the merits, they would suffer no harm because their leave credits would be returned to them. The court denied the firefighters' requests. *Uniform Firefighters of Cohoes v. City of Cohoes*, 669 N.Y.S.2d 492 (N.Y. Sup. Ct. 1998).

• A Boston police officer was injured in a work-related automobile accident and granted disability retirement. Thirteen years later, based upon an evaluation by an orthopedic medical panel, the state retirement board concluded that the officer was no longer disabled. The officer applied for reinstatement, but the city denied the application because of problems with his background check. The officer sued. A trial court ordered the officer's reinstatement. The Supreme Judicial Court of Massachusetts affirmed, noting that **the law removed any discretion on the part of the police commissioner to reinstate retired, formerly disabled officers**. Once a medical panel determines that a retired civil service employee is "qualified for and able to perform the essential duties of the position from which he retired," the employee must be returned to a former or similar position. The law also related the preference specifically to success on the job. Rather than bestow automatic preference on a group, the statute required case-by-case evaluation and was therefore constitutional. *White v. City of Boston*, 700 N.E.2d 526 (Mass. 1998).

• An employee of the New York Transit Authority elected to make his pension contributions to the New York City Employees Retirement System. He retired after suffering a line-of-duty hip injury for which the system granted him ordinary disability retirement benefits. He later accepted a part-time position with the city, and received assurances, including several opinion letters, that his job would not affect his pension benefits because the Transit Authority was legally distinct from the city. However, 10 years later, the system suspended the employee's monthly pension payments and sought to recoup over $89,000 of allegedly improper payments made to him while he was employed by the city. The employee sued to compel restoration of his pension benefits. After the trial court held for the system, the New York Supreme Court, Appellate Division, reversed, holding that **the agency improperly attempted to recoup past disability payments from a pensioner who had relied upon 20 years of prior consistent and contrary city policy**. The city's 10-year delay in seeking to recoup the disability payments was arbitrary and capricious. *Barbera v. New York City Employees Retirement System*, 621 N.Y.S.2d 46 (N.Y. App. Div. 1995).

♦ A Colorado city firefighter responded to an emergency call, which required that he attempt to resuscitate a young boy with whom he was acquainted. In spite of the firefighter's exhaustive efforts, the boy died. The firefighter began having difficulty sleeping, was unable to concentrate, and experienced traumatic flashbacks. He filed a claim for temporary total disability benefits. An administrative law judge granted him the benefits "until terminated by law." The Industrial Claim Appeal Office affirmed. The city appealed, alleging that the firefighter's temporary benefits were limited to 12 weeks. The Supreme Court of Colorado affirmed, ruling that **temporary disability benefits for mental impairments terminated only upon the firefighter's maximum medical improvement**. However, the dollar amount of any temporary benefits that the firefighter would receive for any mental impairment had to be offset against the weekly dollar amounts authorized for permanent disability benefits. *City of Thornton v. Replogle*, 888 P.2d 782 (Colo. 1995).

C. Vacation and Sick Leave

♦ An association representing Los Angeles County peace officers sued for a determination that the county could not force the officers to use excess deferred vacation time rather than receive a cash payout for those benefits. The case reached the California Court of Appeal, which held that the officers could be forced to use vacation time in excess of 320 hours. The officers did not have an unconditional right to accumulate excess deferred hours and be paid for them. The county's policy was not a "use it or lose it" provision and did not cause the forfeiture of any vested vacation time: it was simply an attempt to limit the amount of vacation time that could be accrued. Therefore, **the county could force the officers to use their excess deferred vacation hours** in order to avoid paying them a cash buyout at the end of the year. *Ass'n for Los Angeles Deputy Sheriffs v. County of Los Angeles*, 154 Cal.App.4th 1536, 65 Cal.Rptr.3d 665 (Cal. Ct. App. 2007).

♦ A Massachusetts corrections worker injured his knee restraining an inmate and took two weeks of sick leave. He submitted a letter from his healthcare provider supporting his need for the leave, but the sheriff concluded that because he had already exhausted his sick leave, and because of the way sick leave was defined under the collective bargaining agreement, the officer could be fired for unauthorized use of sick leave. The union filed a grievance on his behalf, and an arbitrator ruled that he ought to be reinstated. The arbitrator determined that **because the officer submitted medical documentation, his absences were not "undocumented" under the bargaining agreement**. A trial court reversed, but the Appeals Court of Massachusetts reinstated the ruling, noting that the arbitrator did not exceed his authority. *Sheriff of Suffolk County v. AFSCME Council 93, Local 419*, 861 N.E.2d 472 (Mass. App. Ct. 2007).

♦ An Indiana not-for-profit penal facility hired a corrections officer as an at-will employee making $9.25 an hour. Its handbook provided that after 90 days, she would be eligible for benefits, including sick time. It also stated that the company did not pay employees for unused sick time upon termination.

Moreover, the handbook described the vacation time policy and stated that employees would not be paid for unused vacation time if they were fired or gave less than two weeks' notice. The officer was fired 45 days later, and was paid only minimum wage for her final pay period. She sued under the state's Wage Claims Statute, asserting that she was entitled to 7.4 hours of accrued sick pay, 14.76 hours of vacation pay and the difference between $9.25 per hour and $5.15 per hour for her final pay period. The Court of Appeals of Indiana held that she was entitled to the difference between her agreed-upon salary and minimum wage, but that **she was not entitled to her accrued but unused sick pay or vacation**. She never met the requirements for vacation pay because she did not work at least 90 days. As for the sick pay, the handbook clearly limited its use and did not allow it to be converted or otherwise made available to the employee. Further, even if the sick pay were analogous to vacation pay, she was still not eligible because she did not meet the handbook's requirements. *Williams v. Riverside Community Corrections Corp.*, 846 N.E.2d 738 (Ind. Ct. App. 2006).

• Three correctional employees in West Virginia sustained work-related injuries and collected workers' compensation Temporary Total Disability (TTD) benefits. During the time they received TTD benefits, they were denied accrual of sick leave time, holiday pay, accrual of credit for years of service and accrual of annual leave under state policy. They sought those fringe benefits at administrative levels unsuccessfully, but a circuit court ruled in their favor. The case reached the Supreme Court of Appeals of West Virginia, which affirmed in part. The court noted that **the policy preventing accrual of sick leave and holiday pay bore a reasonable relationship to a proper governmental purpose** and thus did not violate the equal protection clause of the state constitution. Even though employees on sick leave could continue to accrue sick leave and earn holiday pay (while TTD recipients could not), there was no duplication of benefits because employees on sick leave were depleting their accrued leave on a day-for-day basis, and their holiday pay was not part of the legislatively adopted formula in the state's workers' compensation act (while it was for TTD recipients). However, the policy prohibiting state employees from accruing years of service and annual leave violated equal protection because it treated employees receiving TTD benefits differently than employees on sick leave (who continued to accrue credit for years of service and annual leave) without a rational basis for the distinction. *Canfield v. West Virginia Division of Corrections*, 617 S.E.2d 887 (W.V. 2005).

• A supervisor in the Ohio Attorney General's Bureau of Criminal Identification and Investigation received a notice that because he failed to properly supervise an agent under his control, he would have his vacation leave balance reduced by eight hours or, if he did not have enough of a balance, the reduction would take place as he accrued vacation leave. He challenged the disciplinary action, and the court of appeals held that the attorney general could deduct time from his vacation leave accrued after the date of the disciplinary order, but not any vested vacation time he had earned prior to that date. The Supreme Court of Ohio then held that **the prospective deduction of vacation leave does not affect the vested right of a state employee**. It also ruled that the deduction of prospective vacation leave was a "reduction in pay" under state law and was authorized as a means of disciplining a state employee for neglect of duty. The employee's prospective vacation pay was properly deducted eight hours. *Harden v. Ohio Attorney General*, 802 N.E.2d 1112 (Ohio 2004).

♦ The head of a Connecticut administrative services agency extended the workday from seven to eight hours. After negotiating the longer day with unionized employees, the agency head notified the nonunion employees that their working day would similarly increase, but would do so over a four-year period. The agency head also notified the nonunion employees that they would receive a salary increase to reflect the longer workday and that the value of their future sick and vacation days would be calculated in accordance with the number of hours in the increased workday. Two assistant attorneys general appealed to the employee review board after learning that they would receive only seven hours credit toward sick and vacation leave for each day they had earned prior to when the increased workday began. They claimed that under state law, sick and vacation leave was earned in units of days, not hours. Now that they were working an eight-hour day, they claimed that they still were entitled to a full day of sick or vacation leave for every day of leave earned when they were working a seven-hour day. The Connecticut Supreme Court noted that **an employee who earns one day of sick or vacation leave is entitled to utilize one day of sick or vacation leave regardless of any lengthening of the standard workday**. *Nagy v. Employees' Review Board*, 735 A.2d 297 (Conn. 1999).

♦ A Massachusetts police officer was promoted to sergeant by virtue of a civil service commission order that made the date upon which he was actually promoted retroactive seven years to the date he was initially passed over for the promotion. Because the collective bargaining agreement between the town and the local police union allocated vacation and shift assignments according to preferences based upon length of service in the rank, a dispute arose after the town afforded the sergeant preference in vacation and shift assignments over other sergeants who had been promoted after the date of his retroactive promotion but before the date of his actual promotion. An arbitrator held that under the collective bargaining agreement in effect, **the sergeant was only entitled to a preference as of the date of his actual promotion**. The Appeals Court of Massachusetts upheld the arbitrator's ruling. Because the commission's order promoting the sergeant was ambiguous, and because it did not specifically require that the sergeant's seniority include the right to vacation and shift preference, the arbitrator could reasonably have ruled either way. Even though a court would likely have found that the bargaining agreement contemplated a result in line with the commission's order, the court was nevertheless bound by the arbitrator's interpretation. *Town of Dedham v. Dedham Police Ass'n*, 706 N.E.2d 724 (Mass. App. Ct. 1999).

♦ At one time, a Louisiana city gave all firefighters either double pay or additional time off for 10 designated holidays without regard to whether the firefighters actually worked on those holidays. The city changed its policy and began paying firefighters whose regularly scheduled day off fell on a designated holiday only his or her regular salary for that day. Also, the city began charging a firefighter's sick leave or annual leave account if that firefighter was scheduled to work on a holiday and did not. Finally, the city computed holiday time from 7:00 a.m. to 7:00 p.m. on the holiday. Thirteen firefighters filed a class action suit in state court, alleging that the changes violated state law and were discriminatory. The court rejected the firefighters' claims, except for computation of holiday time. The firefighters appealed to the Court of Appeal of Louisiana, which affirmed, holding that **only firefighters who actually work on specified holidays were entitled to holiday pay**. When read as a whole, the statute required the city to pay the extra compensation only to the firefighters who were actually required to work on holidays. As a discretionary benefit, the city was entitled to grant or remove it. *Perrodin v. City of Lafayette*, 696 So.2d 223 (La. Ct. App. 1997).

♦ An Arkansas city changed its sick leave policy to define a sick day as one eight-hour period. Under the policy, **firefighters working 24-hour shifts who missed their shift were charged three days of accumulated sick leave**. The firefighters sued, challenging the policy as a violation of state law and civil service commission rules and regulations. The court denied relief, and appeal was taken to the Supreme Court of Arkansas. The firefighters argued that the trial court had misinterpreted the term "working day" to mean the hours worked within a 24-hour period and that it had improperly concluded that the new sick leave policy was proper. They pointed out that the city's civil service regulations defined "working day" as meaning "tour of duty." They suggested that "working day" was intended to mean either hours worked within a 24-hour period or a tour of duty. The supreme court disagreed, finding that the terms "working day" and "tour of duty" found in the civil service commission regulations had been omitted from the statute. Further, the regulations as they referred to firefighters' sick leave had little meaning because Arkansas law prohibits such commissions from exercising any control over the normal routine day-to-day operations of a fire department. The city could change its policy by ordinance. *Donaldson v. Taylor*, 936 S.W.2d 551 (Ark. 1997).

♦ When a Texas assistant district attorney (DA) began his employment, the county personnel manual provided that employees with at least five years of continuous employment would be paid, on termination, a half-day's wages for each day of accrued but unused sick leave. However, the county subsequently **adopted a new personnel manual that restricted the right to receive compensation in lieu of sick leave to only those employees who retired**. The DA voluntarily resigned over a year after adoption of the new personnel manual and contended that he had accrued $4,098.70 worth of sick leave under the terms of the original manual. The county denied payment, and the assistant DA sued. The Court of Appeals of Texas noted that the personnel manual expressly provided that the county could unilaterally change its policies and practices. Because the assistant DA continued to work for the county with the knowledge of the changes, he accepted the modified terms of the at-will relationship and gave up his right to claim benefits. *Gamble v. Gregg County*, 932 S.W.2d 253 (Tex. Ct. App. 1996).

• A lesbian employee of the Colorado Department of Health and Hospitals requested family sick leave benefits for three days she took off work to care for her domestic partner. A state Career Service Authority Rule provided that sick leave could be used by an employee to care for a husband, wife or other specified immediate family member. Domestic partners were not included in the rule's definition of "immediate family." Pursuant to this rule, the department denied the employee's request for sick leave benefits. The Career Service Board upheld the denial, but a trial court held for the employee, ruling that a subsequently enacted administrative rule proscribing discrimination based on sexual orientation had invalidated the sick leave provision. The Colorado Court of Appeals reversed, holding that the board's interpretation did not impermissibly discriminate against the employee by reason of her sexual orientation. **Unmarried homosexual employees were treated the same as unmarried heterosexual employees.** Neither were entitled to sick leave benefits to care for their unmarried domestic partners. *Ross v. Denver Dep't of Health & Hospitals*, 883 P.2d 516 (Colo. Ct. App. 1994).

III. EXEMPTIONS

The Age Discrimination in Employment Act (ADEA), as amended by the Older Workers Benefit Protection Act (OWBPA), generally prohibits age-based discrimination by public and private employers but permits employers to maintain employee benefit plans that discriminate on the basis of age when age-based reductions in benefits are justified by significant cost considerations. Qualified governmental benefit programs are exempt from Employee Retirement Income Security Act (ERISA) provisions.

A. Age Restrictions

Congress amended the ADEA by enacting the Older Workers Benefit Protection Act (OWBPA) in 1990. The act prohibits discrimination against older workers with respect to all employee benefits "except when age-based reductions in employee benefit plans are justified by significant cost considerations."

Specifically, age-based discrimination is permitted only when "the actual amount of payment made or **cost incurred** on behalf of an older worker is no less than that made or incurred on behalf of a younger worker."

For example, if the cost of providing a benefit to older workers exceeds the cost of providing the same benefit to younger workers, an employer may provide lesser benefits to the older workers, provided that it spends the same amount on benefits for all workers regardless of age.

Congress provided states and their political subdivisions with the opportunity to preserve benefits provisions rendered unlawful by the amendments if: 1) they implemented new disability benefits that satisfy the

Sec. III   EXEMPTIONS   377

ADEA and 2) they allowed employees covered by the old plan the option to elect the new disability benefits. P.L. 101-433, 104 Stat. 978 (1990). *See also* 29 C.F.R. § 1625.10.

Employers can now coordinate retirees' health benefits with eligibility for Medicare without satisfying the "equal cost/equal benefit" defense in the ADEA. See *AARP v. EEOC*, section VI.A (this chapter).

- The EEOC challenged the Baltimore County pension system that governed employees hired prior to July 1, 2007. Under that system, the percentage of salary that new hires pay into Baltimore County's pension plan varies depending on the number of years to retirement eligibility. For example, a 30-year-old new hire contributes more than a 20-year-old new hire. The EEOC contended that this provision discriminated against older workers. However, a Maryland federal court held that the system did not violate the ADEA. Here, **the system was motivated by the time value of money, not by discriminatory animus**. Thus, older new hires, who had less time until their retirement, accrued benefits faster than younger new hires, and the county actually paid more towards their retirement benefits than it did for younger new hires. *EEOC v. Baltimore County*, 593 F.Supp.2d 797 (D. Md. 2009).

- A Delaware police officer, forced to retire at age 55, had only 13 years of service because he had been hired at the age of 42. He sued for age discrimination, asserting that the county's retirement pension plan improperly paid full benefits only to officers who had accrued 20 years of service. The county sought to dismiss the case. A federal court granted the motion in part, but noted that **the county's retirement plan, which pre-dated the ADEA, could still be a subterfuge to evade the purposes of the ADEA**, and refused to dismiss that portion of the lawsuit. More information was needed on that claim. *Breitigan v. New Castle County*, 350 F.Supp.2d 571 (D. Del. 2004).

- A Massachusetts statute prohibited state and local employees hired after the age of 65 from participating in any public employee retirement system in the state. A part-time town employee who was denied membership in a county retirement system based on this statute filed age discrimination charges with the Equal Employment Opportunity Commission (EEOC), which sued the state and the retirement system, claiming that the statute violated the ADEA. The district court granted the EEOC pretrial judgment. The First Circuit Court of Appeals noted that ADEA regulations permitted an employer to differentiate on the basis of age "where for each benefit or benefit package, the actual amount of payment made or cost incurred on behalf of an older worker is no less than that made or incurred on behalf of a younger worker." The state argued that the exact replication of this language in amendments to the ADEA effectively codified a subsection of the regulation that allowed the exclusion of employees who begin work after the normal retirement age. The court of appeals disagreed, holding that **the statutory exception did not authorize the retirement provision because the state admittedly spent less on older excluded workers than on younger workers**. A contrary holding would be inconsistent with the equal cost/equal benefit principle in the ADEA amendments. *EEOC v. Comwlth. of Massachusetts*, 77 F.3d 572 (1st Cir. 1996).

♦ A Massachusetts statute provided that public employees who were injured on the job and could not continue working receive accidental disability benefits of approximately 72% of their previous wages. However, a 1987 amendment modified the statutory scheme for public employees who had less than 10 years of creditable service and who were at least 55 years old. The amendment allowed disability retirement benefits until the employee turned 65. At that time, benefits were refigured to equal the amount that would have been received based on age and years of service, always a much smaller amount. Two 65-year-old employees whose disability benefits had been reduced pursuant to the amendment and one 56-year-old employee currently receiving disability retirement benefits but subject to a reduction at age 65 sued, alleging that the amendment violated the ADEA, as amended by the OWBPA. The district court granted pretrial judgment to the commonwealth. The First Circuit held that the amendment, as applied to the 65-year-old retirees, was exempt from the OWBPA because the "series" of benefit payments began prior to the OWBPA's effective date. **The OWBPA would not apply retroactively.** However, the OWBPA did apply to the 56-year-old applicant. The trial court ruling with respect to the 56-year-old retiree was reversed, and the case was remanded. *Riva v. Comwlth. of Massachusetts*, 61 F.3d 1003 (1st Cir. 1995).

♦ Members of the Milwaukee Employees' Retirement System were allowed to retire after 25 years of service or upon reaching the minimum retirement age of 57. The amount of an employee's service retirement allowance was calculated based upon years of service. Duty disability allowances provided substantially better benefits than service retirement allowances in most instances. However, the system forced older duty-disabled workers to accept the lower service retirement allowance in lieu of the more attractive disability allowance. After passage of the OWBPA, the city promulgated an optional duty disability plan that provided five years of duty disability benefits for employees disabled "within" five years of the minimum retirement age, and reduced benefits to the amount of the normal service retirement allowance at age 62. Unions representing various city employees sued the city, alleging that the optional plan violated the amended ADEA.

The court noted that under the ADEA, **the regulations allow reductions in benefits where "with respect to disabilities which occur at age 60 or less, benefits cease at age 65"** or "with respect to disabilities that occur after age 60, benefits cease five years after disablement." Alternatively, if the cost of providing the disability benefits to older workers exceeds the cost of providing such benefits to younger workers, the plan will not violate the amended ADEA. Here, a material dispute of fact with respect to cost justification data precluded pretrial judgment for either party. However, because the mandatory reduction at age 62 manipulated benefits in order to force retirement, this provision violated the amended ADEA. *Milwaukee Professional Fire Fighters Ass'n v. City of Milwaukee*, 869 F.Supp. 633 (E.D. Wis. 1994).

B. Service Retirement

♦ A group of tenured teachers over the age of 55 who met the criteria for early retirement under a prior collective bargaining agreement chose to continue working rather than receive the $20,000 lump sum payment offered. When a new bargaining agreement was reached, a second option was presented for older teachers, allowing them to continue working and receive a $7,000 payment each year for three years. The teachers, who were not eligible for this new option, sued their school district, the board of education and the teachers' union, claiming violations of the ADEA and the New York Human Rights Law. A federal court held that **the second option violated the OWBPA because it did not provide some incentive to retire as the OWBPA required**. It ordered the bargaining agreement to come into compliance with the ADEA. The Second Circuit affirmed in part, noting that the second option could be eliminated as a means of complying with the ADEA, even though that would deprive the teachers of extra pay. *Abrahamson v. Board of Educ. of Wappingers Falls Cent. School Dist.*, 374 F.3d 66 (2d Cir. 2004).

♦ A Michigan mental health services facility enacted a severance pay policy that excluded from eligibility those persons eligible for retirement pay at the time they were laid off. Several retirement age employees, who were laid off and denied severance pay, alleged that this reliance on eligibility for retirement pay violated the ADEA because age was one of the factors determining such eligibility. The employees sued the facility. A federal court noted that the Older Workers Benefit Protection Act of 1990 (OWBPA) permits actions otherwise proscribed by the ADEA "where ... the actual amount of payment made or cost incurred on behalf of an older worker is no less than that made or incurred on behalf of a younger worker" or where the bona fide employee benefit plan is a qualified voluntary early retirement incentive plan. Here, **the OWBPA was not effective at the time the employees were denied severance pay**. Because the severance pay policy did not violate the ADEA before it was amended by the OWBPA, the court dismissed the employees' claims. *Barney v. Haveman*, 879 F.Supp. 775 (W.D. Mich. 1995).

C. ERISA

♦ Nine current or retired employees of the Port of Seattle who were eligible to receive retirement benefits under a collective bargaining agreement between the port and the union brought a lawsuit after the bargaining agreement expired and the port stopped making contributions to the welfare benefits trust fund. The employees and retirees asserted that the lawsuit was governed by ERISA, but the Washington Supreme Court disagreed, noting that the question of their vesting rights had to be determined by state law vesting principles. The court also held that **retirement healthcare and welfare benefits provided by the bargaining agreement vested for life with employees who reached retirement eligibility during the term of the bargaining agreement**. Since they did not have the opportunity to bargain for continued benefits after retiring, and since the agreement did not limit benefits on the duration of its term, the port could not cease to provide benefits for the retirees. It did not have to maintain the welfare trust fund, however, if it could find a comparable system for providing benefits to the retirees. *Navlet v. Port of Seattle*, 164 Wash.2d 818, 194 P.3d 221 (Wash. 2008).

♦ A retired employee of the Federal Reserve Bank of St. Louis brought a lawsuit under the ADEA and ERISA, asserting claims related to her retirement. The Federal Reserve Bank sought to dismiss the ERISA claim. A Missouri federal district court granted the motion, finding that the bank was an "instrumentality" of the federal government. The Federal Reserve Banks were established by Congressional legislation for the public purpose of increased control of the nation's currency and banking system. They are supervised by an entity that bears the hallmarks of an agency. Consequently, **the Federal Reserve Bank's employee benefit plans were government plans that were exempt from coverage under ERISA**. *Berini v. Federal Reserve Bank of St. Louis*, 420 F.Supp.2d 1021 (E.D. Mo. 2005).

♦ An Ohio county allowed certain not-for-profit corporations to join its health plan. The plan covered both county employees and those employed by the nonprofits. The expenses were paid from a fund financed by the employers in the plan. Eventually, it was learned that the plan was insufficiently funded, and the county asked the participants for additional contributions. The nonprofits sued in state court, alleging that they were not obligated to make additional payments to the county. In a related federal lawsuit, a U.S. district court held that the plan was subject to ERISA and within the exclusive jurisdiction of the federal court. The state court then dismissed the lawsuit. The county appealed to the Court of Appeals of Ohio, contending that the health plan was a government plan and therefore exempt from ERISA. The court of appeals noted that although the plan was established and maintained for public employees, **the inclusion of nongovernmental employees transformed it into a Multiple Employer Welfare Arrangement subject to ERISA**. Because ERISA applied, the federal court had exclusive jurisdiction over this matter. *Nord Community Mental Health Center v. Lorain County*, 638 N.E.2d 623 (Ohio Ct. App. 1994).

IV. UNEMPLOYMENT AND WORKERS' COMPENSATION

State unemployment compensation systems are designed to compensate displaced workers who become unemployed through no fault of their own. When employees are injured in the course and scope of their employment, they generally become entitled to workers' compensation benefits. However, questions often arise as to whether an injury has arisen out of employment.

A. Unemployment Compensation

♦ A manager with the Pennsylvania Bureau of Driver Licensing accessed driver license records on two occasions to get information about his estranged wife's boyfriend. He printed out the information and took it from the premises.

When his wife discovered a copy in her house, she turned him in. He admitted to the misconduct and was fired, then applied for unemployment compensation benefits. His claim was denied. The Pennsylvania Commonwealth Court held that **he was not similarly situated to other employees fired for accessing confidential information improperly** who had received benefits. In those situations, the employees had been accessing records with the knowledge and consent of friends or family. Here, he not only got the information without the boyfriend's knowledge or consent, but he also printed it out and removed it from the work site. *Walsh v. Unemployment Compensation Board of Review*, 943 A.2d 363 (Pa. Commw. Ct. 2008).

• A Pennsylvania corrections officer heard rumors that a fellow officer was planning to have an inmate under his supervision assaulted by other inmates, but did not know when or whether the attack was to occur. He chose not to report the rumors out of fear that his fellow corrections officers would retaliate against him. When the attack occurred, he did not come to the aid of the inmate, again out of fear of retaliation. After an investigation into his behavior, he was fired. He sought unemployment benefits, which were initially granted, but the Pennsylvania Commonwealth Court ultimately reversed. **The officer's fear of retaliation, no matter how well founded, was not a defense to the charge that he engaged in willful misconduct** when he failed to report the rumors or aid the inmate he was duty-bound to protect. *Dep't of Corrections, SCI-Camp Hill v. Unemployment Compensation Board of Review*, 943 A.2d 1011 (Pa. Commw. Ct. 2008).

• A secretary for the St. Louis Teachers and School Related Personnel Union made arrangements to receive her paycheck via direct deposit. When she received a paper check, she deposited it. However, she also received the same amount via direct deposit. When an audit revealed the double payment, she was told she would have to repay the overpayment. She agreed to repay the money in $100 installments, but was late with the first one. She was then fired. When she applied for unemployment compensation benefits, the Missouri Division of Employment Security denied them because she was discharged for misconduct associated with work. The Missouri Court of Appeals upheld the denial of benefits, **finding the failure to repay the employer in a timely manner to be disqualifying misconduct.** *White v. St. Louis Teachers Union, Division of Employment Security*, 217 S.W.3d 382 (Mo. Ct. App. 2007).

• The director of a public works department in Pennsylvania tested positive for marijuana during a random drug test. After he was fired, he filed for unemployment compensation benefits, asserting that he was not disqualified for them because his drug use had not been while he was on duty and thus did not violate the borough's substance abuse policy. The case reached the Commonwealth Court, which held that **it did not matter that his drug use was off duty.** He was ineligible for benefits because the policy not only prohibited drug use while on duty, but it also required that employees' systems be free of drugs while they were on duty. *Turner v. Unemployment Compensation Board of Review*, 899 A.2d 381 (Pa. Commw. Ct. 2006).

♦ A corrections officer in Mississippi was fired after being absent for three days without notifying the sheriff's department. He filed for unemployment compensation, and the hearing referee apparently failed to notify the sheriff of the upcoming hearing. When only the corrections officer appeared, the referee ruled in his favor. The unemployment compensation review board then sent the sheriff a notice informing him he had 14 days to appeal. He filed the appeal 17 days later, and the review board upheld the claim for benefits. The Mississippi Supreme Court agreed that the corrections officer was entitled to benefits. Even if the sheriff never got the notice about the hearing, **he did receive the notice informing him that he had only 14 days to appeal the findings.** *Mississippi Employment Security Comm'n v. Marion County Sheriff's Dep't*, 865 So.2d 1153 (Miss. 2004).

♦ A temporary placement service hired employees to perform short- and long-term assignments with client companies. The service placed an employee in a long-term assignment with the Small Business Administration (SBA). After the employee's SBA supervisor told her she was going to be reassigned to a work cubicle that the employee believed was totally inadequate, the employee orally resigned. About three hours later, she changed her mind and attempted to withdraw the resignation, but the supervisor refused to rescind it. When the service had no further assignments for her, she applied for unemployment compensation. A hearing officer denied benefits on the grounds that she had quit because of dissatisfaction with standard working conditions. Thus, she was not unemployed through no fault of her own. The Colorado Court of Appeals affirmed the decision against her, noting that **her voluntary resignation set in motion the chain of events that led to her unemployment.** *Cunliffe v. Industrial Claims Appeals Office*, 51 P.3d 1088 (Colo. Ct. App. 2002).

♦ An Iowa county employee plowed snow and spread gravel on county roads. He received an oral warning about poor job performance and the failure to report damaged county property. Several years later, he received another warning. He then hit an overhead electrical wire with a county truck, but was not issued a warning for this incident. Three years after that, while spreading gravel at the recommended speed of 20 miles per hour, he was forced to swerve to avoid an oncoming car. In doing so, he hit and broke an overhead utility wire. Two days later, he hit and broke a support wire for an overhead utility line partially hidden by overhanging trees. Rather than terminate him, the county offered to let him take four drug tests per year, three of which he would have to pay for. He refused and was fired. When he sought unemployment compensation, the Supreme Court of Iowa held that he was entitled to benefits. Even putting all the incidents together, **the county failed to show that the employee had committed work-related misconduct.** Mere inefficiency or inability does not constitute misconduct. *Lee v. Employment Appeal Board*, 616 N.W.2d 661 (Iowa 2000).

♦ A control officer at a county jail monitored surveillance cameras and knew that she was supposed to get relief from her supervisor for bathroom breaks. However, her supervisor never showed up when she asked him to watch the monitors, and when she complained to the department head, nothing was done. She was fired after problems occurred on two of her shifts. She failed to catch the problems because she had gone to the bathroom. When she applied for unemployment compensation, the county challenged her claim. The Mississippi Supreme Court held that the control officer was entitled to benefits for two reasons. First, she had never been told that she would be subject to immediate termination for failing to monitor the cameras or for failing to detect an incident. Second, the sheriff applied the surveillance policy differently to her by taking no disciplinary action against a jail administrator whose job was to review the control officer's tapes after her shift; the administrator had failed to do so. **Though the control officer's conduct had been unsatisfactory, it was not misconduct so as to justify the denial of benefits.** *Coahoma County v. Mississippi Employment Security Comm'n*, 761 So.2d 846 (Miss. 2000).

♦ An employee of the Missouri Department of Natural Resources was transferred to a job site more than 150 miles away from his home. A one-way commute was approximately two-and-one-half hours. Although temporary, the position would become permanent in 30 days if there were no other positions available. The employee attempted to get reinstated to his previous position, but to no avail. The department made a vague offer to pay his travel expenses but did not adjust his work schedule to allow for the lengthy commute. The employee resigned and obtained unemployment compensation benefits. The department appealed to the Missouri Court of Appeals, which held that the employee was entitled to unemployment compensation because he did not voluntarily leave his job without good cause attributable to his work or employer. Here, **it was reasonable for the employee to quit because the department only made a vague offer to pay his travel expenses** without accommodating his workday to allow for his commute. Also, the employee made a good-faith effort to resolve the problem when he unsuccessfully attempted to get reinstated to his former position. The employee's failure to comply with the transfer to a remote job site did not disqualify him from receiving benefits. Unemployment compensation was awarded. *Missouri Dep't of Natural Resources v. Lossos*, 960 S.W.2d 537 (Mo. Ct. App. 1998).

♦ An employee of the Seattle Department of Parks and Recreation had a history of chronic absenteeism from work. Eventually, several conditions for her continued employment were set forth, including 48-hour advance scheduling of all requests for vacation and compensatory time. When she took vacation without obtaining advance approval, the department fired her. She applied for unemployment compensation benefits. The Employment Security Department denied her request on the grounds that she had been discharged for misconduct, but an administrative law judge reversed. The Court of Appeals of Washington held that the employee was disqualified from benefits because she was discharged for misconduct connected with her work. Here, **it was undisputed that the employee took vacation time without obtaining approval 48 hours in advance**. Because this was a requirement for her continued employment, and because the absence was entirely within her control, the employee was guilty of misconduct such that her unemployment in effect was voluntary. *Galvin v. State of Washington, Employment Security Dep't,* 942 P.2d 1040 (Wash. Ct. App. 1997).

♦ A Rhode Island employee of the Department of Children, Youth and Families (DCYF), who served as a superintendent of the Rhode Island Training School for Youth, called the city police department claiming that she had an intruder in her home. The officers did not find an intruder but discovered a white powder that was later determined to be cocaine. Criminal charges were eventually filed against the superintendent, and the director of the DCYF placed her on administrative leave. She was then fired and applied for unemployment compensation benefits, which were denied. The Supreme Court of Rhode Island found that the definition of "misconduct" included a disregard of standards of behavior that the employer has the right to expect from its employees. Here, **the superintendent had a position of high visibility and great responsibility, and she had an obligation to maintain standards of conduct** at least in compliance with the criminal law both on and off the job. Many of the young people committed to her care at the school were confined for drug-related offenses. Accordingly, the employee was not entitled to unemployment benefits. *Bunch v. Board of Review,* 690 A.2d 335 (R.I. 1997).

♦ A Florida correctional officer had several unscheduled absences from work caused by domestic problems with her abusive husband. She was eventually discharged for excessive absenteeism, and she applied for unemployment compensation benefits. The Unemployment Appeals Commission found her ineligible for benefits, and she appealed. The District Court of Appeal of Florida reversed, finding that **the correctional officer's excessive unauthorized absences from work because of her domestic problems did not constitute misconduct**. Specifically, the correctional officer produced sufficient evidence to overcome the presumption that her absences were conduct evincing willful or wanton disregard of her employer's interests, or carelessness or negligence of such a degree or recurrence as to manifest culpability, wrongful intent, or evil design, or an intentional and substantial disregard of the employer's interests or of the employee's duties. Temporary absence from work because of illness or injury or family emergencies does not constitute misconduct that would justify a denial of benefits to an involuntarily terminated employee. *Gilbert v. Dep't of Corrections,* 696 So.2d 416 (Fla. Dist. Ct. App. 1997).

♦ A Louisiana program inspector of low-income housing units received three warnings for incomplete inspections of property, carelessness and work quality violations. The city eventually discharged the inspector, and he applied for unemployment compensation benefits. The Court of Appeal of Louisiana noted that the unemployment statute generally disqualifies employees from benefits upon a finding of misconduct such as a willful or wanton disregard of the employer's interests. However, **substandard work performance alone does not constitute misconduct** unless the employee has the capability to perform the job duties but does not. Here, the inspector's conduct did not constitute a willful and wanton disregard for the city's interests. The inspector's supervisor had stated that she believed he was not capable of performing his job. His inability, not misconduct, prevented satisfactory job performance. The inspector was entitled to unemployment benefits. *Victor v. Administrator, Office of Employment Security*, 676 So.2d 1123 (La. Ct. App. 1996).

B. Workers' Compensation

♦ A Michigan probation officer was accused of sexual harassment by five female attorneys whom he met while attending probation violation hearings. His female supervisor investigated the complaints and recommended a disciplinary conference after the officer denied the allegations. At the conference, he was found to be in violation of Department of Corrections work rules and was suspended for 10 days without pay. When he returned to work, he claimed that he was harassed by his supervisor and by the attorneys he allegedly harassed earlier. He suffered from depression and began seeing a psychologist, then filed a claim for workers' compensation benefits. The Supreme Court of Michigan ruled that he was not entitled to benefits. Here, **the officer was injured "by reason of" his misconduct**. The disciplinary proceedings that caused the mental disability were necessitated by the alleged sexual harassment, and the officer's denials of misconduct were not believed at any level of the proceedings. The officer could not collect workers' compensation. *Daniel v. Michigan Dep't of Corrections*, 658 N.W.2d 144 (Mich. 2003).

♦ A police officer informed his superiors that he suffered from on-the-job depression and that he could no longer continue as a police officer. They assured him that they would handle the filing of his workers' compensation claim, and the city attempted to negotiate a settlement with its insurer for over a year. Nearly two years later, it decided to contest the claim. When the officer filed a petition challenging the city's action, the workers' compensation commission found the petition untimely and dismissed it. The Mississippi Supreme Court held that even though the statute of limitations had passed, the officer could continue his action against the city because **the city had assured him that it would file his claim for him, and the officer had reasonably relied on those assurances**. Further, the city had failed to file a notice challenging the claim within two weeks of learning of the injury, as required by state law. *McCrary v. City of Biloxi*, 757 So.2d 978 (Miss. 2000).

♦ A Pennsylvania police sergeant began to suffer from posttraumatic stress syndrome after over 30 years on the force. He had experienced a number of incidents during his tenure, but nothing unusual for a law enforcement officer. He applied for workers' compensation benefits and obtained an award, which was appealed to the state supreme court. The court reversed the award of benefits, finding that **his physical ailments were a subjective reaction to normal working conditions**. Having a gun pointed in his face, receiving threats against him and his family, being involved in a standoff with 25 neo-Nazis, and having to take over the department when the chief unexpectedly died of a heart attack did not amount to such unusual conditions that made an award of benefits justifiable. *Davis v. Workers' Compensation Appeals Board*, 751 A.2d 168 (Pa. 2000).

1. Arising From Employment

• Two years after a Maryland police officer retired, he filed a claim for workers' compensation, alleging that he had injuries to his knees and hips from getting in and out of his patrol car repeatedly over his 26-year career. A trial court and the Court of Special Appeals of Maryland ruled against him, noting that **he failed to prove he was incapacitated by the pain of getting in and out of his car**. He worked up until his retirement, and even though his doctor testified that he would need treatment to continue doing his job, the officer did not prove that he was avoiding doing his job partially or completely because of the pain. Rather, he continued to work, despite the pain, until he retired. *Smith v. Howard County*, 935 A.2d 450 (Md. Ct. Spec. App. 2007).

• A firefighter for the city of North Las Vegas worked for 15 years before spending a number of years in other jobs. He then became a firefighter again for a private company. During his second stint as a firefighter, he began taking medication for a heart condition and possible silent heart attack. Later he suffered a disabling heart attack. When he filed for workers' compensation benefits, the company's administrator denied the claim. The case reached the Supreme Court of Nevada, which noted that the firefighter had worked at that job for two different employers for five or more continuous years. It also noted the statutory presumption that the disability arose from employment. It then had to determine which of the two employers was liable for medical and disability payments. It decided that **the last injurious exposure rule applied**, requiring the private company (not the city) to defend the claim. *Employers Insurance Co. of Nevada v. Daniels*, 145 P.3d 1024 (Nev. 2006).

• A Connecticut school superintendent with a history of heart problems learned that his contract was not going to be renewed. On the day before his contract was set to expire, he attended a school board meeting at which a last-chance agreement for another employee was considered. He recommended accepting the agreement, but a number of board members harshly criticized him for his stance. When the chairman announced that the board would not accept the recommendation, the superintendent had a heart attack and died. His widow filed for workers' compensation death benefits and the Appellate Court of Connecticut ruled that she was entitled to them. His cardiologist's testimony established that **the board members' attack created the stress that caused the heart attack, making it work-related and compensable**. *Chesler v. City of Derby*, 899 A.2d 624 (Conn. App. Ct. 2006).

• Fifteen years after joining the Philadelphia fire department, a firefighter with a tattoo and a history of alcohol problems contracted hepatitis C. He notified the fire commissioner and stated that **he believed he contracted the disease on the job**. Three years later, he filed a workers' compensation claim, seeking payment for his medical bills. His doctor conducted a biopsy of his liver that did not show alcohol causation. Also, his liver disease was more advanced than would be expected if he had contracted the virus from his tattoo. The firefighter testified that he did not always have gloves available when he was treating bleeding individuals. A workers' compensation judge and the Pennsylvania Commonwealth Court ruled in his favor, awarding him reasonable and necessary medical expenses for his occupational disease. *City of Philadelphia v. WCAB (Cospelich)*, 893 A.2d 171 (Pa. Commw. Ct. 2006).

♦ Juneau County, Wisconsin officers were involved in the pursuit of a murder suspect and requested helicopter assistance from Milwaukee County. Two Milwaukee County deputies flew the helicopter to Juneau County to assist in the search and were killed on the way back afterwards. Milwaukee County made workers' compensation payments to their families, then sought reimbursement from Juneau County, citing the state's "mutual aid" law. The law says that deputies performing police duties outside the county are entitled to the same workers' compensation as for services rendered in the county, and that the employing county will be reimbursed by the county commanding the services out of which the payments arose. The Wisconsin Supreme Court held that Juneau County had to reimburse Milwaukee County because it requested the deputies' services, and Juneau County's insurer had to cover the amount. *Milwaukee County v. Juneau County*, 676 N.W.2d 513 (Wis. 2004).

♦ A paramedic supervisor in a county fire and rescue department responded to about 10 emergency calls a day, including airplane crashes, amputations and decapitations, automobile accidents with multiple victims, shootings, stabbings and house fires where the entire family was killed. After 10 years, he was assigned to various administrative posts and only worked one 24-hour shift every two months to maintain his paramedic certification. On March 10, 1996, he responded to a house fire, pronounced a woman dead, then had to treat her 5-year-old stepdaughter. This reminded him of a fire he responded to more than 15 years earlier where everybody died. He encountered difficulty breathing and later consulted a psychologist. She diagnosed posttraumatic stress disorder, which later worsened into major depression. By December 1996, he was suicidal and had to be hospitalized. When he made a claim for temporary total disability benefits, the workers' compensation commission denied them. The case reached the Virginia Supreme Court, which ruled that he was entitled to benefits. Here, **the paramedic suffered an occupational disease as a result of repeated exposure to traumatic stressors**, which caused reactions in his neurobiological systems. The court remanded the case to the workers' compensation commission for a calculation of benefits. *Fairfax County Fire and Rescue Dep't v. Mottram*, 559 S.E.2d 698 (Va. 2002).

♦ A New York 911 operator was required to work rotating shifts. Eventually, she began experiencing mental health problems that resulted in three separate hospitalizations. She permanently left her employment and filed a workers' compensation claim, contending that her condition was caused by work-related stress. The workers' compensation board ruled that she did not sustain an accidental injury or suffer from an occupational disease within the meaning of the state's workers' compensation law because **the stress to which she was exposed was no greater than that normally encountered in the workplace**. It denied her claim. The appellate division court reversed, finding that the board erred when it denied the operator's claim. On further appeal, the New York Court of Appeals reversed the appellate division. It noted that substantial evidence supported the board's determination. Therefore, its decision was binding on the courts. *Leggio v. Suffolk County Police Dep't,* 96 N.Y.2d 846, 754 N.E.2d 766, 729 N.Y.S.2d 664 (N.Y. 2001).

♦ A trooper with 22 years of service for the Michigan State Police became the subject of an internal affairs investigation after his wife filed a complaint against him for assault and battery. He was placed on administrative leave and had his badge and gun taken away from him. He also was told that he could return to work if he met with a psychologist or psychiatrist and agreed to undergo counseling. Later, it was determined that the charges against him were not credible. However, he did not return to work and, six months later, was placed on disability retirement. He filed for workers' compensation benefits for the mental injuries he had suffered. His claim was dismissed based on a 1984 case that disallowed workers' compensation for mental injuries arising out of termination (because those injuries could not arise out of and in the course of employment). The Michigan Supreme Court reversed, finding that **the officer could file for workers' compensation benefits here because the action taken against him was not a termination.** *Calovecchi v. Michigan,* 611 N.W.2d 300 (Mich. 2000).

♦ A case technician for the New Hampshire Department of Health and Human Services had frequent medical and psychological problems as well as attention deficit disorder. Her work suffered, and she was subjected to justified criticism from her superior. Eventually, she left work, was diagnosed with major depression and applied for workers' compensation benefits. A hearing officer denied her claim, and an appeals board reversed. The Supreme Court of New Hampshire held that she was entitled to workers' compensation benefits because **her depression was an unexpected consequence of good-faith criticism of her performance.** It did not matter that the cause of the injury was routine (and not accidental) because the effect on the employee was unexpected. The court left it to the legislature to decide whether to bar recovery for stress-related injuries arising from good-faith employment actions. *In re New Hampshire Dep't of HHS,* 761 A.2d 431 (N.H. 2000).

♦ A North Dakota law enforcement officer eventually became the chief of police and then suffered a heart attack. He underwent bypass surgery and applied for workers' compensation benefits under a state law that presumed heart disease-related impairments were suffered in the line of duty for police officers with at least two continuous years of service. The North Dakota Supreme Court **granted him benefits despite his past history of smoking, high cholesterol, hypertension and a family predisposition to heart disease.** At the time of his 1982 hire, the officer's medical records did not reveal that he suffered any heart-related impairment. The court rejected testimony by a physician who refused to recognize stress as a risk factor in law enforcement. *Robertson v. City of New England,* 616 N.W.2d 844 (N.D. 2000).

Sec. IV   UNEMPLOYMENT AND WORKERS' COMPENSATION   389

♦ **A nonsmoking physical education teacher who developed tonsil cancer after sharing an office with a chain smoker for 26 years** applied for workers' compensation benefits. A workers' compensation judge concluded that the cancer arose out of, and to a material degree was caused by, conditions peculiar to the teacher's place of employment. The teacher had never smoked and had never lived with anyone who smoked. His alcohol consumption (also a factor in tonsil cancer) was limited to two drinks a year. The teacher was awarded past and future medical expenses, temporary disability benefits and attorneys' fees. The school district's board of education was also directed to reimburse the teacher for all accumulated sick time. The board sought review in a New Jersey court, which affirmed the compensation award but vacated the sick time directive. The evidence supported the award of workers' compensation benefits. However, only the Commissioner of Education could decide how sick leave associated with a work-related illness should be applied. *Magaw v. Middletown Board of Educ.*, 731 A.2d 1196 (N.J. Super. Ct. App. Div. 1999).

♦ A Washington Department of Transportation (DOT) employee sustained injuries when a DOT vehicle hit him after work in a DOT parking lot. The parking lot was also used as a work area to prepare DOT vehicles for service. The employee was awarded workers' compensation benefits, which he later attempted to reject (so that he could sue for his injuries). The state board affirmed the award, and the employee sought judicial review. The Court of Appeals of Washington noted that even though the parking lot was a mixed-use area, the determinative factor was not so much whether the parking lot was a "job site," but **whether the employee was acting in the course of his employment when he was injured**. Here, if the employee had been directed to be in the parking lot, or had been performing work duties there in furtherance of DOT business, he would have been covered. However, because he had not been so directed, he was not entitled to workers' compensation. *Bolden v. State of Washington Dep't of Transportation*, 974 P.2d 909 (Wash. Ct. App. 1999).

♦ A veteran Pennsylvania police officer shot and killed an individual who had barricaded himself inside a building. He sustained injuries to his neck in the ordeal and was compensated for them under workers' compensation. Initially, the officer was praised for his actions. However, it was later learned that the suspect had been unarmed. Public demonstrations began calling for his suspension or termination. He was then indicted and tried on criminal charges. After his acquittal, he sought compensation for his posttraumatic stress injuries. The Pennsylvania Commonwealth Court held that **abnormal conditions were not present so as to justify workers' compensation benefits**, and the Supreme Court of Pennsylvania affirmed. Even if the investigation and trial were abnormal, they were not related to the officer's employment. *City of Philadelphia v. WCAB*, 728 A.2d 938 (Pa. 1999).

♦ A Georgia man was employed as a park maintenance supervisor. During a flood, he was required to manually recover caskets and corpses that floodwaters had carried away from a cemetery. As a result, he suffered vivid, recurring nightmares and was eventually diagnosed with posttraumatic stress disorder.

The employee filed a workers' compensation claim, which was denied by an administrative law judge. The Supreme Court of Georgia affirmed the denial of the claim. The Georgia Workers' Compensation Act defines a compensable injury as a discernible physical injury, and a psychological injury is compensable only if it arises naturally and unavoidably from some discernible physical occurrence. The physical injury need not be the precipitating cause of the psychological injury, but **the psychological injury is compensable only if the physical injury contributed to the continuation of the psychological trauma**. While the employee did endure gruesome physical contact with corpses and did suffer a psychological trauma, the act did not authorize a recovery for purely psychological injuries. *Abernathy v. City of Albany, Georgia*, 495 S.E.2d 13 (Ga. 1998).

♦ A Wisconsin woman became employed as a city engineering technician and was required to provide her address and telephone number to the city's payroll department. Concerned about her abusive former husband, she expressed her desire to have the information remain confidential. However, when the former husband called impersonating a bank representative, a supervisor authorized release of the information without verifying his credentials. The former husband then regularly telephoned the woman at work informing her that he knew her home address and telephone number, and that he would kill her and their two children. She suffered severe emotional distress and sued the city to recover damages for negligent infliction of emotional distress arising from the city's disclosure.

The Supreme Court of Wisconsin first determined that receiving a personal phone call at work constituted a circumstance of employment that was incidental to employment, and was therefore within the course of employment. Next, the court found that when an attack occurs during the course of employment and arises from personal animus imported from a private relationship, the incident arises out of the claimant's employment if employment conditions have contributed to or facilitated the attack. **Because the woman was required to provide her residential information to the city as a condition of employment**, and that facilitated the release of the information, the accident causing her injury arose out of her employment. Accordingly, the exclusive remedy provision of the Worker's Compensation Act barred her common law tort action against the city. *Weiss v. City of Milwaukee*, 559 N.W.2d 588 (Wis. 1997).

♦ A Maryland county paramedic responded to two emergency calls involving serious injuries and fatalities that occurred within a few days of each other. A few years later, she requested a demotion to firefighter but was required to act as a paramedic on several occasions, including one particularly gruesome motorcycle accident. After the motorcycle accident, she remembered the earlier traumatic accidents and began suffering from posttraumatic stress disorder (PTSD). She filed a workers' compensation claim, seeking compensation for 110 hours of missed work. The workers' compensation commission denied benefits, concluding that she had not suffered an occupational disease arising out of and in the course of her employment. The Court of Appeals of Maryland held that PTSD may be compensable as an occupational disease under the Workers' Compensation Act if the claimant can present sufficient evidence to meet the statutory requirements. PTSD is not as a matter of law excluded from compensable occupational diseases, and the nonphysical nature of her claim did not automatically exclude her from coverage. Rather, **she had to prove that she contracted PTSD "as a result of and in the course of employment,"** that the mental illness was due to the nature of a paramedic's job, and that employment as a paramedic entailed the hazard of developing PTSD. The court remanded the case for further proceedings. *Means v. Baltimore County, Maryland*, 689 A.2d 1238 (Md. 1997).

♦ Within six months of beginning work for the Idaho Department of Parks and Recreation as a caretaker, a 67-year-old employee suffered two industrial injuries. After the second injury, she was unable to continue working. She had limited education and work experience, no transferable skills, and an extensive history of preexisting medical conditions including previous industrial injuries. She filed for workers' compensation, contending that the preexisting conditions combined with the subsequent injuries to render her totally and permanently disabled. The Industrial Commission referee ruled against her, and the Supreme Court of Idaho affirmed. **The caretaker was an odd-lot employee who already was totally and permanently disabled coming into the subsequent injuries.** The odd-lot doctrine expands the definition of the term "total disability" to include a claimant for whom there is no employment regularly and continuously available. Here, the caretaker was an odd-lot employee because she performed no more than light-duty work and even this was beyond her diminished abilities, thereby equating it to work provided by a sympathetic employer or friend. *Bybee v. State of Idaho, Industrial Special Indemnity Fund*, 921 P.2d 1200 (Idaho 1996).

2. Exclusivity

♦ A Rhode Island volunteer firefighter burned his hand and wrist while following the instruction of a fire district representative who told him to dump gasoline from a foam cup near a fire during a training exercise. He filed a claim with the fire district's insurer and then sued for negligent supervision. A lower court granted pretrial judgment to the district, but the Rhode Island Supreme Court reversed. It held that **the state's "injured on duty" statute did not cover the volunteer firefighter because he was not employed by the district.** Thus, workers' compensation was not his exclusive remedy and he could pursue his tort lawsuit against the district. *Angell v. The Union Fire Dist. of South Kingstown*, 935 A.2d 943 (R.I. 2007).

♦ Several state hospital employees in Washington who were injured in assaults by patients with mental illnesses sued the hospital for their personal injuries, claiming that it knew the assaults would occur and that it disregarded that knowledge, such that workers' compensation was not their exclusive remedy. The Washington Court of Appeals noted that **the state did not follow the "substantial certainty" test of most other states**. A plaintiff must show that an employer was actually certain that an injury would occur. Here, that threshold was not met. The employees failed to show that the hospital knew any particular assault would occur. Further, even if they could show that, they could not show that the hospital willfully disregarded that knowledge. The hospital in fact offered training in how to respond to patient assaults, demonstrating that it took steps to solve the problem. Workers' compensation was the employees' exclusive remedy. *Brame v. Western State Hospital*, 136 Wash.App. 740, 150 P.3d 637 (Wash. Ct. App. 2007).

◆ A Pennsylvania state trooper was investigating a car accident on an interstate freeway when part of the road collapsed. He fell into a hole and was injured. After collecting workers' compensation benefits for his injuries, he sued the state department of transportation (DOT) for additional damages, asserting that it was a separate entity from the state police. The Commonwealth Court of Pennsylvania disagreed. Under the workers' compensation act, the state and its agencies were not separate, and **the trooper could not sue the DOT for additional compensation**. *Kincel v. Pennsylvania*, 867 A.2d 758 (Pa. Commw. Ct. 2005).

◆ An Idaho physical therapist incurred injuries while helping a wheelchair-bound student off a bus. She tried to help the student because the aide provided by the school for assisting the student had a bad back. She sued the district for negligence, asserting that she was not limited to workers' compensation because she was an independent contractor and not an employee. The case reached the Supreme Court of Idaho, which first noted that the therapist was not entitled to workers' compensation because she was not an employee of the district. However, she also could not succeed on her negligence claim because the school district did not owe her a legal duty. The school could not have foreseen that she would try to maneuver the wheelchair off the bus. Thus, **even though she was an independent contractor, she could not sue the district for negligence**. *Daleiden v. Jefferson County Joint School Dist.*, 80 P.3d 1067 (Idaho 2003).

◆ A Connecticut police officer was a member of the town's tactical response team. While the team was executing a search warrant on an auto sales business, one of the team's members accidentally fired his weapon, hitting the officer. The officer sued the town and various officials to recover for his injuries. However, a state trial court ruled against him, holding that **his exclusive remedy was workers' compensation**. On appeal, the officer argued that the town intentionally created a dangerous situation that made his injuries substantially certain to occur. The Appellate Court of Connecticut affirmed the ruling against the officer. He failed to show that the town engaged in wrongful misconduct such that his injury was substantially certain to result. Even if the team was inadequately staffed, trained, managed and supervised, the town's wrongful failure to act constituted negligence and not intentional misconduct. As a result, the officer was only entitled to recover workers' compensation benefits. *Melanson v. Town of West Hartford*, 767 A.2d 764 (Conn. App. Ct. 2001).

* A Virginia postal worker was involved in a physical altercation with a co-worker over work-related duties. The postal worker sustained a closed-head injury as a result of the co-worker's physical assault. She sued the co-worker under the Federal Tort Claims Act in state court. The co-worker sought to dismiss the action on the ground that the Federal Employees' Compensation Act (FECA) is the sole remedy for a federal employee who is injured in the course of her employment. The matter was then removed to a Virginia federal court, which ruled that since the FECA covers all work-related injuries, the postal employee's state tort actions were barred, and her exclusive remedy was with the FECA. The Fourth Circuit reversed for procedural reasons, holding that **because the co-worker failed to have the Attorney General certify his actions as within the scope of employment, he was not immune** under the amended FTCA. *Salazar v. Ballesteros,* 17 Fed.Appx. 129 (4th Cir. 2001).

* Two employees of the New Mexico Public Defender's Department, along with one employee's daughter, were traveling to a mental health task force meeting when they were in an accident. One employee was killed. Her daughter and the other employee sustained injuries and obtained workers' compensation benefits from the state (the daughter received workers' compensation death benefits). They joined the deceased employee's husband in a lawsuit against the highway department for negligence in failing to properly stripe and place signs along the highway. The Supreme Court of New Mexico held that the exclusive remedy provision of the state's workers' compensation act barred the lawsuit against the highway department. Because the state was the employer of all employees in its various agencies, the highway department was not a different legal entity that could be sued. The court joined such jurisdictions as New York, California, Pennsylvania and Michigan in determining that **a state could not be subdivided into various departments for the purpose of asserting common law rights** on behalf of an employee of one department against another. *Singhas v. New Mexico State Highway Dep't,* 946 P.2d 645 (N.M. 1997).

3. Off-Duty Occurrences

* While with friends in a rural area at night, an off-duty Arizona police officer heard gunshots about a mile away. He and his friends decided to leave and began packing up. A car then approached and shined its lights at them, and its occupants started firing. The officer dove for cover behind his vehicle, but saw that one of his friends had frozen. He ran over to protect the friend and as he tried to push the friend into cover, he was shot in the back. He told his friends to try to memorize the license plate number of the vehicle. He later sought workers' compensation benefits, which an administrative law judge denied. The Arizona Court of Appeals reversed, **finding the officer was entitled to benefits because he was acting in the course and scope of his employment at the time of his injury.** The police department code required him to take official action, even when off-duty, to save life or property, or to prevent the escape of a felon or violent criminal. *Lane v. Industrial Comm'n of Arizona,* 178 P.3d 516 (Ariz. Ct. App. 2008).

• An Arkansas school custodian went to the bank on his lunch break. On his way back to work, he noticed that the lot he liked to park in was blocked by a truck. He drove around to the back entrance and unlocked the gate there, intending to enter that way. However, the gate fell on him, breaking his leg in two places and causing him to miss more than seven months of work. He sought workers' compensation benefits, but was turned down. The Arkansas Court of Appeals held that he was not providing services to the school district at the time of his injury. Rather, he was attending to a personal need – trying to park in a convenient location of his choice – and acting contrary to his employer's interest in keeping a locked entrance. The Supreme Court of Arkansas reversed, ruling that the custodian was entitled to benefits. Here, **he was attempting to return to work at the time of his injury, and he was on call whenever he was on school premises**, even during his lunch break. Further, by unlocking the gate at the back entrance, he was advancing his employer's interests by allowing other employees to enter or exit by that gate. *Texarkana School Dist. v. Conner*, 373 Ark. 372 (Ark. 2008).

• A Montana sheriff's deputy traveled with his supervisor to a hotel for a police conference. While there, the deputy began drinking with fellow conference attendees at a reception. The reception ended at midnight, but the deputy continued to drink with a group of other attendees. Subsequently, he fell off a balcony overlooking the indoor courtyard and died from his injuries. His blood-alcohol level was .203. His widow sought workers' compensation benefits, arguing that he had been acting within the course and scope of his employment at the time of his death, and the Supreme Court of Montana agreed. Here, **the employer knew about the alcohol consumption and did nothing to stop it**. And the after-reception drinking was an extension of the employment-related activities he engaged in during the conference. *Van Vleet v. Montana Ass'n of Counties Workers' Compensation Trust*, 103 P.3d 544 (Mont. 2004).

• A Philadelphia transit police officer ran in a park near his home about twice a week to try to ensure that he would be able to pass the transit authority's running standard of 1.5 miles in 12 minutes or less. During one of his runs, he suffered a knee injury when he hit a depression on the running path. He underwent surgery and then received physical therapy. The question of his entitlement to workers' compensation benefits then arose. The Commonwealth Court of Pennsylvania upheld an administrative ruling in the officer's favor. The court agreed that the officer's injury was directly related to his performance for several reasons. First, the transit authority tested its police officers four to six times a year to see if they met its physical standards. The officer would be subject to progressive discipline if those standards were not met. Second, although the transit authority provided its officers with the use of a downtown sports clinic for exercise, the officer did not know about the facility. Third, the authority provided all officers with a document suggesting that they perform a self-test, where they mark off a one-and-one-half mile course near their home. **Because the officer ran in the park solely to meet the transit authority's running standard, he was entitled to benefits.** *SEPTA v. WCAB*, 730 A.2d 562 (Pa. Commw. Ct. 1999).

♦ A reserve officer of a county sheriff's office was assigned to the position of "rover." His primary duties were patrolling the county jail grounds, providing jail security, and transporting prisoners. Although his car radio only allowed him to hear the sheriff's dispatcher's transmissions, he had a personal police scanner with him in the car. While on the way to dinner, he heard two transmissions from a city police officer regarding gunshots. Although the city officer did not request backup, the reserve officer left his assigned post to provide backup without notifying the sheriff's dispatcher. He was injured in a car accident en route to the scene. The Workers' Compensation Court denied him benefits, and the Supreme Court of Oklahoma upheld the denial. **A compensable work-related injury must both arise out of and occur in the course of the worker's employment.** Here, sufficient evidence supported the conclusion that the officer was outside the course of his employment when he was injured. *Lanman v. Oklahoma County Sheriff's Office,* 958 P.2d 795 (Okla. 1998).

♦ A Maryland police officer participated in a departmental program that permitted, under certain conditions, officers to maintain a personal patrol vehicle. The program was established to provide a higher level of police service to the community. While operating her personal patrol vehicle off duty and on her way to her mother's home, the officer was hit from behind by another vehicle and sustained injuries. She filed a claim with the Workers' Compensation Commission, which awarded temporary total disability benefits. The Court of Appeals of Maryland affirmed, finding that the officer's injuries fell within the state Workers' Compensation Act. **The officer's injuries arose from her employment because they stemmed from her use of the personal patrol vehicle** within the department's guidelines. The officer was acting within the course of her employment because any time she placed the vehicle into operation while she was not on scheduled duty, she was bound to act within the departmental guidelines, which included responding to certain types of calls. Also, the dual purpose doctrine and special errand doctrine supported the conclusion that the officer's injuries resulted in the course of her employment. *Montgomery County v. Wade,* 690 A.2d 990 (Md. 1997).

♦ A Washington corrections officer was placed on administrative home leave for disciplinary reasons. The Department of Corrections instructed him to remain available for contact by phone at all times during his scheduled work shift and to perform no department work unless specifically assigned by his supervisor. He was paid his normal salary and accrued sick and vacation leave. If the officer wanted to be away from his home during his scheduled work hours, he had to use his leave. One day, the officer accidentally amputated three fingers while working on a personal project at his home workbench. The Department of Labor and Industries rejected his claim for benefits because he was not in the course of employment when injured. The Court of Appeals of Washington found that **the officer was not covered because he was acting for his personal benefit at the time of the injury**. The activity was more than an incidental, minor deviation from his normal work activities. It was not required by his employment or done at the direction of his employer. *Washington State Dep't of Labor & Industries v. Johnson,* 928 P.2d 1138 (Wash. Ct. App. 1996).

♦ A police department implemented a physical fitness policy that granted a three-year grace period to permit officers to comply with the physical fitness requirements. A 330-pound officer failed to satisfy the requirements and chose to undergo stomach stapling surgery in an attempt to lose weight. He died of complications from the surgery. His widow filed a petition for workers' compensation benefits and funeral expenses under the Florida Workers' Compensation Act. The District Court of Appeal of Florida held that the officer's death did not occur within the course and scope of his employment. **The officer's death did not occur in a place where he would reasonably be or while he was reasonably engaged in activity incidental to his employment** as a law enforcement officer. Moreover, his supervisors' knowledge or awareness of his efforts to meet the fitness standards or lose weight, and their approval of his voluntary leave for surgery, did not amount to an endorsement or control over the procedure he elected. *City of Kissimmee v. Dickson*, 694 So.2d 143 (Fla. Dist. Ct. App. 1997).

♦ Two Colorado employees, **a prison guard and a police officer, suffered injuries while engaged in off-duty exercise not on the employers' premises** and applied for workers' compensation benefits. Their cases reached the Supreme Court of Colorado, which noted that some off-duty exercise injuries might be compensable under the Workers' Compensation Act. The court applied the following factors: 1) whether the injury occurred during working hours; 2) whether the injury occurred on the employer's premises; 3) whether the employer initiated the employee's exercise program; 4) whether the employer exerted any control or direction over the employee's exercise program; and 5) whether the employer stood to benefit from the employee's exercise program. Factors one and two should be given more weight. The court held that neither claimant satisfied the test, and it affirmed the denial of benefits. *Price v. Industrial Claim Appeals Office*, 919 P.2d 207 (Colo. 1996).

♦ A Michigan county deputy sheriff fell asleep at the steering wheel of his official police vehicle while commuting between his home and the county jail. His car struck an embankment, and he suffered severe personal injuries. During his commute, the deputy was driving the only active county patrol car and was required to respond to police matters if he observed a need for law enforcement or if requested to do so by radio dispatch. A workers' compensation magistrate concluded that his accident "arose out of and in the course of" his employment and awarded workers' compensation benefits. The Court of Appeals of Michigan noted that, as a general rule, employees going to or from work are not covered by the workers' compensation act. However, under the dual purpose exception, travel to and from work may be covered by the act if at the time of the trip "the employer derived a special benefit from the employee's activities at the time of the injury." Here, because the county received the benefit of deterrence of traffic violations and because the deputy was expected to respond to all incidents and remain subject to immediate dispatch, **the deputy was entitled to workers' compensation benefits under the dual purpose exception to the coming-and-going rule**. The commission's ruling was reversed. *Botke v. Chippewa County*, 533 N.W.2d 7 (Mich. Ct. App. 1995).

♦ A state traffic officer employed by the California Highway Patrol **suffered an injury to her right thumb at home, off duty, while she was practicing the standing long jump,** a required part of her annual physical fitness test. She filed a claim for workers' compensation benefits, which was denied on the grounds that her injury did not arise out of and in the course of her employment. The California Court of Appeal found compelling evidence that the officer was under indirect or subtle employer pressure to pass the test. Accordingly, it was objectively reasonable for her to believe that she was required to practice the jump during off-duty hours. A number of officers had testified that the test could not be successfully passed without some prior preparation, and several officers admitted that they had told the officer to practice and had given her tips on how to perform the jump. The officer's injury was thus compensable. *Kidwell v. WCAB*, 39 Cal.Rptr.2d 540 (Cal. Ct. App. 1995).

♦ A New Jersey police officer experienced blurry vision caused by his multiple sclerosis. He was placed off duty and reported to a cardiologist pursuant to department regulations requiring all officers absent for more than three days to submit to a physical examination. The physician determined that he was not yet capable of returning to work because of his condition. However, he was ordered to return for further examination three weeks later. The officer was injured in an automobile accident while driving home from this exam and sought workers' compensation benefits. The Superior Court of New Jersey, Appellate Division, noted that **the officer was not engaged in the direct performance of his police duties,** and the department did not have any control over the course of his travel or manner in which he was transported to the exam. Although the department arguably benefited from the examinations, the benefits were too remote to transform the officer's compliance with department directives into a "special mission." Thus, the officer was not entitled to benefits. *Carberry v. State of New Jersey, Division of State Police*, 652 A.2d 232 (N.J. Super. Ct. App. Div. 1995).

4. Amount of Compensation

♦ In five separate cases, California workers sustained work-related disabilities on top of previous injuries. In one case, a firefighter suffered back and spine injuries resulting in 74% permanent disability after already having been awarded 44.5% permanent disability for similar injuries earlier. The California Supreme Court had to decide whether 2004 legislation reforming workers' compensation changed the formula for apportioning compensation between an employee's past and present injuries. The court determined that the 2004 legislation did not change the apportionment formula. Thus, the firefighter was only entitled to $20,867 – the 29.5% difference between the prior and present injuries. *Brodie v. WCAB*, 156 P.3d 1100 (Cal. 2007).

♦ An Arizona county laborer injured his back while lifting a rock out of a manhole. He had back surgery and injections to relieve the pain so he could work full time. He also received workers' compensation benefits. Later, he was in an industrial vehicle accident and the injections became less effective.

Eventually the pain forced him to stop working. He sought to reopen the workers' compensation claim because of the increased pain, but his request was denied. The Arizona Court of Appeals noted that he failed to prove the pain was the result of medical changes to the injury. Subjective pain by itself does not constitute an injury. **Without showing an organic or structural change in the body, he was not entitled to have the claim reopened.** *Polanco v. Industrial Comm'n of Arizona*, 154 P.3d 391 (Ariz. Ct. App. 2007).

♦   A volunteer EMT for a Pennsylvania city fractured her heel while engaged in her EMT duties. She filed for workers' compensation wage loss benefits even though she was receiving Social Security retirement benefits. The workers' compensation judge awarded her benefits, and the Commonwealth Court upheld that determination. It cited to the workers' compensation statute, which explicitly included members of the volunteer ambulance corps as "employees" entitled to benefits for lost wages. **Her employment status outside her volunteer job was not relevant to her entitlement to wage loss benefits.** *Borough of Heidelberg v. Workers' Compensation Appeal Board (Selva)*, 894 A.2d 861 (Pa. Commw. Ct. 2006).

♦   A city of Erie police officer broke his leg in a work-related motorcycle accident, which prevented him from working his two part-time jobs as a security guard. Under the Pennsylvania Heart and Lung Act, the city paid him his full salary as well as workers' compensation for the part-time jobs. It then sought reimbursement for the workers' compensation benefits, and the Pennsylvania Supreme Court ruled in the city's favor. Although the Heart and Lung Act required the city to pay workers' compensation benefits for the supplemental jobs, it also contained a provision requiring employees who receive workers' compensation under the act to turn such benefits over to their governmental employers. *City of Erie v. Workers' Compensation Appeal Board*, 838 A.2d 598 (Pa. 2003).

♦   A Kansas firefighter suffered two injuries to his back while moving emergency rescue equipment and underwent surgery for a herniated disk. When he returned for light duty, he was told to fill out applications for retirement benefits under two plans: an age-based retirement plan and a service-related disability benefit plan. An administrative law judge then awarded the firefighter workers' compensation benefits after finding that he had suffered a permanent partial disability. The judge, however, offset the award by the amount the firefighter was receiving under the city's disability retirement plan. The state workers' compensation board upheld the award but reversed the ruling to offset benefits, and the Kansas Court of Appeals affirmed. Under Kansas law, cities may offset the payment of workers' compensation benefits by the retirement benefits the employee receives, either under the federal Social Security Act or under any other city retirement plan or system. Here, however, **the firefighter was receiving benefits pursuant to the disability-based retirement plan**, not the age-based retirement plan. Accordingly, the benefits could not be offset. *Green v. City of Wichita*, 977 P.2d 283 (Kan. Ct. App. 1999).

Sec. IV UNEMPLOYMENT AND WORKERS' COMPENSATION 399

◆ While on duty, a Connecticut police officer was exposed to HIV and later tuberculosis. He underwent testing for the two diseases, incurring bills for medical treatment and laboratory work, but paid only for the laboratory services. He then filed for workers' compensation, seeking past treatment and future medical testing and treatment expenses. At a hearing, a physician specializing in infectious diseases testified that exposure to HIV similar to that sustained by the officer would, for at least one year thereafter, require regular testing, drug therapy and potentially psychological counseling. She also testified that his exposure to tuberculosis would require testing and preventative drug therapy for at least six months. The workers' compensation review board denied compensation. The Supreme Court of Connecticut concluded that where a claimant has sustained **actual exposures to life-threatening infectious diseases** in incidents that arose out of and in the course of his employment, he has suffered compensable injuries and may recover the expenses associated with reasonable medical testing and treatment. Here, the officer was entitled to medical expenses for testing and treatment without a showing of incapacity or disability. *Doe v. City of Stamford*, 699 A.2d 52 (Conn. 1997).

◆ An employee of the Arkansas Department of Correction was bitten by an HIV-positive inmate. The injury was accepted as compensable, and payment was made to cover the cost of treating the bite wound. The treating physician at the hospital emergency room recommended that the employee be tested for and receive treatment to prevent the development of tetanus, hepatitis and AIDS. The employer refused to pay for the tests and treatments, and the employee filed a complaint with the state workers' compensation commission. The commission held that the injury was compensable, and that the exposure to the AIDS virus arose directly from a work-related injury. Furthermore, the tests and treatments were reasonably necessary. Thus, the employer was required to pay for them. The employer appealed to the Court of Appeals of Arkansas, which affirmed. **The employee was entitled to the medical treatment prescribed.** *Arkansas Dep't of Correction v. Holybee*, 878 S.W.2d 420 (Ark. Ct. App. 1994).

◆ A Minnesota city police officer was rear-ended by an underinsured motorist while writing a speeding ticket. He collected workers' compensation benefits and settled a claim against the driver's insurer for $42,500. A panel of arbitrators ruled that the officer had suffered $90,152 in damages, but it deducted all monies paid by the driver's and the city's liability insurers. However, it concluded that monies paid by the workers' compensation carrier should not be deducted as a setoff from his award. The officer moved to confirm the arbitration award in a Minnesota district court. The district court reduced the award by the amount paid in the subrogation claim, and the officer appealed to the Court of Appeals of Minnesota, contending that **the arbitrators intended the total damages to be offset only by the amount received by him**. The court of appeals held that language in the arbitrators' ruling evidenced an intent to deduct only monies paid directly to the officer. Thus, the amount was offset only by the amount he actually received. *Ray v. City of Maple Grove*, 519 N.W.2d 466 (Minn. Ct. App. 1994).

V. FAMILY AND MEDICAL LEAVE ACT OF 1993

The Family and Medical Leave Act of 1993 (FMLA), 29 U.S.C. § 2601 et seq., grants eligible employees the statutory right to take up to 12 weeks of unpaid leave per year under specified circumstances related to family health care and childbirth.

The FMLA authorizes eligible employees to take leave upon the birth of a child by the employee or the employee's spouse, the placement of a child for adoption or foster care with the employee, and when the employee is needed to care for a child, spouse or parent who has a serious health condition. An employee unable to perform employment duties because of a serious health condition also may qualify for leave.

The FMLA regulations were amended in 2008 (taking effect in mid-January 2009) to provide that employees with a family service member who suffered a serious injury or illness while on active duty can take up to 26 workweeks of leave in a 12-month period to care for the service member.

The new regulations also state that employees with family in the National Guard or the Reserves can take FMLA-protected leave to help the family member during "qualifying exigencies," which the rules define as 1) short-notice deployment, 2) military events and related activity, 3) childcare and school activities, 4) financial and legal arrangements, 5) counseling, 6) rest and recuperation, 7) post-deployment activities, and 8) additional activities where the employer and employee agree to the leave.

To be eligible for coverage under the FMLA, an employee must have worked for the employer for at least **12 months** and must have worked at least **1,250 hours** during the 12-month period preceding the leave. Spouses employed by the same employer are limited to a total of 12 weeks of leave for childbirth, adoption, or the care of a sick parent.

The FMLA establishes special rules governing the availability of employee leaves for local educational agency employees principally employed as instructors. Employees who receive paid leave from their employers may elect to (and certain employers may require their employees to) substitute accrued paid leave for the 12-week statutory minimum.

The FMLA obligates employees to provide their employers with reasonable prior notice for foreseeable leaves. They also must prove that they have a serious health condition by documenting the condition with sufficient certification from a healthcare provider.

Employers are entitled to obtain a second opinion on the employee or employee family member's health condition when the validity of the certification is in doubt. The FMLA covers employers with 50 or more employees for each working day during 20 or more calendar weeks in a current or preceding calendar year and extends coverage to federal civil service employees. Employers may require eligible employees to periodically report their status and intentions during leave periods.

The taking of a family or medical leave by an eligible employee shall not result in the loss of any employment benefit accrued prior to the commencement date of the leave, but **the FMLA does not entitle employees to accrue seniority rights or employment benefits during leave periods**. Although eligible employees who take leaves for purposes described in the act are entitled to be reinstated to equivalent positions upon their return from leave, restored employees are not entitled to rights, benefits or positions other than those to which they would have been entitled had they not taken leave. The FMLA provides for enforcement through civil actions for damages in the amount of lost wages, employment benefits, interest and attorneys' fees and costs.

* When an employee of the Nevada Department of Human Resources (DHR) sought FMLA leave to care for his wife, who was recovering from a car accident and neck surgery, the DHR granted his request for the full 12 weeks of FMLA leave and authorized him to use the leave intermittently as needed. He used the leave but failed to return to work by the deadline set by the DHR, and was fired. He filed this lawsuit seeking damages and other relief for the department's alleged FMLA violations. A Nevada federal court granted summary judgment to the DHR on the grounds that the Eleventh Amendment barred the employee from recovering damages against the state. The U.S. Court of Appeals for the Ninth Circuit reversed. The U.S. Supreme Court affirmed the ruling against the state. Although the Court previously had held that states could not be sued for money damages under the ADA and the ADEA, **the FMLA was different because it was designed to prevent employers from engaging in gender-based discrimination** against primarily women who take time off work to care for ill family members. Here, Congress had appropriately abrogated states' immunity under the Eleventh Amendment by creating a law that was narrowly tailored to achieving the end of equal protection for employees of both sexes. *Nevada Dep't of Human Resources v. Hibbs*, 538 U.S. 721, 123 S.Ct. 1972, 155 L.Ed.2d 953 (2003).

* After an Arkansas employee was diagnosed with cancer, she requested medical leave. Her employer granted her request and allowed her to take seven months of leave. However, the company did not inform her of her eligibility under the FMLA, nor did it inform her of her right to have the leave designated as FMLA leave. When she exhausted the seven months of company-provided leave, she was fired. Her request for additional FMLA leave was denied. She sued, and a federal court ruled for the employer. The Eighth Circuit affirmed, holding that the employer's failure to designate any part of the leave as FMLA leave did not prevent the FMLA leave from expiring. The court struck down the Department of Labor regulation that required the employer to provide more than 12 weeks of leave because of its failure to designate the leave as FMLA leave. The court refused to penalize the employer because its leave program was more generous than the FMLA. The U.S. Supreme Court also affirmed, noting that **employers**

who provide more than 12 weeks of family and medical leave cannot be penalized for failing to give proper FMLA notice. *Ragsdale v. Wolverine World Wide, Inc.*, 535 U.S. 81, 122 S.Ct. 1155, 152 L.Ed.2d 167 (2002).

A. Eligibility Issues

♦ A Maryland public employee asked for three weeks off to visit her ailing grandmother in Jamaica. She was given only one week off, but told her supervisor she was planning to take three weeks off anyway because her husband had already bought the tickets. When she got to Jamaica, she discovered that her grandmother had suffered a small stroke. She called her supervisor to explain that she needed more than the one week off to care for her and get her into an assisted living facility. Her supervisor did not believe she was FMLA eligible. When she tried to return to work, she was told that she was fired for being AWOL for more than three days. She sued under the FMLA and won. The Fourth Circuit held that **the post-termination evidence she offered clarifying her relationship with her grandmother was relevant to the determination of her FMLA eligibility.** *Dillon v. Maryland-National Capital Park and Planning Comm'n*, 258 Fed.Appx. 577 (4th Cir. 2007).

♦ An Illinois postal employee with a history of attendance problems signed a last chance agreement, then missed several more shifts and was fired. She sued, asserting that she was protected by the FMLA and that her absences were to go to the emergency room and receive medical treatment. However, during the 12 months prior to her emergency room visit, she had 1,249.8 clocked hours – or **0.2 hours short of the 1,250 needed to qualify** for FMLA protection. As a result, the Seventh Circuit ruled that she had been properly fired. *Pirant v. U.S. Postal Service*, 542 F.3d 202 (7th Cir. 2008).

♦ A Florida school district employee was placed on a six-week performance improvement plan at the same time his daughter (in the Army Reserves) was notified that she was being called to active duty overseas. He requested FMLA leave to care for his infant granddaughter, for whom he acted "in loco parentis." His FMLA leave was approved through the end of his contract. However, he was told that his contract would not be renewed if he failed to fulfill his PIP. When his contract was not renewed, he sued under the FMLA. A federal court granted pretrial judgment to the district, but the Eleventh Circuit reversed, finding **issues of fact as to whether he qualified as a stand-in parent under the FMLA** and whether the school district had properly refused to renew his contract. *Martin v. Brevard County Public Schools*, 543 F.3d 1261 (11th Cir. 2008).

♦ A Texas transit authority employee developed diabetes and began taking a medication that caused diarrhea as a side effect. As a result, he went to the bathroom frequently but did not tell his supervisor why. After his supervisor sent him an e-mail questioning his time in the bathroom, he finally gave her a note from his doctor explaining that diarrhea was a side effect of his medication but refused to explain further. After he was put on a corrective action plan, he asked for intermittent FMLA leave. A week later he was fired. When he sued, a federal court and the Fifth Circuit ruled against him. First, **his diarrhea was not a serious health condition** and, second, he failed to cooperate with his supervisor so that flexible bathroom breaks could be provided. *Mauder v. Metropolitan Transit Authority*, 446 F.3d 574 (5th Cir. 2006).

◆ An employee of the Denver Public Schools with a history of abusing sick leave visited his doctor and took five days off work because of a back injury. The following week, he caught the flu and missed two more days. When he returned to work, he was fired. He then made a follow-up visit to his doctor and sued the school district for violating the FMLA. **He claimed that his back injury amounted to a "serious health condition" because he visited the doctor twice.** The Tenth Circuit disagreed. To qualify for FMLA protection, an employee must obtain treatment from a healthcare provider at least twice during his period of incapacity (or one time, followed by a regimen of continuing treatment). At the time the employee returned to work, he had only undergone one treatment on his back, with no regimen of continuing treatment. *Jones v. Denver Public Schools*, 427 F.3d 1315 (10th Cir. 2005).

◆ A teacher in Alabama during her first year of employment notified her principal that she was pregnant and that she was due on August 2. However, on May 15, the school board decided not to renew her contract for the following year because she did not establish a proper relationship with parents or students, and sent students to the office over matters she should have been able to resolve herself. She gave birth July 27, less than a year after she started work, and a federal court determined that she was not eligible for FMLA leave because she had not yet worked for the school district for 12 months. The Eleventh Circuit affirmed, noting that even though she would have been eligible under the FMLA a few days after her leave would have started, **the request was made by an ineligible employee for a leave that would have started while she was still ineligible**. She was not protected by the FMLA. *Walker v. Elmore County Board of Educ.*, 379 F.3d 1249 (11th Cir. 2004).

◆ An Illinois woman began working for a village and received an employee manual advising her generally of her rights under the FMLA. She also received a separate document detailing her rights more specifically, and stating that the village was using the "rolling" 12-month period to determine eligibility for FMLA leave. Over the course of her employment, she missed a great deal of work due to illness – 221 hours in 1998; 591 hours in 1999; and 132 hours in 2000. She was granted both paid and unpaid (FMLA) leave. However, she was eventually fired because she took more leave time than was allowed under the FMLA. She sued the village under the FMLA, and the village sought to dismiss the case. A federal court refused to dismiss the action because the village had not complied with the notice requirements of the regulations. The village should have included the specific eligibility information in the employee manual. By failing to do so, **the employee was entitled to use the calendar year method for computing leave rather than the "rolling" method** the village had sought to implement. Under this method, she would have been entitled to FMLA leave in 2000. The employee could pursue her wrongful discharge claim under the FMLA. *Dodaro v. Village of Glendale Heights*, 2003 WL 1720030 (N.D. Ill. 2003).

B. Documentation and Notice Issues

• A Louisiana crime lab employee took FMLA leave for shoulder and knee surgeries. The sheriff charged her with 424 hours of FMLA leave, leaving her with 52 hours remaining. She then reinjured her knee and took another leave to have knee surgery, but the sheriff didn't notify her that he was charging her with FMLA leave for her absence. When she returned to work, the sheriff reassigned her to the corrections division, where she lost overtime and the use of a car. She sued the sheriff under the FMLA, and the Fifth Circuit ruled in her favor. Here, **the employee was prejudiced by the sheriff's lack of notice**. She could have delayed her surgery until the start of a new FMLA period, and she would have been able to complete her duties in the crime lab during that time. The court of appeals upheld the jury's award of $16,400 in back pay and the trial court's award of $13,128 in front pay. *Downey v. Strain*, 510 F.3d 534 (5th Cir. 2007).

• A postal worker in Oklahoma with a history of attendance problems asked for intermittent leave under the FMLA to treat his chronic back pain. A postal service FMLA coordinator conditionally approved the leave, dependent on his submission of a completed medical certification. He submitted the medical certification, but it was not complete, so he was given an additional 15 days to re-submit it. Two weeks after the second deadline passed, he re-submitted the completed certification. **The postal service decided to enforce the second deadline and refused to accept the certification.** It fired the worker for violating his second last-chance agreement. Over two years later, he sued the postal service for violating his rights under the FMLA. A federal court and the Tenth Circuit ruled against him. Because the postal service did not willfully violate his rights under the FMLA, he was subject to the FMLA's two-year statute of limitations and had sued too late. *Bass v. Potter*, 522 F.3d 1098 (10th Cir. 2008).

• A Maryland Transportation Authority employee fell and injured her knee. She did not report to work afterwards, but a few days later she requested FMLA leave. Her supervisor told her she had to submit to another medical evaluation by a physician of the authority's choosing, which she did. However, the authority didn't notify her of the status of her leave request until the leave was over. She sued and a federal court ruled that even though the authority's lack of notice made her feel "inconvenienced, confused and upset," **she was not entitled to relief under the FMLA because she experienced no loss of job, benefits or compensation.** *Kent v. Maryland Transportation Authority*, 2006 WL 3931648 (D. Md. 12/21/06).

• A Texas firefighter had to stay home to care for his wife, who had flu symptoms and chronic back pain. He submitted a standard leave form as well as an exam form from his doctor and three receipts for prescriptions. The assistant fire chief rejected the leave form but refused to say what documentation the firefighter needed to submit. After the firefighter was fired, he sued under the FMLA. A jury awarded him more than $1 million. The Fifth Circuit Court of Appeals upheld the ruling against the city, but held that the amount had to be recalculated. The jury had sufficient evidence to find that the wife had a serious health condition and that **the city failed to notify the firefighter of what he needed to document his absence.** *Lubke v. City of Arlington*, 455 F.3d 489 (5th Cir. 2006).

* A maintenance technician with the city of Philadelphia used enough sick time that he was placed on the city's "sick abuse list," which required him to obtain medical certification for all sick days. Under the city's sick leave policy, he also had to stay home during work hours unless required to leave for personal reasons related to the sick leave. Further, he had to call the city's sick leave hotline if he was going to be gone during work hours. He failed to do so on three occasions while he was on FMLA leave, and he received a warning and two suspensions. He sued the city for violating the FMLA, but a federal court and the Third Circuit ruled against him. **The city's sick leave policy did not deny or interfere with his FMLA rights.** It merely attempted to prevent employees from abusing their sick leaves. *Callison v. City of Philadelphia*, 128 Fed.Appx. 897 (3d Cir. 2005).

* An Illinois postal employee took FMLA leave after falling ill. He provided two certification forms from his doctor, the latter one estimating when he would be able to return to work. Because he was absent for more than 21 days, the postal service required him to submit to an exam by a postal service physician, and provide documentation about the nature and treatment of his illness, the medications he was taking and his medical restrictions. He instead obtained a certification from his doctor stating that he would be able to return to work without restrictions. The postal service fired him and he sued. The Seventh Circuit Court of Appeals determined that the postal service's 21-day rule, although more burdensome than the FMLA, did not violate the act because it was arrived at through collective bargaining, which the FMLA allowed for. **A collective bargaining agreement may impose more stringent terms on employees than the FMLA.** *Harrell v. U.S. Postal Service*, 445 F.3d 913 (7th Cir. 2006).

* A California corrections department employee asked his supervisor for a one-week vacation to spend Christmas with his parents. Although his written request mentioned his parents' significantly deteriorating health and his speculation that they did not have long to live, he did not make a request for time off under the California Family Rights Act (CFRA) or the FMLA. Nor did he state that he wanted the time off to care for his parents. His request was denied. He later sued the department for violating the CFRA by failing to tell him that he might be eligible for leave under the statute. A state court granted pretrial judgment to the department, finding that **no reasonable employer would think the employee's request for vacation triggered a duty to notify him of his leave rights** under the CFRA. The California Court of Appeal affirmed. Here, the employee's request gave no hint of a desire to care for his

parents. Even though the employee did not have to mention the CFRA or the FMLA by name, he did have to give the employer sufficient information for it to conclude that the CFRA was applicable to the situation. *Stevens v. California Dep't of Corrections*, 132 Cal.Rptr.2d 19 (Cal. Ct. App. 2003).

• An employee of the city of Birmingham claimed that he was fired after leaving the job site because he was suffering from a diabetes attack. He claimed that he told his supervisor this, and he sued the city under the FMLA. The city asserted that he walked off the job and that he had been insubordinate. A federal court granted pretrial judgment to the city, finding that since the employee still had paid leave available under the city's sick leave policy, he could not invoke the protection of the FMLA. The Eleventh Circuit reversed, noting that whether an employee is entitled to receive paid sick leave is irrelevant to his right to FMLA protection. **Employers may require that unpaid FMLA leave be used concurrently with paid leave** taken pursuant to a company policy. The court then stated that there was a question of fact as to whether the employee gave his supervisor notice of his condition. If he did so, he would be entitled to FMLA protection. The court remanded the case. *Strickland v. Water Works and Sewer Board of Birmingham*, 239 F.3d 1199 (11th Cir. 2001).

C. Intermittent Leave

• An Ohio corrections officer was allowed to take intermittent leave to care for his diabetic daughter even though he did not yet qualify for leave under the FMLA. After he had been on the job a year, he continued to use intermittent leave for two years. The following year, after he received a notice that he had used up all his FMLA leave, he continued to take time off to care for his daughter. Some of that leave was with permission. However, he was eventually fired for being away without leave after missing more than 48 hours of work. He sued under the FMLA, claiming the sheriff never informed him that FMLA leave was calculated under the "rolling backward" method. The Sixth Circuit ruled against him, noting that he could not show he was prejudiced by the lack of notice. Here, **the sheriff greatly exceeded his obligation under the FMLA to provide leave.** *Coker v. McFaul*, 247 Fed.Appx. 609 (6th Cir. 2007).

• A city employee in Iowa missed work for all or part of 115 work days, more than 40 of which were for intermittent leave under the FMLA. She suffered from fibromyalgia, diabetes, hypertension and hypothyroidism, and she required the time off whenever one of her conditions flared up. The city advised her to take whatever steps were necessary to improve her attendance and **reassigned her to a position with less responsibility (but the same pay and benefits) until her need for intermittent leave ended.** She sued under the FMLA, but a federal court and the Eighth Circuit ruled against her. The city did not violate the law because the steps it took to ensure that the work got done did not amount to adverse action. *Rodgers v. City of Des Moines*, 435 F.3d 904 (8th Cir. 2006).

• A postal service employee in Ohio won an arbitration award that converted her termination into a 30-day suspension. After she returned to work, she suffered from depression and migraines as a result of her husband's death. She was fired again for failing to maintain a regular schedule. She filed another grievance but lost. She then sued the postal service under the FMLA, asserting that she should have qualified for intermittent leave. A federal court dismissed her lawsuit because she did not have the requisite 1,250 hours of work in the previous year, but the Sixth Circuit reversed. It held that **the hours the employee missed as a result of the wrongful discharge had to be counted toward the 1,250-hour requirement**. The court remanded the case for a determination of whether she qualified for leave after the suspension was taken into account. *Ricco v. Potter*, 377 F.3d 599 (6th Cir. 2004).

D. Procedural Issues

1. Post-Leave Problems

- A Wisconsin teacher took FMLA leave for her pregnancy from April 28 through June 10, 2004, the last work day for teachers. Because of accumulated paid leave, she only had to use 19 days of unpaid leave. The school district paid her health insurance premiums over the summer. However, due to changed circumstances, she decided not to return to work. Although it never notified her that it would require her to repay premiums if she chose not to return to work, the district sued to recover the premiums. The Wisconsin Court of Appeals ruled that she had to reimburse the district about $2,100 (about half what it was seeking). The court noted that the district did not have to create an escrow fund prior to her leave to recoup its premiums. Also, **even though the district failed to provide notice under the FMLA, it could still require her to reimburse it for the premiums**. *Port Edwards School Dist. v. Reissmann*, 750 N.W.2d 519 (Wis. Ct. App. 2008).

- A bookkeeper and treasurer for an Illinois school district missed about 30% of her scheduled hours to care for her terminally ill parents. Her absences became a problem when other employees had to cover for her and she wasn't available to answer questions. At a school board meeting in June, the board discussed hiring a new bookkeeper but took no action. The next fall, the superintendent offered her intermittent FMLA leave after board members contemplated firing her. She continued to miss a great deal of work. Later, the board offered to let her resign or be demoted to a teaching assistant position because she had missed too much work to complete the essential functions of her job. **She was denied reinstatement to the bookkeeper job after the school board found performance issues during her absence.** She sued for retaliation under the FMLA, and a federal court granted pretrial judgment to the board. The Seventh Circuit reversed in part, finding issues of fact as to whether her job performance, unrelated to her absenteeism, justified her removal from the bookkeeper position. *Lewis v. School Dist. #70*, 523 F.3d 730 (7th Cir. 2008).

- As part of her job, a school board employee in Louisiana traveled to various schools in Baton Rouge to help principals and staff with bookkeeping. While she was on maternity leave, the board reorganized the school accounts department. When she returned, she found that **the travel requirement had been eliminated** and that she would have to audit the schools' accounting books from a central office. She sued under the FMLA, claiming that the board failed to restore her to the same or an equivalent position. A federal court and the Fifth Circuit disagreed. This *de minimis* change did not violate the act. She failed to show that she was forced to travel longer or further. *Smith v. East Baton Rouge Parish School Board*, 453 F.3d 650 (5th Cir. 2006).

◆ The head of a Minnesota county's human resources (HR) department took FMLA leave to give birth. When she returned, the board of commissioners decided to keep her replacement in the job. The board chose not to consult an attorney about the change despite advice from the replacement to do so. It kept the employee at her same salary and benefits. After she filed a complaint under the Minnesota Veteran's Preference Act, she was reinstated to her position. Two years and two weeks after being told she was being replaced as the head of HR, she sued under the FMLA. A federal court and the Eighth Circuit ruled against her. Here, the county may have violated the FMLA, but its failure to consult an attorney was not a willful violation, which meant that the **statute of limitations** (two years for violations; three years for willful violations) had passed. *Hanger v. Lake County, Minnesota*, 390 F.3d 579 (8th Cir. 2004).

◆ A sanitation department superintendent with the city of Chicago had a record of poor performance and was suspended for three days for various deficiencies. He relied too heavily on employees underneath him, was difficult to contact via radio or pager, and refused to drive the city van during work hours. Shortly after he took FMLA leave for health problems, he was indicted for mail fraud. When he refused to resign, he was fired – on the same day he returned to work from his leave. He sued the city under the FMLA. The case reached the Seventh Circuit Court of Appeals, which ruled that the city could fire him without violating the FMLA while he was on leave. The FMLA does not protect a problem employee from losing his job when his performance problems are well documented and **the employee would have been fired even if he had not taken the leave.** *Phelan v. City of Chicago*, 347 F.3d 679 (7th Cir. 2003).

2. Concurrent Paid Leave

◆ A Missouri police officer with more than 12 weeks of accrued sick leave injured his shoulder while off duty and underwent surgery. The city sent him a letter informing him that his sick leave would run concurrently with his FMLA leave, that he had 12 weeks and that he had to submit a fitness-for-duty certification before returning to work. When he was unable to return after 12 weeks, he was forced to resign. He sued under the FMLA, and a federal court ruled for the city. The Eighth Circuit Court of Appeals affirmed, finding that **the city could limit the officer to 12 weeks despite the fact that he had accrued more than 12 weeks in sick leave.** *Slentz v. City of Republic*, 448 F.3d 1008 (8th Cir. 2006).

♦ An Omaha police officer took FMLA leave for the three weeks he would be absent from work due to surgery. He elected to have paid sick leave count against the FMLA leave because city employees could not use unpaid leave until all paid leave was exhausted. He had at least 1,000 hours of accrued sick leave. When he returned to work, the city refused to pay him an annual leave bonus because he had used more than 40 hours of sick leave. He sued under the FMLA. A federal court and the Eighth Circuit ruled against him. The annual leave bonus was a benefit, not pay. Therefore, the city could refuse to provide it where he used more than 40 hours of sick leave. Also, **the city could force him to use paid sick leave before unpaid leave** without violating the FMLA. *Chubb v. City of Omaha*, 424 F.3d 831 (8th Cir. 2005).

3. Other Procedural Issues

♦ A Kansas police department clerk claimed she suffered a breakdown after reporting that the chief had pornography on his computer. She took seven months' sick leave. After returning to work, she claimed that the chief and the city manager treated her poorly. She told the chief and the city manager she could not attend any meetings with them unless her husband or doctor could be there to offer emotional support. The city manager agreed, so long as the support person did not speak. At the next meeting, the clerk's husband ignored the directive and entered the conversation. The clerk then refused to attend two subsequent meetings, even though her husband or doctor could have attended to offer support. She was fired, then sued for retaliation under the FMLA. A federal court and the Tenth Circuit ruled against her, noting that she expressly asked not to have her sick leave counted as FMLA leave so she wouldn't have to provide medical certification of her condition. *Ney v. City of Hoisington*, 264 Fed.Appx. 678 (10th Cir. 2008).

♦ A Louisiana couple worked for the corrections department. When the wife sued the department for violating her FMLA rights, the husband stayed out of it, giving his wife moral support but otherwise not getting involved with the lawsuit. He intended to testify on her behalf if the case went to trial, but it settled first. He then applied for a number of promotions, all of which he was denied. The sheriff and the warden told him he would never be promoted and in fact placed him on a less desirable night shift, causing him to lose holiday and overtime pay. He then sued for retaliation under the FMLA, but lost. The Fifth Circuit explained that **he was not entitled to the FMLA's protections because he never "opposed" any practice upon which his wife's claim was based**. Nor was he "about to testify" when the alleged retaliation occurred because the case had settled by that time. *Elsensohn v. St. Tammany Parish Sheriff's Office*, 530 F.3d 368 (5th Cir. 2008).

♦ A Wisconsin corrections worker, fired after taking FMLA leave for anxiety and stress, sued the state, which sought to have the case dismissed, claiming Eleventh Amendment immunity. The Seventh Circuit Court of Appeals granted the state immunity, noting that this case was different than *Nevada Dep't of Human Resources v. Hibbs*, 538 U.S. 721 (2003), where the

Supreme Court held that individuals could sue states under the FMLA's family-care provision because of a history of gender discrimination against women who took time off to care for sick family members. **Under the self-care provision of the FMLA, there was no history of gender discrimination, so states retained their immunity.** *Toeller v. Wisconsin Dep't of Corrections*, 461 F.3d 871 (7th Cir. 2006).

♦ A nurse at an Arkansas county hospital began experiencing emotional difficulties after a divorce and the death of her father. She became disruptive at work, shirked her responsibilities, and finally agreed to take a leave under the FMLA. However, she still came to work, acted disruptively and was asked to resign. She did so, then sued under the FMLA. A jury found that the hospital interfered with her FMLA rights by forcing her to resign while she was on leave, but that she would have been fired even if she hadn't been on FMLA leave. The Eighth Circuit agreed that **the hospital was not liable for forcing the nurse's resignation.** Under the FMLA, an employee has no greater rights than she would have if she had not taken the leave. The jury reasonably found that she would have been fired even without taking leave. *Throneberry v. McGehee Desha County Hospital*, 403 F.3d 972 (8th Cir. 2005).

♦ An employee of an Indiana county auditor's office was fired after she missed a lot of work for personal leave, vacation, sick leave and FMLA-qualified leave. She sued the county auditor's office under the FMLA. A federal court dismissed the case, finding that the county auditor's office, with only 12 employees, was too small to have to comply with the FMLA. The Seventh Circuit reversed, holding that **the county auditor's office was not independent of the county** and that the lawsuit should not have been dismissed. No Indiana state law established the county auditor's office as a separate government entity or as having autonomy over its own management. The "Census of Governments" criteria for identifying independent public agencies dictated a finding of no independence. Those criteria are: 1) existence as an organized entity; 2) governmental character; and 3) substantial autonomy. *Fain v. Wayne County Auditor's Office*, 388 F.3d 257 (7th Cir. 2004).

♦ An Oklahoma postal service employee missed 78 out of 254 days of work for health-related reasons – 49 of which qualified under the FMLA. Because of mental and emotional problems, he then requested 60 days' leave, and after that ended sought a transfer to a Texas office. The Texas office refused to accept his transfer because of the high number of unexplained absences. When he returned to work, he discovered that his job had been re-posted and he had been reassigned. He threatened violence, apologized, was fired, filed a grievance, and had the termination reduced to a suspension. He sued under the Rehabilitation Act and FMLA. The U.S. Court of Appeals, Tenth Circuit, held that there was no Rehabilitation Act violation because the employee had been offered a reasonable accommodation, but that the postal service had **violated the FMLA by withholding his back pay for eight months after his suspension began.** The significant delay in paying the wages meant that the employee was entitled to liquidated damages. *Jordan v. U.S. Postal Service*, 379 F.3d 1196 (10th Cir. 2004).

VI. OTHER EMPLOYMENT BENEFITS CASES

♦ A 21-year veteran of the Birmingham police department borrowed $8,000 from the city's Retirement and Relief System and $4,000 from the police and firefighters' supplement pension system, using his paycheck as security for the loan. When he retired, he had not yet repaid the balance. To secure the loan after his retirement, he continued the credit life insurance policy the city had been paying the premiums on, reduced the policy coverage in half, and agreed to pay the premiums himself. He later sued the system, **asserting that it had required him to obtain the credit life insurance policy in violation of state law**. An Alabama statute provided that with respect to any consumer credit transaction, the creditor cannot require the purchase of credit life insurance. The system asserted that it was not subject to the statute because it did not regularly extend or arrange for loans. However, the Alabama Supreme Court held that the system was a creditor for purposes of the statute because it made over 100 loans a year. Further, there were issues of fact as to whether the system had forced the officer to obtain the credit life insurance policy. The case would have to proceed to trial. *Watkins v. Board of Managers of City of Birmingham Retirement & Relief System*, 802 So.2d 190 (Ala. 2001).

A. Coordination of Benefits

Generally, multiple benefit awards are not allowed. When an employee can receive several types of benefits, the employer will retain a right to set off the award to prevent a double recovery.

♦ After a California firefighter had worked for a city for 28 years, the city's fire department merged with the county's fire department. He worked for the county for another seven years and then applied for service-related disability retirement benefits from the county's retirement system. He also sought retirement benefits from the city's retirement system. Because the city and county used two different systems, his combined benefits would have been 125% of what he would have received had he stayed with the same public employer for all 35 years. The county system reduced his disability retirement benefits so that he would make no more than what he would have received working for just one public employer. He sued and lost. The California Court of Appeal held that **the retirement systems could coordinate benefits so that he did not receive a windfall**. *Block v. Orange County Employees Retirement System*, 75 Cal.Rptr.3d 137 (Cal. Ct. App. 2008).

♦ The EEOC issued a proposed **rule that would allow employers to reduce retirees' health benefits when the retirees became eligible for Medicare**. The proposed rule exempted from the ADEA employer efforts to coordinate retirees' healthcare benefits when the retirees reach 65. The American Association of Retired Persons sued, challenging the proposed rule, and a Pennsylvania federal court found the rule valid. The Third Circuit Court of Appeals agreed, noting that the ADEA grants the EEOC the authority to provide narrow exemptions that are reasonable and necessary and "proper in the public interest." Here the EEOC issued the rule in response to the fact that employer-sponsored retiree health benefits were decreasing. The proposed rule would permit employers to offer retirees benefits to the greatest extent possible. *AARP v. EEOC*, 489 F.3d 558 (3d Cir. 2007).

♦   A Connecticut police officer retired and received a pension. Later, notwithstanding that he had retired, the officer and his former employer entered into a voluntary agreement where he was awarded permanent partial disability benefits because of a heart disability pursuant to the Heart and Hypertension Act. Because the cumulative payments of the pension and disability benefits exceeded the Act's ceiling of 100% of the earnings of an active duty officer, the city limited his benefits payment accordingly. When the officer sought the full amount of his pension and disability benefits, the Connecticut Supreme Court held that the benefits under the act were not workers' compensation payments because the employee did not have to prove that he sustained injuries arising out of and in the course of his employment. Accordingly, **they could be limited where, in combination with the officer's pension, they exceeded 100% of his previous salary**. To allow the officer to avoid the ceiling because he qualified for a nondisability pension would be inconsistent with the general purpose of the ceiling. The ceiling applied to disability and pension benefits when any portion of those payments had been awarded under the Act. *Carriero v. Borough of Naugatuck*, 707 A.2d 706 (Conn. 1998).

♦   A North Carolina county deputy sheriff assisted the U.S. Bureau of Alcohol, Tobacco, and Firearms in the execution of a federal search warrant and a federal arrest warrant. While executing the warrants, the deputy was accidentally shot in the foot by a federal agent who lost his balance. The deputy retired from the county sheriff's department and was entitled to state workers' compensation benefits due to the disability arising from the gunshot wound. He also was granted federal workers' compensation benefits. The Department of Labor determined that the deputy was covered under the Federal Employees' Compensation Act (FECA). However, the deputy sued in a North Carolina federal court under the Federal Tort Claims Act in lieu of accepting the FECA compensation. The district court held that **FECA was the deputy's exclusive remedy** and granted the defendants' motion to dismiss. FECA benefits extend to state and local law enforcement personnel who are injured while collaborating with federal officials in the apprehension of persons committing federal crimes. Moreover, the Secretary of Labor's determination of coverage was not subject to judicial review. *Aponte v. U.S. Dep't of Treasury*, 940 F.Supp. 898 (E.D.N.C. 1996).

♦   After 38 years, a Maryland city firefighter received a "time-earned" service retirement. Later, he applied for workers' compensation benefits for heart disease, hypertension, and lung ailments. The workers' compensation commission applied the firefighter occupational disease presumption provision and awarded temporary total disability benefits. The mayor and city council appealed the award to the state circuit court, which affirmed. However, the court of special appeals reversed, finding that the statute's offset provisions required a reduction of the workers' compensation award so that when combined with his retirement benefits his payment would not exceed his weekly salary while employed as a firefighter. The Court of Appeals of Maryland granted review.

The firefighter argued that the statute's offset provision applied only when workers' compensation benefits and retirement benefits were the result of the same disabling event. The court of appeals rejected this argument. Under the statutory presumption of compensability for heart disease, benefits received had to be adjusted so that the weekly total of those benefits and retirement benefits did not exceed the weekly salary that was paid to the firefighter. The statute applicable to the firefighter made no distinction between retirement benefits accruing by reason of age and service, and those occurring as a result of a disability. As a result, **the firefighter's workers' compensation benefits had to be reduced** to the extent that, when combined with his retirement benefits, the sum did not exceed his weekly salary. *Polomski v. Mayor & City Council of Baltimore, Maryland*, 684 A.2d 1338 (Md. 1996).

♦ A Maine state employee sued the state retirement system because his disability retirement benefits were reduced by the amount of workers' compensation and social security disability benefits that he also received. He alleged that the reduction violated the Equal Protection Clauses of the U.S. and Maine Constitutions. A Maine trial court held for the state retirement system, and the employee appealed. The Supreme Judicial Court of Maine noted that under an equal protection challenge a difference in treatment is constitutional if there are sufficient facts to justify the distinction. The court held that it was reasonable for the Maine legislature to conclude that **state disability retirement benefits serve the same purpose as workers' compensation and social security disability benefits**. Because the legislation encouraged the disabled worker to return to work and controlled the costs of disability retirement benefits, it was not unreasonable. Also, since ordinary retirement benefits derive from the employee's years of work, and required more years of service than disability retirement benefits, it was reasonable that ordinary retirement benefits need not be reduced by workers' compensation and social security disability benefits. The court affirmed the trial court's decision. *Dishon v. Maine State Retirement System*, 569 A.2d 1216 (Me. 1990).

B. Contribution Rates

The U.S. Supreme Court has held that employee contribution rates must not be discriminatory in violation of Title VII of the Civil Rights Act of 1964. Other variations in contribution rates that are nondiscriminatory have been approved by lower courts.

♦ The Los Angeles Department of Water and Power required its female employees to make larger contributions to their retirement pension funds than those made by male employees. The department justified the disparity in contribution because females lived longer than males, necessarily increasing the average pension of retired females. A group of female employees filed a

Title VII discrimination complaint against the department, seeking an injunction against the disparate contributions and a refund of their excess contributions. Meanwhile, the California state legislature enacted a law prohibiting municipal agencies from requiring higher contributions based upon sex. The department then amended its plan so that both sexes paid the same retirement contribution. The court granted the employees pretrial judgment and ordered restitution of the excess funds. The Ninth Circuit affirmed, and the U.S. Supreme Court granted review.

The department argued that the difference in required contributions was not unlawful discrimination because it was based upon mortality tables, which constituted a factor other than sex under the Equal Pay Act. The Court held that while there was a legitimate basis in fact for the distinction drawn by the department, the distinction involved a generalization which was not true in each individual case. **Because Title VII prohibited unlawful employment discrimination against any *individual*, courts were required to focus on alleged discrimination against individuals and to disregard generalizations about classes of persons.** The lower courts had correctly ruled that the distinction drawn by the department was unlawful sex discrimination. However, the lower courts had improperly awarded restitution of excess contributions to the aggrieved female employees. The pension fund had taken the disparate contributions in the good faith belief that the mortality tables would justify them. There was no reason to penalize the funds and possibly jeopardize them for a good-faith error. The Court remanded the case. *City of Los Angeles Dep't of Water v. Manhart*, 435 U.S. 702, 98 S.Ct. 1370, 55 L.Ed.2d 657 (1978).

♦ In 2001, the South Carolina Legislature created a retention incentive program allowing state employees to retire but continue working for up to five years afterwards. During those five years, the state would withhold their normal pension benefits and then either pay them as a lump sum or roll the accrued benefits into a retirement plan. The retirees who participated in the program made no further employee contributions to the state retirement system, were not eligible for group life insurance or disability retirement benefits and received no further service credit for their additional employment. In 2005, the legislature amended the law to require participants to contribute to the retirement system. A lawsuit resulted, and the Supreme Court of South Carolina held that the new requirements breached a contract with the retirees. Although **the legislature could require future retirees to pay into the system**, it could not require retirees who enrolled in the program before the 2005 act was passed to pay in. *Layman v. State*, 630 S.E.2d 265 (S.C. 2006).

♦ Current and former police officers and firefighters sued the city of Chicago, alleging that the city failed to report to the pension boards the full amount of "salary" paid to them, thereby decreasing their total vested pension benefits. The police officers sought inclusion of: duty availability allowance, uniform allowance, overtime pay, holiday pay, optional pay for personal days, pay for baby furlough days, final vacation pay, pay for work out-of-grade, and supplemental pay for sergeants, lieutenants, and captains, as well as a one-time lump sum arbitration award. The firefighters contended that "salary" included:

shift reduction allowance, clothing allowance, overtime pay, holiday pay, final vacation pay, pay received for acting out-of-classification, pay received for attending recertification training seminars during off-duty hours, pay for unused administrative days, training instructor incentive pay, as well as a one-time lump sum payment. The court dismissed the action.

The Appellate Court of Illinois affirmed, finding that the additional items of compensation should not be included in the definition of "salary" for purposes of computing pension deductions, contributions, and benefits. The state pension code did not contain any language indicating an intent by the legislature to depart from the generally accepted definition of "salary," i.e., fixed compensation paid regularly for services. **The disputed items of compensation constituted fringe benefits because they were in addition to the regular wage.** As a result, the benefits were properly excluded under the pension code irrespective of how the appropriation ordinances or collective bargaining agreements treated them. *Holland v. City of Chicago*, 682 N.E.2d 323 (Ill. App. Ct. 1997).

• Similarly, Kansas City firefighters sought recalculation of their retirement benefits to include their one-time lump sum payment for accumulated sick leave, vacation leave, and compensatory time which was received at retirement. The city deducted a 3% contribution to the pension from the lump sum payments, but did not include the lump sum payments as part of the firefighters' monthly salary for purposes of retirement benefit calculations. The firefighters sued for a ruling that the lump sum payments must be included in their final income for the purposes of calculating retirement benefits. The Court of Appeals of Kansas instead found that "salary" meant a periodic payment dependent upon time. More specifically, "periodic" was defined as "occurring at regular intervals" or "occurring repeatedly from time to time." By definition, therefore, **a lump sum payment that occurred once upon retirement could not be a periodic payment.** *Int'l Ass'n of Firefighters, Local No. 64 v. City of Kansas City*, 942 P.2d 45 (Kan. Ct. App. 1997).

• Active members of the District of Columbia Police Department received an increase in their salaries, labeled as a "retention allowance," approved by the legislature. A group of retired officers sought a comparable increase in their retirement plans pursuant to a provision in the District of Columbia Police and Firefighters Retirement and Disability Act. The act allows for equalization of pension benefits in the same percentage as the "scheduled rate of compensation" to which they would be entitled if still active. The superior court granted the retired officers' motion for pretrial judgment. The District of Columbia appealed to the D.C. Court of Appeals, which affirmed the superior court decision and found that **any increase in salary had to result in increased retirement compensation.** *District of Columbia v. Tarlosky*, 675 A.2d 77 (D.C. App. 1996).

• New York's plan for paying retirement benefits to New York City police officers created several categories of retirees: ordinary disability, service-related disability, deferred vested pension, and service retirees. Service retirees were those who served at least 20 years with the department. In addition to the regular pension benefits received by all retirees, service retirees received variable supplements from a special fund. A group of retirees, who did not receive this additional benefit, filed suit in federal court claiming that the practice was unconstitutional. The U.S. Court of Appeals, Second Circuit, concluded that **the plan had a reasonable basis**, and did not violate the Equal Protection Clause, the Due Process Clause or the Contract Clause. *Castellano v. Board of Trustees of Police Officers' Variable Supplements Fund,* 937 F.2d 752 (2d Cir. 1991).

♦ A surviving spouse of an Ohio firefighter and her two minor children were eligible to participate in the Firemen and Policemen's Death Benefit Fund. The fund provided that the spouse and her two minor children each would receive one-third of the decedent's monthly salary. The children were eligible for such benefits until the dates of their emancipation and also were entitled to college tuition reimbursement and other similar programs. After the children became ineligible for further benefits, the spouse continued to receive only one-third of the decedent's monthly salary. A spouse without children, however, was entitled to receive the full monthly salary. The spouse filed suit in an Ohio court of common pleas alleging that this differential treatment violated the Ohio Constitution. The court of common pleas held for the spouse and ordered a reallocation of the benefits paid. The court of appeals affirmed, and the fund administrators appealed to the Supreme Court of Ohio.

The supreme court determined that the woman was not a member of a suspect class. Further, the alleged differential treatment did not implicate a fundamental right. Therefore, the statute only had to be "not arbitrary" to be constitutional. The court noted that the overall purpose of the statute was to provide "an unbroken stream of income to dependents of the decedent." Thus, **the fund's practice of making lesser payments to surviving spouses with emancipated children than to surviving spouses with no children was arbitrary**. The additional expense incurred by the college tuition reimbursement program and other similar programs for the decedent's children did not justify the distinction. The court ordered the fund administrators to recalculate the spouse's benefits. *Roseman v. Firemen and Policemen's Fund,* 613 N.E.2d 574 (Ohio 1993).

C. Taxation

♦ The state of Georgia exempted from taxation retirement benefits paid by the state, but not retirement benefits paid by the federal government. After this practice was declared unconstitutional by the U.S. Supreme Court in *Davis v. Michigan Dep't of Treasury,* 489 U.S. 803 (1989), Georgia repealed its special tax exemption for state retirees. A federal military officer from Georgia sought a refund for the tax years 1980 and after in a state court. He alleged that a Georgia statute providing "clear and certain" post-deprivation relief from unconstitutional state taxes entitled him to a refund. The Georgia statute provided: "A taxpayer shall be refunded all taxes or fees ... illegally assessed and collected from him under the laws of this state, whether paid voluntarily or involuntarily." The court declined to award the refund, and the Georgia Supreme Court affirmed. It found that the availability of adequate pre-deprivation remedies precluded relief under the federal Due Process Clause. The officer appealed to the U.S. Supreme Court.

The Supreme Court noted that the Georgia court had unfairly sanctioned a "bait and switch" scheme when it held the "clear and certain" post-deprivation remedy guaranteed by the state statute not to exist. Because an average taxpayer would not consider the pre-deprivation procedures to be the exclusive remedies for unlawful taxes – especially in light of the refund statute – the Georgia Supreme Court had improperly denied the officer a refund based on these measures. Instead, the statute's "sweeping language" indicated that state taxes assessed in violation of federal law were "illegally assessed." In fact, the Court noted that **states ordinarily prefer taxpayers to "pay first, litigate later." The Court refused to penalize the taxpayer for adhering to this preference.** The holding of the Georgia Supreme Court was reversed and the case was remanded for the provision of "meaningful backward-looking relief." *Reich v. Collins*, 513 U.S. 106, 115 S.Ct. 547, 130 L.Ed.2d 454 (1994).

♦ An Arizona man brought a taxpayer's suit challenging pension benefit increases, insurance premium subsidies, and tax equity allowances for beneficiaries of the designated plans who had retired from public employment before the Arizona legislature authorized the benefits. He claimed that all three types of post-retirement benefit increases violated the Extra Compensation Clause of the Arizona Constitution because the retired recipients provided no additional services in exchange for the increased benefits. The court granted pretrial judgment to the county, and the taxpayer appealed to the Court of Appeals of Arizona. **The Extra Compensation Clause states that a retired employee is entitled to the amount of compensation specified in the pension agreement in effect at the time of retirement.** Any compensation exceeding this contractual amount for which the beneficiary provides no additional services or consideration constitutes extra compensation and is prohibited. The county contended that the Extra Compensation Clause applied to post-retirement benefit increases only if the money belonged to the state. The appellate court agreed and determined that the Extra Compensation Clause did not apply to any expenditures unless they involved state funds paid from the state treasury. In this case, all the post-retirement benefit increases were paid from plan funds, additional employer contributions, or investment earnings. Therefore, no increase was funded by money from the state general fund. The decision for the county was affirmed. *McClead v. Pima County*, 849 P.2d 1378 (Ariz. Ct. App. 1992).

CHAPTER SEVEN

Labor Relations

	Page
I. FAIR LABOR STANDARDS ACT	419
A. Covered Employees	419
B. Overtime Wages	422
1. Exempt Salaried Employees	423
2. Method of Calculation	427
3. Comp and Flex Time	432
4. Compensable Activities	434
5. Commuting Expenses	437
6. Procedural Issues	439
II. PRIVACY OF EMPLOYEE INFORMATION	441
III. WAGE DISCRIMINATION	443
IV. UNION REPRESENTATION	445
A. Duty of Fair Representation	447
B. Collective Bargaining Fees	451
V. UNFAIR LABOR PRACTICES	454
A. Right to Organize	454
B. Terms and Conditions	457
1. Wages and Hours	457
2. Employer Policies	459
3. Procedural Issues	464
C. Arbitration	467

I. FAIR LABOR STANDARDS ACT

The Fair Labor Standards Act, 29 U.S.C. § 201 et seq., (FLSA) sets forth wage requirements and hour restrictions for employees (such as compensation for overtime work and minimum wage requirements).

A. Covered Employees

In 1974, Congress amended the FLSA to extend its coverage to almost all public employees. However, the U.S. Supreme Court, in *National League of Cities v. Usery*, 426 U.S. 833 (1976), held that the amendments were invalid with respect to employees working in traditional government function jobs.

Later, the Court in *Garcia v. San Antonio Metropolitan Transit Authority*, 469 U.S. 528 (1985), below, overturned the *National League of Cities* decision and held that it was permissible to require state and local government employers to comply with the FLSA.

♦ The FLSA requires certain employers to pay their employees a minimum hourly wage and to pay time-and-a-half for hours worked over 40 a week. In 1974, Congress amended the act, broadening its coverage to include almost all public employees. Various cities and states and the National League of Cities brought an action challenging the validity of the amendments, asserting that intergovernmental immunity prevented Congress from amending the act. A three-judge district court dismissed the complaint. Further appeal was taken to the U.S. Supreme Court, which held that the 1974 amendments obstructed the states' abilities to structure their employer-employee relationships with respect to areas of traditional government functions. **The amendments were invalid because they impaired the states' abilities to function effectively in a federal system.** Essentially, the Court determined that Congress could not directly force the states to utilize only Congress' means of conducting integral governmental functions. The Court thus reversed the district court's decision and held the amendments invalid. *National League of Cities v. Usery,* 426 U.S. 833, 96 S.Ct. 2465, 49 L.Ed.2d 245 (1976). This case was overturned by *Garcia v. San Antonio Metropolitan Transit Authority*, below.

♦ The San Antonio Metropolitan Transit Authority (SAMTA) provided transportation to the San Antonio area with the help of substantial financial assistance under the Urban Mass Transportation Act. In 1979, the Wage and Hour Administration of the Department of Labor issued an opinion that SAMTA's operations were not immune from the minimum wage and overtime requirements of the FLSA. SAMTA sued in federal court, asserting under *National League of Cities v. Usery* that it was exempt from the requirements of the FLSA. The district court agreed. However, the U.S. Supreme Court reversed, noting that **drawing boundaries between areas of traditional governmental functions and those areas that were not traditionally run by the government was not only unworkable, but inconsistent** with established principles of federalism. Further, the Court noted that the FLSA requirements did not destroy state sovereignty or violate the Constitution. Accordingly, the Court overruled *National League of Cities*, above. State and local government employers could be compelled to comply with the FLSA *Garcia v. San Antonio Metropolitan Transit Authority*, 469 U.S. 528, 105 S.Ct. 1005, 83 L.Ed.2d 1016 (1985).

♦ Three hundred fire service paramedics in Philadelphia brought a lawsuit seeking overtime compensation under the FLSA. They claimed that they did not engage in fire suppression activities under Section 203(y) and thus were not exempt from overtime. The case reached the Third Circuit Court of Appeals, which agreed that the paramedics were entitled to overtime. **The paramedics were not hired to fight fires, and were not expected to do so.** Their job description made no mention of fire suppression duties, and they were dispatched to fire scenes only when it was necessary to have medical personnel on site. Finally, their training was different than the training received by firefighters. *Lawrence v. City of Philadelphia*, 527 F.3d 299 (3d Cir. 2008).

♦ Anticipating a budget impasse, the governor of Pennsylvania devised a plan to temporarily lay off non-critical employees who were not exempt under the FLSA. The state constitution barred the state from paying money from its treasury if the legislature had not yet passed an appropriations budget by the end of the fiscal year. The governor's plan never took effect because the legislature passed a new budget before the deadline. However, several unions sued the state, claiming that the FLSA superseded the state constitution, preventing the governor from implementing the plan. The Commonwealth Court of Pennsylvania ruled for the state, noting that **the FLSA did not preempt the state constitution**. *Council 13 v. Comwlth. of Pennsylvania*, 954 A.2d 706 (Pa. Commw. Ct. 2008).

♦ A number of police officers for a city/county governmental entity in Kansas also worked as security guards in their off-duty hours for the Housing Authority of Kansas City. They sued both the city/county entity and the housing authority seeking overtime, claiming that the two entities were joint employers under the FLSA so that hours worked for both entities should be combined for the purpose of determining whether they were due overtime pay. A jury ruled for the defendants, and the Tenth Circuit affirmed. Here, the evidence supported the jury's finding that **the officers/security guards were independent contractors of the housing authority and not employees**. The housing authority exercised very little control over the officers/security guards, who could work whatever hours they chose and who were subject to very little supervision. *Johnson v. Unified Government of Wyandotte County/Kansas City, Kansas*, 371 F.3d 723 (10th Cir. 2004).

♦ A Virginia city did not have to provide overtime pay to seven firefighters who, in addition to their full-time responsibilities, volunteered to work with private emergency rescue squads. Each rescue squad in the city was a separately incorporated nonprofit entity that provided emergency medical services to city residents. **The seven firefighters claimed that their work with the volunteer rescue squads should be covered under the FLSA** because they still were "employees" of the city when they did their volunteer work. Firefighters are often dispatched to a medical emergency before the rescue squad's arrival but in 1990, the city created the Department of Emergency Medical Services (DEMS) in response to the rescue squads' growing medical sophistication. The DEMS served as a central training office for the squads as well as a coordinating arm for the city's public and private emergency response services. However, it was the rescue squads, not the DEMS, that had ultimate authority over whether a volunteer was accepted for membership, the Fourth Circuit Court of Appeals said. The rescue squads also maintained control over the number of hours a member could choose to serve, minimum training requirements, scheduling, and attendance at squad meetings. Accordingly, despite the involvement of the DEMS, the city was not liable under the FLSA. *Benshoff v. City of Virginia Beach*, 180 F.3d 136 (4th Cir. 1999).

♦   A Florida woman served on a jury for two days and was paid nothing. On her own behalf and on behalf of all others similarly situated, the juror sued the county in federal court, alleging violations of the FLSA because she was not paid minimum wage and overtime for her service. The county moved for dismissal, and its motion was granted. The juror appealed to the U.S. Court of Appeals, Eleventh Circuit. While there was no dispute that the county was an employer, the appellate court held that the relationship between the county and the juror was not an employment relationship. **Jurors are not county employees** because they do not apply for employment, but are randomly selected from voter registration lists and do not volunteer their labor; they are compelled to serve. Also, unlike county employees, jurors do not receive salary or benefits, and they cannot be fired for poor performance. Finding that jury service is a privilege and duty that cannot be avoided because of inconvenience or decreased earning power, and that it does not constitute employment, the court affirmed the lower court's judgment. *Brouwer v. Metropolitan Dade County*, 139 F.3d 817 (11th Cir. 1998).

♦   Two employees of a South Carolina fire district were elected as president and secretary-treasurer of the newly formed local firefighters' association. Both employees had been the lead plaintiffs and spokespersons in FLSA suits against the district. Around this time, the city and district negotiated a contract under which the district fire department was to disband and the city was to provide fire protection and related services. District employees were allowed to submit applications, but the city had discretion to determine which district employees would have their employment transferred. Neither the president nor the secretary-treasurer were hired. They sued the city and several officials, alleging retaliation for their FLSA claims. The court dismissed the case, finding that the FLSA anti-retaliation provision requires an employer-employee relationship. Although no requirement exists that the defendant be the plaintiff's employer, the statutory "any employee" language mandates that the plaintiff have a current or past employment relationship with the defendant. **Job applicants do not fall under FLSA protection.** The plaintiffs here were job applicants with no prior employment relationship with the city. *Glover v. City of North Charleston, South Carolina*, 942 F.Supp. 243 (D.S.C. 1996).

B. Overtime Wages

Section 207 of the FLSA governs overtime wages and states that an employer must pay an employee working more than 40 hours per week at least one and one-half times his or her regular wage.

Although the FLSA requires employers to pay certain employees for overtime, it allows public employers to provide their employees compensatory time (extra time off) under a collective bargaining agreement or other agreement between the public agency and employee representatives.

The new final regulations to the FLSA change who is eligible for overtime while keeping the "salary basis" and "job duties" requirements, though in modified form. For example, the salary for exempt employees must now be at least $455 per week. Salaried employees earning less than that amount automatically qualify for overtime.

Employees who meet the salary basis test must still meet the job duties requirement to be exempt from overtime. In other words, they must be "executive, administrative, professional, computer [or] outside sales" employees. "First responders" (law enforcement and public safety personnel who have a responsibility to be a first responder) will be eligible for overtime even if they have supervisory duties.

Executive employees must "customarily and regularly direct the work of two or more other employees" and either have the authority to hire, fire and promote, or have their recommendations for hiring, firing and promotion be "given particular weight." This latter requirement allows supervisory employees who can only make suggestions and recommendations about job status to still be considered exempt from overtime in some situations.

The regulations change the allowance for disciplinary deductions to provide that exempt salaried employees can now be suspended without pay for less than a full week and still not lose their exempt status. Other permissible deductions from salary for exempt employees are:

—Absences for one or more full days for personal reasons
—Absences for one or more full days due to sickness or disability if the deductions are made under a bona fide plan, policy or practice of providing wage replacement benefits
—Offset for payments for jury fees, witness fees or military pay
—Penalties imposed in good faith for violating safety rules "of major significance"
—Proportionate rate of full salary for time actually worked in the first and last weeks of employment, and
—Unpaid leave taken pursuant to the FMLA.

1. Exempt Salaried Employees

◆ Several Missouri police officers employed by the St. Louis Police Department filed an FLSA lawsuit against the Board of Police Commissioners in federal court, seeking overtime wages. The officers contended they did not meet the exemption for salaried employees because under the terms of the department manual their compensation could be reduced for disciplinary infractions related to the "quality or quantity" of work performed. They also claimed they did not meet the other requirement for exempt status: that their duties be of an executive, administrative or professional nature. The district court found that the officers were paid on a salary basis, although not all the officers satisfied the duties criteria. The Eighth Circuit Court of Appeals affirmed in part and reversed in part, holding that both the salary basis and duties tests were satisfied as to all the officers.

The U.S. Supreme Court found that the "no disciplinary deductions" element of the salary basis test applied to public sector employees. Moreover, the Secretary of Labor had reasonably interpreted the salary basis test to deny exempt status when either an actual practice of making pay deductions exists or an employment policy creates a "significant likelihood" of such deductions. **An inadvertent deduction or deduction for reasons other than lack of work will not remove the exemption if the employer reimburses the employee for such deductions and promises to comply in the future.** Further, the regulations do not require immediate payment of the reimbursement. The Court affirmed the court of appeals' decision. *Auer v. Robbins*, 519 U.S. 452, 117 S.Ct. 905, 137 L.Ed.2d 79 (1997).

• A Georgia county fire chief asked paramedics to become certified in firefighting and then changed their job classification to reflect fire suppression duties. The county assigned the paramedics to a 212-hour, 28-day work schedule (53 hours a week) to comply with Section 207(k) of the FLSA. It then stopped paying the paramedics for overtime for hours in excess of 40 per week. A number of paramedics sued, claiming they never actually engaged in fire suppression duties and thus were not exempt employees. A federal court and the Eleventh Circuit ruled for the county, finding that **the paramedics had the responsibility to engage in fire suppression even if they were never called upon to perform that duty**. Thus, they met the statutory definition of exempt fire protection employees in Section 207(y). *Huff v. DeKalb County*, 516 F.3d 1273 (11th Cir. 2008).

• Thousands of police sergeants sued the NYPD and the city of New York, seeking overtime compensation under the FLSA. They moved for partial pretrial judgment on the issue of the defendants' liability. A federal court held that under the "short test" for the period prior to August 23, 2004, when the Department of Labor's revised regulations became effective, the sergeants were exempt from overtime as executive employees. Although the sergeants spent much of their time in the field with their subordinates, their primary duties (and principal value to the defendants) were supervisory. However, with respect to the time period after the revised regulations became effective (August 23, 2004), there were questions of fact as to **whether the sergeants had the authority to hire and fire** or whether their recommendations as to hiring and firing were given particular weight. Those questions required a trial. *Mullins v. City of New York*, 523 F.Supp.2d 339 (S.D.N.Y. 2007).

• A former employee of the Triborough Bridge and Tunnel Authority brought a lawsuit seeking overtime. A New York federal court ruled that the employee worked in a bona fide professional capacity, and thus was not eligible for overtime. The employee earned $68,000 a year; he worked in a field requiring professional knowledge and training (engineering); and he regularly exercised discretion and judgment while performing his job duties. On appeal to the Second Circuit, he asserted that under the "duties test" of the FLSA, he spent the majority of his time performing supervisory tasks rather than engineering work; under the "salary test," he was an at-will employee; and he was performing a public service. He also asserted that he was retaliated against in violation of the FLSA. The court held that **the employee clearly fell into the professional capacity exception to the FLSA**. It did not matter that he was an at-will employee, that his work was of a "public service" nature, or that, in addition to his engineering tasks, he was doing supervisory work without the power to hire, fire and promote. His pay did not vary depending on the quality or quantity of work he performed. His retaliation claim also failed because he never filed a formal complaint prior to his termination – a requirement for a retaliation claim under the FLSA. *Aneja v. Triborough Bridge and Tunnel Authority*, 35 Fed.Appx. 19 (2d Cir. 2002).

◆ A South Carolina nuclear station was shut down for routine maintenance every 18 months for a five- or six-week period. During that time, 17 salaried employees, who were otherwise exempt administrative employees under the FLSA, performed nonexempt duties. Claiming they were entitled to overtime, they sued in a federal court and lost. The Fourth Circuit Court of Appeals affirmed, noting that **the employees' primary duties were administrative in nature**, and that the five or six weeks of nonexempt work did not have to be treated independently for purposes of applying the FLSA. The whole 18-month period could be looked at together to determine that the employees were exempt. *Counts v. South Carolina Electric & Gas Co.*, 317 F.3d 453 (4th Cir. 2003).

◆ Under Section 7(k) of the FLSA, employers are allowed a partial exemption from paying overtime for employees engaged in "fire protection services." About 250 Norfolk firefighters sued under the FLSA, seeking to recoup overtime payments they claimed were owed because they performed simultaneous service as emergency medical personnel. According to FLSA regulations, employers forfeit the "fire protection services" exemption if more than 20% of the firefighters' work is not performed as an incident to or in conjunction with their fire protection activities. Here, the firefighters claimed that more than 20% of their time was spent on emergency medical services (EMS) duties at non-fire emergencies, such that the city forfeited the "fire protection services" exemption. The case reached the Fourth Circuit Court of Appeals, which held that **the firefighting and EMS services were so integrated that the firefighters were not entitled to the exemption**. Even when they were at non-fire emergencies, the firefighters had to have their firefighting tools with them in case they were called to fight a fire. As a result, their EMS duties were incidental to or in conjunction with their fire protection activities for purposes of the regulations. The city was not liable for overtime. *Adams v. City of Norfolk*, 274 F.3d 148 (4th Cir. 2001).

◆ A union negotiator for the Public School Employees (PSE) of Washington represented PSE members on job-related issues such as grievances and disciplinary matters, and helped individual bargaining units develop policies and objectives. He was paid an annual salary of $65,000 and regularly worked more than 40 hours a week. However, in weeks where he missed parts of workdays without making up the time during the week, his sick leave was docked under a policy that allowed for sick leave or vacation time to be docked in 15-minute increments. He sued PSE under the FLSA and state law for overtime. A federal court dismissed his lawsuit under the FLSA, and the Ninth Circuit Court of Appeals affirmed. Here, he met the FLSA's "primary duties" test as **an exempt administrative employee because his work was "directly related to management policy** or general business operations of ... his employer's customers," the bargaining units. He also met the FLSA's "salary basis" test because he received a predetermined amount each pay period, and those wages were not subject to reductions because of the quantity or quality of the work. The deductions made to his sick leave did not count as a reduction in salary because under the FLSA, sick leave is a fringe benefit rather than salary. However, under state law, those deductions might make him eligible for overtime. The court remanded the case on that issue. *Webster v. Public School Employees of Washington, Inc.*, 247 F.3d 910 (9th Cir. 2001).

• Over a six-year period, a California county imposed 53 disciplinary suspensions on exempt salaried employees pursuant to a county ordinance. The county employed approximately 5,300 exempt employees. A federal court found that the suspensions violated federal regulations under the FLSA. As a result, the county had improperly classified the employees as exempt salaried employees, and the employees were entitled to overtime compensation. Subsequently, the Supreme Court decided *Auer v. Robbins*, which held that where an employer made an improper disciplinary suspension (even an intentional one), it could correct that violation under the "window of correction" rule and maintain the classification of its exempt salaried employees under the FLSA. The county then sought reconsideration of the order that it pay overtime. The court found that it could not make use of the window of correction, and the Ninth Circuit Court of Appeals affirmed. **The window of correction could not be used here because the county had engaged in a pattern or practice of improper deductions** even though only 1% of its exempt employees had been improperly suspended. The county had to pay the employees overtime. *Klem v. Santa Clara County*, 208 F.3d 1085 (9th Cir. 2000).

• Current and former fire chiefs in Oklahoma sought overtime for hours worked between March 30, 1995 and June 30, 1997. The city asserted that the chiefs were not eligible for overtime because they were "bona fide executive, administrative, or professional" employees under Section 213(a)(1) of the FLSA. The chiefs maintained that their pay was subject to reduction as a means of discipline and that they were not salaried employees as a result. The U.S. Court of Appeals noted that **none of the chiefs had ever been subject to a disciplinary reduction in pay**. Since the city's written policy did not effectively communicate that pay deductions were an anticipated form of punishment for employees in the chiefs' category, it could not be assumed that such sanctions were likely to be imposed on the chiefs. Thus, they were salaried employees who were not entitled to overtime. *Spradling v. City of Tulsa*, 198 F.3d 1219 (10th Cir. 2000).

• In 1996, the Tenth Circuit Court of Appeals concluded that the city of Denver's express policy on disciplining lieutenants, captains, and division chiefs in the Denver Police Department rendered the officers' salaries "subject to" disciplinary or other deductions. This possibility of reduction required the city to pay them overtime. The U.S. Supreme Court vacated and remanded the decision for further consideration in light of *Auer v. Robbins*. On remand, the Tenth Circuit applied the reasoning in *Auer* to hold the officers exempt from the overtime requirements of the FLSA. The court found that the city's policy applied to all members of the classified service, and that **no evidence of disciplinary or other deductions in pay either as an actual practice or as an employment policy existed**. *Carpenter v. City & County of Denver, Colorado*, 115 F.3d 765 (10th Cir. 1997).

2. Method of Calculation

* A group of current and former firefighters brought a lawsuit alleging that their overtime pay had been improperly calculated. The case reached the Court of Appeals of Kentucky, which noted that the firefighters averaged 56 hours per week, and that their overtime hours should be calculated using a 40-hour week as a base. The court also agreed with the firefighters that **Educational Incentive Pay, Longevity Pay, a Salary Supplement and a "July Bonus" should be included for the purpose of calculating overtime** pay. However, the clothing allowance the firefighters received was not remuneration that should be included in the wage calculations. Finally, the firefighters were not entitled to have the statute of limitations tolled, so their claims could not go back more than five years. *Comwlth., Labor Cabinet v. Hasken*, 265 S.W.3d 215 (Ky. Ct. App. 2007).

* Nine Aberdeen, South Dakota firefighters sued the city claiming that **they should be compensated for overtime they were scheduled to work even though they found substitutes to cover their shifts**. The case reached the Eighth Circuit, which noted that firefighters commonly ask other employees to cover their shifts and that Section 207 of the FLSA allows the practice as long as it is voluntary and done with the employer's permission. When a substitution occurs, the employer pays the scheduled employee and not the substitute. The two employees enter into a private agreement as to how to compensate the employee who worked the shift (often by trading shifts). This keeps overtime costs from spiraling out of control and does not require the employer to pay more in overtime than it would have if there were no voluntary substitutions. The firefighters were entitled to overtime pay for the shifts they did not work. *Senger v. City of Aberdeen*, 466 F.3d 670 (8th Cir. 2006).

* A Missouri city had a sick leave buy-back program wherein it paid certain firefighters 75% of their regular hourly rate for unused sick days sold back to the city. To qualify for the program, firefighters had to work 24-hour shifts during the course of the year for several years to amass the necessary six-month leave reserve. Essentially, the program required firefighters to have consistent workplace attendance. A group of firefighters sued the city under the FLSA, claiming that **the buy-back moneys they received should be included in their regular rate of pay for the purposes of determining overtime**. The case reached the Eighth Circuit Court of Appeals, which agreed with the firefighters.

It cited Section 778.223 of the FLSA regulations, noting that the buy-back moneys constituted remuneration for employment because their primary purpose was to encourage firefighters to come to work regularly over a significant period of time. *Acton v. City of Columbia*, 436 F.3d 969 (8th Cir. 2006).

◆ A group of 119 paramedics certified in fire suppression skills brought a lawsuit against the city of Los Angeles under the FLSA for overtime. They asserted that **the city misclassified them as "dual-function" paramedics because they did not in fact perform any firefighting activities** and did not even carry any firefighting equipment with them in their ambulances. Claiming they were employees engaged in fire protection activities and pursuant to Section 207(k), the city had paid them overtime only for the hours they worked in excess of 204 per 27-day work period. After the lawsuit was filed, Congress passed Section 203(y), an amendment to the FLSA that defined "employee in a fire protection activity" as one who "has the legal authority and responsibility to engage in the prevention, control or extinguishment of a fire of any type." The case reached the Ninth Circuit, which ruled in favor of the paramedics, upholding a $5 million award against the city. Even though the FLSA was not amended until after the lawsuit was filed, the regulations in place prior to that time clearly placed the paramedics outside the overtime exemption. *Cleveland v. City of Los Angeles*, 420 F.3d 981 (9th Cir. 2005).

◆ A township in Pennsylvania **agreed to include police officers' non-work pay in the calculation of their regular rate** of pay in exchange for the officers' agreement to relinquish their right to have incentive/expense pay added to their regular rate. Eventually, a lawsuit resulted over the proper method of calculating the regular rate of pay for purposes of overtime compensation. The case reached the Third Circuit, which noted that under Section 207(e) of the FLSA, an employee's regular rate of pay "shall not be deemed to include" non-work pay. However, the township could bargain for such an inclusion; doing so was not illegal. Since the township had agreed to include non-work pay in the regular rate, it had to be included. As for the incentive/expense pay, the township did not qualify for the credits specified in the FLSA. Accordingly, it could not exclude the incentive pay from the regular rate. *Wheeler v. Hampton Township*, 399 F.3d 238 (3d Cir. 2005).

◆ A Nevada city negotiated with the police officers' union a flat fee of $60 every two weeks to compensate canine officers for off-duty care of police dogs. A canine officer sued, challenging the flat fee as a violation of the FLSA, claiming she spent an average of 28 off-duty hours per week caring for and training her dog. Under Section 785.23 of the FLSA regulations, employers and employees can agree on an alternative method of compensating for overtime where the agreements are reasonable and take into account "all of the pertinent facts." A federal court granted pretrial judgment to the city. The Ninth Circuit Court of Appeals reversed. Here, **the negotiated clause did not take into account "some approximation of the number of hours actually worked by the employee"** or the hours she might have to work. The city admittedly did not know how much off-duty time the officer spent caring for her dog when it negotiated the flat fee. The court remanded the case for a determination of whether the clause was reasonable under the FLSA. *Leever v. Carson City*, 360 F.3d 1014 (9th Cir. 2004).

♦ A Massachusetts town entered into a collective bargaining agreement with non-supervisory police officers, which set each officer's salary according to rank. The officers then received 1/52 of that salary each week as base pay regardless of the number of hours actually worked. State law also required the officers be paid shift-differential compensation, longevity pay and career incentive pay. The town did not include these wage "augments" in calculating an officer's regular rate of pay for determining overtime. Instead, it calculated the overtime rate by dividing the annual salary by 1,950 (the expected number of regular shift hours) and then multiplying by 1.5. The First Circuit Court of Appeals held that **the FLSA required the town to include the augmented pay in the calculation of the officers' regular rate.** It remanded the case for a determination of the extent of damages, if any, to which the officers were entitled. *O'Brien v. Town of Agawam*, 350 F.3d 279 (1st Cir. 2003).

♦ Two Indiana city employees (a facilities maintenance supervisor and an employee in the Department of Capital Asset Management) sued the city and mayor for overtime and vacation time credit allegedly owed them under the FLSA. They claimed that because the city's policies required that their pay be docked if they failed to work an eight-hour day, they were not salaried employees. The city asserted that it could dock the employees for partial-day absences under the "public accountability" exception to the no-docking rule of the FLSA. A federal court agreed with the city.

The Seventh Circuit affirmed the ruling for the city, finding that the city had shown that its policy was consistent with the government's efforts to maintain a precise accounting of its employees' hours. **The city qualified for the public accountability exception to the no-docking rule.** Further, while it was true that some other salaried employees received discretionary payments that appeared to be calculated solely based on hours worked in excess of 40 per week, this practice was not necessarily inconsistent with the salary basis test, and it could not be used by the employees here because they did not receive any discretionary payments. They could not use payments to others as a basis for their claims that they were hourly employees. The employees were not entitled to overtime. *Demos v. City of Indianapolis*, 302 F.3d 698 (7th Cir. 2002).

♦ Firefighters in Waco, Texas, worked a regularly recurring schedule of 120 hours in one 14-day period, 120 hours in the next 14-day period, and 96 hours in the third 14-day period. As a municipal employer of firefighters, Waco was entitled to the FLSA's partial exemption from overtime payment in 29 U.S.C. § 207(k). Under that section, where a city adopts a 14-day work period, it does not have to pay overtime until firefighters have worked 106 hours. When the firefighters sued the city for violating the FLSA, a federal court ruled in their favor. It then determined that their regular rate of pay should be calculated by dividing their salary by 120 hours or 96 hours, depending on which period was at issue. The firefighters challenged this determination, asserting that their regular rate of pay should not have included any overtime hours (i.e., that their salary should have been divided by 106 hours). The case reached the Fifth Circuit Court of Appeals, which affirmed the district court's determination. **Regular hours are not limited to non-overtime hours**, but instead are the hours normally and regularly worked by the employee. The court also ruled that the city could offset the overpayments made in the 96-hour work period against the underpayments made in the 120-hour work periods. This did not violate the FLSA. *Singer v. City of Waco*, 324 F.3d 813 (5th Cir. 2003).

♦ A collective bargaining agreement required a New Jersey corrections facility to assign overtime to the union member whose name appeared at the top of the list. The facility assigned overtime to a nonunion supervisor whose name erroneously appeared on the overtime-rotation list. When three union employees challenged the overtime pay to the nonunion member, an arbitrator awarded back pay to the three employees. The case reached the New Jersey Supreme Court, which upheld the award. It abolished the "no work, no pay" doctrine (prohibiting the state from paying for services it did not receive), and held that **the bargaining agreement could be read to require the state to pay for overtime hours that were not actually worked**. This was because the agreement provided that employees would be paid for "overtime hours accrued," and that phrase could be interpreted to mean that employees were eligible for back pay for hours they were entitled to work. Those hours could be said to be accrued even if they were not actually worked. *State v. Int'l Federation of Professional and Technical Engineers, Local 195*, 780 A.2d 525 (N.J. 2001).

♦ Sixteen Georgia firefighters who were also emergency medical services (EMS) employees sued the county for overtime. The county asserted that they were not entitled to overtime because they were engaged in fire protection activities. The Eleventh Circuit noted that under the Department of Labor's 80/20 rule, if the employees spent more than 20% of their time on nonexempt activities unrelated to firefighting, they would be entitled to overtime. However, the employees here were dual-function employees – that is, they performed both firefighting and EMS activities. Thus, **their EMS activities were exempt from overtime compensation under Section 207(k) of the FLSA**. The court remanded the case for a determination of how much time the employees spent on nonexempt activities unrelated to either firefighting or EMS activities. If it amounted to more than 20%, the employees would be entitled to overtime. *Falken v. Glynn County*, 197 F.3d 1341 (11th Cir. 1999).

♦ A number of Washington police officers questioned whether a city established a "7(k) exemption" to overtime requirements, as allowed in the FLSA for public employers of law enforcement personnel. The 7(k) exemption slightly increases the number of hours that must be worked before overtime is paid, giving law enforcement employers greater flexibility to select the work period. Under Department of Labor regulations, **if the employer selects an eight-day work period, overtime begins to accrue after 49 hours**. The officers, who worked four 12-hour shifts every eight days, claimed the city owed them compensation for 10-minute briefings they were required to attend before their shifts began. They claimed that they were either entitled to overtime for the briefings because the city failed to show that it had, in fact, established a 7(k) exemption, or that their salaries did not compensate them for the briefings. The case reached the Ninth Circuit Court of Appeals, which noted that the officers could not succeed on their overtime claim. The employer's intent to adopt a 7(k)-work cycle was established by the parties' collective bargaining agreement, which stated that the work period would be eight days, and by the fact that the officers actually worked those cycles. However, there was an issue as to whether the officers' regular salaries adequately compensated them for the briefings. The court remanded the case for a determination on that issue. *Adair v. City of Kirkland*, 185 F.3d 1055 (9th Cir. 1999).

♦ South Carolina emergency medical services (EMS) employees provided medical assistance when dispatched to fires, crime scenes, and automobile accidents. When an EMS vehicle was already on call, another EMS vehicle in an adjacent area was required to cover both areas and be on "stand by." The EMS employees were compensated under the FLSA law enforcement exemption, which paid overtime after 43 hours of work within a one-week period, and were paid an annual salary even though the actual number of hours worked during each week varied. Several past and present EMS employees sued the county in federal court, alleging denial of overtime compensation in violation of the FLSA.

The court held that the EMS employees did not qualify under the fire protection or law enforcement exemption of the FLSA. The county did not meet the "substantially related" test of the federal regulations implementing the FLSA because the EMS employees did not regularly respond to fire protection or law enforcement calls. Approximately 30% of the EMS calls and only about 10% of the total number of working hours were spent on fire and law enforcement calls. The county also **failed to meet the 80/20 rule of the regulations because over 20% of the EMS employees' time was spent on other nonexempt activities**. Thus, the EMS employees were not exempt from the overtime requirements and were entitled to compensation on a 40-hour per week basis. On appeal, the Fourth Circuit Court of Appeals affirmed. *Roy v. County of Lexington, South Carolina*, 141 F.3d 533 (4th Cir. 1998).

♦ Police officers and certain civilian employees of an Illinois village police department had to attend a 15-minute roll call before beginning their shift each day. The employees' eight-hour shift included two paid 15-minute breaks and a paid 30-minute meal period, during which they remained on call. The village's police department policy and procedure manual required roll call attendance but did not require compensation for this time. The manual also provided that employees had to work 30 minutes or more before being entitled to overtime. The employees sued, seeking compensation for time spent at roll call. The Seventh Circuit held that there was neither an express nor an implied contractual right to compensation attending roll call. The 30-minute minimum precluded overtime compensation for the 15-minute roll call. Next, the court held that **the village qualified for an exemption under Section 7(k) of the FLSA**. This exemption is available to public agencies that elect to establish "work periods" from seven to 28 days for employees engaging in law enforcement or fire protection activities. Employers utilizing this exemption are only required to pay overtime to employees who work more than 43 hours in a seven-day work period. Although the department's 28-day schedule predated the enactment of Section 7(k) of the FLSA, it lawfully met the criteria for the exemption. Finally, because the meal periods were not compensable under the FLSA, and the village could offset the meal break against the compensable roll call time worked by the employees, the employees were not entitled to overtime. The city could pay them for 30 minutes of "non-work" time each day and reserve the right to offset 30 minutes of "work" time beyond regular working hours. *Barefield v. Village of Winnetka*, 81 F.3d 704 (7th Cir. 1996).

3. Comp and Flex Time

♦ A Texas county became concerned that it would have to pay cash for accrued compensatory time by certain employees. It adopted a policy requiring employees to schedule time off in order to reduce the amount of comp time they had banked. A number of deputy sheriffs sued, asserting that the policy violated the FLSA, because Section 207(o)(5) of the act provided the exclusive means of using compensatory time in the absence of an agreement otherwise. That section requires employers to honor employees' requests to use comp time within a reasonable period unless doing so would unduly disrupt the employers' operations. Accordingly, the deputies argued, the county could not tell them when they had to use their comp time. A federal court agreed with the deputies, but the Fifth Circuit Court of Appeals reversed, finding that the FLSA did not speak to the issue and thus did not prevent the county from implementing the policy. The U.S. Supreme Court affirmed. It noted that **nothing in the FLSA or its regulations prohibits an employer from compelling the use of compensatory time**. Section 207(o)(5) was designed to ensure that employees receive a timely benefit for overtime work. It was not intended to set forth the exclusive method by which comp time could be used. As a result, the county could force the deputies to use comp time. *Christensen v. Harris County*, 529 U.S. 576, 120 S.Ct. 1655, 146 L.Ed.2d 621 (2000).

♦ A sheriff's union represented more than 400 deputy sheriffs. However, the union was prohibited by Texas law from entering into collective bargaining agreements with a Texas county. Each employee was bound by form agreements individually entered into with the county. These form agreements provided in part that employees working overtime would be compensated with extra time off. The union filed suit in federal court, alleging that the representation by the union precluded the individual agreements providing for comp time rather than overtime pay. The district court entered pretrial judgment for the county and the Fifth Circuit affirmed, albeit on different reasoning. The union appealed to the U.S. Supreme Court, which determined that **individual agreements were precluded only when an elected labor representative had the authority to negotiate the use of comp time via a collective bargaining agreement**. Since the union did not have authority under local law to enter into a collective bargaining agreement, individual agreements authorizing comp time were permitted. The holding of the court of appeals was affirmed. *Moreau v. Klevenhagen*, 508 U.S. 22, 113 S.Ct. 1905, 123 L.Ed.2d 584 (1993).

• Social Security employees brought a lawsuit in the Court of Federal Claims, asserting that the Social Security Administration's practice of granting employees credit hours and compensatory time for overtime work violated the FLSA. Among their arguments was that the comp time they received for work in excess of 40 hours a week should not be hour-for-hour. They claimed they should receive one-and-a-half hours of comp time for each hour of overtime worked. The case reached the United States Court of Appeals, Federal Circuit, which held that the plain language of **the Federal Employees Pay Act allows the head of an agency to grant an employee comp time for an "equal amount of time spent in irregular or occasional overtime work."** This was different than Section 207(o) of the FLSA, which requires state or local agencies to grant comp time of at least one-and-a-half hours for each hour of employment. The employees remained free to take overtime pay rather than comp time if they so chose. *Doe v. U.S.*, 513 F.3d 1348 (Fed. Cir. 2008).

• A group of airport police officers in Michigan sued for overtime because they were required to wear pagers while off duty following the 9/11 terrorist attacks. After they filed the lawsuit, airport management collected the pagers and implemented a number of changes, including requiring them to use vacation days for vacations, rather than substituting comp time and later exchanging the unused vacation time for pay. A federal court and the Sixth Circuit found no overtime violation and no retaliation by the airport authority. The officers were not seriously restricted in their personal pursuits while off duty. Also, **the decision to remove the pagers and disallow further comp time did not result in materially adverse employment action.** *Adair v. Charter County of Wayne*, 452 F.3d 482 (6th Cir. 2006).

• A group of past and present police officers sued the city of Cleveland under the FLSA, **alleging that the city improperly denied them compensatory leave** under Section 207(o)(5)(B). That section allows employers to deny comp time where it would "unduly disrupt the operations" of the agency. The city claimed that it would have to pay substitute officers overtime to cover the shifts of the officers taking comp leave, creating an additional payroll expense. A federal court granted pretrial judgment to the city, but the Sixth Circuit reversed and remanded the case. Here, the bargaining agreement did not identify "financial impact" as a basis for denying requests for comp time. To succeed at trial, the city had to show that the officers' timely requests for comp time would saddle it with a financial burden that would unduly disrupt its ability to provide police services. *Beck v. City of Cleveland*, 390 F.3d 912 (6th Cir. 2004).

• The Sacramento County Sheriff's Department used a leave book to schedule compensatory time off (CTO). A correction center deputy sheriff requested 12 hours of comp time on a particular day, but his supervisor denied the request because the leave book was full for that day. He sued under the FLSA, asserting that his overtime rights under Section 207(o)(5)(B) were violated because he was not allowed to take comp leave when he wanted. A federal court and the Ninth Circuit ruled against him. The court of appeals held that **public employers, not employees, had the discretion to choose the days on which comp time leave would be granted.** The FLSA clearly states that when an employee requests CTO, the employer has a reasonable period of time to grant the request. There were 18 alternate days with open leave slots available within the two-month period surrounding his request. Also, the county did not have to grant CTO where another employee was willing to work overtime to cover the shift. *Mortenson v. County of Sacramento*, 368 F.3d 1082 (9th Cir. 2004).

♦ Employers must provide requested comp time within a reasonable time after the employee makes the request. The Houston Police Department did so using a log book, wherein any officer wishing to use accrued comp time had to sign the book for the day or days off desired. The department generally limited time off to 10% of a unit's staff. The police officers' union challenged the log book system under Section 207(o)(5) of the FLSA because of its inflexible 10% limit on the number of officers who could be off work on any given day. It asserted that Section 207(o)(5) required the department to make an individualized assessment of any inconvenience an officer's absence on any particular day would cause. The Fifth Circuit disagreed. It held that **the FLSA's mandate of a "reasonable period" for use of comp time was not the same as mandating the employee's chosen dates.** Making an exception to the log book practice could create public safety issues. The city did not have to give the police officers the exact days off they requested. *Houston Police Officers Union v. City of Houston*, 330 F.3d 298 (5th Cir. 2003).

4. Compensable Activities

♦ Two canine handler police officers sued a Tennessee city for overtime for their off-duty care of their police dogs. After they won, the city stopped using canine handlers for a time. When it began doing so again, two officers assigned to the police dogs asked about overtime for taking care of their dogs. The chief told them that they couldn't have any comp time and that they had to keep quiet about it or the city council would get rid of the dogs. The chief told the officers they could take time off from their regular shifts to care for the dogs, though this would have meant less pay. When one of the officers sued for overtime, a federal court ruled in his favor, awarding him $21,000 in overtime and $21,000 in liquidated damages for bad faith. **The city knew from the prior lawsuit that it should have paid for the off-duty care of the dogs.** And the officers could not agree to accept less pay than the FLSA requires. *Letner v. City of Oliver Springs*, 545 F.Supp.2d 717 (E.D. Tenn. 2008).

♦ A former police officer in New Hampshire filed a lawsuit against the town, alleging that he was required to attend a police academy for a 12-week period instead of performing his regular duties, and that he was not compensated for time beyond 40 hours per week. The town sought to dismiss the case, contending that the training was required for certification by state law, and thus was not compensable under 29 C.F.R. § 553.226(b). A New Hampshire federal court refused to dismiss the case, noting that 29 C.F.R. § 553.226(c) was the appropriate regulation for this situation. That regulation stated that police officers attending a training facility "are not considered to be on duty during those times when they are not in class or at a training session, if they are free to use such time for personal pursuits. Such time is not compensable." This was a more specific regulation and took precedence over the more general regulation on training required for certification by state law. *Olsen v. Town of Loudon*, 482 F.Supp.2d 177 (D.N.H. 2007).

• An Illinois emergency dispatcher was ordered to stay for a second shift because of a staff shortage. She became angry and left a half-hour into the second shift. When she returned to work, the city required her to submit to a fitness-for-duty evaluation. The doctor found her fit for duty, but recommended she see a psychotherapist once a week for six months as a condition of employment. The city required her to see its therapist, rather than her own, and paid for 90% of the session costs. After she resigned, she sued the city for FLSA violations, asserting that **she was owed for the time she spent visiting the therapist**, because the time went beyond her normal 40-hour week. A federal court and the Seventh Circuit agreed with her. The sessions were primarily for the city's benefit and were a requirement of her continued employment. *Sehie v. City of Aurora*, 432 F.3d 749 (7th Cir. 2005).

• Maryland law defines compensable work time to include the time during which an employee participates in activities that are "job-related immediately before the beginning or immediately after the end of an assignment." Non-uniformed prison case managers cited the law when they challenged the mandatory security checks put in place after September 11, 2001. They claimed that the new procedures caused them to be late for reasons outside their control. An administrative law judge agreed, and the Maryland Court of Appeals affirmed. Here, management mandated the security checks, maintained supervisory control over the case managers while they were in line, and could unduly delay the time it took to go through the line. Thus, the **case managers had to be paid for their time going through the security line** at the beginning and end of each shift. *Dep't of Public Safety and Correctional Services v. Palmer*, 886 A.2d 554 (Md. 2005).

• Eight Omaha paramedics sued to recover overtime for hours they worked over 40 per week. Although they had initially been hired as firefighters by the city, they had since undergone nine months of extensive medical training. They were dispatched to traffic accidents as well as crime and fire scenes. They claimed they were not engaged in firefighting activities because their duties involved only medical care. Thus, they were entitled to overtime for all time worked over 40 hours. The city maintained that they were firefighters and so subject to the Section 207(k) exemption of the FLSA, which allows public employers to schedule fire employees for up to 216 hours of work in a 28-day period before becoming liable for overtime. After a bench trial, the district court ruled for the city, and the Eighth Circuit Court of Appeals affirmed. **Even if the paramedics here performed nothing other than medical duties at a fire,**

they fell within the Section 207(k) exemption because they were trained and sworn as firefighters, who could, if the situation required, be pressed into a firefighting function. In addition, the paramedics' response to medical calls or automobile accidents was still exempt activity related to fire protection; as such, they also failed to show that more than 20% of their time was spent on nonexempt activities. *Lang v. City of Omaha,* 186 F.3d 1035 (8th Cir. 1999).

♦ Some Pennsylvania county sheriff's deputies were assigned to on-call duty, during which they were not required to wear their uniforms or stay at the sheriff's office. Instead, they had to wear pagers when not at home and, if called, had to report within a reasonable time. Because they were not compensated for their on-call time, they sued the county under the FLSA. The Third Circuit Court of Appeals noted that the FLSA does not dictate whether time spent waiting on call, as opposed to time spent responding to a call, is compensable. Courts have followed regulations promulgated by the Department of Labor, which state that on-call time is compensable if the employee is required to remain on the employer's premises. Alternatively, **if the employee finds his on-call time so restricted that it interferes with personal pursuits, the time is compensable**. Here, the deputies were allowed to carry pagers, and the frequency and urgency of the calls did not preclude them from using their on-call time for personal activities. Also, there was no evidence that any deputies were disciplined for late call responses. Finally, they were allowed to trade on-call shifts. Thus, on-call duty did not limit their personal activities to such a degree that their time was spent primarily for the county's benefit. *Ingram v. County of Bucks,* 144 F.3d 265 (3d Cir. 1998).

♦ Corrections officers at a Maryland detention center were not compensated for their meal times during their eight-and-a-half-hour shifts. During their 30-minute meal period, the officers were required to wear their uniforms, were not allowed to leave the grounds, were subject to being recalled to their posts, were not allowed to use the gym, and could not sleep. The officers sued for overtime compensation for the 30-minute meal period. **FLSA regulations provide that employees need not be compensated for bona fide meal periods** – where the employees are completely relieved from duty for the purposes of eating regular meals. The officers in this case were part of a collective bargaining agreement, which stated that meal periods were not to be included while computing compensation. However, the court refused to defer to a collective bargaining agreement where that agreement was a violation of the FLSA's overtime requirements. Here, the officers were subject to being called to their posts at any time during their meals, they were not free to leave the facility, and they were not free to engage in any other type of activity. Therefore, their meal periods had to be included in the computation of overtime pay. *Abendschein v. Montgomery County, Maryland,* 984 F.Supp. 356 (D. Md. 1997).

♦ Employees of the Kansas Department of Corrections were on the job five days a week, eight-and-a-half hours per day, for a total of 42.5 hours per week. However, the department contended that on each of the eight-and-a-half hour days, the employees received a half hour bona fide meal period which, under 29

C.F.R. § 785.19, was not work time. It argued that the employees only had 40 hours of work time per week and were therefore not entitled to overtime under Section 207(a) of the act. The employees sued for overtime under the FLSA. The evidence at trial indicated that many of the meal periods were not scheduled and did not occur at regular times. A jury found in favor of the department, and the U.S. Court of Appeals, Tenth Circuit, affirmed. **Section 785.19 did not require meals to be scheduled or to occur at a regular time.** *Bates v. Dep't of Corrections of Kansas*, 81 F.3d 1008 (10th Cir. 1996).

5. Commuting Expenses

♦ New York City fire inspectors were required to carry their files from their homes to the job sites they inspected and back home again. They were not allowed to store the files overnight at unit headquarters. The inspectors lugged briefcases weighing up to 20 pounds, and they sometimes missed their buses because the extra weight slowed them down. They then had to wait up to 30 minutes for the next bus. Six inspectors sued the city under the FLSA, asserting that they were entitled to pay for the time added to their commutes. A federal court and the Second Circuit ruled against them. The court of appeals noted that even if carrying the files was "integral and indispensable" to the inspectors' primary duties, **any increase in commuting time caused by the files was *de minimis* (minimal) as a matter of law.** *Singh v. City of New York*, 524 F.3d 361 (2d Cir. 2008).

♦ Public works employees in a Florida county sought overtime compensation under the FLSA for commuting in county vehicles to and from secure county-owned or county-operated locations to their job sites, where they inspected the work of subcontractors. Because county policy prohibited employees from taking the vehicles home at the end of the work day, they were required to drive their personal vehicles to the secure parking sites to pick up the county vehicles and drive them to the work sites. They then had to return the vehicles to the secure parking sites before returning home. A federal court ruled for the employees, and the Eleventh Circuit affirmed. The Employee Commuting Flexibility Act amended the Portal-to-Portal Act to clarify that commuting to work in the employer's vehicle rather than the employee's vehicle did not make the commute compensable. However, it did not change the fact that **where the employer requires the employee to report to the employer's premises before and after the work day, that commute is compensable.** *Burton v. Hillsborough County, Florida*, 181 Fed.Appx. 829 (11th Cir. 2006).

♦ Former employees of the Department of Health and Human Services, whose jobs involved the construction of water, sewer and solid waste facilities in Alaska, usually in rural Native Alaskan villages, brought a lawsuit seeking per diem pay. They claimed they were entitled to an allowance based on duty at remote worksites. They cited to regulations under 5 U.S.C. § 5942, which provided that employees were eligible for remote worksite pay if: a) the duty post is farther than 50 miles from the nearest established community of suitable place of residence; b) daily commuting to the duty post is impractical and employees are required to remain at the duty post during the workweek; or c) the duty post can only be reached by boat, aircraft, or other unusual conveyance. The Court of Federal Claims held that **the employees were not prohibited from obtaining remote worksite pay simply because they did not commute**. Further, all the locations except one qualified as remote work locations under the statute. Finally, the employees showed that they remained at their worksites at the direction of management because daily commuting was impractical. *Agwiak v. U.S.*, 64 Fed.Cl. 203 (Fed. Ct. Cl. 2005).

♦ Some California police officers were required to attend mandatory peace officer training outside their city. They were paid for all time spent in training courses. When they were required to report to the police department prior to and after attending off-site training, they were compensated for their travel time even though they performed no police duties while traveling to the training site locations. However, they were not compensated for time spent commuting directly from their homes to the off-site training locations unless it cut across the normal workday. The officers sued the city alleging violations of the FLSA. The court ruled for the city, and the Ninth Circuit affirmed.

The FLSA was amended by the **Portal-to-Portal Act**, 29 U.S.C. §§ 251-262 in part to protect employers from responsibility for commuting time. Under the act, employers are not required to compensate employees for "walking, riding, or traveling to and from the actual place of performance of the [employee's] principal activity or activities." 29 U.S.C. § 254(a)(1). The court held that law enforcement training was such an activity because it was an integral and indispensable part of the principal activity of law enforcement. Further, normal home-to-work travel, even when the employee was expected to report to work at locations away from the employer's premises, was not compensable. **The training did not fall into the unusual assignment exception of the FLSA.** It was normal, contemplated and even mandated by their collective bargaining agreement. Although the training benefited the city, it was equally beneficial to the officers because they needed it to maintain their certification. The city did not violate the FLSA. *Imada v. City of Hercules, California*, 138 F.3d 1294 (9th Cir. 1998).

♦ Under a collective bargaining agreement, the Montana Department of Transportation and a union agreed that the department would pay certain employees a "district construction allowance" for their commute from their homes to their reporting stations. The union sued for a ruling that the allowance should be treated as an element of an employee's base pay when calculating overtime. The court held that the allowance was a travel reimbursement and could not be included in base pay. However, the Montana Supreme Court reversed. The FLSA, at 29 U.S.C. § 207(e)(2), provides that "reasonable payments for traveling expenses, or other expenses, incurred by an employee in the furtherance of his employer's interests and properly reimbursable by the employer" are excluded from the base pay of an employee. Here, the allowance was not an expense incurred on the department's behalf. Instead, it was a reimbursement for normal everyday expenses incurred by employees for their own benefit. Therefore, **the allowance could not be excluded from base pay** as reimbursement for travel expenses. *Montana Public Employees' Ass'n v. Dep't of Transportation,* 954 P.2d 21 (Mont. 1998).

6. Procedural Issues

• Bus drivers, custodians, clerical workers and other employees of a Georgia school district sued the district for violating the FLSA, alleging that they were not properly paid for overtime work they performed. They offered testimony that they were told the school board would not pay overtime, so they shouldn't report it on their time sheets. A principal also allegedly told an employee to use comp time instead of overtime, but then refused to let her take the comp time. And a supervisor allegedly erased overtime hours from another employee's time sheet. A federal court granted pretrial judgment to the school district on the grounds that the time sheets did not show any unpaid overtime. However, the Eleventh Circuit Court of Appeals reversed, finding issues of fact that required a trial. Here, **the employees' statements were admissible to show that the district's written records could not be trusted.** A jury would have to decide whether to believe the employees or district officials. With respect to bus driver overtime rates, the court held that the district properly paid overtime to bus drivers based on blended rates for different types of routes. The FLSA did not state that blended rates were available only when employees performed different types of work. *Allen v. Board of Public Educ. for Bibb County,* 495 F.3d 1306 (11th Cir. 2007).

• A Texas city relied on "volunteers" to staff its police force. Apart from the chief and two part-time officers who were paid, all the other officers were volunteers who had their police "commissions" maintained. This meant that they were able to keep their licenses so as to maintain their status as peace officers. When the paid officers sued for overtime under the FLSA, a federal court and the Fifth Circuit ruled against them. **The city did not have to comply with the FLSA because it had fewer than five employees.** Maintaining the commissions for the volunteer officers did not amount to payment so as to make the volunteer officers employees. *Cleveland v. City of Elmendorf, Texas,* 388 F.3d 522 (5th Cir. 2004).

• Current and former Department of Justice (DOJ) lawyers brought a class action lawsuit for overtime pay under the Federal Employees Pay Act (FEPA). A federal court ruled against them, and the Federal Circuit Court of Appeals affirmed. Although the FLSA requires overtime pay where an employer "suffers or permits" employees to work overtime, there is no similar provision in the FEPA. A regulation barred overtime pay under the FEPA unless managers ordered the work and approved it in writing. Here, DOJ managers may have induced the lawyers to work overtime by telling them they were expected to work until the job was done, even if that meant regularly putting in overtime, but that did not comply with the requirements of the FEPA. *Doe v. U.S.,* 372 F.3d 1347 (Fed. Cir. 2004).

♦ A union filed a grievance against a New Jersey utilities authority on behalf of 12 sludge dewatering machine operators for overtime they claimed they lost when the authority assigned their work to sewage plant operators. They asserted that the authority did this to avoid paying overtime as required by the collective bargaining agreement. An arbitrator held that **the employees were entitled to back pay for the lost overtime**, and the New Jersey Superior Court, Appellate Division, upheld that decision. The arbitrator acted within his power even though the bargaining agreement did not expressly allow back pay as a remedy. Nothing in state law prohibited an award of back pay. Also, the "no work, no pay" rule had been abolished by the state supreme court in 2001, so the employees could be paid for work they did not perform. *Office & Professional Employees Int'l Union, Local 32 v. Camden County Municipal Utilities Authority*, 828 A.2d 927 (N.J. Super. Ct. App. Div. 2003).

♦ Supervisory employees with the Immigration and Naturalization Service (INS) were suspended without pay for disciplinary reasons pursuant to a federal statute. They sued under the FLSA, asserting that because of the disciplinary pay deductions, they were not actually exempt executive employees. Thus, they argued, they were entitled to overtime. The U.S. Court of Appeals, Federal Circuit, ruled that they still were exempt executive employees. Even though the federal regulations interpreting the FLSA only allow deductions for infractions of safety rules of major significance, the INS supervisors' situation here was different because **the suspensions meted out against the supervisors were provided for by federal statute**. The supervisors were not entitled to overtime. *Billings v. U.S.*, 322 F.3d 1328 (Fed. Cir. 2003).

♦ A North Carolina school board secretary sued the school board under the FLSA for overtime, claiming that she often worked more than 40 hours per week and that she had not been compensated for the extra work. A federal court dismissed her lawsuit after determining that any damage award she received would come from state-controlled funds. The Fourth Circuit Court of Appeals reversed, finding that the school board was not a state agency. It exercised general control and supervision of its schools, and it had a sufficient degree of autonomy from the state education board. As a result, the Eleventh Amendment did not bar the lawsuit under the FLSA. *Cash v. Granville County Board of Educ.*, 242 F.3d 219 (4th Cir. 2001).

♦ In 1994, 43 commanding officers in the Portland, Oregon, police bureau sued the city in federal court for taking impermissible deductions from their weekly pay in violation of the FLSA. The case was consolidated with a lawsuit filed three years later by 19 managerial employees from several other city departments, charging similar violations. The U.S. Court of Appeals upheld a pretrial judgment for the city under the FLSA's "window of correction," which enables employers to avoid liability if they reimburse the employee for such deductions and promise to comply with the act in the future. The Ninth Circuit focused on language in the Department of Labor regulations that make the window of correction available to an employer only if the deduction was either "inadvertent or made for reasons other than for lack of work."

Here, only two employees actually had been suspended and had deductions taken from their weekly pay. Four other employees were threatened but never received suspensions. The remaining 57 employees were neither threatened with nor actually subjected to any impermissible deductions. During the litigation, however, the city acknowledged that the two actual deductions might have been improper, reimbursed the employees who had been suspended and promised to comply with the FLSA in the future. Thus, even if it had illegally imposed suspensions, **the city was entitled to resort to the FLSA's "window of correction" to avoid liability.** Further, a pattern or practice of making impermissible deductions could not be surmised from only two instances of actual deductions being taken. *Paresi v. City of Portland*, 182 F.3d 665 (9th Cir. 1999).

II. PRIVACY OF EMPLOYEE INFORMATION

In many cases, labor unions representing public employees have sought to have different government agencies provide them with the names and home addresses of agency employees working in relevant bargaining units.

◆ Two local unions asked various federal agencies to provide them with the names and home addresses of employees whom the unions sought to represent. The agencies refused to disclose the home addresses and the unions filed unfair labor practice charges with the Federal Labor Relations Authority. The authority required the agencies to disclose the home addresses. The Fifth Circuit affirmed, holding that the Freedom of Information Act (FOIA) required disclosure of the home addresses. The U.S. Supreme Court noted that the Federal Service Labor-Management Relations Statute requires federal agencies to provide unions with collective bargaining data to the extent not prohibited by law. However, **the Privacy Act of 1974 prohibits agency disclosure of records unless disclosure is required by the FOIA.** The FOIA generally requires full disclosure unless an express statutory exemption applies. Exemption six of the FOIA provides that these broad disclosure requirements do not apply to "personnel and medical files and similar files the disclosure of which would constitute a clearly unwarranted invasion of personal privacy." The Supreme Court determined that employee addresses were records and therefore protected by the Privacy Act. The employees had substantial privacy interests in avoiding unwanted union mailings and telephone calls. Their privacy interest in nondisclosure outweighed the negligible public interest in disclosure. **The Privacy Act prohibited the release of employee addresses to the unions.** *U.S. Dep't of Defense v. Federal Labor Relations Authority*, 510 U.S. 487, 114 S.Ct. 1006, 127 L.Ed.2d 325 (1994).

◆ When a Washington newspaper sought the records of any teachers accused of, investigated, or disciplined for sexual misconduct in the past 10 years, a school district notified 55 current and former teachers that records had been gathered in response to the request. Thirty-seven teachers filed suit to prevent the release of information, claiming invasion of privacy, and the newspaper joined the lawsuit. The case reached the Supreme Court of Washington, which ruled that when there is an allegation of sexual misconduct against a public school teacher, **the identity of the accused teacher may be disclosed to the public under the public disclosure act (PDA) only if the misconduct is substantiated or the teacher's conduct results in some form of discipline.** Further, the PDA mandates the disclosure of letters of direction, but where a letter simply seeks to guide future conduct, does not mention substantiated misconduct, and a teacher is not disciplined or subject to any restriction, the name and identifying information of the teacher should be redacted. *Bellevue John Does 1-11 v. Bellevue School Dist. # 405*, 189 P.3d 139 (Wash. 2008).

♦ A newspaper, under Pennsylvania's Right to Know Act, requested information from the State Employees' Retirement Board relating to the salaries and service history of Joe Paterno, the legendary Penn State University head football coach, as well as several other Penn State employees. When the board granted the request, Penn State and the employees appealed. The Supreme Court of Pennsylvania held that the salaries and service histories were public records subject to disclosure. Further, **the privacy rights of the coach and the other employees were outweighed by the public interest** in learning the factual bases for, and details of, guaranteed disbursements of state funds. Although the records requested might impair the reputation or personal security of the employees, that impairment did not outweigh the public interest in dissemination of the information. *Pennsylvania State Univ. v. State Employees' Retirement Board*, 935 A.2d 530 (Pa. 2007).

♦ A California school district's board of education hired an investigator after allegations of misconduct and sexual harassment against the district's superintendent arose. Portions of the investigator's report were released to a newspaper by persons the investigator had interviewed. After the board received the full report, it entered into an agreement with the superintendent that it would pay him money and keep the report private in exchange for his resignation. The public and media smelled a "sweetheart deal" and demanded the board release the report. The board refused and a lawsuit resulted. The California Court of Appeal held that the state Public Records Act required disclosure of the report, subject to redacting identifiable information on other persons. Although the superintendent had a significant privacy interest in his personnel file, **his position as a public official and the public nature of the allegations outweighed his interest in keeping the allegations confidential.** *BRV, Inc. v. Superior Court*, 49 Cal.Rptr.3d 519 (Cal. Ct. App. 2006).

♦ A number of off-duty police officers pelted a car with eggs while celebrating a fellow officer's bachelor party. The officers admitted their involvement, cleaned up the car, and reimbursed the owner for damage to the vehicle. They also accepted disciplinary actions in varying degrees. Two newspapers sought the names and personnel files of the officers involved under the state's Freedom of Information Law (FOIL). When the city clerk refused to disclose the files because of the state's Civil Rights Law requiring that the officers first provide consent, the papers sought a court order. The newspapers claimed that New York's consent requirement did not apply to them because the records were being used to provide newsworthy information to the general public, not for litigation. The New York Court of Appeals disagreed. The decisive factor in determining **whether an officer's personnel record was exempted from FOIL disclosure** under the Civil Rights Law was the potential use of the information contained therein, not the specific purpose of the particular individual requesting access or whether the request actually was made in contemplation of litigation. *Daily Gazette Co. v. City of Schenectady*, 688 N.Y.S.2d 472 (N.Y. 1999).

♦ A public employee union was the exclusive bargaining representative for employees at a Kansas public hospital. Under the Public Employer-Employee Relations Act the union requested the names and addresses of all persons in the bargaining unit. The hospital provided the names, but refused to provide the home addresses. The union filed a complaint with the Public Employee Relations Board (PERB). The hospital argued that a state statute prohibited it from disclosing the home addresses to the public. The PERB found that the statute did not apply in this instance, since the disclosure was not made to the general public. It adopted the hearing officer's recommendations and ordered the hospital to disclose the addresses. The Supreme Court of Kansas held that **the public disclosure statute did not give the hospital discretion to refuse to provide the addresses**. The law provided that all public records were open to the public unless the agency could show that certain records were exempt from this requirement. *State Dep't of Social & Rehabilitation Services v. PERB*, 815 P.2d 66 (Kan. 1991).

III. WAGE DISCRIMINATION

The following cases consider wage discrimination in public employment. Public employers are held to the same standards as private employers with respect to rights of employees to receive equal pay for equal work. For cases that involve other types of discrimination in public employment, see Chapter One, Employment Discrimination.

♦ A Georgia Department of Public Safety employee had never been a uniformed officer and had never made a greater contribution to the state's Employees' Retirement System than employees who were not eligible for early retirement. However, he was reported to the system as eligible for early retirement and he believed he was eligible. In March 2005, the system notified the commissioner of the department about the ongoing improper designation of employees as eligible for early retirement. The employee sought to obtain early retirement benefits and was told that he was not eligible. He sued the system, and a trial court ruled in his favor. However, the Georgia Court of Appeals reversed the lower court, noting that the statute providing for early retirement limited its availability to those employees who had served in the uniform division. Moreover, **the employee was not similarly situated to other non-uniformed employees who had retired early** because they retired before the department and the system corrected the improper designation of early retirees. Thus, there was no equal protection violation. *Employees' Retirement System of Georgia v. Melton*, 669 S.E.2d 692 (Ga. Ct. App. 2008).

♦ An Alabama county sheriff qualified for the supernumerary sheriff program and became a supernumerary sheriff, in which position he received an enhanced salary. As part of that compensation, he received cost-of-living increases pursuant to state statutes. Subsequently, the Alabama Legislature amended the law to provide that "[a]ny laws to the contrary notwithstanding, no person holding supernumerary office shall be entitled to any increases in compensation or expenses as a result of the implementation of any salary adjustments provided for in this chapter." The sheriff then was denied cost-of-living adjustments. A lawsuit resulted and the Alabama Supreme Court held that the legislature could limit the compensation of a supernumerary sheriff without impairing the obligation of contract as guaranteed by the Alabama Constitution. Accordingly, **the sheriff was prohibited from receiving cost-of-living adjustments** contemporaneously with other county employees. *Cleburne County Comm'n v. Norton*, 979 So.2d 766 (Ala. 2007).

♦ A group of current and former employees of a New York county district attorney's office brought a lawsuit alleging that their equal protection rights were violated when they were denied cost of living raises and required to contribute 10% of the cost of their health insurance premiums. They were classified as managerial/confidential employees. **Union employees with identical job grades but not the same classification were not so targeted.** The plaintiffs claimed that the reason for the discrepancy was because they were not union employees. The U.S. District Court for the Western District of New York upheld the action, noting that there was a legitimate cost-saving reason for it, and that it was rationally related to a legitimate governmental purpose. Thus, it did not violate equal protection. *Flaherty v. Giambra*, 446 F.Supp.2d 153 (W.D.N.Y. 2006).

♦ A retired public employee in Alaska who moved out of state joined with a group of retired public school teachers who were planning to move out of state in bringing a class action suit against the state's public employees' retirement system and teachers' retirement system, **alleging that the residency requirement for the cost of living adjustment was unconstitutional**. The case reached the Supreme Court of Alaska, which held that the COLA's residency requirement did not violate the equal protection clause of the Alaska Constitution. The state had a legitimate purpose in compensating retirees who chose to continue living in Alaska (with its high living costs) more substantially than retirees who moved out of state, as a means of encouraging retirees to stay in Alaska. *Public Employees' Retirement System v. Gallant*, 153 P.3d 346 (Alaska 2007).

♦ Under a state law, Rhode Island provided incentive pay to corrections officers who met certain educational qualifications. To get the pay, officers had to work for the department for four years. In 1996, the state amended the law to mandate that the extra pay would be a flat sum rather than a percentage of the officers' salary. This had the effect of decreasing the pay because salaries tend to rise over time. In 2001, the officers' union filed a lawsuit to maintain the percentage formula that had been used in the past, asserting that the change violated the Contract Clauses of the state and federal constitutions. A federal court dismissed the lawsuit, and the First Circuit affirmed. Since **the statute did not create any contractual rights to have the extra pay determined in any particular way** (e.g., salary-based incentive pay), there was no violation of the Contract Clauses. *Rhode Island Brotherhood of Correctional Officers v. State of Rhode Island*, 357 F.3d 42 (1st Cir. 2004).

• A number of former and current judges in Monroe County, New York filed suit against the state, asserting that they were improperly paid $4,000 less per year than judges in neighboring counties. A trial court dismissed their lawsuit, but the appellate division reversed, finding the salary disparity unconstitutional under the Equal Protection Clause. The case reached the New York Court of Appeals, which held that there was a rational basis for the salary discrepancy because the median home values in Monroe County were at least 34% lower than home values in the neighboring counties. Further, judges in Monroe County had a lighter workload than judges in the neighboring counties. As a result, **there was sufficient statistical evidence to support the geographic pay difference**. The court reversed the lower court's decision and ruled for the state. *Barr v. Crosson*, 711 N.Y.S.2d 145 (N.Y. 2000).

• After the Louisiana Department of Wildlife and Fisheries (DWF) supplemented the pay of officers in its law enforcement division, a group of non-enforcement DWF officers sued in state court, claiming they were denied equal protection of the law. The non-enforcement officers had tangential enforcement duties: they carried a gun and had the authority to arrest anyone they saw violating the law. The trial court found that the non-enforcement officers were "similarly situated" to the enforcement officers and ordered the state to pay them supplemental wages.

The Louisiana Court of Appeal affirmed that decision. Because DWF enforcement division officers were paid the supplements to compensate them for the hazardous conditions they faced on the job, and because both the non-enforcement and enforcement officers engaged in hazardous responsibilities, **they were "similarly situated" for equal protection purposes**. There was no rational reason for treating the two groups differently, such as a problem recruiting DWF enforcement officers. *Marceaux v. State of Louisiana*, 720 So.2d 29 (La. Ct. App. 1998).

IV. UNION REPRESENTATION

Labor associations work to negotiate the terms and conditions of employment for their members. A collective bargaining agreement serves to represent the substantive and procedural rights of the employees. Labor associations must represent their members fairly in their negotiations as well as in their grievance procedures. For cases discussing disciplinary action or termination such as union representation during investigations, refer to Chapter Two, Discipline, Suspension, and Termination.

• A New Hampshire city hired police officers pursuant to individual three-year training agreements, which provided that the city would pay them during and after training as specified in the city's compensation plan. The plan included annual step increases and was identical to the pay schedule incorporated in the 1991 collective bargaining agreement. The officers became bargaining unit members after completing their one-year probationary period. In 1994, the collective bargaining agreement expired. For the next three years, until a new agreement was signed, the city did not pay step increases to any bargaining unit employees. The new agreement did not provide for retroactive adjustments or payments, and the officers sued. They asserted that their individual contracts were enforceable such that they should receive retroactive pay increases for the three years at issue. The Supreme Court of New Hampshire disagreed. Complying with the terms of the individual contracts would result in a conflict with the collective bargaining agreement. The U.S. Supreme Court has stated that **the National Labor Relations Act does not allow individual employment contracts to limit the terms of collective bargaining agreements**. The officers were not entitled to retroactive pay. *Collins v. City of Manchester*, 797 A.2d 132 (N.H. 2002).

• Two New Jersey statutes required public employers to grant paid leave to duly authorized representatives of specifically enumerated associations attending annual union conventions. When a fire department refused to provide paid leave to several firefighters attending the annual convention, their union sued. A state court ruled that the statutes were unconstitutional, and the New Jersey Superior Court, Appellate Division, affirmed. Here, the statutes improperly delegated to private organizations (unions) the power and authority to determine how many delegates a fire department must provide with paid convention leave. Also, there was no rational basis for granting paid leave to the members of certain organizations while excluding the members of other organizations. *New Jersey State Firemen's Mutual Benevolent Ass'n v. North Hudson Regional Fire & Rescue*, 775 A.2d 43 (N.J. Super. Ct. App. Div. 2001).

• A Louisiana woman worked for one union as a field representative; was represented by another union; and took a leave of absence to work for a third union under an individual contract containing the same terms as the collective bargaining agreement (CBA) that governed her employment with the first union. After the third union fired her, she sought reinstatement with the first union and tried to file a grievance with the second union. She was unsuccessful. She then sued both the first and the third unions for breach of contract, asserting that the first union should have reinstated her and that the third union had improperly fired her. She also alleged a violation of the Labor Management Reporting and Disclosure Act (LMRDA). A jury awarded her over $100,000, and the unions appealed. The court held that the Labor Management Relations Act (LMRA) preempted the employee's breach of contract claim against the first union because resolution of the claim depended on how the CBA was interpreted. However, **the LMRA did not preempt her claim against the third union because her employment contract with that union was an individual contract**. With respect to the LMRDA claim, the court remanded the case for a determination as to whether either union actually bargained with the private sector so as to bring them within the act's coverage. *Meredith v. Louisiana Federation of Teachers*, 209 F.3d 398 (5th Cir. 2000).

A. Duty of Fair Representation

Labor associations have a duty to represent their members fairly. Disgruntled employees who lose employment-related cases often add claims against their labor association for breach of this duty.

• The Defense Language Institute (DLI) is a federal agency. A course developer for the DLI was demoted to instructor when his position was abolished. Five years later, the DLI reopened and advertised the position. The former course developer did not reapply, and another instructor was awarded the job. The developer filed a grievance against the DLI, asserting that he should have been assigned the position and that there should have been no competitive application process. The developer's union accepted his claim and successfully arbitrated the matter. The developer was reassigned to the job. The previously selected instructor was demoted. The employees' union then refused to handle the instructor's grievance, claiming that it had a conflict of interest because it had previously represented the developer.

The instructor filed an unfair labor practice charge with the Federal Labor Relations Authority (FLRA) claiming that the DLI had violated the collective bargaining agreement and that the union had breached its duty of fair representation to him. The FLRA's general counsel upheld only the fair representation claim. The FLRA and union reached an agreement in which the union posted notice that it would represent all employees. The instructor contended that this settlement gave him no relief and sued the DLI and union in federal court. The court dismissed the charge against the DLI but permitted the unfair labor practice charge against the union as a private action for breach of the duty of fair representation.

The union appealed to the Ninth Circuit Court of Appeals, which reversed. The U.S. Supreme Court then ruled that although the federal Civil Service Reform Act was patterned after the National Labor Relations Act, it did not imply a private right of action. **Because Congress expressed no intention to provide a private legal remedy to enforce the duty of fair representation, the instructor had no recourse.** Since the FLRA had final authority to issue unfair labor practice complaints, the appeals court had correctly denied the instructor's private action against the union. *Karahalios v. National Federation of Federal Employees, Local 1263*, 489 U.S. 527, 109 S.Ct. 1282, 103 L.Ed.2d 539 (1989).

• A U.S. Postal Service employee was suspended without pay for fighting with a co-worker. He was a member of the American Postal Workers Union. After the employee was formally discharged, he filed a grievance with the union as provided by the collective bargaining agreement. The union chose not to take his grievance to arbitration. He then sued the union and the postal service, asserting that the postal service had violated the bargaining agreement by dismissing him without just cause, and that the union had breached its duty of fair representation. A jury found for the employee and against both defendants and apportioned the damages between the two. On appeal, the Fourth Circuit affirmed except for the award of damages against the union. The U.S. Supreme Court reversed, holding that where damage had been caused by both the employer and the union, **it was proper to apportion liability between the two** according to the damage each had caused. Here, requiring the union to pay damages would not impose on it a burden inconsistent with national policy, but rather would provide an additional incentive to unions to process members' claims where warranted. The Court thus allowed apportionment of the damages between the postal service and the union. *Bowen v. U.S. Postal Service*, 459 U.S. 212, 103 S.Ct. 588, 74 L.Ed.2d 402 (1983).

♦ The Federal Labor Relations Authority (FLRA) determined that the Federal Labor Relations Act did not require federal employers to bargain over proposals that would bind the parties to mid-term bargaining. But the FLRA reversed its position after the U.S. Court of Appeals, D.C. Circuit, held that the statute required such bargaining. The Fourth Circuit took a contrary view. It held that the act did not require mid-term bargaining, and set aside the FLRA's order to the Department of the Interior to negotiate a proposal for mid-term bargaining with a union. The Supreme Court reviewed the case and found that **the act neither absolutely prohibited, nor absolutely compelled, the parties to bargain about midterm bargaining**. It remanded the case to the FLRA for a determination as to whether the Department had to negotiate over the proposal. *NFFE, Local 1309 v. Dep't of the Interior*, 526 U.S. 86, 119 S.Ct. 1003, 143 L.Ed.2d 171 (1999).

♦ After the Utah Transit Authority added light-rail service to Salt Lake City, the local union that represented mass transit workers began representing light-rail workers as well. One of the bargaining agreement provisions it negotiated **allowed senior bus employees to transfer to light-rail jobs and displace less senior employees**. Two light-rail employees sued under the Urban Mass Transportation Act and state law, alleging that the transit authority and the union violated the law by including light-rail and bus employees in the same bargaining unit. The Tenth Circuit ruled against them, holding that even though the collective bargaining agreement allowed for the displacement of some light-rail workers by more senior bus employees, the union was not an inappropriate bargaining unit. *Burke v. Utah Transit Authority and Local 382*, 462 F.3d 1253 (10th Cir. 2006).

♦ The Nevada Supreme Court held that a union representing employees at a state university medical center **could charge nonunion employees for handling individual disciplinary grievances** even though state law made the union the exclusive representative of all employees, whether they were union members or not. The court noted that another law (explicitly authorizing nonunion members to act on their own behalf with respect to employment matters) lent support to its conclusion that the union could legitimately charge the fees. This language implied that the union could charge for such services. The union's policy did not interfere with employees' rights not to join a union. Further, even though the union provided exclusive representation to employees, nothing in the statute prevented the union from picking and choosing which representational services it would provide free of charge. *Cone v. Nevada Service Employees Union*, 998 P.2d 1178 (Nev. 2000).

• A fire inspector for the city of Anchorage resigned because of hypertension. After being denied benefits for a permanent occupational disability, he sought to return to his job. The fire chief agreed to rehire him as a Firefighter III, but not in the higher-level fire inspector position. In a letter written by the chief documenting that agreement, the union president signed his name under the notation, "CONCUR." After the fire chief refused to let the firefighter "leapfrog" other eligible employees on the fire inspector promotion list, the firefighter asked the union to file a grievance. An arbitrator refused to order a preferential promotion, and the union did not appeal that decision. The Alaska Supreme Court held that **factual issues existed as to whether the union breached its duty of fair representation**. Union affidavits did not explicitly explain why the union president originally signed the letter. Thus, the firefighter could attempt to prove that the union had acted in bad faith or in a discriminatory manner by doing so. *Wilson v. Municipality of Anchorage*, 977 P.2d 713 (Alaska 1999).

• A Kansas City, Missouri letter carrier had a number of problems with a co-worker. She threatened to bring a gun to work if the co-worker continued to make more remarks about her deceased mother. The carrier was then sent to an employee assistance program and placed on emergency leave without pay. Although two psychiatrists later determined that she was fit to return to work, the postal service decided to fire her. She promptly filed grievances regarding the suspension and termination, and an arbitrator ultimately found just cause for both actions. The letter carrier sued the postal service, alleging that it had breached its collective bargaining agreement with her union. The court ruled for the postal service, and the U.S. Court of Appeals, Eighth Circuit, affirmed. To prevail on a claim for breach of the bargaining agreement, **the letter carrier had to show that the union discriminated against her by breaching its duty of fair representation** in the way it handled her grievance. However, mere negligence, poor judgment, or ineptitude will not establish a breach of duty claim. Here, the union had treated the carrier in a fair manner and diligently pursued her complaints throughout the entire grievance procedure. *Buford v. Runyon*, 160 F.3d 1199 (8th Cir. 1998).

• A laid-off county hospital employee was denied his "bumping" rights under a collective bargaining agreement. His union helped him complete a grievance form, requested certain documents, and met with the hospital's personnel director. Shortly thereafter, the union received a letter from the employee's attorney, requesting that both he and the employee be notified of progress and be provided copies of management responses. When the hospital denied the employee's grievance, the union did not pursue it; nor did it notify the employee or his attorney of the hospital's denial or its decision to refrain from pursuing the matter further. The employee filed a prohibited practice charge with the Labor Relations Commission against his union, claiming a violation of its duty of fair representation. The Commission ruled for the union, and the employee appealed to the Appeals Court of Massachusetts.

A union has a duty to represent its members fairly in connection with issues that arise under a collective bargaining unit. Although ordinary negligence may not amount to a denial of fair representation, lack of a rational basis for a union decision and egregious unfairness, reckless omissions, or disregard for an individual employee's rights may have that effect. Here, the union's obvious failure to follow its own policies governing its processing of the employee's grievance, its failure to inform him of the status of his grievance, and its failure to respond to his attorney's requests for more information constituted grossly inattentive or grossly negligent conduct, thereby mandating a finding that **the union violated its duty of fair representation.** *Goncalves v. Labor Relations Comm'n*, 682 N.E.2d 914 (Mass. App. Ct. 1997).

♦ A Wisconsin county parks department employee failed the written jailer examination and was not hired by the county corrections department. However, another applicant was hired even though he also failed the exam. The successful applicant became a member of the union after his probationary period expired. The union filed a grievance on behalf of the unsuccessful applicant, noting that the successful applicant also had failed the test. The county and the union entered into a settlement agreement that instated the unsuccessful applicant and required the successful applicant to pass the test in order to keep his job. The union and county rejected the successful applicant's request for a grievance hearing. The Court of Appeals of Wisconsin noted that the union had properly listened to the successful applicant, discussed the merits of the grievance, and elected not to pursue it. **The fact that the union had previously represented the unsuccessful applicant did not make its conduct arbitrary, discriminatory or in bad faith.** The Wisconsin Supreme Court has held that unions have the freedom to represent one union member whose interests are opposed to another's. Because the union did not breach its duty of fair representation, the union and the county were not liable. *Gray v. Marinette County*, 546 N.W.2d 553 (Wis. Ct. App. 1996).

♦ A South Carolina postal worker witnessed a killer, who had just killed the station's owner, fleeing out of a service station. Fearing for his life, the employee resigned and planned to leave the state. The killer was captured three days later, and the employee sought to rescind the resignation. His supervisor refused because it already had been processed. The employee asked the union to file an appeal on his behalf, but the union declined because the postal service had done nothing wrong. The employee ultimately attempted suicide and was treated for alcohol addiction and posttraumatic stress disorder. A year later, the union again refused to file an appeal on his behalf, noting that the employee had failed to produce evidence that his psychological problems had precluded rational thought at the time of his resignation. The employee sued the union and the postal service under Section 1208 of the Postal Reorganization Act, alleging breach of the duty of fair representation.

The court noted that the six-month statute of limitations applicable to claims brought under the analogous Labor Management Relations Act also was applicable to Section 1208 claims. **The statute of limitations** begins to run when an aggrieved employee first obtains actual or imputed knowledge of a decision by union officials not to address the alleged cause of action. Because over a year had passed since this time, the statute of limitations barred the employee's claim. Nor did his alleged mental incompetence justify equitable tolling. Even if the claim had been timely filed, the court held that the union had no duty to file a meritless grievance on the employee's behalf. The court dismissed the suit. *Mincey v. U.S. Postal Service*, 879 F.Supp. 567 (D.S.C. 1995).

B. Collective Bargaining Fees

Employees who choose not to join collective bargaining associations where the workplace is subject to a collective bargaining agreement must pay a service fee, also known as an agency fee or "fair share" fee, to the association. Courts uphold these fees, but have stated that it is impermissible for the labor association to use the fees for political purposes.

Recent cases have challenged the way in which non-union members are allowed to opt out of having their fees used for political purposes.

• A local union representing employees of Maine's state agencies charged nonmembers a fee for "national litigation" over non-political collective bargaining issues that didn't directly affect the local union. Nonunion members of the Maine State Employees Association (MSEA) claimed the $1.34 per month fee, which the MSEA paid to its national affiliate, the Service Employees International Union, violated their First Amendment rights because the fees did not directly benefit the local union. The case reached the U.S. Supreme Court, which said that **the local could charge the fee if the services ultimately benefited local union members** by virtue of their membership in the national union. Here, the subject matter of the national litigation was of a kind that would be chargeable if the litigation were local, and the local reasonably expected other local unions to contribute similarly to the national union's resources, making the charge reciprocal in nature. *Locke v. Karass*, 129 S.Ct. 798 (U.S. 2009).

• The faculty at a Michigan state college elected the Michigan Education Association as its exclusive bargaining representative. A group of nonunion employees sued, challenging the requirement that they pay a service or "fair share" fee to the union for representing them in collective bargaining. A federal court found that certain activities objected to by the nonmembers could be charged to them. Those activities included lobbying and electoral politics, bargaining and litigation on behalf of members of other bargaining units, public relations, union meetings and conventions, and strike preparations. The nonunion employees appealed to the Sixth Circuit Court of Appeals, which concluded that the activities sufficiently related to the union's collective bargaining activities to warrant requiring nonmembers to subsidize them. The U.S. Supreme Court agreed to review the case.

It noted that requiring private sector employees to subsidize lobbying would not be permissible. However, public employee unions often must lobby in order to obtain benefits or have contracts ratified. Because such lobbying is not for ideological purposes, nonmembers could be required to fund such activities. The Court next held that **it was permissible to require nonmembers to contribute to the parent organization**, provided that the funds would be used in a manner that would be of potential benefit to the nonmembers. Public relations expenditures could not be charged to nonmembers, but the Court held that they could be required to subsidize the costs incurred by delegates from their bargaining unit in attending national conventions. Despite the fact that Michigan teachers were barred by state law from striking, the Court concluded that the costs of preparing for an illegal strike could be assessed against the dissenting nonmembers. The Court affirmed part of the appeals court decision and remanded the case for further consideration. *Lehnert v. Ferris Faculty Ass'n*, 500 U.S. 507, 111 S.Ct. 1950, 114 L.Ed.2d 572 (1991).

♦ The state of Washington and a class of nonunion public school employees sued the Washington Education Association, claiming that the union had used nonmember agency shop fees to make political expenditures without their affirmative authorization, as required by state law. Instead, the union had sent out *Hudson* notices, notifying nonmembers that they could "opt out" of paying fees for certain politically related expenses. The state supreme court held that the law requiring affirmative authorization (an "opt in" requirement) to make political expenditures violated the First Amendment. The U.S. Supreme Court reversed. It held that **a state could require its public-sector unions to receive affirmative authorization from a nonmember before spending that nonmember's agency fees for election-related purposes**. The unions had no constitutional entitlement to the fees of nonmember employees and therefore no right to force nonmembers to opt out of political spending. *Davenport v. Washington Educ. Ass'n*, 551 U.S. 177, 127 S.Ct. 2372, 168 L.Ed.2d 71 (U.S. 2007).

♦ The California State Employees Association sent "fair share" notices to nonunion members, setting the fair share fee at 95% of union dues and giving nonunion employees an opportunity to object to paying for activities not germane to collective bargaining. The notice included a report on the association's previous year's expenditures, dividing them into those that were chargeable, those that were not, and those that were partially chargeable to nonunion members. It also informed the recipients that the numbers were taken from an independent audit, but did not contain a copy of the complete auditor's report. A lawsuit resulted when a number of nonunion members alleged that the notice should have included an "allocation audit" – verification by the auditors not only that the money was spent the way the union said it was spent, but that the union properly allocated costs between those that were chargeable and those that were not. The Ninth Circuit joined the Second, Fourth, Sixth and Seventh Circuits in holding that an allocation audit was not required. However, **the "fair share" notice did have to include independent verification** from the auditor that the breakdown accurately reflected the auditor's report. *Cummings v. Connell*, 316 F.3d 886 (9th Cir. 2003).

♦ Eleven education professionals in a Pennsylvania school district chose not to be union members and instead paid fair share fees to the local union, the state union and the National Education Association. All three unions provided collective bargaining services, and the 11 nonmembers had to pay for their share of such costs. Six of the nonmembers filed a lawsuit under the First Amendment and 42 U.S.C. § 1983, alleging that the local union improperly assessed them for litigation costs associated with the other two unions and with health care workers represented by the state union. A federal court ruled in their favor, holding that they could not be charged for litigation expenses not related to the local union. The Third Circuit reversed in part, finding that **a local union can charge nonmembers for collective-bargaining-related litigation expenses incurred on behalf of another bargaining unit** pursuant to an expense-pooling arrangement. It also held that a union can charge nonmembers for pooled resources available to all local affiliates even though some of the affiliates represent employees in different positions. *Otto v. Pennsylvania State Education Ass'n*, 330 F.3d 125 (3d Cir. 2003).

♦ A group of California teachers, who were not members of their local unions but were required to pay agency or "fair share" fees to the unions under collective bargaining agreements, claimed that the **unions failed to provide them with adequate notice** of agency fee deductions. They sued the unions and a number of school superintendents in federal court for violating the financial disclosure requirements set forth by the Supreme Court in *Chicago Teachers Union v. Hudson*, 475 U.S. 292 (1986). There, the Supreme Court held that agency fee payers are entitled to an adequate explanation of the basis for the fee and a reasonably prompt opportunity to challenge the amount of the fee. Here, the court held that the unions and the superintendents violated the *Hudson* requirements. The Ninth Circuit Court of Appeals reversed, noting that while employers owe nonunion member employees the general duty set forth in *Hudson*, employers do not owe employees a specific duty to ensure that proper *Hudson* notice is received by each employee before agency fees are deducted. *Foster v. Mahdesian*, 268 F.3d 689 (9th Cir. 2001).

♦ A number of public school teachers and state university instructors sued the Massachusetts Teachers Association for charging them agency fees for activities that were not part of doing business as a collective bargaining representative. The state Labor Relations Commission examined the union's expenditures to determine which were chargeable to nonunion members and which were not. It concluded that each of the nonunion members had been charged excess service fees of $26.77. The Supreme Judicial Court of Massachusetts largely upheld the commission's ruling, noting that **only those expenses germane to the union's duties as a collective bargaining representative may be charged to**

nonunion members as agency fees. Political speech and public relations activities are not chargeable, whereas union officials' salaries are. Further, expenses related to the withholding of services by faculty members at a state university were not chargeable even though the action was taken to protest the lack of funding of their bargaining agreements. The withholding of services amounted to an illegal strike. *Belhumeur v. Labor Relations Comm'n*, 735 N.E.2d 860 (Mass. 2000).

♦ The Oregon Public Employees Union (OPEU) was authorized under state law to collect "fair share" costs from nonunion members for collective bargaining done on their behalf. These payments could not be used to fund political candidates or otherwise espouse political views. The OPEU sent a notice to all nonunion members regarding the amount of their fair share payments due. After paying the fees, the nonunion members alleged that the OPEU fair share collection procedures did not comply with First Amendment safeguards. The Employment Relations Board agreed and ordered the OPEU to refund the amount already paid. The court of appeals affirmed. The Oregon Supreme Court then noted that **the OPEU's procedural violation itself did not result in any financial harm to the nonunion members**. However, the OPEU was required to refund that which was taken unconstitutionally regardless of financial harm. Also, the board had the authority to order restitution as a remedy for an unfair labor practice. The U.S. Supreme Court had interpreted the National Labor Relations Act (NLRA) to give the board this authority. Since the state law was modeled after the NLRA, the court determined that the board should be given similar remedies. Thus, the OPEU was required to return the fair share payments, and the court of appeals' decision was affirmed. *Elvin v. Oregon Public Employees Union,* 832 P.2d 36 (Or. 1992).

V. UNFAIR LABOR PRACTICES

Public employment is highly regulated by state legislation. Generally, public employers have a duty to bargain with employee representatives in good faith. However, they need not bargain over matters of inherent management policy. Failure to bargain over terms that affect employment or conditions of employment can result in the filing of unfair labor practice charges. For cases discussing the privatization of public employment positions, refer to Chapter Eight, Employment Practices.

A. Right to Organize

♦ The District of Columbia police department has a reserve corps of unpaid volunteers who assist police officers in their law enforcement duties. In 1996, the chief issued an order to bring the reserve corps in line with regulations interpreting the district's volunteer services act. Among the order's provisions: **volunteers were not eligible for benefits like insurance or retirement, nor did they have the right to organize for collective bargaining purposes**; finally, the order stated that volunteers did not have the right to due process before being discharged. Two reserve corps members sued to prevent the order from taking effect. They asserted that the collective bargaining provision kept them from exercising their First Amendment rights, and that they had a due process right to keep their positions until they received notice and a hearing. The U.S. Court of Appeals, D.C. Circuit, disagreed with them. The officers were not deprived of the chance to talk about their working conditions. The chief simply did not have to discuss their views with them. Also, there was no statute or ordinance that granted the reserve officers a property right to continue in their positions. *Griffith v. Lanier*, 521 F.3d 398 (D.C. Cir. 2008).

♦ In 1978, the Florida Supreme Court ruled that deputy sheriffs were not public employees entitled to collective bargaining rights because they served as managerial-level employees who could take charge in the sheriff's absence. However, the issue arose again and the court held this time that **sheriff's deputies are public employees. As such, they have the right to bargain collectively.** Noting that deputies work for their sheriffs in much the same way that police officers work for their chiefs, the court stated that "a clerk of court today might employ a score or more of skilled workers as bookkeepers, archivists, filing clerks, typists and receptionists ... such employees are often still called deputies, but ... [they] look surprisingly like other public employees." Since the state constitution guarantees the right of collective bargaining to all employees, public and private, and since the state failed to show it had a compelling interest in keeping sheriffs' deputies from collectively bargaining, the deputies were entitled to bargain as public employees. *Coastal Florida Police Benevolent Ass'n v. Williams*, 838 So.2d 543 (Fla. 2003).

♦ The governor of Maryland issued an executive order that **granted to employees of the executive branch the right to unionize and bargain collectively**, but also provided that any agreement reached that required legislative approval or the appropriation of funds would result in a recommendation to the legislature for approval or appropriation as necessary. Also, any agreement had to be consistent with applicable law, and the order could be revoked or amended by the governor at any time. A group of taxpayers sued the governor to prevent implementation of the order. They alleged that it was invalid and unconstitutional because it violated the separation of powers doctrine, exceeded the statutory powers of the governor, and conflicted with the legislature's repeated rejection of similar collective bargaining bills. The trial court upheld the order.

The Court of Appeals of Maryland affirmed, determining that **the order did not violate the separation of powers doctrine** because the governor had significant discretionary powers to set policies and supervise state employees. Further, the order did not purport to make any agreement legally binding or to divest the governor of discretion given him by law. It merely envisioned a process in which employment-related disputes could be resolved through open, candid and good-faith discussion. If the state failed to negotiate in good faith, the employee unions would have no identifiable remedy. This did not exceed the statutory powers of the governor. Finally, although the legislature had created employee/management teams for the resolution of workplace conditions, this did not mean that the legislature intended them to be the exclusive means of addressing employee/management relations. *McCulloch v. Glendening*, 701 A.2d 99 (Md. 1997).

• An administrative employees association petitioned the Michigan Employment Relations Commission (MERC) to represent five supervisory city employees – clerk, treasurer, assessor, police chief and fire chief. MERC found that public policy prevented allowing the proposed bargaining unit. The court of appeals reversed. The Supreme Court of Michigan found that the court of appeals failed to give the necessary deference to MERC's expertise and long-standing practice. Prior MERC decisions indicated that **public supervisory employees who formulate, determine and effectuate management policies fall in the category of "executive."** Accordingly, though they were not barred from belonging to a collective bargaining unit, MERC had the authority to determine their appropriate bargaining unit. The court vacated and remanded the case to MERC. *Grandville Municipal Executive Ass'n v. City of Grandville*, 553 N.W.2d 917 (Mich. 1996).

• A union member employed by a New Hampshire fire department provided to the press an alcoholic rehabilitation agreement between the department and another union member. The union's executive board authorized the release of the agreement to the press in retaliation for the member's criticism of the union for failing to help him after he was suspended for losing his driver's license. One of the fire commissioners later told a reporter that what the union had done was "reprehensible." She also made negative comments about the union and its leadership and stated that she believed that the leadership had hurt members during recent contract negotiations. The union filed an unfair labor practice charge against the city and the Board of Fire Commissioners with the Public Employee Labor Relations Board. The case reached the Supreme Court of New Hampshire, which noted that the commissioner's comments properly addressed the competence and honesty of elected union representatives. Because **the commissioners' statements constituted fair comment on the question of union representation** and did not contain elements of intimidation, coercion, or misrepresentation, they did not violate the Unfair Labor Practices Statute. *Appeal of City of Portsmouth, Board of Fire Commissioners*, 667 A.2d 345 (N.H. 1995).

• New Jersey state investigators fall under a state statutory classification of "confidential" employees. The classification removes them from the statutorily created right to collectively bargain in the public sector. The New Jersey Division of Criminal Justice State Investigators petitioned for representation, which was dismissed by the Public Employment Relations Commission (PERC). The PERC found no obligation to collectively bargain, and the investigators appealed the PERC order. The investigators alleged constitutional violations including the right to organize under the New Jersey Constitution, the right of association and assembly under the U.S. Constitution, and equal protection. The court of appeals found that **the New Jersey Constitution does not grant a constitutional right to bargain collectively to public employees.**

Any rights to bargain collectively have been statutorily created. The statutes creating and limiting those rights do not prevent the organization, association or assembly of employees but rather limit the employer's duty to collectively bargain. The court also found no equal protection violations because the statute's classification served a legitimate government interest of protecting the Attorney General's ability to perform its duty in the state's criminal justice system. *Matter of Division of Criminal Justice State Investigators*, 674 A.2d 199 (N.J. Super. Ct. App. Div. 1996).

♦ A union filed a petition for a representation election with the State Employment Relations Board. The petition named an Ohio County Department of Human Services Children's Division (which included nine social workers, five child care workers, two aides, one screener, two investigators and one part-time social worker) as the affected public employer. The department did not propose an alternative bargaining unit but stated only that the 20-employee unit was not proper. A hearing officer found for the union but the board dismissed the union's petition for a representation election, stating that the proposed bargaining unit was not appropriate. The Supreme Court of Ohio ordered the board to conduct a representation election. An employer that fails to include an alternative bargaining unit proposal must establish by substantial evidence that the proposed unit is not appropriate. Here, the employees in the division shared sufficient collective bargaining objectives to justify the creation of the smaller bargaining unit. Specifically, the division was functionally distinct and **the proposed bargaining unit would not compromise the division's efficiency**. *State ex rel. Glass Workers v. SERB*, 638 N.E.2d 556 (Ohio 1994).

B. Terms and Conditions

1. Wages and Hours

♦ The Hawaii Legislature passed a law allowing the governor to convert the predicted payroll system to an after-the-fact payroll system so that public employees, instead of being paid on the fifteenth and last day of every month, would be paid on the fifth and twentieth days. When the governor tried to implement the new payroll system for faculty members at the University of Hawaii, several faculty members and the union sued to prevent it, asserting that implementing the lag violated the Contract Clause and that the state had to bargain over the change. The case reached the Supreme Court of Hawaii, which held that although the lag did not violate the faculty members' right to bargain collectively, **the governor could not implement the new payroll system for the faculty members** because the purpose of the lag was to save $6.2 million from the university's budget, which had already been accomplished, and because the specific time mandated for implementing the lag had passed. *Malahoff v. Saito*, 140 P.3d 401 (Haw. 2006).

♦ Over a four-year period, the city of Buffalo eliminated 800 teaching jobs and 250 teaching assistant positions. The city also approved tax increases amounting to $6.3 million. However, it still faced a predicted budget gap in excess of $250 million over the next four years. As a result, the Buffalo Fiscal Responsibility Authority froze the wages of all city employees to preserve essential services while keeping taxes affordable. The teachers union sued, claiming that the freeze violated the Constitution's Contract Clause because the union contract with the city called for a 2% wage increase. The Second Circuit found the wage freeze legal. **In the midst of a financial crisis, the city could temporarily freeze wages as a last resort.** It was the least drastic measure, taken to avoid eliminating more jobs and closing more schools. *Buffalo Teachers Federation v. Tobe*, 464 F.3d 362 (2d Cir. 2006).

♦ Billings, Montana, negotiated a post-1995 collective bargaining agreement (CBA) with its firefighters' union. The city intended to compensate firefighters the same way it had in the past, but the old CBA identified the annual rate of pay and provided that the hourly rate was to be determined from that annual rate. The new CBA listed the hourly rates on an attached schedule and provided that the annual base salary could be reached by multiplying the hourly base by a set of annual numbers. The problem resulted from the fact that firefighters were paid for 2,080 hours each year, while actually working 2,272 hours based on their 27-day cycle. Seventeen firefighters sued the city for breaching the new CBA. The Montana Supreme Court upheld the lower court's decision in favor of the firefighters, awarding them more than $3 million in damages. The old CBA provided exact annual wages regardless of the number of hours actually worked, while **the new CBA required firefighters to be paid for each hour worked**. *Kuhr v. City of Billings*, 168 P.3d 615 (Mont. 2007).

♦ Under a collective bargaining agreement, the Nashua, New Hampshire police department had to provide employees with 24 hours' advance notice of the need to appear in court, or of a canceled court appearance. If the department failed to provide the required notice, the employee would be entitled to one hour of overtime. While the agreement was in effect, the department unilaterally changed the notification procedure by posting notices near the employees' entrance and making employees responsible for checking on the status of the cases themselves. After a grievance was denied, the police officers' union filed an unfair labor practice charge with the New Hampshire Public Employee Labor Relations Board. The board ruled that **the new notification procedure violated the bargaining agreement** as well as the city's obligation to bargain over wages and hours. The New Hampshire Supreme Court upheld the board's ruling. Since notifying employees promptly of court appearances and cancellations directly affects their terms and conditions of employment, the city had a duty to bargain before changing its notification policy. *Appeal of Nashua Police Comm'n*, 827 A.2d 1013 (N.H. 2003).

♦ A 1979 collective bargaining agreement (CBA) between the city of Boston and the police officers' union contained a compensation provision stating that captains serving day shifts as district commanders would receive an additional $27 pay differential. Another "Stability of Agreement" provision stated that no agreement, understanding or variation of the terms of the CBA would be binding unless made and executed in writing. Five captains in the Boston Police

Department served as commanders of special units. The city paid the differential to the five captains from 1980 until the summer of 1993, when it discovered that it had made an error by issuing the payment. After the city stopped the payment, the union challenged the action before the Massachusetts Labor Relations Commission, which found that the city had committed an unfair labor practice and ordered the city to bargain in good faith with the union over the issue. The state court of appeals affirmed. It disagreed with the city that the compensation provision contained clear language limiting the payment of a differential to day district commanders. Rather, the provision was simply an affirmative statement that the day commanders were to receive a differential. The provision was silent on the issue of differentials for the special unit captains. Even though the differential payments were not included in the CBA, **they were a past practice that did not conflict with the CBA and thus could not be unilaterally stopped.** *City of Boston v. Labor Relations Comm'n*, 718 N.E.2d 875 (Mass. App. Ct. 1999).

• A Florida city entered into several collective bargaining agreements with the local firefighters' union. Each bargaining agreement provided for individual performance increases on each respective employee's merit date. In 1991, the bargaining agreement expired before a new agreement had been reached. The city ceased paying individual performance increases during this time (the status quo period). The union filed an unfair labor practice charge against the city with the Public Employees Relations Commission. The commission held for the union, and the city appealed, contending that the union waived its right to individual performance increases during the status quo period. The court of appeals disagreed, ruling that **employers are prohibited from unilaterally altering wages** (including individual performance increases) while negotiations for a new collective bargaining agreement are pending. Only if the bargaining agreement contained language that unambiguously allowed the city to unilaterally change terms and conditions of employment would the employees have waived their right to maintain the status quo. Here, the mere reference in the bargaining agreement to the effective years of the contract did not limit the payment of increases, where these increases had endured for a significant time. The union was entitled to attorney fees because the city should have known its actions violated established law. Since there was no waiver, exigent circumstances or a contrary legislative resolution, the city violated the CBA by unilaterally altering individual performance increases. *City of Delray Beach v. Professional Firefighters*, 636 So.2d 157 (Fla. Dist. Ct. App. 1994).

2. Employer Policies

• **The U.S. Supreme Court upheld the constitutionality of an Ohio law placing the teaching workload of state university faculty outside the purview of collective bargaining.** In 1993, the Ohio legislature passed a law to ensure that teaching standards remained consistent among state universities. The law directed each state university to develop workload standards that took precedence "over any conflicting provisions of any collective bargaining agreement." In 1994, Central State University adopted its policy and notified the faculty's union (AAUP) that the policy would not be subject to bargaining. The AAUP sued to stop the policy from being enforced, arguing that the law violated the Equal Protection Clauses of the Ohio and the U.S. Constitutions by creating a class of public employees not entitled to bargain over their workload. Finding no evidence linking "collective bargaining with the decline in teaching over the last decade," the Ohio Supreme Court concluded that there was no rational basis for singling out faculty members and that the law violated both constitutions. The U.S. Supreme Court, reviewing the federal issue, reversed. It said the Ohio court misconstrued the rational basis test. Even though it had not been shown that past collective bargaining had led to the decline in classroom time for faculty, that did not detract from the rationality of the legislative decision. *Central State Univ. v. American Ass'n of Univ. Professors, CSU Chapter*, 526 U.S. 124, 119 S.Ct. 1162, 143 L.Ed.2d 227 (1999).

♦ A Pennsylvania city passed an ordinance that banned smoking and the use of tobacco products on city-owned property. The ordinance applied to employees and citizens alike. When the union challenged the ban, a hearing officer and the labor relations board held that the city had committed an unfair labor practice. The Pennsylvania Commonwealth Court reversed, noting that the ban was a management concern that was not subject to collective bargaining. **Smoking at work was not a term or condition of employment because the ban applied to both employees and citizens,** and because the city had the power to regulate the health and welfare of its citizens while they were on public property. *Borough of Ellwood City v. Pennsylvania Labor Relations Board*, 941 A.2d 728 (Pa. Commw. Ct. 2008).

♦ After September 11, 2001, the Washington Metropolitan Area Transit Authority notified the union representing its employees that it was going to close the 30-year-old cafeteria at its downtown D.C. headquarters. When the union objected, the authority asserted its management rights with respect to the decision, but offered to discuss how the closure would affect employees. The union demanded arbitration. An arbitrator ruled for the union and a Virginia federal court upheld that decision. The Fourth Circuit affirmed, noting that **the closing of the cafeteria was not a "management" decision that could be made without bargaining** because the authority was not in the business of selling food to its employees. Thus, the decision to run or close the cafeteria was not at the core of managerial control of the authority. The authority had to arbitrate or bargain over the decision to close the cafeteria. *Washington Metropolitan Area Transit Authority v. Local 2, Office Professional Employees Int'l Union*, 465 F.3d 151 (4th Cir. 2006).

♦ The old collective bargaining agreement between a Michigan city and its public safety officers' (PSOs') union specified minimum staffing and layoff provisions. During negotiations for a new bargaining agreement, the city indicated it would not negotiate minimum staffing or layoff provisions because they were not mandatory subjects of bargaining. The union sought to retain the provisions and, after an impasse, filed for compulsory arbitration. The city filed an unfair labor practice charge. An administrative law judge and the state employment relations commission found that the provisions were not inextricably tied to the PSOs' safety. The Michigan Court of Appeals agreed. **The union failed to show that minimum staffing levels or layoff provisions would have a significant impact on its members' safety.** Thus, they were not a mandatory subject of bargaining. *Oak Park Public Safety Officers Ass'n v. City of Oak Park*, 277 Mich.App. 317, 745 N.W.2d 527 (Mich. Ct. App. 2007).

♦ An Oklahoma city required 36 police officer applicants to sign individual fitness contracts as a condition of employment in 1994. However, it did not try to enforce the contracts until 1999, long after the applicants had become full-time police officers covered by the collective bargaining agreement. The Oklahoma Court of Appeals held that the fitness contracts were subsidiary to the bargaining agreement, which did not condition employment on successful completion of a physical exam or set forth particular fitness requirements. As a result, **the city's desire to enforce the fitness contracts was a mandatory bargaining subject** over the terms and conditions of employment. The city could not enforce the fitness contracts. *City of Midwest City, Oklahoma v. Public Employees Relations Board*, 69 P.3d 1218 (Okla. Ct. App. 2003).

♦ A union representing certain employees of the Department of Veterans Affairs proposed that a union representative be allowed to observe performance-based interviews conducted to fill vacancies for bargaining unit positions. Performance-based interviews ask applicants how they would deal with situations commonly arising on the job, then compare the answers to the expectations for how the job should be performed. The Federal Labor Relations Authority determined that the proposal dealt with management's right to "make selections for appointments" and was therefore not a subject over which the union could bargain. The U.S. Court of Appeals, D.C. Circuit, agreed. **The unwanted presence of a union rep would infringe upon management's authority to fill positions**, and was not a negotiable bargaining subject. *American Federation of Government Employees, National Veterans Affairs Council 53 v. FLRA*, 352 F.3d 433 (D.C. Cir. 2003).

♦ A Pennsylvania corrections officer was notified that an investigation was going to be conducted into whether he violated a code of ethics when he reported being injured on the job. A union representative attended the fact-finding meeting and also met with the officer prior to the meeting. However, the questioner refused to let the officer take a break to confer with the union rep before answering a question. The union filed an unfair labor practices charge against the state, and the case reached the Commonwealth Court of Pennsylvania. The court ruled that where there are reasonable grounds for doing so, **the state cannot refuse to allow an employee to consult with a union representative during an investigatory meeting**. Doing so constitutes an unfair labor practice under state law (which mirrors the National Labor Relations Act). Here, the state Labor Relations Board properly held that the state violated the officer's rights by refusing to allow the officer to confer with the union rep during the investigatory meeting. *Comwlth. of Pennsylvania v. PLRB*, 826 A.2d 932 (Pa. Commw. Ct. 2003).

♦ A New Hampshire school district had a three-year collective bargaining agreement (CBA) with its custodians and maintenance workers. Following projections that the district could save $91,000 a year if the custodial and maintenance work was subcontracted out, **the district terminated all 11 bargaining unit members**. It then subcontracted the work to independent contractors, who, at the district's urging, hired three of the 11 bargaining unit members. The union filed an unfair labor practice complaint with the state Public Employee Labor Relations Board. The board ruled in the union's favor, and the case reached the New Hampshire Supreme Court. The district argued that the CBA's management rights clause gave it the authority to: 1) lay off employees for any reason, including budgetary or quality concerns; 2) modify its organizational structure by providing services through independent contractors; and 3) reduce the number of employees by laying off all employees in a bargaining unit. The court disagreed. First, the district's action did not result in a true layoff or reorganization. Second, the CBA did not specifically give the district the right to subcontract work during the term of the contract (something the district could have bargained for had it wanted to). The district's action was an **unfair labor practice**. *Appeal of Hillsboro-Deering School Dist.*, 737 A.2d 1098 (N.H. 1999).

♦ An expiring collective bargaining agreement (CBA) between an Ohio county sheriff and the union provided that detectives in the criminal investigations division (CID) would not normally be scheduled for holidays but could schedule themselves to work to get overtime. During negotiations for a new CBA, the sheriff's office proposed to replace the Columbus Day holiday with the day after Thanksgiving. The union then proposed that both days be holidays. About three weeks later, the CID patrol commander issued a directive, stating that the detectives would not be allowed to schedule work on any holiday listed in the CBA. The State Employment Relations Board (SERB) found that an unfair practice had been committed. The Ohio Court of Appeals upheld that ruling. During negotiations, the chief CID detective, who reported directly to the patrol commander, told a detective that union objections could hurt union employees in the long run. In addition, the patrol commander made a rare appearance at a morning briefing session, stating that it was the fault of the union negotiator if the detectives lost their holiday pay structure. Based on these statements and the timing of the directive, it was reasonable for SERB to conclude that **the directive was issued to interfere with, restrain, or coerce the union in the exercise of its bargaining rights**. *Hamilton County Sheriff v. State Employment Relations Board*, 731 N.E.2d 1196 (Ohio Ct. App. 1999).

♦ The University of Alaska's Board of Regents adopted a policy barring smoking in all university facilities open to the public, and in motor vehicles. An employee censured for smoking in a vehicle circulated a petition, signed by 30 union members, asking the union to negotiate the non-smoking policy. The union presented the proposal to the university, which refused to bargain, asserting that the policy was a permissive subject for which it had no obligation to bargain. The parties reached a collective bargaining agreement that was ratified by the union members. The agreement contained no express reference to the **non-smoking policy**. The agreement contained a reservation of rights clause stating that bargaining unit members agreed to follow all university policies not specified in the agreement and reserving the right to change university policies. The union filed an unfair labor practice complaint against the university, asserting that the non-smoking policy was a mandatory subject of bargaining. The case reached the Supreme Court of Alaska, which observed that because the collective bargaining agreement contained no specific reference to the non-smoking policy, **the union had contractually waived its right to bargain on that issue by agreeing to the contract.** *Univ. of Alaska v. Univ. of Alaska Classified Employees Ass'n*, 952 P.2d 1182 (Alaska 1998).

♦ Two nurses employed at a county jail's health facility returned from extended leaves and were required to provide a urine specimen for purposes of drug testing. Neither nurse had any history of drug abuse or disciplinary problems associated with substance abuse. Although policies for probable cause and reasonable suspicion testing existed, the policy requiring drug testing of employees returning to work after leaves of more than 30 days was never written down and no notification of its implementation was provided to any labor organizations. A nurses association filed an unfair labor practice charge against the county. The case reached the Appellate Court of Illinois, which found that an unfair labor practice had occurred. **Drug testing in employment has been recognized as a condition of employment** by the National Labor Relations Board, which has found that unilateral implementation by an employer of drug testing certain employees constitutes an unfair labor practice. Here, the drug testing at issue should have been subject to mandatory bargaining. The city failed to establish any link between the 30-day leave test and jail security needs. *County of Cook v. Licensed Practical Nurses Ass'n of Illinois*, 671 N.E.2d 787 (Ill. App. Ct. 1996).

♦ A New Mexico fire chief issued a memorandum forbidding union organizational activities in any city fire department facility. The firefighters' union complained that the chief's directive constituted a practice prohibited by the Public Employee Bargaining Act (PEBA) and a similar city ordinance. However, the ordinance also stated that an employee, labor organization or its representative could not solicit membership for an employee or labor organization during the employee's duty hours. The city contended that the entire 24-hour shift constituted "duty hours" for a firefighter and therefore union solicitation was banned from fire stations at all times. The local board ruled in favor of the union. The Court of Appeals of New Mexico affirmed, holding that the chief's non-solicitation rule constituted a prohibited employer practice. **A no-solicitation rule that encompassed rest breaks, lunch time, and residential hours was presumptively contrary to the PEBA.** *Las Cruces Professional Fire Fighters v. City of Las Cruces*, 938 P.2d 1384 (N.M. Ct. App. 1997).

♦ The New Jersey governor initiated a plan to save $6.7 million by eliminating numerous state employees' 40-hour-a-week positions and moving them into 35-hour-a-week positions instead. The employees would not lose benefits or seniority rights, and would receive a higher hourly rate of pay for the hours actually worked. However, the increase would not offset the loss caused by the reduced number of hours. The employees' union demanded that the state negotiate this issue. The state refused, and the union filed an unfair practice charge with the Public Employment Relations Commission. The commission ruled that the governor's comprehensive scheme preempted negotiations. The union appealed to the New Jersey Superior Court, Appellate Division, which held that **the governor's statutorily created comprehensive demotional layoff scheme did not require negotiation with respect to layoffs and demotions.** The state had properly considered the public's interests over those of the employees. *State of New Jersey v. Communications Workers of America, AFL-CIO,* 667 A.2d 1070 (N.J. Super. Ct. App. Div. 1995).

3. Procedural Issues

• In 2006, in the midst of collective bargaining efforts, several unions representing Sacramento County workers threatened a strike. The county asked a trial court to prevent 200 employees who were essential to providing critical health and public safety services from joining the strike. The court granted a temporary restraining order to keep the unions from encouraging the critical employees to participate in the strike. However, the California Court of Appeal reversed. It ruled that the county had to exhaust its administrative remedies with the public employment relations board before seeking an injunction in court. *County of Sacramento v. AFSCME Local 146,* 80 Cal.Rptr.3d 911 (Cal. Ct. App. 2008).

• A Massachusetts police officer was notified that his sergeant wanted to interview him as part of an internal investigation into allegations that the officer had made disparaging remarks to other supervisory personnel. The officer contacted his union representative, who was busy during the scheduled interview time and asked a union attorney to take his place. The sergeant did not allow the union attorney to be present at the interview, and the officer and union filed an unfair labor practice charge. The state labor relations committee upheld the charge, as did the Massachusetts Court of Appeals. **The union attorney had to be allowed to represent the officer** because the attorney's role was not only to protect the officer's rights, but also to safeguard the interests of the union and its other members. The union attorney, acting as a *Weingarten* representative, could make certain the employer did not initiate or continue unjust punishments. *Town of Hudson v. Labor Relations Comm'n,* 870 N.E.2d 618 (Mass. App. Ct. 2007).

• After the New York City Transit Authority received a complaint that a worker had used a racial slur, it asked the worker to prepare a written statement in response. He met with a union official and submitted a statement, but the transit authority believed the union official had prepared the statement rather than the worker. It required him to prepare another statement in the superintendent's office without assistance from the union official. The union filed improper labor practice charges with the Public Employment Relations Board, which ruled in its favor. The transit authority sued. The Supreme Court,

Appellate Division, upheld the ruling for the union. It compared New York's law to the *Weingarten* rule set forth by the U.S. Supreme Court, explaining that public employees have the right to have a union representative present at an investigative interview if the interview might result in discipline. However, the Court of Appeals of New York reversed, noting that **New York public employees do not have the same protections enjoyed by private sector employees during interviews and discussions with their employers.** *New York City Transit Authority v. New York State PERB*, 8 N.Y.3d 226 (N.Y. 2007).

• The union representing Department of Labor and Training employees in Rhode Island included in its collective bargaining agreement the terms of a "parity letter," which said that when another union negotiated a wage or benefit increase, its rights to the same terms were triggered. After the state entered into a bargaining agreement with another union, a third union claimed that its parity letter was triggered. The state disagreed, and the matter went to arbitration. The arbitrator awarded the third union an increase in wages. Based on that ruling, the labor employees union then submitted its own grievance seeking a wage increase. An arbitrator ruled in its favor, but the Supreme Court of Rhode Island disagreed that the parity letter applied. Here, **the increase to the third union did not result from "negotiations" but from an arbitrator's ruling.** *State v. Rhode Island Employment Security Alliance, Local 401, SEIU*, 840 A.2d 1093 (R.I. 2003).

• The Milwaukee County Board of Supervisors passed an ordinance that required certain contractors doing business with the county to negotiate "labor peace agreements" with unions attempting to organize their work places. A business association brought a lawsuit challenging the ordinance, asserting that it was preempted by the National Labor Relations Act and that it violated the First Amendment. A Wisconsin federal court granted pretrial judgment to the county, holding that the case was not ripe for review because the ordinance had not yet been enforced. However, the Seventh Circuit reversed. The action was not premature because the county already had refused to enter into contracts with association members who expressed their objections to the ordinance. Also, the county had delayed payment on several preexisting contracts where contractors refused to sign a new contract containing the requirements of the ordinance. Moreover, just by being in effect, **the ordinance altered the balance of bargaining power between unions and association members**, strengthening the position of the former and weakening the position of the latter. The case required a trial. *Metropolitan Milwaukee Ass'n of Commerce v. Milwaukee County*, 325 F.3d 879 (7th Cir. 2003).

• During the course of contract negotiations with the union representing Massachusetts' Finance Department employees, someone with the governor's office sent the employees a survey to determine their views on and usage of sick leave. After the negotiations ended, the state announced changes in the procedures by which finance department employees would report and verify sick leave. The union objected and the changes were not made. The union then charged the state with violating Massachusetts labor statutes, and the state supreme court found the survey unlawful. **The state had a duty to refrain from circumventing the union** by dealing directly with bargaining unit employees as to mandatory subjects of negotiation. Since sick leave, as a term or condition of employment, was a mandatory subject of bargaining, and since negotiations had begun at the time of the survey, the survey was an unfair labor practice. *Service Employees Int'l Union, Local 509 v. Labor Relations Comm'n*, 729 N.E.2d 1100 (Mass. 2000).

♦ In November 1997, after a series of rapes against school children, a New York fire chief ordered all firefighters to patrol the streets in the district from 6 a.m. until 8 a.m. on school days. The purpose of the patrols was to assist the police department, and the order was effective until January 1, 1998. The firefighters were directed not to intervene, but only to notify their dispatcher of suspicious activity. The firefighters' union filed a grievance stating that the order was tantamount to changing the firefighters' work rules, which violated their collective bargaining agreement (CBA). Although the CBA required that the matter be arbitrated, the union sought judicial review to vacate the chief's order without exhausting its administrative remedies, alleging that the grievance procedure would outlast the duration of the order. The city moved for dismissal.

The court found that **the union had met the requirements to have its case judicially reviewed without exhausting its administrative remedies**. While it was doubtful that the firefighters faced physical harm, the patrols were not "incidental or necessary to the protection of life and property during fires and other emergencies" as dictated by the city charter. The court vacated the chief's order and denied the city's request for dismissal. *Rochester Fire Fighters Ass'n v. Griffith*, 671 N.Y.S.2d 593 (N.Y. Sup. Ct. 1998).

♦ An Iowa county hospital negotiated a collective bargaining agreement with its employees' union. The agreement contained a re-opener provision on wage and insurance benefits. When the union requested the contract be reopened for negotiations and requested information on the salaries of hospital administrators and supervisors (non-bargaining unit employees), the hospital refused. The union filed a prohibited-practice complaint with the Public Employment Relations Board (PERB).

The PERB ruled that the salary information requested was relevant. The Supreme Court of Iowa agreed, noting that state law imposes a **duty on public employers and employees to negotiate in good faith**. The duty carries an obligation on the employer to supply the union with information relevant and necessary to effectively represent the employees in contract negotiations. Instead of adopting the more narrow standards established by the National Labor Relations Board for the private sector, the PERB established broader relevancy standards that include information that "may be relevant" to the bargaining process. *Greater Community Hospital v. PERB*, 553 N.W.2d 869 (Iowa 1996).

C. Arbitration

Most collective bargaining agreements provide for arbitration of disagreements; however, not all issues are arbitrable. Additionally, an arbitrator's authority to resolve disputes may be limited by state statute.

♦ The Philadelphia Housing Authority fired an employee after determining that he had sexually harassed a female co-worker. He filed a grievance, and an arbitrator ruled that he should be reinstated because: 1) management was aware of and condoned sexual horseplay, and 2) the employee stopped his harassment after being warned by a supervisor. The authority objected to the arbitrator's ruling. It appealed to the Commonwealth Court of Pennsylvania, which agreed that the employee did not have to be reinstated. The arbitrator had found that the employee engaged in lewd, lascivious and extraordinarily perverse behavior. Thus, reinstating the employee undermined public policy and effectively precluded the housing authority from satisfying its legal obligation to protect against sexual harassment in the workplace. *Philadelphia Housing Authority v. AFSCME*, 956 A.2d 477 (Pa. Commw. Ct. 2008).

♦ A California county and a public employee union reached an impasse during negotiations over compensation for employees of the probation department. The union requested that the dispute be submitted to binding arbitration pursuant to a state law that required counties and firefighter or law enforcement unions to submit wage and salary issues to binding arbitration upon reaching an impasse. The county refused to do so, claiming that the law violated the California Constitution, which mandates that a county's governing body provide employee compensation and prevents the state legislature from delegating the function to private individuals or entities. The union filed a lawsuit to compel arbitration, and a state court ruled in its favor. However, the Court of Appeal reversed, noting that **even though a county could choose to delegate its salary-setting authority to an arbitrator, the legislature could not compel it to do so.** *Riverside Sheriff's Ass'n v. County of Riverside*, 131 Cal.Rptr.2d 454 (Cal. Ct. App. 2003).

♦ A city employee threatened to shoot a fellow employee and his family. This resulted in the employee's arrest for making terroristic threats and an injunction requiring the employee to stay at least 100 yards away from the threatened employee. It also prevented him from approaching the threatened employee's workplace. When the city fired him, an arbitrator ordered his reinstatement on the grounds that 1) the city had not properly followed its disciplinary procedures, and 2) the employee did not intend to carry out his threat. The California Court of Appeal noted that because there was an injunction requiring the employee to stay away from the workplace, **the arbitrator's award could not stand because it required violating a court order**. Thus, even if reinstating the employee would not violate public policy requiring an employer to provide a safe workplace, public policy requiring compliance with court orders would be violated by the reinstatement. *City of Palo Alto v. SEIU, Local 715*, 91 Cal.Rptr.2d 500 (Cal. Ct. App. 1999).

• Three municipalities formed a regional police department (RPD) and delegated to it the power to hire, supervise, discipline and discharge police officers, and the power to determine wages, benefits and terms and conditions of employment. The municipalities also agreed they each would delegate two representatives, appointed by their own governing boards, to sit on a board of directors that would control the RPD. After the officers' union and the RPD reached an impasse during contract negotiations, an arbitration panel ordered the municipalities to consolidate their pension plans and give their pension monies to the RPD for the development of a single pension plan. One municipality claimed that the state Police Pension Act prevented it from delegating its pension responsibilities to the RPD. After a retiring RPD officer was told that he could not receive his pension benefits because the municipality had refused to distribute its pension funds to the RPD, the union filed an unfair labor practice charge against the RPD and the municipality. The case reached the Pennsylvania Supreme Court, which held that the municipality, through its designated representatives on the RPD board, had exercised powers demonstrating that it had an employer-employee relationship, as a joint employer with the RPD, with the officers. **As a joint employer, the municipality was deemed to have participated in the arbitration proceedings** in which the RPD was involved. Further, its refusal to pay its pension funds to the RPD was an unfair labor practice. *Borough of Lewistown v. Pennsylvania Labor Relations Board,* 735 A.2d 1240 (Pa. 1999).

• Previous collective bargaining agreements (CBAs) between a New Hampshire county and the union that represented county employees had contained a five-step wage schedule for annual increases within each labor grade. The CBAs established the effective date for annual step increases to be the employee's anniversary date – the exact anniversary date for employees hired after a specific date – and a July 1 effective date for all other employees. A new CBA added several more step levels to each labor grade, but did not modify the existing provision establishing the anniversary date for each annual increase. The union requested that the more senior employees receive an immediate step increase on July 1 in addition to their anniversary date increase. When the county refused, the union demanded that the county submit the dispute to binding arbitration. The county filed an unfair labor practice complaint with the public employment labor relations board. The board ordered the parties into arbitration. The county appealed to the Supreme Court of New Hampshire.

The CBA contained a clause that required the parties to arbitrate any grievance "arising from an alleged violation, misinterpretation or misapplication" of any provision in the CBA. However, the court held that the clause applied only when the dispute arose over an existing contract provision. Here, the CBA did not indicate that employees would obtain their annual wage increases at any time other than their anniversary date. Also, the court disagreed with the union that the language regarding the date of the increase was mistakenly excluded from the CBA and therefore subject to arbitration. The court held that **arbitration could not arise on the basis of an omitted term** because such a term cannot be violated, misinterpreted, or misapplied. A dispute over the reformation of the CBA to include an alleged term that was inadvertently omitted was not arbitrable under the arbitration clause. The board's decision was reversed. *Appeal of Merrimack County Board of Commissioners,* 709 A.2d 775 (N.H. 1998).

* Health care employees of the state of Rhode Island negotiated a collective bargaining agreement (CBA). The agreement provided that the employees could not be compelled to work more than 16 consecutive hours except in an emergency. However, there was no express contractual limit on the number of overtime hours for which employees could volunteer. Thus, some employees would volunteer to work 24 consecutive hours. Concerned about adverse health risks for its patients, the state department of mental health, retardation, and hospitals limited the employees to two consecutive eight-hour shifts except in an emergency. The health care employees' union filed grievances protesting the state's new policy, and the parties submitted the matter to arbitration. The arbitrator found that the state had violated the CBA, and a state superior court affirmed.

The Supreme Court of Rhode Island found that **the arbitrator exceeded his powers** because the dispute at issue was non-arbitrable and the submission to arbitration usurped the exclusive statutory authority of the department and its director to ensure the comfort and promote the welfare of the patients. The state's obligation to arbitrate regarding its health care employees' hours of work was circumscribed by the statutory obligations to protect disabled, custodial patients entrusted to the department's care. Thus, neither the department nor its director could delegate to arbitrators the department's statutory obligation to take all steps necessary to provide for the health and welfare of the patients. The case was reversed, and the arbitrator's award was vacated. *State of Rhode Island v. Rhode Island Council 94,* 692 A.2d 318 (R.I. 1997).

* An Illinois city discharged an emergency medical technician (EMT). His union agreed to allow the EMT to pursue arbitration against the city in exchange for his agreement to pay the union's share of the arbitration costs. The union agreed that the EMT and his attorneys would have sole discretion as to the arbitration procedure, presentation of evidence and any and all decisions concerning the prosecution of the grievance and/or arbitration procedure. The EMT then released the union from all representational responsibility regarding the arbitration of his grievance. The city refused to engage in arbitration, claiming that its only obligation under the collective bargaining agreement was to arbitrate with the union. The EMT sued to compel arbitration.

The Appellate Court of Illinois found that **the personal nature of the roles of each party prevented either party from assigning to a third party the right to demand arbitration**. First, the reference in the bargaining agreement to the union as the exclusive bargaining agent for all city employees made clear that the intent of the parties was that arbitration would take place solely between the union and the city, and that the city specifically agreed not to bargain or arbitrate with any other parties, including a third party such as the EMT. Second, the terms of the National Labor Relations Act and its respective case law mandated that the union could not validly assign to the EMT its right to demand arbitration. *Martin v. City of O'Fallon*, 670 N.E.2d 1238 (Ill. App. Ct. 1996).

• Two Ohio police officers struggled with a suspect, and one officer applied pressure to his neck and face. The pressure caused the suspect's death. The city charged the officers with violating departmental rules. After a disciplinary hearing, the officers were suspended without pay. Their union filed a grievance, and the matter was sent to arbitration. When the arbitrator denied the grievance, the union appealed to a state trial court alleging that the arbitrator imperfectly executed his powers because he failed to consider a disparate treatment issue. The trial court reversed the arbitrator's decision, although it found that the disparate treatment issue had been addressed. The city appealed, arguing that the trial court went beyond the scope of the statutory basis for the appeal and used an incorrect standard for review. **Judicial review of arbitration decisions is statutorily restricted** and limits vacation or modification of awards to certain enumerated grounds. The Court of Appeals of Ohio found that the trial court correctly reviewed the disparate treatment issue, but incorrectly overturned the award on a new basis not presented or specifically enumerated in the statute. The trial court's actions were fundamentally unfair and exceeded the court's authority. Accordingly, the arbitrator's award was reinstated. *Cleveland Police Patrolmen's Ass'n v. City of Cleveland*, 668 N.E.2d 548 (Ohio Ct. App. 1995).

CHAPTER EIGHT

Employment Practices

	Page
I. APPOINTMENTS AND PROMOTIONS	471
A. Eligibility Lists	472
1. Examinations	474
2. Review of Test Materials	476
3. Preference Points and Credits	477
B. Classifications	479
1. Creation of Classifications	480
2. Temporary Assignments	481
3. Reclassification	483
C. Privatization	486
D. Nepotism	489
II. RESIDENCY REQUIREMENTS	491
III. VETERANS' RIGHTS AND PREFERENCES	495
IV. EMPLOYER POLICIES AND RESTRICTIONS	500
A. Secondary Employment	501
B. Employment Testing	504
C. Legal Fees Reimbursement	506
D. Marital Restrictions	508

I. APPOINTMENTS AND PROMOTIONS

Public employees generally enter public service through appointments pursuant to civil service examinations. Once appointed, public servants may be reclassified to higher or lower classification levels or removed from the public system because of privatization.

Promotions also follow a civil service examination procedure, which produces an eligibility list for appointments.

♦ A Fort Worth fire chief notified a fire engineer that she would be indefinitely suspended, effectively losing her job the following day. However, he failed to follow the suspension up with a written statement to the Civil Service Commission within 120 hours, as required by the local government code. When the fire engineer appealed her suspension and the error was realized, she was returned to the job. Meanwhile, the firefighter who was next on the promotion eligibility list asserted that he was entitled to be promoted to fire engineer within 60 days. The fire department disputed that assertion, and a lawsuit resulted. The case reached the Court of Appeals of Texas, which noted that **the indefinite suspension created a vacancy that the chief had to fill from the promotion eligibility list**. The chief had no discretion in the matter. Therefore, the firefighter was entitled to the promotion within 60 days of the vacancy. *Carr v. City of Fort Worth*, 266 S.W.3d 116 (Tex. Ct. App. 2008).

♦   A politically appointed city clerk in Illinois learned from the mayor-elect that he was not going to be reappointed to the position after the mayor was inaugurated the next day. Believing that he had been fired, the clerk vacated his office immediately. He sued the city under 42 U.S.C. § 1983, claiming that his due process right to progressive discipline had been violated, and that he had lost pension benefit money as a result. The Seventh Circuit held that **the advance notice to the clerk that his appointment would end did not amount to a premature termination**. Further, the mayor-elect was not acting "under color of state law" when he told the clerk of his decision not to reappoint him. He had no power to terminate the clerk before his inauguration. *Burrell v. City of Mattoon*, 378 F.3d 642 (7th Cir. 2004).

♦   A group of individuals employed by the Boston housing police department and the Boston municipal police department, whose duties included protecting Boston's public properties and buildings, sued the city after being rejected for positions with the Boston police department. A state statute **allowed cities to reject applicants over the age of 32 for original appointments to the police department**. The Appeals Court of Massachusetts held that the statute applied to the applicants here. Even though they were already civil service employees, they still had to take examinations to become eligible for original appointments to other civil service positions. And they were not entitled to promotional appointments because they never took promotional exams for police officer positions. *Goncalves v. City of Boston*, 845 N.E.2d 1201 (Mass. App. Ct. 2006).

A. Eligibility Lists

Upon taking a civil service examination, applicants are placed on an eligibility list from which the department may choose to hire or promote the applicant. Placement on the eligibility list, however, does not ensure hiring or promotion. Usually, employers have the option of hiring any of the top three or five employees on the eligibility list.

♦   A New Jersey fire department captain served as the acting deputy fire chief after scoring the highest on the promotional exam. However, he was not named to the position permanently because the city was in the process of arranging for another candidate to receive the promotion – a fellow captain who had sued the city for wrongfully denying him a promotion to captain two years earlier. As part of the settlement, the city had agreed to relax the rule that he spend a year as a captain before being allowed to try for the deputy chief position. The settlement also stated that he would get the deputy chief job if he scored highest on the next promotional exam. When he scored the highest on the exam, he was given the permanent deputy chief job over the acting deputy chief, who was returned to the rank of captain. A lawsuit arose challenging the automatic appointment as violating the rule of three. The Superior Court of New Jersey, Appellate Division, held that **the city could relax the one-year-in-grade requirement, but that the automatic promotion violated the rule of three**. The court remanded the case so the city could select a new permanent deputy chief from among the two employees here and whoever was next on the list. *In re Martinez*, 956 A.2d 386 (N.J. Super. App. Div. 2008).

• The bargaining agreement between a police union and a Maryland county provided that the police department had to fill a vacancy within 90 days or pay the first person on the eligibility list for the position as if he or she had been promoted on the 91st day. The chief, believing he did not necessarily have to promote the top person, issued a memo stating that he would be instituting a "Rule of 3," allowing him to consider other variables in promoting from among the top three candidates. The union filed a grievance and an arbitrator ruled for the union, requiring the chief to promote the top candidate. The Maryland Court of Special Appeals upheld the arbitrator's decision, noting testimony from past officials who **understood the agreement to require the promotion of the top-ranked candidate and who had followed this "Rule of 1"** by promoting the top candidate in the past. *Prince George's County, Maryland v. Fraternal Order of Police, Lodge 89*, 914 A.2d 199 (Md. Ct. Spec. App. 2007).

• Sixteen firefighter candidates were **disqualified from an eligibility list based on their responses during a polygraph examination**, which was part of the pre-employment screening process. During the exam, they answered questions regarding various matters, including residency, education, military service, employment history, driving record, history of illegal drug use or sale and criminal background. Although none of them were deemed to have been untruthful, some provided more complete or more accurate information during the polygraph than they did on an information-gathering form they filled out. After they were disqualified, they sued, challenging the use of the polygraphs, and the Pennsylvania Commonwealth Court ruled against them. They could not challenge the information-gathering procedures used by the city; they could only challenge whether there was just cause for their disqualification. *City of Pittsburgh v. Bachner*, 912 A.2d 368 (Pa. Commw. Ct. 2006).

• An Illinois police officer who also served as a union representative ranked fourth on a promotion eligibility list. The three candidates above him were promoted, but he was passed over for the next candidate on the list. After another sergeant retired, the chief chose not to fill the position until the list expired. The officer claimed retaliation and sued. The Appellate Court of Illinois held that **he had no vested right in a promotion** and that the police department could legitimately reduce the number of sergeants in the force from 7 to 6. Such action was legislative in nature, providing absolute immunity to the decision-makers. However, there was a question as to whether other actions taken by the chief were a retaliatory response to his union activity. This claim required a trial. *Schlicher v. Board of Fire and Police Commissioners of Village of Westmont*, 845 N.E.2d 55 (Ill. App. Ct. 2006).

♦ A 15-year volunteer firefighter in a New Jersey borough took a civil service exam and physical to become a paid firefighter. He ranked number one on the eligibility list. He became an "inactive" volunteer firefighter and applied for paid firefighter positions as they became available. However, the borough council refused to appoint him on three occasions, instead selecting active volunteers without informing him that they considered active status to be a necessary precondition to a paid position. When he challenged the borough's actions, the Superior Court of New Jersey, Appellate Division, held that **the use of a secret criterion not mentioned to the volunteer firefighter warranted a reversal of the administrative decision denying his appointment**. The court remanded the case for reconsideration of appointments with active volunteer status to be used as only one factor in deciding the merit of the candidates. *In re Hruska*, 867 A.2d 479 (N.J. Super. Ct. App. Div. 2005).

♦ Three police officers in Edmond, Oklahoma were promoted to sergeant based on a promotion eligibility list that was challenged by an officer who did not receive a promotion. An arbitrator later determined that the eligibility list was invalid under the collective bargaining agreement (CBA) because the oral exam was not conducted properly. The police chief then notified the three officers that they were being demoted and that they would have to take the next oral exam to be considered for promotion. They filed a grievance, then sued under 42 U.S.C. § 1983, alleging that the chief violated their constitutional rights to due process by demoting them without a hearing. The case reached the Oklahoma Supreme Court, which ruled that the chief violated their procedural due process rights. Here, **the officers had a property right to their rank of sergeant** because the CBA only allowed demotions for cause. The officers should not have been demoted. *Barnthouse v. City of Edmond*, 73 P.3d 840 (Okla. 2003).

1. Examinations

♦ A Pennsylvania fire department's chief engineer took the examination for a vacant captaincy. He received a score of 82.28, the highest score on the exam, while the acting captain received a score of 75.5. After the fire department selected the acting captain for the position, the engineer sued, asserting that a state statute required the highest-scoring candidate to be selected for the job. The fire department argued that it could use the rule of three to select from among the top three candidates. The case reached the Pennsylvania Commonwealth Court, which held that **the department was required to promote the top-scoring candidate to the job**. A promotion was not like an original appointment, which allowed for the use of the rule of three. Promotions were to be based strictly on merit, removing discretion from the process. *Borough of Wilkinsburg v. Colella*, 961 A.2d 265 (Pa. Commw. Ct. 2008).

♦ A provisional New Jersey police officer with an unblemished record of service applied for a permanent appointment with the sheriff's department. After an interview, he was given a conditional offer of employment, contingent on his successful completion of a background investigation, stress test, psychological evaluation, medical examination, and police academy basic training. After a psychological evaluation, the officer was determined to be unfit for the position, partly for his low score on the Wonderlic personnel test (a brief test of intelligence consisting of traditional items such as vocabulary, arithmetic, and logic), and partly for lack of "honesty and integrity," based on inconsistent information he provided about his juvenile record during the application and interview process. When he appealed, **an independent psychological evaluation confirmed that he was unfit for the position**. The New Jersey Superior Court, Appellate Division, upheld the administrative decision. The evidence supported the determination that he was psychologically unfit to be a police officer. *In re Tulko*, 2007 WL 1452513 (N.J. Super. Ct. App. Div. 5/18/07).

♦ The mayor of a Massachusetts city requested that 10 city police officers (who had been reserve police officers before the reserve police force was disbanded) be declared eligible to take a promotional exam for sergeant. They were allowed to take the exam. Other officers challenged that decision, asserting that they hadn't been on the police force for three years, as required for eligibility. The case reached the Appeals Court of Massachusetts, which held that **the eligibility list could include officers with less than three years of experience** by allowing them to tack on full-time service in the reserve force so as to meet the statutory requirement for eligibility for the sergeants' exam. *City of Lawrence v. Civil Service Comm'n*, 847 N.E.2d 360 (Mass. App. Ct. 2006).

♦ Connecticut police officers who were passed over for promotions sued the city and various officials, alleging that the methodology used for promoting officers violated city charter provisions limiting the exercise of discretion in making promotions. The city used a method that **rounded up civil service exam scores to whole numbers and then treated them as score groups** for application of the rule of three. The case reached the Supreme Court of Connecticut, which held that the city's method violated the city charter by potentially allowing more than the top three candidates to be considered for a position. This broadened the exercise of discretion beyond what was allowable. *Kelly v. City of New Haven*, 881 A.2d 978 (Conn. 2005).

♦ Three public employees sought a promotion to the positions of Health Program Administrator I and II. They took the exams and were placed in the first or second zone, but they were not selected for promotion. They challenged the use of zone scoring (wherein all scores within a certain range received a single zone score, which included seniority credits, but not veteran's credits, which were added to the zone score before the eligibility list was generated). **They claimed that candidates ought to be ranked exclusively by raw score.** The New York Supreme Court, Appellate Division, held that the Civil Service Commission's decision to use zone scoring had to be accorded substantial deference. The commission set forth its reasons for using such scoring (including that there were limitations on the role of testing to accurately reflect the nuances of the diverse positions), and the zones were narrowly drawn. Thus, the employees were not entitled to relief. *Benson v. New York State Dep't of Civil Service*, 745 N.Y.S.2d 329 (N.Y. App. Div. 2002).

♦ An Arkansas police officer took a promotion exam and was ranked second on the three-person eligibility list for promotion to corporal. During the one-year span that the list was in effect, three other police officers were promoted to corporal. He sued, alleging that he was entitled to be promoted because of his ranking, and that the city failed to advertise the competitive examination for promotion to corporal in the following year, foreclosing him from taking that exam. Before the Supreme Court of Arkansas, he argued that it was a mathematical impossibility for three promotions to be made in one year without all three people originally named as the three highest-ranking persons being selected. The court disagreed. Under state law, each time a position becomes available, the civil service commission is required to submit the names of the three applicants with the highest exam scores to the chief of police. As a result, **the officer was only entitled to consideration as one of three candidates each time a promotion was made from the eligibility list**. The court then addressed the issue of notice and held that state law did not require newspaper notice for examinations to decide promotion to a higher rank. It was sufficient to post dates for exams on the officers' bulletin board in the department. Newspaper notice was only required for initial hiring of police officers and firefighters. The court affirmed the trial court's decision in favor of the city. *Burcham v. City of Van Buren*, 954 S.W.2d 266 (Ark. 1997).

2. Review of Test Materials

♦ A Cincinnati police sergeant took a promotional exam for lieutenant and after seeing the results, **challenged the grading of the exam**. The civil service commission denied his request for a hearing, stating that challenges to specific questions were not permitted. When he sued, a trial court retroactively promoted him to lieutenant. The city appealed. The Court of Appeals of Ohio held that the commission should have addressed the merits of the sergeant's challenge to the exam. It further noted that the trial court should have remanded the case to the commission for it to determine the merits of the sergeant's challenge to the promotional exam. It reversed the lower court's decision and remanded the case. *State ex rel. Fern v. Cincinnati*, 832 N.E.2d 106 (Ohio Ct. App. 2005).

♦ A New Jersey city police sergeant took a competitive civil service exam for the position of police captain. The written part of the examination consisted of problems arising from factual situations typical of those likely to confront a police captain. The sergeant passed the exam but was dissatisfied with his score and appealed to the supervisor of the selection appeals unit. **The sergeant was allowed one hour to review his answers, the examination instructions and the scores**, along with the brief descriptive statement of his performance on each question, but was not allowed to remove the materials from the room where he examined them. The supervisor and the Merit System Board affirmed the results of the exam, and the sergeant appealed to the Superior Court of New Jersey, Appellate Division, which reversed.

On further appeal, the Supreme Court of New Jersey held that under the state's Civil Service Act, the department of personnel has substantial discretion in determining the appropriate level of access to test materials by examinees. The department's reuse of examination questions justifies limiting access to the actual test questions and the scoring key in order to ensure security and confidentiality. The expense involved in formulating entirely new questions for each test, the consistency that recycling questions achieves among exams at different times, and the ability to evaluate the effectiveness of questions that results from providing them to a large pool of examinees supported the department's reuse of questions. Moreover, the department's procedures accommodated the competing goals of examination security and examinee access. **Although the examinees did not have full and complete access to their exam materials, they had sufficient access to judge whether the grading process was arbitrary.** The judgment of the appellate division was reversed. *Brady v. Dep't of Personnel*, 693 A.2d 466 (N.J. 1997).

♦ A police officer employed by a city in Iowa took two civil service examinations for promotion to the rank of lieutenant. Although he was placed on the eligible promotional list twice, he was not promoted and began to suspect that the Civil Service Commission was not following its own rules in establishing the promotional lists. Pursuant to the state's open records law, he requested a review of the raw scores of each person who took the two examinations and the grading scales used in scoring. The Commission denied his request, contending that the records fell within exceptions to the disclosure requirement. The officer then sued in state court, which granted pretrial judgment to the officer and ordered disclosure. The city and Commission appealed.

The Supreme Court of Iowa affirmed, although it modified the disclosure to allow for redacting the names of the individuals. The court interpreted the disclosure requirement broadly and determined that the exemptions for trade secrets, personal records, and examinations were inapplicable with the exception of redacting the individual names. Under the personal information exemption, the court balanced the public interests served by disclosure against invasions of privacy. Here, **the public's interest in grading accuracy outweighed the privacy sacrificed by disclosing the scores of the successful candidates**. The court noted that the invasion of privacy was tolerable because the candidates scored well enough to qualify for promotion and the public knew their rank relative to other successful candidates. The redaction of the individuals' names also helped to protect the candidates' privacy. *DeLaMater v. Marion Civil Service Comm'n*, 554 N.W.2d 875 (Iowa 1996).

3. Preference Points and Credits

♦ Two applicants for Game Conservation Officer Trainee positions were **entitled to preference in hiring as a result of the Rule of Three** (where the promotion must come from the three highest-ranking persons on the eligibility list), and under the **Veterans' Preference Act**. However, after their interviews, the Game Commission sought to have them removed from the eligibility list – one for showing too much interest in deadly force, and the other for violating state Game Law. The Civil Service Commission denied the request and ordered that the applicants be kept on the eligibility list. When the Game Commission challenged the order, the Commonwealth Court of Pennsylvania held that the Rule of Three and the Veterans' Preference Act were intended to prevent public employers from imposing additional hiring criteria upon civil service applicants. The Game Commission wasn't deprived of a legally protected property right by the refusal of a hearing on the removal request. The applicants had to be kept on the eligibility list. *Pennsylvania Game Comm'n v. State Civil Service Comm'n*, 789 A.2d 839 (Pa. Commw. Ct. 2002).

♦ Several firefighter candidates took and passed a civil service examination for the New York City Fire Department. The eligibility list created from the examination was extended because of a hiring freeze. Subsequently, the city announced that a residency credit would be instituted on another examination. The city stopped appointments from the old eligibility list and let it expire so that appointments from the new list, which contained the residency credit, could be made. Several firefighter candidates on the old list sought a court order to stop the city from using the residency credit, from appointing candidates from the new eligibility list without discounting the credit, and from terminating the old eligibility list. The court granted the defendants' motion to dismiss, finding that the firefighter candidates lacked standing because they did not take the new examination. The Court of Appeals of New York agreed that the candidates lacked standing to challenge the use of the residency credit in the subsequent examination because **the only persons aggrieved by application of the residency credit were the non-city residents who took that examination**. The appeals court also noted that although the candidates had standing to challenge the allegedly improper expiration of their own eligibility list, they failed to establish the necessary arbitrariness or bad faith that would entitle them to relief. *Altamore v. Barrios-Paoli*, 90 N.Y.2d 378, 660 N.Y.S.2d 834, 683 N.E.2d 740 (N.Y. 1997).

♦ A Pennsylvania man on the eligibility list for the position of corrections officer trainee was charged with resisting arrest, public intoxication, and disorderly conduct. Although the record of the arrest was expunged by court order after he completed a program of accelerated rehabilitative disposition, the Department of Corrections (DOC) removed him from the eligibility list. However, the state civil service commission concluded that the DOC's reliance on the expunged arrest record discriminated against him based on non-merit factors, in violation of the Civil Service Act. The Commonwealth Court of Pennsylvania reversed, finding that the DOC had not discriminated against the applicant. The DOC's removal of the applicant's name was based on the result of a criminal background investigation, which indicated a disregard for authority and rules, an inability or lack of inclination to comply with orders, a lack of self-discipline, and poor judgment. Because the appointing authority has the exclusive judgment to determine the merit of an applicant's background, **the DOC's determination that under some circumstances an arrest record may** be a merit factor in an applicant's qualification for a corrections officer position did not constitute an abuse of discretion. The assistant chief stated that the arrest alone did not result in the applicant's disqualification but that the events surrounding the arrest – resisting authority and violent behavior – were the primary factors in his disqualification. *Comwlth. of Pennsylvania, Dep't of Corrections v. Krempowsky*, 698 A.2d 144 (Pa. Commw. Ct. 1997).

• A county in California maintained a practice of awarding five preference points to permanent county employees whose scores on open examinations did not initially place them in the top three ranks of those taking the tests. In an open examination for the position of underground construction and maintenance supervisor, a permanent county employee placed in the first rank. However, the county adjusted the scores of the permanent employees who scored in the fourth through the sixth ranks, making those employees eligible for promotion along with the employees in ranks one through three. As a result, the top-ranking employee was passed over in the initial selection process. The union sought an order to prevent the county from continuing its practice of awarding preference points and asking for monetary damages for lost wages and benefits due the employee. The case reached the California Court of Appeal, which held that the policy violated both the county charter and the county's civil service rules. **The preference points were intended to favor employees who already had achieved permanent employment status over those who had not.** Here, by awarding five preference points to only those employees outside the first three ranks, the county was favoring certain permanent employees over others. *Stationary Engineers Local 39 v. County of Sacramento*, 69 Cal.Rptr.2d 598 (Cal. Ct. App. 1997).

B. Classifications

Most public employees receive a classification that defines their job duties and compensation. However, temporary assignments do not necessarily entitle an employee to that particular classification. Likewise, an employee may be reclassified for a variety of reasons, including mis-classification.

• A Pennsylvania corrections officer was promoted to sergeant – a CO2 classification. Ten years later (fifteen years after he started as a corrections officer) he was promoted to lieutenant – a CO3 classification – which took him out of his bargaining unit. Thus, he lost all seniority for purposes of both furloughs and promotion. Soon after taking the promotion, for personal reasons, the officer requested to return to the CO2 position. After he was transferred back, in accordance with the collective bargaining unit, he was assigned a seniority start date that made him essentially like a new employee. A lawsuit resulted. The officer claimed that where the State Civil Service Act conflicted with the collective bargaining agreement, the act trumped the agreement. The Supreme Court of Pennsylvania agreed. **The officer retained his seniority for purposes of promotions and furloughs after his brief appointment to the CO3 classification.** *Pennsylvania State Corrections Officers Ass'n v. State Civil Service Comm'n*, 939 A.2d 296 (Pa. 2007).

1. Creation of Classifications

♦ A New York police officer who had been working out-of-title as a detective in the county's district attorney's office brought an administrative challenge, seeking to be designated a detective along with any other similarly situated officers. **He claimed that the out-of-title work created a right to reclassification** under Civil Service Law §§ 58(4)(c)(ii) and (iii). The case reached the Supreme Court, Appellate Division, which ruled against him. It stated that the civil service law in question expressly excluded the investigatory personnel of the office of the district attorney in any county from the right of reclassification. *Lake City Police Club v. City of Oswego*, 818 N.Y.S.2d 703 (N.Y. App. Div. 2006).

♦ The New York City Transit Authority assigned several level I supervisors to more highly compensated level II supervisory positions without requiring them to take an additional civil service examination. Assignment between the two levels, both within the same pay grade, was at the discretion of the authority, depending on its needs. Level I employees who were eligible for but not assigned to the level II positions filed suit against the city in a New York trial court, seeking to nullify the promotions and to require the city to develop, administer and grade a level II competitive examination. The trial court dismissed the claim, and the New York Supreme Court, Appellate Division, affirmed. The employees appealed to the Court of Appeals of New York. The court of appeals held that **individuals within the supervisory pay grade were properly assigned to either level I or level II duties** and that such an assignment between levels was neither a promotion nor a demotion under the state Civil Service Law. The reassignment or consolidation of assignments under a single title with a written competitive examination had been held permissible in previous rulings. Also, the requirement that level II supervisors serve a probationary period did not render the reassignment a promotion under Civil Service Law Section 63. Accordingly, the lower court rulings were affirmed and the case was dismissed. *Kitchings v. Jenkins*, 628 N.Y.S.2d 36 (N.Y. 1995).

♦ A Texas city categorized its police officers into four classes: class A – uniformed and detective class; class B – technical class; class C – communication class; and class D – park police. A group of park police officers filed a lawsuit against the city in a Texas trial court, seeking a declaration that they were entitled to maintain their current seniority and be transferred to class A status. The officers contended that the city had improperly created a fourth class and that they performed substantially the same duties as class A officers. The trial court granted pretrial judgment to the city, and the officers appealed to the Court of Appeals of Texas. The court of appeals noted that the Texas Constitution authorized cities to create positions, adopt classification plans, set the rate of pay, and abolish positions. The Texas Local Government Code did not expressly prohibit the creation of a fourth classification but merely required that all officers be placed within the protection of a civil service system. Thus, the current classification scheme did not authorize park police officers to be transferred into class A while maintaining their current level of seniority. Even if there was a statutory requirement that the park police officers be entitled to the same rate of pay as the class A officers if they performed the same duties, **there were substantial differences in the authority and functions of the two classes**. For example, the park police officers were required to summon a class A officer to handle major crime investigations and were specifically hired to provide security only within the parks. The trial court ruling was affirmed. *Jones v. City of Houston*, 907 S.W.2d 871 (Tex. Ct. App. 1995).

♦ A New Jersey fire district was served by a volunteer fire company. In 1989, township fire commissioners adopted a resolution creating two permanent firefighter positions. Two volunteer firefighters, among others, applied for the positions. They received the firefighter positions under grandfather provisions of the state Civil Service Act. The act provided that any employee who was actively employed by a political subdivision for a period of one year prior to the adoption of the position would continue to hold the position. One of the other applicants appealed to the state Department of Personnel, challenging the classification of the firefighters as permanent employees. The New Jersey Merit Systems Board issued a final decision determining that the firefighters had been improperly classified and were required to take the civil service exam. The firefighters appealed to the Superior Court of New Jersey, Appellate Division.

Although the volunteer firefighters were not paid regular salaries, they were covered by workers' compensation and life insurance. Volunteers also were reimbursed for training courses, fire drills and fire calls. The court noted that **the purpose of the Civil Service Act was to fill public service positions according to individual merit and fitness**, demonstrated through a competitive examination process. This purpose would be frustrated if volunteers were accorded the status of permanent employees. The volunteers might be entitled to compensation in accordance with state and federal minimum wage laws, enrollment in public employees' retirement systems, and protection under the New Jersey Public Employees' Occupational Safety and Health Act. Thus, the court affirmed the board's determination that the firefighters were not grandfathered into regular paid positions. *Matter of Tavani*, 624 A.2d 75 (N.J. Super. Ct. App. Div. 1993).

2. Temporary Assignments

♦ A police officer in Texas became eligible for promotion to senior police officer. When a senior police officer who was also in the Army Reserve was recalled to active duty and was granted a military leave of absence, the officer was temporarily appointed to fill the senior police officer position. He demanded that he be appointed to the position permanently, and a lawsuit resulted. The Court of Appeals of Texas ultimately ruled against him, noting that the involuntary recall was not the same as leaving the police force to join the military. The senior police officer intended to return to the job after his military service expired. Thus, **there was no "vacancy" so as to require that the officer be permanently appointed** to the senior police officer position. *McElroy v. City of Temple*, 208 S.W.3d 471 (Tex. Ct. App. 2006).

* Two Ohio firefighters took the promotion exam for lieutenant and made the eligibility list. By the time the list expired, they were the next two firefighters in line to be promoted. Shortly after the list expired, a lieutenant who had been promoted ahead of them asked that his promotion be rescinded. The city's director of public safety, rather than promote one of the two firefighters, made a temporary appointment of another firefighter without consulting the expired eligibility list. The firefighters sued, claiming that they should have been considered for the temporary promotion, and seeking to prevent further temporary promotions outside the expired list. The case reached the Ohio Court of Appeals, which ruled against them, noting that **civil service rules allowed the director to make temporary promotions without reference to the expired eligibility list.** *Wollman v. Cleveland*, No. 85548, 2005 WL 2590250 (Ohio Ct. App. 10/13/2005).

* Two employees challenged a city's receipt of waivers for three civil service positions after examination and the creation of eligibility lists. For the first position, Program Monitor, the city sought a waiver after the provisionally appointed employee resigned. The city asserted that no one was currently performing the job, and that a financial crisis prevented it from making a permanent appointment. The Superior Court of New Jersey, Appellate Division, upheld the grant of a waiver for that position. However, it reversed the grant of a waiver for the other two positions at issue: Community Service Aide/Senior Clerk and Code Enforcement Officer. For those positions, an insufficient record had been created as to **whether the city improperly kept provisional employees in the positions by changing the classifications of the jobs**. If the separately titled jobs were actually the same or functionally equivalent to the positions the employees had tested for, it would not matter that the city was in a financial crisis. By keeping provisional employees in the jobs rather than appointing permanent employees from the eligibility lists, the city would have violated the civil service requirements. The court remanded for a determination as to whether the provisional jobs were the same as the jobs applied for. *In re Code Enforcement Officer*, 793 A.2d 839 (N.J. Super Ct. App. Div. 2002).

* When two junior officers were assigned to a drug task force, two senior officers challenged the assignments. The drug task force was run out of the federal building in Anchorage and allowed the officers assigned there to work the morning shift rather than the afternoon shift. They also reported to a Drug Enforcement Administration supervisor. The two senior officers claimed that they should have been given the assignments based on seniority. A trial court granted pretrial judgment to the city, but the Supreme Court of Alaska reversed and remanded the case. It noted that there was a question of fact as to **whether the assignment was a "job assignment"** under the collective bargaining agreement that required the department to take officers' seniority into account, or whether it was more of a "case" assignment that only involved differing duties. *Larsen v. Municipality of Anchorage*, 993 P.2d 428 (Alaska 1999).

* A New York police officer, who temporarily served as a detective for more than 18 months, sought a promotion to the rank of detective in the Rochester

Police Department. He argued that under the New York Civil Service Law Section 58(4)(c), the 18-month period he had spent performing investigative duties matured automatically into a permanent detective appointment. The city argued that the law violated the Merit and Fitness Clause of the New York Constitution. The Court of Appeals of New York held that **appointment by the alternative statutory route improperly allowed temporarily assigned officers to be promoted** without submitting to the competitive examination mandated by the Merit and Fitness Clause. The employee contended that the detective position was not a true appointment under the Merit and Fitness Clause because no tenure attached until the appointee had held the position for three years. The court of appeals disagreed, ruling that the appointment or promotion "sprang to life" when the appointee earned the rank, benefits, and preferred status of detective. Because a legislative determination of impracticability of testing could not be found in the legislative history, the law was unconstitutional. Also, the constitutional testing requirement could not be summarily evaded simply on the basis of satisfactory performance during the officer's temporary service. *Wood v. Irving*, 623 N.Y.S.2d 824 (N.Y. 1995).

♦ An Oklahoma police detective was temporarily assigned to the position of lieutenant and received an increase in pay. He performed the duties of a lieutenant for more than a year, and then was reassigned to his former detective position. He filed a grievance against the city, claiming that the assignment was actually a promotion and that the reassignment was a wrongful demotion. The city's merit board voted in favor of the detective and reinstated him as a lieutenant. The city appealed, and the case reached the Supreme Court of Oklahoma. The court noted that at the time of the assignment to the lieutenant position, an eligibility list contained the names of three police officers who were eligible for promotion to that position. The detective was not on that list. The detective had merely been assigned out of his normal classification to fill a need that existed. Accordingly, **his assignment was only temporary, and he was not entitled to reinstatement to the lieutenant position**. *City of Muskogee v. Grayson*, 818 P.2d 491 (Okla. 1991).

3. Reclassification

♦ The New York Department of Corrections proposed having its education supervisors, plant superintendents and assistant industrial superintendents conduct tier III inmate disciplinary hearings as part of their job duties. The employees' union filed a grievance, and the Division of Classification and Compensation determined that conducting the hearings constituted out-of-title work. The division then determined that the job titles needed updating and reclassified the jobs to include conducting tier III hearings. When the union challenged the reclassification, the New York Supreme Court, Appellate Division, **upheld the reclassification, finding that it was not wholly arbitrary or without any rational basis**. There was no potential conflict here like there would be if the division tried to force senior correction counselors to conduct tier III hearings. *Criscolo v. Vagianelis*, 856 N.Y.S.2d 265 (N.Y. App. Div. 2008).

• Three California probation officers left their jobs with the county and took deferred retirement – an option that allowed them to keep their accumulated contributions in the county retirement fund. After they left, a new collective bargaining agreement made a state statute applicable in the county. This statute made probation officers "safety members" for retirement purposes rather than "general members" as the probation officers were when they left their jobs. They sued to be reclassified as safety members so that they could partake of the greater benefits available. The California Court of Appeal ruled against them, holding that **they were not entitled to the benefit of the reclassification**. They were only entitled to the benefits of their prior classification as general members. *Bonner v. County of San Diego*, 44 Cal.Rptr.3d 116 (Cal. Ct. App. 2006).

• An appointed employee of one political party in Puerto Rico asked to have her position reclassified as a career job. After that was done, a new governor was elected from the other major party. The employee then claimed that she was harassed and summarily fired after the new head of her department determined that the reclassification was null and void. When she sued the department head under the First and Fourteenth Amendments, he sought pretrial dismissal, claiming she was not entitled to due process before her firing, and also asserting qualified immunity as a defense. The court denied his request, finding issues of fact that required a trial. When he tried to appeal, the First Circuit held that it did not have jurisdiction. A trial would be held over **whether the reclassification was valid and whether she was fired for political reasons**. *Cruz-Gomez v. Rivera-Hernandez*, 444 F.3d 29 (1st Cir. 2006).

• A Tennessee county posted a job opening for a fire/EMT dispatcher at an annual salary of $29,998. A medical center employee applied for the job and was hired. However, **before she started work, the job was reclassified** so that the salary became $23,949. After she started work, she learned about the reclassification and lower salary. Her attempts to talk to various officials about receiving the salary she had been offered or at least when she might expect to receive raises were unsuccessful. Five months later, she quit and returned to her old job, but with less benefits and seniority. She sued the county for breach of contract and was ultimately awarded $2,971.68 – the difference between the promised and actual salaries for the five months she was on the job. *Sircy v. Metropolitan Government of Nashville and Davidson County*, 182 S.W.3d 815 (Tenn. Ct. App. 2005).

• The city of Newark transferred a variety of clerical duties from police officers to civilians and returned the officers to operational duties. The transfers took place as the result of a grant the city was awarded under the COPS MORE program of the federal Violent Crime Control and Law Enforcement Act. The local union (FOP) filed a grievance over the transfer of duties. An arbitrator ruled that the transfer of duties did not violate the bargaining agreement because the "displaced officers" continued to function as police officers in their core duties. However, he also concluded that the clerical positions could not be removed from the FOP unit. The Public Employment Relations Commission (PERC) ruled that the arbitrator's decision violated a state law prohibiting police and non-police from being in the same bargaining unit. The Superior Court of New Jersey, Appellate Division, affirmed. **The transfer of clerical duties to civilians in order to free up police officers for operational duties was clearly a management prerogative** and not subject to bargaining. Also, state law required placing police officers in a separate category from other public employees. The civil service employees' union could adequately represent the civilian clerks. *City of Newark v. Newark Council 21*, 726 A.2d 942 (N.J. Super. Ct. App. Div. 1999).

♦ Three applicants for managerial positions within the Kentucky Department of Education (DOE) sued after the DOE hired two other people who did not meet the jobs' minimum qualifications. The DOE advertised for the two classified positions through an internal announcement. After rejecting the three applicants, the DOE director sent a memo to the state personnel board requesting that the title of the first position be changed to accommodate a fourth applicant who did not meet the first position's requirements. The director wanted to hire this person because she had a law degree and experience evaluating administrative hearings. Through a written memo, the director hired a second lawyer as an unclassified employee to carry out the duties of the other position. After the personnel board dismissed the applicants' complaint, they appealed to a state trial court. The court held that the DOE had acted improperly, and the Kentucky Court of Appeals affirmed. **The DOE attempted to circumvent the state's reclassification procedure** with respect to the first position and failed to follow state law procedures with respect to the second position. *Comwlth. of Kentucky v. Gobert*, 979 S.W.2d 922 (Ky. Ct. App. 1998).

♦ An Alabama employee of the state Department of Transportation worked as an auditor II. He accepted a transfer to the state Medicaid Agency and a promotion to auditor III, with the understanding that there was a probationary period regarding the auditor III classification. While on probation, the employee was discharged and his name was placed on the reemployment list at the lower classification. He contended that he should have been demoted to any accountant I or auditor II vacancy at Medicaid and that he was entitled to back pay for the period of time that such a position was not offered to him. The Court of Civil Appeals of Alabama disagreed. If an employee's promotion has been in a state agency other than the one in which he held regular status, and there is no vacancy to which he may be demoted, his name shall be placed on the reemployment list for the class of the position in which he was a regular employee. **Where the promotion to the higher class is in another agency, the employee has no right of return to the lower class.** The employee was not entitled to the demotion to a vacant job within the lower classification. *State Personnel Board v. Wallace*, 682 So.2d 1357 (Ala. Civ. App. 1996).

♦ The West Virginia Division of Human Services promulgated job specifications for social workers. The specifications provided that level-one social workers perform entry-level professional social service work in program areas such as daycare, personal care homes, health care and other services at that level. A level-two social worker performed professional social service work in such program areas as nursing home placement, adult family care, pre-institutionalization, admission and aftercare. However, level-two social workers also provided "generic social services." The word "generic" was not defined, but five years later a level-three position description defined the term "generic" to mean social work in a variety of program areas such as daycare, foster care and protective services. **Several level one social workers initiated a grievance, contending that their classifications should be changed from level one to level two.** An administrative law judge held that they had been properly classified, but a circuit court reversed and ordered reclassification. The Supreme Court of Appeals of West Virginia agreed with the lower court that the social workers were entitled to reclassification. *Watts v. Dep't of Health & Human Resources*, 465 S.E.2d 887 (W.Va. 1995).

C. Privatization

Lawsuits often arise when public employers transfer civil service work to the private sector. Some challenges to privatization allege violation of the civil service laws and unfair labor practices.

♦ California's governor, faced with massive overcrowding in the state's prisons, sought legislation to rectify the problem, but the legislature rejected the measures. He then declared prison overcrowding a state emergency and, invoking the state's Emergency Services Act (ESA), **contracted with a private company to house California inmates out of state until new prisons could be built**. The corrections officers union filed suit to stop the outsourcing, and a trial court found the contracts unlawful. However, the Court of Appeal reversed. It noted that prison overcrowding was covered by the ESA even though prisons had been overcrowded for years. Also, the governor wasn't importing independent contractors; he was exporting prisoners due to the lack of prison facilities, which made it difficult for corrections officers to adequately perform their duties. The solution was only temporary, and it addressed the emergency facing the state. *California Correctional Peace Officers Ass'n v. Schwarzenegger*, 77 Cal.Rptr.3d 844 (Cal. Ct. App. 2008).

♦ A Washington appropriations bill directed the state department of social and health services (DSHS) to close a state-run program for mentally ill patients and contract those services out to the private sector. A union alleged that the law violated the state constitution's prohibition against impairment of contracts. It sued on behalf of an employee who was laid off. One provision directed the agency to phase out the voluntary residential treatment program and another directed the DSHS to establish a privately operated program at another site that provided involuntary treatment for both the mentally ill and chemically addicted. The court of appeals found that taken as a whole, the bill effectively transferred civil service work to the private sector and therefore **impaired the state from following through with its obligations under the collective bargaining agreement**. The legislation was unconstitutional, and the employee was entitled to get her job back. *Johanson v. Dep't of Social & Health Services*, 959 P.2d 1166 (Wash. Ct. App. 1998).

♦ The Vermont Police Academy's food service was staffed by civil servants employed under the State Employees Labor Relations Act and a collective bargaining agreement. For economic reasons, the academy laid off the civil servants and contracted their work out to a private company. Before the academy contracted with the company, it consulted the attorney general to see whether such a private contract was contrary to merit system principles. The Vermont State Employees' Association filed a complaint in a state trial court requesting that the employees' layoffs be declared illegal and an order restoring them to their former positions. The trial court dismissed the claim, and the union appealed to the Vermont Supreme Court.

The court's review focused on whether the attorney general abused his discretion in certifying that the private contract did not violate merit system principles. The court found that by privatizing the work, the academy would realize a significant cost savings and promote efficiency. The proposal also was endorsed by the legislature. The court found that the fundamental purpose of the merit system was to insulate public employees from political influence as well as to improve the effectiveness and efficiency of state government. It rejected the union's argument that cost savings was not an appropriate factor to consider in determining whether privatizing state work was within the spirit and intent of merit system principles because cost savings was not specifically listed as a considering factor. The responsibility of the attorney general was to determine whether the contract was contrary to the merit system, not whether it furthered the system. Finding that **the attorney general did not abuse his discretion in regard to the privatization of state jobs** and finding that there was no suggestion that privatization undermined the state merit system, the court affirmed the dismissal of the suit. *Vermont State Employees' Ass'n v. Vermont Criminal Justice Training Council*, 704 A.2d 769 (Vt. 1997).

♦ A Hawaii county privatized the construction and operation of a new landfill designed to replace an existing landfill operated by the county. The workers at the old landfill were given the option of relinquishing their civil service status and working for the new private landfill or being reassigned to other civil service positions. The actual work performed by the workers at the new landfill was virtually identical to the work performed at the old landfill, except for a minor change in the duties of equipment operators. The workers' union sued, claiming that the privatization of the landfill violated constitutionally mandated merit principles and civil service statutes. The case reached the Supreme Court of Hawaii, which applied the "nature of the services" test to determine that the protection of civil service laws extended to the landfill services that had been customarily and historically provided by civil servants. Under the test, **services that have been customarily provided by civil servants cannot be privatized** absent a showing that civil servants cannot provide those services. The landfill worker positions and actual work performed were essentially the same at the new landfill. Thus, the workers were performing a service that had been customarily and historically provided by civil servants, and merit principles under the state constitution and the civil service statutes applied. Privatization of the new landfill violated constitutionally mandated merit principles and civil service statutes. *Konno v. County of Hawaii*, 937 P.2d 397 (Haw. 1997).

♦ An Illinois city fire department did not have emergency medical technicians (EMTs) who were paramedics. When paramedic services were needed, city EMTs worked with paramedics from private ambulance companies. In their collective bargaining negotiations, the city and the firefighters' union were unable to agree upon an in-house paramedic program. The city decided to upgrade its emergency medical services to the paramedic level by contracting with a private company to provide such services. The union requested to bargain over the decision to contract out paramedic services, alleging that it was a mandatory subject of collective bargaining. When the city refused, the union filed an unfair labor charge with the state Labor Relations Board.

The board ordered the city to bargain with the union over its decision. The city appealed, and the Illinois Supreme Court held that the city only had a duty to engage in good-faith collective bargaining over issues that affected "wages, hours, and other conditions of employment." Here, **since private companies had historically provided paramedic services to the fire department, the city had not made a change in a previously established practice**. Also, the city's decision did not change the firefighters' employment conditions because there was no elimination of positions and no reduction in their wages or hours. Finally, the city's decision did not deprive firefighters of potential work or promotional opportunities because they had not performed such services in the past and were never qualified to do so. The city did not have to bargain with the union over the issue. *City of Belvidere v. Illinois State Labor Relations Board*, 692 N.E.2d 295 (Ill. 1998).

♦ The New York Department of Correctional Services implemented a program that grouped geographically close correctional facilities under one controlling administration. The provisions included civilianization of some correction officer positions and transfer of some supervisory positions to civilians. The correction officers, joined by other intervening parties, filed an improper labor practice charge against the department. An administrative law judge (ALJ) held that the transfer of supervisory responsibility violated the Civil Service Law, but that the civilianization of positions was not a violation. Several exceptions to the ALJ's decision were filed by the parties, leading to the New York Public Employment Relations Board (PERB) decision that **both the transfer of supervisory responsibilities and the civilianization of certain positions were violations**. The PERB ordered the positions to be reestablished and required reinstatement with back pay. The department challenged the PERB's decision and order, and the PERB asked for an enforcement order in the Supreme Court, Appellate Division.

The appellate division, limited to determining whether the PERB's decision was supported by substantial evidence, referred to a previous decision by the PERB regarding a transfer of unit work. The court outlined the analysis as requiring threshold inquiries to determine whether: 1) the work was performed exclusively by unit employees, and 2) the reassigned tasks were substantially similar. Affirmative answers to these inquiries would result in a violation unless the job qualifications for the positions changed significantly. A significant change in job qualifications would result in a balancing test of the interests of the public employer and unit employees. The court found that the transfer of the supervisory responsibilities and the civilianization of the positions amounted to a violation and were improper employer practices. *State of New York v. Kinsella*, 642 N.Y.S.2d 720 (N.Y. App. Div. 1996).

♦ The Alaska Department of Transportation responded to declining state revenues by adopting a privatization plan designed to cut costs. The department awarded a one-year airport maintenance contract to the lowest bidding private firm. As a result, several rural airport positions were eliminated. One employee who worked under a contract between the state and the local public employees union challenged his discharge in state court, alleging that the merit principle set forth in the Alaska Constitution precluded the privatization plan. The trial court granted pretrial judgment to the department, and the employee appealed. The Supreme Court of Alaska noted that the main reason for the merit principle was to ensure that employees were hired and retained on the basis of their merits rather than on their politics. A secondary purpose was to establish qualifications and conditions of employment. Agencies are given broad discretion to eliminate positions for economic reasons. The employee argued that privatization violated public policy by allowing the state to avoid employment costs that it should properly bear. The supreme court disagreed, ruling that **the relatively slight danger to the merit system did not justify the absolute constitutional proscription of all privatizations**. The social costs of privatization were best dealt with on a case-by-case basis. Thus, the Alaska Constitution did not categorically bar privatization of state jobs for economic reasons. *Moore v. State, Dep't of Transportation*, 875 P.2d 765 (Alaska 1994).

D. Nepotism

♦ An Ohio housing authority employee was promoted to an at-will supervisory position and given an employment manual that expressly disclaimed it created any contractual rights. The manual also provided for a pre-disciplinary conference, written notice of charges and an opportunity to be heard before termination. She was fired shortly after she questioned a purchase order signed by the director's brother, whom she believed did not have the authority to sign such orders. She sued, claiming due process violations and asserting that the termination violated Ohio's public policy against nepotism. A federal court found no constitutional violation because the manual did not alter the at-will nature of her employment. As for the nepotism claim, **she never invoked the anti-nepotism policy when she questioned the purchase order; she only questioned the brother's authority to sign it**. The court ruled for the housing authority. *George v. Fairfield Metropolitan Housing Authority*, 2008 WL 3008663 (S.D. Ohio 8/1/08).

♦ A communications technician for an Oregon county became romantically involved with a male co-worker who belonged to a different union. Later, the co-worker's position was reclassified and he joined the technician's union. They started living together and decided to get married. When they asked for time off for their honeymoon, their supervisor checked with his superiors to determine **whether they were violating the county's nepotism policy, which** prohibited an employee from supervising or reviewing the duties of a spouse. The county also had an unwritten policy prohibiting lead workers from working in the same department as people they supervised. After the county fired the technician, she sued under 42 U.S.C. § 1983, alleging a violation of her privacy and associational rights. She sought pretrial judgment, but a federal court found issues of fact that required a trial. There was a question as to whether the co-worker had supervisory duties with respect to the technician, and whether the county acted prematurely in firing the technician while she was unmarried. Further, the county's interests in avoiding the appearance of impropriety and favoritism seemed to be legitimate, and the nepotism policy seemed to be rationally related to those interests. *Gouveia v. Sears*, 2006 WL 2882826 (D. Or. 10/6/06).

♦ A Kansas county corrections department hired a black applicant for a position. During the interview, the applicant stated that his daughter also worked for the department in a different facility. Two supervisors approved the hire despite the county's anti-nepotism policy. However, when the department's director learned that the hiring violated the anti-nepotism policy, he fired the employee while he was still on probationary status and hired another black applicant. The fired employee sued for discrimination and lost. The Tenth Circuit held that **the anti-nepotism policy was a legitimate non-discriminatory reason for the firing**. Also, the county could grandfather in spouses hired before the anti-nepotism policy took effect, and it could allow siblings who had gained permanent status to remain on the job, as well as spouses who worked in different programs from each other. *Anderson v. Sedgwick County*, 150 Fed.Appx. 754 (10th Cir. 2005).

♦ The daughter of a Cape Cod town selectman applied for a seasonal police officer (SPO) position for the upcoming summer. Unlike permanent officers, SPOs were not subject to the state civil service process. To avoid the appearance of hiring improprieties, the town followed an unwritten anti-nepotism policy, whereby children of permanent police officers, town selectmen and the town administrator's staff were deemed ineligible for the SPO positions. When the administrator rejected her application, she sued, claiming gender and ancestry discrimination. A Massachusetts federal court granted the town pretrial judgment. **The town's anti-nepotism policy provided a legitimate non-discriminatory reason for denying her application.** Even if the policy was inconsistently applied, as shown by evidence that the children of other town employees, including a school employee's daughter, were selected, that still did not prove the policy was a pretext for illegal discrimination. *Roche v. Town of Wareham*, 24 F.Supp.2d 146 (D. Mass. 1998).

♦ A Minnesota firefighter applicant earned the highest written examination score and was ranked first on the employment eligibility list. He was passed over twice and was never offered a job. He eventually learned that the fire department had hired four firefighters, three of whom were related to either present or former fire department employees. He sued, claiming that the fire department had discriminated against him in violation of the Equal Protection

Clause of the U.S. Constitution because he was not related to any past or present employees. The district court granted pretrial judgment to the city, but the Eighth Circuit reversed and remanded, finding that the U.S. Supreme Court in *Kotch v. Board of River Port Pilot Commissioners*, 330 U.S. 552 (1947), **required nepotism in hiring to have a rational basis**. Specifically, there must be some measure of justification connecting the challenged hiring criterion to the capacity of the applicant to perform the duties of the job. In *Kotch*, the Court upheld nepotism in hiring river pilots, finding that river pilotage was a unique institution and that communities populated by relatives and friends from which new pilots were appointed provided an opportunity to acquire special knowledge of the locality and ambition to become pilots. Here, the record contained nothing about the culture of firefighting and the firefighters, or the unique requirements, if any, of the job. The lower court's decision was reversed, and the case was remanded. *Backlund v. Hessen*, 104 F.3d 1031 (8th Cir. 1997).

• A New York mail clerk/messenger for a public bus service corporation was promoted several times and ranked third on a list of nine candidates considered for two foreman positions. The corporation promoted the fifth-and seventh-ranked candidates and indicated that promotion of the mail clerk would violate the anti-nepotism policy because both his father and uncle worked as foremen at the corporation. However, **the job listings and application forms did not warn or disclose the existence of an anti-nepotism policy**, and the mail clerk was never advised before or during the application process that he was ineligible. The corporation's approved policy/instructions did not mention any anti-nepotism policy; in fact, the corporation first distributed a memorandum on nepotism after the mail clerk was rejected, which stated that the policy would apply prospectively. Finally, several people previously were hired for positions where they were either supervised by or working in the same department as family members. The mail clerk sued the corporation, seeking an order directing the corporation to appoint him to the foreman position with back pay and benefits. The New York Supreme Court, Appellate Division, found that the decision to deny the mail clerk's promotion on the basis of the unsubstantiated anti-nepotism policy of the corporation was arbitrary and capricious. *Gabriele v. Metropolitan Suburban Bus Authority*, 657 N.Y.S.2d 761 (N.Y. App. Div. 1997).

II. RESIDENCY REQUIREMENTS

Many public entities maintain residency requirements for their employees. To survive constitutional challenges as a violation of employee equal protection rights, residency requirements must be reasonably related to the public employer's stated purpose. Legitimate public interests in imposing residency requirements include shorter emergency response time, loyalty to the community and support for the local tax base.

• A New Jersey sergeant, who had recently moved out of a borough, sought a promotion to the position of lieutenant. After the first two phases of the promotional process, he was ranked slightly ahead of another sergeant.

However, after the final stage (the oral interview), he was rated below the other officer and was not promoted. **His union challenged the borough's decision, asserting that the real reason was his non-residency.** An arbitrator and appellate court agreed, noting that the borough failed to offer evidence as to why the leading candidate, who also had more seniority and education, suddenly dropped below the second-ranked candidate. And testimony from borough witnesses that it must have been the sergeant's move out of the borough that caused him to drop in the rankings was properly considered to be the real reason. This was an inappropriate factor. However, the New Jersey Supreme Court held that the sergeant was not yet entitled to the promotion because not all phases of the promotion procedure had been completed. The court remanded the case for further proceedings. *Borough of Glassboro v. Fraternal Order of Police, Lodge No. 108*, --- A.2d ---, 2008 WL 5103187 (N.J. 2008).

◆ The city of Cleveland had a residency rule that did not explain when a waiver could be granted. Three firefighters sought waivers of the rule. When their requests were denied, they sued the city for violating the Equal Protection Clause and their constitutional right to travel. They also claimed that the rule was unconstitutionally vague. An Ohio federal court and the U.S. Court of Appeals, Sixth Circuit, ruled against them. Their right-to-travel claim failed because **the firefighters did not have a constitutional right to be employed by Cleveland while living elsewhere**. Also, there was no Equal Protection Clause violation because the city could enforce the residency requirement against public safety officers, while choosing not to enforce it against other workers. The rule was not unconstitutionally vague because it gave the city council the flexibility it needed to deal with unforeseen but meritorious requests. *Ass'n of Cleveland Firefighters v. City of Cleveland, Ohio*, 502 F.3d 545 (6th Cir. 2007).

◆ A Michigan police officer applied for a job with another city and was informed that he was likely to obtain a position if he met the residency requirements and passed the physical and psychological exams. He bought property that he determined was within the 20-mile limit. However, the police chief informed him that his new home was 23 road miles from the city limits. Thus, he would not be offered the job. He sued and the case reached the Michigan Supreme Court, which held that **the state statute restricting governmental entities from imposing residency requirements as a condition of employment allowed governmental employers to require employees to live within 20 miles**. This meant 20 miles as the crow flies, not via roads. Because the city's residency requirement obligated employees to reside within 15 radial miles or 20 road miles, it violated the state statute. Finally, the court held that the police officer could not sue for money damages under the statute. *Lash v. City of Traverse City*, 479 Mich. 180, 735 N.W.2d 628 (Mich. 2007).

◆ A Rhode Island city had a residency requirement applicable to all city and school board employees, but it did not enforce the requirement for substitute teachers. When a substitute teacher who lived in another town became a full-time teacher, the school board refused to renew his contract for the following year. The teacher and his union sued the city and school board for reinstatement, claiming that other teachers who did not meet the residency requirement had not been terminated. The case reached the Supreme Court of Rhode Island, which noted that although **the city had inadvertently allowed four other nonresident teachers to remain employed**, it did not violate the Equal Protection Clause by singling out the teacher. The inconsistent treatment was due to disorganized files and poor record-keeping, and therefore it was not unconstitutional. *Providence Teachers' Union, Local 958 v. City of Council of City of Providence*, 888 A.2d 948 (R.I. 2005).

• A number of Scranton, Pennsylvania, police officers sued the city to challenge its residency requirement. A court upheld the constitutionality of the requirement. The city then conducted an investigation into residences of its employees and fired only five people, including three who had been involved in the earlier lawsuit. Those three sued the city under 42 U.S.C. § 1983, claiming retaliation for exercising their First Amendment right to petition the government. A federal court granted pretrial judgment to the city, but the Third Circuit reversed. Here, there were factual questions as to **whether the city knew other employees were in violation of the residency requirement and yet allowed them to remain on the job**. Also, the city's investigatory process was flawed, and no employee was ever disciplined for violating the requirement before the first lawsuit ended. *Hill v. City of Scranton*, 411 F.3d 118 (3d Cir. 2005).

• An Illinois city had a residency requirement for its employees. It hired a parks and recreation mechanic who lived outside the city limits and gave him a year to comply with the residency requirement. When he could not get the price he wanted for his house, his wife continued to live there, and he stayed in the city with his aunt two days a week. City managers knew about this arrangement for 20 years but did nothing about it. After a new parks and rec director learned about the two residences, he obtained the city council's authorization and fired the mechanic. The mechanic sued under the Age Discrimination in Employment Act, claiming he was technically in compliance with the residency requirement and that the real reason for the termination was age discrimination, but the Seventh Circuit ruled against him. **It did not matter whether his living arrangement violated the residency requirement.** What mattered was that the city council believed it did. Thus, there was no age discrimination, and the mechanic was properly fired. *Gusewelle v. City of Wood River*, 374 F.3d 569 (7th Cir. 2004).

• An Ohio city had a residency requirement in place until 1995, at which time it allowed nonresidents to obtain employment with the city if, within 18 months of being hired, they moved to within 15 miles of the city's borders. One of the reasons it eliminated the residency requirement was because of a lawsuit filed by the National Association for the Advancement of Colored People alleging that the city had kept the requirement to avoid hiring blacks. A federal court dismissed the lawsuit, but the Sixth Circuit reversed, finding that there were issues of fact regarding whether the city was continuing to enforce the requirement. **As late as 1997, the city still was asking job applicants how** long they had resided in the city. Further, its practice of hiring through word-of-mouth advertising and posting openings in city buildings had a tendency to perpetuate the all-white composition of the work force. The court remanded the case for further proceedings. *Cleveland Branch, NAACP v. City of Parma*, 263 F.3d 513 (6th Cir. 2001).

♦ A Milwaukee firefighter lived with his family within the city boundaries until he built a home in another town. At that point, he rented an apartment in the city while his wife and children moved to the new home. He also moved a family business, which had been operated out of the Milwaukee home, to the new home outside the city limits. When a tip was received regarding the possibility that he might be violating the city's residency requirements, an investigation was conducted. The Fire and Police Commission used **a nine-factor guideline to determine that the firefighter's actual or "bona fide" residence was in the home he owned outside the city.** Included in the factors against him were: 1) his wife and children lived outside the city, 2) most of his personal items were located outside the city, 3) his home-based business was located outside the city, and 4) he was only renting the apartment inside the city limits. The Wisconsin Court of Appeals upheld the firefighter's discharge for violating the residency requirement. The nine-factor guideline was an appropriate method for determining residency. *Golembiewski v. City of Milwaukee*, 605 N.W.2d 663 (Wis. Ct. App. 1999).

♦ A Missouri man was hired by Kansas City as a carpenter. He resided in the city but eventually purchased a home in a suburb, where his wife and son moved. When the city investigated his residency, he represented that he continued to live in the city at his parents' house and that he was in the process of getting a divorce. Four years later, the city again investigated his residency and found that he spent 90% of his time at the suburban address. The city fired him for violating its residency requirement, and he filed for unemployment compensation. The issue of his eligibility for unemployment compensation eventually reached the Missouri Court of Appeals, which held that the carpenter had committed misconduct connected with his work so as to disqualify him from receiving unemployment benefits. Here, **the carpenter knew he was required to reside within the city** and went to great lengths to persuade the city that he was doing so. This was work-related misconduct. *City of Kansas City v. Arthur*, 998 S.W.2d 870 (Mo. Ct. App. 1999).

♦ A North Carolina city adopted an ordinance requiring city employees to live within the county. An administrative personnel policy was later promulgated, giving the city manager additional authority to grant extensions or waivers of the residency requirement in cases of extreme hardship. A county resident became employed by the city as a police officer and subsequently moved his residence to another county. The chief of police advised him that he would be fired if he did not move into the county. The officer sued the city, seeking a judgment declaring the city ordinance and administrative policy unconstitutional. The case reached the Court of Appeals of North Carolina, which held that the city ordinance and administrative policy violated the officer's right to equal protection under both the U.S. and North Carolina Constitutions. **The residency requirement did not bear a rational relationship to a legitimate state purpose** because the requirement forced city employees to reside not within the city but within the county. Further, the residency requirement did not ensure rapid emergency assistance. Finally, the administrative policy was unconstitutional on its face because it granted the city manager unlimited discretion in approving or disapproving requests for exemption from the residency requirement without any objective standards or criteria. *Lewis v. City of Kinston*, 488 S.E.2d 274 (N.C. Ct. App. 1997).

* A New York city had a residency requirement for all of its employees. The city conferred upon its own municipal civil service commission jurisdiction to enforce the residency requirement. However, the city also had a collective bargaining agreement (CBA) with the employees' union, which limited discharge procedures. Despite the CBA, the commission held hearings and terminated union city employees who had violated the residency requirement. The union sued the city in a state trial court, seeking a declaratory judgment that the commission did not have jurisdiction to terminate any union city employee without following the procedures of the CBA. The trial court disagreed and held that the commission had jurisdiction to remove union city employees who violated the residency requirements. The union appealed to the New York Supreme Court, Appellate Division. Because it was the commission, not the city, that discharged the employees, the court held that the commission, an independent body that was not a party to the CBA, was not bound by the bargaining agreement's terms. Finding that **the commission had the authority to direct the termination of a union employee for violations of the residency requirements**, the lower court's judgment was affirmed. *De Franks v. City of Buffalo*, 670 N.Y.S.2d 282 (N.Y. App. Div. 1998).

III. VETERANS' RIGHTS AND PREFERENCES

The Uniformed Services Employment and Reemployment Rights Act (USERRA) grants veterans certain rights because of their military service. The rights include reemployment after military service and hiring preferences. Some state and local laws also allow for veterans preferences.

* A Tennessee police officer and longtime member of the Army Reserves was sent to Kuwait in 2004. A few months later, he resigned from active duty to avoid a court martial for giving alcohol to an enlisted soldier. He then sought his patrol job back, but the police department had an extensive return-to-work process for all officers who are gone for an extended time. He was required to fill out a personal history form and take a voice-stress test. The department believed he showed deception but eventually cleared him, placing him in a desk job while it investigated. He sued under the USERRA, and the Sixth Circuit ruled in his favor. The county violated Sections 4312 and 4313 by forcing him to undergo a return-to-work evaluation and by delaying his reinstatement. **He met USERRA's requirements for reinstatement**, including: 1) giving timely

notice of his need for military leave, 2) spending less than five years on leave, 3) requesting reinstatement in a timely fashion, 4) being honorably discharged, and 5) providing proper documentation. As a result, he should have been reinstated to his job or one with similar pay, seniority and status within two weeks of his request. *Petty v. Metropolitan Government of Nashville-Davidson County*, 538 F.3d 431 (6th Cir. 2008).

♦   A San Diego police officer also served as a Naval Reservist. After his deployments abroad in Bosnia and Operation Desert Storm, he was disciplined for alleged misconduct that his supervisor never verified. He was also given a negative evaluation for the first time in 23 years after returning from active duty in 1998. **His supervisor even recommended his termination after he took his third tour of duty.** Even though he was not fired, he was suspended, transferred and then placed on a 90-day probation by his old supervisor, who no longer had direct command over him. He resigned and sued under USERRA. A jury awarded him $256,800, and the Ninth Circuit upheld the award. *Wallace v. City of San Diego*, 479 F.3d 616 (9th Cir. 2007).

♦   A Kentucky police officer also served as a reservist in the Marine Corps. He claimed that as soon as he started working for the county, his supervisors criticized him for being in the military and also singled him out for discipline while other officers engaged in similar conduct were not targeted. He resigned, then sued the county for subjecting him to a hostile work environment in violation of USERRA. A federal court held that **although USERRA does not specifically bar harassment, the officer could still bring his claim**. The right to be free of a hostile work environment is a benefit of employment. Although his claims might be difficult to prove, he was entitled to a jury trial. *Steenken v. Campbell County*, 2007 WL 837173 (N.D. Ky. 3/15/07).

♦   A disabled veteran worked for a Massachusetts agency as a level-one investigator until severe budget cuts forced his layoff, along with other level-one investigators. When the agency recalled some non-disabled, non-veteran level-one investigators who had previously been provisionally appointed to higher-level positions, he sued, claiming that the state had violated veterans' preference laws. The case reached the Supreme Judicial Court of Massachusetts, which clarified that provisionally promoted employees are in a higher title position for purposes of state personnel laws. Thus, the agency properly recalled the non-veteran investigators for the higher positions because **the disabled veteran had no entitlement to a promotion under the state's veterans' preference laws**. *Andrews v. Civil Service Comm'n*, 846 N.E.2d 1126 (Mass. 2006).

♦   San Antonio firefighters and emergency medical services (EMS) employees worked 168 hours every 21 days, thus earning nine hours of overtime each pay cycle. They were covered by a collective bargaining agreement that capped at 27 hours the number of overtime hours they could lose per year because of previously scheduled vacation leave. However, military leave, unlike vacation or other related leave, did not count toward the 27-hour cap. The bargaining agreement also provided that employees who were not working because of military leave "in excess of 15 days" in a calendar year would not be entitled to receive the "perfect attendance" bonus leave. In a discrimination lawsuit filed under the Uniformed Services Employment and Reemployment Rights Act (USERRA), a Texas federal court ruled against the city. Here, the fact that the policies existed allowed the firefighters and EMS employees to meet their burden of proving that their military status was a motivating factor in the decision to deny them benefits available to other employees. The Fifth Circuit Court of Appeals ruled in favor of the city on the first three claims. Under USERRA, **they were not entitled to preferential treatment compared to non-military employees** with respect to non-seniority rights and benefits. They were only entitled to equal treatment, which they received. However, they could pursue their final three claims because there were issues of fact as to whether non-military firefighters received those benefits when they did not. *Rogers v. City of San Antonio*, 392 F.3d 758 (5th Cir. 2005).

* Suppression firefighters in Indianapolis worked 24-hour shifts, while non-suppression firefighters work eight-hour shifts. Under Indiana law, public employees are granted up to 15 days of paid leave per year for military service. The fire department converted those 15 days into hours (using an eight-hour shift as a base) and provided 120 hours of paid leave to firefighters with military obligations. A number of suppression firefighters who also were military reservists or members of the National Guard **sued the city for discriminating against them in violation of USERRA**. They claimed that the city's policy forced them to alter their work schedules more often than non-suppression firefighters or be forced to take unpaid leave to fulfill their military obligations. They asked to have the city grant them 15 24-hour days of leave. A federal court ruled for the city, and the Seventh Circuit affirmed. Here, the rule did not discriminate against the suppression firefighters because of their membership in the armed services. Any disparity arose from their work schedules. As a result, there was no USERRA violation. *Miller v. City of Indianapolis*, 281 F.3d 648 (7th Cir. 2002).

* A Florida man employed by a county sheriff's department joined the United States Coast Guard Reserves and was ordered to report for special active duty training in support of Operation Desert Shield/Desert Storm. During the eight-day assignment with the Coast Guard, the man received his regular salary and full benefits from the sheriff's department. He then returned to the sheriff's department and continued his employment. Subsequently, he applied for the position of sergeant and was promoted without receiving a veteran's preference although he had requested it. Approximately two years later, he unsuccessfully applied for promotion to lieutenant and requested a veteran's preference. His request was denied. This time he filed a complaint with the Public Employees Relations Commission (PERC), which determined that he was not entitled to the preference when he applied for the lieutenant's position because the preference expired when he was previously promoted to sergeant. The sergeant appealed to the District Court of Appeal of Florida, Fifth District. The court agreed with the PERC, finding that the plain meaning of the statute clearly

provided that **the preference applied only to a veteran's first promotion after reinstatement or reemployment**. When the officer applied for the preference the first time and it was disallowed, his right to appeal was available then. Neither the denial of the preference nor his promotion without the preference entitled him to save or "bank" the preference for future promotions. *Keller v. PERC*, 691 So.2d 36 (Fla. Dist. Ct. App. 1997).

* An Illinois veteran applied for a position with the State Police and sought a veteran's preference. He received a category grade of "A" and was placed on an eligibility list. Although he was interviewed for the position, the state police hired a non-veteran who also had received a category grade of "A." The veteran contacted the state Civil Service Commission, contending that the failure to hire him violated the state administrative code. The code required that veteran eligibles in each category be preferred for appointment before non-veteran eligibles in the same category. The commission responded that the non-veteran's overall credentials were superior and that the administrative code had been interpreted to permit an agency to bypass a veteran when the qualifications of the eligible non-veteran were superior. The veteran challenged that decision, and the case reached the Supreme Court of Illinois.

The veteran asserted that the administrative code unambiguously mandated an absolute hiring preference for veterans in the same grade category as non-veterans. The supreme court agreed, finding that **the administrative code mandated an absolute hiring preference over non-veterans** because the term "preferred" mandated appointment. No value would exist in a preference for appointment that did not result in appointment over non-veterans in the same class. Organizing eligibility lists on the basis of category ratings requires that a veteran receive an offer for the job before non-veterans of the same grade category. The court noted, however, that if numerical eligibility lists were used (ranking the candidates), the employing agencies could consider the three highest applicants on the list for appointment. *Denton v. Civil Service Comm'n of the State of Illinois*, 679 N.E.2d 1234 (Ill. 1997).

* Several Pennsylvania applicants took the civil service examination for city firefighter positions. Pursuant to the state Veterans' Preference Act, the city awarded additional points to the grade scores of any applicant qualifying as a soldier under the act. After establishing the initial eligibility list, the city began to award preference points to applicants who had obtained honorable discharges after successfully completing only reserve training but who had not yet served their full reserve and/or national guard commitment. This was possible because the reservists were awarded honorable discharges after completing only the basic training part of their commitment. Several veterans who had completed their full service commitment sued in state court, alleging that the applicants who completed training but had not yet provided service did not qualify for the veteran's preference points.

The court ruled for the veterans, and the Commonwealth Court of Pennsylvania affirmed. **An honorable discharge after completing only reserve training did not equate to an honorable discharge from service** for purposes of the act. The act's definition of "soldier" requires that the individual fulfill his or her military service commitment and receive an honorable discharge from such service. *Sicuro v. City of Pittsburgh*, 684 A.2d 232 (Pa. Commw. Ct. 1996).

♦ A Texas assistant district attorney and reserve officer was called to active duty for Operation Desert Storm. During his absence, the staff discovered very explicit sexual materials throughout his office. When the reservist returned, the district attorney (DA) sought to terminate his employment because the DA believed the materials could subject his office to a Title VII hostile work environment lawsuit and a negative public image. The reservist refused to retire and was fired. He then filed suit alleging violation of the Veterans' Reemployment Rights Act (VRRA), seeking back pay as well as reinstatement. The district court entered judgment for the DA's office and awarded costs. The reservist appealed to the U.S. Court of Appeals, Fifth Circuit.

The court of appeals upheld the discharge, finding that the DA's office had sufficient cause to terminate the reservist at the time he left for active duty. It determined that **the VRRA does not require employers to reinstate an employee before terminating him or her for cause**. An employer can terminate a veteran or reservist for cause if the discharge satisfies two criteria of reasonableness. First, it must be reasonable to discharge the employee because of certain conduct, and second, the employee must have fair notice, express or fairly implied, that such conduct would be grounds for discharge. The reservist in this case met both criteria because he knew the receipt and collection of sexually explicit materials in the office was prohibited by his employer. *Jordan v. Jones*, 84 F.3d 729 (5th Cir. 1996).

♦ An honorably discharged veteran with a 10% physical impairment was employed by the U.S. Navy in an electrical shop. His impairment prevented him from performing any shipboard work. The veteran applied for a promotion, and was rated among the 15 "best qualified" candidates, but was not selected for the position. Three of the candidates who were promoted previously had held a higher rank, and the remaining promoted candidates had six and four years more experience, respectively. All of the candidates selected for the promotion had taken advantage of volunteer training opportunities that were available to all employees. The veteran had not enrolled in these courses. He filed Rehabilitation Act and Vietnam Era Veterans' Readjustment Assistance Act (VEVRA) claims against the Navy, alleging that he was not selected because the promotion system did not provide an alternative route for veteran employees with disabilities to advance or to obtain experience commensurate with shipboard experience which, he argued, was necessary to be promoted. At trial, two Navy employees testified that several promoted applicants had never worked on board a ship, that shipboard experience was not a paramount consideration, and that the inability to go on board ship did not prohibit attaining the necessary experience.

The U.S. District Court for the Eastern District of Virginia held that **the veteran's lack of training and experience were the predominant factors in the Navy's decision not to promote him**. The Navy had offered adequate opportunities for the veteran to acquire the skills necessary to receive the promotion. Even without considering shipboard experience, the successful candidates were more qualified then the veteran. It was not the lack of accommodation, but the veteran's own lack of experience and initiative to pursue voluntary training programs, that hindered his advancement. The district court dismissed the veteran's VEVRA and Rehabilitation Act claims. *Blizzard v. Dalton*, 905 F.Supp. 331 (E.D. Va. 1995).

♦ A New York village police chief allegedly cursed at an officer, who also was a U.S. Air Force reservist, and twice threatened to "get" him. The officer submitted his official written military orders, which stated that he was to report to a base on a designated day at 7:30 a.m. Because he was scheduled to work until 7:00 a.m. on his day of departure, he submitted a written request for military leave from that shift. The chief told him to either trade shifts with another officer or obtain another official written military order. He was unable to obtain another order and left work early. The chief fired him and he sued, alleging that he had been fired in violation of the Veterans' Reemployment Rights Act. The district court granted pretrial judgment to the village, but the Second Circuit reversed. Given the department's antipathy toward the officer's enforcement of his statutory rights under the act, **a jury could reasonably infer that the allegedly nondiscriminatory reasons for the denial of the leave request were pretextual**. For example, the same month the chief allegedly threatened the officer, he complained to a local official about the special treatment given to reservists and requested legislation to end what he called "double dipping in its most flagrant form." These and other statements established a *prima facie* case under the act and precluded pretrial judgment in favor of the department. However, the department's policy of not granting leave without the reservist's presentation of written orders did not violate the act. *Gummo v. Village of Depew, New York*, 75 F.3d 98 (2d Cir. 1996).

IV. EMPLOYER POLICIES AND RESTRICTIONS

Public employees work under laws specific to public employment, which restrict certain types of conduct such as secondary employment. For cases on ethics codes, refer to Chapter Two, Discipline, Suspension, and Termination. Additionally, public employees may be subject to restrictions often found in private employment, including marital restrictions and employment testing.

♦ The state of Indiana could make Good Friday a legal holiday for state employees, the U.S. Court of Appeals, Seventh Circuit, held. It agreed that **the state had a legitimate secular purpose for offering the holiday**: to provide a long spring weekend for its employees. An Indiana resident claimed the state violated the Establishment Clause, which prohibits the government from making laws respecting an establishment of religion. But like Hawaii and Kentucky, the Seventh Circuit said, "Indiana also justifies its Good Friday closing as accomplishing the secular purpose of providing a spring holiday." *Bridenbaugh v. O'Bannon*, 185 F.3d 796 (7th Cir. 1999).

A. Secondary Employment

Most public employers have established limitations on secondary employment, such as approval from superior officers. Violation of secondary employment restrictions may result in disciplinary action or termination.

♦ A Pittsburgh police officer formed a company to schedule police officers' secondary employment doing block parties, special events and traffic obstruction jobs. The chief then created a pilot program to govern secondary employment of that nature, requiring all such permit requests to go through an office in the department. The police officer sued, claiming that the policy was unconstitutional because it did not target all secondary employment, but only the kinds of work his company arranged. A federal court ruled against him, noting that **the chief could rationally decide to regulate only certain kinds of secondary employment** while leaving the more difficult and massive undertakings (like providing security at Steelers football games and nightclubs) outside the department's pilot program for the present. *Novak v. City of Pittsburgh*, No. 2:05-CV-00897, 2006 WL 3420959 (W.D. Pa. 11/27/06).

♦ Two Maryland park police officers formed a company to run a secondary business activity. This resulted in an investigation into **whether they were using their official positions and government property and resources to further conflicting private interests**. They resigned during the investigation. When the park and planning commission's general counsel sought to debar them from any procurement activity before the commission, they asserted that they were entitled to the protections of the Law Enforcement Officers Bill of Rights (LEOBR). The case reached the Court of Appeals of Maryland, which held that the LEOBR procedures did not apply to the commission's debarment proceedings because those proceedings were not punitive in nature. *Boyle v. Maryland-National Capital Park and Planning Comm'n*, 867 A.2d 1050 (Md. 2005).

♦ A Tennessee police officer who also owned a company that provided security services sued the county and the police department challenging **an order forbidding police officers from arranging for security employment for other metro police officers**. He claimed that the order violated his due process rights. A federal court and the Sixth Circuit ruled against him. Here, the mayor's order stated that the rule was needed to prevent interference with duties, conflict of interest, preferential treatment, the appearance of impropriety, the loss of independence and impartiality, and the loss of public confidence. These were rational reasons, thus making the order constitutional. *Jones v. Smith*, 74 Fed.Appx. 482 (6th Cir. 2003).

♦ Although Maryland law allows police officers to engage in off-duty employment, the law also **allows police departments to set rules regarding how off-duty employment will be handled**. Therefore, the Court of Special Appeals of Maryland held that no violation of law occurred when a county police chief required his officers to get his permission before engaging in such activity, and he was justified in disciplining two officers who failed to do so before selling T-shirts at a local concert. During the concert, the officers seized the T-shirts of an unauthorized vendor. The chief charged them with violating a department order that required them to secure his written approval before engaging in security-related secondary employment. The disciplinary hearing was put on hold after the officers and their union filed a lawsuit in state court seeking to have the order declared invalid. The court found that the order was issued in accordance with the county code, and the court of appeals affirmed. The code gave department heads the authority to issue rules regarding internal management without approval from the county council. The police chief clearly had the authority to issue the rule without first obtaining the council's approval, and he also was justified in disciplining the officers for disobeying the rule. *Howard County Police Officers Ass'n, Inc. v. Howard County*, 728 A.2d 795 (Md. Ct. Spec. App. 1999).

♦ A Maryland police officer worked a second job as a security officer without obtaining written permission from the chief of police and approval by the county ethics commission, as required by departmental rules. When his second job became known, the department initiated proceedings against him in accordance with the state Law Enforcement Officers Bill of Rights (LEOBR). After a hearing, the board found a violation and recommended a reprimand letter and a three-month suspension from engaging in secondary employment. The chief followed the recommendations and refused requests to reconsider or rescind the suspension. Pursuant to the LEOBR, the officer appealed to the circuit court, which affirmed the suspension.

The Court of Appeals of Maryland held that **the chief lacked the authority to prohibit officers from engaging in secondary employment**. Under the LEOBR, a law enforcement agency may not prohibit secondary employment but may promulgate reasonable regulations as to a law enforcement officer's secondary employment. In the instant case, no regulations mentioned the prohibition or suspension of the right to engage in secondary employment. The police department's function code, which expressly authorized the chief to cancel, temporarily or permanently, permission of any employee to engage in secondary employment, was neither properly adopted nor approved. The ethics commission regulations were properly adopted, but the regulations did not authorize the chief to prohibit secondary employment or suspend an officer as a sanction for violations. Thus, the chief lacked authorization for his actions. The circuit court's decision was reversed and remanded. *Fraternal Order of Police, Montgomery County Lodge No. 35 v. Mehrling*, 680 A.2d 1052 (Md. 1996).

♦ A North Carolina police officer held **a second job as a teacher of firearms safety**. The police department prohibited officers from holding secondary employment without first seeking the chief's permission. Because the officer did not do so, he was suspended. He sued the city in the U.S. District Court for the Eastern District of North Carolina under 42 U.S.C. § 1983, claiming violations of his First Amendment right to association, Second Amendment right to bear arms, due process and equal protection. After he sought to amend his complaint, the employer filed a motion for dismissal, which the district court granted. The officer appealed. The Fourth Circuit Court of Appeals held that the district court should not have dismissed the officer's Section 1983 claims alleging a violation of his First Amendment rights to free speech and freedom of association. Also, the court should have allowed the officer to amend his complaint. However, the other claims had been properly dismissed. *Edwards v. City of Goldsboro*, 178 F.3d 231 (4th Cir. 1999).

* An Atlanta police officer had a second job as a coordinator for an organization that trained clients to deal with stressful situations, such as being kidnapped, held hostage, imprisoned, or interrogated. In videotaped "training sessions," the officer was shown shocking a client with a stun gun, holding a client upside down in a urinal, and using racial slurs. After concluding that some clients participated in the "training sessions" for purposes of self-gratification, he quit this second job. Eventually, the police department obtained copies of the videotaped "training sessions." Despite the policy of progressive discipline, the police chief immediately fired him for violation of departmental work rules. After unsuccessfully appealing to the civil service board and a state trial court, he appealed to the Court of Appeals of Georgia. Even though the police department had a policy of progressive discipline, the court found that **it was proper to fire the officer immediately when his presence impaired the "effectiveness of others" by hurting the image of the police department**. The court also rejected his contention that he was fired without due process because he was afforded a hearing before the chief where he addressed evidentiary and job performance issues. The court agreed with the civil service board and found that his behavior was unsuitable for a police officer. The immediate firing of the officer was upheld. *Hanrahan v. City of Atlanta*, 495 S.E.2d 324 (Ga. Ct. App. 1997).

* A Louisiana fire chief was elected to the position of alderman while continuing to serve as the fire chief. As a result, he was one of the people responsible for appointing himself to the full-time fire chief position. Also, the fire department received partial funding from the city through a budget voted on by the board of aldermen. The mayor requested an opinion from the state attorney general regarding the propriety of the alderman's concurrent service in both positions. Although the opinion suggested that the alderman resign one of his positions, he ran for and won reelection. The attorney general sued to compel the alderman to resign one of his positions. The trial court denied relief. However, to remedy any conflicts of interest or ethical dilemmas, the court ordered the alderman to recuse himself from voting on matters regarding the fire department budget. The attorney general appealed to the Court of Appeal. **Louisiana law prohibits an elected official from simultaneously holding employment in the same political subdivision in which he holds elective office.** Here, because the position of fire chief was a full-time, appointed position, the concurrent holding of both offices in the same political subdivision clearly was prohibited. Further, since the board participated in the appointment of the fire chief and funded the fire department budget, this also violated the statute. The lower court's judgment was reversed, and the case was remanded to make the determination as to which office would be declared vacant. *Ieyoub v. Polito*, 712 So.2d 692 (La. Ct. App. 1998).

B. Employment Testing

Public employees also may be subject to testing requirements such as medical and psychological testing. For cases involving blood and drug testing, refer to Chapter Five.

♦ An Illinois corrections officer was suspended without pay for 120 days for insubordination because she refused to comply with a superior officer's order that she submit to a polygraph examination. She appealed the suspension, and the case reached the Appellate Court of Illinois. Although the officer was not entitled to the protections of the state's Uniform Peace Officers' Disciplinary Act because she was not a "peace officer," the Illinois Supreme Court ruling in *Kaske v. City of Rockford*, 450 N.E.2d 314 (Ill. 1983), provided an independent basis for challenging her administrative suspension. Polygraph evidence violates the requirement of a fair hearing because the examinations do not produce results that are more probative than prejudicial. And polygraph examinations are no more reliable when the subject is a corrections officer instead of a police officer. Thus, **the corrections officer could not be forced to submit to the polygraph or punished for refusing to submit to it.** *Kelley v. Sheriff's Merit Comm'n of Kane County*, 372 Ill.App.3d 931, 866 N.E.2d 702 (Ill. App. Ct. 2007).

♦ A military veteran applied for a job as a police officer and received a conditional offer of probationary employment. She underwent a medical examination. After conducting the exam, the city's doctor cited her medical history, including her military medical records (which diagnosed her with an incurable condition known as Raynaud's syndrome and restricted her activity) in deciding that she failed the qualifying medical examination. After the job offer was revoked, she brought an administrative challenge, asserting that she didn't in fact have the disease. The case reached the New York Supreme Court, Appellate Division, which held that **the city's doctor was entitled to rely on her medical history and records**. The decision to withdraw the offer of employment was not arbitrary or irrational. *Thomas v. Straub*, 818 N.Y.S.2d 90 (N.Y. App. Div. 2006).

♦ The chief of the New Jersey Transit Corporation issued an administrative order requiring all police officers to submit to annual medical examinations as well as blood and urine testing. Officers refusing to be tested could be suspended or fired. The officers' union sued to prevent the examinations, claiming they were unconstitutional. The Superior Court, Appellate Division, disagreed. **Public employers have the right to determine whether their police officers are fit to perform their jobs.** Also, even though the exam was a search, the officers had a diminished expectation of privacy because of the uniform, nondiscretionary nature of the exams. Further, the exams were permissible under a recognized exception to the warrant requirement for administrative searches of highly regulated industries. *New Jersey Transit PBA Local 304 v. New Jersey Transit Corp.*, 895 A.2d 472 (N.J. Super. Ct. App. Div. 2006).

♦ An Iowa City police department extended a conditional offer of employment to a reserve officer, subject to his satisfactory performance on medical and psychological examinations adopted pursuant to state statute. The results of the officer's psychological test indicated that he was not well-suited to serve in the position of police officer. The chief revoked the conditional offer of employment and also revoked his status as reserve police officer. The officer appealed the chief's action to the city Civil Service Commission, which upheld the discharge and expressly took action to remove the officer's name from the list of certified candidates. An Iowa trial court reversed, and the commission appealed.

The Supreme Court of Iowa noted that the screening process should include personal interviews, strength and agility tests, and other matters that fairly test the mental and physical ability of the applicant to perform police duties. Although a state statute expressly sanctioned post-employment medical examinations only, the court held that **the commission properly determined that the department also could delay psychological testing until a conditional offer of employment had been extended**. Even assuming that there had been a failure to follow statutory procedures applicable to psychological testing, the maximum relief that the commission could grant to a probationary employee such as the officer would be to order that his conditional appointment be reconsidered under altered procedures. Because the delayed psychological examination was proper, the district court ruling was reversed and the chief's decisions were reinstated. *Bahr v. Council Bluffs Civil Service Comm'n*, 542 N.W.2d 255 (Iowa 1996).

♦ The city of Los Angeles required applicants for sensitive law enforcement positions, including the anti-terrorist and narcotics divisions, to submit to a polygraph examination. Those who failed were allowed to retake the exam and meet with division commanders to discuss why the results were unfair and should be disregarded. The questions asked during the exam all related to the particular position for which the candidate applied and did not address personal matters. The Los Angeles Police Protective League sued the city in a California trial court, alleging that the polygraph requirement violated state constitutional and statutory provisions. It sought an order declaring the polygraph procedures illegal and an injunction prohibiting their further use. The trial court entered a preliminary injunction prohibiting further use of the polygraph tests, and the city appealed to the California Court of Appeal.

The state Public Safety Officers Procedural Bill of Rights Act provided that "no public safety officer shall be compelled to submit to a polygraph examination against his will." The act was primarily intended to address abuses connected with disciplinary investigations. Although prior case law had interpreted the act to prohibit polygraph testing as a condition of continued employment when employees were under investigation for suspected criminal activity, the court held that the present case lacked the requisite government compulsion. **Officers voluntarily applied for the transfers with full knowledge of the polygraph requirement.** Because the city did not coerce applicants to apply for the transfers, the constitution did not require that the polygraph test be justified by a compelling government interest. However, the city's interest in hiring the most dependable, incorruptible, and finest individuals was sufficiently compelling even under this heightened standard. The polygraph requirement was upheld. *Los Angeles Police Protective League v. City of Los Angeles*, 42 Cal. Rptr. 2d 23 (Cal. Ct. App. 1995).

♦ Members of specialized drug enforcement units within the Baltimore City Police Department were required to submit to a routine polygraph examination. As a result of these examinations, several officers were reassigned from the drug enforcement unit into other units within the department. Some of these officers submitted to voluntary urinalysis drug tests, which indicated no drug use. Their requests to retake the polygraph examination were denied. The officers sued, alleging that the department had violated their rights to an administrative hearing guaranteed under the state Law Enforcement Officers' Bill of Rights (LEOBR). The court granted the department's motion for pretrial judgment, and the officers appealed. The Court of Special Appeals of Maryland noted that the department had properly administered the polygraph examinations as a means to evaluate the competency of the drug enforcement officers, using established departmental procedures that were applied consistently to all officers in those units. **The polygraph examinations were not investigations or interrogations sufficient to trigger the protections of the LEOBR.** Because the officers' reassignments were neither punitive in nature nor intended to punish them for specific acts of misconduct, the due process protections of the LEOBR were not implicated. The circuit court's ruling was affirmed. *Calhoun v. Commissioner of Baltimore Police*, 654 A.2d 905 (Md. Ct. Spec. App. 1995).

C. Legal Fees Reimbursement

In some states and localities, a public employee may be reimbursed for legal fees spent in defense of actions taken by the employee within the scope of his or her employment.

♦ A Michigan police officer was certified to inspect "salvage vehicles." When he conducted inspections in the city, he gave the $25 fee to the city. But when he conducted inspections outside the city, he kept the fee. After conducting two inspections outside the city, he verified that certain repairs had been made and that the vehicles were roadworthy. In fact, he was wrong. He was charged with false certification, a felony, and fired. However, a jury acquitted him. He then sought reimbursement of $205,000 in attorneys' fees. **The city council denied reimbursement because his actions had not been for any public purpose of the city.** When he sued, the case reached the Supreme Court of Michigan, which held that the discretionary decision of the city council was not reviewable by a court. The officer was not entitled to reimbursement. *Warda v. City Council of City of Flushing*, 696 N.W.2d 671 (Mich. 2005).

♦ Two Florida police officers were charged with felony battery and official misconduct, but were acquitted. They applied to the city for the fees and costs of defending themselves. The city commission denied their payment requests, and they then submitted their applications to a court pursuant to state statute. The city sought a ruling that the court did not have jurisdiction over it because it had not been properly served, but the Florida District Court of Appeal ruled against the city. Under the statute, **the officers did not have to provide service of process when they applied to the court for their fees**. The court refused to dismiss the case against the city. *City of Sweetwater Florida v. St. Germain*, 943 So.2d 259 (Fla. Dist. Ct. App. 2006).

♦ A New York man allegedly assaulted by a police officer sued the officer and city. The city initially defended both the officer and itself, but later determined a potential conflict of interest existed and advised the officer he would have to be represented by separate counsel. It agreed to reimburse the officer for his reasonable attorneys' fees provided he chose one of three attorneys from a list provided to him by the city. He rejected the attorneys on the list and retained another attorney. In a pretrial conference, the attorney raised the issue of who would pay for the officer's representation. The magistrate judge found that the officer was entitled to the attorney of his choice; however, the city was entitled to limit the choice of attorneys for which they would reimburse him. The officer appealed to a New York federal court, which affirmed. Municipal law required indemnification of police officers for attorneys' fees incurred in defending negligence and tort actions arising out of the officers' official acts; however, **the municipality did not have to allow the officer to select counsel of his choosing even if a potential conflict of interest existed**. Also, the state statute requiring the city to reimburse officers for counsel of their choosing had not been adopted by local law and therefore did not create any rights in favor of the officer. *Mothersell v. City of Syracuse, New York*, 952 F.Supp. 112 (N.D.N.Y. 1997).

♦ Former Illinois city commissioners and corporate counsel were found guilty of official misconduct and conflict of interest charges. They filed suit in state court against the city pursuant to a city ordinance granting indemnification for any criminal action or proceeding seeking reimbursement of attorneys' fees and litigation expenses incurred in defense of the charges. The city filed a motion to dismiss, which was granted. The appellate court reversed, and the city appealed to the Supreme Court of Illinois. The supreme court reversed, holding that **the city had neither the duty nor the authority to reimburse plaintiffs for legal fees incurred in the unsuccessful defense of criminal official misconduct and conflict of interest charges**. Although public entities may indemnify their employees in certain situations, the expenditure of public funds must be for a public purpose. Because an unsuccessful criminal defense of a public official for conduct outside his lawful duties constitutes purely private litigation, absorbing the costs cannot be considered a proper public purpose. As a result, plaintiffs such as the former commissioners and corporate counsel in this case were not eligible to recover the expenses of the unsuccessful criminal defense. *Wright v. City of Danville, Illinois*, 675 N.E.2d 110 (Ill. 1996).

D. Marital Restrictions

• An applicant for a probation officer position was married to a former inmate. At her interview, she stated that she resigned from her previous position at a correctional facility on bad terms, but did not mention who her husband was. After a judge offered her the job, he learned she was married to a former inmate and requested more information about the circumstances surrounding her departure from the job. Upon examining the information, he withdrew the offer of employment. She sued, claiming that he violated her First Amendment right to intimate association. A Michigan federal court ruled against her, noting that **it was not an undue intrusion into her marital relationship for the judge to withdraw the employment offer after learning she was married to a former inmate**. Further, the judge provided other legitimate reasons for withdrawing the offer, including whether she made a full disclosure of the circumstances surrounding her resignation from her previous job. *Clark v. Alston*, 442 F.Supp.2d 395 (E.D. Mich. 2006).

• A black correctional employee became involved with a convicted murderer after the convicted murderer left her supervision and transferred to another facility. She later married him without informing her superiors. When they discovered the marriage, they **fired her for violating the county's anti-fraternization policies**. She challenged the discharge, alleging race discrimination and asserting that the firing was based on her marital status in violation of state law. The case reached the Eleventh Circuit, which upheld the ruling against her. She failed to show that she was similarly situated to any other correctional officers who were not fired after having relationships with inmates. Also, the county fired her for violating that policy, not because of her marital status. *Burke-Fowler v. Orange County, Florida*, 447 F.3d 1319 (11th Cir. 2006).

• A former deputy district attorney in Orange County claimed that she had received unfavorable assignments as a result of dating and then marrying a high-level management attorney in the office. She also asserted that she was denied promotions because of her marital status, her race and her gender. In her lawsuit against the county, she stated that because her husband was not in the good graces of the then-district attorney, she did not receive any plum assignments. The California Court of Appeal ruled that **the origin of any animus was the political disfavor her husband was in at the time, not her marital status**. Further, there was no antipathy toward her being married to a co-worker. It was only because she was involved with one particular co-worker that any adverse action was taken against her. This was not discrimination on the basis of marital status. *Chen v. County of Orange*, 116 Cal.Rptr.2d 786 (Cal. Ct. App. 2002).

• A married couple employed as police officers by the state of Illinois was informed that an unwritten policy prohibited them from working on the same shift in the same patrol area. They could remain in the same patrol area but on different shifts. Alternatively, one of them could transfer to another county patrol area but work the same hours with the same days off. The couple filed charges with the Department of Human Rights, alleging unlawful discrimination based on marital status. An administrative law judge sustained the charges and recommended an award of damages and attorneys' fees. The state Human Rights Commission held that marital status discrimination under the Illinois Human Rights Act included policies restricting married couples. However, it held that no unlawful discrimination had occurred. The case reached the Supreme Court of Illinois, which affirmed, holding that the statutory definition of marital status discrimination did not encompass employment policies based on the identity of one's spouse. As defined under the act, prohibited marital status discrimination included discrimination based on an individual's "legal status" as married, single, separated, divorced, or widowed. **A policy prohibiting spouses from working together presented an entirely different kind of harm than discrimination based on an individual's legal status.** *Boaden v. Dep't of Law Enforcement*, 664 N.E.2d 61 (Ill. 1996).

♦ A male captain and a female sergeant discussed their marriage plans with a Georgia city chief of police. The chief informed them that a city ordinance prohibited relatives of city employees in supervisory positions from working in the same department. If the two married, the less senior member would have to leave the department. The couple postponed their marriage and filed a lawsuit in a U.S. district court, alleging that the city's anti-nepotism policy violated the First Amendment as well as the Due Process and Equal Protection Clauses of the Fourteenth Amendment. The district court ruled that the policy was not a direct restraint on marriage and held for the city. The officers appealed to the Eleventh Circuit, which noted that the right to marry is a constitutionally protected fundamental right. However, reasonable regulations that do not significantly interfere with decisions to enter into marriage do not violate the Due Process Clause. Because the anti-nepotism policy did not absolutely prevent a class of people from marrying, it would be valid if rationally related to a legitimate government interest. Here, several legitimate interests, including the reduction of favoritism, the prevention of family conflicts and decreasing the likelihood of sexual harassment, justified the anti-nepotism policy. **The policy did not "order" individuals not to marry and did not prevent the less senior spouse from working in another department** or outside the municipal government. Consequently, it was valid under both the First Amendment and the Due Process Clause. Even if the policy had a disparate impact on females, the equal protection claim failed for lack of a showing of discriminatory intent. The holding of the district court was affirmed. *Parks v. City of Warner Robins, Georgia*, 43 F.3d 609 (11th Cir. 1995).

APPENDIX A

UNITED STATES CONSTITUTION

[Relevant provisions with respect to employment law]

ARTICLE I

Section 1. All legislative Powers herein granted shall be vested in a Congress of the United States, which shall consist of a Senate and House of Representatives.

* * *

Section 8. The Congress shall have Power To lay and collect Taxes, Duties, Imposts and Excises, to pay the Debts and provide for the common Defence and general Welfare of the United States; but all Duties, Imposts and Excises shall be uniform throughout the United States;

To borrow money on the credit of the United States;

To regulate Commerce with foreign Nations, and among the several States, and with the Indian Tribes;

To establish an uniform Rule of Naturalization, and uniform Laws on the subject of Bankruptcies throughout the United States;

* * *

To promote the Progress of Science and useful Arts, by securing for limited Times to Authors and Inventors the exclusive Right to their respective Writings and Discoveries;

* * *

To make all Laws which shall be necessary and proper for carrying into Execution for the foregoing Powers, and all other Powers vested by this Constitution in the Government of the United States, or in any Department or Officer thereof.

* * *

Section 9.

* * *

No Bill of Attainder or ex post facto Law shall be passed.

* * *

Section 10. No State shall ... pass any Bill of Attainder, ex post facto Law, or Law impairing the Obligation of Contracts, or grant any Title of Nobility.

ARTICLE II

Section 1. The executive Power shall be vested in a President of the United States of America.

* * *

ARTICLE III

Section 1. The judicial Power of the United States, shall be vested in one supreme Court, and in such inferior Courts as the Congress may from time to time ordain and establish. The Judges, both of the supreme and inferior courts, shall hold their Offices during good Behaviour, and shall, at stated Times, receive for their Services a Compensation, which shall not be diminished during their Continuance in Office.

Section 2. The judicial Power shall extend to all Cases, in Law and Equity, arising under this Constitution, the Laws of the United States, and Treaties made, or which shall be made, under their Authority; - to all Cases affecting Ambassadors, other public Ministers and Consuls; - to all Cases of admiralty and maritime Jurisdiction, - to Controversies to which the United States shall be a party; - to Controversies between two or more States; - between a State and Citizens of another State; - between Citizens of different States; - between Citizens of the same State claiming Lands under the Grants of different States, and between a State, or the Citizens thereof, and foreign States, Citizens or Subjects.

* * *

ARTICLE IV

Section 1. Full Faith and Credit shall be given in each State to the public Acts, Records and judicial Proceedings of every other State.

* * *

Section 2. The Citizens of each State shall be entitled to all Privileges and Immunities of Citizens in the several States.

* * *

Section 4. The United States shall guarantee to every State in this Union a Republican Form of Government, and shall protect each of them against

Invasion; and on Application of the Legislature, or of the Executive (when the Legislature cannot be convened) against domestic Violence.

ARTICLE V

The Congress, whenever two thirds of both Houses shall deem it necessary, shall propose Amendments to this Constitution, or, on the Application of the Legislatures of two thirds of the several States, shall call a Convention for proposing Amendments, which, in either Case, shall be valid to all Intents and Purposes, as part of this Constitution, when ratified by the Legislatures of three fourths of the several States, or by Conventions in three fourths thereof, as the one or the other Mode of Ratification may be proposed by the Congress; Provided that no Amendment which may be made prior to the Year One thousand eight hundred and eight shall in any Manner affect the first and fourth Clauses in the Ninth Section of the first Article; and that no State, without its Consent, shall be deprived of its equal Suffrage in the Senate.

ARTICLE VI

* * *

This Constitution, and the Laws of the United States which shall be made in Pursuance thereof; and all Treaties made, or which shall be made, under the Authority of the United States, shall be the supreme Law of the Land; and the Judges in every State shall be bound thereby, any Thing in the Constitution or Laws of any State to the Contrary notwithstanding.

The Senators and Representatives before mentioned, and the Members of the several State Legislatures, and all executive and judicial Officers, both of the United States and of the several States, shall be bound by Oath or Affirmation, to support this Constitution; but no religious Test shall ever be required as a Qualification to any Office or public Trust under the United States.

* * *

AMENDMENT I

Congress shall make no law respecting an establishment of religion, or prohibiting the free exercise thereof; or abridging the freedom of speech, or of the press; or the right of the people peaceably to assemble, and to petition the Government for a redress of grievances.

* * *

AMENDMENT IV

The right of the people to be secure in their persons, houses, papers, and effects, against unreasonable searches and seizures, shall not be violated, and no Warrants shall issue, but upon probable cause, supported by Oath or affirmation, and particularly describing the place to be searched, and the persons or things to be seized.

AMENDMENT V

No person shall be held to answer for a capital, or otherwise infamous crime, unless on a presentment or indictment of a Grand Jury, except in cases arising in the land or naval forces, or in the Militia, when in actual service in time of War or public danger; nor shall any person be subject for the same offence to be twice put in jeopardy of life or limb; nor shall be compelled in any criminal case to be a witness against himself, nor be deprived of life, liberty, or property, without due process of law; nor shall private property be taken for public use, without just compensation.

AMENDMENT VI

In all criminal prosecutions, the accused shall enjoy the right to a speedy and public trial, by an impartial jury of the State and district wherein the crime shall have been committed, which district shall have been previously ascertained by law, and to be informed of the nature and cause of the accusation; to be confronted with the witnesses against him; to have compulsory process for obtaining witnesses in his favor, and to have the Assistance of Counsel for his defense.

AMENDMENT VII

In Suits at common law, where the value in controversy shall exceed twenty dollars, the right of trial by jury shall be preserved, and no fact tried by jury, shall be otherwise re-examined in any Court of the United States, than according to the rules of the common law.

AMENDMENT VIII

Excessive bail shall not be required, nor excessive fines imposed , nor cruel and unusual punishments inflicted.

AMENDMENT IX

The enumeration in the Constitution, of certain rights, shall not be construed to deny or disparage others retained by the people.

AMENDMENT X

The powers not delegated to the United States by the Constitution, nor prohibited by it to the States, are reserved to the States respectively, or to the people.

AMENDMENT XI

The Judicial power of the United States shall not be construed to extend to any suit in law or equity, commenced or prosecuted against one of the United States by Citizens of another State, or by Citizens or Subjects of any Foreign State.

* * *

AMENDMENT XIII

Section 1. Neither slavery nor involuntary servitude, except as a punishment for crime whereof the party shall have been duly convicted, shall exist within the United States, or any place subject to their jurisdiction.

Section 2. Congress shall have power to enforce this article by appropriate legislation.

AMENDMENT XIV

Section 1. All persons born or naturalized in the United States, and subject to the jurisdiction thereof, are citizens of the United States and of the State wherein they reside. No State shall make or enforce any law which shall abridge the privileges or immunities of citizens of the United States; nor shall any State deprive any person of life, liberty, or property, without due process of law; nor deny to any person within its jurisdiction the equal protection of the laws.

* * *

Section 5. The Congress shall have power to enforce, by appropriate legislation, the provisions of this article.

APPENDIX B

TABLE OF RECENT AND IMPORTANT UNITED STATES SUPREME COURT EMPLOYMENT CASES

Affirmative Action

Adarand Constructors, Inc. v. Pena, 515 U.S. 200, 115 S.Ct. 2097, 132 L.Ed.2d 158 (1995).
Martin v. Wilks, 490 U.S. 755, 109 S.Ct. 2180, 104 L.Ed.2d 835 (1989).
City of Richmond v. J.A. Croson Co., 488 U.S. 469, 109 S.Ct. 706, 102 L.Ed.2d 854 (1989).
Johnson v. Transportation Agency, Santa Clara County, 480 U.S. 616, 107 S.Ct. 1442, 94 L.Ed.2d 615 (1987).
U.S. v. Paradise, 480 U.S. 149, 107 S.Ct. 1053, 94 L.Ed.2d 203 (1987).
Wygant v. Jackson Board of Educ., 476 U.S. 267, 106 S.Ct. 1842, 90 L.Ed.2d 260 (1986).
Firefighters Local Union No. 1784 v. Stotts, 467 U.S. 561, 104 S.Ct. 2576, 81 L.Ed.2d 483 (1984).
County of Los Angeles v. Davis, 440 U.S. 625, 99 S.Ct. 1379, 59 L.Ed.2d 642 (1979).

Discrimination

Crawford v. Metropolitan Government of Nashville and Davidson County, 2009 WL 160424 (U.S. 1/26/09).
CBOCS West, Inc. v. Humphries, 128 S.Ct. 1951 (U.S. 2008).
Meacham v. Knolls Atomic Power Laboratory, 128 S.Ct. 2395 (U.S. 2008).
Sprint/United Management Co. v. Mendelsohn, 128 S.Ct. 1140 (U.S. 2008).
Ledbetter v. Goodyear Tire & Rubber Co., Inc., 127 S.Ct. 2162, 167 L.Ed.2d 982 (U.S. 2007).
Ash v. Tyson Foods, Inc., 546 U.S. 454, 126 S.Ct. 1195, 163 L.Ed.2d 1053 (2006).
Burlington Northern and Santa Fe Railway Co. v. White, 126 S.Ct. 2405, 165 L.Ed.2d 345 (U.S. 2006).
Smith v. City of Jackson, 125 S.Ct. 1536, 161 L.Ed.2d 410 (U.S. 2005).
Pennsylvania State Pollice v. Suders, 542 U.S. 129, 124 S.Ct. 2342, 159 L. Ed.2d 204 (2004).
Chevron U.S.A. v. Echazabal, 536 U.S. 73, 122 S.Ct. 2045, 153 L.Ed.2d 82 (2002).
Edelman v. Lynchburg College, 535 U.S. 106, 122 S.Ct. 1145, 152 L.Ed.2d 188 (2002).
EEOC v. Waffle House, Inc., 534 U.S. 279, 122 S.Ct. 754, 151 L.Ed.2d 755 (2002).

Toyota Motor Manufacturing v. Williams, 534 U.S. 184, 122 S.Ct. 681, 151 L.Ed.2d 615 (2002).

US Airways v. Barnett, 535 U.S. 391, 122 S.Ct. 1516, 152 L.Ed.2d 589 (2002).

National Railroad Passenger Corp. v. Morgan, 536 U.S. 101, 122 S.Ct. 2061, 153 L.Ed.2d 106 (2002).

Clark County School Dist. v. Breeden, 532 U.S. 268, 121 S.Ct. 1508, 149 L.Ed.2d 509 (2001).

Board of Trustees of Univ. of Alabama v. Garrett, 531 U.S. 356, 121 S.Ct. 955, 148 L.Ed.2d 866 (2001).

Reeves v. Sanderson Plumbing Products, 530 U.S. 133, 120 S.Ct. 2097, 147 L.Ed.2d 105 (2000).

Kimel v. Florida Board of Regents, 528 U.S. 62, 120 S.Ct. 631, 145 L.Ed.2d 522 (2000).

Albertsons, Inc. v. Kirkingburg, 527 U.S. 555, 119 S.Ct. 2162, 144 L.Ed.2d 518 (1999).

Murphy v. United Parcel Service, Inc., 527 U.S. 516, 119 S.Ct. 2133, 144 L.Ed.2d 484 (1999).

Sutton v. United Air Lines, Inc., 527 U.S. 471, 119 S.Ct. 2139, 144 L.Ed.2d 450 (1999).

Cleveland v. Policy Management Systems Corp., 526 U.S. 795, 119 S.Ct. 1597, 143 L.Ed.2d 966 (1999).

Kolstad v. American Dental Ass'n, 527 U.S. 526, 119 S.Ct. 2118, 144 L.Ed.2d 494 (1999).

Faragher v. City of Boca Raton, 524 U.S. 775, 118 S.Ct. 2275, 141 L.Ed.2d 662 (1998).

Burlington Industries, Inc. v. Ellerth, 524 U.S. 742, 118 S.Ct. 2257, 141 L.Ed.2d 633 (1998).

Bragdon v. Abbott, 524 U.S. 624, 118 S.Ct. 2196, 141 L.Ed.2d 540 (1998).

Oncale v. Sundowner Offshore Services, Inc., 523 U.S. 75, 118 S.Ct. 998, 140 L.Ed.2d 201 (1998).

Oubre v. Entergy Operations, Inc., 522 U.S. 422, 118 S.Ct. 838, 139 L.Ed.2d 849 (1998).

Walters v. Metropolitan Educ. Enterprises, Inc., 519 U.S. 202, 117 S.Ct. 660, 136 L.Ed.2d 644 (1997).

Robinson v. Shell Oil Co., 519 U.S. 337, 117 S.Ct. 843, 136 L.Ed.2d 808 (1997).

O'Connor v. Consolidated Coin Caterers Corp., 517 U.S. 308, 116 S.Ct. 1307, 134 L.Ed.2d 433 (1996).

Commissioner of Internal Revenue v. Schleier, 515 U.S. 323, 115 S.Ct. 2159, 132 L.Ed.2d 294 (1995).

McKennon v. Nashville Banner Publishing Co., 513 U.S. 352, 115 S.Ct. 879, 130 L.Ed.2d 852 (1995).

Harris v. Forklift Systems, Inc., 510 U.S. 17, 114 S.Ct. 367, 126 L.Ed.2d 295 (1993).

Hazen Paper Co. v. Biggins, 507 U.S. 604, 113 S.Ct. 1701, 123 L.Ed.2d 338 (1993).

St. Mary's Honor Center v. Hicks, 509 U.S. 502, 113 S.Ct. 2742, 125 L.Ed.2d 407 (1993).

Astoria Federal Saving and Loan Ass'n v. Solimino, 501 U.S. 104, 111 S.Ct. 2166, 115 L.Ed.2d 96 (1991).

Gilmer v. Interstate/Johnson Lane Corp., 500 U.S. 20, 111 S.Ct. 1647, 114 L.Ed.2d 26 (1991).

Stevens v. Dep't of the Treasury, 500 U.S. 1, 111 S.Ct. 1562, 114 L.Ed.2d 1 (1991).

EEOC v. Arabian American Oil Co., 499 U.S. 244, 111 S.Ct. 1227, 113 L.Ed.2d 274 (1991).

Int'l Union, UAW v. Johnson Controls, 499 U.S. 187, 111 S.Ct. 1196, 113 L.Ed.2d 158 (1991).

Public Employees Retirement System of Ohio v. Betts, 492 U.S. 158, 109 S.Ct. 2854, 106 L.Ed.2d 134 (1989).

Jett v. Dallas Independent School Dist., 491 U.S. 701, 109 S.Ct. 2702, 105 L.Ed.2d 598 (1989).

Patterson v. McLean Credit Union, 491 U.S. 164, 109 S.Ct. 2363, 105 L.Ed.2d 132 (1989).

Lorance v. AT&T Technologies, Inc., 490 U.S. 900, 109 S.Ct. 2261, 104 L.Ed.2d 961 (1989).

Wards Cove Packing Co., Inc. v. Atonio, 490 U.S. 642, 109 S.Ct. 2115, 104 L.Ed.2d 733 (1989).

Price Waterhouse v. Hopkins, 490 U.S. 228, 109 S.Ct.1775, 104 L.Ed.2d 268 (1989).

Watson v. Fort Worth Bank and Trust, 487 U.S. 977, 108 S.Ct. 2777, 101 L.Ed.2d 827 (1988).

Goodman v. Lukens Steel Co., 482 U.S. 656, 107 S.Ct. 2617, 96 L.Ed.2d 572 (1987).

School Board of Nassau County, Florida v. Arline, 480 U.S. 273, 107 S.Ct.1123, 94 L.Ed.2d 307 (1987).

Ansonia Board of Educ. v. Philbrook, 479 U.S. 60, 107 S.Ct. 367, 93 L.Ed.2d 305 (1986).

Local No. 93, Int'l Ass'n of Firefighters v. City of Cleveland, 478 U.S. 501, 106 S.Ct. 3063, 92 L.Ed.2d 405 (1986).

Local 28 of Sheet Metal Workers v. EEOC, 478 U.S. 421, 106 S.Ct. 3019, 92 L.Ed.2d 344 (1986).

Meritor Savings Bank, FSB v. Vinson, 477 U.S. 57, 106 S.Ct. 2399, 91 L.Ed.2d 49 (1986).

Western Air Lines, Inc. v. Criswell, 472 U.S. 400, 105 S.Ct. 2743, 86 L.Ed.2d 321 (1985).

Connecticut v. Teal, 457 U.S. 440, 102 S.Ct. 2525, 73 L.Ed.2d 130 (1982).

County of Washington v. Gunther, 452 U.S. 161, 101 S.Ct. 2242, 68 L.Ed.2d 751 (1981).

Texas Dep't of Community Affairs v. Burdine, 450 U.S. 248, 101 S.Ct. 1089, 67 L.Ed.2d 207 (1981).

Int'l Brotherhood of Teamsters v. U.S., 433 U.S. 324, 97 S.Ct. 1843, 52 L.Ed.2d 396 (1977).

Dothard v. Rawlinson, 433 U.S. 321, 97 S.Ct. 2720, 53 L.Ed.2d 786 (1977).
Trans World Airlines, Inc. v. Hardison, 432 U.S. 63, 97 S.Ct. 2264, 53 L.Ed.2d 113 (1977).
Massachusetts Board of Retirement v. Murgia, 427 U.S. 307, 96 S.Ct. 2562, 49 L.Ed.2d 520 (1976).
Albemarle Paper Co. v. Moody, 422 U.S. 405, 95 S.Ct. 2362, 45 L.Ed.2d 280 (1975).
McDonnell Douglas Corp. v. Green, 411 U.S. 792, 93 S.Ct. 1817, 36 L.Ed.2d 668 (1973).
Griggs v. Duke Power Co., 401 U.S. 424, 91 S.Ct. 849, 28 L.Ed.2d 158 (1971).

Employee Benefits

Kentucky Retirement Systems v. EEOC, 128 S.Ct. 2361 (U.S. 2008).
Nevada Dep't of Human Resources v. Hibbs, 538 U.S. 721, 123 S.Ct. 1972, 155 L.Ed.2d 953 (2003).
Ragsdale v. Wolverine World Wide, Inc., 535 U.S. 81, 122 S.Ct. 1155, 152 L.Ed.2d 167 (2002).
Eastern Enterprises v. Apfel, 524 U.S. 498, 118 S.Ct. 2131, 141 L.Ed.2d 451 (1998).
Geissal v. Moore Medical Corp., 524 U.S. 74, 118 S.Ct. 1869, 141 L.Ed.2d 64 (1998).
Bay Area Laundry and Dry Cleaning Pension Trust Fund v. Ferbar Corp. of California, Inc., 522 U.S. 192, 118 S.Ct. 542, 139 L.Ed.2d 553 (1997).
California Division of Labor Standards Enforcement v. Dillingham Construction N.A., Inc., 519 U.S. 316, 117 S.Ct. 832, 136 L.Ed.2d 791 (1997).
Boggs v. Boggs, 520 U.S. 833, 117 S.Ct. 1754, 138 L.Ed.2d 45 (1997).
DeBuono v. NYSA-ILA Medical and Clinical Services Fund, 520 U.S. 806, 117 S.Ct. 1747, 138 L.Ed.2d 21 (1997).
Inter-Modal Rail Employees Ass'n v. Atchison, Topeka and Santa Fe Railway Co., 520 U.S. 510, 117 S.Ct. 1513, 137 L.Ed.2d 763 (1997).
Lockheed Corp. v. Spink, 517 U.S. 882, 116 S.Ct. 1783, 135 L.Ed.2d 153 (1996).
Varity Corp. v. Howe, 516 U.S. 489, 116 S.Ct. 1065, 134 L.Ed.2d 130 (1996).
Peacock v. Thomas, 516 U.S. 349, 116 S.Ct. 862, 133 L.Ed.2d 817 (1996).
Milwaukee Brewery Workers' Pension Plan v. Jos. Schlitz Brewing Co., 513 U.S. 414, 115 S.Ct. 981, 130 L.Ed.2d 932 (1995).
Curtiss-Wright Corp. v. Schoonejongen, 514 U.S. 73, 115 S.Ct. 1223, 131 L.Ed.2d 94 (1995).
John Hancock Mutual Life Insurance Co. v. Harris Trust and Savings Bank, 510 U.S. 86, 114 S.Ct. 517, 126 L.Ed.2d 524 (1993).
Mertens v. Hewitt Associates, 508 U.S. 248, 113 S.Ct. 2063, 124 L.Ed.2d 161 (1993).

Commissioner of Internal Revenue v. Keystone Consolidated Industries, Inc., 508 U.S. 152, 113 S.Ct. 2006, 124 L.Ed.2d 71 (1993).
Bath Iron Works v. Director, OWCP, 506 U.S. 153, 113 S.Ct. 692, 121 L.Ed.2d 619 (1993).
District of Columbia v. Greater Washington Board of Trade, 506 U.S. 125, 113 S.Ct. 580, 121 L.Ed.2d 513 (1992).
Nationwide Mutual Insurance Co. v. Darden, 503 U.S. 318, 112 S.Ct. 1344, 117 L.Ed.2d 581 (1992).
Ingersoll-Rand Co. v. McClendon, 498 U.S. 133, 111 S.Ct. 478, 112 L.Ed.2d 474 (1990).
FMC Corp. v. Holliday, 498 U.S. 52, 111 S.Ct. 403, 112 L.Ed.2d 356 (1990).
Mead Corp. v. Tilley, 490 U.S. 714, 109 S.Ct. 2156, 104 L.Ed.2d 796 (1989).
Massachusetts v. Morash, 490 U.S. 107, 109 S.Ct. 1668, 104 L.Ed.2d 98 (1989).
Firestone Tire and Rubber Co. v. Bruch, 489 U.S. 101, 109 S.Ct. 948, 103 L.Ed.2d 80 (1989).
Fort Halifax Packing Co. v. Coyne, 482 U.S. 1, 107 S.Ct. 2211, 96 L.Ed.2d 1 (1987).
Connolly v. Pension Benefit Guaranty Corp., 475 U.S. 211, 106 S.Ct. 1018, 89 L.Ed.2d 166 (1986).
Central States, Southeast and Southwest Areas Pension Fund v. Central Transport, Inc., 472 U.S. 559, 105 S.Ct. 2833, 86 L.Ed.2d 447 (1985).
Metropolitan Life Insurance Co. v. Massachusetts, 471 U.S. 724, 105 S.Ct. 2380, 85 L.Ed.2d 728 (1985).
City of Los Angeles Dep't of Water v. Manhart, 435 U.S. 702, 98 S.Ct. 1370, 55 L.Ed.2d 657 (1978).

Employer Liability

Engquist v. Oregon Dep't of Agriculture, 128 S.Ct. 2146 (U.S. 2008).
Scott v. Harris, 127 S.Ct. 1769, 167 L.Ed.2d 686 (U.S. 2007).
Town of Castle Rock v. Gonzales, 545 U.S. 748, 125 S.Ct. 2796 (2005).
Cook County v. U.S. ex rel. Chandler, 538 U.S. 119, 123 S.Ct. 1239, 155 L.Ed.2d 247 (2003).
Lapides v. Board of Regents of Univ. System of Georgia, 535 U.S. 613, 122 S.Ct. 1640, 152 L.Ed.2d 806 (2002).
Haddle v. Garrison, 525 U.S. 121, 119 S.Ct. 489, 142 L.Ed.2d 502 (1998).
Metro-North Commuter Railroad Co. v. Buckley, 521 U.S. 424, 117 S.Ct. 2113, 138 L.Ed.2d 560 (1997).
Atchison, Topeka and Santa Fe Railway Co. v. Buell, 480 U.S. 557, 107 S.Ct. 1410, 94 L.Ed.2d 563 (1987).
O'Connor v. Ortega, 480 U.S. 709, 107 S.Ct. 1492, 94 L.Ed.2d 714 (1987).

Employment Practices

Osborn v. Haley, 127 S.Ct. 881, 166 L.Ed.2d 819 (U.S. 2007).
Brogan v. U.S., 522 U.S. 398, 118 S.Ct. 805, 139 L.Ed.2d 830 (1998).
California Federal Savings and Loan Ass'n v. Guerra, 479 U.S. 272, 107 S.Ct. 683, 93 L.Ed.2d 613 (1987).
Attorney General of New York v. Soto-Lopez, 476 U.S. 898, 106 S.Ct. 2317, 90 L.Ed.2d 899 (1986).

Free Speech

Garcetti v. Ceballos, 547 U.S. 410, 126 S.Ct. 1951, 164 L.Ed.2d 689 (2006).
Dun & Bradstreet, Inc. v. Greenmoss Builders, Inc., 472 U.S. 749, 105 S.Ct. 2939, 86 L.Ed.2d 593 (1985).
Brockett v. Spokane Arcades, Inc., 472 U.S. 491, 105 S.Ct. 2794, 86 L.Ed.2d 394 (1985).
Connick v. Myers, 461 U.S. 138, 103 S.Ct. 1684, 75 L.Ed.2d 708 (1983).

Labor Relations

Locke v. Karass, 129 S.Ct. 798 (U.S. 2009).
Davenport v. Washington Educ. Ass'n, 127 S.Ct. 2372, 168 L.Ed.2d 71 (U.S. 2007).
Christensen v. Harris County, 529 U.S. 576, 120 S.Ct. 1655, 146 L.Ed.2d 621 (2000).
Marquez v. Screen Actors Guild, 525 U.S. 33, 119 S.Ct. 292, 142 L.Ed.2d 242 (1998).
Wright v. Universal Maritime Service Corp., 525 U.S. 70, 119 S.Ct. 391, 142 L.Ed.2d 361 (1998).
Air Line Pilots Ass'n v. Miller, 523 U.S. 866, 118 S.Ct. 1761, 140 L.Ed.2d 1070 (1998).
Allentown Mack Sales and Service, Inc. v. NLRB, 522 U.S. 359, 118 S.Ct. 818, 139 L.Ed.2d 797 (1998).
Textron Lycoming Reciprocating Engine Div., AVCO Corp. v. United Automobile, Aerospace and Agricultural Implement Workers of America, Int'l Union, Local 787, 523 U.S. 653, 118 S.Ct. 1626, 140 L.Ed.2d 863 (1998).
Auciello Iron Works, Inc. v. NLRB, 517 U.S. 781, 116 S.Ct. 1754, 135 L.Ed.2d 64 (1996).
United Food and Commercial Workers Union Local 751 v. Brown Group, Inc., 517 U.S. 544, 116 S.Ct. 1529, 134 L.Ed.2d 758 (1996).
Holly Farms Corp. v. NLRB, 517 U.S. 392, 116 S.Ct. 1396, 134 L.Ed.2d 593 (1996).
Brotherhood of Locomotive Engineers v. Atchison, Topeka & Santa Fe Railroad Co., 516 U.S. 152, 116 S.Ct. 595, 133 L.Ed.2d 535 (1996).

NLRB v. Town & Country Electric, Inc., 516 U.S. 85, 116 S.Ct. 450, 133 L.Ed.2d 371 (1995).

North Star Steel Co. v. Thomas, 515 U.S. 29, 115 S.Ct. 1927, 132 L.Ed.2d 27 (1995).

NLRB v. Health Care & Retirement Corp., 511 U.S. 571, 114 S.Ct. 1778, 128 L.Ed.2d 586 (1994).

ABF Freight System, Inc. v. NLRB, 510 U.S. 317, 114 S.Ct. 835, 127 L.Ed.2d 152 (1994).

Livadas v. Bradshaw, 512 U.S. 107, 114 S.Ct. 2068, 129 L.Ed.2d 93 (1994).

Hawaiian Airlines, Inc. v. Norris, 512 U.S. 246, 114 S.Ct. 2239, 129 L.Ed.2d 203 (1994).

Thunder Basin Coal Co. v. Reich, 510 U.S. 200, 114 S.Ct. 771, 127 L.Ed.2d 29 (1994).

Lechmere, Inc. v. NLRB, 502 U.S. 527, 112 S.Ct. 841, 117 L.Ed.2d 79 (1992).

Litton Financial Printing v. NLRB, 501 U.S. 190, 111 S.Ct. 2215, 115 L.Ed.2d 177 (1991).

Air Line Pilots Ass'n Int'l v. O'Neill, 499 U.S. 65, 111 S.Ct. 1127, 113 L.Ed.2d 51 (1991).

Martin v. OSHRC, 499 U.S. 144, 111 S.Ct. 1171, 113 L.Ed.2d 117 (1991).

Groves v. Ring Screw Works, 498 U.S. 168, 111 S.Ct. 498, 112 L.Ed.2d 508 (1990).

English v. General Electric Co., 496 U.S. 72, 110 S.Ct. 2270, 110 L.Ed.2d 65 (1990).

NLRB v. Curtin Matheson Scientific, Inc., 494 U.S. 775, 110 S.Ct. 1542, 108 L.Ed.2d 801 (1990).

Trans World Airlines v. Independent Federation of Flight Attendants, 489 U.S. 426, 109 S.Ct. 1225, 103 L.Ed.2d 456 (1989).

Communications Workers of America v. Beck, 487 U.S. 735, 108 S.Ct. 2641, 101 L.Ed.2d 634 (1988).

Fall River Dyeing & Finishing Corp. v. NLRB, 482 U.S. 27, 107 S.Ct. 2225, 96 L.Ed.2d 22 (1987).

Icicle Seafoods, Inc. v. Worthington, 475 U.S. 709, 106 S.Ct. 1527, 89 L.Ed.2d 739 (1986).

NLRB v. Int'l Longshoremen's Ass'n, AFL-CIO, 473 U.S. 61, 105 S.Ct. 3045, 87 L.Ed.2d 47 (1985).

NLRB v. Action Automotive, Inc., 471 U.S. 1049, 105 S.Ct. 984, 83 L.Ed.2d 986 (1985).

Tony and Susan Alamo Foundation v. Secretary of Labor, 471 U.S. 290, 105 S.Ct. 1953, 85 L.Ed.2d 278 (1985).

Allis-Chalmers Corp. v. Lueck, 471 U.S. 202, 105 S.Ct. 1904, 85 L.Ed.2d 206 (1985).

Barrentine v. Arkansas-Best Freight System, 450 U.S. 728, 101 S.Ct. 1437, 67 L.Ed.2d 641 (1981).

NLRB v. Weingarten, 420 U.S. 251 (1975).

Termination

U.S. Postal Service v. Gregory, 534 U.S. 1, 122 S.Ct. 431, 151 L.Ed.2d 323 (2001).

Baker v. General Motors Corp., 522 U.S. 222, 118 S.Ct. 657, 139 L.Ed.2d 580 (1998).

Lingle v. Norge Division of Magic Chef, Inc., 486 U.S. 399, 108 S.Ct. 1877, 100 L.Ed.2d 410 (1988).

United Paperworkers Int'l Union v. Misco, Inc., 484 U.S. 29, 108 S.Ct. 364, 98 L.Ed.2d 286 (1987).

Caterpillar Inc. v. Williams, 482 U.S. 386, 107 S.Ct. 2425, 96 L.Ed.2d 318 (1987).

Unemployment Compensation

Frazee v. Illinois Dep't of Employment Security, 489 U.S. 829, 109 S.Ct. 1514, 103 L.Ed.2d 914 (1989).

Hobbie v. Unemployment Appeals Comm'n of Florida, 480 U.S. 136, 107 S.Ct. 1046, 94 L.Ed.2d 190 (1987).

Baker v. General Motors Corp., 478 U.S. 621, 106 S.Ct. 3129, 92 L.Ed.2d 504 (1986).

Thomas v. Review Board of Indiana Employment Security Division, 450 U.S. 707, 101 S.Ct. 1425, 67 L.Ed.2d 624 (1981).

Workers' Compensation

American Manufacturers Mutual Insurance Co. v. Sullivan, 526 U.S. 40, 119 S.Ct. 977, 143 L.Ed.2d 130 (1999).

Metropolitan Stevedore Co. v. Rambo (Rambo II), 521 U.S. 121, 117 S.Ct. 1953, 138 L.Ed.2d 327 (1997).

Ingalls Shipbuilding, Inc. v. Director, OWCP, 519 U.S. 248, 117 S.Ct. 796, 136 L.Ed.2d 736 (1997).

Director, Office of Workers' Compensation Programs, Dep't of Labor v. Newport News Shipbuilding and Dry Dock Co., 514 U.S. 122, 115 S.Ct. 1278, 131 L.Ed.2d 160 (1995).

Chandris, Inc. v. Latsis, 515 U.S. 347, 115 S.Ct. 2172, 132 L.Ed.2d 314 (1995).

Metropolitan Stevedore Co. v. Rambo, 515 U.S. 291, 115 S.Ct. 2144, 132 L.Ed.2d 226 (1995).

Director, Office of Workers' Compensation Programs v. Greenwich Collieries, 512 U.S. 267, 114 S.Ct. 2251, 129 L.Ed.2d 221 (1994).

Thomas v. Washington Gas Light Co., 448 U.S. 261, 100 S.Ct. 2647, 65 L.Ed.2d 757 (1980).

Wengler v. Druggist Mutual Insurance Co., 446 U.S. 142, 100 S.Ct. 1540, 64 L.Ed.2d 107 (1980).

THE JUDICIAL SYSTEM

In order to allow you to determine the relative importance of a judicial decision, the cases included in *Deskbook Encyclopedia of Public Employment Law* identify the particular court from which a decision has been issued. For example, a case decided by a state supreme court generally will be of greater significance than a state circuit court case. Hence a basic knowledge of the structure of our judicial system is important to an understanding of public employment law.

Almost all the reports in this volume are taken from appellate court decisions. Although most employment law decisions occur at trial court and administrative levels, appellate court decisions have the effect of binding lower courts and administrators so that appellate court decisions have the effect of law within their court systems.

State and federal court systems generally function independently of each other. Each court system applies its own law according to statutes and the determinations of its highest court. However, judges at all levels often consider opinions from other court systems to settle issues that are new or arise under unique fact situations. Similarly, lawyers look at the opinions of many courts to locate authority that supports their clients' cases.

Once a lawsuit is filed in a particular court system, that system retains the matter until its conclusion. Unsuccessful parties at the administrative or trial court level generally have the right to appeal unfavorable determinations of law to appellate courts within the system. When federal law issues or constitutional grounds are present, lawsuits may be appropriately filed in the federal court system. In those cases, the lawsuit is filed initially in the federal district court for that area.

On rare occasions, the U.S. Supreme Court considers appeals from the highest courts of the states if a distinct federal question exists and at least four justices agree on the question's importance. The federal courts occasionally send cases to state courts for application of state law. These situations are infrequent and, in general, the state and federal court systems should be considered separate from each other.

The most common system, used by nearly all states and also the federal judiciary, is as follows: a legal action is commenced in district court (sometimes called trial court, county court, common pleas court or superior court) where a decision is initially reached. The case may then be appealed to the court of appeals (or appellate court), and in turn this decision may be appealed to the supreme court.

Several states, however, do not have a court of appeals; lower court decisions are appealed directly to the state's supreme court. Additionally, some states have labeled their courts in a nonstandard fashion.

In Maryland, the highest state court is called the Court of Appeals. In the state of New York, the trial court is called the Supreme Court. Decisions of this court may be appealed to the Supreme Court, Appellate Division. The highest court in New York is the Court of Appeals. Pennsylvania has perhaps the most complex court system. The lowest state court is the Court of Common Pleas. Depending on the circumstances of the case, appeals may be taken to either the Commonwealth Court or the Superior Court. In certain instances the Commonwealth Court functions as a trial court as well as an appellate court. The Superior Court, however, is strictly an intermediate appellate court. The highest court in Pennsylvania is the Supreme Court.

While supreme court decisions generally are regarded as the last word in legal matters, it is important to remember that trial and appeals court decisions also create important legal precedents. For the hierarchy of typical state and federal court systems, please see the diagram below.

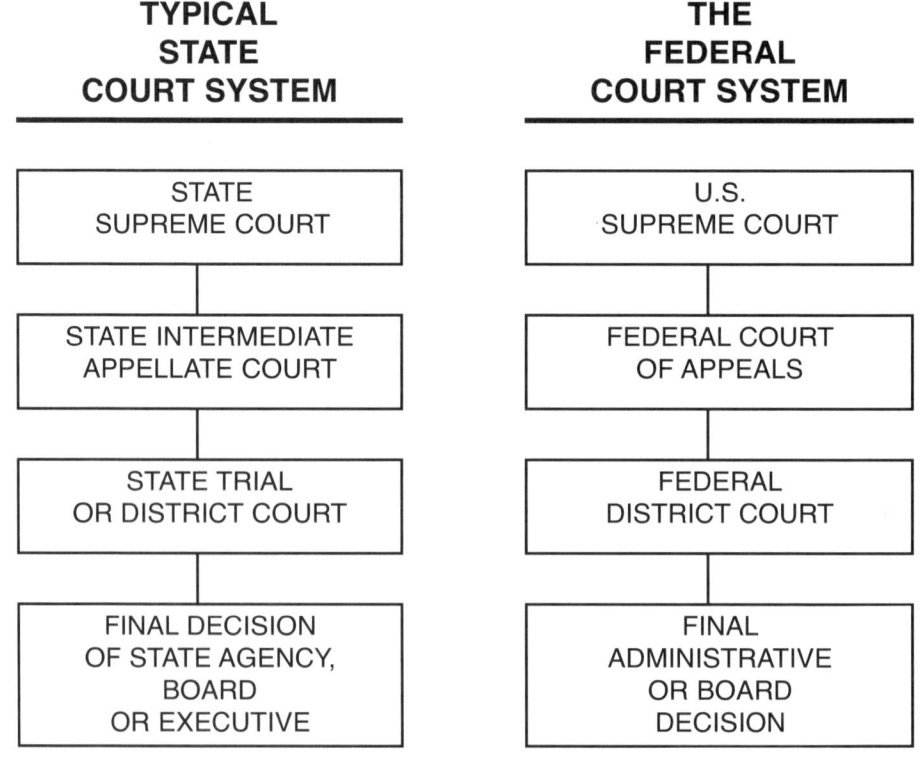

Federal courts of appeals hear appeals from the district courts that are located in their circuits. Below is a list of states matched to the federal circuits in which they are located.

First Circuit	—	Puerto Rico, Maine, New Hampshire, Massachusetts, Rhode Island
Second Circuit	—	New York, Vermont, Connecticut
Third Circuit	—	Pennsylvania, New Jersey, Delaware, Virgin Islands
Fourth Circuit	—	West Virginia, Maryland, Virginia, North Carolina, South Carolina
Fifth Circuit	—	Texas, Louisiana, Mississippi
Sixth Circuit	—	Ohio, Kentucky, Tennessee, Michigan
Seventh Circuit	—	Wisconsin, Indiana, Illinois
Eighth Circuit	—	North Dakota, South Dakota, Nebraska, Arkansas, Missouri, Iowa, Minnesota
Ninth Circuit	—	Alaska, Washington, Oregon, California, Hawaii, Arizona, Nevada, Idaho, Montana, Northern Mariana Islands, Guam
Tenth Circuit	—	Wyoming, Utah, Colorado, Kansas, Oklahoma, New Mexico
Eleventh Circuit	—	Alabama, Georgia, Florida
District of Columbia Circuit	—	Hears cases from the U.S. District Court for the District of Columbia.
Federal Circuit	—	Sitting in Washington, D.C., the U.S. Court of Appeals, Federal Circuit hears patent and trade appeals and certain appeals on claims brought against the federal government and its agencies.

HOW TO READ A CASE CITATION

Generally, court decisions can be located in case reporters at law school or governmental law libraries. Some cases also can be located on the Internet through legal Web sites or official court Web sites.

Each case summary contains the citation, or legal reference, to the full text of the case. The diagram below illustrates how to read a case citation.

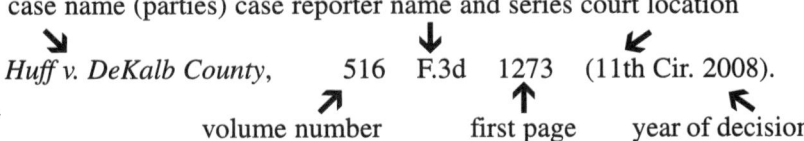

Some cases may have two or three reporter names such as U.S. Supreme Court cases and cases reported in regional case reporters as well as state case reporters. For example, a U.S. Supreme Court case usually contains three case reporter citations.

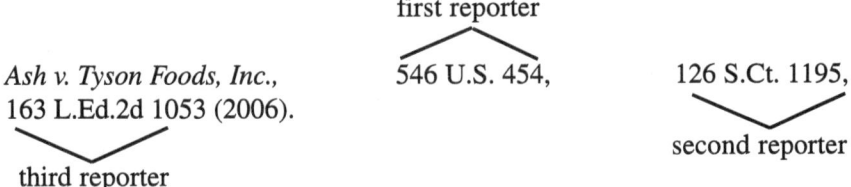

The citations are still read in the same manner as if only one citation has been listed.

Occasionally, a case may contain a citation that does not reference a case reporter. For example, a citation may contain a reference such as:

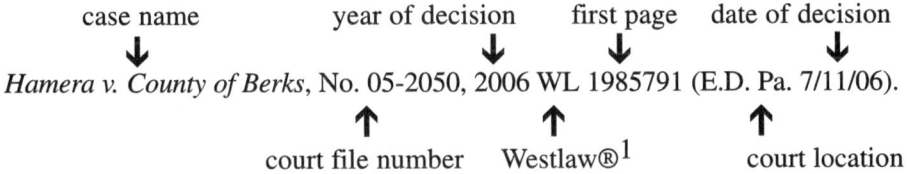

The court file number indicates the specific number assigned to a case by the particular court system deciding the case. In our example, the U.S. District Court

---

[1] WESTLAW® is a computerized database of court cases available for a fee.

for the Eastern District of Pennsylvania has assigned the case of *Hamera v. County of Berks* the case number of "No. 05-2050," which will serve as the reference number for the case. Locating a case on the Internet generally requires either the case name and date of the decision, and/or the court file number.

Below, we have listed the full names of the regional reporters. As mentioned previously, many states have individual state reporters. The names of those reporters may be obtained from a reference law librarian.

P. **Pacific Reporter**
Alaska, Arizona, California, Colorado, Hawaii, Idaho, Kansas, Montana, Nevada, New Mexico, Oklahoma, Oregon, Utah, Washington, Wyoming

A. **Atlantic Reporter**
Connecticut, Delaware, District of Columbia, Maine, Maryland, New Hampshire, New Jersey, Pennsylvania, Rhode Island, Vermont

N.E. **Northeastern Reporter**
Illinois, Indiana, Massachusetts, New York, Ohio

N.W. **Northwestern Reporter**
Iowa, Michigan, Minnesota, Nebraska, North Dakota, South Dakota, Wisconsin

S. **Southern Reporter**
Alabama, Florida, Louisiana, Mississippi

S.E. **Southeastern Reporter**
Georgia, North Carolina, South Carolina, Virginia, West Virginia

S.W. **Southwestern Reporter**
Arkansas, Kentucky, Missouri, Tennessee, Texas

F. **Federal Reporter**
Decisions of the 13 federal judicial circuit courts of appeals. *See The Judicial System, p. 525,* for specific state circuits.

F.Supp. **Federal Supplement**
District court decisions from the 13 federal judicial circuits. *See The Judicial System, p. 525,* for specific state circuits.

Fed.Appx. **Federal Appendix**
Contains unpublished decisions of the U.S. Circuit Courts of Appeal.

U.S. **United States Reports**
S.Ct. **Supreme Court Reporter** — U.S. Supreme Court Decisions
L.Ed. **Lawyers' Edition**

GLOSSARY

Administrative Law Judge (ALJ) - an officer who presides at administrative hearings. ALJs are empowered by employment and agency statutes to serve as initial fact finders in many employment cases, including workers' compensation and unemployment benefits claims and many labor disputes. Although courts must give ALJ findings of fact considerable weight, they are not bound by an ALJ's conclusions of law.

Age Discrimination in Employment Act (ADEA) - The ADEA, 29 U.S.C. § 621 *et seq.*, is part of the Fair Labor Standards Act. It prohibits discrimination against persons who are at least 40 years old, and applies to employers that have 20 or more employees and that affect interstate commerce.

Americans with Disabilities Act (ADA) - The provisions of the ADA, 42 U.S.C. § 12101 *et seq.*, that relate specifically to employment took effect on July 26, 1992. Among other things, the ADA prohibits discrimination against a qualified individual with a disability because of that person's disability with respect to job application procedures, the hiring, advancement or discharge of employees, employee compensation, job training, and other terms, conditions and privileges of employment.

Bona fide - Latin term meaning "good faith." Generally used to note a party's lack of bad intent or fraudulent purpose.

CBA - Collective bargaining agreement.

Class Action Suit - Federal Rule of Civil Procedure 23 allows members of a class to sue as representatives on behalf of the whole class provided that the class is so large that joinder of all parties is impractical, there are questions of law or fact common to the class, the claims or defenses of the representatives are typical of the claims or defenses of the class, and the representative parties will adequately protect the interests of the class. In addition, there must be some danger of inconsistent verdicts or adjudications if the class action were prosecuted as separate actions. Most states also allow class actions under the same or similar circumstances.

Collateral Estoppel - Also known as issue preclusion. The idea that once an issue has been litigated, it may not be re-tried. Similar to the doctrine of *Res Judicata* (see below).

Due Process Clause - The clauses of the Fifth and Fourteenth Amendments to the Constitution that guarantee the citizens of the United States "due process of law" (see below). The Fifth Amendment's Due Process Clause applies to the federal government, and the Fourteenth Amendment's Due Process Clause applies to the states.

Due Process of Law - The idea of "fair play" in the government's application of law to its citizens, guaranteed by the Fifth and Fourteenth Amendments. Substantive due process is just plain *fairness*, and procedural due process is accorded when the government utilizes adequate procedural safeguards for the protection of an individual's liberty or property interests.

Employee Retirement Income Security Act (ERISA) - Federal legislation that sets uniform standards for employee pension benefit plans and employee welfare benefit plans. It is codified at 29 U.S.C. § 1001 *et seq.*

Enjoin - (see Injunction).

Equal Pay Act - Federal legislation that is part of the Fair Labor Standards Act. It applies to discrimination in wages that is based on gender. For race discrimination, employees paid unequally must utilize Title VII or 42 U.S.C. § 1981. Unlike many labor statutes, there is no minimum number of employees necessary to invoke the act's protection.

Equal Protection Clause - The clause of the Fourteenth Amendment that prohibits a state from denying any person within its jurisdiction equal protection of its laws. Also, the Due Process Clause of the Fifth Amendment that pertains to the federal government. This has been interpreted by the Supreme Court to grant equal protection even though there is no explicit grant in the Constitution.

Establishment Clause - The clause of the First Amendment that prohibits Congress from making "any law respecting an establishment of religion." This clause has been interpreted as creating a "wall of separation" between church and state. The test now used to determine whether government action violates the Establishment Clause, referred to as the *Lemon* test, from *Lemon v. Kurtzman,* 403 U.S. 602, 91 S.Ct. 2105, 29 L.Ed.2d 745 (1971), asks whether the action has a secular purpose, whether its primary effect promotes or inhibits religion, and whether it requires excessive entanglement between church and state.

Ex Post Facto Law - A law that punishes as criminal any action that was not a crime at the time it was performed. Prohibited by Article I, Section 9, of the Constitution.

Exclusionary Rule - Constitutional limitation on the introduction of evidence, which states that evidence derived from a constitutional violation must be excluded from trial.

Fair Labor Standards Act (FLSA) - Federal legislation that mandates the payment of minimum wages and overtime compensation to covered employees. The overtime provisions require employers to pay at least time-and-one-half to employees who work more than 40 hours per week.

Federal Employers' Liability Act (FELA) - Legislation enacted to provide a federal remedy for railroad workers who are injured as a result of employer or co-employee negligence. It expressly prohibits covered carriers from adopting any regulation, or entering into any contract, which limits their FELA liability.

Federal Tort Claims Act - Federal legislation that determines the circumstances under which the United States waives its sovereign immunity (see below) and agrees to be sued in court for money damages. The government retains its immunity in cases of intentional torts committed by its employees or agents, and where the tort is the result of a "discretionary function" of a federal employee or agency. Many states have similar acts.

42 U.S.C. §§ 1981, 1983 - Section 1983 of the federal Civil Rights Act prohibits any person acting under color of state law from depriving any other person of rights protected by the Constitution or by federal laws. A vast majority of lawsuits claiming constitutional violations are brought under § 1983. Section 1981 provides that all persons enjoy the same right to make and enforce contracts as "white citizens." Section 1981 applies to employment contracts. Further, unlike § 1983, § 1981 applies even to private actors. It is not limited to those acting under color of state law. These sections do not apply to the federal government, though the government may be sued directly under the Constitution for any violations.

Free Exercise Clause - The clause of the First Amendment that prohibits Congress from interfering with citizens' rights to the free exercise of their religion. Through the Fourteenth Amendment, it also has been made applicable to the states and their sub-entities.

Incorporation Doctrine - By its own terms, the Bill of Rights applies only to the federal government. The Incorporation Doctrine states that the Fourteenth Amendment makes the Bill of Rights applicable to the states.

Injunction - An equitable remedy (see Remedies) wherein a court orders a party to do or refrain from doing some particular action.

Issue Preclusion - (see Collateral Estoppel).

Jurisdiction - The power of a court to determine cases and controversies. The Supreme Court's jurisdiction extends to cases arising under the Constitution and under federal law. Federal courts have the power to hear cases where there is diversity of citizenship or where a federal question is involved.

Labor Management Relations Act (LMRA) - Federal labor law that preempts state law with respect to controversies involving collective bargaining agreements. The most important provision of the LMRA is § 301, which is codified at 29 U.S.C. § 185.

National Labor Relations Act (NLRA) - Federal legislation that guarantees employees the right to form and participate in labor organizations. It prohibits employers from interfering with employees in the exercise of their rights under the NLRA.

Negligence per se - Negligence on its face. Usually, the violation of an ordinance or statute will be treated as negligence per se because no careful person would have been guilty of it.

Occupational Safety and Health Act (OSHA) - Federal legislation that requires employers to provide a safe workplace. Employers have both general and specific duties under OSHA. The general duty is to provide a workplace that is free from recognized hazards that are likely to result in serious physical harm. The specific duty is to conform to the health and safety standards promulgated by the Secretary of Labor.

Overbroad - A government action is overbroad if, in an attempt to alleviate a specific evil, it impermissibly prohibits or chills a protected action. For example, attempting to deal with street litter by prohibiting the distribution of leaflets or handbills.

Preemption Doctrine - Doctrine that states that when federal and state law attempt to regulate the same subject matter, federal law prevents the state law from operating. Based on the Supremacy Clause of Article VI, Clause 2, of the Constitution.

Pretrial Judgment - (see **Summary Judgment**).

Prior Restraint - Restraining a publication before it is distributed. In general, constitutional law doctrine prohibits government from exercising prior restraint.

Pro Se - A party appearing in court, without the benefit of an attorney, is said to be appearing "pro se."

Religious Freedom Restoration Act - Federal law that creates a statutory prohibition against governmental action that substantially burdens the exercise of religion, even if the burden results from a rule of general applicability, unless the government can show that the action is the least restrictive means of furthering a compelling governmental interest.

Remand - The act of an appellate court in returning a case to the court from which it came for further action.

GLOSSARY

Remedies - There are two general categories of remedies, or relief: legal remedies, which consist of money damages, and equitable remedies, which consist of a court mandate that a specific action be prohibited or required. For example, a claim for compensatory and punitive damages seeks a legal remedy; a claim for an injunction seeks an equitable remedy. Equitable remedies are generally unavailable unless legal remedies are inadequate to address the harm.

Res Judicata - The judicial notion that a claim or action may not be tried twice or re-litigated, or that all causes of action arising out of the same set of operative facts should be tried at one time. Also known as claim preclusion.

Section 504 of the Rehabilitation Act of 1973 - Section 504 applies to public or private institutions receiving federal financial assistance. It requires that, in the employment context, an otherwise qualified individual cannot be denied employment based on his or her handicap. An otherwise qualified individual is one who can perform the "essential functions" of the job with "reasonable accomodation."

Section 1981 & Section 1983 - (see 42 U.S.C. §§ 1981, 1983).

Sovereign Immunity - The idea that the government cannot be sued without its consent. It stems from the English notion that "the King can do no wrong." This immunity from suit has been abrogated in most states and by the federal government through legislative acts known as "tort claims acts."

Standing - The judicial doctrine that states that in order to maintain a lawsuit a party must have some real interest at stake in the outcome of the trial.

Statute of Limitations - A statute of limitation provides the time period in which a specific cause of action may be brought.

Summary Judgment - Also referred to as pretrial judgment. Similar to a dismissal. Where there is no genuine issue as to any material fact and all that remains is a question of law, a judge can rule in favor of one party or the other. In general, summary judgment is used to dispose of claims that do not support a legally recognized claim.

Supremacy Clause - Clause in Article VI of the Constitution, which states that federal legislation is the supreme law of the land. This clause is used to support the Preemption Doctrine (see above).

Title VII, Civil Rights Act of 1964 (Title VII) - Title VII prohibits discrimination in employment based upon race, color, sex, national origin, or religion. It applies to any employer having 15 or more employees. Under Title VII, where an employer intentionally discriminates, employees may obtain money damages unless the claim is for race discrimination. For those claims, monetary relief is available under 42 U.S.C. § 1981.

U.S. Equal Employment Opportunity Commission (EEOC) - The EEOC is the government entity that is empowered to enforce Title VII, the ADA and other federal laws through investigation and/or lawsuits. Private individuals alleging discrimination must pursue administrative remedies with the EEOC before they are allowed to file suit under Title VII.

Vacate - The act of annulling the judgment of a court either by an appellate court or by the court itself. The Supreme Court generally will vacate a lower court's judgment without deciding the case itself, and remand the case to the lower court for further consideration in light of some recent controlling decision.

Void-for-Vagueness Doctrine - A judicial doctrine based on the Fourteenth Amendment's Due Process Clause. In order for a law that regulates speech, or any criminal statute, to pass muster under the doctrine, the law must make clear what actions are prohibited or made criminal. Under the principles of the Due Process Clause, people of average intelligence should not have to guess at the meaning of a law.

Writ of Certiorari - The device used by the Supreme Court to transfer cases from the appellate court's docket to its own. Since the Supreme Court's appellate jurisdiction is largely discretionary, it need only issue such a writ when it desires to rule in the case.

INDEX

Abandonment and resignation, 138-143
Affirmative action, 93-101
    Affirmative action programs, 93-98
        Employment terminations, 97-98
        Hiring decisions, 93-95
        Promotions, 95-97
    Procedural issues, 98-99
    Race and national origin discrimination, 40-54
    Termination and modification of, 99-101
Age Discrimination in Employment Act (ADEA)
    Burden of proof
        Adverse employment action, 6-7
        Age factor, 3-6
        Pretext for discrimination, 7-9
    Defenses, 12-16
    Employee benefits, 2-3
    Filing requirements, 9, 10-11
    Older Workers Benefit Protection Act, 2, 9, 10
    Procedural issues, 9-12
    Waiver of ADEA claims, 9, 10
Agency fees, 451-454
AIDS, 17-18, 20, 155, 308, 399
Americans with Disabilities Act (ADA)
    Defenses, 26-29
    Drug and alcohol use, 35
        Current drug abusers, 36-37
        Rehabilitation programs, 37
    Essential job functions, 23-25
    Physical or mental impairment, 17-20
    Procedural issues, 25-26
    Reasonable accommodation, 30-35
        Types of accommodation, 31-33
        Unreasonable accommodations, 33-35
    Regarded as disabled, 29-30
    Substantial limitation, 20-23
Arbitration, 467-470

Bivens action, 253, 292
Blood testing
    See Search and seizure

Civil Service Reform Act (CSRA), 107
Classifications, 479-486
    Creation of classifications, 480-481
    Reclassification, 483-486
    Temporary assignments, 481-483
Collective bargaining agreements
    Fees, 451-454
    Investigatory interviews, 136-137

Procedures for discipline under, 134-136
Workload, 459-460
Commuting expenses, 437-439
Compensatory time, 432-434
Constructive discharge, 120, 171
Criminal violations and discipline, 147-149

Defamation, 210-214
Demotions, 191, 197
Disciplinary action
    See Termination and suspension
Discrimination
    See also Affirmative action and harassment
    Affirmative action, 93-101
        Affirmative action programs, 93-98
        Procedural issues, 98-99
        Termination and modification of, 99-101
    Age, 2
        Adverse employment action, 6-7
        Age as a factor, 3-6
        Defenses, 12-16
        Mandatory retirement, 14-16
        Pretext for discrimination, 7-9
    Disability, 16-40
        Defenses under ADA, 26-29
        Drug and alcohol use, 35-37
        Reasonable accommodation, 30-35, 39-40
        Rehabilitation Act and Americans with Disabilities Act, 17-30
        State statutes, 37-40
    National origin, 51-54
    Procedural matters, 101-104
    Race, 40-51
        Burden of proof, 40-46
        Harassment, 46-48
        Judgments and settlement decrees, 48-51
    Religious, 80-86
        Burden of proof, 80-82
        Reasonable accommodation, 82-86
        Seniority systems, 86-87
    Retaliation, 87-93
    Sex discrimination, 54-80
        Burden of proof, 54-58
        Defenses, 60-62
        Equal pay, 62-66
        Generally, 54-62
        Harassment, 67-80
        Legitimate reasons for adverse action, 58-60
        Pregnancy, 66-67
        Sexual orientation, 75-77
    Sexual orientation, 367
Dress codes and personal appearance, 233-238
Drug and alcohol use: discrimination, 35-37

Drug testing
    See Search and seizure
Drugs: possession of, 107, 112, 113
Due process rights, 105-137
    Collective bargaining agreements, 133-137
    Employment handbooks and policies, 126-129
    Evidentiary issues, 110
    Hearing rights, 106-115
    Impartial decision maker, 113-115
    Notice and opportunity to respond, 108-110
    Property and liberty interests, 115-126
    Statutes and ordinances, 129-133

Employee benefits, 352-417
    Contribution rates, 413-416
    Coordination of benefits, 411-413
    Disability benefits
        Eligibility, 364-368
        Modification and termination of, 368-372
    Exemptions
        Age restrictions, 376-378
        ERISA, 379-380
        Service retirement, 379
    Health insurance, 366-367
    Holiday pay, 374-375
    Pension benefits, 352-363
        Benefit calculations, 357-361
        Disqualification for misconduct, 361-363
        Eligibility, 352-354
        Overtime wages and, 359-360
        Statutory amendments to, 354-357
    Severance pay, 379
    Sick leave, 374, 375-376
    Taxation, 416-417
    Vacation pay, 356, 358-359, 373-374, 414-415
Employee Retirement Income Security Act (ERISA), 379-380
Employment practices
    See also Hiring practices
    Appointments, 471
    Legal fees reimbursement, 506-507
    Marital restrictions, 508-509
    Privatization, 486-489
    Promotions
        Affirmative action, 95-97
        Classifications, 479-486
        Eligibility lists, 472-479
        Nepotism, 489-491
    Residency requirements, 491-495
    Secondary employment, 501-503
    Veterans preferences, 495-500
        Hiring, 498-499
        Promotions, 497-498, 499-500
        Terminations, 499

Equal Pay Act (EPA), 62-66
Ethics in Government Act, 180-181
Expression, freedom of
    See First Amendment and Freedom of Speech

42 U.S.C. § 1983
    Firefighters' and other employees' actions, 300-303
    First Amendment, 186, 190-191, 192
    Personal capacity employees, 263
    Police officers' actions, 295-300
    Prison guards, 263
    Supreme Court cases, 293-295
Family and Medical Leave Act, 400-410
    Documentation and notice, 404-406
    Eligibility, 402-404
    Intermittent leave, 406-407
    Procedural issues, 407-410
Federal Employees' Compensation Act, 412
Federal Labor Relations Authority, 447, 448
Federal Tort Claims Act, 303-305
Fifth Amendment
    Immunity and, 279
    Retaliation and, 269-270
First Amendment
    Immunity and, 271-273
    Loyalty oaths, 230-232
    Political activities and patronage
        Managerial and discretionary positions, 219-224
        Participation in the political process, 224-227
        Running for public office, 227-229
    Privacy rights and, 242-250, 291
    Religious freedom and, 238-242
    Speaker's interest vs. government's interest, 186-190, 194-199
    Speech and expression issues under, 177-250
Fourteenth Amendment
    Immunity and, 273-276
Fourth Amendment
    Immunity and, 276-278
    Search and seizure issues under, 311-350
Freedom of association, 207-210
Freedom of speech
    See also First Amendment
    Defamation, 210-214
    Internet access, 198-199
    Matters of public concern, 184-186
    Prior restraint, 192-193
    Protected speech, 177-193
    Speaker's interest vs. government's interest, 186-190, 194-199
    Speech of a personal nature, 199-204
    Speech reporting criminal activity, 190-191
    Supreme Court cases involving, 178-181
    Unprotected speech, 193-207

Handbooks, 126-129
Harassment
    Racial, 46-48
    Sexual, 67-80
        42 U.S.C. § 1983, 77-78
        Burden of proof, 68-72
        Same-sex and sexual orientation issues, 75-77
        State statutes, 78-80
Hatch Act, 227-228
Hiring practices
    See also Employment practices
    Affirmative action, 93-98
    Appointments, 471-491
        Classifications, 479-486
        Eligibility lists, 472-479
        Nepotism, 489-491
        Privatization, 486-489
    Residency requirements, 491-495
    Veterans' preferences, 495-500
Holiday pay, 373, 374-375, 414-415
Holiday: Good Friday as, 500

Immunity
    See also Liability
    Absolute, 258-262
        Attorneys general, 258-259, 261-262
        Legislators, 259-260, 261
        Police officers, 259
        Presidential aides, 258
    Constitutional violations, 271-279
        Eighth Amendment rights, 278
        Fifth Amendment rights, 279
        First Amendment speech rights, 208, 271-273
        Fourteenth Amendment rights, 273-276
        Fourth Amendment rights, 276-278
    Fair Labor Standards Act, 252
    Qualified immunity
        Emergency calls, 264-265
        Improper office behavior, 265-267
        Police misconduct, 267-270
    Sovereign
        Generally, 252-256
        Insurance as waiver, 256-258
    Special duty to prtotect, 279-283
        Other public employees, 281-283
        Police officers, 280-281
        Supreme Court cases, 279-280
Ionscan drug test, 319-320

Labor relations
    Arbitration, 467-470
    Disciplinary pay deductions, 423-424
    Fair Labor Standards Act (FLSA), 419-441

542 INDEX

        Applicability to public employment, 419-422
        Overtime wages, 422-441
        Window of correction, 426
    Unfair labor practices, 454-470
        Right to organize, 454-457
        Terms and conditions, 457-466
    Union representation, 445-454
        Collective bargaining fees, 451-454
        Duty of fair representation, 447-451
    Wage discrimination, 443-445
    Wages and hours, 457-459
Layoffs for financial reasons, 159-161
Liability
    Domestic disputes, 285-287
    Firefighter's rule, 287-288
    Generally, 284-293
    Suicides, 284-285
    Vicarious liability, 288-291
Loyalty oaths, 230-232

Mandatory retirement, 14-16
Marital restrictions, 508-509
Misconduct
    Criminal violations, 147-149
    Employer rules and policies violations, 149-156
    False statements, 106-107
    Off-duty misconduct, 156-159
    Official misconduct, 143-147
        Ethics codes violations, 143-145
        Neglect of duty, 145-147

National origin discrimination
    See Discrimination
National security, 173-175
Nepotism, 490-491

Occupational Safety and Health Administration (OSHA), 171-172
Older Workers Benefit Protection Act, 2, 9, 10, 376-378
Overtime wages, 422-441
    Commuting expenses, 437-439
    Comp and flex time, 432-434
    Compensable activities, 434-437
    Disciplinary pay deductions, 423-424, 426-427
    Exempt salaried employees, 423-427
    Method of calculation, 427-432
    Procedural issues, 439-441

Personal appearance and dress codes, 233-238
Political activities and patronage
    Managerial and discretionary positions, 219-224
    Participation in the political process, 224-227
    Retaliation against same party members, 229-230
    Running for public office, 227-229

Polygraphs, 112, 155-156, 505-506
Portal-to-Portal Act, 438
Postal Reorganization Act, 450-451
Pregnancy discrimination, 66-67
Privacy, 242-250, 441-443
Privatization of work, 486-489
Probationary employees, 117-119
Promotional exams, 474-477
Property and liberty interests, 115-126
Psychological testing, 505

Race discrimination
    See Discrimination
Rehabilitation Act
    See Americans with Disabilities Act (ADA)
Rehabilitation Act, 17-30, 34, 36-37
Religious discrimination
    See Discrimination
Religious freedom, 238-242
Religious Freedom Restoration Act (RFRA), 232, 235
Reputation interests, 121-123
Residency requirements, 491-495
Resignation, 140-143
Retaliatory actions
    Title VII, 87-93
    Whistleblower protection acts, 162-170
    Wrongful discharge, 170-173
Retaliatory actions
    Fifth Amendment rights, 269-270

Search and seizure
    Blood and drug testing, 321-350
        Adequacy of testing procedures, 346-350
        Balancing public and individual rights, 321-337
        Corrections officers and court employees, 340-342
        Direct observation, 333-336
        Overbroad testing policies, 322-325
        Police officers and firefighters, 338-340
        Post-accident testing, 336-337
        Random drug tests, 330-333
        Safety-sensitive positions, 325-330
        Standards for reasonable suspicion, 337-344
        Transportation employees, 342-344
        Unemployment benefits, 344-346
    Generally, 311-350
    Reasonable expectation of privacy, 312-313, 315-316, 317-321
    School searches, 312
    Supreme Court cases involving, 312-313
Secondary employment, 501-503
Seniority systems, 86-87
Severance pay, 379
Sex discrimination
    See Discrimination

Sexual harassment
    See Harassment
Sick leave, 374, 375-376
Smoking, 152, 389, 462-463
State tort claims acts, 305-309

Taxation of employee benefits, 416-417
Tenure, 172-173
Termination and suspension
    Abandonment and resignation, 138
    Application falsification, 106-107, 118, 152
    Due process rights, 106
        Collective bargaining agreements, 133-137
        Employment handbooks and policies, 126-129
        Evidentiary issues, 110-113
        Hearing rights, 106-107
        Impartial decision maker, 113-115
        Notice and opportunity to respond, 108-110
        Property and liberty interests, 115-126
        Statutes and ordinances, 129-133
    Layoffs for financial reasons, 159-161
    Misconduct, 143-159
        Criminal violations, 147-149
        Employer rules and policies violations, 149
        Off-duty misconduct, 156
        Official misconduct, 143-147
    National security, 173-175
    Retaliatory discharge, 162-173
        Whistleblower protection acts, 162-170
        Wrongful discharge, 170-173
    Suspensions, 107, 111, 112-113, 133, 135, 136, 146
    Whistleblower protection acts, 162-170
Title VII
    Affirmative action, 94-95, 95-96, 96-97
    Religious discrimination, 80-86
    Retaliation, 87-93
    Sex discrimination, 54-58, 58-61, 62, 66, 67-68, 70, 71-72, 75-77
Transfers, 119-121

Unemployment compensation, 380-385
Unions
    Arbitration, 467-470
    Collective bargaining fees, 451-454
    Duty of fair representation, 447-451
    Speech issues and, 215-218
    Unfair labor practices, 454
        Right to organize, 454-457
        Terms and conditions, 457-467
    Wages and hours, 457-459

Vacation pay, 356, 358-359, 373-374, 414-415
Veterans preference, 495

Wage discrimination, 443-445
Whistleblower protection acts, 162-170
Workers' compensation, 385-399
    Amount of compensation, 397-399
    Arising from employment, 386-391
    Exclusivity, 391-393
    Off-duty occurrences, 393-397